LETTERS OF
Mari Sandoz

LETTERS OF

Mari Sandoz

Edited and with an introduction

by Helen Winter Stauffer

UNIVERSITY OF NEBRASKA PRESS

LINCOLN & LONDON

ANSI Z39.48–1984.
Library of Congress
Cataloging-in-Publication Data
Sandoz, Mari, 1896–1966.
[Correspondence. Selections]
Letters of Mari Sandoz /
edited and with an introduction
by Helen Winter Stauffer.
p. cm.
Selected letters, 1928–1966.
Includes bibliographical references
(p.) and index.
ISBN 0-8032-4206-9
1. Sandoz, Mari, 1896–1966—
Correspondence. 2. Authors, American—
20th century—Correspondence.
3. West (U.S.) in literature.
I. Stauffer, Helen Winter, 1922–
II. Title.
PS3537.A667Z48 1992
813′.52—dc20
[B] 91-46762 CIP
The photograph of Mari Sandoz that appears
on the title page is by Halsman.

CONTENTS

PREFACE, VII

ACKNOWLEDGMENTS, XI

INTRODUCTION, XIII

LETTERS, 1

BIBLIOGRAPHY, 463

INDEX OF ADDRESSEES, 469

SUBJECT INDEX, 474

PREFACE

The great majority of the letters reproduced here are from the correspondence files of the Sandoz Collection at the University of Nebraska–Lincoln, the repository of Mari Sandoz's letters, files, manuscripts, maps, and working papers. The letters between Edward Weeks and A. E. Sheldon cited in the Introduction are found at the Nebraska State Historical Society, in the A. E. Sheldon Collection. For the June 15, 1935, letter from Mari Sandoz to her mother, permission is given by Flora Sandoz. In addition I have seen correspondence, family papers, and documents at the homes of Caroline Sandoz Pifer and Flora Sandoz, Mari's sisters. I have examined letters at Syracuse University, Chadron State College (Chadron, Nebraska), and the Denver Public Library. The University of Wyoming has a series of letters that are duplicates of some held by the University of Nebraska–Lincoln. I have also seen letters or photocopies of letters held by other individuals.

The Sandoz Collection contains forty years of letters: the originals sent to

Sandoz and carbon copies of her answers. Usually her letters are typed, but often Sandoz has added notes and marginalia in pen. On occasion I have been able to compare the carbons with the originals, and I find that she was conscientious in her additions, although the wording was not always identical. For example, in a letter to B. A. Botkin, September 14, 1953, she added "the K.P." in pen to the original and two copies (she often had multiple carbons). Later in that letter she inserted "with four" to the original and the two carbons. But with another addition, her original holograph reads, "Were really five others, M.S". Carbon one reads, "Really turned out to be five M.S.", and carbon two reads, "Really were five MS". Thus there is evidence that her written additions vary in minor ways.

The carbons have been catalogued by individuals who, for one reason or another, have sometimes identified the recipient or added a date. Sandoz often used only partial addresses or names, and when a researcher can identify either, it is, of course, helpful. But though Sandoz's own distinctive penmanship can be recognized in her additions, the accuracy of other entries is less certain. In those cases I have not speculated but have given only the information I was sure of. Complete identification of those to whom Sandoz wrote has at times proved impossible. Many of her letters were written to fans—she was as conscientious in her answers to them as to people she knew personally. Many she never met, but because her reply incorporates some aspect of her writing career the letter is included. The cataloguers also removed to other files the enclosures Sandoz sometimes refers to. I have not included them.

Sandoz did not save the envelopes she received. When she included the recipient's address in the heading I have included as much as necessary to aid in identifying either the addressee or the subject matter. When she did not include that information, but the address was possible to identify and seemed pertinent, I have included it in brackets.

The early letters were typed by Sandoz herself; later she dictated to secretaries. That she proofread is obvious; she caught a good many spelling errors and marked them with brown ink, but inevitably some slipped through. Because I worked, in the main, with Sandoz's carbons rather than her originals, I sometimes felt it useful to make editorial corrections I would not have made if working with originals. I could not be sure, for instance, that she had not corrected an occasional misspelling on her original while leaving the error on the carbons. This was also true for the rare occasions of faulty or missing punctuation. Therefore, I have silently corrected misspellings and occasionally made the minor adjustment of a comma or period for clarity. I have also included diacritical marks. In the matter of her consistent punctuation, however, such as spaces before and after her dashes, her end punctuation falling after quote marks rather than before, her use of asterisks to indicate omissions, and her inconsistencies from letter to letter in underlining book titles or using all capital letters, I felt that keeping to her usage would avoid unnecessary editorial interference between the writer and the reader. These variations on modern usage are not apt seriously to distract attention from the content.

As a strong proponent of individuality in language usage, Sandoz quite intentionally broke some standard rules of grammar, as in her consistent use of *lay* for *lie* and in a deliberate use of misplaced modifiers. More rare was an occasional invented word, such as *diminuting* (Sandoz to Karl Shapiro, September 15, 1956). These are part of her style and therefore, I think, worth keeping without the disconcerting insertion of [*sic*]. In the last few years of her life, Sandoz often wrote letters by hand, rather than dictating them. I have made no distinction in this matter.

Because these letters are selected for the insights they give into Sandoz's writing, researching, and publishing, I occasionally deleted matter that did not relate to those areas, that did not seem to add to our knowledge of Sandoz herself, or that was repetitive. In those instances I indicated the deletion by four ellipses. If a word or phrase could not be definitely clarified, my reasoned guess is in brackets.

Since Sandoz moved infrequently, I have included her address only when she first used it. Because she usually did not sign her name to her carbons, I have also omitted that signature whenever she did. If there is a sequence of letters to an individual, I have included the information for only the first letter of the series.

The collection at the University of Nebraska–Lincoln, large and valuable as it is, does not include every letter Sandoz received. Occasional references by Sandoz to numbers or to specific letters not now in the collection indicate that she disposed of some, probably a considerable number. Although an occasional reference to "hundreds of letters" she received in response to a specific issue is almost certainly an exaggeration, surely her comment to her mother in February 1936, in which she stated that she had received over two thousand letters regarding *Old Jules*, is not fabrication. However, there are not that many letters from 1935–36 in the collection now.

My aim in providing explanatory notes is to avoid overdocumentation while providing enough background to clarify Sandoz's references. The notes relating to people, places, or events are intended to help put Sandoz's letters in a clear context for modern-day readers. Because she read so extensively, her letters often refer to books now out of print or unfamiliar to today's public; I have endeavored to give pertinent publication information for the less familiar titles.

I have used the following abbreviations in the notes to the letters:

AM *Atlantic Monthly*
CA *Cheyenne Autumn*
CH *Crazy Horse*
MS Mari Sandoz
NAR *North American Review*
NH *Nebraska History*
NSHS Nebraska State Historical Society
OJ *Old Jules*
PrS *Prairie Schooner*
SEP *Saturday Evening Post*
UNA University of Nebraska Archives

ACKNOWLEDGMENTS

My appreciation for help with this book extends to many, both within and without the academic community. At the University of Nebraska at Kearney, thanks go to Kenneth Nikels and the Nebraska State College Research Services Council, to English Chair Harland Hoffman, to Dean of Fine Arts and Humanities Betty Becker-Theye, and to my fellow academicians Tom Godfrey, Dick Cloyed, and Charles Peek. At the University of Nebraska–Lincoln, I thank Fred Link for courtesies extended while I was adjunct professor there.

I received splendid help from archival and library staffs: at the University of Nebraska at Kearney, Anita Norman and Ray Barnard, particularly; at the University of Nebraska–Lincoln, the archives staff, Jerry Rudolph, Joe Svoboda, Dean Waddell, and especially Lynn Beideck-Porn, who worked with me throughout this project and earlier ones as well; Emily Levine, my research assistant; at the Nebraska State Historical Society, John Carter and Anne Billesbach; and the staff at the University of Nebraska Alumni Office.

Mari Sandoz's friends, among them Volta Torrey, Tip Stanley, Edwin Van den Bark, Kay Rogers, and Henry S. "Tom" Smith, sent vital information.

Marjorie Neill and Patricia McLaughlin, steady friends, gave me support. Flora Sandoz and Caroline Sandoz Pifer, Mari's sisters, opened their homes and family records to me. Their unfailing courtesy and interest have been indispensable. Some of the letters in this volume were first published by Caroline Sandoz Pifer in the *Gordon* (Nebraska) *Journal* between 1967 and 1971.

My special appreciation goes to Susan J. Rosowski for her careful reading and interest, and for her wisdom and friendship. A number of ideas discussed in the Introduction have come from our conversations. And I would like to thank also Paul Mattern, for turning over to me the materials left at the death of his wife, Claire Mattern, who first began the work of publishing these letters.

Commendation goes to Gina Christianson and Chris Godfrey for their hours spent committing the letters to the word processer, and also to Chris for his patience with technical problems.

And once again, my thanks to my husband and family, who have accepted with good grace the fact that research must sometimes take precedence over family plans.

Both the west and the

writing are really my life.

– Mari Sandoz to Benn Hall

and John Barkham,

April 5, 1958

INTRODUCTION

A fire in the Greenwich Village apartment house in which Mari Sandoz lived drove the tenants from the building—all, that is, but Sandoz. Determined, that January night in 1956, to protect her irreplaceable research material, she carried her huge collection of notes, file cards, manuscripts, and correspondence out to the fire escape, ignoring the flames and the water pouring into her rooms from the fire hoses. She was too busy and concerned for her historical material to think of her own danger.

In her search for a new and safer home, she looked first for protection and ample room for her files, rather than for personal comfort. To a friend she listed the amenities of the new location at 422 Hudson: a virtually fireproof brick building, basement storage for her files, a safer, more private entrance—less chance that someone could in any way disturb her records. This was a typical attitude and reaction for Sandoz, since historical sources formed the basis of almost all her writing. Fortunately she saved her letters also from that fire, for in those letters she reveals the story of her work and much of what is known of her life.

WHEN EDWARD WEEKS, editor of Atlantic Monthly Press, wrote A. E. Sheldon in June 1935 in "quiet confidence" for authentic details about Old Jules Sandoz, "who was, I understand, a famous old character in the settlement days of Nebraska," he was being merely prudent. Weeks was about to present the press's 1935 nonfiction award to Mari Sandoz for her biography of her father, and it behooved him to check with Dr. Sheldon, superintendent of the Nebraska State Historical Society, professor of history, state legislator, and newspaper editor. This trepidation concerning her western truths, however, would mark much of Sandoz's later relationships with eastern editors and publishers as well. "I do not wish in the least to challenge her word," Weeks wrote Sheldon, but "it is in a sense my responsibility to our readers to make sure that the character and description of Old Jules is as secure and authentic as care can make it" (Weeks to Sheldon, June 11, 1935, NSHS).

Sheldon's response was immediate and positive: he had known Jules during the twelve years he, Sheldon, had lived in the Sandhills, and Jules was all Mari claimed him to be. Furthermore, Sheldon noted that Mari Sandoz herself was also "an interesting character, an original genius in her own way, which is something different from that of her father, but none the less engaging." He noted that she had worked at various times for the society and was at that time giving him some assistance in his own historical work. He had observed her research work and had read a considerable part of her manuscript, and he concluded, "From what I know of Jules Sandoz and Mari Sandoz, . . . the story is a reliable and accurate picture of life in the Northwestern Nebraska region" (Sheldon to Weeks, June 13, 1935, NSHS).

Weeks accepted Sheldon's recommendation; a few days later he telegraphed to Sandoz that she had won the 1935 Atlantic Nonfiction Prize of five thousand dollars. National recognition of her writing, so long in coming, finally would be hers. Her determination to portray the West as she knew it, however, meant that this was only one obstacle she had overcome on her way to acceptance as an author of significance. Eventually she published twenty-one books, won a number of national prizes, and became a noted public speaker and a radio and television personality. Throughout her life she battled the misconceptions and stereotypes of the West held by those in the East.

She was well qualified for that role. Born in 1896 on a primitive homestead near the Niobrara River to Swiss immigrant parents, during the settlement of

Nebraska's northwestern frontier, she was concerned with America's past, particularly with the history of the Great Plains during the Indian wars. She lectured everyone, from editors at *Encyclopaedia Britannica* to various Hollywood producers and directors, about accuracy. Her letters indicate that she was just as involved with twentieth-century problems: the perception that the West was still considered only a colony of the East; the farm crises of the 1920s and 1930s; the events leading up to World War II, including the growth of fascism, both in Europe and in America; the postwar excesses; the government policies that drove the Indians from their reservations into urban ghettos; the defoliation of Vietnam. She was often involved in attempting to rectify some of the world's ills, both directly and through her writing. Her writing dominated her adult life.

The letters selected here illustrate primarily those aspects of Mari Sandoz that relate to her writing, researching, and publishing. They are not intended to convey the entirety of this complex woman's life experiences. The Sandoz Collection at the University of Nebraska–Lincoln, in which the majority of the letters are to be found, is huge but incomplete. The earliest letter in the collection is dated 1926, when Sandoz was already a woman of thirty, with an eventful youth behind her. Some of those early years are still largely unknown to the researcher; some were deliberately obscured by Sandoz.

Her memory for dates in her own history was always hazy, perhaps at times intentionally so, although she was conscientious about dates in her historical research. In a number of her biographical sketches, for instance, she gave her birth date variously as 1901 to 1903. She claimed that lack of a birth certificate made it impossible to verify her age, but the family Bible, as well as a Lutheran baptismal certificate, confirms her birth date as May 11, 1896. Other dates may have been missed more innocently. "We moved into the hills in 1911," she wrote an inquirer. It was actually 1910, the autumn after her youngest sister, Caroline, was born.

She was also less than forthcoming about her early, five-year marriage to Sandhills rancher Wray Macumber. "I am single," she replied when asked her marital status—and indeed she was single. She was also divorced, but that fact never appeared in the thousands of letters she wrote. Although she used the name Marie Macumber for her writing until she settled on Mari Sandoz in 1929, she so thoroughly and successfully hid the marriage that only after her death did it become known even to many of her closest acquaintances.

Sandoz's recollection of her early desire to be a writer is verified by memories of her brothers, close to her in age, and by schoolmates. Her first published story, written for the children's page of the *Omaha Daily News*, appeared when she was eleven and precipitated a violent scene with her father. Using various pen names, she published five more stories. Though this hardly guaranteed that she would become an adult author, she recalled that seeing her name in print convinced her of her future career.

She suppressed her writing, at least for publication, during her adolescence, her teaching in country schools, and her marriage, but after her divorce in 1919 and her flight from the Sandhills to Lincoln, she vigorously sought publication. By 1922 she had become a permanent resident of Lincoln and began to send out her short stories to editors of magazines, always to have them returned to her. Shortly after that, Mari began to save her correspondence.

Until the publication of *Old Jules* in 1935, Sandoz suffered periods of stress, frustration, and severe poverty. She later recalled these apprentice years in Lincoln positively. In "I Remember Lincoln" (*Lincoln Journal*, 8 May 1959), she referred to the young intellectuals with whom she shared hours of talk over five-cent cups of coffee at a local meeting place or at her tiny apartment. But the article was written long after she had achieved renown. There were other experiences: resentment at what she saw as snubs by important people, illness caused by malnutrition, despair at lack of publishing success, and her extremely negative view of Lincoln itself. That view is inscribed in her 1939 *Capital City*, no matter how she denied it.

Sandoz's publishing problems were exacerbated by the region she first wrote about—that small area of the high plains, the Nebraska Sandhills. Most eastern editors had never heard of it; some apparently did not believe it existed. Those who did were not sure it was worth writing about. Yet Mari was determined that the Sandhills, the settling of that region, and the battles over its use—ethical, ecological, social and economic problems—were of importance, locally of course, but at a much more general level. The frontier as she knew it, the development and settlement of formerly Indian lands, was as important as the settlement of Jamestown and Plymouth, as she pointed out to Frank C. Hanighen (September 21, 1933). But how to attract the eastern publishers to this idea, especially when the Sandhills, along with the entire Midwest, was in a drouth cycle that seemed to doom it to insignificance agriculturally and economically? Her letters limn her efforts, her methods, and her unshakable faith in her message. They also reveal her determination to tell her message in her own way, in her voice, the authentic voice of her region—sometimes raspy, scratchy, raucous, sometimes softly lyrical, but always unmistakably western and Sandoz.

Although she worked independently of others—she did all her own research, writing, and revising — she had one goal in common with other serious western writers: she was committed to telling an alternative version of history. The white adventurers who came into the Great Plains were not, in her view, always heroic. Rather, to the Indians who first occupied the territory, they were interlopers. The whites could be treacherous, liars and thieves, destructive of the land and its inhabitants. In *Old Jules,* her history of the settlement period, the whites were the protagonists, but the settlers displayed all the frailties of humankind; they could be weak as well as brave. Some were flawed, unpredictable, niggardly, murderous, and often unattractive, though seldom dull. Old Jules himself was villainous at times. And in her fine histories of the Plains Indian wars of the 1870s, Sandoz depicted the scenes from the Indians' perspective. In her judgment, the U.S. Army and government were seldom admirable; contrary to conventional treatment of the time, she often debunked them as aggressors. Although this view is more common today, Sandoz was one of the few to advance it then and to treat Indians as important individuals. She carried her ideas even further in three books in her Great Plains series: *The Buffalo Hunters* (1954), *The Cattlemen* (1958), and *The Beaver Men* (1964). She focused on the animals and the ecology they affected. Particularly in *The Beaver Men,* she recognized the little-known real heroes of human history as well, those who were far from sources of government power but who actually lived and explored in the West. Such ideas led to occasional criticism by readers, reviewers, and historians.

In her letters, Sandoz revealed her relish for a good conflict. After *The Cattlemen* was published, she noted to a friend that she was receiving a goodly number of hostile letters from families of characters she had portrayed in the book: "a good fight brewing." Although she could not tolerate close interpersonal conflicts, battle on a larger landscape suited her just fine. During her early Lincoln years it was the entrenched oligarchy as she saw it, along with the complacent Republicanism of the 1920s and 1930s, that her liberal spirit deplored. Once *Old Jules* was accepted for publication in 1935, her battles moved to the East. Her skirmishes from then on were primarily with the eastern establishment, not just with publishers, editors, and critics — personal battles for the integrity of her writing and for sales of her books — but also on a broader level, with bureaucrats and financiers.

The letters tell also of battles with Hollywood, most of which Sandoz lost. *Miss Morissa* (1955) was originally conceived and written for Greer Garson, then at Warner Brothers, but Garson moved to a different studio before the script could be completed. A short time later she was the star of a film titled

Strange Lady in Town. The similarities between this film and Sandoz's proposal are considerable, although the setting moved from Nebraska to New Mexico. A film titled *Chief Crazy Horse* drew heavily from Sandoz's *Crazy Horse* (1942), but she was given neither credit nor money. When Universal Studio's Gregory Ratoff insisted that material in the film was in the public domain, although unquestionably it could have come only from her book, she was angry enough to challenge Jacques Chambrun, then her agent about it. Because the film violated a number of Sioux tribal taboos and was historically inaccurate, Sandoz would have nothing to do with it, although friends urged her to sue the studio for plagiarism. When the film came out, she contented herself with writing a fiery letter and repudiating any connection with the movie. Later, Warner Brothers bought the rights to *Cheyenne Autumn* (1953). They used its title and little more. The film was, finally, a travesty of her book and of history. Seldom did she speak with such vehemence as in her letters to James Webb, the scriptwriter. In spite of these experiences, and in spite of illness, in January 1965 she was discussing the possibility that Blanche Yurka would play the role of the villainous Gulla in a filming of *Slogum House* (1937).

Sandoz's letters are remarkable for their extent. They cover forty years, from 1926 to Sandoz's death in 1966, and number between twenty-five and thirty thousand. Sure of the importance of her work long before anyone else was, Sandoz methodically began keeping carbons, even of her holograph notes, for some years before she was published nationally. In addition to correspondence on her own writing, many letters relate to her concerns as a mentor to aspiring writers. She contributed her time and interest with almost inconceivable generosity, writing long and frequent letters to them. Fully one-fourth to one-third of her correspondence is with or about these fledging authors, many of whom she helped to publication. To include more than a fraction of so extensive a collection is impractical; therefore, one winnows. Only a few examples of Sandoz's correspondence as a teacher of and guide to other writers are published in this volume.

On the other hand, some aspects of Sandoz's life are barely recorded in her letters. At times she led a busy social and cultural life. She was always interested in the theater, in music and art, but there are only fleeting references to these interests. An early letter from Sandoz in Lincoln to her sister Flora mentions a George Bernard Shaw play she had to miss. Her letters include references to an occasional play or art show, sometimes a "thank you" for a lovely weekend at someone's country home, enough to indicate that she could break her strenuous writing schedule to lunch with critics, writers, and journalists. Sandoz wrote of trips to Washington, D.C., for hearings relating to the Indians of the plains and sent notes to various members of the New York Posse of the Westerners, a group dedicated to preserving the history of the West and of which she was a charter member. She was not living the life of an anchorite all the time.

Contrary to what one might expect from a prolific reader and writer, Mari seldom wrote in detail about either theories or specifics of the books she read at the rate of six or seven a week. She talked about them, but she seldom wrote about them. Nor did she often share many details of the emotional or psychological aspects of her own writing.

Sandoz's letters reveal little of her inner life or close emotional relationships. She wrote once of her father, "Jules was no Hamlet" (Sandoz to Hanighan, November 21, 1933). He never questioned himself. This could be applied to Mari as well. She read Nietzsche, Freud, and Jung and considered their theories. She clearly accepted Freud's explanation of the Oedipus complex, Jung's collective unconscious, and Nietzsche's will-to-power. But if her introspection included consideration of her own subconscious or libido, she did not write about it. If there was self-searching, she kept it out of her letters. Even her earliest extant letters suggest a personality fully formed and, usually, at ease with itself.

Two, possibly three, letters referred to marriage proposals. Not one word mentioned her marriage and divorce. Although the letters, particularly those between Sandoz and her longtime Lincoln friends, give glimpses of her personality not otherwise revealed, even here Sandoz displays considerable reserve. Their letters to her were often gossipy, breezy, funny, and clever. Her answers tended to be straightforward—interested but direct. As one friend of many years wrote her, "I shall never be the detached person you are—heaven knows I'd like to be" (from "Marie," n.d., Sandoz Collection, UNA).

Sandoz changed in the forty years covered in her correspondence. Still, the letters reveal a remarkably stable personality, a woman dedicated to her writing. She never deviated from her major purpose, to bring knowledge of western history to the attention of American readers and to draw attention to the evils, past and present, of our civilization, so that they could be corrected. Her letters emphasize that she judged people by their integrity in following their own goals. She had no use for those who wasted their time in a futile or frivolous life. Her friends, both men and women, were those who strove to accomplish something, whatever it might be.

Only in the letters to her sisters, particularly to Flora, did she let down her reserve. These letters, however, are not in the University of Nebraska collection; Mari's sisters graciously allowed me to read the letters but asked that I not quote directly from them. Although there is little in them pertaining to her writing or career not found elsewhere, she discussed her work more fully and frankly here. In the early years, particularly, she attempted to draw Flora into the creative world and shared her emotional highs and lows with her.

Mari was ten years older than Flora, but she had had charge of her sister since Flora's birth, even naming her, as Mari reminded her (Sandoz to Flora Sandoz, October 23, 1965). When Flora entered the University of Nebraska after high school, she lived with Mari in the 1226 J Street apartment one semester, and when she returned to the Sandhills after graduating from the University of Minnesota, Mari continued to use her as a sounding board for writing ideas.

The letters to Flora reveal Mari's early struggles as she endured them, as poignantly as do her letters to Eleanor Hinman included here. Perhaps because Flora was less likely to intrude on Mari's jealously guarded private space, these letters reveal a much less prickly character. In December 1931, Mari reported to her sister that times had been so bad for so long that she was comfortable with them; she was so poor and writing so diligently that she had not been out of the house for three weeks except to go to the grocery store. She spoke often and matter-of-factly about her migraines; Flora had been aware of them all her life. Mari had no reason to impress Flora, so when she spoke of working fourteen to sixteen hours at the typewriter on days when she could work at all, there was no sense of exaggeration or forced drama. Although Mari eventually gave up on Flora as a writer, her letters continued throughout the years to discuss aspects of her own writing and revealed her feelings more openly than elsewhere.

SANDOZ'S FRIENDS remembered her as a gifted conversationalist, a raconteur, and an authority on almost any subject mentioned, from American history to biology, from folk medicine to big- and little-league baseball. If she had never written a book, she would be remembered by many as a talented storyteller.

Fortunately, we have the letters to augment the recollections of those who knew her as full of verve, energy, curiosity, and esoteric knowledge. Except in times of illness (and sometimes then as well) she drove herself hard and expected others to follow the same regime. Her letters also provide valuable evidence of this writer's patterns of work. Sandoz attributed her work habits to her Swiss ancestry, particularly to the work ethic of her mother's German-Swiss antecedents. There was also the Calvinist background of her father's family. Considering her own difficult childhood and youth, she may well have equated her personal worth with her ability to work. Certainly, when she went to Lincoln after her divorce in 1919, she knew that whatever became of her and her goals would be dependent entirely on her own ability to achieve them.

From her description of her method of writing, it is clear that writing was never easy for Mari. As her sisters attest, she worked harder than anyone else they knew. Her ideas, however, came easily. She seems never to have had a "dry spell." Usually she worked on more than one book at a time; she had three books clearly in mind or contracted for at the time of her death—a book on oil on the Great Plains and one on the Dog Soldier societies of the Plains Indians for Hastings House and a book on the Sioux for Harpers.

The research too, though challenging and sometimes frustrating, was interesting and rewarding. She enumerated her typical range of research in her letters: almost every archival repository on the Great Plains, the New York Public Library and other eastern repositories, government records, historical societies, and of even more importance, her personal contacts. Some of the latter gave privileged information; some notes she referred to (from Wild Hog and He Dog, for example) are not now in her files. She may have destroyed them before her death, as she sometimes hints. The value and extent of Sandoz's sources have not yet been thoroughly explored.

In her correspondence, Sandoz revealed not only her belief that place was an essential element in her writing but also her methods for achieving geographical authenticity. She needed more than authenticity, however; she wanted to capture the aura, as she described it eloquently in her letter to the *New York Times* (January 21, 1931). Places shape the memory, as Sandoz knew well. She almost always began her books with a description of the setting. In *Old Jules, Crazy Horse, Cheyenne Autumn, Love Song to the Plains,* and many others, she described the places she knew, remembered, and returned to again and again—the West, the Great Plains, the Sandhills of Nebraska. These places shaped her life and molded her as a writer. She saw her region as a microcosm of world history, containing within its boundaries prototypes of universal happenings—geological, historical, and natural.

SANDOZ CREATED her adult self; the metamorphosis from the apprentice to the nationally recognized expert on the West is unfolded in her letters. By themselves, however, because they deal largely with her career, they may give the impression that she was consistently direct, forthright, and to the point; less often do they reveal her considerable charm, her sense of fun, her hearty laugh, or her gregariousness, which she usually held in check but which was nevertheless strong. A friend from her university years described her as "high spirited, friendly, and sociable." A few letters, such as that to Edward Weeks (November [?], 1935), detailed her sociability, which she enjoyed all her life. Her wry humor surfaced only occasionally, as in her answer to the woman who wanted to review her book without reading it (January 5, 1936) or in her comment that *Old Jules* would live long after she was dead, if it had been published by then (to Hanighen, May 31, 1933).

The letters illustrate the changes in her self-image as well as her status, reflected in her relationships with the publishing establishment. Before *Old Jules,* her letters were sometimes coy, certainly arch, as she attempted to make some impression. She complemented *Forum* on Faulkner's "A Rose for Emily" (August 25, 1933), wrote an exceedingly lengthy letter to the editors of *Harpers* in response to an essay on the importance of sex in biography (October 19, 1932), and sent H. L. Mencken an impassioned proposal for an opera based on the life of Crazy Horse, the Oglala Sioux chief killed in 1877 at Fort Robinson, Nebraska (February 13, 1933). What must those men have thought of this brash young woman whose short stories they always rejected as "not quite suitable for our magazine"?

The correspondence amply illustrates that Sandoz went to considerable lengths to draw attention to herself as a person and a writer, but she did not, even in her most desperate moments, compromise her ideas. When Margaret Christie, her first agent, criticized her short story "Victorie," saying it was bad for her as a writer and would hurt her reputation, Sandoz refused to change it. In spite of the fact that she experimented endlessly with the form of *Old Jules,* she refused to fabricate details to strengthen scenes or characterization. Responding to changes suggested by Frank C. Hanighen of Dodd, Mead, she was polite but firm (November 21, 1933). Caxton Press, in Idaho, was seriously interested in the manuscript, but their reader also wanted fictionalization, and Mari would not agree. Most of the thirteen publishing companies who saw the manuscript were not interested at all. During this time, Sandoz became so discouraged that she vowed to give up writing altogether—a vow that lasted only a brief time—but she did not back down on what she had to say and how she wanted to say it.

Her early responses to critical suggestions indicate that she was willing to be more flexible about her short stories, but eventually she refused to do more with them either. She claimed to be bewildered by the conflicting advice given by different readers; there seemed to be no way she could please the editors. Easterners could not conceive of the Sandhills and the frontier as a real place, and almost everything she wrote was set there. She finally burned most of the "seventy five or so" stories that had circulated for several years—a melodramatic solution, but memorable to those who watched or heard of it.

Sandoz tended toward the dramatic and, in common with many writers, was something of an actor in her own scenes. Her early letters in particular reflect this sense of drama. To Eleanor Hinman, her most devoted friend, she moaned, "I did feel as helplessly driven as Hardy's *Tess*. . . . Now I must stagger on, I presume, with some semblance of notice to the Kantian duty whip that hangs over me for the remainder of my life!" (January 10, 1930). This is in marked contrast to her concurrent accounts, written to publishers, in which she pictured herself as the local "chaplain," her little apartment or favorite booth in a local coffee shop called "agony corner" because so many poured out their troubles to her. But time seems to have softened her memories; later recollections of her childhood and her apprentice years were usually filled with detachment and humor.

Detachment and humor were her saving grace during most of her career, but on occasion they vanished. When she became angry or concerned about an issue, she dealt with it head-on, as in her arguments with Atlantic Press and their publisher, Little, Brown, about *Slogum House*. In her letter to Alfred McIntyre (March 22, 1937), she blamed the East for the flaws in westerners' characters and threatened to take her book from Little, Brown to another publisher.

She seldom held grudges. She might have been angry often ("my Old Julesian temper"), but there were few longtime feuds. The one person she never forgave for what she considered a breach of trust was Howard Fast, whose *The Last Frontier* (1941) was written about the same incident she had been researching for years. She maintained that Fast and his publishers knew—had to know—that she was writing about the 1878 Cheyenne Indians' trek from their Oklahoma reservation back to their old home in Montana. Fast did his research in months, and when his book came on the market Sandoz did the only thing possible: she put aside her research and began another book. Years later she took up her Cheyenne work again, and her *Cheyenne Autumn*, published in 1953, is one of her finest works. It was nonfiction, whereas Fast's work was fiction, but she could never achieve any equanimity about the affair. She had no correspondence with Fast; there is no evidence she ever met him, but his name appeared periodically throughout her correspondence, and she was always angry.

There were innumerable opportunities for Sandoz to take umbrage, to brood, and to cherish wounds, but that seems not to have been her nature. Most of her life she seemed to operate on the premise of "sufficient unto the day. . . ." Although her letters, particularly those to Eleanor Hinman, showed her despair at times during her early Lincoln years—after all, thirteen or fourteen years of steady effort that seems never to succeed is cause for depression—and periods of economic distress, she was usually resilient and resolute, of good cheer.

She had inherited her father's paranoia to some extent, however, as well as her mother's sense of drama and imminent disaster. Although this translated into what some called overreaction (sometimes to personal crises but more often to national and international events), there is evidence that she had some basis for her concern. She may have sounded melodramatic in her letter to the chief of police in Lincoln (December 10, 1937) stating that she had been threatened and that her files had been rifled, but friends verified both instances. Her remarks on the dust cover of *Crazy Horse,* published in 1942, noted that members of one of the many "shirt" groups (blackshirts, brownshirts, etc., generally fascist organizations) had rung her doorbell and warned her that she could be eliminated; again, friends offered corroboration. In fact, her letters contain little that link her to the work she was doing for the government at that time; as she often said, she knew more than she told.

But her sense of imminent doom was most dramatically expressed when she wrote of her fears for the United States. Her first mention of Hitler and his *Mein Kampf* appeared in the 1930s. Her fear of Hitler's fascism, stronger than her fear of either Stalin or Mussolini, permeated her letters during the later 1930s and during the war years. In 1940 she bet a friend that the Germans would be in North America by July 4. Although she was happy to pay off the dollar bet, she still feared that Hitler would be able to form a puppet government in North America, "perhaps with the Duke of Windsor and his American wife" to rule, after England had capitulated to Germany (Sandoz to Bob Ferguson, July 17, 1940, Sandoz Collection, UNA). Perhaps because of her Swiss ancestry, she was much more concerned about the European theater than the Pacific war. Both *Capital City* (1939) and *The Tom-Walker* (1947) are centered on twentieth-century problems leading to and resulting from World War II.

Sandoz's letters reveal her very human imperfections. She could be sharp, on occasion patronizing. In her early years she was sometimes cloying. She was opinionated, and as she became older, surer, and perhaps more verbose, she found it difficult to accept contradiction. Early in her career she sought criticism, but after she had authored a number of highly respected books, she took criticism badly, whether from an editor, reviewer, or friend. She changed agents when Harold Ober was unenthusiastic about *The Tom-Walker,* for instance, and later broke with her friend Thomas Hornsby Ferril because of his criticism of *Son of the Gamblin' Man* (1960). This absolute assurance in her own view, so significant for the integrity of her early work, may have hurt the quality of some later work. By then she had so much self-confidence and presence that she simply overrode any opposition.

On the other hand, the letters also give glimpses of Sandoz's talent for friendship. Although she was a self-contained woman in many ways, and few could claim any real intimacy with her, she had a strong bent for congeniality and maintained some of these relationships from early years until her death. Her friendships with both men and women were usually in some way related to literature, the fine arts, or western history. Her strongest longtime friendship, formed in 1925 in Lincoln, was with Melvin Van den Bark, the man she always credited with teaching her how to write. Coming to the University of Nebraska from the University of Iowa in 1925, he taught short story writing courses, and it was in his class that Sandoz learned, after years of unsuccessful writing, how to organize her material.

"Van" was a bachelor with responsibility for an ailing mother and various nieces and nephews (these were depression years; social security was nonexistent). Mari, desperately poor but with ambition, optimism, and drive, spent a great deal of time with him while in Lincoln, and their close friendship continued until her death. Mari was something of an oddity in Lincoln, and Lincolnites were always interested in university professors, so their relationship was gossiped about. People often assumed that they were "going together"; some believed they were engaged, others suspected an illicit affair. Sandoz later laughed about it all. There was apparently nothing sexual, but a deep and abiding friendship. One of the emotions she expressed, not surprisingly, was gratitude for his early guidance in her writing, and she dedicated her *Love Song to the Plains* (1961) to him, the highest honor she could bestow. Sandoz did not as a rule approve of dedicating books to individuals.

Although she learned from Van how to organize her material, the writing itself never became easy. Letters written even late in her life emphasize that it was a tedious, laborious process, but style was every bit as important to her as the subject matter. Although her desire to write stories first lured her into research and the field of history, she struggled with problems of style throughout her life. A determined "plodder," as she more than once described herself, she worked from file cards through revision after revision—

often ten or more reams of paper for a book — as amply demonstrated in the manuscripts in the Sandoz Collection.

Her belief that writing could be taught, that anyone could learn to write, came from her own experience, and she preached this tenet constantly. Her letters explain in detail the method she worked out for herself through years of experimentation and striving. The first step, as she described it in a *Saturday Evening Post* column "Keeping Posted" (March 4, 1939), was the most important. Before beginning any writing, she would type a simple declaratory sentence stating her theme. This would go on the wall in front of her typewriter. Two or three of these statements can still be found in her files.

When she moved to Denver in 1940 to complete her research and the writing of *Crazy Horse* and to work on *Son of the Gamblin' Man,* she continued her Lincoln friendships through correspondence. And in Denver she met others — again often connected with literature, history, or art — and these friends too she kept through later years. The Denver years were her "glamour period." The years from 1940 to 1943 are the leanest in numbers of letters but were among the busiest in her life. The fact that she completed *Crazy Horse* during that time, along with leading an active social life and becoming increasingly involved in committee and government duties brought about by World War II, is an indication of her enormous energy and dedication. She knew Lenore Fitzell, the poet; Thomas Hornsby Ferril, the poet and columnist, and his wife Hellie, the owner of the *Rocky Mountain Herald;* Alan Swallow, the professor, writer, and publisher of Swallow Press; Mary Chase, the playwright and author of *Harvey.* Close — as close as one could get — was Caroline Bancroft, a socialite, book editor for the *Denver Post,* and expert in Colorado history. Here too she met the Lynn Van Vleets, who were not writers but were hosts par excellence to celebrities at their Arabian horse ranch near Nederland. She remained friends with most of them after her move to New York, although she eventually broke with Ferril.

There were New York friends too, notably Marguerite Young, whom Sandoz aided, with encouragement and pragmatic means such as locating grants and fellowships, to her publication of the monumental *Miss MacIntosh, My Darling.* And she met Kay and Joe Rogers, journalists both. Kay often accompanied her friend on the long walks mandated by daily injections of the medicine Sandoz had finally found helpful for her migraines. There was James Carr, a rare-book dealer who published several of her books in beautiful, leather-bound special editions. She maintained friendly relations with a number of editors as well, which is surprising considering her generally negative attitude toward the profession. One of her longest friendships was with Paul Hoffman. She met him in 1935 at Atlantic Monthly Press, followed him to Knopf, and eventually worked with him when he went to Westminster. That friendship had its crises and was broken off at least twice but was patched up in each instance. Both breaks came about because of editorial differences. Her New York friendships, however, included few close associations with major established writers of the time. She belonged to no school, group, or clique of writers there.

Through her correspondence Sandoz also traced her travels. Her research took her on extended excursions all over the West; she always scouted the areas she wrote about in order to be geographically correct. With the exception of a couple of trips to the Southwest and Mexico, almost all of her treks had to do directly with her writing or lecturing.

When she was not traveling to investigate a potential scene of historical significance, she was often lecturing at book fairs, author luncheons, or some historical society. Originally reluctant to speak in public, she eventually came to view this as good public relations for her books; she was also interested in promoting historical knowledge for its own sake. Convinced that humans could learn from the past, her letters continually prodded individuals to write what they knew of their area or about their own experiences.

She actively promoted and marketed her books. The East, she learned, quickly forgot the reviews—her market was in the West. "Yesterday I had two requests for my new books and I couldn't give the name of even *one* bookstore in all of Manhattan that carries my most recent work," she complained to the editor Mary Pfeiffer (April 22, 1962). Every year or so she would go on a round of autographing sessions at midwestern bookstores; at the same time she would sandwich in lectures, often free of charge, at public libraries. If she could manage it she would swing into western Nebraska to visit her family in the Sandhills.

She continued her concern for her writing even during the last pain-filled years before her death. *Old Jules Country* (1965) was conceived by Walter Frese and Mary Abbot, but Sandoz listed the possible selections (January 25, 1965), and later she was discussing her small recollection *The Christmas of the Phonograph Records* (1966) with Bruce Nicoll of the University of Nebraska Press.

PERHAPS MORE than anything else, the letters reveal that for Sandoz, being a serious western writer meant doing battle. She was fond of remarking that whereas some people were promiscuous about marital partners, she was promiscuous about publishers. Eventually she had nine; at the end of her life she was still under contract to five. Her most volatile relationship was with Atlantic Monthly Press and its publisher, Little, Brown. Her letters show her at first thrilled and grateful to have won the 1935 nonfiction award and also show how quickly she became disenchanted with the press. There is a curious mixture of almost simultaneous positive and negative attitudes. Shortly after receiving the award, she wrote to Edward Weeks, "I can't thank you enough for understanding our westernisms" (June 14, 1935, Sandoz Collection, UNA). But shortly thereafter she was telling people that her ten days in Boston, while the editor and she went over the manuscript word by word, had been about the most harrowing experience of her life. The continuing questions and emendations in the next few months reinforced the feeling that her world and that of Boston were almost incompatible.

The next few years, during which she was lionized in the East as a new and exotic author, were exhilarating — she was probably as euphoric at this time as she ever was. Never again would she write with the enthusiasm and frank pleasure about the literati of the metropolitan East as she did in the letters telling of her introduction to the critics, writers, and publishers during her first two visits East in 1935. At the same time, and perhaps symptomatic of her reservations about and hostility to the establishment, she suffered more severely from her migraines than ever before or after. The pain was so excruciating while she was in New York in November that she caught an early flight back to Lincoln, canceling meetings with friends old and new.

Although migraine is too complex a medical condition to attribute entirely to one cause, stress had much to do with the headaches she had suffered from since infancy. So severe were her attacks that she would be incapacitated for two to three days a week. Eventually she found a medical remedy to control the migraines, but that would not occur until some time after *Old Jules* was published and she had had some continued success with her writing.

Because she was eager to have *Old Jules* published, and probably in part because of her lack of experience in working with a prestigious press, Sandoz made a number of compromises in the book, but she was not happy about it. Almost from the beginning she criticized the press in letters to her friends, notably to Paul Hoffman, himself an editor there. When Paul left Atlantic Monthly Press not long after, Sandoz not only congratulated him but also bewailed the fact that she did not see how she could honorably break her contract giving the Atlantic an option on her next book. That book was *Slogum House*.

Whenever Editor Weeks questioned any part of that book Sandoz responded angrily, and before long Alfred R. McIntyre, the president of Little,

Brown, the Atlantic Press publisher, was involved in the discussion. Both Weeks and McIntyre wrote long, patient letters to her, but she was difficult to mollify. By this time, two years into the relationship, she realized that it was more difficult than she had at first imagined for their East and her West to meet.

Less and less happy with Atlantic Press, Sandoz found more and more to complain of—often, however, to someone other than the company. Letters to Jacques Chambrun, her literary agent for short stories, conveyed many of the complaints, as did those to Paul Hoffman and others. After publication of her third book, *Capital City,* which she felt Atlantic Press had not promoted as well as it should have, she found a way out. She offered the press a collection of her short stories; when the Atlantic rejected it she determined that she had carried out the requirements of her contract and she found another publisher for her next book, *Crazy Horse.* As a neophyte author, Sandoz may well have taken that option clause much too seriously, thereby causing herself several years of unnecessary anguish.

Alfred A. Knopf, where Paul Hoffman was now an editor, contracted for *Crazy Horse* in 1940, and at first Sandoz thought she had found publishers she could work with. But conflicts arose during publication, and shortly afterward Hoffman left Knopf for Westminster in Philadelphia. Mari and Blanche Knopf, her next editor, could not agree, so she set about looking for another. Dial published her *The Tom-Walker,* but that was all. At McGraw-Hill she had an old friend, Edward Aswell, formerly at Atlantic Monthly Press, as editor for *Cheyenne Autumn,* but by the time *Miss Morissa* was at the press in 1955 he had gone. The man now in charge was once more an easterner, and her letters to the publishers emphasize her dismay that that book was badly handled too.

Sandoz did not maintain her anger at Atlantic Press, as her amicable letters during the 1940s to Edward Weeks and other editors there attest. She assumed they were to publish *The Tom-Walker;* when, for reasons now unclear, the arrangement fell through, she was once again angry, but when her *Cheyenne Autumn* was ready, she tried Atlantic again. At the manuscript's rejection, she blamed her agent rather than the press.

The letters between Sandoz and her later editors and publishers show a more experienced and tougher author. With the exception of her troubles with Clarkson Potter, who published *Son of the Gamblin' Man* in 1960 (in her mind the most disastrous of any of her publishing relationships), she had considerably more influence on the fate of her books.

Hastings House, specializing in Americana, was from the beginning more sympathetic to her point of view than earlier publishers had been. But Hastings too sometimes failed to produce as well or as promptly as she expected, and she pulled no punches when she felt disappointed. She also introduced a weapon that she used more than once: the threat to quit writing and take on another kind of work. It might be teaching, lecturing, or serving as a regular member of a TV quiz show. At any rate, in every case she was coaxed back to writing, and she usually won the concession she sought.

Eventually Sandoz was invited to write for Lippincott, Harpers, and others and worked with their editors amicably, but it seemed that with each book she was confronted with a different and frustrating problem—not always due to the fact that she was a westerner working with easterners but often enough to make it obvious that there were different points of view or standards. Once it was a cartographer, whose map got into *The Buffalo Hunters* without her supervision; he located Bismarck, misspelled, in Minnesota. More than once it was an officious copy editor, who in one instance substituted an incorrect date and on other occasions changed spellings and thus meanings (*breaks* for *brakes,* for instance). Often there was trouble with Sandoz's use of language. She knew she was an expert in this field and took umbrage whenever there was tampering. Even the artwork and photographs were at times inaccurate.

Sandoz's correspondence shows quite a different relationship with the University of Nebraska Press. She was always concerned for its success, but it was against her better judgment that she agreed in 1957 to let the press publish a collection of her short work to help its faltering finances. She could not imagine that there would be interest in her early work. She wrote to Virginia Faulkner (August 8, 1957), "I am also struck . . . with the inadequacy of my short writings as any gauge to me as a writer, or at least I hope so." That *Hostiles and Friendlies* (1959) was so successful was because of Faulkner's skillful editing, according to Sandoz. Later, when her friend Bruce Nicoll was director of the press, she became an unofficial advisor, and her letters regularly and enthusiastically proposed books for the Bison Books imprint of paperbacks. One of her first suggestions was John G. Neihardt's *Black Elk Speaks,* at that time out of print and remaindered. Until her death, she kept close ties with the University of Nebraska Press, but even here she occasionally had to correct interpretations of her language. "Never say 'milch' cows about cattle on western ranches," she once was compelled to inform the press (Sandoz to Virginia Faulkner, January 20, 1959, Sandoz Collection, UNA).

About agents Sandoz was somewhat less critical, but she sometimes was at odds with them too. One of the earliest letters in the collection is written to a New York agent, who she hoped would take her as a client because she was so unsuccessful in selling her short stories herself. This attempt had no result, but she was successful later in hiring Margaret Christie, just starting her own agency and willing to take on an unknown. Christie's one success, selling Sandoz's two-part "The Kinkaider Comes and Goes" to *North American Review*, brought typical Sandoz comment. She wanted to know what she had done right, so she could continue to sell her work.

In spite of a consistent effort on Christie's part, and in spite of Sandoz's making changes in many of her stories at Christie's suggestion, there were no more sales. Sandoz rather abruptly terminated that relationship, striking out once more on her own. Although she engaged other agents later—Jacques Chambrun and Harold Ober after *Old Jules* came out, McIntosh and Otis when she became disenchanted with Chambrun and Ober—she pointed out to a friend that she herself sold almost all her books. The agents took care of the contracts and details.

In 1950, when Sandoz engaged McIntosh and Otis, a company staffed by women, she finally found the personnel to her liking and agents she felt were truly in sympathy with her work; in the years of correspondence between author and agent, there is not one letter critical of McIntosh and Otis. Sandoz began working with Elizabeth Otis, the president, but shortly Mary Abbot, who specialized in handling longer works, was assigned to her. This arrangement lasted the rest of Sandoz's life. There is no evidence in the letters to indicate whether they shared any social life other than the regular luncheons, teas, and cocktail parties related to business, but the association between agent and client was obviously compatible.

Mary Abbot worked actively in Sandoz's behalf; perhaps her most notable contribution was her introducing Walter Frese, the president of Hastings House, to the author. Hastings House wanted Sandoz to write a book about buffalo hunters; it was Mary Abbot who promoted the idea. Sandoz was at first reluctant to take on a book at a publisher's order; *The Buffalo Hunters* was not in her original plan for the Great Plains series. But in spite of problems with copy editors and cartographers, Sandoz found the Hastings House people good to work with, and subsequently they published the following two books of her Great Plains series, as well as *These Were the Sioux* (1961) and *Old Jules Country* (1965).

Sandoz apparently went to McIntosh and Otis because she felt the agents were competent and not because the company was made up of women. To her, the division between the sexes in American society was artificial. She was familiar with the psychological theories discussing the importance of sex, but she had little tolerance for them. Sex, she said, was important to everyone, but other drives were even more so (Sandoz to *Harper's*, October 19, 1932). She stressed more than once that gender differences in people were less significant than other characteristics. Why, she asked David Susskind, did the guests on his television show concern themselves so much with "this childish division of mankind down the middle" (March 22, 1961)? Nor did she believe that either sex should have special treatment. She had made her own way in a world dominated by men, knew other successful women at the University of Nebraska and in the business and art worlds, had seen women succeed on the frontier of her youth. She had some sympathy with organized women's groups attempting to give women better opportunities, but she did not wish to be involved with them. Although she had argued with her father during World War I days that women should have the vote, her later energies were directed to another group of underprivileged, the American Indian. Her admiration was directed toward individuals who succeeded or were creative, whether male or female. She could be just as angry with Blanche Knopf, the president of Alfred A. Knopf, as she was with Edward Weeks. She was as persistent in giving help and information to Father Peter J. Powell in his Cheyenne Indian research as she was to Marguerite Young in her long years of writing *Miss MacIntosh, My Darling*. Her friends and associates were chosen because of mutual interests and included both men and women.

It is true that most of the historical characters she wrote of were men; in the mid–twentieth century, historical focus was still, in the main, on what men had done. The most obvious comparison can be seen in the time and attention she gave to the stories of her father and mother. Old Jules himself consumed her interest for years, with the resulting book named for him. Her mother, who, she claimed more than once, was typical of the heroic women of the frontier, was the subject of one article. On the other hand, among her memorable fictional characters, both villainous and heroic, are several women: Gulla, Miss Morissa, and Lecia in *Winter Thunder* (1954).

THE READER of Sandoz's letters in the University of Nebraska collection must keep in mind that the author herself intended that they be read and used for study. They are, of course, an extension of her personality, but of only a carefully guarded, usually controlled part of that personality. Nevertheless, they are a valuable resource for exploring Sandoz's professional life and the world in which she lived. Through her own retrospective letters she furnished glimpses of her youth, growing up in a family and a culture antagonistic to her literary aspirations; of even more value, perhaps, are her letters written about contemporaneous circumstances, from personal situations to world events.

The letters delineate Sandoz's eventual success in her chosen field as a well-established literary and historical authority, but they also are a valuable record of the many obstacles she faced. Although she eventually came to terms with most of the eastern publishing world, she could comment to Bruce Nicoll as late as 1963 that she would like to write about the destructive influence of publishers on the writing of the 1940s through the 1960s "and on the paucity of criticism in America except the monastic type from the colleges, written for other monastics and their employers" (July 7, 1963).

In addition to elucidating the history of Sandoz's career as a western writer and historian, her correspondence also points up problems in the broader field of western writing, for her experiences, her struggles and successes, reflect those of others in this genre. Mary Austin fulminated against the East; Vardis Fisher was often without a publisher for his books and railed at what he called the immature eastern establishment for its ignorance of and patronizing attitude toward the West. Walter Van Tilburg Clark reputedly was devastated by critics. Alan Swallow eventually started his own western press in order to publish outstanding western writers. Other western writers did as Willa Cather and Mari Sandoz did, moving to the East in order to write about the West. Sandoz's letters thus give us the portrait of an individual's literary life, and they illuminate the broader perspective of western writing as well.

LETTERS OF *Mari Sandoz*

To Robert Baldwin

Lincoln, Nebraska

1126 Q Street
February 23, 1928

My Dear Mr. Baldwin:

I do not see what effect I have had upon the development of Lincoln. However, if you desire what information I can give you, you are welcome to use it.

I am a member of the Jules A. Sandoz family of Sheridan County Nebraska. My mother's maiden name was Marie Fehr. I attended country school, business college, and the University of Nebraska, where I lack a few hours of graduation, not over one semester's work. I am a member of Chi Delta Phi, women's literary organization. I have taught rural school, done stenographic work, been English assistant in the university, and am now in the editorial offices of the American Educational Digest, strictly writing.[1] I write short stories under my name and under various pen names. My religious preference is the Methodist church, and I am a Democrat, with reservations of liberalistic leanings. My residence in Lincoln has been fairly constant for the last eight years. The only bid for distinction that I could attempt is my inclusion in O'Brien's roll of honor of American Writers, and nobody knows that Mr. O'Brien exists, far less that he compiles rolls of honor.[2] My office address is 1126 Q Street, my home address is 1226 J, telephone B 3146.

If this has bored you and not profited you, remember you *insisted.*

I wish you success in your rather daring adventure.

Sincerely,

1. *American Educational Digest,* later titled *School Executives Magazine,* was published in Lincoln. MS was with the journal from 1927 to 1929 and became assistant editor in 1929. Her name (Marie Macumber) was on the masthead from February 1929 to September 1929.

2. Edward J. O'Brien edited the annual *Best Short Stories and the Yearbook of the American Short Story* from 1914 to 1940 (New York: Small, Maynard; Dodd, Mead; Houghton Mifflin). MS eventually had three stories on his roll of honor: "The Vine," *PrS* 1.1 (January 1927); "Old Potato Face," *PrS* 2.1 (Winter 1928); and "Pieces to a Quilt," *NAR* (May 1933).

To August Lenniger

Box 922, Lincoln, Nebr.
August 30, 1928

My dear Mr. Lenniger:

I have decided that I need a literary agent. I may be mistaken — what I need may be a junk man. If that is true, well, I should know it, and now.

I have thirty some stories in what seems to be a completed stage. These range from the 1,500 word "short" to a 10,000 word story that is rather interesting in spite of its length. These stories range from mere flippancies to the acutely painful story, represented by "The Vine" which pleased Mr. E. O'Brien sufficiently to bring my name upon his Roll of Honor, if that means anything.

In addition to the mess enumerated, I have a novel in its embryonic and cynical stage, and some essays, informal, on informal subjects.[1] I spend eight hours a day in the editorial offices of the Digest, where I read, revise, and ghost write manuscripts, including the editorials for the editor, whose activities are generally restricted to handling the office correspondence and editing what I write.

My life began in the homesteading era of the Sand Hills of western Nebraska, when the professional killer officially deleted the ranks. I learned to ride, shoot, and drive wild horses. Also to toss bewildered rattlesnakes from the hay I was stacking if they were so unfortunate as to be thrown up to me. I have charge, also "ghost" of the short story writing course offered by the University of Nebraska by extension. In addition to all of that, I — sh — have taught country school. Of course I want information concerning your service.

Sincerely,

1. This first novel, titled variously "Ungirt Runner" and "Murky River," was never published.

To *The Forum*

January 1, 1929

Editorial Offices
The Forum
Gentlemen:

I have submitted short stories to the Forum before but they were invariably backed by a Sandhill locale, something apparently very distasteful to the editorial world. And that is as it should be. If I cannot make that land beautiful or significant enough to sell despite all prejudices, I should go on, unheard except in my capacity as associate editor of the Digest.

But "The Dime" has a small city locale, and for that reason, I am moved to try it, rather than the forty odd stories that contain too much sand.

Sincerely,

To Margaret Christie

June 29, 1929

My dear Miss Christie:[1]

You really can't suspect what boredom you are wishing upon yourself and your readers when you say you wish to see *all* my stories. I will, however, send you six or eight sandhill stories as soon as I get time to look them over, sometime during the next week. They haven't been out of the files for ages, have been keeping company with FEARBITTEN. I assume that you prefer stories with my special locale. I have many others.

I am interested in what you say about FEARBITTEN.[2] I see that you are probably right—that in my last revision I considered story more than emotional content. The carbon is in the hands of a globe-trotting friend of mine, and while I have the major changes on an old carbon, I couldn't hope to do justice to the story from that. Will you please return the Old Lady to me? I'll sharpen the drama from page 12 on. Mr. Allen at Harpers said nice things about the original draft of that story, which is three years and about a score of revisions ago.

You and the market are to set the price of anything that you can sell, which I still doubt, ungrammatically but emphatically. If there ever is a time when I can hope to set a price, that will be soon enough to worry about values from my end of the business. I don't seem to have a very definite notion of your method of compensation—.

Your frankness is admirable, but I see no need for apology. I believe in youth, either in age or in a field. It has a zest that overcomes what might well be insurmountable obstacles to experience.

About coming to New York—I have been advised by several writers who have made their mark, as the advertisements say, to go to New York, not because it is usually done, but because my definite "sandhilliness" lends authenticity to my locale. At the present it is impossible. If I ever dare resign my deadening business of writing educational bromides and voodooisms, I am coming. Besides, there is a sister in college who depends upon me for financial augmentation.

Sorry. I have never written a play, that is, what was intended as a play. I am writing a story now, very sophisticated and very naive, which is told almost entirely by dialogue. I feel the need of the practice, as I am no Hemingway, and so the first draft is play-like. But I have no plays.

Your frankness and sincerity are very pleasing, as is your enthusiasm. I hope it isn't misplaced. Please do not feel that you need to explain that you can't write every few days. I've been in the business world too long to imagine that I am quite the center of the universe.

By the way, I am sending some copies of the Prairie Schooner that contain copies of my stories, also a bit about my father. I hope that you won't let me bore you to extinction.

Sincerely,

P. S. When my first novel is ready, sometime during October or November, I hope, do you want a look at it? M.

1. Margaret Christie (1872–1967) was suggested as a literary agent to members of Quill, a women's writing club in Lincoln, by Dr. Leo Jacks, a professor of classics at Creighton University in Omaha and an active member of the Nebraska Writers Guild.

2. Also called "Hounds of Fear," this short story won honorable mention in Harpers' Intercollegiate Short Story Contest in 1926. It went through many revisions but was not published in MS's lifetime. It can be found in Caroline Sandoz Pifer, ed., *The Making of an Author: From the Mementoes of Mari Sandoz* (Gordon, Nebr.: Gordon Journal Press, 1972).

July 11, 1929

My dear Miss Christie:

Evidently *Argosy* did not want "The Smart Man."[1] I am frankly glad because I have enough Sandhill characterizations and conflicts for a volume—some day, and I would regret the necessity of having to give Argosy credit for the publication of any of them. The lesser ones—well, I don't care where they go. I don't intend to use them any more if they do sell.

Of the attached stories, "The Swan Song" is based upon actual occurrences.[2] Killers were "kept" on many ranches or else were immediately available in Western Nebraska until about 1912. The last homesteader shot in our locality was my Uncle, Emil Sandoz, shot at sundown while milking his cow. That was in 1907. I remember the excitement, the attempt to form a posse, the fear of being mixed into the affair, with further killings and the fruitless search, since darkness and the hills make a strong protagonist. The killer was finally caught, through his carelessness, in Oklahoma, tried here, and spent two and one-half years in the penitentiary. Not a profitable deal at $500 a man. That was also the first conviction in our district. It was commonly considered that the man was a bungler, or he would have been turned scott free. Before that, killers were rather more than tolerated. Often they were the most likable sort, friendly to everyone, even to their victims—who were usually given a choice between leaving or fighting it out.

"Fearbitten" arrived.

Stories will come to you as rapidly as I can find time to look them over. Do you prefer any special type first?

Sincerely,

1. Published in *PrS* 33.1 (Spring 1959).

2. Sometimes titled "Swan Song of Simmons Flat," this was never published, but the material appears in *OJ* and elsewhere.

July 17, 1929

My dear Miss Christie:

I made an attempt at revising FEARBITTEN but found that there was little that I could honestly do without subordinating the man's plunge into the night. I tried another dramatic situation but through it, the contrast between the comparative lull and the climb to the exit was lost, and I am so fond of contrasts in any art! If you feel dissatisfied with it now, return it and I'll add another contribution to my hopeless chest.

Probably the SWAN SONG IN SIMMONS FLAT and THE TWO JASPER RINGS have reached you by this time. That, with the attached FEARBITTEN, makes seven stories, I believe, in your hands, and they cover, in a general way, every type of narrative that I have to offer except the alleged humorous and the American magazines are tragic with that type of thing now, so I'll withstand any urge I might have to place mine.

Have you had any encouragement for my work?

Perhaps the wiser course would be to hold the rest of my stories here for the present. It seems such a waste of your time and my postage to send them all on a futile trip to New York. If you find those you have unsalable, there seems little reason to expect the rest to be of greater commercial value. In the meantime I am losing my contacts with editors, contacts that cost much time and effort.

I hope that New York isn't too unbearable this summer.

Sincerely,

September 5, 1929

My dear Miss Christie:

Well, back to the city—and I am being very curious—what has happened to my brain products during the last two weeks?

I am sorry that I could not write sooner, especially regarding my reaction to the article in the *Century*, but I found myself in the most impossible situation! I went to the Sandhills to gather material. When I arrived at home, haying was not done, the fruit was being picked, with miles of hot yellow sand, ankle deep, to be waded up and down the orchard rows Sundays and week days alike from six in the morning to dark. There was scarcely time and never the inclination for more than a glance at the lovely russet bunchgrass blowing in undulations up long hills and across mauve gullies. Then there was a three weeks' laundry to be done—hay hands' greasy shirts and overalls—all in the hot sun on a wash board.

My mother absolutely squelched my getting information. She is as antagonistic to my writing as ever. So we wisked her off for a three-day trip, hectic as a ginned kaleidoscope, through the Black Hills. So here I am, raw with sunburn and callouses until the mere contemplation of action brings waves of aches. I shall have to reconstruct the scenes of "Old Jules" from memory, which is too bad.

Thanks for letting me see the note from The Country Gentleman. I suppose arousing "some rather heated controversy" in an editorial office is something, but it's not enough. I am, of course, always pleased with such notes even though I've learned to know all the adjectives "by heart" long ago.

"What Makes Teachers Cranky" in the August *Century* is in no way overdrawn, nor is the writer, in my opinion, an alarmist. Those of us who have been even remotely connected with public education and have given the matter any thought at all are aware of the situation—and disturbed or frankly cynical. I wonder, however, if the cause does not lie deeper than emphasis on buildings or organization. It would be comparatively easy to shift emphasis; to change the educational philosophy practiced in a nation is more difficult.

Public education in America, I fear, has become the world's prize voodooism. Its fetishes are many,—extracurricular activities, exploratory courses, vocational guidance, citizenship practice, and so on and on. Its voodoo words are impressive—integration, socialization, standardization, individualization—without a visible end. At frequent intervals these are repeated pompously to impress subordinates and the public. Even the voodooisms of the Rotarians: Service, Idealism, Achievement, Cooperation, etc., have been annexed by the enthusiastic high priests who administer, measure, counsel, and guide the public school charges, all with a high hand and an absolutism seldom equalled even in the history of religion. Public education also has its evangelistic outposts — institutes and teachers' meetings of various kinds — where missionaries are sent to spout undigested but none the less extensive banalities and stupidities, with much flattery, in the face of the teacher audience, compelled to attend. Even though these speaking tours draw some of the high names of the country, who can deny that this sort of thing is mostly emotionalism, sporadic "pepping up" all with a vocabulary of many syllabled abstractions that would make the tent meeting artist green if he heard them?

But, someone says, this state of things is the fault of the public. Is it? Or is the public, at least to a large extent, the product of the community educational leadership, or lack of it? The expenditures of the public school system of America are surely great enough to justify such an assumption if the effects are sometimes vague. The attitude, the entire outlook of the school administrator is too often the result of fallacious training by our pseudo-psychologists, our teacher training institutions, and the educational press. He follows these too closely, and why not? Are not they, presumably, the final authorities on the dwelling place of education and the mode of its attainment — not dispensation, as pop or goupe sundaes — but attainment? And all except a mere handful of educational psychologists, the few genuine searchers after truth, hope to remedy the recognized evils of universal standardization in the classroom by that synonymous procedure — universal individualization! Can much be expected of their further suggestions?

As for the teacher training institution — Dr. Judd knows and tells us freely what is wrong with them. In addition to his good natured condemnation I want to say that to me most of the teacher training institutions seem the worst voodooism dispensers imaginable. It is one thing to coin words and terms to be used by those who grasp their theory and spirit. It is quite another thing to cram these terms indiscriminately into the mouth of every student, without regard to the mental concept it does or does not arouse, giving him the words and the air of an expert educator with which to clothe his ignorance.

Another thing: the courses in school administration that are usually offered place so much stress upon diplomatic handling of the community that too many administrators have done everything by devious routes, entirely missing the place of legitimate diplomacy. The result is often a situation akin to the old salesman and buyer relationship. Too often all the tricks discarded by even the most obvious panhandlers have been picked up by educators and used in their absurd,—worse—ridiculous and tragic "selling" campaigns. Through these practices a false measure of executive fitness has grown up. After the recent election of Carroll Reed to the Minneapolis superintendency every educational journal, save one, that carries any news or comments on personalities gave Mr. Reed one qualification for his new position, and one only! He had been a leader in Kiwanian work in his last position as superintendent of schools!

[The remainder of this letter is missing.]

October 12, 1929

My dear Miss Christie:

Your violent reaction to VICTORIE is exceedingly gratifying to me.[1] Evidently my evaluation of the story is correct. I suspected that it would not appeal to an agent, who must, of necessity, be guided by the commercial value of a story rather than its artistic value. And that's that. Of course, I shall not change the story, nor put it aside. I shall get it into print by some expedient and keep it always before me as a mark to shoot at, a theme I can never hope to exceed, force that I shall probably never equal again if I write fifty years. As for that sort of thing harming my mind—children, dogs, and old people are still inordinately fond of me, even since I wrote the "desperate tragedy" which is not a tragedy at all, not technically, because like Clara Bow, Kate gets her man not only once but twice.

However, I do appreciate your position, and to prove it, I have written a cow country skit for you in native "talk" which is the only virtue the story possesses. My study of philology under Miss Pound, one of the editors of *American Speech* and an internationally accepted authority convinces me that the "talk" is consistent and authentic.[2] The cook is a real character. I am very fond of Shorty, who is getting stiffer in the knees but not in his tongue. As a story, I am ashamed of A COW COUNTRY CURE[3] by either name, and therein lies my tragedy—my literary taste will probably always be my undoing.

In the future I shall use better judgment in what I send to you. I am trying to concoct a story for the *Sat. Eve. Post* but I'm frankly dubious—.

Referring to the SMART MAN,[4] I have no objection to making minor changes in any of my stories if they promise a sale. If the occasion for any such changes arises, fire the mss. back to me with instructions.

Sincerely,

1. "Victorie," a long short story, won the 1929 Omaha Women's Press Club state contest award. MS continued to work with the material, based on events in her neighborhood. Parts of the story appear in *OJ;* one version appears as "River Polak," *AM,* September 1937.

2. Louise Pound (1872–1958), one of the most brilliant of the university professors, received her Ph.D. from the University of Heidelburg in 1900. The author and editor of books on linguistics, literature, education, and folklore, first woman president of the Modern Language Association, and founder of *American Speech,* she was a strong influence on MS. She encouraged MS to use the Sandhills vernacular and later often consulted her on folklore for Pound's presentations. A friend of H. L. Mencken's, Pound may have encouraged MS to send stories to him. She was one of those proposing MS for the honorary doctorate at the University of Nebraska in 1950.

3. "A Cow Country Cure" has not been identified.

4. "The Smart Man" appeared in *PrS* 33.1 (Spring 1959).

October 27, 1929

My dear Miss Christie:

I am disappointed but not surprised at Mr. Howland's decision on my reaction to WHAT MAKES TEACHERS CRANKY. I had hoped that he would choose some particular phase of my criticism and let me try an article on that. Perhaps I should have followed my inclination and written the article without permission but that seemed too presumptuous. However, if you find anyone who's sufficiently interested to give me an opportunity at an article on some phase of public education, I'd like that. If the Macumber is preferable because of its connections—let's humor them.[1]

You paralyzed my writing arm as far as the novel is concerned.[2] I just can't touch it any more without an overwhelming sense of futility. If I finish it as it is written, you'll fire it back—and I can't write it any other way, not for any amount of money that it might bring me. I'd rather stack hay or teach, or even scrub floors. Unless I can shake this lethargy there won't be a novel—ever. It all seems such a lot of work to lie around in my cabinet to yellow, and the files are full now.

Just read [Erich Maria] Remarque's *All Quiet* [*on the Western Front*] in the German. Now there's a novel. If Remarque were only ten years older! More maturity would have given him sufficient detachment to make the book one of the twenty-five greatest. As it stands it is remarkable, but I can't imagine its being published, originally, in English any more than I can [Sigrid] Undset's *Kristin Lavransdatter, ad infinitum.* In the meantime we feed on the artificial happy ending, or to show the height of our brows, on an occasional equally artificial unhappy ending and wonder why we are temperamentally so discontented with most of the world's things in our laps or where our laps once were. But what's the use?

Thanks for sending the letter from the *Century.* I am returning it for your files.

Sincerely,

Afterthought:

How about a series of four or five personal narratives, about 2500 or 3500 words in length? Something like this:

SNAKEBITE

My first trip into the sandhills proper, twenty-five miles from home. My father was bitten by a rattler. I was eleven. We had a gun, a lumber wagon, and a team of bronchs. The nearest neighbor was seven miles over the hills and I hadn't the remotest idea in which direction.

SNOWBLIND

Our first spring in the hills. The cattle that were to pay off a $1700 mortgage (it wasn't funny then) drifted away in a May blizzard. My brother, eleven, and I, thirteen,[3] followed them horseback, found, dug out, and saved all but two cows. It took us twelve hours to go seven miles and I was totally blind for six weeks, still blind in one eye.

THE KILLING

Jules Sandoz's reaction to his brother's death by the bullet of a hired killer, knowing that he, the locater, was the logical one to be bumped first because he was the locater of the family, bringing in dozens of families every year. Our fear, the ridiculous things we children did, and the shading off into comedy when the killer was caught by an absurd trick, to be sentenced to ten years in prison because Uncle Emil lived three days with a bullet in his lungs.

If you feel that there might be a market for such a series, I'll try a couple and let you see them. . . . I would, of course, be willing to give the names and addresses of various well-known people who could testify to the truth of these sketches. Papa was the only government witness in the famous Richards-Comstock cattleman case under Roosevelt, which ended in opening the entire hills to homesteaders and got local protection for them.[4] The days were hectic and there's no amount of conflict, color, and comedy.

I am enclosing a short ditty written for a class exercise under Professor [Sherlock Bronson] Gass,[5] whose article on the modern novel appeared in the *Forum* last year. He suggested that I send it to an Omaha daily, which I did, but realizing that its center of interest was weak, I never tried it further. I am enclosing it merely to give you some idea of the probable style I would employ. I am certain there can be no market for that particular one.

Well, it seems that the afterthought was longer than the forethought.

1. MS was still writing under her married name, Marie Macumber. At Christie's encouragement she changed to Mari Sandoz in 1929 and used that name both professionally and socially from that time on.

2. MS is referring to "Murky River." Although Christie urged MS to send the novel, she had commented that the last stories sent to her sounded as though MS had "metaphorically flung" her "hands against a flaccid world and found it ashes—they are not sound writing—but do read like states of mind" (October 17, 1929).

3. MS was fifteen in May 1911, Jules thirteen.

4. Bartlett Richards (1862–1911) was a target of Jules's long-standing animosity in the cattleman-settler struggles. He was co-owner of the vast Spade Ranch, stretching from Gordon, Nebraska, to Ellsworth, Nebraska, extending over eight hundred square miles. Richards and his partner, William Comstock, along with other ranchers, were convicted of illegally fencing government land and filing illegal homestead entries; they were fined and jailed. Richards died while in jail, in Hastings, Nebraska. Comstock returned to ranching after completing his sentence, but the vast Spade holdings were broken up; Jules's own Sandhills homestead was on land that had once been fenced, and he located many settlers there. See Ruth Van Ackeren and Bartlett Richards, Jr., *Bartlett Richards: Nebraska Sandhills Cattleman* (Lincoln: NSHS, 1980).

5. Sherlock Bronson Gass (1878–1945) was Professor of Journalism at the University of Nebraska. MS took his class, "Magazine Article Writing." The article MS sent Christie was "Sandhill Homes," later titled "Sandhill Sundays," first published in B. A. Botkin, ed., *Folk-say: A Regional Miscellany,* vol. 3 (Norman: U of Oklahoma P, 1931).

[To an Unidentified Friend]

November 3, 1929

My dear Lady:

I am very, very sorry to hear that you have been ill. How long has this been going on? And even in a phenomenal recovery you should not be writing much, especially things that demand introspection—.

Under no circumstances would I permit my presence where hemorrhages are the fashion. Perfectly well people are prone to them if over-exposed to me. I'm glad that I'm too far away to call. . . .

Your reaction to *Wolf Solent* is very good.[1] It is stylistically beautiful but lacks power in my estimation. However, the reading time is well spent because the style is so finished even if the critics were evidently partial. More truth and beauty, intrinsic, is to be found in many novels of lesser praise, even in unknown things like Haldeman-Julius's *Dust,* which no one knows at all.[2] *Farewell to Arms* is a vast improvement in style over the Early Hemingway but it lacks the force of, say, "The Killers." Of course, reading it immediately after Remarque's *All Quiet,* etc., in German, which lacks only ten years of maturity in the author to be one of the world's greatest twenty, *Farewell* was bound to be hopelessly subordinated. You read it in English, as I remember. I've written to Remarque and I hope he opens it, instead of burning the letter unopened, as he apparently does. Oversensitive, as a genius must be, he has thrown down his pen and refuses to write any more, saying that he has nothing to say that the world understands. What great artist ever did?

Yes, I'm reading, violently, of course, in my first taste of Utopian existence.[3] Only two or three select souls are permitted entrance without protest to my *sanctum.* Bertrand Russell's *Marriage and Morality*—which is clear and lucid if you've missed it, but is only a step or two toward emancipation from cavemen conventions.[4] I'm peering into the mist for more—regulated reproduction in laboratory incubators, growing freedom from sex engrossment—with greater freedom from crime, maladjustment, hampering laws or conventions, crowd domination—in short, a place of perfection which will seem as imperfect then as this does now. Mere contemplation of such an existence stirs me to action.

In order to see my way more clearly I hope to go to Heidelberg within the next few years for some academically free study, or as academically free study as our faulty conception of freedom permits.

Your study of style is an excellent idea and an essential one. Why should a writer pass up the opportunity to learn from the masters any more than the musician or the painter? . . .

I've stopped reading "thinking" books. Some one is always trying to commercialize Dimnet's publicity, which I consider undeserved, another heretic, you see.[5] Of course, I'm following *Don Juan* in the *Forum.* By the way, did you notice the two [Rockwell] Kents in the October issue? The "Man at the Mast" is framed and hangs over my study-work table. The original "man", I understand, was one of the two who went with Kent to Greenland this summer in the three-man sail boat which was wrecked and the men cast up on the cold and rocky coast. They had a hectic time saving themselves, almost froze and starved. One week after his return, the "man" was killed by an auto in New York. One of life's little ironies!

Well, that's about all I've to say. I'm writing my novel. The bitterness of the last two years so permeated it that I was compelled to re-do it from the first word. The improvement seems worth the bother. In one or two more months now, I'll start the second, *Old Jule,* which I will have to reconstruct from memory, because mother absolutely refused to give me one word of information or to permit me to gather any material there.[6] Customary parental accommodation and understanding. I'll never be a parent. I'll think of other ways of being nasty, more original ones, I hope. Which reminds me, my special abettor in my formulation of the conflict theories, Mr. Wilcox, has departed from the faculty and gone to Macmillans. I'm very glad for him but it's hard on the few rebels on our campus. He was a brilliant defender in time of need.

As for yourself, take things slowly and don't let your mind — temporarily freer from the physical, race itself to invalidism. That has happened, you know.

Now for the story:

It is excellent, so much sounder than the short short story usually can be. Much sounder than my last attempt, carbon enclosed, which is a mere incident. I realize that the short is not my *forte.* I believe that your story is more a *Collier* type than *Liberty.* However, I'd try L first; Colliers have so many contracted for that the chances are not so good. If these should both reject it, be of strong heart and consider the *Pictorial Review* market, also *Scribners.* The future short story, I believe, will be more compact, in keeping with our accelerated tempo of life, with all excess baggage swept away. That's the type of writing we will be compelled to turn out. *Vanity Fair* wants stories of about 1800 words. If you need more markets, there will be others by that time.

Suggestions are indicated on the carbon, and they are suggestions only. Remember that. Interrogation points mean consider changing something. On page 4 the office girl makes a discovery that's too abrupt, I believe. Shouldn't the reader feel the rising emotions in Constance more surely — and the foreshadowing of the climax? Think about it. And the headlines — make them tabloid.

The title is good enough — but not sufficiently arresting for the short. It will do, however, if nothing more attractive presents itself.

Well, be nice to yourself and stop doing whatever has caused the gallstones and the ulcers, even if it be eating.

Regards to the family, *et al.*

1. John Cowper Powys, *Wolf Solent* (New York: Harper and Row, 1929).

2. Emanuel Haldeman-Julius, *Dust* (New York: Brentano, 1921).

3. MS had quit her job in September and was attempting to write full time.

4. Bertrand Russell, *Marriage and Morals* (New York: H. Liveright, 1929).

5. Ernest Dimnit, *The Art of Thinking* (New York: Simon and Schuster, 1928).

6. Mary later relented and gave detailed interviews to MS.

To Margaret Christie

December 8, 1929

Dear Miss Christie:

Your comments on THE LAST EMBER mystify me.[1] I never dreamed that you would like anything like that. In fact, last week I burned a dozen stories as good in their peculiar various ways. Nothing remains except a few stories that I have given to a handful of loyal souls, such as everyone accumulates, no matter how unpromising their object of devotion may be.

I suppose that this seems foolish to you, and I would agree with you if I had financial backing or were free from responsibilities to those girls. As it is, they are losing their enthusiasm for college rapidly and I dare not endanger their careers further. Only a definite break with this writing business will insure them against my time-wasting habit. After all, sisters are sisters.

By January 1 I must decide definitely upon a two year contract for a school, a position I am to take February 1. In the meantime I'll attack the article for Mr. Payne.[2] I believe that I see quite clearly what he wants. So I'll spend my holiday season on that. It should be in your hands by the first of the year.

Sincerely,

1. Never published. The manuscript is in the Sandoz Family Corporation Archives at the home of Caroline Sandoz Pifer, Gordon, Nebraska.

2. Kenneth Wilcox Payne was the editor of *NAR*.

January 6, 1929 NO 1930

My dear Miss Christie:

My personal jinx is working again—this time in the shape of a bank failure, leaving me with $1.83—hardly enough to get me to Nevada, where I was to begin teaching the first of February—and live for a month without wages. While I can think of several ways to get to Nevada on that sum, none of them are compatible with the dignity required of a high school English instructor. So that's out. In the meantime I'll live on my friends, etc., until I get the novel finished, if they last that long.

Am enclosing two shorts. "Hot Iron" was at *Radio News* so long I'd forgotten it existed at all. "Lothario's Pajamas"—that's the first title I ever concocted to my taste, was at *Colliers* in 1926, in a friend's files since. I lifted it and copied it today. Quillers report that you won't handle shorts.[1] If that is true, send them back. If, however, you don't particularly object to them, I can scare up a few more, I should judge, among the acquaintances. Everything I wrote from 1924 to 1926 seems to have been abbreviated.

And, since there's no job, I'll peg away at the novel.

Hope that THE KINKAIDER COMES AND GOES arrived.

Sincerely,

1. Neither story was published. The "Hot Iron" manuscript is in the Sandoz Family Corporation Archives. "Lothario's Pajamas" is not, but the archives have a story titled "Striped Pajamas," which may be the original, retitled. Quill, a women's writing group organized in the 1920s (and still in existence), met twice a month. Members read their works and shared publication information.

To Eleanor Hinman

January 10, 1930

Dear Eli:[1]

Why did you call just when you did, just when I was reading a letter from Allie with the news that they also banked at the First State of Alliance?[2] I did feel as helplessly driven as Hardy's *Tess*. Had you called a day sooner or later you would never, in all probability, have known. And I would have been free forever from a sense of responsibility to a human being or a man-made principle. Now I must stagger on, I presume, with some semblance of notice to the Kantian duty whip that hangs over me for the remainder of my life!

Not that I'm not grateful—very, for the rope that you threw to me, but after having gone down for the last time, suffered all the misery of drowning and having arrived at that blissful state of semi-consciousness when everything has a lovely greenish translucence, to be dragged back to hard realism is not particularly agreeable. Especially not when the suspicion that chance will compel a drowning sooner or later anyway persists.

Which doesn't mean that I contemplated suicide—far from it. I had, for the first time in my life, attained a complete detachment, a disinterest in material things, the ability to see how very comical all my struggles have been. I had at last glimpsed the ideal that every hobo lives by. Misfortune had ceased to exist as that old hag has for all those who have no more to lose. Whatever happens, I have had one week of absolute freedom in a fetter-weary world.

You are gratifyingly optimistic about the N[orth] A[merican] REVIEW. I looked over the article this morning and by no stretch of imagination can I see it between the canary yellow covers of that voice of the intellectual aristocrats. And the fault does not lie with my imagination—a notoriously elastic one. Of course it will sell, the article, I mean, after I have lost interest in it. Everything comes to mere man after he ceases to desire it in this funny business we call life. That is one of the laws of the world, evidently, and another reason for my belief in a Supreme Being. No law of chance could act [with] such unfailing malice. Of course, there are the kindly souls who believe that the bitterness in the world lies in the cup of achievement—but that's saying the same thing. You don't want a thing when you get it. What difference whether the achievement brings the bitterness or the bitterness the achievement so long as they arrive simultaneously?

But I've saved one thing. It's still funny.

Gratefully,

Attached I.O.U for $50.00 due Oct. 1, 1930.

1. Eleanor Hinman (1898–1982) was one of MS's most loyal supporters. Daughter of the chairman of the Philosophy Department at the University of Nebraska, she was a journalist, poet, and novelist; she probably met MS at Quill. In the early 1920s she was a feature writer for the *Lincoln Star* and *Omaha Bee* and later became a research assistant in the College of Agriculture; she was a WAC during World War II.

2. Allie Sandoz was a second cousin. The bank at Alliance, Nebraska, had been closed, and patrons lost most of their deposits.

To Margaret Christie

February 16, 1930

My dear Miss Christie:

I am glad, glad.

Of course, I was out of town when the telegram was delivered, the second time this winter! But how I appreciated it!

I am especially glad that Mr. Payne took the sandhill article.[1] It gives us a toe-hold or, to mix my metaphors, something to point to. More than that, I have always suspected that editors, even Mr. Bridges, felt that there wasn't really such a place as the sandhills as I wrote about them. That is, I know, a serious indictment of my writing, but I'm afraid a pertinent one, if indictments can be pertinent.

Now I wonder if you will tell me one thing: What was the quality, in addition to your salesmanship, that put the article across? Trying to eliminate my faults, you see, by developing what virtues I may possess. That is good pedagogy, I hope.

I don't see how Mr. Payne made room for so much material on such short notice. However, I'm properly thankful, whatever the circumstance. In the meantime, *thank you* until something more tangible manifests itself.

Sincerely,

P. S. By the way, my street address is 1226 J Street, which might facilitate delivery of telegrams if the occasion should arise again—.

1. "The Kinkaider Comes and Goes," *NAR* (April–May 1930).

February 20, 1930

My dear Miss Christie:

Am returning Mr. Payne's letter. There is always a carbon of everything I send out, and, since the FEARBITTEN incident, always within reach of my long arm. So send the MS along and I'll tackle it immediately.

I feel confident that I can write up one of the various incidents untouched into two type-written pages. If they didn't leave me disfigured, as the snowstorm did, they are interesting. There is, for instance, a settler who burglarized us while Father was away. He was an ex-convict, we found out that through our Jim.[1] His bullet clipped a goodly nick out of my upstanding roach. The bullet still is embedded in the wall. It would have been too much to expect all that scum to carry no reptiles, as my mother said. Then there is a gorgeous prairie fire, one that began at the railroad near Bingham in the forenoon. By 3:30 PM it trailed sooty smoke over our claim, recalling the two boys that were burned to death in the Osborn, the valley north of us, in the reeds of the swamp, only a few years before. And the hail storm that peeled all our young orchard, pounded the rye, just beating down until it looked like a mowed meadow. Or the time Papa became infuriated at our neighbors, budding cattlemen, in a small way, and I, grown bold by all my experiences, jerked the rifle from his hand. If I ever faced Death, it was for the next few minutes as he stood, the muzzle of the thirty-thirty to my heart. Believe me, the Statue of Liberty does a Black Bottom daily compared to my immobility for the aeon that Father's anger lasted.

Anyway, send the MS and I'll do what I can.

Sincerely,

1. Jim was a Nebraska convict paroled to Jules for some years.

[To an unidentified recipient]

March 29, 1930

My dear Pete:

I received your letter. Yes, I was surprised, how could I have helped being surprised?

I agree—you should get married, but not to me. I'm temperamental, and haven't the slightest inclination to housekeeping at all. I hate anything domestic. You deserve a pleasant, dependable companion. I'm none of these things.

The fact that I'm not married is no indication that I couldn't be. This minute a bowl of roses stands on my table—from a man prominent in business in Omaha, a man who drives a Packard car and offers me a honeymoon trip around the world. And I'm not interested in him either. My writing is my life. Nothing else can exist. So far, I've been more successful than other writers of my age usually dare hope to be.

Peggy was right.[1] I am coming home—to gather material for a biography of Papa.

Let us forget your letter, say nothing about it, and go on being nice acquaintances.

Sincerely,

1. "Peggy" was a family pet name for MS's youngest sister, Caroline.

To Joseph Conrad Fehr

April 1, 1930

My dear Mr. Fehr:[1]

I must apologize. In my enthusiasm over your letter I dispatched it to Mother, without keeping a notation of your address. (That's not a Fehr trait—rather a seeping in of the French from the West). And Mother, with the best intentions in the world, could not return it before last week. Living forty miles from a railroad with only semi-weekly mail service in *nice* weather does have its disadvantages, especially during such winters as this Our Lord 1929–30.

Mother considers you a very interesting Swiss—but then who isn't interesting, etc.? Even the bleary eyed old Berner from whom I buy my evening paper had his "high" moments.

Your career has been an interesting one. A newspaper fluency, law clarity of thought, and native ability to turn a fine phrase—what an excellent combination! The government bulletin you sent reveals a splendid command of argumentative English. You have done so much.

My preference is short story writing, but because the Family disapproved of writing as a career for a woman, I assumed a pen name, Marie Macumber, which I used for a considerable length of time before the truth "outed."[2] Under that title I made O'Brien's Roll of Honor of American short story writers in 1927—and nothing much else. But before Father died he asked me if I would write up his experiences, which I am doing, in a fictionized biography. I suppose that you are heartily tired of that sort of thing. Well, so am I, but it might be made fairly interesting and my narrative style isn't quite as lurid as you would suppose.

Have you ever tried fiction? But of course you have, who hasn't? I should ask: Do you prefer to deal with facts and ideas? Somehow, I assume that you like abstract topics. Philosophic discussions are my pet reading, but of course I would never attempt to write that sort of thing.

Thank you—If I ever pass through Washington, I shall call on you for a moment, and be delighted to have the opportunity.

Sincerely,

1. J. C. Fehr, a lawyer in Washington, D.C. MS was interested in whether they might be related; her mother's maiden name was Fehr.

2. This is MS's first explanation for changing her name.

To Margaret Christie

June 6, 1930

Dear Miss Christie:

Your suggestions for a story to enter in *Scribners* contest is doubtless a good one but it would require two months of full time and several thousand dollars worth of material—all on a very, very risky gamble. So long as I must do proof reading for my existence I can't undertake such a task even if I cared to do so. The *N. A. R.* article cut the heart from my material with certainly very little profit to me.

No. I've spent nine months trying to write to another's measure—the last hour I'll ever waste in that way.

And that goes for revision upon outside suggestions unless I have some definite agreement that the revision has a good chance of acceptance.

July 1, 1930, ends one year, approximately, of our business relationship, a most unfortunate one for both of us. I suggest that unless something tangible materializes by that date, the relationship be definitely terminated.

Sincerely,

To Kenneth Wilcox Payne

North American Review

June 21, 1930

My dear Mr. Payne:

As Miss Christie seems to have blown up with a bang audible even out here, I take the liberty of eliminating the middleman.

Would you be interested in an article of about 3000 or 3500 words called "Stalking the Ghost of Crazy Horse in a Whoopie"?

Eleanor Hinman, daughter of Dr. Hinman, head of the Philosophy Department, University of Nebraska, is writing a fictionalized biography, book length, of Crazy Horse, an Indian war chief killed at Fort Robinson. In the eyes of the Indian he was murdered and it appears that the Indian saw straight that day. But in order to find the truth and the motivation, if any, for the apparently deliberate miss-interpretation by the scout and interpreter, Frank Grouard and the still more apparently silly confidences and fears of General Crook which ended in the killing of Crazy Horse after he and his people had "come in" and surrendered their arms, we shall do some personal research work. We intend to interview all the Indians, scouts, and military men available who were in any way connected with the killing or the incidents leading up to it.

We are going in an old Ford, a creature unfamiliar to both of us. The trip will cover a call at the Rosebud Reservation, S. Dak., where an old priest who is writing a dictionary of the Dakotah language resides.[1] Then to the Pine Ridge Reservation, also in South Dakota, where Old He Dog, one of the few surviving members of the fraternal organizations to which Crazy Horse belonged, resides. He is blind, speaks no English, but has a vivid memory. From there we go to Sheridan, Wyo., to interview some old timers, and then on to the Custer Battlefield and the locale of the Battle of the Rosebud, both in Montana. Fortunately we have access to the pictograph manuscript, the sole surviving Indian history of those battles, which Helen Blish is deciphering for the Carnegie Foundation.[2] Our trip covers the Fourth of July celebration at Pine Ridge, with its mixture of Indian war dances, reading of the Declaration of Independence, broncho busting, Indian wrestling and feats of strength, concession grafts, and barbecued beef, bunting, and bootleg. Altogether the event is reported very colorful if the bi-annual rain doesn't hit the reservation the Fourth.

We hope to keep our feet clear of the Indian agents but of course, we won't. No one ever has. Their fingers are in every pie except possibly the ton of the Eskimo variety that will be consumed during the celebration.

I have neglected to thank you for the fine way you handled my article on the Kinkaiders.[3] It was well received here, although there was some disgruntlement evident among the cattlemen after the first installment. But after the second came out all was peace once more.

While in an editorial position I learned how vastly important an occasional subscriber reaction to the contents of the magazine can become. I suppose that not even the *North American Review* is entirely aloof. If not, I wish to say that the June number gave me more satisfaction, stimulation, entertainment, edification and, if I may use that much maligned word, inspiration, than I imagined possible in so small a space. "Hungry River" by Overbeck is one of the few magazine short stories that pleased my jaded taste. As my chief and almost constant dissipation is short story reading, or giving courses in their writing, I am rather blasé. Even so, I was delighted with "Hungry River." Spots in that are superbly done.

About the article again: We are leaving the first of July. If you can, will you use the enclosed stamped envelope and let me know your reaction? I might as well slant my material as I collect it for my possible markets.

Thank you.

Sincerely

1. Father Eugene Buechel, S.J. (1874–1954), a Catholic priest at St. Francis, South Dakota, published *A Grammar of Lakota: The Language of the Teton Sioux Indians* (St. Louis: John Swift, 1939).

2. Amos Bad Heart Bull, *A Pictographic History of the Oglala Sioux*, text by Helen Blish, introduction by Mari Sandoz (Lincoln: U of Nebraska P, 1967).

3. "Kinkaiders" were people who settled on claims made available through the Kinkaid Act of 1904, which allowed settlers in northwest Nebraska 640 acres, more than in previous acts, because Congress recognized that the area was not well adapted to intensive cultivation.

To the *New York Times*[1]

1226 J Street,
Lincoln, Nebr.,
January 21, 1931

Gentlemen:

Would you be interested in a 3000 to 4000 word article, "Stalking the Ghost of Crazy Horse," to be used as you see fit, and with a large number of good illustrations, photographs taken in 1930?

Last summer Miss Hinman, whose father is head of the philosophy department, University of Nebraska, and I made a 3000 mile trip in a $45 ford through the old Sioux country: Rosebud and Pine Ridge agencies, the Black Hills, Rawhide Creek and Powder River, Wyo., and the Crow and Northern Cheyenne Reservations in Montana. We camped on the ridge along which Custer's men retreated, burned out our clutch band in Reno Creek, and saw the canyon where the battle of the Rosebud took place, reported to be both "deep, dark, and tortuous," and "at no place less than two miles wide," which we found to be neither.

But our main interest was Crazy Horse, the Ogalala war chief said to be the first to break the lines of Custer and later bayonetted through the kidney at Fort Robinson after he had been promised security, the victim, we suspected, of betrayal by his own people. But as Miss Hinman is writing a biography of Crazy Horse, we needed evidence. So we lived among his people, interviewing the old warriers, through interpreters, particularly He Dog, a fellow chieftan, and the followers of Red Cloud, who had had reason to fear supersession by the younger Crazy Horse. We uncovered much new material, were suspected of being spies from Washington tracing the guilt of the Custer affair, saw the first Sundance permitted at Pine Ridge since the Ghost Dance troubles of 1891, and ended by being called the grand daughters of He Dog. We stood on the spot where Crazy Horse fell, heard the modern soldier's opinion of Custer. "He was looking for Indians; he found them," Capt. Ginsburgh told us. "A general is never surprised."

But it was at night, out upon the sagebrush plains of the Rawhide where the brown-haired, never photographed chief had hoped to establish a refuge for his people that we seemed closest to the spirit of this silent, powerful war chief of the Ogalalas.

I believe that your readers would be interested, particularly now that vacations, with the hope of something different, come to mind. We got far from the tourist routes, were stared at, questioned, and treated with the fine courtesy of the uncommercialized Indian. We saw something of his struggles, heard his hopes and dreams.

Perhaps I should say, by way of reference, that a two-part article on my western childhood appeared in the North American Review, April and May, 1930.

Sincerely,

1. Similar letters were sent to *Omaha World-Herald, Chicago Tribune, Portland Oregonian,* and *Boston Transcript.*

To Mr. Smith, Credit Manager

Gold and Company
Lincoln, Nebraska

April 23, 1931

My dear Mr. Smith:

I am writing regarding my account of approximately $15, long overdue. This bill I had hoped to pay when due but the publishing market went to pieces completely during the early winter and stories of mine that had been accepted were returned unused. I looked for employment but everywhere the first choice was naturally given to people having dependents or those who would be permanent. I was not particular. I would have taken anything, but it was so obvious that I would not be content to remain in an ordinary position forever that I had no success at all.

About your account: Either I can give you a note to be paid next winter or perhaps I might work it out. I do most types of office work and know a great deal about current books, what people like to read, where they can find particular information. I realize that you have a regular employment department, and also how utterly hopeless my case would be there. But I would appreciate the opportunity to work enough to settle this bill at least.

In any case I appreciate your many kindnesses in the past. The enclosed clipping will give you some idea of what I am trying to do if you are not too busy to glance over it.[1]

Sincerely,

1. Gold's response is not known.

To H. L. Mencken

AMERICAN MERCURY

May 28, 1931

Dear Mr. Mencken:[1]

Please glance over "Victorie". I realize that the story may be too long to interest you. Perhaps I'm only using it as an excuse to write, for I do want to tell you how much I enjoyed your review of Dr. Morf's new volume on Joseph Conrad.[2] Your evaluation and my consequent reading of the book help explain why I was so attracted to the author of Lord Jim and the Nigger at twelve, when my associates read Harold Bell Wright and the backless remains of Mary J. Holmes. My taste did not strike me as eccentric in a child until, as English assistant in the university here, I found that Conrad, if he was to be read by them at all, had to be crammed down the students' throats as a goose might be fattened, only the readers remained lean, at least spiritually!

Although it was years before I discovered his nationality, the Pole in Conrad evidently attracted me from the first. We lived on the edge of the Polish settlement, with the lanky Pete of "Victorie" as our playfellow. We saw but did not understand the terrific conflicts that arose as the glitter of the American environment attracted the more susceptible of the younger Poles, conflicts that must be resolved in spiritual isolation as complete as that of Conrad's characters, for these people, too, were outcasts on a sea, a sea of endless, undulating hills, stretching in yellow-green monotony toward a remote and unfriendly horizon.

In fact, we were all outcasts. My father left his beloved Lake Neuchatel because he must have room for his elbows and his gun; the Poles and Bohemians sought homes free from political oppression; the native Americans came to escape the high rentals and the sharp practices exposed in [Hamlin] Garland's "Under the Lion's Paw". Who can say how much of the shocking violences committed in the sandhills are generically related to the tragedies of Lord Jim and Nostromo?

As to the authenticity of the locale, I refer you to my two part article in the *North American Review*, April and May, 1930.

Sincerely,

1. H. L. Mencken (1880–1956), famed American iconoclast, was the contributor and/or editor of *Smart Set*, the *Nation*, and *American Mercury* as well as the author of several books. He knew a number of faculty members at the University of Nebraska, including Louise Pound and Lowry Wimberly.

2. Gustav Morf, *The Polish Heritage of Joseph Conrad* (Neuchatel: Thèse, 1930).

June 24, 1931

My dear Mr. Mencken:

After taking a very provocative course in social progress under Dr. Hertzler of the University of Nebraska,[1] I began to wonder about the growing practice of curb pick-ups in Lincoln. Surely not all of these apparently very ordinary men could be evil-intentioned, not even by my grandmother's most tight-lipped definition.

The result has been a most amusing study, if I may dignify my procedure by calling it a study. The attached article, "The Stranger at the Curb," grew out of the tables and the jottings.[2]

Because the article does not seem to lend itself to my descriptive powers, I am sending the whole to you rather than an inadequate synopsis or outline. The tables are not intended for publication. If any portion of the article seems dull or objectionable to you, I would be glad to revise or delete, as you might direct.

Sincerely,

1. Joyce Hertzler (1895–1975), Professor of Sociology from 1923 to 1961, was the author of *History of Utopian Thought* (New York: Macmillan, 1933).

2. The article was rejected by Mencken. "Stranger at the Curb," with editorial notes by Michael R. Hill, was published in *Mid-American Review of Sociology* 13.2 (1988).

To John Collier

AMERICAN INDIAN DEFENSE ASSOCIATION

July 27, 1931

My dear Mr. Collier:[1]

I am interested in the suit brought by the Sioux Indians against the United States, May 1923, particularly with the section dealing with the breaking up of the Black Hills Treaty—1868.[2]

Last summer I visited the Rosebud and Pine Ridge agencies with Eleanor Hinman, daughter of Dr. Hinman, head of philosophy, University of Nebraska. Miss Hinman is writing a biography of Crazy Horse and we camped on the reservations for several weeks, interviewing old timers through interpreters. And always there was talk of the Black Hills Settlement—with apparent problems of money distribution, if any was forth coming, talks of conferences, past and future. This summer I went back to check up on some genealogy for Miss Hinman and I was told that nothing much was accomplished last summer about the Black Hills matter—but this summer—.

Can you give me any enlightenment on the present status of the suit and the aim of the conferences and what has been accomplished to date?

It seems to me that even the generally well-informed citizen has not an inkling of the Indian situation or the tactics the white man used to reduce him to his present unhappy state. Our public is either vaguely sentimental or totally uninformed and disinterested on anything pertaining to the Indian. I, for one, don't intend to stay so. Please give me what information you can.

Sincerely,

1. John Collier (1884–1968) was long active in Indian concerns. He was the editor for *American Indian Life* from 1926 to 1933 and served at different times on the Board of Indian Affairs and the Board for Indian Arts and Crafts and as the director of the National Indian Institute of the U.S.A. He was U.S. commissioner of Indian affairs from 1933 to 1945.

2. MS was seeking information for a full-length feature article titled "Black Hills Become a Stake in a $700,000,000 Lawsuit," *Lincoln Journal and Star*, September 27, 1931, detailing the history and current status of the suit brought by the Sioux against the U.S. government asking payment for illegal seizure of the Black Hills.

To Ben A. Botkin

University of Oklahoma

September 8, 1931

Dear Mr. Botkin:[1]

I am glad that the 1931 *Folksay* is off your desk, at least until the proofs come in.[2] To bring order out of the chaos of material that must drift in, particularly at the last minute, seems a hunk of an undertaking on this day of 102 degrees with humidity.

About "Sandhill Sundays"—"logey" strikes me as a very common colloquialism. It seems to me I've seen it endlessly in western "literature" but just where I can't say today. I use it freely, in the sense of *slow, dumb, dull.* When applied to a person we say he is "logey with misery, grief, fatigue, cold, even food." Some fat farm women never wash the dinner dishes until three o'clock because they are too logey before. A "knot-head," one who seems to resist teaching, is "logey," as is anyone slow-witted. A spirited horse is never logey unless he is sick or too fat. Oxen, plow critters, are often described as "logey" by old timers who tried to cover our vast distances with them. The *o* is long, which, I suspect, prevents the double *g*. However, I won't quibble over the sound of a vowel. Spell the word as you prefer, and the chaps as well.

About the ambiguous phraseology—either you have the wrong copy of page eight or I saved the wrong carbon. Will the sentences as they stand on the enclosed carbon do? If still ambiguous, clarify them, or anything else that seems too involved for rapid reading.

All four of the personal narratives dragged back eventually. I've had four or five nice notes from Mencken this summer. He still has "The Smart Man with Hogs" but will surely return the ms. this week. "Grubline Riders" is out but you may see it again upon its return if you like.

I've read proof most of the summer, since July 25. So there has been little writing except Sunday features, which invariably sell the first time out but pay so little and are so bad for any latent talent I might possess.

I hope Mrs. Botkin is shopping freely in the grocery stores, without an inferiority complex.

Sincerely,

1. Benjamin Albert Botkin (1901–75), a graduate student under Louise Pound, was one of the preeminent folklorists of America. The editor of many collections of folklore and a professor at the University of Oklahoma from 1921 to 1940, he was national folklore editor for the Federal Writers' Project in 1938–39 and later head of Archives of American Folk Song at the Library of Congress.

2. B. A. Botkin, ed., *Folk-say: A Regional Miscellany,* 4 vols. (Norman: U of Oklahoma P, 1929–32).

To Willa Cather

October 10, 1931

Dear Miss Cather:[1]

At last I have found a book that gives me a highly significant section of life in a style that never once threatens the illusion of reality. More, it shows me new and unsuspected facets of the actualities about us. Because of this achievement, *Shadows on the Rock* becomes a part of the life the reader lives, not for the short span of the reading but for his always.

May I thank you for the rare experience?

Sincerely,

1. MS and Cather (1873–1947) apparently never met. Cather responded with a brief, one-sentence acknowledgment of MS's appreciation.

To Mr. Merriam

December 7, 1931

My dear Mr. Merriam:[1]

I was interested in your comment on the rejection slip of "The Swan Song of Simmons Flat." "Melodramatic" is a new word to add to the long list of characterizations editors have given my work—on paper to me. Just what they thought is something else again.

Unfortunately the story I sent you is a true one, and proper objectiveness comes harder in such cases, particularly as one of my uncles was shot by such a killer. Yet I admired the man who is the "Blackie" of the story.

The Sandhills is a comic-opera land, even now, and always smacks of the "Never-never" business, even to the eye. I find that quality creeps into my writing of the Hills—despite my sincere effort to be coldly objective. Even my articles are saturated with it—for instance the one in the *North American Review,* April and May, 1930, and in the one to appear in the 1931 *Folk-say,* probably off the press by now.

I don't suppose that you are interested in the "Spent Storm" sort of thing, but I'm sending it anyway. It is a sort of a synopsis of a life in the Hills. The book manuscript on Old Jules will be completed by January 15, 1932, I hope.

Thanks for the "melodramatic."

Sincerely,

1. Mr. Merriam is an unidentified editor.

To Mr. Frank G. Dodd

DODD, MEAD & COMPANY

January 28, 1932

Dear Mr. Dodd:

I am tired to death of novels that seem only painted figures on gauze or perhaps even exquisite chiffons, but transparent, lifeless save for the wind of the author's agitation. I want American novels in which the push of life thrusts itself upon the reader, even if there is only one character in a desert. For you know and I know that the push is there and to me it seems highly significant.

But enough—

The incidents and characters of *Old Jules* are historically factual. I read every newspaper of the north Panhandle from 1884, the earliest, to 1929, read all references in the larger state papers to the Panhandle from 1880 up, and compiled fifteen hundred pages of notes before I wrote a word of *Old Jules*. From this mass of information I tried to bring some reason, some pattern,—to make a book artistically and philosophically as well as historically true.

After an afternoon's discussion of my problems with the editor of the *State Journal*, Mr. Williams,[1] an old newspaper man and a shrewd and frank one, I compiled a file of fictitious names. I made some of the geographic locations vague and was not too damagingly specific in the personal descriptions of potentially dangerous characters. Throughout I've been as objective, just, and fair as it is in me to be.

The title of the book seems inadequate to me. The book purports to be one of a place and a people as well as of a man. Once I considered *Thunder in the Morning*.

Tomorrow I register in the university, going back to teaching next fall. Monday I start working for my board and shall probably eat my employer out of his home and into the poorhouse.[2]

Sincerely,

1. Frank L. Williams (1866–1943), a veteran newspaperman and an editor in central and northwestern Nebraska in the late 1800s, advised MS on the accuracy of some of her material.

2. MS may be referring to a brief stint as housekeeper for Louise Austin, a university art instructor living at the same address, 1226 J Street. It seems likely that at some time she also worked in the home of Sarah Douglas Bristow, 3041 N Street. MS and Bristow were registered in several of the same university classes in the early 1920s.

To Ben A. Botkin

[April 1932?]

Dear Mr. Botkin:

Pardon the delay. With my 14 hours of school work and the four hours a day research in Red Cloud for the [Nebraska State] Historical society, I took on another job, proof reading on the [Nebraska State] Journal at night, which just about fills up the day.

Your summer itinerary sounds most interesting. I think you will both enjoy Missoula in the summer. Let me warn you about the nights. They are not only cool but cold. . . .

The fragments [of the *Old Jules* manuscript] are enclosed, also two chapters, carbons and in scandalous shape, for I never make corrections on carbons. No one is supposed to see them. The reaction to Old Jules seems to indicate that it should be labeled a novel. Pretty strong meat, seems to be the verdict, and that seems to be one of the permissible qualifications for novels only. It's not been anywhere except to the people I knew were broke. Somehow it doesn't seem worthwhile sending anything out now, under the present conditions. I've not decided upon a novel title yet for the book. If you find that the fragments, or what you [think] are not too terrible, you may list them or whatever you use of them as you like. I am sure no chapter of the book would lend itself to reproduction intact, in *Folksay*. Do whatever you like with this business. I'll be not in the least disturbed if you find that none of it fits the 1932 Folksay, for art must be served.

If you come through Lincoln this summer, don't forget to call me up. I'd like one of our long lunch hours down at the Lincoln [Hotel] or some other quiet place and shall expect you to call when you go through and I'll arrange it. It would seem good to have one of those talk-fests. Nothing like that this winter. Just work, work.

Well, I see by the papers that they found your Alfalfa Bill this morning. I wasn't convinced he was really lost. I went to hear him last fall. Was agreeably surprised and a little envious. Our Bryan was quite subordinated by Bill and his handle-bars.[1]

Hope the 1932 Folksay is lining up nicely.

Sincerely,

1. William ("Alfalfa Bill") Murray (1869–1956) was governor of Oklahoma, 1931–35. His nickname derived from his consistent promotion of cultivation of alfalfa. A colorful, "down home" politician, he was known to contrive a number of

incidents in order to keep himself in the public eye. Charles Bryan (1867–1945), brother of William Jennings Bryan, was governor of Nebraska, 1923–25, 1931–35; mayor of Lincoln, 1915–17; and Democrat candidate for vice-president in 1924. Although he spent a lifetime in state and national politics, he never attracted the public attention and adulation of his brother.

To Mr. George Lorimer, Editor

SATURDAY EVENING POST

July 23, 1932

Dear Mr. Lorimer:[1]

The attached LITTLE BIG MAN'S HEART IS BAD is one of a series of articles on Sioux conflicts I am writing.[2]

My qualifications for this sort of work are, first, and most important, a childhood in the northwestern corner of Nebraska, where all the old timers look back to the golden days, sometimes literally golden, of mining, and Indian fighting and freighting. My father spent eight months in the hospital at Camp Robinson, Fort now, in 1884 and knew [Billy] Garnett and Little Bat (Garnier) very well. They and others about the fort helped amuse him during the long winter while a crushed ankle drained with stories centered about that region. My father had many friends among the Sioux and these spent part of every summer on the Niobrara, camped before our house. Those young Indians were our best playmates. In addition to that young start, I've spent much of the last three summers on the Pine Ridge and Rosebud agencies where many of the Oglala and the Brules are. Much of last winter I spent going through the entire Ricker Collection for Dr. Sheldon of the state Historical Society.[3]

The Ricker Collection was brought together by the late Judge Ricker of Chadron, Nebraska, which is near Fort Robinson.[4] He spent twenty years of his life gathering material for a series of works on plains Indians, interviewing every one he could find who might know anything of the conflicts and the conditions: military, traders, bad men, Indians, etc., and gathered all the historical records, reports, etc., he could. And after twenty years of this he died, without [*sic*] writing only a few sketchy bits.

My writing experience will interest you less. It varies from the associate editorship of the School Executives Magazine to writing articles for feature sections and even for the *North American Review* and short stories three-starred by O'Brien. I have also finished two novels, unpublished, and am starting a third, on the Oglalas this time.

Other articles in this series which I have planned are: The treaty of 1876, where Minor Sitting Bull, who was given a gold mounted rifle for bravery in defending the stockade in 1874, defies the Indians with his notorious three butcher-knife bladed weapon of which they are very superstitious; The killing of Conquering Bear in 1854, by the drunken Grattan over the foot-sore Mormon cow; The flagpole and Frank Appleton affairs at Red Cloud; The Killing of Crazy Horse at Ft. Robinson, and any others that seem interesting from among a long possible list, including the Fetterman Massacre, the Ghost Dance troubles, which have never been written with the undercurrent of Indian conflicts, etc.

One more word. In this article I have taken the liberty to make of the early word for whiteman, *Wasicun,* what the Indians made of it, *Wasicu* and *Wasicus,* following the whiteman's scheme of pluralization as I have heard it all my life. *Lakota,* is, as you know, the Indian name for Sioux used by the western branch that have *l* in their speech in place of the *d* of the Sioux who say *Dakota.* A variant is *Lakotah,* an earlier spelling which I really prefer.

If anything else seems to require explanation for your consideration, please do not hesitate to inquire.

Sincerely,

P.S. Illustrations for this sort of thing, I suppose, should be done by an artist rather than cuts from photographs. There are very fine photographs of Young Man Afraid of His Horses, Red Cloud, and Spotted Tail, taken while at Washington, available as guides for an artist, either there or at our historical Society. If you need these I'll make arrangements to have them sent to you. I have photographs of Crow Butte and maps of the early Camp Robinson and like things in my files, but they seem unadapted to the use required here.

1. George (Graeme) Lorimer (b. 1903) was editor of *Country Gentleman* and *Ladies' Home Journal* before coming to *SEP,* 1932–38. He returned as editor to the *Journal* in 1939.

2. Little Big Man was a Cheyenne-Oglala Sioux prominent in the Indian wars of the 1860s and 1870s. This article dealt with his behavior during a U.S. government–Indian council held in 1875 in northwestern Nebraska. The council broke up without agreement. MS revised the article many times, but it was not published during her lifetime. One version, *The Great Council,* was published after her death by her sister,

Caroline Sandoz Pifer (Rushville, Nebr.: News/Star Press, 1970). Little Big Man appears in both *Crazy Horse* and *Cheyenne Autumn.*

3. Addison E. Sheldon (1861–1943) homesteaded in western Nebraska in 1886 and was a newspaper correspondent at the time of the Wounded Knee Massacre (1890); he was a journalist for several Nebraska newspapers and the author of a number of Nebraska history books. The longtime secretary (director) of the Nebraska State Historical Society, he edited the *NH* magazine from 1917 to 1941. An active Populist in the 1890s, he served in the Nebraska House of Representatives in 1897 on the Populist ticket. He worked for a state unicameral system from 1918 until it was adopted in 1934. He encouraged MS in her historical research and writing; as her employer, he gave her a number of responsibilities.

4. Eli Ricker (1843–1926) was a lawyer, judge, editor of the *Chadron Times,* and historian in Dawes County, Nebraska. From 1905 until his death he researched local history and interviewed soldiers, Indians, cowboys, trappers, and generally anyone with knowledge of the frontier and frontier incidents. The collection in the NSHS consists of thirty-six manuscript boxes. Most important to MS were his interviews, written in pencil on Big Chief tablets. In many cases she could use the material almost verbatim. All of the people and events mentioned here appear in her books.

Editorial Offices

THE ATLANTIC MONTHLY PRESS

October 5, 1932

Gentlemen:[1]

On October four I sent you the manuscript of OLD JULES, The Man from the Running Water, which I wish to enter in your Non-Fiction Contest. To establish, in a measure at least, the authenticity of the book, I enclosed a few of the two thousand letters and documents pertaining to the main character and his community that my father, Jules Sandoz, left behind him. You may, of course, see any or all of the rest.

In addition I refer you to Mr. Frank Williams, managing editor, *Nebraska State Journal,* Lincoln, a Nebraska journalist for over forty years, beginning in the western half of the state. Mr. Williams knew Jules Sandoz personally, knew of his work and of the situation in the Panhandle. I have written many features on that section of the state for Mr. Williams's *Journal* and he usually discussed his editorials on the "cow counties" with me before writing them. Because of his canniness about libel, I showed him an early draft of the book, the only time in my life I have ever thrust a manuscript of mine upon an acquaintance. For information, then, as to my personal integrity, the dependability of the factual content of my writing and my knowledge of the locale I refer you to Mr. Williams.

For evaluation of my historical sense and my ability to check and weigh sources I refer you to Dr. Addison Sheldon, secretary of the State Historical Society, Capitol, Lincoln, Nebraska. I spent several months this spring researching in the Ricker Collection for Dr. Sheldon's forthcoming book on a great Sioux chief. He also knew my father, particularly in the early days of the late Eighties and the Nineties about Rushville and Chadron, where Mr. Sheldon was a newspaper man and a good Populist in those days.

For an estimation of my seriousness as a student of literature and literary values I refer you to Dr. Wimberly, editor, *The Prairie Schooner,* University of Nebraska, Lincoln,[2] and to Miss Louise Pound, co-editor of *American Speech,* University of Nebraska. Mr. Benjamin Botkin, Norman, Oklahoma, (University of Oklahoma) knows more of my ability or inability to take criticism and work out suggestions than any one else. Mr. Botkin, as you know, is editor of *Folksay,* a regional Miscellaney. The 1931 *Folksay* included a sketch, "Sandhill Sundays", and the 1932 is to open, I believe, with the first chapter of OLD JULES.[3]

Mr. Botkin took his Ph. D. under Miss Pound here in 1931. I spent many pleasant evenings in hot discussions of regionalism in literature with the Botkins.

As to the book itself: I spent all my spare time for five years and two full-time years on it. I followed as faithfully as I could the actual sequence of events, choosing, of course, from an unusually unwieldy profusion of events and incidents those that seemed to me most revealing and those intrinsic parts of the rhythmic pattern of life on the Running Water [Niobrara River] during the last forty years. My last ten years, spent in Lincoln, have given me some perspective, enough I hope. I have kept myself, the Marie, as subordinated as seemed possible, considering that I was somehow inextricably entangled with the rather dramatic moments of the book from my childhood on. Not, I hasten to say, and hope I made clear in the book, by intention was I so entangled, or by any volition. It seems to have been sheer chance. However, if you feel that I have intruded at any time in an unwarranted manner I shall be glad to change the emphasis. I deserve no credit other than that of narrator.

Although there was apparently no affection between us, my father somehow talked more sincerely to me, particularly when we went hunting, than was his custom. During these stories he never looked at me — almost as though he were talking to himself, without feeling any compunction to "throw in another grizzly." Perhaps it was because of my cringing cowardice from ridicule, (I'm well over that now). He could be certain that I would not laugh.

Outside of our family and the uncles, cousins, and grandparents I have used no real names except for well-known characters as Roosevelt, Governor Mickey, etc., Doc Middleton, and father's friend Nippel. There seemed no other name so good as Doc's and Nippel played such an incidental part in the story. I have a complete file of the names and their counterparts, at your disposal. I tried to improve upon them, with little success. However, I preserved the nationality, with as pronounceable a substitute as possible. For instance Staskiewiecz becomes Zaluski, not as good but sayable. Surber I called Schimmel; Westover, Eastman; Charles Schmidt, Carl Swartz; the Greens, Blacks; Sturgeon, Pike; Aubert, Acherd; Tissot, Jollet; Degaillez, Debray, etc. Jules' various wives and the members of our family fortunately had pronounceable names, without too great duplication. I preserved the actual names of the towns because Mr. Williams thought the definite localization a good point, but that would be as you desired it. The Rushville *Standard* I called the *Banner*, only slightly veiled. But nothing could hide the spiciness of that grand old gossip of the Panhandle. One side of every conflict, every bit of gossip got into its columns and no abuse was too libelous to print.

Before I wrote one word of OLD JULES I took notes on all references to the Panhandle in all the important papers of the state from 1880 to 1929, and more complete notes on every Panhandle or near Panhandle paper from its establishment to the end. The gleanings fill three heavy notebooks. All quotations from documents, letters or papers are actual specimens and the original is still in existence. Then of course I read all the frontier literature and history obtainable, with a study of frontier economics and politics. I studied the history of the west under our former dean of the arts college, John Hicks, author of THE POPULIST MOVEMENT,[4] and recently departed to Wisconsin to take the post vacated by Dr. Paxson, to our irreparable loss. Last fall and winter I went through the entire Ricker Collection, containing interviews with all the old timers the late Judge Ricker of Chadron could find in twenty years of diligent search. Most valuable were the tremendous files, no, boxes of Old Jules himself, a little moldy from the leaky flat roof of our Kinkaid home but generally intact. His habit of revising has saved many of his violent letters for me, in his own characteristically forceful push-and-pull penmanship.

From this material I worked out an outline, a skeleton of actual incidents and actual people to give as authentic a picture of a man and a community as I could. At all times I struggled for detachment, for the gossamer of reality, unpleasant, amusing, sentimental at times, tragic often as life was in our Panhandle. I tried to draw contrasts between the different waves of settlers, that swept in and receded, leaving only a few staunch rocks or poor driftwood too weak to ride the out-going tide. I tried to give the book the texture of life there, with its monotony, the dull, sordid struggle for petty existence shattered by swift events that might be either tragic or comical and none could say until the end which it would be. Large hatreds and loves were blasted; little loves, little hatreds bore large fruits. And under it all was the country of the Running Water, which never accepts the intruder unless he gives himself wholly. Even though the mowers shave the valleys, the plows and the wells disturb the surface, fires blacken it and the wind moves the dunes about nothing ever changes the land. No one who has ever been into the land has ever forgotten it. He may hate it, probably does hate it, but he can never be indifferent to it.

The two short manuscripts enclosed with this letter seem to contain the germs of further books. My preference is the Indian one, written from as nearly the Indian point of view as I can get, but the more judicious Indian, Young Man Afraid of His Horse, a great warrior and a great if deliberately humble figure on the agencies. He dropped dead at Newcastle, Wyoming, in the early twentieth century, still a comparatively young man. And to the Indians therein lies a tale also.[5]

Now I am revising a novel tentatively accepted in 1930 "if times get better by the fall of 1931." The manuscript came back and has gathered little slips with ideas for revision while I did the actual writing of OLD JULES. Now I return to the novel.

Pardon the lengthy and meandering discussion. Somehow there seems something else I should say. Perhaps OLD JULES will say the rest for me, good or bad.

Sincerely,

1. The Atlantic Monthly Press used this letter, together with a later version of April 6, 1935, in the foreword to *OJ*.

2. Lowry Wimberly (1890–1959), an English professor at the university, strongly encouraged creative writing. He founded and was for many years editor of *PrS*, the prestigious quarterly. A prolific writer himself, he was directly responsible for the publication success of a number of his students, including MS.

3. The chapter from *OJ* did not appear in the 1932 *Folk-say.* A May 16, 1932, letter from Botkin gave high praise to the *OJ* material, but in an October 11, 1932, letter Botkin told MS that he had been forced to omit her story and three others in order to keep the publication to the required three hundred pages. He added, "I am holding the story for the 1933 Folksay," but that volume was never published.

4. John Hicks (1890–1972) was a disciple of Frederick Jackson Turner. MS took his class, "History of the Frontier since 1829," in 1932. He published a number of books and essays, his most notable being *The Populist Revolt: A History of the Farmers' Alliance and the People's Party* (Minneapolis: U of Minnesota P, 1931). He was with the University of Nebraska from 1923 to 1932.

5. One manuscript cannot be identified. The other was probably a version of "The Great Council." The Man Afraid family had MS's respect; she considered them the aristocrats of the Sioux and contemplated writing a book about them.

To Mr. B. A. Botkin

October 15, 1932

Dear Mr. Botkin:

Folksay just arrived and while I've only looked through it as one might see a river from a hill top, I liked the glimpse. . . .

Anyway, I am looking forward to a fine evening with *Folksay.*

About omitting Old Jules—I was sorry because it put you into a hole. Otherwise—pfutt! What does matter? I confess now that once or twice I wished I had the courage to ask for it back. You know I never quite approved of this business of publishing parts of a book here and there. I remembere how cheated I felt when I found that I had read the best incident of *Prairie Women*[1] as a short story.

Furthermore, the book has been completely rewritten, less salable, I suspect, but I've ceased to look into the future. At last I'm writing as nearly what I want to write as my equipment permits.

I had an opportunity to go to New York and almost went but it didn't seem quite worth while. I can't see it as my business—this pushing myself, trying to "put myself across". Oh, me, how did I get on that subject.

Under no circumstances are you to feel bad about omitting any material from *Folksay.* Your first responsibility is to the book. I do wish I had known it a little sooner but I took the liberty of sending your letter to the publishers who are considering the volume now. I don't think they liked the idea and it would have been easier if I had never needed mention it. Just forget about the business. Haven't I edited a magazine and know how those things happen? And now thanks for the book. I'll write about it when I've read it and the results have settled.

Sincerely,

1. Ivan Beede, *Prairie Women* (New York: Harper and Row, 1930).

To Editorial Offices

HARPERS MONTHLY MAGAZINE

October 19, 1932

Gentlemen:

I just read Mr. Boyd's article, "Sex in Biographies" in the November *Harpers* and am lost in a greyish rose mist of agreement and doubt.[1] When the author suggests that, the post-Freudians to the contrary, sex isn't everything, I heartily agree. True, I've been exposed to the teachings of Freud and sloshed through the dregs of his theories in dissertations, novels and biographies. But I was, to an extent at least, immunized by a childhood in a new country, in a late frontier, where the veneer of civilization was thin and convention a sleazy thing of little warp and practically no woof. It was not suspected that underlying every act is the great sex urge and so everyone went unself-consciously about his business and the current sex manifestations were discouragingly simple and direct. In fact, as I look back, sex never seemed primary there, not even with animals, for stronger than all else was the urge of self-preservation and even mating animals fled before the threat of death or injury with a scandalous lack of hesitation. Man, having a wider capacity for fear, feared more, feared not only the immediate hunger, cold, claws and steel; he projected himself into the future and desire often died within him before the threat of dangers that could never be more than imaginary, died for unfathomable reasons, and, for all I can see, often unaccountably. But that was before they heard of Freud. It's probably different there now.

Mr. Boyd's statement: "Sex in biography, as in life itself, is simultaneously essential and unimportant, save when nothing else is afoot," seems curiously effective at first glance. But upon closer inspection I can't get a true picture. Admitting that sex is not the strongest factor in the determination of character and destiny, few who are close to life in the raw would so underestimate the place of sex as a formative and determining factor. They have seen lives destroyed, families broken, communities torn, the work of a life-time lost in a moment through the power of sex. The same things happen every day in any metropolis but we are too far removed from reality. We are inclined to think of sex as something in certain magazines, night clubs, leg shows, and movie houses.

Perhaps because I was almost without fear as a child, I was often sent to stay with this or that Kinkaider's wife while her husband was gone on the long trips to the railroad. Often these women were so afraid of every sound or lack of sound about the lonely soddies that they trembled all night, even with me sleeping soundly beside them. Yet they would be near their men. Sometimes it was not convenient that I go, for there were always babies to tend and much work to do. We let one woman, a former school teacher with a life certificate stay alone one night.[2] Haggard and jumpy, she walked four miles to plead with mother the next day.

"You must let her come. Another night alone and I'll go crazy."

Some of them did go crazy and yet, realizing what was happening to them, they stayed on, with men who were usually worried by drouth and crop failures, often lacking in understanding, crude, even brutal creatures, men they made no pretence now of either respecting or loving. Some of these women had good homes, positions, security awaiting them where the grass was green more than three months a year, with trees and neighbors and no demonic coyotes echoing from hill to hill about them. Perhaps these women were perverts, but if so there are millions like them, men and women, and sex could not be omitted from any biography they might merit. Perhaps there was, as Mr. Boyd suggests, nothing else afoot.

No, I can't admit that sex is unimportant in the life of the normal individual. I do not find that true in my experience with people, not true of the great characters of fiction or of history. Not even the lives of the saints are free from it. Surely, anything that conditions the character or influences his destiny is not only pertinent but essential in his biography, even if it is not more pathological than the normal producing of a son or a daughter. The son may make his parent happy or sad, may keep him from a throne, may even terminate his life by accident. A prominent W.C.T.U. may be stopped at the last pitch of her climb to a national office by a gin-drinking daughter. Even in the most virtuous lives normal sex is important.

To say that "Where sex is not pathological its importance is slight almost to the point of non-existence," seems a bit sweeping, particularly after the admission: "There are, needless to say, biographers who are compelled to take cognizance of the sexual problem presented by their subject when it is patent that such a problem lies at the very root of the latter's life and work." Apparently the implication is that the biographers are then dealing with pathological material, and "If pathological, the biographer becomes the scientist, * * * * and biography as a work of art, as a means of expression, ceases to concern us." Are we to assume that any great novels that hinge somewhere or another upon sex, or if it "lies at the very root" of the work, should also "cease to concern us"?

To me the creation of a character that moves and breathes and lives upon the printed page is a high literary achievement be he created in the image of an actual character or from the imagination. And be he ever so pathological. Was not Hamlet pathological—and Prometheus, Cain, Medea, and Becky Sharp? What would remain of Shakespeare, of any great literature if the pathological characters caused it to cease to concern us?

Perhaps Mr. Boyd wishes to restrict his use of "sex" to those submerged manifestations that demand case-history study. Here, I should have to depend upon the new voodoo of Freud and his over-interpreters for my experience with such people has been singularly limited. I suspect that my acquaintances now are abnormally normal and for all the sex-saturated phraseology current in my home community, only one was remotely applicable to a pervert and that was so specific that it left no doubt in my seven year old head as to its meaning. It had the concreteness and bald terseness some of our so-called franker realists strive for and never quite attain.

Then, too, I find that there is some rather prevalent disagreement as to what constitutes the normal in sex relations, depending upon the group one follows. Probably the solid ground lies somewhere between the muck of untrammeled animal lust titillated by man's superior imagination, the arid sand of sex for premeditated procreation only, and the deep bogs the psychoanalysts propose to probe for us. Or it may even come to mean, as a learned professor once pointed out to his class, of which I was a member, that most wide-spread and universal manifestation of sex, masturbation.

I'll readily agree with Mr. Boyd that this sex-obsession business has been vastly over-played, not only in biographies, everywhere. Even the victims of the Oedipus complex might discover, if the stigma of incest were suddenly and completely blotted from the world, that the satisfaction fails the anticipation. It seems to me that such folk are spoiled children who, when they find that for man there is no complete satisfaction this side of the grave, not sexually, not in anything, desire to flee to the fictions of childhood and the parent who healed all hurts, made all things well. I suspect there will always be a crying in the wilderness with nothing more satisfying for the incomplete soul alone than a frank facing of the inescapable isolation of life as every adult and most children must live it. It's probably hard for the romantics but I don't see what's to be done about it.

Mr. Boyd says, "Sex is essential * * * *" and I'll endeavor to restrain myself and not be as obnoxious as I can be. One might, you know, demand "Essential to what or to whom?" Essential to the continuation of the human race, yes, at least at the present, but considerably less essential to the individual, it seems to me, than food or rest or shelter from the blizzard winds. Often it is not even as essential as power, or money, or a job, and yet we have all seen instances where all these things were risked, even permanently renounced for sex by people who are not usually considered pathological, unless everyone between twelve and fifty be so considered and I'll admit, with Mr. Boyd, that the current stress in biographies suggests such a state of affairs. On the other hand, where is the man or woman worthy a biographer's pen who may not be suspected of at least temporary vergings upon the pathological?

No, sex isn't all there is to biography, not so long as we have such good complicators as the will-to-power, the Messiah complex, and endless mechanisms and compensations, unless we are going to consider all these sex. And the experts are coining new terms faster than we can familiarize ourselves with the old. But I still maintain that there was never a man or a woman worth writing a book about whose character and destiny was not at one time or another modified or changed by sex. Have not politicians, military leaders, statesmen, emperors and even the comparatively less susceptible Indian chiefs, when otherwise invulnerable, been brought low by sex? When all else fails fate and their enemies can usually muster at least one onslaught of the temptress and kingdoms have crumbled and peoples have vanished off the earth thereby.

And for some of the less obvious results of sex: Who can say how many of our great men broke from mediocrity for a woman or through the determination to bring remorse to one who held herself too high or became less kind?

And in answer to Mr. Boyd's statement that "The happiest sex life is one that has no history * * * *" one might point out that not only has happy sex life no history but it has been said in many languages and with much more grace than I can muster that happy people never have any history at all, and, apparently, are never good candidates for biographies.

Evidently I found the article interesting!

Sincerely,

1. MS may have been hoping this would be published as a rebuttal to Ernest Boyd's article, but it was not.

2. A life certificate entitled a teacher to teach for his or her lifetime. It was the ultimate certificate, attained after meeting all required standards.

To Mr. C. C. Calhoun

Washington, D. C.

November 17, 1932

Dear Mr. Calhoun:[1]

I am glad to hear that the government has at last finished the lengthy audit of their transactions with the Sioux and I sincerely wish you Godspeed with the case.

Miss Hinman is not the best source of information in the world. She has a fine historical sense and an excellent memory for dates and facts, but she never remembers to answer letters. Perhaps she felt that she had little to contribute. Her research, as a biography of Crazy Horse would suggest, has been mostly among the hostiles, the old men who knew or pretended to know little of what the Loaf-About-The-Forts were doing. Just now her book rests, much to my regret, for the theme is not only a vital and significant one but the four chapters she has written reveal more of the true nature of the Plains Indian than anything so far, not excepting Vestal, Neihardt, and Linderman.[2] Whether she could sustain such writing only the actual execution would tell.

Whether I have any information or can direct you to any that would be of value depends. I spent several months last winter going through the Ricker Collection, at the State Historical Society for Dr. Sheldon, secretary of the organization, taking notes for his forthcoming book on a prominent Sioux chief. . . . It contains all the usual books, pamphlets, leaflets, etc., and a great many clippings on the Plains Indians. Most valuable, it seems to me, are the several unpublished manuscripts of varying length on various phases of the Sioux struggle and even more valuable the forty odd pencil tablets containing personal interviews with all the old Indians, breeds, and white men of prominence and strategic position from 1851 to 1906–7 that the judge could find. The interviews were taken during the later dates. These cover the hostile struggles, the battles, etc., but even more revealing, it seems to me, are those on the Black Hills councils, 1875 and 1876 with the frontier opinion of the commissioners, the contract-hungry white men, and other hangers-on as well as the jealousies and suspicions of the Indians among themselves, with some disconcerting side-lights on the tactics used to get the treaty of 1876 signed. There is, of course, considerable on the state of affairs that led to the drawing away of Red Cloud and Red Leaf and their capture and dismounting later in the fall. There is a great deal of material on the later treaties for land cession and the sharp practices of Dr. Hinman, no relative, I am glad to say, of my Eleanor Hinman.

The pertinency and the legal status of such material I am, of course, unable to weigh. I suppose that the disinterestedness and the integrity of the interviewer, the interpreter, where one is used, and the individual interviewed might bear upon its value to you, even if the information itself had pertinency. The interviews have this value: Many of them are with men and women in positions to know the actual situation at the time of treating, men and women now dead, in most cases, at least. It may be said that Judge Ricker had no ulterior purpose beyond writing an authentic volume on the Plains Indians, and the material he accumulated became so over-whelming in volume that he never got more than a classification started before his death. The interviews are with such people as: American Horse, chief under Red Cloud in 1876; Herbert Bissonnette, son of Joseph, full-blood French, long with the Sioux and official interpreter at Camp Robinson; Louie Bordeaux, breed interpreter at Red Cloud, member of the 100 who went to the northern camps with Young Man Afraid in 1875 with the council tobacco; Mrs. Ellis Brown, daughter of Big Bat Pourier and raised with the Sioux; Slim Jim Burdick, chief of dog scouts for Custer and Stanley, back and forth from Black Hills to Red Cloud and Laramie; Mrs. Charles Clifford, relative of Little Bat, daughter-in-law of Hank Clifford; Louis Chardon, son of Chardon after whom Chadron, creek and town, were named, always lived with Sioux; James H. Cook, of Agate, Nebraska, strong Red Cloud man; George Colhoff, breed working at Yates store in 1874–8; Cornelius A. Craven, with beef herd at Red Cloud 1875, etc.; Mrs. John Farnham, daughter of Big Mouth, wife of saloon keeper between Red Cloud [Agency][3] and Camp Robinson; William Garnett, raised by Sioux, scout and interpreter, son-in-law of Nick Janis; Mrs. Nettie Goings, half-sister of Frank Grouard, famous scout of "Sandwich Island" fame; Mrs. Nick Janis, wife of trader for American Fur Co., whose first daughter was born at Horse Creek during treating of 1851; Mrs. Maggie Palmer, daughter of Antoine Janis, son of Nick; R. O. Pugh, married to breed, agency hand 1876, etc; Red Cloud, the chief; Rev. Amos Ross, Episcopal minister with early Sioux; Jack Russel, Buckskin Jack, bullwhacker at Richards bridge over Platte in 50's, later assistant farmer for Pine Ridge; Richard Stirk, charge of beef herd, with

Ben Tibbitts, 1875–6; Mrs. Emma Stirk, sister of Little Bat Garnier; Ben Tibbitts, wagon master with Custer, with Indians to Pine Ridge from Sod agency and from Red Cloud; Wm. Young, mule skinner about Red Cloud; Sword, Indian capt. of police, on dog council, etc. These interviews go on endlessly. Those I mention here happen to be among my notes I am using to write two narrative articles on the treaties of 1875 and of 1876. I intend to reconstruct the situation as much in actuality as possible, the characters, the stakes, and the conflicts among the ambitious tribesmen, from the Indian point of view.

Some day, unless some one else beats me to the time and funds, I intend to write a book on the Man Afraid dynasty. Against my will I have become convinced that they were the embodiment of genuine aristocracy, so secure that they did not feel driven to stoop quite as far as some of their contemporaries in the struggle to grasp and maintain power through the stupid, vicious, and vascilating Indian Policy of the white man.

I apologize for taking so much of your time. I hope that it has not been a complete loss to you. I wish you luck. You will need it—to get anything out of Congress for many years.

Sincerely,

1. C. C. Calhoun was a lawyer representing the Sioux in their suit against the U.S. government asking for indemnity for the Black Hills area they claimed was taken illegally.

2. Walter S. Campbell (Stanley Vestal) (1887–1957) was a professor of history at the University of Oklahoma. Under his pen name he wrote a number of western histories and biographies, among them *Sitting Bull: Champion of the Sioux* (Boston: Houghton Mifflin, 1932); *Warpath* (Boston: Houghton Mifflin, 1934); and *New Sources of Indian History, 1850–1891* (Norman: U of Oklahoma P, 1934).

John G. Neihardt (1881–1973) had a lifetime of writing to his credit. An epic and lyric poet, novelist, and literary critic, he was an expert on western history, having intimate knowledge of the exploration and settling of the West. Among other works, he published *Black Elk Speaks* (New York: Morrow, 1932) and *Cycle of the West* (New York: Macmillan, 1915–41).

Frank Linderman (1868–1938), a Montanan, wrote a number of books on western history and studies of Crow Indians, including *American: The Life of a Great Indian* (New York: John Day, 1930) and *Red Mother* (New York: John Day, 1932), retitled *Pretty Shield* in 1972.

3. MS sometimes refers to Red Cloud (1822–1909), the man the U.S. Government appointed chief of the Oglala Sioux, and the Indian agency named for him, near Fort Robinson, Nebraska.

To Mr. Edwin C. Hill

"The Human Side of the News"

December 2, 1932

Dear Mr. Hill:

I've listened to your "Human Side of the News" with considerable interest for some time but the story you told of the killing of Custer set me to wondering. Just how much stock should one put in radio commentators?

Chief Standing Bear, I'm sure, is a fine "ole" Indian but if he told you the story you repeated over the radio, he's been at the white man's version of it and took a credulous newspaper man for a sleigh ride. You said the battle was no surprise to the Indians. That depends upon what you mean by surprise. The Oglala, etc., under Crazy Horse had tasted victory on the Rosebud a week before and so knew that soldiers were after them but their scouts also knew where Crook, the commander at Rosebud, had gone. They had no immediate fear of him. Those who believed in the old signs knew that victory was coming, for they knew the vision of Sitting Bull promised a complete overcoming of their enemy. But they did not look for a battle on the Little Big Horn. Indians never deliberately exposed their women and children to the mercies of the soldiers. Sand Creek and lesser butcheries had not been forgotten. The accidental finding of a fresh soldier trail by young Sioux about their own business saved the camp from a complete surprise. Even so, when the first column of dust was sighted from the camp the ponies were still out in the hills, many men were bathing, the chiefs sitting about with their fly brushes discussing the news the boy had just brought—a soldier trail. The old Indians tell a story of panic—of women leaving their tipis standing and fleeing to the hills with the children, old men shouting advice, warriors rushing for the ponies. It is significant that the chieftains were of such caliber that they brought order out of chaos and managed their forces with such telling effect.

Your words of Standing Bear's doubt as to who killed Custer are right. Not one of the hundreds of Indians whose stories I've heard or read knew who killed Custer, for his long hair was cut before the last push. These same Indians deny that Rain in the Face was even in the Camp on the Little Big Horn, let alone killed Custer. Rain in the Face had contact with the white men before, understood their cravings for a good story and wasn't without fondness for a little gory glory. Learning of the catastrophe early, he told his story. There may be better story tellers than the whiteman-contaminated young Sioux but evidently our newshawks never discovered them. I am not acquainted with Standing Bear but if he is of the caliber of the fine old Sioux on Pine Ridge, He Dog, Little Killer, Short Bull, and so on, and I suspect he is, I'm sorry his name was ever used in connection with such a tale. To be sure the booklets put out by the Custer Battlefield people give the story of Rain in the Face, but if you want to know how inaccurate they can be up there, go to the turn of the road towards the battlefield of the Rosebud in Montana and unless my loud protests brought a change you will see a sign at least twelve feet long and four to six feet wide saying that this road takes you to the battlefield of the Rosebud where the Sioux fought the whiteman under the leadership of Red Cloud.[1] And Red Cloud was an agency Indian from 1869 on, poor soul, and was too demoralized to do anything but intrigue and jockey for power by 1876!

Sorry this had to be said, but you know how it is.

Sincerely,

P.S. I'm thankful you left out the tale about Rain—etc., cutting out Tom Custer's heart and eating it!

1. John A. Doerner, Custer Battlefield Park Ranger, reports, "The sign is no longer in place at the junction of Montana highway 212 and 314" (October 13, 1990).

To Alfred A. Knopf, Publishers[1]

February 11, 1933

Gentlemen:

I wish to thank you for your admirably frank admission in the March *Mercury.* Now if other publishers would only be equally frank and publish the number, if any, of manuscripts bought direct from unknown and unvouched-for authors. Apparently it would be an advantage for them, relieving them of the expensive, I presume they are expensive, reading staffs and save endless fuss writing letters to the thousands, perhaps millions of not-too-flush citizens who are spending money trying to market their manuscripts. To be sure the postal deficit would be considerably greater but a little more deficit couldn't make much difference now.

Perhaps publishers should cite more than figures, for beginning writers are so incurably optimistic. Of the dozen I sent to the March *Mercury* not one saw any particular significance in your statement. Couldn't you point it a bit?

Perhaps because publishers' readers must handle a tremendous volume of mediocre manuscript their critical faculties become undependable, as seems only reasonable. Publishers seem to find themselves in the position of the sandhill housewife after a good old frontier cloudburst that scattered the local grocery and soaked the labels off all the cans. She was afraid to buy anything for fear the can that looked like Libby's pineapple might turn out to be only watery tomatoes. Under such circumstances it is only prudent to depend upon the advice of people who seem to know what's in the can.

But all this gives me a most uncomfortable feeling. For nearly ten years I've stoutly maintained to all the hopeful and struggling writers I met that a good manuscript will find a market sooner or later and that the thing to do is to keep writing and to keep buying stamps. Perhaps I should have advised them to cultivate personages with strategic acquaintances and reputations and pass out mimeographed lists of agencies.

Anyway, your announcement had done much to simplify my existence.

Thank you.

Sincerely,

1. Alfred A. Knopf (1892–1984) started his own publishing firm in 1915; he published outstanding authors such as Thomas Mann, Sigmund Freud, Albert Camus, and Willa Cather. His firm was known for its high standards of workmanship and production. MS's *CH,* published by Knopf in 1942, won an award for bookmaking quality.

To H. L. Mencken

AMERICAN MERCURY

February 13, 1933

Dear Mr. Mencken:

Perhaps because you have made the Mercury a sort of clearing house for ideas, I approach you. It seems to be what others do.

Anyway, I think it is high time that some one wrote an opera on the American Indian. Perhaps I can guess your reaction. We have heard of the precarious position of the Metropolitan and are grieved. To see our lawmakers haggle over inanities and worse at a cost to the taxpayer that would set up several projects like the Metropolitan is somehow no longer infuriating. Even fury dies in the end.

Every time I go to the Sioux reservations I see fewer of the old aristocrats, fewer of the lean old meat-eaters who made fortitude their *wakan* tree of their existence through the tribulations of vanishing hunting grounds, whiskey traders and forked-tongue treaty makers, even to starvation. Soon (Ah, this is about the only topic on this earth that can bring a mist to my eyes) soon they will all be gone. Their seamed faces, the faded eyes, the toothless gums emphasize the need for haste. It is not comforting to know that their kind will never walk this earth again.

But enough of sentimentality. What concerns me now is that something more than a few moth-eaten war-bonnets and scalps should be preserved of this magnificent people. And if this is to be anything more than the "noble Redman" sort of thing, something that indicates his virility, the menace, the magnificence of his presence on the plains, it must be gathered now. If the composer and the librettist would picture anything more than the agency Indian they must hasten while there are still such haughty, arrogant Sioux as Neihardt's friend, Black Elk and Short Bull, Little Soldier and He Dog of my acquaintance.

He Dog was born in the same village as Crazy Horse, the famous Oglala war chief; they grew up together, became Shirt-Wearers together, and chiefs. It is this Crazy Horse I suggest as the central character of an Indian opera, Siouan because over a long period of years they were the whiteman's fast friends; they were the most feared fighters if not as foolhardy as the Cheyennes and their resistance was the most prolonged, the most spectacular and the most successful. Recency too is an element, for there are still pre-agency Indians at Rosebud and Pine Ridge, men and women mature when the whiteman first drove the Sioux to war.

The life of Crazy Horse offers a great deal of material, humorous, romantic, dramatic, tragic. He was an outstanding youth called Curly because his hair was fuzzy and the color of young prairie chickens, which suggests white blood to me, coming greatness to the Indians. Then came his coups; the event that gave him his father's name, Crazy Horse; the vision saying he would never be harmed by bullets; the jealousies of brother chiefs; the wooing of his wife, already in No Water's tipi, (Black Shawl must have been attractive, for No Water, no mean Indian, failed in the old Siouan test of fortitude, the leave-taking of his wife, and tried to compel her to return, injuring Crazy Horse with a knife.[1] There is a legend that he aimed at his face but his pistol misfired.);[2] the desertion of Man Afraid of his Horse and Red Cloud for the powers and annuities of the agencies; the shortage of buffaloes, pressure of the whiteman; soldiers; the death of his only child and his fast of four days at her grave; the constant harrying of his people by soldiers.

And through these difficulties a legend arose among the Sioux that if the white soldiers were surprised, their horses stolen, and the dead on the field mostly rifle-armed soldiers, Crazy Horse had been there. Often it happened so swiftly that the wagon guns were of no use at all. Anyway they could never harm him. It was Crazy Horse who planned an ambush that would have cost Crook his life had he not listened to his Arapahoe scouts, who frankly rebelled. It was the same chief's band that came up the coulee and cut off the retreat of Custer a week later.

But after these victories he made no talks. Even in council he let others speak and look to him for the final decision. He never painted, wore only one feather, as ordered in his vision. Even after the days of mourning on the Little Big Horn were over and the wild victory dance proceeded, Crazy Horse sat apart. He had never heard of manifest destiny but he understood its essence. He knew that starvation of his people was inevitable, starvation or surrender—and under the regimes of that day, sometimes both on the agency.

Then came the disheartening news that the Black Hills had been sold by the agency Indians, under coercion, of course, but he could not understand selling the home of his fathers this side of death. One after another his brother chiefs were hunted down and defeated and yet they must separate to hunt for winter was near. It came, so cold that the soldiers froze. There was no joy in the tipis, for a summer spent in defeating the Army of the Plains yields no meat and robes, only scalps and badly fitting blue uniforms, full of holes. To test him still further, the Cheyennes, driven from their beds in a forty-below blizzard, came for help in their nakedness. He was compelled to commit the Indian's greatest discourtesy, turn away a guest, ever so uninvited.[3] His own camp was raided. When spring came the agency chiefs brought peace tobacco and promises of fine things if he would come in. He could not deny his people food any longer, although he retreated to a hill-top for a day in his tribulation.

At Fort Robinson he was stripped of arms and ponies and inveigled into taking another wife, a breed, because the officers hoped it would reconcile him to the hated whites. Then came his betrayal, partly through the new wife's bad council, and the lies of [Frank] Gruard who squatted many months at his tipi fire, and by his own people. Promised that he was to go to Washington and be given a reservation for his people he left Black Shawl with his uncle, Spotted Tail, and went to Fort Robinson with the officers, only to discover that he was not a guest but a prisoner in the guardhouse. He made one last bid for freedom and was bayoneted in the kidney, died that night. And all about on the knolls and buttes rose a keening of women and a mourning from self-mutilated braves. They knew that this was the end.

Sitting Bull was in Canada. They were unwelcome strangers at the agency where there was not enough food for those who belonged there. Crazy Horse was dead. The keening lay heavy on the wind.

The next morning his father and mother moved slowly northeastward towards the breaks of Pine Ridge, out of the valley of the White Earth [River], on two ponies, a buckskin drawing the travois with their dead son. They left behind them, in the purple mourning dress of the Indian woman, the faithful Black Shawl who left her husband and followed him through the starvation years from 1868 to 1877.

He Dog saw the killing, and as he speaks of it to me, a white woman, dangerous fires glow in his fading eyes. He throws the cigarette I brought and lighted from him. But in his generosity he soon forgets and as I leave I am once more his grand-daughter, his white grand-daughter, Little Boy.

The Sioux offers a great variety of "ballet" material, ranging from the dance of the virgins to the wild sundance on the Little Big Horn and the wilder victory dance a week later. The problem, it seems to me, is two fold: finding a librettist willing to take the trouble to avoid the misstatements of frontier narrators, work out an authentic Siouan atmosphere, and avoid the ghastly sentimentalities of present day Indian songs; the even greater problem of a composer technically capable and temperamentally fitted for the scope, the grandeur, the ruthless dignity of the tragedy.

I don't expect you to be interested—or anyone else for fifty years. Then it will be too late. Every year is that much too late. But in spite of the frowns I meet I shall keep agitating. It seems vastly important to me that the Plains Indians be given a place in opera, if not the Sioux then the Cheyenne, in all the violence, ferocity, humor, courtesy, generosity, poise and tragedy of his nature.

If you care to suggest victims I shall attempt to convince them.

And I do thank you for your patience.

1. MS's later research corrected a number of misstatements made here. Black Buffalo Woman, No Water's wife, returned to her husband after he shot Crazy Horse. Crazy Horse later married Black Shawl; he was her only husband. For the clearest explanation of these relationships, see Eleanor Hinman, "Oglala Sources on the Life of Crazy Horse," *NH* 57.1 (Spring 1976):1–51. The material is based on interviews with old friends of Crazy Horse's in 1930. MS was present at these interviews, and she returned to the Pine Ridge Reservation in 1931 and 1932 for further interviews. MS uses the situations as described in the interviews in *CH*. The information revealed intratribal conflicts that white historians had never known about.

2. MS established that No Water shot Crazy Horse in the face, leaving a scar. Apparently No Water did not use a knife.

3. Crazy Horse's village aided the stricken Cheyennes, as MS's further investigation proved.

February 22, 1933

Dear Mr. Mencken:

I owe you an apology about the Indian opera. Had I realized that Victor Herbert's "Natoma" was considered either opera or Indian in the East, I should not have presumed upon your time.

Thank you,

Sincerely,

To Frank C. Hanighen

May 31, 1933

Dear Mr. Hanighen:[1]

It was very kind of Mr. Stepanek to introduce me and kinder of you to write.[2]

I have two book length manuscripts, one, a novel, UNGIRT RUNNER, which Dodd-Mead held for four months and returned with the enclosed note. Upon rereading the ms. I was thankful it was safely back in my hands. There [is] some good material in it but it's so evidently amateurish. Nothing further has been done with that book.

In the meantime I wrote another one, the story of a community in the Panhandle of Nebraska, with Jules Sandoz the central character. This, in an early, very rough draft, was also at Dodd Mead, although I find no letter in my files from Mr. Dodd about it. At least I think I sent it to them, early in 1932. Since then I spent six months giving the book a thorough rewriting and entered it in the Atlantic Monthly Press Non-fiction contest, where it remained almost eight months, went to the final judges, and came back some time in May, 1933. Now I'm looking it over, cutting a little here and there, etc., and expect to start it out again in a week or so.

I am not usually given to conceit. My critical faculties never let me believe that anything I write is good, but good or bad, I believe this OLD JULES, THE MAN FROM THE RUNNING WATER, or whatever the final title is to be, will remain in print long after I am dead, provided it is published by then. It is, as nearly as I could make it, a true picture of our last actual frontier, turbulent, comic, tragic, in a most unfriendly environment, with a highly individual central character who speaks and reads five languages, believes that the way to freedom from oppression in this world is through home-owning, with a good strong wife and sturdy children. He married four times, never the woman he loves, planted several communities that stand solidly today, but left them after feuding with every one, going to jail for shooting at his neighbors, was a crack shot, agitated the cattlemen situation until [President Theodore] Roosevelt sent soldiers to cut their fences, fought the sheep-men, was never safe, (his brother was shot down by a hired killer in 1908), was the good friend of men like Dr. Barbour, Dr. Brunner [*sic*], Dr. Bessey, and Dr. Condra[3] and never took a bath unless compelled to it. And with it all was not without the salt of humor, even when he held up court with 30 Winchesters.

All of which raises the question: should the book go as biography or fiction? The names of all the people are fictitious, except those of our own family, and their last name is never used. Every one mentioned actually existed, every event is authenticated by the account in some newspaper, by an old timer, by my mother or in my own recollection.

I asked Mr. Williams, of the *State Journal* to read the rough draft. He is the most cautious soul in the world where libel is concerned and he seemed to think there was no danger of such trouble. It is true that no people ever see anything the same and I find that no one ever recognizes my word picture of him.

Before beginning to write I put in seven years, spare time, etc., reading all the papers of the Panhandle from '80 to 1928, and all the pertinent references in all the state papers, kept on file at the Historical Society. I went through our letter files, containing thousands of letters, etc. and interviewed all the available old timers.

But enough of this.

You can, if you are interested, find some of my work in the *North American Review,* April and May, 1930, and May 1933. *Nature* has a personal narrative accepted for early publication and the *Prairie Schooner, Folksay,* etc., have published my work. For two years I was associate editor of the *School Executives Magazine.* Have boxes of unpublished short stories, good, bad, indifferent.

What a dull lot of tripe!

I might send you Old Jules if you are interested.

Sincerely,

P.S. Pr. Schooner stories published under the "Macumber".

1. Frank C. Hanighen (1900–1964), originally from Omaha, was on the editorial staff of Dodd Mead. He had asked MS to submit a manuscript to his company at the suggestion of Orin Stepanek (see next note). Later he was the founder and editor of *Human Events,* a conservative Washington newsletter.

2. Orin Stepanek (1888–1955), a professor of comparative literature and Slavic languages, was one of the best-loved professors at the university. Although he was often at odds with the administration, his recommendation that MS receive the Honorary Doctor of Letters was a strong influence in her receiving the degree in 1950.

3. All eminent professors at the university: Ervin Hickly Barbour (1856–1947), State Geologist, Director of the University of Nebraska State Museum; Lawrence Bruner (1856–1937), Professor of Entomology; Charles Edwin Bessey (1845–1915), Professor of Botany and Dean of the Industrial College, Acting Chancellor; George Evert Condra (1869–1958), Dean of the Conservation and Survey Division.

To Nebraska Credit Company

Lincoln, Nebr.

July 12, 1933

Gentlemen:

Apparently it was your representative who annoyed my landlady today and put her through a lengthy questioning. Mrs. Boston has been bedfast much of the time for four months and the entire business seems singularly inexcuseable to me.

I assume this is the rather tardy aftermath to my request July 3 for a few days credit at Mr. Moeller's store, where I have been known by sight at least for ten years. Only hunger drove me to ask for credit then and I endeavored to make it very clear that I was not interested in credit then unless I got it that day. In fact, I was promised a call that afternoon. If my delayed publishers' checks had not arrived I would be starved into the hospital long before this; either that or I would have been driven to borrow from my friends. Luckily I have a few.

I hope I may be forgiven if I seem to consider this procedure needlessly dilatory and inquisitional. My father, the late Jules A. Sandoz of Ellsworth, Nebraska, never went through such procedure before he let the rankest stranger have groceries on credit.

Please drop this matter immediately. I could not be interested in trading at Moeller's now under any circumstances.

Very respectfully,

To Mamie Meredith

July 17, 1933

Dear Mamie:[1]

Your letter arrived uncensored and unopened this morning. I was pleased, but scarcely as pleased as I was to see you so vitally yourself, more so than you've been for two years. Freed, somehow, of the gradual inversion that was taking place, if *inversion* is the word. Now if I could rid myself of the menace—.

Big business today. A letter from Mother. Girls are both home, both teaching somewhere near this fall, etc. The twisters lifted the roof off the old barn I helped Papa build in 1913, sixty feet long and forty feet wide, with lean-tos on both ends, and not a stick of it heavier than two by fours. My god, what a shell. I remember when we put up the plate, (yes you do know what that means) sixteen feet high, I teetered up there in every puff of wind and Papa shouting "By golly, don't let me that fall or I lick hell out of you!" And when we found that the roof hadn't enough slope to shed water well with shingles and I, armed with a brush and old overshoes, spread hot roofing tar over it all, on a blistering hot day, something like these chaps who spread the tar on the streets—and every drop that hit me raised a blister. Them was the days! (Mama picked up and went to the south orchard, after the third good cussing around the family, and the boys ran away to the swamp, and there I was, uninsulated, so to speak, against the heat of the tar and the paper.)

By the way, Mama's to have $350 to put a new roof on the old shell, unpainted, but lovely and soft now against the hills, when the insurance moratorium is over, if ever.

There are some cherries, she says, and apples. She gave up the store and the gas business, so I'll be isolated this winter, with nobody but John, our bachelor neighbor and perhaps Pahl, the hero of "The Smart Man" for company.[2] My god some more.

Also got a check from the W. *Herald* for the Reed story.[3] It, the story, seems to have been well received, as the check is, I assure you.

Got the enclosed note from Scribners today. That's the kind of thing that will drive me out to Bailey's some day,[4] but to the other end of the establishment. Rejection slips are nothing but potential twisters for my cigarettes but *them damned* notes that show me how far I must go to conform before I can sell! By the way, the Devil's Lane has been rewritten into a story half as long as when you heard it, with a serious ending, told in strictly chronological order, beginning with the two old duffers and their mania to divide everything. . . .[5]

Love,

1. Mamie Meredith (1888–1966) taught Business English at the university. Active in a number of professional organizations, she was a charter member and organizer of the American Name Society and contributor to folklore societies. MS and Meredith met early in MS's Lincoln years, and although Mamie Meredith never had MS as a student, the professor was her staunch supporter.

2. "The Smart Man," *PrS* 33.1 (Spring 1959).

3. "Frontier Days of an Immortal Man of Science," *Omaha World-Herald*, June 25, 1933.

4. Dr. Benjamin F. Bailey's Green Gables, a private sanitorium for the mentally ill, was located at 5515 South Street in Lincoln.

5. "The Devil's Lane," *Ladies' Home Journal*, April 1938: 17.

n.d. [1933]

Dear Mamie:

Glad to hear you are out of the hospital. No wonder they sent you home, insisting upon seeing the worst thing in the world for a surgeon—an emergency case, with spectators.

To see the scene between the man and woman in the room the morning after was a real privilege—one of those rare moments when all the reticences of an inarticulate person have fallen away. The queer thing about it seems to be the lack of anything at all remaining when the same thing happens to more articulate souls. Perhaps because we have no reticences nothing remains in us to be guarded.

That has always been one of my chief concerns with human nature. That's why Dr. Gibson's sudden entrance into the room out there upset me so. In one flash I seemed to see something the man has possibly been driven to great lengths to preserve, the essential essence within him. The sort of thing one would never see again if one saw him every day for a hundred years. The sporting thing would have been for me not to mention it at all and usually I don't, but I was so unprepared for his type of man.

The 21st century child will be so versed in psychology, and perhaps not too insulated against those psychic flashes, and so sensitive to human conflict that even the most aloof of us today will seem obvious. All I can see to do is to raise the threshold of one's mind, sort of a dyke-building process, or give it up as lost, as most people do now. That's why I feel that even fifty years from now all of us today will seem to be vastly overwriting, over-acting, just over-obvious, plain, doddering bores to the alert reader. Consequently I write as tersely as I dare, hoping not to escape the grasp of my contemporaries entirely and not to be too over-obvious to those that come after.

I know how conceited this writing for posterity seems, but nobody today has the remotest idea what I am driving at, and, so far as I can discover, only a few in the past have ever bothered about what I find important, so, consequently I am forced to look to the future for understanding.

Not that my stand is without precedence—there is the very popular Samuel Butler who seems to have had a little difficulty with his contemporaries and yet today I find him guilty of all the things his contemporaries committed, flamboyant, melodramatic, but fortunately to a lesser degree than his contemporaries.

Oh, me, how did I get off on that? Almost as bad as the "My Operation," habit, which, by the way, will be making an attempt to creep up on *youououou* about now.

I'm rather sorry I brought you that book of Neumann's.[1] It doesn't suggest his power and scope at all. For that one should read *The Devil* or *The Rebel,* and get a little pain and horror free. Of course the underlying purpose of the *Mirror* is serious enough. Who of us is there that isn't trying to be king of some Poland, and going at it in similar ways? Only most of us get less fun from the pilgrimage.

1. Alfred Neumann, *Mirror of Fools* (New York: Knopf, 1933); *The Devil* (New York: Huntley Paterson, 1928); *The Rebel* (Stuttgart: Verlags-Anstett, 1927).

To THE FORUM and CENTURY

August 25, 1933

Editorial Offices

Gentlemen:

I am pleased to see the enthusiasm shown in the September *Harpers* over "A Rose for Emily" by William Faulkner.

No sitter on my hassock has escaped without Emily thrust upon him sometime since the story appeared. From the first reading the story seemed to me to have unusual significance for the young American, whether a writer, a teacher or the intelligent consumer of literature. My two copies of the April 1930 *Forum* are in tatters but Emily keeps going.

At the time I applauded your courage in publishing this story, for there's no denying that Emily has a certain unpleasantness—an unpleasantness very conspicuous in life, it seems to me, and perhaps therefore banned from so many magazines. The fact that Faulkner was then a comparatively unknown writer made the publication more daring.

Incidentally, may I say I regret the passing of the era of controversy in the life of the *Forum?* I'd like a good, caustic pro and con controversial discussion of the NRA and incidentally one on the idea of feeding the poor unemployed piggy sow meat.[1]

You see my fancy runs to the taboo and the unpleasant.

However, I still wonder if you can't dig up someone who doesn't give a damn about his financial future to write an article on the possible loss of foreign markets through drastic curtailment in the production of wheat and cotton. Yes, of course I know about the international conference on wheat, but does anybody expect much from that? Wheat curtailment seems particularly cruel when half the world is starving for bread. Then, too, there's the little matter of what to do with the corn if you sell off all the little pigs. And the suggestion to make fertilizer of the little pigs. Shades of Charles Lamb!

I think an investigator might find that the farmer is in a desperate state of uncertainty. How can he tell what to plant, spring or fall, when there's no telling what the government may do to interfere with the prices? I was raised on an experiment station, in a community where the better farmer asked only a fair shake in the world market. Even today our bankrupt farmers don't want bonuses and crutches. They want the right to battle the elements and the earth with some promise that all this post-war helping of agriculture will cease so they can pull themselves out of a decade of poverty and pauperism. They did not leave their European homes, their jobs and their plots in York state or the packing houses of Chicago to be peasants. They did not battle with the heat and the drouth and grasshoppers and early frosts and wind and discouragements to be pauperized by the mismanagements, to put it mildly, of men in high places, political and financial.

In our community, and I do not think that we are unique, there has always been acreage curtailment. Until the government started pegging wheat the good farmer could predict with considerable success what would be his best paying crop at planting time.

But as unemployment increased in the east, the west and mid-west was flooded with amateur farmers, men who would not serve the apprenticeship required by the world's most complex occupation. They wanted to come from their clerkships and their mills and make money immediately, and when it wasn't to be done that way, they howled to high heaven for cash. I don't insist that the farmer has ever had a fair deal. Of course he hasn't, but the adaptable survived, even made money.

Now? Well, all we are hoping for now is to hang on somehow until the government gets done with helping us.

Sincerely,

P.S. I do think you might dig up someone to write an article for us that doesn't pussy-foot around, afraid of disturbing the sleeping agriculturist. The agriculturist worth the rocksalt his cows lick is never asleep.

And couldn't we have a story, now and then, by William? There won't, perhaps, be any more Emilies, but something?

1. The NRA (National Recovery Administration) was established in 1933 to take measures to give the nation economic stimulation. However, MS probably refers to the AAA (Agricultural Adjustment Administration), also operating under a 1933 act. In an attempt to raise farm prices and reduce surpluses, the agency ordered the destruction of six million piglets and two hundred thousand sows.

To Eleanor Hinman

Ellsworth, (soon) Nebraska
September 12, 1933

Dear Eleanor:

I've thought your proposition to send me to New York over for a week now, although the verdict was final from the first. I could not possibly go with the understanding that I'm to "get in with some publisher and find out what they want, get their point of view." Literature is not made that way and there's really very little of the journalist in me, even now, after all these years of trying to produce what my acquaintances expected of me.

I'm grateful, but would be much more grateful for even one person in Lincoln who could give me the comfort of if not understanding at least tolerance for my purpose in writing.

But no matter. I really didn't ever expect it and I am certainly not down hearted over its failure to materialize. In fact I'm more convinced that I'm right. So I'll go home, eventually teach myself free from my financial bondage to my acquaintances, and be free to write what I want to write.

Thank you,

Sincerely,

Sandoz, via Ellsworth, Nebr.
November 5, 1933

Dear Eleanor:

I found your telegram yesterday, Saturday, when I came home from hunting—too late to answer on the same mail.[1] No letter received yet.

I admire your persistent efforts to rescue me but don't you see the futility of it all? I know you feel I should be available to publishers, etc., this winter and of course you refuse to believe that if I had remained in Lincoln for twenty years Hanighen would never have asked to see me. Very well. Say it is superstition—certainly more real to me than any reality I've ever encountered—this idea of mine that somehow I've run afoul of the rhythm of circumstance—that on the down beat I always seem to be coming up—the lot of the inadequate. Call it rot or whatever you like but that does not invalidate my repeated experiences. In the future if circumstances defeat me it will be negatively and not positively, for I've made my last effort at adequacy.

Now, will you please give my apologies to Mr. Filley and to yourself.

My failure was inevitable. Please let it rest there.

Sincerely,

1. Eleanor Hinman urged MS to return to Lincoln; she found a job for MS in her own office, under Horace Clyde Filley, a professor of farm management at the College of Agriculture.

Sandoz, via Ellsworth, Nebr.
November 7, 1933

My dear Eleanor:

Will you please go to Hell?

If I'm tired and disgusted and want to lay down with my face in the sand, please remember that sand is plentiful and the face is after all, mine, and not even you, my creditor, can stop me.

In the future I shall label both advice and commands as deliberate violations of personality and I shall tolerate neither from anyone. As for telling me my book should have been done earlier and to make the fall market—finish a book and see how well you can time its completion.

Furthermore, I've made no secret of my opinion of Lincoln as the last word in decadent middle class towns, sterile, deadening. Only by a constant isolation of conscious defensiveness did I exist there at all. While the sandhillers are equally antagonistic to the creative mind they at least are not superior or patronizing about it; do not set themselves up as beings of supreme culture. They openly consider me an amusing fool but assume no responsibility for my reformation, which, incidentally, is something. The sandhills have nothing more to give me, true, but neither has Lincoln or perhaps any other spot on earth. And at least the sandhills do not pretend that they have.

You speak of dissolution — has it ever occurred to you that my dissolution took place in Lincoln — that any traits you Lincolnites may have found interesting in me are Panhandle survivals forceably conserved by deliberate retreat, rudeness, and "busy" signs.

As for writing — what do you expect of one after three years as those I just passed? Suppose that I am dormant — even all winter? Haven't I earned that?

Yes, quite evidently I've lost personality seriously during the last few years. No one would have dared, until recently, the familiarities you dare. Only serious dissolution on my part can account for your presumption. But now my manners are gone too, as they should be when people take advantage of them.

Now will you please get to work on your novel?

To Frank Williams

Editor, THE STATE JOURNAL
Lincoln, Nebr.

November 9, 1933

Dear Mr. Williams:

I have a very nice letter from Longman Greens', saying you recommended my manuscript. I am deeply indebted to you, particularly as I realize that praise from you means something. (But I like the cuss words too.)

I'm wondering if you are keeping your nice brown color and if you are faithful to your cod liver tablets. This winter promises to be a hard one and preparation for it seems rather important. I reached this conclusion after helping with the branding, vaccinating, and emasculating, which, as you probably know, is a bloodless process by now. Not that it would make any difference to me. I often helped with the older operation without any particular embarrassment for anyone concerned. Thick skinned that way.

From the reports of the theater receipts, etc., in New York and Wash. I presume that either people have more money or are spending more. Out here life has settled pretty well to its simplest terms. Women with pink-ruffled bedspreads are picking cowchips — more, making conversation and competition with it. I understand that 60 triple box loads will keep a heater and a cookstove going through the worst winter known. They figure 40 tubs to the loads, 3 loads per person per day — with the cactus or cacti in the fingers sheer profit.

Still, things seem a little better than they apparently have been. Jule has paid off $4000 debts with a deflated dollar. They seem to figure about $60 a year outlay for the family, 4, clothing, the little food they cannot grow, drugs, etc. In the meantime overalls have quadruple patches and razor blades are sharpened in a smooth water glass. But there's not a saner, clearer eyed man in all the town of Lincoln for all the patches. Instead of talking hard times and *hemorrhagic septicemia* and contagious abortion, etc., diseases that have decimated his stock from chickens to horses, he wants to know if there's any new "dope" on the origin of the sand hills and on the theories of heredity control.

Most of the cattlemen are gone or choring for eastern capital — but that's the inevitable story of the west, apparently. However there's patience here, and confidence in the administration, whether the sandhiller is republican or democrat. As for state government, the theory here seems to be that it must be tolerated something like a club foot, not desirable, but not conveniently remediable.

Mother had a fair crop of apples despite the late storm and frost and could have sold many more if she had them. Her Delicious were nice but for me, not particularly an apple fancier, I'll take her McIntosh Reds, easily the best apple, to my way of thinking, I've ever tasted. Up to October 20 we had all the fresh strawberries, everbearings, of course, that we wanted, but finally an ice frost blighted the blossoms.

Yes, life is simpler here, reduced to keeping warm and fed, and now taxes are due. Everyone has learned to live as our fathers did — few use their cars much. Gas lamps, gas irons, etc., are put away for the older, cheaper ways. Yet its comforting to know that most of the country will eat even if the cheap money hounds run away with the administration and although cultural contacts are *nil,* its comforting to know that you can still take a dally around a post fast enough to keep a bellering weaning calf from rope-burning your hands.

Well, thanks again for the letter to Longmans. Trust in God and keep the cod liver tablets handy.[1]

Sincerely,

1. Frank Williams quoted from or paraphrased parts of this letter in his "More or Less Personal" column in the *Lincoln State Journal,* November 19, 1933. He prefaced

it with this introduction: "Our special sandhills correspondent gives a sandhills region picture that seems rather important, indicating that people do live there, enjoy life, study and think. Having time to think, they probably think more, think deeper and give more time to working on problems not necessarily their own than busy city people."

To Frank C. Hanighen

November 21, 1933

Dear Mr. Hanighen:

I appreciate your criticism of the Thunderer very much and see both its generosity and its validity.[1] Perhaps if I were in New York Dodd Mead and I could come to an understanding. Or if I could have seen you in Lincoln. However, the Thunderer will probably go better in a couple of years than just now, in this period of "happy" literature.

Parenthetically, I wish to say it is not precarious to write a criticism of anything to me. Two years as associate editor on an educational magazine would have served to sicken me with the prima donna attitude of beginning writers if it had ever come natural to me.

But to return to your criticism. The major ones I anticipated in the early drafts of the story. First I told it with American poverty of incident, with more introspection and considerable emotional elaboration. This method, which I used in my first novel and in my early short stories, seemed incompatible with my material and therefore I deserted it. Gradually I solidified the environment, objectified the point of view, and increased the restraint. I must confess that I like it better so—which is not necessarily a good reason for changing a book. Writers, like mothers, are often blind to the faults of their children. This came home to me during my five years as reader for the University's extension course in fiction writing.

Even granting that my taste is good, I know that it is not that of the book buying public. Instead of considering the possibilities of making a popular book I tried to make one giving one way of life, bringing an experience to the reader that he could get no other way, a book that will be as authentic and worth reading ten, twenty, even fifty years from now as today. Such books usually deviate from the accepted in structure and in treatment as well as in theme.

Your letter shows me that in certain ways I have failed utterly in my presentation of the main characters of the book. You want more of the estrangement with Henriette etc. Had I succeeded in my characterization you would recognize the lack of Jules' realization of an estrangement as revelatory of character. Jules was no Hamlet. He did no soul searching. He was almost never conscious of wrong or fault in himself. Others made mistakes and compelled him to make them. His anger was never against himself.

About using the populist disorders more conspicuously in the Thunderer—I tried to show that only those comparatively comfortable can get very excited about state and nation. The settlers on the Flats in the Nineties were concerned with the more immediate things of wind and rain, fuel and food—the actual things the body needed immediately. To be sure I might distort my material, giving the picture others want just now. Perhaps because I'm intensely interested in a new novel, *Slogum House,* which does not concern itself with the unconquerableness of environment, keeps very close to the incidents within one household, and should have considerable good old-fashioned suspense.[2] There is someone to hate heartily, someone to pity, someone to feel superior to, and a pretty girl. Oh, yes, and enough of the forbidden experiences to give "the old lady of Madison Avenue" considerable kick. All the characters of the Slogum family go about thinking things that must not get out instead of busying their heads about world news and national problems, as in the Thunderer.

But I will not go on like this any farther. You, of necessity, are looking for books that will make money next spring and summer. I, by nature, am writing what I hope has a certain validity for some time.

Oh, by the way, you would hardly expect anyone of my temperament to "emphasize the hopelessness of the struggle in the sandhills." I don't recognize any hopelessness in any struggle with nature. Defeated we are, of course, for death is inevitable, but to the people that seem interesting to me the struggle is a magnificent one in any event.

You see how antagonistic our aims and ends are, yours and mine.

Thanks for the trouble. Please don't feel that I am unappreciative. Perhaps I am just rationalizing myself out of the necessity of redoing that long manuscript. Just now the task seems beyond me.

Thank you,

P. S. I'm having Dodd-Mead send the Thunderer over to Longman Greens. They asked to see it. Not that they are venturesome either, but who is in these days?

1. "The Thunderer" was an early title and version of *Old Jules.*

2. *Slogum House* (Boston: Little, Brown, 1937).

To Tyler Buchenau

December 6, 1933

Dear Buck:[1]

Your letter has motivated me to do the unprecedented—not only answer a letter but answer it promptly. Indeed, it lets me in for a day of the business, for my conscience won't permit partiality in correspondence.

But to return to you. Is there an undertone of disappointment in your letter? Don't be too despondent about it. It is the inevitable that is happening to you. The west has always been so much freer for its superior people than the east that the change is bound to be depressing, both for you and for Alice,[2] whom I happen to know because she belongs to Chi Delta Phi, etc., (and admire for other reasons). I suspected that the Raysorian type of mind prevailed in the east in the colleges,[3] only one reason I would never make much effort to go east for an education. You are so much more disciplined that I hoped the adjustment would be less difficult. But you'll make it; of that I am certain.

As for me—I've been out here in the hills since the first of November and found things so comfortable that I was compelled to build myself a shack in which to live and make an attempt at writing another novel. *Col. Pomroy,*[4] which I hoped to do this winter, requires a good-humored attitude from me and for that reason the Col. is shelved and another novel is going strong. *Slogum House,* the story of a family at one of the 1890 roadhouses, with all the intrigue and the family hatred, etc., followed up to 1933. The scenes are singularly unified, almost entirely at the House, and the treatment threatens to be bitter. However, my mood may mellow. At any rate, I should like to make it a story as ruthless as Feuch[t]wanger's are.[5] My failure in that is foreordained, but it may have more strength than the average American's novel and that's a worthy aim for my caliber any day. It's not a pretty story.

As for my novel: Hanighen, reader for Dodd, Mead showed up in Lincoln looking for me the Sunday after I left. Probably came to town primarily to see Stepanek. Anyway, no one could tell him where I had gone. Nice bit of irony, since I had become tired of waiting on him and sent the ms. to New York to his address and gone home. However, he read the ms. [and] sent me his reasons for rejection. I was amused. It was almost verbatim the things Stepanek once told me eight years ago, when I was reading for Van [den Bark][6] and his attitude towards me was every bit as antagonistic as it is now. Hanighen lauded my writing as writing, but suggested that I rewrite the book to give it structure, say by having the main character tell it as a journey, in imitation of some book just out this fall, a story of a Catholic mission in the west. If he knew my opinion of artificial structure! In addition he thought that I should inject good old fashioned suspense at the end of the chapters as it is done in the westerners. His criticism was legitimate enough from the book-selling point of view. Suicidal from the art standpoint. Anyway, long before that I had a request from Longmans, Green, company, and they have the book now. If you really want to bother with it, I'll have it sent to you when they are tired of looking at it, if you are still in New York. I think I'd like to try Farrar and Rinehart next. Farrar is some sort of relative of Gilbert Doane here and he suggested that I use his name as an excuse for sending it.[7] Say he advised me to try them. Of course, Mr. Doane has not seen the book but that seems to be a minor matter in this book-selling business.

Would you like to pack it over there? It would be fine if you get to meet Farrar himself. I understand he's about thirty and very cosmopolitan. Rinehart is a son of Mary K. Did you know Leslie Dykstra, the poet, who used to live here? She's a friend of Farrar. (meaning Lincoln.)

However, don't let me bother you. Don't do it at all unless you think it might be diverting.

Your reading sounds interesting. Wharton I've always taken a snooty attitude towards. Somehow I can't remember to forget her imitation of Henry James. She is certainly more readable, I believe, but imitations have a way of breaking down in the crucial spots. However, she seems to keep the east impressed with her type of realism, as they seem to call it. However, I admire old Edith too. There's a fine surface polish to every thing she does.

I'm disappointed that you haven't seen any plays. Had you seen Dinner at Eight? I should be interested in Pursuit of Happiness, "a play about bundling." I think I should have liked to see Rene Clair's film, July 14. O'Neill in a "delightful comedy" would be beyond my appetite, I fear. However, you will regret not going to something while you are there. Have you taken spiritual sides in the Eva La Gallienne-Ethel Barrymore versus the Philadelphia club women fight? Old Ethel must have had some good rye to stimulate her so to the defense of a sister actress. This is flippancy. I know she is really responsible for Eva's ever getting a chance at all; or so I hear. . . .

We had a family reunion at the house here Thanksgiving. Every one and the in-laws. Then we went to a country dance en masse. My first one here in ten years and my last, unless I frankly go to exploit the situation. When we got there there seemed a certain lightness, a rustic frivolity, about the business. A very bad "by-ear" orchestra was playing Christine LeRoy, (you wouldn't remember it) and some long necker yelling changes in a quadrille.

Very gay. Before supper there was plenty staggering, even among the women. A former beau of my sister's was being chased about the place by his wife, club in hand, and in his state was having a very difficult time of it. Two little boys, fourteen and fifteen, were revoltingly sick and their parents up in arms, telling them they could not return to high school for their antics. Must pitch hay all winter. Every now and then I noticed some wife tolling her husband away from our direction probably because I am, after all, one of them city women. And outside a woman who has always been jealous of her older daughter was encouraging her to elope to Alliance with an eight dollar a week Skaggs-Safeway, clerk. But the girl kept saying, "I don't know. I guess I ought to ask papa first." And every few minutes some acid-voiced woman would say, so we could hear it, that it was Steve who brought the liquor to the dance. Steve, until this fall, having been our hired hand and evidently our responsibility. But there are no jobs for his type of loafer and even Steve must eat. Besides, nothing short of a tank wagon could have brought *all* the liquor there.

And at no time could you be sure of a whole square foot of the old pine board floor for your feet.

Country dance, but with a Russian undertone. Fortunately our escorts and our brothers remained arid as a blowout, so we could *act* superior, anyway. . . .

I'm disappointed in the lack of good conversation you find in New York. Evidently the disease is a national one. I had always hoped that conversation, like the blue bird of happiness, was just beyond my finger tips somewhere, say east of the Mississippi, or at least of the banks of the Hudson. Surely it isn't among Seth Parker's Mainers. I'm here to testify it isn't in the sandhills, although I ran across one glimmer of it. Two weeks ago three hunters stopped here. I happened to have a lot of stuff laying around, such as the *New Yorker, American Speech,* the new *Esquire,* etc., and a bit of radical stuff, such as *New Masses,* etc. The three dirty-overalled chaps fell upon it avidly, scarcely waited for the gallon of coffee they had asked Mother to make for them. I wasn't much impressed, as the shortest of them, and the lightweight, was about six feet two and ap. 220 lbs. But they finally cornered me, and got it out of me that I was Mari, and for three hours we went through the only conversation or approximate approach to it I've found out here. They had read everything that remotely touches border history and, better than I, one of the three always remembered all the fine points, the controversial points. One of them had an inside story, another one, about the Mencken departure from the *Mercury,* etc. It never occurred to anyone to introduce us, and so not until they were gone did I know that they were nephews of Judge Glass, a real character out in this region, and that the two men possessed the only real approach to a library west of Lincoln. Furthermore, one of them is a professional boxer and he never mentioned it. Phenomenon I calls it. Of course, the hunting season is over.

My shack, to which I referred earlier, was an old garage one of our passing show of hired hands built for his Chevy. I dug up a lot of old lumber from the barn last spring's tornado wrecked here, doubled it all over, made myself a closet, a dressing room, and a little hall, sent for a trash burner stove, made a roof saddle, put in a floor, lined the whole with building paper, trimmed the inside with barky slabs, and have a bunk house all my own, with no welcome sign anywhere. So far only sight-seers have been inside. If I only had a radio the whole thing would be fine. Music is my only lack here, now. But when I had to live in the house I was always in the way, everywhere, although there are five big rooms and only Mother in it. (Hired man has a bunk house of his own.) There's no discounting the antagonism the average woman feels for the eldest daughter. The infuriating thing is that most mothers blame the daughters for their hatred when it's just what makes the mother pig eat her first batch of young. Of course one can't tell them that.

However, I sally houseward near mealtimes, help cook, wash the dishes, help gather the fuel, chop all the wood, spend Mon. A.M. washing, Tues. A.M. ironing, and wait on the gas tank customers, etc., between times. I aim to spend two hours just plain visiting with mother, singing old songs with her, listening to her accounts of her childhood and of the early days here. Eight hours a day I put on *Slogum House*. Not a bad situation, if it weren't for the lack of conversation and music. Oh, I forgot. I've blossomed out into quite a good hunter. Get grouse, pheasants, rabbits, and ducks, the latter in season, right along. Most fun, or funniest shot is me being so struck with the beauty of a cock pheasant I forget to raise my gun until he's out of range. Much merry making among the rustics over this point, as well as other unaccountable traits I seem to have developed, such as an aversion to tooth picks at the table. Jokes on them. I never did pick my teeth. Have other methods of concentration.

But enough of this chatter. Be nice to yourself. New Yorkers will be agreeable before spring. I wish I had some very gay and not too shallow acquaintances in New York. Unfortunately I know only a very few there, and even them remotely, such as the former Josephine Gund, who married somebody, God knows who. With your hair and personality, they can't keep you down.

Sincerely,

1. Tyler Buchenau (d. 1988) had been a student at the university; when he moved to New York he offered to take MS's *OJ* manuscript to a publisher there.

2. Alice Geddes was at Bryn Mawr.

3. Thomas Raysor (1895–1974), an English professor at the university, was the chairman of the English Department from 1930 to 1940. MS took his class on romantic poets.

4. "Colonel Pomroy" was never completed, or at least is no longer extant. The name appears in several fragments of MS's unpublished short stories. Sandoz once described her concept as that of a mythical character in a mythical town between Hay Springs and Chadron or Alliance, Nebr.: a vigorous, lusty, bluff man who makes his early money from beef contracts with the Indians, with the usual graft. He makes only one mistake in his life—marrying "a good woman."

5. Lion Feuchtwanger, a German author, published books from 1918 to 1958. MS may be referring to *Josephus* (New York: Literary Guild, 1932).

6. Melvin Van den Bark (d. 1974) was an English professor at the university. MS took his short story class in 1925 and credited him with giving her a successful method of organizing her material. She was a reader for his classes for some time (she states it variously as one and a half to three years). They were lifelong friends.

7. Gilbert Doane (b. 1897) was Director of Libraries at the university from 1925 to 1937.

To Eleanor Hinman

December 6, 1933

Dear Eli,

Write I must, although there doesn't seem to be anything to say. Family Reunion Thanksgiving, which I lived through because I now have my own shack, which took me two weeks and most of the skin of my hands to build, as Fred was using the only good saw and the only square of any kind in his carpentry about the barn. So with a tape measure and a tree saw and a bone saw I converted one of the numerous old shacks, the old garage east of the road, here in the yard, into a habitation, living room, dressing room, closet, and hall. Needless to say, only one of my dimensions could get in, but as there are no welcomes printed on my door mat, I've had no difficulty with my place of escape. Actually, with a little good conversation, some reading matter when I'm dull, and a radio it would come as near being a writer's heaven as could be imagined. I have a new trash burner, earned by writing a speech, a day bed, formerly in the bunkhouse, five pillows, my filing case, a rustic table, a rustic bookcase, and my pictures, all against a back ground of building paper, pink speckled, you know the stuff, but not as impossible as it sounds when trimmed with pink-barked pine slabs from Pine Ridge. These were too rotten to use, Mother said, and they were scandalous to saw, but they make a fine rustic touch on table, casing, and bookcase. Really I've had many sight-seers. No visitors, however.

I'm working on *Slogum House*. The bitter, tragic portions will work out well here and as the book is nothing else but, I expect to do all but the last portions, that is, the final revisions here. Imagination and rhythmic writing I'll never produce here. Drudgery of writing can probably go as well here as anywhere. It's all drudgery anyway, this business of existence, to one of my temperament.

How is the novel coming?[1] Well, I hope.

By the way, one of the girl's friends brought over old Tom Milligan, who rode with trail herds in 72. Came up to Standing Rock with cattle in 78. Remained in South Dakota, near Standing Rock, in 1879. Still rides any horse his rope settles on "of a morning." He was the chap who helped Jack Zully, of *The Last Frontier* out of jail, and to Canada.[2] He helped hide Zully when he got tired of the Queen's domain and came back to his Indian wife on Standing Rock. Very reliable narrator seems to me. First old timer I ever struck who never saw Calamity Jane, was not in Deadwood when McCall killed Wild Bill Hickock and never shot an Indian, unless he did it accidentally one night through the Indian strip, but he's certain most of the trail herd depredations were done by white "Indians" with a few feathers in the hair. Makes no flat statements, etc. Just my luck to have a bronch throw him and kill the lean bellied old timer. Nobody at the Fawn Lake [Ranch] knows how old he is but the general guess is 80, from his stories, although you'd never guess it except that he does what only the ancient, ancient cowboy ever does — he wears overshoes over his boots.

Clyde tells me he still cleans out the bunkhouse at poker. I'm to have a whole day with him soon. Clyde, by the way, has been in love with Flora for about ten years.[3] Told me once he was all through with such stuff but Thanksgiving night when his illumination began to wear off a little he came around with a sob in his voice. He just had to find Flora, even if she was eating supper somewhere out in a car with another man. In order to prevent what looked like a flood, I told him where to find her, daring to incur a fight, but it turned out all right. Now he'll drag old Tom over by the heels if I say so. No telling how long that will last, so I'll be ready to snap up the occasion.

Have you read *Broken Arrow*?[4] Old Tom has, he says, and thinks its pretty good, but a little bellyachey, if you know what he means. I could guess. I see [John] Collier is to be up at Pine Ridge this week.

I've quit sending out manuscripts. The change in address from Lincoln to Ellsworth made the difference of letters to purely rejection slips. More and more am I convinced that the actual product has almost nothing to do with either the reception or the sale of a manuscript. Stop me if I seem to be wrong.

Not that it matters. The book is unreported and I don't expect anything to sell anyway.

Sincerely,

1. Eleanor Hinman was writing a novel based on the life of Crazy Horse. She never completed it.

2. Zachary Taylor Sutley, *The Last Frontier* (New York: Macmillan, 1930).

3. Clyde is unidentified. Flora is Mari's sister.

4. Robert Gessner, *Broken Arrow* (New York: Farrar and Rinehart, 1933).

To Anne Longman

December 6, 1933

Dear Anne:[1]

Thanks so much for the kind words. They are scarce out in these regions. Also for the sheets with Horgan's story. That seemed a little more like the Horgan I expect. Another thing that interested me even more and did much for my morale was the article on Rockwell Kent. Did you read it?

But there's no denying that I was just a bit disappointed when I opened the bulky envelope and found nothing at all of ONE SUMMER in it. Am I entitled to any more of it or am I entitled to it?

Now I won't take no for an answer. You must write and I think you should let me see it, at least before you let that bunch of Quillers deflate you. How far would Sherwood Anderson, or Jane Austin, or Shakespeare have gotten with any group? They want the usual, the accepted. The more certainly that you feel depressed after reading them anything the more promising I should say the work is, all things being equal.

As a marketing address Ellsworth, Nebraska, seems to be the last word. People that never fail to send me letters with my manuscripts now return them with a polite rejection slip. So it wasn't the work after all, only the address.

I hope that you are keeping the old liver going these bad days. At least I judge the days are bad by the papers. Here we've only had one snow that was sufficient for jack rabbit tracking. Never have done this before, I had beginner's luck, brought home 19 pounds of meat, a Texas jack and a grey one. Had Hasenpfeffer from the hind quarters of one, the rest was chopped for the chickens to encourage a little producing for Christmas fruit cakes, etc.

Still no report on the book.

Tell me what you are reading and writing. Have you noticed the change in the story policy at Household? Last spring I took it for Crawford spring fever but it seems to continue. Try some of your stories on old Nelson Antrim.[2] I believe he'll like them.

Oh, I must tell you about my shack. My own domain, made it my self. Sleep in it, stay up as late as I like, rattle the typewriter, strut up and down when I've hit a snag, pile the maggoty remains of cigarettes high, and no one says one word. All to the fragrance of burning cowchips!

Sincerely,

1. Anne Longman was a journalist with the *Lincoln Journal* and a member of Quill.

2. Nelson Antrim Crawford (1888–1963) was the editor-in-chief of *Household* magazine from 1928 to 1951. He was also a professor of journalism at Kansas State College and professor of scientific writing at the Menninger School of Psychiatry.

To Helen Mary Hayes

December about the 9
[c. 1933]

Dear H.[1]

I have a general, suffused feeling of gratitude towards you only also another feeling, a guiltiness that I don't remember the causes of my gratitude. Ain't that a state?

First and foremost I presume its all those chatty letters, with the dirt of Igenfottem, as Marie[2] calls her, and her male admirers. How times have changed, but not so much that most of the admirers are still anything but mail here. There, that's almost up with Lorraine [Kuse],[3] wouldn't you know it? . . .

By the way—I got motivated to the extent of going up in the blowout for you, this time, and found the snow covering all the nice sharp, silicate sand. However, it was bad tracking rabbits today, so maybe, if the clouds don't bust again, there may be a little dry sand soon.

Almost everybody, including Buck, has written. . . . He hasn't even been to one play or concert, and him living at the International House! Says everybody else there is like he, looking for interesting conversation and there's none. Metterlinck knew that was no way to find little apples.

Your men sound interesting and damned envy-provoking. Who, by the way is Perry, or rather, where and what is it or he? Sounds like one a them naughty places, but I hope not.

Marie reports, 2 times, that John and Eck are still playing cards at your house.[4] Here and there, but no writing. Still, Marie seems to be doing a bit, of something. Sounds interesting. I'm looking forward to seeing a lot when and if I ever get back. Chances get remoter and remoter. Rather interesting to be where you're not wanted and not be able to leave. Sort of tree between cement blocks feeling. (Ribbon stuck here.)

Family Reunion Thanksgiving, with all the inlaws and all the hired hands and corn pickers, and the usual act of group singing about the organ, with Peggy at the keys. God! There's only one pump or pedal or whatever you call those carpet strip things, and act of jumping furiously on one foot. That's Peggy. Fred, hired hand, has not only no ear but a contrary one. Ear is so bad he can't even sing cowboy songs, although he's never discovered it. Jules tries manfully but trusts to memory on words, often not of song he's singing. Marie has taught school and knows how it ought to be only unfortunately it's never like that in our books. Fritz retires to store and swings feed from counter and entertains John, (Who's come over to show me his new lumber jacket and too bashful) (56 or thereabouts,) to come in. James does better.[5] He's the one who knows he doesn't know anything much about music so he tunes his fiddle with a pitchpipe and when he's not sure of a song he just stops and hopes someone else keeps on. Which leaves a couple of hired hands, one who sings fair but doesn't reach much, Flora, who's been told she can't carry a tune, slanderously, but just as effective as though she couldn't, and *me*. Well, was our sing a success! Oh, I forgot, there are others too, but I don't remember any noises from them, perhaps because of mine. Anyway, we sang for three hours and did we have fun! Then to a community dance, en masse, that night. . . .

But enough. I must to the house for my ten o'clock cup of tea before the mater puts the grounds out and to bed. (When I first moved out she said, "Well, it looks like I'll have a lot of little houses around the place, and have to live alone after all," rather tearfully. But she sure picks on me about the place when I'm in. Now she's half better.)

Say, you and everybody around here, keep referring to the footnotes in the Journal made of my letter. It would just happen that that Sunday's issue was sent to Peggy before I saw it and she burnt it. You couldn't clip me a copy? I would like to know what everybody's mad about. Not that I care, only I would like to know the extent of my "treason," as they term it. Particularly potent is a man with 20,000 acres of land to sell.[6]

As to the weather — best fall I've ever seen. Only one snow that more than just whitened the ground, and that only kept a day or so.

By the way, what's everybody reading? I've done nothing literate unless you call Slogum House, or the writing of it, literacy.

Yesterday Mother went to Alliance and I had to stay home, and in the house to crank out gas, and what not. And suddenly it dawned on me that I'd give a lot for one hour with the radio and the mob, just any mob. Instead, I cooked for Fred, who likes gravy so thick you can spread it like cheese, and conversed on the state of the turkey market with neighbors, etc. Gosh, I got homesick for the old two by-four across from the bathroom.

Well, I don't seem to know anything. Sorry.

1. Helen Mary Hayes (d. 1963) studied at the Chicago School of Music, was art and music critic for the *Lincoln State Journal,* and later was Assistant City Editor. She and MS lived at the same 1226 J Street house in their early Lincoln days and maintained their friendship for many years. She may well have been a major influence on MS's interest in both music and modern art.

2. Among MS's Lincoln friends there were several named Marie, Martha, Dorothy, and John. MS is probably speaking here of Marie Cronley, whom she first met in Van den Bark's university English classes. A businesswoman, Cronley was also a poet and member of Quill.

3. Lorraine Kuse, a member of Quill, was later associated with the Voice of America in Washington, D.C.

4. Eck was Elinor Gustin Crancer. John may have been Marie Cronley's nephew. He worked on the *Lincoln Journal,* later on the *Omaha Bee.*

5. Jules, Fritz, and James were MS's brothers. Marie was James's wife.

6. See the footnote to MS's letter to Frank Williams, November 9, 1933, p. 61.

Dr. A. E. Sheldon

State Historical Society

December 16, 1933

Dear Dr. Sheldon:

Your kind letters arrived safely on our not so rapid post. I have no words to express my appreciation. All I can say is Thank you.

The applications you suggested were made immediately, first to Miss Wolford and now to Mr. Thomas.

Evidently you are your normal vigorous and optimistic self this fine winter. A good winter for your birds too, I suspect. There are still a few Canada geese here and flocks of mallards. The fall has been beautiful here but life without library facilities and without music is no life to me. I hope the work in your department materializes, and the sooner the better for me.

I am deeply indebted to you.[1]

Sincerely,

1. MS was hired by Dr. Sheldon to work at NSHS under a federal grant program, the Civil Works Administration (CWA). She assisted him in research for a book he was working on—*Land Systems and Land Policies in Nebraska* (Lincoln: NSHS, 1936)—and handled general office duties. The CWA shortly was discontinued; in its place, under somewhat different funding, was the Federal Emergency Relief Administration (FERA). Later MS was also made director of personnel, sometimes with as many as thirty or forty FERA employees under her guidance as they organized archival material; she was also named associate editor of *NH*. MS returned to Lincoln in January 1934 and to her old address at 1226 J Street.

To Tyler Buchenau

March 19, 1934

Dear Buck:

Well, bless my soul 'n garter, if you ain't a comin' on up there in NYC, speakin' familiar like of the "Strachey school!" Don't you remember my enthusiasm last spring over the "Coming Struggle,"[1] terming it extravagantly, as everyone but Ted Shane said, the most important book of any country for the year. Frankly, of course, I find Strachey's discussion of the problem before society much more profound than his solution. I'll admit that he does his solving half-heartedly, or so it seems to me. Once more no one agrees with me. I can see the imperialism, God knows it's plain enough, but man being what he is, how long could you keep any state, communistic or otherwise, from falling into the hands of the few for profit—shekels, privilege or whatever the profit of the times is measured in. Perhaps that's why communism was given up that other time it got a serious trial—when our ancestors skulked among the rocky bluffs along the rivers of, say, Europe. Somebody with more power to his arm and more club just naturally took what he wanted regardless to the communism that was prevalent. There is always, at least during historic times there has always been a huge herd of sheep-like creatures who are willing to let the ambitious man accumulate privilege. I'm afraid we'll have to expose humanity for the groveling thing it is as a rule and try to remedy it. Then perhaps communism may work — when we have attained the place where my dreams can begin to become actuality — when every one is capable of self-government without encroaching upon his neighbor. Enlightened anarchy.

I knew H[arcourt] B[race] had turned the book down. A completely strange man, I assume it is a man, from down in Arkansas on a rural route wrote me so. He happened to be in NYC for a few weeks and knew somebody over at the HB stables. He heard about my manuscript — "naturalo-regionalism" he calls it and suggests Covici-Friede. Nor did he take the trouble to write his name legibly. "Bachelor Stork Party" is back so the novel will be back from Harpers probably before now. As some one told me: "That about uses up the hide-bound conservatives, doesn't it?" I'm all in favor of Farrar and Rhinehart [*sic*]. [Gilbert] Doane recommended them in 1932, said I might use his name, and so I wrote with considerable enthusiasm but ever since then the ms has been out or someone has had another conservative publisher to send it to. Viking Press is a good bet too. [Howard] Erickson wrote me to try them. They published his "Son of Earth" last spring — unleavened story of Iowa toil and scheming; you must be tired of the book by now.[2] If so, return it collect and I'll send it out.

And now to you. Your Jenny Lee sounds like a story, a nice version of the woman in *Union Square*. Have you read it? I have read "Moral Man and Immoral Society." Somehow it seems to me Dr. [Reinhold] Niebuhr used to be at Cleveland or Cincinnati or some place like that. He is frequently quoted, and with telling effect, by the young intellectuals on everything from literature to war (or is that so far?) in their raft of fat books put out by such publishers as Covici-Friede. "Recovery through Revolution" is one of these compilations, wherein appear such people as Calverton, the man who analyzes American literature from the bourgeois influence, petty and upper.[3] Cole, etc. Niebuhr is quoted in such books almost as frequently as Marx.

I love your description of the music at his church. The comment about "insincere choir with damned little cooperation from the virgins" is perfect. Anyone would know just what sort of music it produced, and what the virgins were like. Which brings me to the idea dearest to my heart concerning you: I've always seen latent talent for writing in you, but I knew that it couldn't be forced or even urged and that only an upheaval of your inner poise would probably ever bring the need for creative expression. Evidently it has come, sufficient that your music will no longer suffice, and so I wish you luck and not too much agony and grief. Articles would be a good place to begin and if you could detach yourself sufficiently from the ego, a frank, honest, terse article on the upheaval might go. Articles and ideas for them seem to spring from the individual. I have ideas for a dozen at least buzzing in my brain but not a one of these would do for anyone else—the material is either personal experience or of primary personal importance. If one had syndicate connections International House might make one for the writer gifted in unearthing the purpose behind the student there. Your impressions from New York—that is, many things one who reads anticipates but there are always perfectly obvious things that no one ever tells us or writes about that slap the newcomer in the face. The *New Yorker* was originally built upon that idea, I am told, and I'm sure it's not entirely exploited. An interesting article might be made from the restricted books and manuscripts, as for example, the difficulties one has getting to look at *Banditti of the Plains,*[4] written on the Johnson County War (Wyo.), in the N. Y. City library. There are only a few copies left, two or three, and it is very difficult, I am told, to get a look at it. You might try it. There are other, similar books that for one reason or another have systematically been destroyed by fanatics or people who have something to lose by their circulation. There are various religious books of that type, an exposé of Masonry, etc.

I like your notion that you can out-Stein Stein. And probably you can, at that. I've tried it, but mine becomes automatic writing, almost immediately, and turns out much too coherent only I don't know what it's about. "Did that come out of me"ish, you know. Even the mode of expression is not mine. Sounds a little psychopathic, wouldn't you say? I'm sure yours will be symbolism. You are a symbolic person, if I may be permitted the looseness in terminology.

Yes, I read the [Oswald] Spengler article. He amuses me, after he has depressed me to the complete desaturation point. And [John] Dewey of the Dewey system gives me the pip, you know, what chickens get when they have no feathers and get rained on. Most disagreeable disease.

Jack Conroy, editor of Anvil and author of "Disinherited"[5] wrote me there was an interesting young communist in town by the name of Hoorwich, gave me his address, and laments that there are so few literature minded souls in this town, apparently. I jotted the man a line and then I had the uncomfortable feeling that I should not have done it. I do believe he was one of the guests at Mrs. Deutch's dinner, the one who got up from the table and left, oh, properly excused, of course. But he was so completely bored with us.

Impulsive, that's me. There's a bit of humor to the situation. He's an inactive communist investigating the American farmer for the government or some such thing. . . .

From appearances now I shall be trekking westward about the first or the fifteenth of April. The C[ivil] W[orks] A[dministration] stops and there seems nothing else to do that guarantees meals with fair regularity.[6] I have been sending manuscripts out in the hope of staving off the evil day but all I collect is complimentary letters. Someday I shall get me a gun and kill every editor who tells me how good my stuff is and then returns it. This business has held up the novel, which Harcourt Brace would *not* like. I've landed several short stories with the new mushroom magazines (no pay) and having more fun with the contacts with editors. They almost invariably take me to their immature bosoms and write me their aims and ambitions in life, their troubles with publishers, with contributors, with this and that, even the mother-in-law (not in every case.)

Dorothy Thomas must be selling for she hasn't been over for weeks.[7] That's always an index. The unhappy and confused seek me out. Probably makes them feel happy by contrast. Happy [Thomas] is in love and so long as Sally Green is available he's not going anywhere to report on his sisters' progress in the writing game. . . .

Well, report at intervals.

1. John Strachey, *The Coming Struggle for Power* (New York: Covici Friede, 1933).

2. Howard Erickson, *Son of Earth* (New York: Dial, 1933).

3. Reinhold Niebuhr, *Moral Man and Immoral Society* (New York: Scribner, 1932); Samuel Schmalhausen, ed., *Recovery through Revolution* (New York: Covici Friede, 1933).

4. Asa Shinn Mercer, *Banditti of the Plains* (Cheyenne, Wyo.: A. S. Mercer, 1894). MS's edition was published in San Francisco by Grabhorn Press in 1935.

5. Jack Conroy, *The Disinherited* (New York: Covici Friede, 1933).

6. Although the Civil Works Administration was a relatively short-lived program and federal funds were periodically in doubt, money from one source or another, including a modest stipend from the state, was found, and MS stayed with NSHS until after *OJ* won the *Atlantic Monthly* prize in 1935.

7. Dorothy Thomas, from a large and talented family, was a member of Quill. The winner of an O. Henry award, she published over two hundred short stories, books for children, and two novels, *Ma Jeeter's Girls* (New York: Knopf, 1933) and *The Home Place* (New York: Knopf, 1936).

Sunday evening
n.d. [1934]

Dear Buck:

The novel has come. I have not opened it yet, for I know what I'll find—cigarette burns, ashes, hair, queer markings, pages folded back and the whole thing out of sequence. Publishers' readers are like that.

Not that it matters.

As for the reason for my telegram—Have you read the introduction to Kafka's "The Castle"?[1] If Kafka could not command enough loyalty from his closest friend to insure the carrying out of his wishes, surely I could expect no more of a casual acquaintance. Being by nature less trusting than Kafka I shall look after the minor details for myself.

And thanks for the bother and everything.

Good luck,

1. Buchenau had asked MS what she wanted him to do with the *OJ* manuscript after he collected it from its latest rejection. She told him to burn it. When he mailed it to her instead, she responded with this note. "Buck" failed to understand her allusion to Kafka.

April 30, 1934

Dear Buck:

Once more I see how sadly my words misconvey my intentions. It was nothing you did—you have been the most considerate and generous person and—

But perhaps, much as I dislike doing so, I should tell you the real reason. Kafka was a struggling German writer of Slavic intermixture. He wrote in a manner and of a matter unpalatable to German publishers, starved, finally died, indirectly, of the hardship. Because he did not die at home he had to depend upon his friend, Broad [*sic*], I believe it was, to destroy his spurned manuscripts. Broad agreed, and then when Kafka was safely dead and buried—and suddenly a *good* writer in the eyes of the German book makers—Broad managed to get his manuscripts published.[1] Perhaps it was not a selfish act. Perhaps he really believed, as he says he did, that Kafka's work was great and must not cease to be. Anyway, while it leaves people like me, who find a certain fourth dimension in his work glad, it angers me too. Somehow it is as though Kafka had been denied burial, as though I, by reading, were a conspirator to defraud the dead.

It looked as though I could not possibly survive much beyond the 20th of

April. I know my resistance to starvation rather well by now and can predict when collapse will come. I knew, also, that to ask you to burn the book would be asking something of you that I had no right to ask of anyone. Consequently there was only one thing to do — get the book into my own hands.

I dislike saying these things. I know how ghastly and melodramatic they sound. Only because an explanation seems necessary and certainly due you can I get myself to consider mailing this letter at all.

Please believe me — I hoped to spare you an unpleasant task.

1. Franz Kafka (1883–1924) was from a German-Jewish family, but was born and lived most of his life in Prague. His most famous works include *The Metamorphosis* (1915), *The Castle* (1926), *The Trial* (1925), *Amerika* (1927), and *The Judgement* (1928). Max Brod (1884–1968), also a German Jew living in Prague, was a longtime friend. When Kafka died he left two notes for Brod, one requiring his friend to destroy all unpublished manuscripts and one to refrain from republishing material already in print. Brod refused to do so.

To Editorial Offices

THE SATURDAY EVENING POST

February 21, 1935

Gentlemen:

THE GREAT COUNCIL is the story of the first Black Hills council, the Bad Council as the Indians call it, the first attempt to strip from the Sioux their most valuable possession. The Homestake mine alone yielded $200,000,000 in gold. The next council, 1876, was more successful. Annuities were cut off; the council held in the stockade; the chiefs literally held prisoners until 41 of them signed. It was an exciting time, and even here Young Man Afraid of His Horse avoided actually "touching the pen" to the treaty. I am writing the story of this one also.

My work has appeared in such publications as *Nature, North American Review,* etc. For some time now I have been doing research in Indians for the Nebraska State Historical Society here and am also associate editor of the Nebraska *History Magazine.*

Thank you,

P. S. Attached sources are for your information only. Good photographs of Red Cloud, Spotted Tail, Young Man Afraid are available for your artists, as well as some of the locale.

To Editorial Offices

Non-Fiction Contest
THE ATLANTIC MONTHLY PRESS[1]

April 6, 1935

Dear Sirs:

April 1, 1935, I sent you a manuscript, HOME ON THE RUNNING WATER, and apologetically, for almost at the last minute the manuscript was destroyed and only a rallying of my more durable friends and their equally durable typewriters for a wild Saturday night and Sunday of typing got the book out on April 1 in any shape at all. I am sorry.[2]

An earlier draft of this book, with fictional names, was entered in your 1933 non-fiction contest and held approximately eight months. The manuscript, after two years of reconsideration, a complete and thorough rewriting and with the actual names of the characters used throughout, is re-entered with the written permission from your offices.

And now for the manuscript: I have tried to make *Home on the Running Water* the biography of a community, the upper Niobrara country in western Nebraska, and of a man, my father, Jules Ami Sandoz.

The book grew out of a childhood and adolescence spent among the story tellers of the frontier, for the frontier, whether by Turner's famous definition or any other, is a land of story tellers and in this respect remains frontier in nature until the last original settler is gone.

It grew, then, out of the long hours in the smoky old kitchen on the Running Water, the silent hours of listening behind the stove or in the woodbox, when it was assumed that of course I was asleep in bed. So I heard all the accounts of the hunts, the well accident, the fights with the cattlemen and the sheepmen, given hints here and there of the tragic scarcity of women, when a man had to "marry anything that got off the train," as Old Jules often said; the drouths, the storms, and the wind and isolation. At school we heard other versions, partly through the natural cruelty of childhood, partly because a feud was on and we were actually outsiders in the school.

But the most impressive stories were those told me by Old Jules himself, perhaps on the top of Indian hill, overlooking the spot where a man was hung under his leadership, and the scene of six years of lawing that drove his second wife into the insane asylum. Perhaps he limped through the orchard as he talked, with me close behind, my hands full of ducks or grouse or quail. Perhaps I followed among flowering cherry trees, carrying the plats to the orchard. Perhaps I drove the team on long trips while he smoked and talked of his own dreams and his joys and his disappointments. And always was I too frightened of him to voice either approval or surprise.

Sometimes it seems that a quirk of fate has tied me to this father I feared so much even into my maturity. The three crucial moments in his life after I could take part in our family life involved me as an unwilling participant: the snakebite, the near-killing of the Strasburgers, and my near-ending with the same gun, and the final moment when he died.

Out of these events came the need to write this book, augmented by the one line my father wrote me in 1925 [1926], when I received honorable mention in the Harper Intercollegiate short story contest, guarded by the name of Marie Macumber. He discovered my activities, sent me one line in his emphatic up and down strokes: "You know I consider writers and artists the maggots of society." The book became a duty the last day of his life, when he asked that I write of his struggles as a locater, a builder of communities, a bringer of fruit to the Panhandle.

Always a notebook keeper, after his death I began methodically to cover the entire period from 1880 to 1928. I read every newspaper reference to northwest Nebraska printed during the period and made available through the splendid newspaper files of the Nebraska State Historical Society, every one of the 4000 letters and documents in the files of Old Jules, exposed my mother to months of inquisitional inquiry and interviewed everyone available. And as I read, the stories of my childhood came back to me with new significance. And as I arranged and rearranged the bits of information in what seemed the closest verisimilitude of life as those people lived it in the Running Water country, the duty became a privilege. Not one character, included or regretfully put aside, would I have one whit different. Not my mother, who had the courage and the tenacity to live with this man so many years, or the Surbers, to whom many of us owe what joy we derive from music and from art, not Nell Sears, Jim the convict, the Peters, Andy Brown the yellah boy, the Smiths, who constituted the bit of glamour of our community, Tissot, Freese, Dr. Walter Reed and Old Jules himself. These people have endured and as I review them from the vantage point of twice knowledge, my eyes mist. A gallant race, and I salute them.

It was only after Old Jules was dead and his portrait hung in the Nebraska Agricultural Hall of Achievement that I discovered that his family were to celebrate the 450th anniversary of the family foundation in Switzerland. The long line of men were usually professional, veterinaries and doctors, and so on, but always with agriculture as their hobby, the furthering of agricultural fairs their enjoyment, — a family of men. Yet long before women talked much of careers the Sandoz women pushed out into the world. One is said to have made periodic trips to Sweden in the Eighteenth century for iron. Later there were such women as Madam Rosat, governess, perhaps I should say tutor, to Franklin D. Roosevelt in the '90's. My father often spoke of her and of his only sister who taught French in Toronto with pride and maintained with the next breath that woman's place was in the home.

As for the events and the people pictured in HOME ON THE RUNNING WATER, I can promise affidavits from the Society on any event of moment, as for instance, the Niobrara feud, the cattleman murder of the brother of Old Jules, etc., from newspapers of the period. As to my historical and personal integrity as well as my portrait of the time and the community I refer you to Dr. A. E. Sheldon, Superintendent, Nebraska State Historical Society, State Capitol, Lincoln, with whom I have worked at various times for years and for the last year in the capacity of associate editor of the Nebraska *History Magazine* and director of much of the research, or to Frank L. Williams, Managing Editor, Nebraska State *Journal,* Lincoln. Mr. Williams knew Old Jules also, and he spent his cub reporter days in western Nebraska in the Eighties.

My published work is inconsequential: historical features, a two part article in the *North American Review,* April and May, 1930, an article of the first few months in the hills in October 1933, *Nature,* another, on Sandhill Sundays, an attempt to show the changing folk ways by the changing Sundays published in *Folksay,* 1932, and several stories, one in the N[orth] A[merican] *Review,* May 1933 and the others in the *Prairie Schooner.* I am very prolific as a writer, not so fortunate in selling. Now I am revising my first book, a novel, and have two others well outlined, with sections in first draft.[3] Besides these I have an Indian historical novel planned, or rather another biography, of a family this time—the Man Afraid of His Horse people, last of the great Sioux chieftain lines. I am enclosing a carbon of a treaty council from the material. The original is out.

But surely I must take up no more of your time. If there is anything that requires further explanation, I shall be glad to do what I can.
Thank you,

1. Atlantic Monthly Press used much of this letter almost verbatim as the forward to *OJ,* but with an earlier date of March 23, 1935.

2. MS experimented with several titles for the biography: "The Thunderer," "Thunder on the Running Water," and "Home on the Running Water." The manuscript fell into a full scrub bucket. It was unsalvageable.

3. The revised novel was the never published "Murky River." Of the two novels outlined, one was *Slogum House.* The other may have been "Col. Pomroy."

To Edward Weeks

ATLANTIC MONTHLY PRESS[1]

June 14, 1935

Dear Mr. Weeks:

There are no words in my vocabulary to express my appreciation of the honor and recognition the Atlantic Monthly Press, through you, has bestowed upon me. It is almost exactly ten years since I was given honorable mention in Harpers' Inter-Collegiate Contest, a long Nebraska drouth.

Regarding the photographs: During the week-end I'll go through my stock of photographs and collect all that might be of use to you directly or as guides to illustrations. Dr. Condra of the Soil Conservation Department, a firm friend of Old Jules, has a series of fine photographs of him in his orchard, etc. I'll obtain these for you.

Unfortunately I do not have a photograph of myself. My acquaintances always expect the play of facial expression that they know to be suggested somehow and our photographers are not equal to the task. I had a sheaf of exposures taken Thursday with the sad results enclosed. I am sorry. Surely there must be more to me than that photograph suggests to make my room the center of the writers and artists—a gathering and discussion place. Perhaps it is just because one can loaf there.

About the revision: I am one of those Very Capable persons, a crutch, nothing much, but habit forming. However, there is no reason why I cannot come to Boston for the revising almost any time after July 1, if any of the prize money is available for my use by that time. Just now I am finishing the editorial work on a book for Dr. Sheldon.[2]

I look forward to working with the editorial staff of the Press, I expect to profit a great deal through the knowledge gained.

Thank you,

1. MS is responding to the telegram notifying her that *OJ* had won. It read:

13 June 1935

HAPPY TO ANNOUNCE THAT YOUR MANUSCRIPT WINS ATLANTIC CONTEST STOP PRIZE AWARDED ON CONDITION IT BE EDITED AND REDUCED TO APPROXIMATELY ONE HUNDRED THIRTY FIVE THOUSAND WORDS HOPE YOU

CAN COME EAST TO ASSIST WITH EDITING PERSONALLY STOP WISH TO ENTITLE BOOK OLD JULES STOP KEEP THIS NEWS STRICTLY CONFIDENTIAL UNTIL JUNE SEVENTEENTH WHEN ANNOUNCEMENT RELEASED TO NEWSPAPERS BE PREPARED FOR INTERVIEWS LINCOLN STOP SEND ALL AVAILABLE PHOTOGRAPHS YOURSELF AND JULES ACKNOWLEDGE THIS WIRE HEARTY CONGRATULATIONS — EDWARD WEEKS

2. Sheldon, *Land Systems and Land Policies in Nebraska.*

To Mrs. Jules Sandoz

June 15, 1935

Dear Mother:

Wouldn't Old Jules snort if he knew that his story won the $5,000 Atlantic Monthly Press prize?

Love,

More details later.

Yes *Five thousand dollars!*

To Miss M. A. LeHand

[Secretary to President Franklin D. Roosevelt]
The White House

July 20, 1935

Dear Miss LeHand:

A communication from Roger L. Scaife of Little-Brown at last caught up with me. He tells me that the President expressed a desire that I make a short call while in Washington.

May I say how very sorry I am that I missed receiving the telegram at New York? A continuous migraine of two weeks standing and word that the editor I hoped to see at Washington was out of town altered my plans. Of course I did not dare hope that President Roosevelt would really wish to see me or my original plans would most certainly have remained unaltered.

All through my childhood I heard of the remarkable youth whom Tante Rosat[1] had taught at Hyde Park, and for a long time there was a photograph of him in my father's stamp album, a photograph that was most delightful to our eyes, for my brothers wore overalls that my mother made and their feet were usually bare. But now and then Father would let us see the boy with such fine clothes and such neat hair. "A fine young gentleman!" my father would remark. "And don't forget that a Swiss woman was his teacher, and a Sandoz!" Then for a long time our protests against our foreignness and strangeness would be stilled.

Old Jules did not live to see the Roosevelt Program launched, but he would have approved most heartily. He spent his life obtaining homes for the landless, bringing trees and fruit to the bare hills of western Nebraska. In the Nineties he saw the entire community he built in the wilderness foreclosed by eastern capital that in its turn went under. (All through my childhood we paid 12 and what even amounted to 14 percent on eastern loans.) Father saw the need of greater opportunity for the individual and at least a semblance of social security. He died in 1928, the gloom of agricultural calamity already about him.

But we, his children, have seen the "Fine young gentleman" save Nebraska from a chaos that will always be inconceivable to all those who do not realize how long our farmer has staggered along under the heavy load of tariff discrimination. By 1929 he was already at the precipice of dire need, at least in many instances, and the combined calamities of depression and drouth did the rest.

I have no words to express my regret that I missed my opportunity to see President Roosevelt. If an appropriate moment arises, will you convey my apologies to him?

Thank you,

1. Jeanne Rosat, Mari's paternal great-aunt, was Franklin Roosevelt's governess.

To Edward Weeks

July 31, 1935

Dear Mr. Weeks:

I apologize for the length of this letter at the outset. And now to business:

> I've made such corrections as seemed best under the circumstances, on the proof. I hope that they are not too unintelligible and not too antagonistic to your policy. You have made some very fine compromises in this manuscript and I do appreciate it.
>
> The proper names, as Oglala, Ogallala, Vetterli, etc., I have checked once more with undisputable sources. They are correct. Suzanna I find is spelled *Susanna* by Sears in his digest of songs. Our old songbook, backless for thirty years, uses the *z*. The *s* is without doubt safer here.

The Reed letter contained several abbreviations that were not clearly written and strange to me and my guess may well be wrong. If the letter, God forbid, is really lost, I suggest that you have the abbreviations checked by a surgeon. And do tell me the worst about the letter, please. I'd much rather know that it was gone than be kept in suspense.[1]

Schwartz—I was under the impression that I used Swartz. Not that it matters in the least except that we shall have to be very thorough in our checking, both in the introductory letter and the ms. proofs.

Court *sits,* I know, but never in my work unless it is intended as a jibe. Who but a lawyer clings to such silly business in the face of universal mispronunciation?

I hope you'll approve of the circumlocution, galley 46.

I feel that I've not made the changes and improvements you expected of me but somehow the ms. is getting beyond the cobbling stage, or don't you think so? No more places to hold patches. Only a complete rewrite would help it much now. Some of the cobbled paragraphs are among the very worst in the book, it seems to me.

Now about more general matters:

Credit for the Dwight Kirsh pictures—Have you written to him about them?[2] Please do this if you have been too busy. And will you return the others to me please. I don't want him to think that I am unappreciative.

Credit to the Nebraska State Historical Society for the "D. H. Lawrence" photograph of Old Jules. And return the original as soon as possible for their files.

"River Polak"—I should like this story returned if convenient.[3] I can, however, make another copy from my carbon if it is not easily available. This story went in with the MS last spring.

Harriet Ashbrooke, publicity, Coward-McCann, sends word that you are doing very well by me. The Atlantic spread is fine. I hope that it won't raise too many expectations.

My work at the Society will have to terminate soon. There are really a surprising number of articles, etc., for me to write right now, and perhaps they won't be wanted later. You see, I still can't see Atlantic Monthly Press readers liking Old Jules. Quite likely no readers would. I hope that I am wrong. I never feel that way about my work or rather I never have before. I certainly don't feel that way about SLOGUM HOUSE.

Sincerely,

1. MS had included with her book manuscript a letter written by Dr. Walter Reed. It later was misplaced, and she feared it had been permanently lost (the facsimile appears in the pictures following p. 206 in *OJ*, 1935 edition).

2. Frederick Dwight Kirsch (1899–1981) was chairman of the Department of Fine Arts and director of University Galleries. His photographs of the sandhills were used for the endpapers of the 1935 Atlantic Monthly Press edition.

3. The story appeared in *AM* in September 1937.

To Carlton Wells

University of Michigan
Ann Arbor, Michigan

November 12, 1935

Dear Mr. Wells:

I am interested in your question: Have there been two strikingly different pioneer Nebraskas?

Pioneer life has at least four great similarities.

First: The pioneer himself was a misfit, either by nature, inclination, or ambition, or necessity, in his home community. That is—he wanted something more than it could give him even if it didn't deny him freedom and a livelihood.

Second: All pioneer communities are, by definition, remote from the advantages of settlements.

Third: The region is untried and unfamiliar, and usually conquered only by many tragic trials and errors.

Fourth: Being "open" and "free" it is the region where conflicting ambitions have their, if not most unrestricted, at least their most undisguised manifestation, and where emotions are less restricted by the conventions of organized society, where amusements are more often group activities, as the free for all [?], picnic, house raising, etc.

The pioneer region of Willa Cather was never so close to the frontier in her time as my region was in my life. Nor was it ever so close to the frontier in any of her stories. The Red Cloud region, home of Willa Cather, had as many settlers in the 1860's as my region had in 1884. The really tragic period then was the period of the Indian wars, 1864 to 1867, when Sioux and Cheyenne kept the scattered settlers in terror. When the Indian was removed the homesteader swept in. He found the land more or less free, with the cattleman foothold a very insecure one because the hungry Indian had made cattle growing a precarious business. In one decade the region was settled and while stragglers deserted, the problem was what one finds so superbly portrayed in *My Antonia* and *O Pioneers*—one of adjustment rather than one of staying at all at any price. The land was fertile, similar in climate and altitude to that settled successfully not far to the east; the crops it produced were similar; the roads were passable and the railroad no farther after 1868 than it is from my home in the sandhills today. The altitude is approximately 1,200 to 1,800 feet while we are over 4,000 feet—with half the rainfall and real blizzards, not snow storms. Altogether, you see, there is little actual duplication of conditions between the material of Willa Cather and that in *Old Jules*.

Of course, one real difference lies much deeper than the material—the difference between an artist of the caliber of Miss Cather, and an ordinary plug frontier historian with a craving to write!

Thank you for the very fine compliment you pay *Old Jules*.

Sincerely,

To Edward Weeks

November [?], 1935

Dear Mr. Weeks:

This letter promises to be as itemized as a tailor's bill, so be prepared.

First, I hope that your speaking dates in the middle west went off without too many hitches. The weather was apparently at its very bad worst. The plane was grounded for two hours the night of the tenth and at no time would the pilots promise to get us farther than the next air port. But west of Chicago the clouds broke and gave the Stratosphere a rather decent day.

I look back on my two weeks in New York as a period of almost undiluted joy. The luncheon with Miss Bolton went rather well, except that the critics were disappointed in me personally, as I knew they would be. Lewis Gannett made me show the broken bone in my hand to prove my identity. I liked them all except Soskin, who seems so strange I felt compelled to look at him. And then I couldn't make Harry Hansen talk about his own writing—which I consider a major defeat and was impressed accordingly.[1]

After that the high point in the New York stay was the Marshall party for the Russian Consul (whom, incidentally, I never got around to see at all, partly because of Dr. Cohn, Ben Stolberg, Canby, Hindus, etc.). Harry

Sherman was there and since we couldn't talk, he had Whit Burnett and Martha Foley and Mrs. Sherman to lunch and we had a fine visit.[2]

The thing I will never forget was the Van Gogh exhibit. I found myself returning to it several times. How could anyone fail to recognize the man as a genius? His self-portraits are masterpieces, of course, but for myself I should like to have "The Potato Eaters" accessible at all times. Is there another painter, I wonder, who suffers so much from reproduction? After everyone thought I had gone home I went down to the Battery and started up town, working from gallery to gallery. Here and there I would hear of some obscure little show of new art and be tramped over to see it. There were several of these around Union Square. Anyway, I saw practically all of them to the Metropolitan.

Mr. Studin, remotely from Pueblo and apparently mostly a party giver, got together a little group at his apartment, including Dr. Alvin Johnson and Rollin Kirby. In Dr. Johnson I discovered an individual willing to go almost as far in human experimentation as I and much more willing to generalize. I like him very much. No one has any business being as handsome as Kirby.[3]

I spent a week-end at Darien, Conn, with the Reids. We ran into a post Dartmouth victory party with some brilliant conversation between slightly happy philosophers and with a man who knew all the Gilbert and Sullivan airs "by heart". His wife, a former Lincoln woman (although we didn't discover this until late) accompanied him unfailingly, also by memory. It was a feat. For variety a former actor swallowed lighted cigarettes. It was a mad house. John Hyde Preston and his wife were there and the next day we all went to see Konrad Bercovici, who was just what I once, long ago, expected him to be. He was the only person in New York who seemed to genuinely like me and I was pleased with him accordingly.[4]

To my infinite disgust I found that *Tobacco Road* is being burlesqued.[5]

Enough gossip. This seems to be the reaction from too much book autographing. I did two hundred for the public, at a tea, this afternoon. Sacrifice upon the altar of commerce.

By the way, to whom do I owe thanks for the copy of Charles Dawes *Notes*?[6]

And now to the book: Its reception appalls me, although Bernard De Voto pointed out the probabilities of all this flubdubbery. The only really sensible criticism I've seen was that in the [Boston] *Transcript* and unfortunately it had the sound of carping. Of course I'm swamped with letters. Not from the sad, frustrated, rhyme-making women who wrote last summer but from former dwellers in the Panhandle, from history teachers and college instructors. Incidentally there are dozens of requests for a rough map to help follow the meanderings. If the book is ever redone I think a map might be advisable, if maps are still used then.

And Mr. Kirsch and the Society want their pictures. I should have the letters, etc., back also, as I'm responsible for them to the family, particularly the Reed letter and the documents. Paul [Hoffman] is to have one of Old Jules' own letters if he wants it,[7] preferably not one essential to the historical background of the book. In case you want one for any purpose, help yourself.

Another incidental: I want to thank you for recommending Harold Ober.[8] He seems thoroughly sympathetic with my point of view. You may be interested and amused to know that *Pictorial Review* and *Cosmopolitan* turned out with food for me. Miss Whiting of the *Cosmopolitan* wants a look at *Slogum House* for serialization. I told her they wouldn't want it as I'm writing it and I won't have it changed. Nevertheless she insists that I get your opinion on the subject. That is, if you were to find it acceptable what would be your attitude toward serialization in the *Cosmopolitan?* Personally I'm very certain it will never do for them.

There are other things I intended to ask, but my mind has gone flat. Monday I'm putting up my "Busy until July 1" sign.

Sincerely,

1. Laetitia Bolton was in Public Relations for the Atlantic Monthly Press. The men mentioned were critics. Lewis Gannett (1891–1966) was on the staff of the *Manchester Guardian* and *New York Herald-Tribune.* William Soskin (1899–1952) was literary critic for *New York American* and later a Book-of-the-Month Club editor. Harry Hansen (1884–1977), the author of numerous books, was with *New York World-Telegram* and later was a vice-president of Hastings House Publishers.

2. The Marshalls are unidentified. The four men mentioned were writers. David Cohn published "We Fight No More" in *AM* in November 1937. Ben Stolberg, an author-journalist and professor, was the associate editor of *Bookman,* columnist for *New York Evening Post,* and coeditor (with Warren J. Vinton) of *Economic Consequences of the New Deal* (New York: Harcourt Brace, 1935). Courtland Canby wrote "A Letter from Persepolis," *AM,* July 1937. Maurice Gershon Hindus was an authority on Russian Armenians, Doukhobors, and Russian collective farms. His work includes *Red Bread* (New York: Cape and H. Smith, 1931) and *The Great Offensive* (London: Gollancz, 1933).

Harry Sherman may have been Harold M. Sherman, a free-lance interviewer, radio writer, and prolific writer of sports fiction and "how-to" books. Whit Burnett (1899–1973), an editor (*Scholastic Magazine*), essayist, and short story writer, founded *Story* in 1931 with Martha Foley, at that time his wife. Martha Foley (1897–1977) was a newspaperwoman in California and New York and later edited *Best American Short Stories* (Boston: Houghton Mifflin, 1942–75).

3. Mr. Studin is unidentified. Alvin Johnson (1874–1971), a Nebraska-born writer and economist, was a professor of economics at Yale, editor of the *New Republic* from 1917 to 1923, director of the New School for Social Research, and a prolific writer. His autobiography was *Pioneer's Progress* (New York: Viking, 1952). Rollin Kirby (1875–1952) was a cartoonist for magazines and New York newspapers, winning Pulitzer prizes in 1921, 1924, and 1928 for his political cartoons. He was also a poet and essayist.

4. James Reid was with Harcourt Brace. John Hyde Preston (1906–80) was a novelist, essayist, biographer, and writer-in-residence at Black Mountain College in the 1930s. He published *The Exploits of Anthony Wayne* (New York: Book League of America, 1930). Konrad Bercovici (1882–1961), a Romanian, was the author of numerous novels as well as nonfiction about gypsies. His autobiography was titled *It's the Gypsy in Me* (New York: Prentis Hall, 1941). He was on the staff of *New York World* and *New York Post*.

5. Erskine Caldwell, *Tobacco Road* (1932; London: Hunemann, 1955). The play was scripted by Jack Kirkland in 1932.

6. Charles Dawes (1865–1951) practiced law in Nebraska, 1886–94, and later was vice-president under Coolidge. He created the Dawes Plan for a budget for Germany after World War I and in 1925 was awarded the Nobel Peace Prize.

7. Paul Hoffman (d. 1960) was a young editor at Atlantic Monthly Press who first recommended *OJ* for publication. He wrote a personal letter of congratulation to MS shortly after the book was accepted and thereby began a long, close friendship. As with so many editors, he moved frequently from one publisher to another. After leaving Boston, he was with Alfred A. Knopf, later joined Westminster Press in Philadelphia, and did some free-lancing. A graduate of Syracuse and Harvard universities, he willed his MS correspondence and manuscripts to Syracuse.

8. Harold Ober was a highly respected literary agent who represented such distinguished authors as F. Scott Fitzgerald, William Faulkner, Pearl Buck, Catherine Drinker Bowen, and J. D. Salinger. Sandoz chose him to represent her for her book-length works.

To Will H. Johnson

December 30, 1935

Dear Mr. Johnson:

You ask for something a little different from what is on the flap of *Old Jules*. Unfortunately, I don't know just what is there. I learned early in this business that if you never read what people say about you you can be much happier. But I can't go into detail for you—Old Jules fan mail still runs around 200 letters a week, with very few that do not require an answer of some sort. And, incidentally, I'm to have another manuscript in the hands of my publishers by July 1, 1936. Only a miracle can help me now.

But about me. Well, I'm lean, thin-faced, with a large, elastic mouth that laughs much of the time, sometimes inwardly, at me, sometimes outwardly. It is so seldom still, (to either ear or eye) that when I have a picture taken everyone shouts "That's not you! Your mouth isn't right!"

I'm about five feet five, weight around a hundred pounds, can still shoulder a hundred and a quarter fairly easily and when I was home three years ago I found I could still take a dally around a post with sufficient dispatch to keep my hands from being rope burned when a fractious yearling was on the other end of it. I like to hunt; can usually get all the game I can carry home and have been known to cache some. I'm not so good on target practice. Probably because I need the urge for speed and shoot better on drop sight than when I have the time to get choicy. I can build a fire in a rain and can take a model T Ford apart on an Indian reservation to put in a new ring gear or new bands if necessary. I'm not afraid of Indians, gun men, wild cows or critics but I don't like teas and when people begin to talk about inspiration in writing I feel like an infidel.

But enough. Perhaps the enclosed carbon of a letter to a woman in a predicament similar to yours will help you.

And don't let the business bore you too much.

Sincerely,

Of course I'll be glad to inscribe the book for you.

To Mrs. O. W. Adams

December 30, 1935

Dear Clara Adams:

The charge made by one of your acquaintances that I wrote *Old Jules* to vent my bitterness amuses me. First, because there is no reason for bitterness at all. No family of my acquaintance has been better equipped against the vicissitudes of life as it must be lived than his six children. Don't forget that we got our ability to dream dreams far above our surroundings from him. Further, tell your friend that she would have to go a long ways to find anyone more uniformly gay than I—or at least as I was until all this hullabloo over the book began to dissipate my time so seriously.

You ask my reason for writing *Old Jules*. Naturally, it goes far beyond his permission to do so, which was a mechanical requirement before I could begin, but no more. I have always been interested in man and his way of life, which, to me, means history, and writing—literature, if possible, never writing merely to amuse.

I looked around me for the most promising material and I saw rather early that it was unquestionably Old Jules and his community. That in itself should indicate my respect for the man and his ambitions.

As I worked with the material, three years in research and two in writing, it gradually dawned upon me that here was a character who embodied not only his own strengths and weaknesses but those of all humanity—that his struggles were universal struggles and his defeats at the hands of environment and his own insufficiencies were those of mankind; his tenacious clinging to his dream the symbol of man's undying hope that over the next hill he will find the green pasture of his desire which he has never yet deserved. I looked around me in life and in history and literature and I saw that there were two kinds of men, the defeated and the undefeated and that surely the last were first.

Unfortunately, Old Jules' daughter was not equal to her task. The grandeur of her conception escaped her and the result is the mediocre one you see in *Old Jules*. But even so, it was not written for squeamish souls. If asked, I might have estimated that there should be about 10,000 people in the United States who might be interested in what I tried to do in the book. Unfortunately it is falling into the hands of some people who have, by our modern civilization, been spared the necessity of facing actual reality at all. They should have been further spared by good advice in their reading. In fact, that, it seems to me, is one of the most necessary steps in a civilization such as ours. Reality in literature is disturbing to the sheltered mind and is therefore bad for our whole scheme we seem to be trying to build up. As the hull is taken from our foods the hull should also be taken from any food for the mind.

Only I happen to disapprove of the whole process of infantilizing our citizenry. I like the strong things of life, the strong individuals whose passing

Dr. Carroll [*sic*] bewails in his *Man, the Unknown.*[1] I like bone and muscle in my literature and what passes for literature.

However, I have no desire to offend anyone and I hope that all those who are inadvertently disturbed by *Old Jules* will avoid any further books from my typewriter. Nor have I any desire to defend Old Jules. He needs no defence.

Now I've probably beclouded the issue for your gentle lady more than ever. I'm sorry.

And a good 1936 to you all.

1. Alexis Carrel, *Man, the Unknown* (New York: Harpers, 1935).

To Mrs. E. S. Baxendale

January 5, 1936

Dear Madam:

I am interested in your letter, particularly as you are "asked to review" my book but add "Please understand I am not reading the book—". That's something, anyway. I knew it was done that way often but you are the first one to frankly tell me so and so I shall break my usual custom and answer your letter, giving you the little information that I can.

I am single, trying to write another book but with little success as *Old Jules* fan mail still runs better than 200 letters a week, many from those who knew him at one time or another and must be answered. I have no photos of myself. Such as appear are taken by newspaper photographers and I see a print of them in the paper as the rest of you. There were some in the *News-Week, Time,* etc., about the second week in November. If you must see one look at one of these in the city Library. Better still, just make me up, as the non-readers do the book they review. I think it would be fun.

And here's luck to you.

Sincerely,

To Lewis Gannett

THE NEW YORK HERALD-TRIBUNE

January 9, 1936

Dear Mr. Gannett:

To enumerate, as you suggest, six or a dozen books whose memory "is particularly fresh" in my mind leaves me in the embarrassing position of a cow hand with a thousand long horns to cull down to a dozen for a model farm. Cow hands being what they are, the farmer would be in for a complimentary run for his money.

So, instead of insulting my acquaintances by recommending such monumental and easily available books as *War and Peace,* I more often find myself suggesting such books as:

Story of a Country Town—Howe
Ritual—Reik
Confessions of Zeno—Schmitz
A Mirror of Fools—Neumann
Twelve Against the Gods—Bolitho
Journey to the End of Night—Celine
Between Red and White—Dwinger
In Tragic Life—Fisher
Tall Tales of the Southwest (collection)
McTeague—Norris
Memoirs of a Fox Hunting Man—Sassoon
Black Elk Speaks—Neihardt
The Castle—Kafka

But when I really want to make my acquaintances ride hard I advise them to read the works of Aristophanes, Josephus or Lucian. Recently I've added Pareto's *The Mind and Society.* Not that any of them ever do, but they'd be impressed if they did.[1]

Please forgive the flippant air of this letter. I really am serious about the books listed and I was so pleased to hear from you. You, if it's any satisfaction to you, are one of the few people I can recall at all from my hectic two weeks in New York. If you knew my genius for forgetting faces, you'd be properly flattered.

And I do think your idea for a substitute for best seller lists is a good one. Certainly a book that you can recall is of more importance, personally at least, than just any one that has been read. It might be interesting to know how many best sellers each of us has read and can't recall more than a few weeks.

A good new year,

1. Edgar W. Howe, *Story of a Country Town* (Atchison, Kans.: Howe, 1883); Theodore Reik, *Ritual: Psycho-analytical Studies* (New York: Norton, 1931); Ettore Schmitz [Italo Svevo, pseud.], *Confessions of Zeno* (New York: Knopf, 1930); Alfred

Neumann, *A Mirror of Fools* (New York: Knopf, 1933); William Bolitho, *Twelve Against the Gods* (New York: Simon and Schuster, 1929); Louis-Ferdinand Celine, *Journey to the End of Night* (New York: New Directions, 1934); Edwin E. Dwinger, *Between White and Red* (New York: Scribner, 1932); Vardis Fisher, *In Tragic Life* (Caldwell, Idaho: Caxton, 1932); Franklin J. Meine, ed., *Tall Tales of the Southwest: An Anthology of Southern and Southwestern Humor, 1830–1860* (New York: Knopf, 1930); Frank Norris, *McTeague: A Story of San Francisco* (Garden City: Doubleday Doran, 1928); Siegfried Sassoon, *Memoirs of a Fox Hunting Man* (Garden City: Sun Dial Press, c. 1931); John G. Neihardt, *Black Elk Speaks* (New York: Morrow, 1932); Franz Kafka, *The Castle* (New York: Knopf, 1930); Vilfredo Pareto, *The Mind and Society: A Treatise on General Sociology*, ed. Arthur Livingston (New York: Dover, 1935).

To W. Keith Peterson

PETERSON & BARTA
Center, Nebraska

January 22, 1936

Dear Mr. Peterson:

Thank you for your most interesting letter, particularly for the additional data on Old Jules. Both the affidavits are very probably his.[1] He never was very certain of his age, or of that of any of his children, so the age discrepancy is no obstacle at all. The discrepancy in his mother's name is perfectly understandable. Her name was Ida Dessoulavy but his writing must have been very foreign as well as his pronunciation and the clerk probably did the best he could.

Among Old Jules' letters (unfortunately stored away in a safety deposit box down town) are some from a Mlle. Balmer, in Switzerland at the time, as I recall. She does indicate that she is coming to America, but the letters are all formal and distant. When I made my survey of the correspondence I found nothing in them to indicate that Mlle. Balmer was more than one of the hundreds of settlers, men and women, he wrote to in an effort to bring them to the new land. However, he always seemed to be in need of a wife and probably "had hopes" as he put it.

At any rate, the incident seems perfectly in keeping with Old Jules as I knew him and tried to picture him.

I appreciate your alertness. We need more individuals in public life like you. There is, incidentally, material for a grand book in your region. Have you ever thought of yourself as the author?

And thank you for the kind things you say of *Old Jules*.

Sincerely,

1. An attorney in Knox County, Peterson had discovered two applications for marriage licenses, dated 1883 and made out to Jules Sandoz. Details of the two were inconsistent. One named Estelle Thompson as the intended wife, the other a Mlle. Balmer. Estelle was Jules's first wife.

To Jay Amos Barrett

February 4, 1936

Dear Jay Barrett:[1]

Dr. Sheldon and I talked over the early days of the Society last week, and the energy of the men connected with it in those days.

I joined "the force" as a part-time researcher in Sioux and Cheyenne Indian history in 1931, after most of the *Old Jules* research was done and my roomrent was far behind. I was taking a course under Hicks, History of the West, at the time. At that time the Society was divided between the old basement Library on the campus where (due to space limitations at the Capitol) Mrs. [Clara] Paine still has the Society's library—the 9th floor in the Capitol tower and the newspaper files in the basement of the capitol. Now the main offices are with the Historical Museum (latter in charge of A. T. Hill)[2] in the west wing of the Capitol ground floor, with the newspapers and the duplicate books in the capitol basement. The regular staff in the capitol is Dr. Sheldon, Mr. Hill and Miss [Martha] Turner, with a part-time stenographer and bookkeeper. Most of the time since 1934 there has been a government project. I was supervisor of a CWS, a CWA and FERA project, in charge of Dr. Sheldon and some of my workers trained under the earlier projects. Much of the old accumulations has been at least roughly organized and the work is going forward nicely. I'm no longer over there—as my own work keeps me very, very busy, but I do run over every day or so for this or that—advisory business or information. My two years with the Society were very happy ones. Dr. Sheldon gave me considerable responsibility and leeway and was an ideal superior in every way. My relations with Mr. Hill were typical western—he felt like swearing at me at times and often did. We had gay times in the Museum. Miss Turner has several government workers to help her with the newspapers and seems to have a very good time too. Historical work should be a joy. It is to me.

Most of the research on *Old Jules* (three solid years) was done in the old Library basement. Several months I worked in the Society's old basement on Jay street, with "gullaches" because the floor was wet and unheated and a flashlight for light.[3] You see, I really did read all available panhandle newspapers and all references to the panhandle in the papers from 1880 to 1929.

The English department in your day was exceptional. Now it is just ordinary—or so it seems to me. Of course I came here with a strange and conglomerate background. My real help came from such people as Miss Pound, who said, "You have your own things to say, say them your own way,"—really masterly advice for me, don't you agree. Then there was Mr. Gass who said, "You know where you are going better than I." And Melvin Van den Bark, who teaches short story writing at night—he taught me everything one can be taught about writing, which is not much after all. I was his reader for a year and a half. There I learned that even the "feel" for a good sentence is a gift that no one can confer upon you.

I typed a manuscript for Dr. Sherman (never published),[4] but he was already vague and wandering in his sentence structure. I followed his work word for word and did not try to make sense from it. One learns to do that with other people's manuscripts. . . .

No, I have no degree. You see, I have no high school credits at all. I just "went" to college.

One of my favorite teachers in the English department is your friend Dr. Stuff.[5] In Boston Mr. Weeks, of the Atlantic Press, said to me, "Your feeling for subordination and your skill in closing scenes are remarkable." Only then did it dawn upon me that I *had* learned about those things—in studying *Anthony and Cleopatra* under Dr. Stuff. Odd how I hadn't been conscious of any technical knowledge about the business until it was brought up by Mr. Weeks. . . .

Of course, being an historian yourself and a writer, you know that I had to write *Old Jules* in something of the manner in which it stands. The canons of history and of literature must come first with me and shall be preserved to the best of my ability in everything that I write. Any personal feeling I might have must be subordinated,—or at least saved until I write an autobiography, which I hope to spare the public.

It was nice of you to write me so much of the background of the Historical Society. And the Rosemary—I've put it into my own copy of the *Old Jules*, under a bit of cellophane.

A good winter to you.

1. Jay Amos Barrett (1865–1937) was a historian, librarian, and for many years curator at the NSHS before retiring in California. He published books on war ordinance and on Nebraska history.

2. A. T. Hill (1871–1953), a self-taught archaeologist, discovered and excavated a number of prehistoric Indian sites in Nebraska. His methods were in several instances adopted by the Smithsonian Institution. A successful businessman, he became a member of the NSHS Board in 1926, became curator in 1933, business manager in 1934, and, on the death of Dr. Sheldon, director in 1943. He worked without pay.

3. For many years the NSHS collections were scattered in numerous buildings throughout Lincoln. In the 1920s the society bought a lot at 16th and H streets and built a basement. Further construction on the building was stopped because of the state's depressed economy. The basement housed some of the NSHS material, but no utilities were installed. In 1931, when the state capitol was completed, the NSHS main office and some materials were assigned space in the tower, with more space allotted on the first floor. The main history library, museum, and current maps were still in the university library at Bessey Hall. In 1932, NSHS holdings were still scattered around at five different locations in Lincoln. The society's own building was erected at 15th and R streets in 1953. MS maintained her interest in NSHS affairs throughout her life.

4. Lucius Adelno Sherman (1847–1933), was Chairman of the Department of English, later Dean of General Faculty, Dean of the Graduate College, and then Chairman of the Board of Deans at the university.

5. Frederick Ames Stuff (1865–1943) was a professor at the university from 1904 to 1937. Chairman of (Professional) English in Teachers College, he later returned to the College of Arts and Sciences.

To C. P. Parsley

February 16, 1936

Dear Mr. Parsley:

First of all I must thank you for the most novel compact I've ever had. I've showed it all around with the most satisfying results. Everyone is envious. . . .

Incidentally, I've read the interesting material you sent me. I'm particularly intrigued by the story of Dorothy and her Indian chief. This is splendid material for an historical novel if it hasn't been done. In any case it might be perfectly usable as an idea because no two writers would interpret the material alike.

I can't imagine more significant material—material that reveals the innate nature of both white man and red,—the story of a white girl who makes her difficult choice and lives to see it through. Her adjustments to her situation and her evident reward in the chief's complete love are a story and so is his deliberate act which lost her to him.

Of course, letting a woman go home to see her people is so very in keeping with Indian usage. An Indian of any standing in his community always treated his wife as a free agent—much more so than the average white man. At least among the Plains Indians and among most of the others the young man left his tribe for his wife's, becoming of her people. At no time could a man of standing show lack of fortitude to the extent of displaying annoyance if his wife went visiting or departed for good.

Considering this usage, it was perfectly in keeping with traditional conduct for a chief of standing to let his wife return to her people, even if he suspected she might never return.

There is something magnificent in the material and well written there would be no difficulty at all in finding a good publisher.

As a family story you might have to finance the book yourself but not as the story of Dorothy and her Indian.

Sincerely,

To Rose Rosicky

February 22, 1936

Dear Rose Rosicky:[1]

How many times have I hauled out your historical folio of Bohemians of Nebraska for "customers" at the state Historical Society. Last Spring, Mr. Folda put in half a day looking for it. Researchers are always using your Bohemian collection. It is invaluable.

Of course I knew of Chladek at Dunlap,—many grand stories. I never knew him personally. Old Jules settled many of your people! Dr. Juren, Fischer, Dukat, Bolik, Drbal, etc.[2]

The decay of the foreign "language press" is a sad thing to behold but it seems inevitable.

Thank you for your kind letter.

Sincerely,

1. Rose Rosicky (1875–1954) was active in preserving ethnic culture in Nebraska; she was associate editor of a Czech newspaper in Omaha, did a good deal of translating, and wrote *A History of Czechs (Bohemians) in Nebraska* (Omaha: Czech Historical Society, 1911).

2. Flora Sandoz recalls that Dr. Juren homesteaded two miles north of the Sandoz ranch. Nick Dukat lived between the Sandoz ranch and the Wray Macumber ranch; Bolik married Joseph Fischer's widow; and Drbal lived three miles northwest of the Sandoz ranch.

To Julia Blanchard McGillycuddy

March 4, 1936

Dear Mrs. McGillycuddy:[1]

Your letter stands out from the hundreds that pour in every month because Dr. McGillycuddy is one of the most interesting characters of the Nebraska and Dakota frontier.[2] His book should be in print, of course, and if you've tried only two publishers, you haven't scratched the surface. *Old Jules* sold on the fifteenth trip out. The Doctor's life covers some of the most dramatic incidents of the frontier—the culmination of a Manifest Destiny, the last defeat of a virile race through the destruction of their food, home, and clothing—the buffalo.

Indeed, I am very anxious to see what you have done with the material and while I'm an amateur, myself, perhaps I might help you place the book. Send me the carbon, if you have one—after all, the express companies are not infallible.

Sincerely,

1. The second wife of Dr. Valentine McGillycuddy.

2. Dr. Valentine McGillycuddy (1849–1939) was Chief Engineer with the U.S. Survey and Exploration Expedition in the Black Hills, 1875–76, was surgeon for the cavalry, and was the U.S. Indian agent in charge of the Pine Ridge Agency during the Indian wars and later. MS gave his wife encouragement and help for several years regarding his book, which was published as *McGillycuddy Agent,* (Stanford: Stanford U P, 1941), but deplored its inaccuracies.

To Bernard De Voto

HARPERS MAGAZINE

April 9, 1936

Dear Mr. De Voto:[1]

Every time an Oh-you-poor-dear-how-you-must-have-suffered letter about *Old Jules* comes in I am tempted to write you a note of thanks for seeing that the Running Water of my childhood was a paradise, a paradise beyond anything the horrified can conceive, let alone attain, in even the best of their conventionalized, dehumanized, civilized society. Your reply to [Louis] Adamic's "Education on a Mountain" in the current *Harpers* helps overcome my last scruple about writing.

You see, I studied Greek history under John Rice at the University of Nebraska ten or eleven years ago. In those days he specialized in deflating the fatuous undergraduate with swift, well-aimed thrusts. That is, he did when he wasn't quarreling with Dr. Fling.[2]

Judging by Adamic's account, my professor has softened considerably, but even so I can imagine the hell the newcomer at Black Mountain must endure if he stays.

Perhaps I suspected John Rice of sophistry back in those days when I occupied a second row seat and looked up at the patches on his soles usually on top of his desk. Anyway, he irritated me to extensive reading in Greek literature in an attempt to find material for silent rebuttal. So while I remember almost no Greek history from the course I did develop an abiding taste for Athenian literature. Aeschylus and Aristophanes have been my best bed books ever since.

I wonder if John Rice can do any more for his students at Black Mountain.

Thank you,

1. Bernard DeVoto (1897–1955), as editor for *Saturday Review*, had written a favorable review of *OJ*. He was the author of novels and histories, and his *Across the Wide Missouri* (Boston: Houghton Mifflin, 1947) won a Pulitzer Prize for history in 1948. DeVoto wrote a monthly column, "The Easy Chair," for *Harper's*.

2. John Rice (1888–1968) was a professor of classical history at the university from 1919 to 1928. Frequently at odds with fellow instructors and the world in general, he wrote his autobiography, *I Came out of the Eighteenth Century* (New York: Harper and Brothers, 1942). In 1933 he was a founder of Black Mountain College. Fred Fling (1860–1934), as Chairman of the History Department at the university, brought "scientific history" methods to Nebraska from German universities. He worked out an elaborate filing system that MS adapted for her own use.

To Lewis Gannett

April 14, 1936

Dear Mr. Gannett:

In looking through your *Sweet Land* again (great fun)[1] I noticed once more your reference to Crazy Horse, the Minor, with the same amusement but not the annoyance I felt when I found his full regalia picture in the "official" history of Fort Robinson as "The great war chief who cut off the retreat of Custer", true enough, and only half the story, if it hadn't been the wrong chap.

The gentleman to whom you refer was probably Crazy Horse right enough, so named because he married the widow of the greatest Sioux war chief of all time. As is not uncommon among nomadic warrior peoples, the Sioux usually left his band for his wife's — by way of insuring proper care for his wife and her children in case of his very probable early death. It's only a step from that to taking the name of the deceased husband if he happened to be an outstanding character. Crazy Horse, the Minor, lived an uneventful life on Pine Ridge between "shows" I understand.

I noticed this particularly in your book because I'm notoriously hipped on Crazy Horse, Major — have believed for years that it is a ready made theme for a great Indian opera. When I mentioned it in a note to H. L. Menken [*sic*] years ago he referred me to *Natoma,* which I, with characteristic western lack of tact, replied was not opera, so far as I could judge and certainly not Indian.

Just forget this.

1. Lewis Gannett, *Sweet Land* (Garden City: Doubleday, 1934).

To William Hooker

May 19, 1936

Dear Pizen Bill:[1]

No other character has been mentioned in my mail more often than Bartlett Richards and very often the mention was a protest against my kind treatment of him. I was accused of "suppressing" the reason for his going to Germany — namely, to marry his niece — which I guess is true, also that he had a negro mistress and four children — which I had heard but had no intention of using, true or not. Had he been my main character these things would have had pertinence. Not otherwise and certainly not without checking for fact.

I always looked upon Richards as an aristocrat—with the temper of an aristocrat. His mother, I understand, was really a *grande dame*. Everyone rose at her entrance, etc. Richards in the nineties, was seldom at the Spade [Ranch]. He had a foreman who was efficient as a cow man—but apparently of a notorious outlaw family. This connection, with the isolation of the ranch made it a hangout for all kinds of shady characters. Several times Richards is reported to have ordered the ranch cleared but such people are soon replaced by others of their kind so long as the foreman remains the same. And he *was* a good cowman—not too plentiful a species at any time. To the cattleman using free land any way they liked was not dishonest, anymore than despoiling the public domain in any other way was considered dishonest—or is now.

Richards and all his contemporaries thought they were in the right. They had the land—had always had it. Why should they give it up? To be sure [President] Cleveland had fussed about the fencing of government land but he was only a democrat and didn't count. Unfortunately [President Theodore] Roosevelt knew the cattle game and saw the pressure of unemployment growing in the east. Western land was the solution—and it *was* a solution so long as it lasted.

Old Jules always considered Richards a gentleman and not in anyway comparable to many of the lesser ranchers who used every means to exterminate the settler. When father shot the greywolf the Spade ranch check for their share of the bounty came very promptly, with a congratulatory letter.

I was very careful to point out that Richards was not accused of "intimidation of settlers" as the Krauses were and to show that the Spade treated the settlers very well, even suffered at their hands, when the little fellow once took over the country. And it is true that Richards' pride and his aristocratic stubbornness got him sentenced. And I'm not without admiration for his stand.

Of course I know who Mr. Seymour is.[2] Those interested in preserving the history and the wild life of the west are not so numerous that I would miss knowing of one so prominent as he.

Your suggestion about the buffalo and cattle day article is a good one and I'm taking it up with Dr. Sheldon. Have you heard from him? Just at the present I'm so pressed for time with my book that I'm not over there only on "call."

I see Mr. Seymour's point perfectly and I admire his stand. The facts are that I had no intention to malign such a colorful character as Bartlett

Richards at all. Did you know that a fine photograph of him is in Dr. Sheldon's *Land Systems and Land Policies of Nebraska,* off the press June 1?

We're looking forward to your sojourn in Nebraska in the near future.

Thank you, and

Be nice to yourself,

1. William "Pizen Bill" Hooker (1856–1938) had been a teamster in the late 1800s and was familiar with northwestern Nebraska. His letters to MS contain a great deal of information about his adventures. He wrote *The Prairie Schooner* (Chicago: Saul Brothers, 1918) and "Bill Hooker, Bull Whacker," *NH* 16.4 (October–December 1935).

2. Edmund Seymour was a Wall Street banker and broker once associated with Bartlett Richards in Wyoming and Nebraska cattle business. A western historian and collector, he was the president of the American Bison Society.

To Mr. B. A. Botkin

University of Oklahoma
Norman, Oklahoma

May 19, 1936

Dear Mr. Botkin:

It was fine to have word from you and the family through Betty Cottam. She brought very good reports and Van and I sat around and plied her with questions in very good imitation of the Botkin manner.

Dorothy Ann must be a delight—and just a bit of a caution—as we say in middle Nebraska.

Sear's *Deserts on the March*[1] is a very interesting book. Of course deserts march both ways. Long before white man came, the "dust" cycles seem to have been well established. I recall when plains historians were a little patronizing about the dust stories of the Mormons and the Oregon Trailers. They were just eastern softies. But now we all know something of what they probably meant when they wrote that for two days they had not seen their captain except in camp. The dust was everywhere, and the sun hidden. They saw something more than just trail dust—which would have been bad enough.

Our dust clouds are from far away and probably the cause is prolonged drouth plus ground winds. In the sandhills we classify our winds into two varieties. Ground winds, that begin in little puffs along the earth or on the snow, and gradually rising, carry anything loose upward, without necessarily attaining very great velocity. Ordinary winds blow sixty miles an hour without lifting either sand or snow far into the air and the moment they die down the air is clear as though rain-swept.

Just now I'm frantically trying to make a deadline I foolishly agreed to a year ago—when I had no intimation of the thousands of letters I should be compelled to answer, lost relatives I should help locate, disputes about frontier life I should be asked to settle.—The latter I usually only heighten.

I'm writing a novel, not because I prefer to do so but because if I wrote two fairly successful books of non-fiction I should have to do it the rest of my life and I would run out of good topics. Next I hope to do the Man Afraid of His Horse Family, father and son, one of the greatest chieftain families of the Teton Sioux and covering the transitional period from the buffalo hunt to the walking plow, the boarding school and the political agent. It's a heart-breaking story, and a magnificent one of two men who tried to act with wisdom and foresight for their people and finally came to the place where they saw that death with a bullet in the heart would have been preferable.

Thanks, too, for the clipsheet from the *English Journal*. It's a fine statement and goes into my file on Regionalism. And what are the prospects for the revival of *Folksay?* I know of no recent books that are as constantly fresh and reward rereading as these volumes. I hope the prospect for the continuation is not too dark.

Betty tells me of your gloomy prospects for the summer. Following the instructions of my admirable Christian Science landlady (who died of cancer) I'm holding the right thought for you for a surprise and a pleasant summer in a cooler climate. And if it brings you in this direction, let us know.

Sincerely,

It would be nice to sit around, with you and the Mrs. and just talk talk.

1. Paul Bigelow Sears, *Deserts on the March* (Norman: U of Oklahoma P, 1935).

To Mrs. L. A. Hornburg

June 3, 1936

Dear Mrs. Hornburg:

No, I'm not afraid to open letters—in fact, among the thousands of complimentary ones, only two objected in any way to the book.

People who are disturbed by *Old Jules* forget that only the strong and the ruthless stayed—that the squeamish may be nicer to live with but they conquer no wildernesses. If you look into history you will find that vision is always accompanied by a degree of thoughtlessness, impatience, and even intolerance for others.

I am surprised that anyone would imagine I hated my father. Does one spend five years of his life in an effort, no matter how puny the effort, to immortalize a man one hates?

You are one of those who can look life squarely in the face and still say "It is good." Thank you.

Sincerely,

To Fred Howard

Clay County *Sun*
Clay Center, Nebraska

June 10, 1936

Dear Fred Howard:[1]

I'm sorry I missed you when you called. I was tracking down some authentic "Ohio" lingo for the 80's and 90's, such as a homeseeker from Ohio might use—really a necessary business. I'm one of those unimaginative people who want everything as authentic as possible. Then if you do get it right, nobody notices. . . .

Sincerely,

1. Fred Howard (1868–1939) was the publisher and editor of the weekly *Clay County* (Nebraska) *Sun.* His column, "Sunbeams," covered a wide range of subjects, often humorously incorporating the views of two fictitious women.

August 21, 1936

My dear Fred Howard:

Pardon the long delay. I feel especially apologetic because your letter came at a most opportune time—I was in a very low state. I suppose that I'll have that to go through with every book I ever write. I was so desperately disappointed in *Old Jules,* after about a year of writing on it, that I could have jumped off the capitol too, but it wouldn't have improved the book particularly. There is, however, no denying that I can't approximate anything in my writing that approached the first fine conception I catch of it.

And in that desperate slough your grand letter came. And immediately things began to look up. I said to myself, says I: "Why should you swelter here and try to write a book? Why not go to a cool climate and at least give yourself a chance to deliver a decent piece of work?" so I ups and to the mountains.[1] There I rewrote the entire book, with an eye to giving it the swiftness and inevitability the theme seemed to demand.

And while still no masterpiece, it certainly is improved. Among my references were a Webster's, a German dictionary, a box of historical notes, on dress, food, etc., and your letter. The latter by way of food for the ego.

And the evening before I left there were 48 elk down out of the timber, three big bulls and several baby elks—three weeks early, the old timers said, and indicative of an early fall—

But aren't they magnificent creatures—and so oblivious to man so long as he stays in a car and hurries along the silly road they don't mind crossing any more.

Tomorrow I'm going to the Historical Society to read up on your column and beware if it runs too much to politics. The political issues are things of the hour, made things of the hour, but the better items of your column are sometimes things for all time.

Sincerely,

1. MS rented a cabin at Estes Park, Colorado, for three weeks.

To Edward Weeks

September 19, 1936

Dear Mr. Weeks:

Thank you for your letter about *Slogum House*. Yes, of course the book is not done. Nothing I write ever is, and this book was written under peculiarly inauspicious circumstances.

However, most of your criticisms strike me exactly as your objection to the vigilante shooting in the first chapter of *Old Jules* did and I'm as firmly set to preserve the criticised points as I was that incident.

For example: It seems to me that it is obviously the contrast with the William Penn Slogums that makes the western family seem strong. If your strong reaction is any indication it is an effective contrasting of American civilizations. Of course, I realize that you are looking out for your eastern readers and the critics, which is unfortunately your business but not mine. I don't give a good goddamn about the whole raft of readers and critics. I found the latter a very nice lot with a living to make by a unique method of torture that demands reviewing a dozen times more books than it's humanly possible for anyone to read. Fortunately I'm in the writing business for the writing and the rest is certainly very incidental.

However, you have put your finger upon what I consider the most serious weakness in *Slogum House*—in addition to its present slovenly writing. The throw-back material in Chapter II has given me more trouble than all the rest of the book together. I tried it as the introduction; I sifted it in like pepper in milk gravy and always it showed up for what it was, just plain necessary information. Now I'm working with it once more and I hope to build it in so securely that it cannot be torn from its place any more than the silly business of the birds flying around in the tent in the *Mayor of Casterbridge* which so profoundly influenced the mayor's life. Only in my book the contrast of civilizations is both the foundation and the framework of the book and must be made to be that to the reader if I have to point it out in one of those damned quotation things that I finally had to use in *Old Jules* when I discovered that no publisher's reader knew what I was driving at. But you cannot be blind to the part the entrenched east has played in the building of huge holdings in the west at the sacrifice of all human decency through its thrusting of an inferiority complex upon its less fortunate individuals. Look at Astor, Vanderbilt, Rockefeller, and so on, through the whole list of exploiters of the west, from 1800 on. Why did they do it? So they could go east and show those who had looked down upon them that they were as good as anybody.

Fannie must stay in the story because she is exactly what you see her to be. I've seen dozens of her come out of the east to their families. Libbie?—I gave her a much stronger part once but she either steals the story and makes it into an ordinary love rental or else runs it into a semblance of the slaughter of a more serious final curtain in Shakespeare. The truth of the matter is that most of us side-step the drama in our own families much as Libby did, and for equally incredible lengths of time. There were Ward and Ruedy to be considered and she was never ready to permit herself to be tested. I intend to bring that fact out a little more strongly.

Dodie is a story in himself in my mind and I had to clip him out here and there. He gets too much sympathy and I'm not asking for sympathy, no matter what the version you have may suggest to you. I despise a story that bids for sympathy more than I do the earth worm who lets himself be washed out upon a cement walk and lays there to bake in the sun.

* * *

Well, that just about brings the business to a draw—and only touches upon one of the problems I'm facing in my revision. Believe me, the others are every bit as real and important to me.

As for my coming to Boston: I'm sure it would be unwise. This time I would not need to face unpleasant publicity as I should have if I had followed my inclination and walked out with *Old Jules* under my arm. In fact, I gave the walking out very serious consideration all that terrible time in Boston but I saw that there was only one thing I could do—disappear permanently with the manuscript, and there was obviously only one way to do that—and me wanting to write a dozen books.

This time there would be nothing to keep me from throwing you a kiss and departing in my highest manner when my Old Julesian temper got to boiling as it did all the ten days in Boston once.

I'm giving the book a complete rewriting, and while it may take only six weeks, it may take all winter and I want to be absolutely free to do it my way. Of course you are under no obligation to spend any more time looking at it even then unless you particularly want to.

Sorry,

To Bernard DeVoto

December 22, 1936

Dear Mr. DeVoto:

A long deferred visit into the sandhills, with some good hunting in the old manner, afoot, gun across the arm, etc., has taken up considerable of the last few weeks and helped delay all my plans, including my New York vacation and this reply to your fine letter.

I've given your suggestions considerable thought while pursuing the wily pheasant through the weeds and always I am reduced to a return to the gray matrix of my own reactions to the dedication of the monument at Winter Quarters. Worse, nothing crystalizes from the matrix, no matter how much heat and pressure I exert upon it.[1]

The dedicatory exercises were the usual sort of thing: a car-fringed knoll capped by a crowd of people about a tall, veiled monument. Off to one side was the roofed platform for the dignitaries of the Church and the U. P. railroad, the mayor of Omaha, etc., with a choir, trumpeters from Fort Crook, (near Omaha), the usual crop of microphone men and photographers, and loud speakers blaring out the details of a child lost on the grounds or a message for so-and-so at the platform. And then, inevitably, the general uneasiness that some old timer is wandering in his speaking and will never be able to stop. This time it was (for you only), Apostle Heber himself. I felt this situation acutely. In our historical affairs I'm usually given charge of the old Indian fighters and am supposed to maneuver them into speech and out of it.

The fine moment of the exercises was not the unveiling, although the monument is a much stronger piece of work than the badly lighted cut on the enclosed invitation would indicate. It was the arising into view of the sculptor, a tall and exceedingly earnest young man, with far-focusing blue eyes that might, under other circumstances, have blazed with divine fanaticism instead of creative fire.

But I couldn't keep my mind on the crowd, the story the speakers were telling, already familiar to me, or even the low rolling, September-hazed breaks of the Missouri before me, cut by paved roads and shadowed by the airplanes overhead. I thought of the region as it must have been in those years from 1804 to 1847, when the Missouri river region was the most important literary locale on the western continent and almost everybody who wrote about it had actually been there, no matter how inaccurate his observation. In fact, journal-keeping adventurers, explorers, cartographers and missionaries, in addition to what might be termed professional writers and artists must have been as thick along the Missouri in those years as buffalo gnats about the ears of a visiting Englishman.

Many of these accounts reached a large public, particularly the work of such men as Irving, Audubon, (a more convincing individual in the incidental frontier mentioning of him than in Peattie or Rourke), Catlin, with his exciting narrative and 300 engravings, and Prince Maximilian of Wied. The work of Maximilian's artist, Charles [*sic*] Bodmer, is still most interesting to the visitors of our Historical Society here. His "Snags in the Missouri" recalls my first intrigued chills at a sight of hell as offered by my grandmother's illustrated Bible.

To be sure these accounts were mostly the work of visiting narrators, etc., inaccurate in detail, sometimes in very important detail. The man who knew the frontier was a man of action with no gift or patience for the pen. The Irvings, the Catlins and the visiting princes interpreted the astonishing things as they saw them, often with complete innocence of the powerful factions that were setting the stage for their eager and undiscerning eyes. Of course there were authentic accounts, many of them buried in the reports of the war department, many more in the books of the fur and whiskey traders. Recently many of the latter are reaching publication. A fine example is Chardon's *Journal of Fort Clark*, 1834–39, edited by [Annie Heloise] Abel.[2] This journal alone establishes half a dozen traders in the Council Bluffs region, simultaneously.

The flood of literature in the 1830's and 40's on the Missouri and its drainage basin should convince anyone of its vast news value, but it is the journals of the traders that make one see the huge commercial importance of the lower Missouri and the region around Winter Quarters in the 1840's. It was not only the chief artery of the fur trade, with its cut-throat competition, its strings of bull boats rounded with beaver hides, its canoes, rafts, snag boats and steamboats puffing against the current, often with world celebrities and social lions aboard, well chefed and champagned; the banks of the river deep-pathed by the cordelling; the foothills stumpland, cleared of timber for the rafts and for fuel for the engines and the stills. But there was more than fur trade and sight-seeing in this period. There was the huge and growing Indian segregation, with its trade in weapons and whiskey, the army expeditions necessary for a show of force, the flocks of agents and agencies. There was the colonizing of the west, with the trails necessary for both trade and protection. For these purposes it did not matter so much that the picture in a book which everybody read was not really of a great and dangerous Indian chief but only a whiskey-sodden Loaf-about-the-Fort dressed up for the occasion. Nor did the accounts of the hardships and the danger matter. Here was adventure for those who sought it and the economic and social pressure in the settled regions was strong enough to drive those without homes out to face any hardship for the promise of a bit of land, a refuge. Every newspaper played up the west. Altogether it was the most colossal build-up that any region without an actual gold strike ever had. And even that came later.

And so, to the knoll west of the Missouri, overlooking what was the world's most famous water highway, the fleeing Mormons came, with winter hard on their heels. Here they dug in for the most trying season of their history, with cold, hunger and disease always among them, until the graveyard was no longer an orderly thing of mounds and paths but a desperate chaos, the sick and dying covering those who went before as well as they might.

With the region before them so well publicized in all its danger and hardship and camped within walking distance of half a dozen trading posts where breeds, traders, trappers and frontier riff-raff talked the winter away, the Mormons still held to their resolution to push onward. They must have known of the wide reaches where water was days apart, the dust so dense they could see no sun from one night to another, scarcely the yokes of the oxen they would goad along. Their diaries tell what they found on the long way.

"Softies" we used to say, good-humoredly of the trailers, those of us who lived long in Nebraska wind and like it. Then came the dust clouds of 1934 out of the southwest and from my office window on the 9th floor of the capitol I could not see the street lights burning all day below me. And once more we had to admit that the last word in the history of any region or period is never in. Now we know something of the dust the traveler upon the trails of the 1840's probably faced.

And so when the grey swathing fell from the tall bronze figures of the father and the mother mourning the child they must leave behind at Winter Quarters, it was not only the dead child but a dead era, a heroic, tragic era I mourned. It is an era we can know very well if we care to read the most exciting accounts of travels ever written in the western hemisphere, accounts of that time when every spring brought into this land of the Indian and the fur-trader, of hardship and danger and isolation, homeseekers by the ten thousands. And before them and behind them came the writers and the artists, depicting the danger and the adventure so glowingly that more and more wagons came for the land that lay beyond. More dressers and cottage organs were thrown out along the trail when the oxen became footsore, the waterholes dried, the wheels of the wagons broke down, winter came extra-early. And all the long way were mounds, large mounds and small, such as those at Winter Quarters.

Yet, knowing all these things, there was [no] slacking of feet upon the trails.

Well, there's the matrix. I feel very apologetic about it and see that there is no promising crystalization that you might select for my enlargement or shaping and polishing. But I had fun thinking about this once more.

A good 1937 to you,

1. Winter Quarters, where Mormons spent the winter of 1846–47 before continuing to Salt Lake City, is now within the city limits of Florence, Nebraska, near Omaha. MS had attended, on September 20, 1936, the dedication of a statue in the Mormon Pioneer Cemetery there, honoring the more than six hundred Mormons who had died in 1846–47 and were buried in the cemetery. Bernard De Voto had asked Sandoz to write an article on the dedication for *Saturday Review,* but MS did not complete it.

2. Francis A. Chardon, *The Journal of Ft. Clark,* ed. Annie Heloise Abel (Pierre, S.D.: State Department of History, 1932).

To Harold Ober

January 11, 1937

Dear Mr. Ober:[1]

Your sale of *Old Jules* to Chapman & Hall pleases me very much. I know very little about the firm but you do, and I have absolute confidence in your judgment.

Too bad Little-Brown let all of last winter slip away for us. You could have done this last year and with less bother, I'm sure.

A good 1937 to you, and if I ever dig out of this drift of work I've let myself settle into I'm coming to New York.

Sincerely,

1. Harold Ober, who had become MS's agent for subsidiary rights in 1935, had contracted with Chapman and Hall for British publication of *OJ*. MS complained that Little, Brown was not vigorous enough in marketing her book.

To M. I. McCreight

January 27, 1937

Dear Tchanta Tanka:[1]

Thank you so much for the fine little book, *Chief Flying Hawk's Tales*. It is a beautiful thing, and very valuable historically but more than that—you have caught the essence of the laconic Indian tale. "We met Crows. The Crows killed one of our men, and we chased them a long ways. We got back." There is a lot to be learned in the stiff tale telling of the Indian. A thousand pages have been written on much less than the three sentences I copied from your story.

There is considerable verification in this book for my file material, and some things I'd like more information on, if you have it.

I assume that when Flying Hawk speaks of the Custer battle on the Big Horn he means not the river but the Little Big Horn, or the Greasy Grass as the Lakotah called it. Could the soldier Crazy Horse pursued half a mile, p. 29, have been Harrington, who was never accounted for until about ten years ago, when the skeleton of a soldier was found down the river, in a thicket? Of course he doesn't literally mean that the soldiers rounded up Big Foot's band in the Bad Lands and brought them in, p. 37. Big Foot never was in the Bad Lands at all.

I didn't get up to Rosebud for the 1928 Sundance but I saw the one at Pine

Ridge in 1930. We camped out on White Clay creek about nine miles out from the agency, in White Calf's pasture for several weeks. They were very friendly to us. We spent all the time we could with Old He Dog up beyond Oglala. You mention his camp on the Rosebud in 1928. Must be another He Dog. The one I mean died last winter — a brother chieftain and shirt-wearer of Crazy Horse, one of the hostile leaders who came in the spring of 1877. He was blind in 1930, and his legs were bad, but he always recognized my step and told us long stories of his youth. We brought him the two things he loved, cigarettes and fresh beef. And once he had stood with Crazy Horse and Sitting Bull and Gall against the entire nation. It makes my vocabulary inadequate to think of these things. And now he is dead, and with these old plains Indians dies a culture and a courtesy that will never be seen again.

It is enough.

1. An old cattleman from around Chadron, Nebraska, and a western history buff, M. I. McCreight had been adopted into the Sioux tribe and given the Indian name Tchanta Tanka — Great Heart or Big Heart. He published *Chief Flying Hawk's Tales: The True Story of Custer's Last Fight* (New York: Alliance Press, 1936).

To Bill Hooker

February 9, 1937

Dear Bill Hooker:

You're one grand person, Pizen Bill, do you know it? Just when I'm thoroughly disgusted with myself for ever getting tangled up with a Boston publisher and feeling pretty small potatoes, you put such little annoyances right in their place and flatter me into feeling pretty good.

You see, my publishers are always trying to tell me what I'm to find in my material. They're always afraid of any reflection on the East, the book buying region. Damn it, you and I know the East has long bled the west white, is still doing it, and I'm to distort facts to please a book public. Why, I'd rather write my own way and dig ditches for my soup and hard tack than write lies for a yacht and sables. Row boat and rabbit's more my style anyway. Now about you:

About all the early day material, Bill, why don't you and the Mrs. do it? You have first hand knowledge. The material is yours by squatters rights. More, you actually helped create it.

Yes, there's a story in Julesburg [Colorado], which I've not planned to touch. So far, I've outlined two Indian biographies. One, Young Man Afraid of His Horse, I've put off a while because two people to whom I'm obligated are writing related biographies and I don't want to take advantage of my earlier publishing connections. Besides, Young Man, etc., had a great decision to make and never, until his death, was he convinced for any length of time that he had made the right decision by coming in when he did. This demands great familiarity with Indian psychology and for that reason I am doing the combined and contrasted biography of Dull Knife and Little Wolf first. I'm calling it *Flight to the North*. I hope you approve. I hope to get down to Florida before the book is done for a long talk with you about the agency, politics, etc., if you'll be kind enough to give me some of the information you have on this subject, always assuming it's not something you plan to use yourself.

Yes, I have a book in the hands of the publishers, a novel. But it's these true stories that interest me more.

Sincerely,

February 17, 1937

Dear Pizen Bill:

Whew! Like the burr in the saddleblanket, I seem to've started something.

But first—I'm glad that the *Atlantic* saw fit to get a little iron into its blood, even if only by the back door route. When're you appearing?[1] About that Barber kid who's running the magazine now—I met him, scarcely dry behind the ears and no experience in writing, editing and surely not in life. "Good family connections" they told me in Boston, by way of explanation. Family connections, hell. That's no justification for cutting your stuff that he admits is "pungent" and that's more than one can say for the usual run of eastern tripe. They mean well but they just don't know what life's all about.

Now about you. You know my notions about us human beings. I figger that this world runs on a pretty even keel and those of us who are cursed with fine virtues, like courage and sincerity, have faults as strong. Frontiersmen had to have courage, tenacity, resourcefulness, and determination and the sap of life in superlative degree or they'd high-tailed it back east long before they got to be frontiersmen. To balance these virtues you and your kind are permitted any faults you may care to entertain and it's all right with me.

And as for killing a man—I think it is more ethical to kill outright than to warp for life millions of children through a starvation wage for the breadwinner or no wage at all. To me the world's worst criminals are the psychopathic killers like the Dillingers and the robber barons who stole the earth's surface, raped it of its resources, its timber, its minerals, etc., resources that were not there for one generation but for all time. And between the two types I have only pity for the poor Dillingers, who have no choice in being what they are and don't go around making such a damned sanctimonious noise to the heavens to cover up their rottenness of soul. Last night Alec Woollcott talked about the Andy Mellon gift of paintings. A fine thing, yes, but one the public is certainly entitled to. Those paintings were paid for in starved bodies and stunted souls so Andy Mellon can make the grand gesture.

But to get back to your crime. And you have committed one, or at least I think so. That was the destruction of your autobiography. There are some things that we owe to our fellowmen. I owed them the story of Old Jules, written as well as it was in me to write it. You owe us your story. I know it's difficult to admit that you or one you loved has perhaps committed acts attributable to a skunk but who hasn't? Only he who has never had the opportunity.

Yes, I see *Pizen Bill* the name of a book, not a novel, no. PIZEN BILL, the Story of a Man. And you're the one to write it. In fact, you're writing the synopsis of it now, and I'm saving it for you.

And don't worry about me and the *Atlantic* set. I've me another publisher the minute I can get foot-loose there. I will not have my Indian books "denaturized". That is the field in which I've spent much of my life and I am an authority in it. If any one doubts it, he should see my correspondence. For ten years I've been consulted on Sioux history, family relationships, etc. And it seems I've barely scratched the surface in what is a great lost culture, a culture that made it possible to live in small villages, with food always a doubtful thing, with house space the reaches of a skin tipi, and still make courtesy for your fellows, your guest and your family the keynote. Just look at the careful way in which everything was planned to further a calm, reasonable existence. A man left his band for his wife's people, so if he were killed in the precarious business of hunting or war, she and her children would not be far away among strangers. Because of the surplus of women always found in a nomadic warrior people, there was plurality of wives, so every woman would have a hunter, but the custom was to take in the sister of your wife if her husband was killed, because the sisters were accustomed to living with each other, had affection and common childhood experiences to bind them together and help make the life in close confines pleasanter. Look at the established custom that a mother-in-law never addressed her son-in-law directly, not that she didn't like him but it just worked out better if the talk went through a third person. Etc., etc. I like the old survivers of the buffalo days. The transitional Indian is a sad mess. He has lost the culture that fits his traditions and his temperament and the white man has given him nothing to take the place of the loss. Yet even so, nowhere but in an Indian community would I feel like leaving my camp unguarded, my typewriter, etc., in the open tent all day while I was thirty, forty miles away. I've done this many, many times. And because I usually camp along a wagon road for traveling facility, I usually find some curious Indians awaiting my return to camp, waiting to see the white woman who has no man but uses the writing machine on her knee and makes the words very fast and can also shoot a gun well. And is not afraid. Particularly is not afraid. They know if you are. One old Indian took me aside once and told me to tell a friend of mine, a young Lincoln woman who was with me, not to be afraid. He knew that she was, although she had made a very brave noise all the week we were around.

About Man Afraid of His Horse: I'm glad to have your version of his name. I'm always collecting additional evidence on every question of western history. Indian contemporaries of the old chief say he was named Man-They-(His enemy)-Are-Afraid-of-(The-sight)-His Horse. It seems to have grown out of a battle in his youth with the Arapahoes or Snakes (in my notes) wherein he and his horse, a strikingly marked colt, literally tore holes in the enemy until the warriors fled before the sight of his horse. The name passed on to his son. From what I can gather they are the last of one of the finest old Sioux families. Man was named chief of all the Sioux by the dying Conquering Bear, 1854 (after Grattan affair) but Man modestly refused the position, saying he was not a great man, as such a chief must be.

Power to you and family,

1. Hooker's material was not published in *AM*.

To Edward Weeks

March 15, 1937

Dear Mr. Weeks:

I'm sorry that I didn't make myself clear about the time required for my Indian book earlier. I was under the impression that I had written my estimation of the time to you, and that I had elaborated my ideas on biography writing at very great length at luncheon at Boston. That is the only place I've ever spoken much of my writing and I don't remember speaking of such serious business to Paul [Hoffman] there. But no matter. Three years is a short time for a frontier research book for me, and it may well run into another year. So far the waters have been becoming more clouded by conflicting accounts by the army until I'm becoming very suspicious of everything I read and hear. Fortunately the government is sending much of the archival material I need to Oklahoma, not quite so low a climate and politically much more congenial, I suspect, to good researching.

But that's not the purpose of this letter. The last week I've skimmed over the version of SLOGUM HOUSE that I took to the mountains for cutting to conform to the editorial policy of the Atlantic Press or what it seemed to be from my experience with OLD JULES. Now I'm putting this earlier draft into the hands of my secretary for a clean copy, without the mutilations, so I can get a good look at the book as I wrote it for myself. After May 1 I hope to put some time on it.

However, I doubt very much whether the Atlantic and I can ever agree on the book. It is evidently full of dynamite so far as the class and the region the Press represents are concerned, a circumstance gratifying enough to me as the purveyor of the theme and treatment of the book but a very unhappy one for me as an unwise benefactor [*sic*] of one of the Atlantic's prizes.

Frankly, I like the idea of the book. I'm satisfied there's something in it that American novels have rather consistently lacked, with a very few exceptions, from the very beginning, and I should like to have the book published. Not for the money. I've had tremendously flattering offers to write for money. I want it published because I believe there are a few people who will see something of the implications I hoped that the book would carry.

I should like to be released from my obligation to withhold the book from publication.

Sincerely,

To Alfred R. McIntyre, President

Little, Brown & Company

March 22, 1937

Dear Mr. McIntyre:[1]

I am sorry that you were troubled with my difficulties with the Atlantic people, particularly as you seem to misunderstand my complaint as much as they.

I do not want such *carte blanche* as you seem compelled to offer me on *Slogum House*. That appears as stupid to me as the other extreme: letting the publisher do anything he likes with my work. True, with the Indian biographies a publisher will have to depend upon me as a reliable researcher and historian or not at all, for it will be impossible for him to know much about my material. If he considers me reliable then the most he can say will be that the work is uninteresting, unconvincing or has no probable market.

With a novel the situation seems entirely different to me. Suppose that the publisher finds that the characters and the life the author has tried to create violate his conscious or unconscious taboos. The writer can't trot out evidence (as I fortunately could for many disputed points in *Old Jules* and as I will be able to do for the Indian books). All that the novelist can do is consider the criticism, and if it seems unjustified, try elsewhere. But only after careful consideration of the criticism, for, barring an attack upon himself for being what he is, any intelligent reader's criticism deserves consideration. Only a few writers can adequately judge the effects they are getting, either in kind or degree. I certainly do not care to forego a dispassionate criticism of any fiction I write.

Now to clear up this business of "strong meat." At no time, that I recall, has there been the slightest difficulty with the Atlantic people about my work as strong meat in the sense of Celine's stark treatment of horror and sex.[2] It has always been over the natural "strongness" of my meat, inevitable in work authentically grounded in a flavorsome environment, it seems to me, much as the "strongness" of the meat of fresh bear or sage hen.

My understanding of the Atlantic's objections to my work simmers down to two points: First, their quarrel with my use of colloquialisms, unjustified in my eyes because my terms seem to express more precisely my meaning than the language of the scholars, built up for an entirely different purpose; Second, my conception of the west and the middlewest in the period of *Old Jules* and *Slogum House* as a ravished colonial region, beginning with the Indian dispossession, running through the period of the settler-farmer and the small land owner, including, with or without their connivance, the rape of the earth of its resources, and finally to the small owner's dispossession, as shown by the increased large land holdings and the alarming rise in tenancy.

At no time have the Atlantic people objected to an unattractive portrait of the dwellers of my region but when I dare suggest that they are at least in part so because they are exploited colonials then they complain, finding all evidence of this idea that is so repugnant to them as highly unconvincing, melodramatic, etc. It was so with *Old Jules* and again with *Slogum House*. It would be doubly true with my Indian work, which I will not have emasculated, even unconsciously, by my connection with an unsympathetic publisher.

Please understand that I do not quarrel with the attitude of the Atlantic people. I believe that a publisher's imprint should mean something to the potential reader. I think they should keep to writers whose meat is not "strong" with the natural flavor of my bitter prairie sage. Unfortunately I have no intention of deodorizing my work.

Sincerely,

1. Alfred McIntyre (1886–1948) was president of Little, Brown from 1926 to 1948. In 1925 Little, Brown arranged with *AM* to publish the magazine as well as other material generated by *AM* editors. McIntyre's distinguished career included publication of Erich Maria Remarque, Ogden Nash, Walter Lippmann, and many others.

2. Louis-Ferdinand Celine, *Journey to the End of Night* (New York: New Directions, 1934). MS mentions this author and Franz Kafka more frequently than any others.

Little, Brown and Company

April 5, 1937

Gentlemen:

A German friend of mine brings me the January 1937 *Atlantic,* containing a first instalment of *Old Jules,* translated by Marie von Schoen, copyrighted by Atlantic-Verlag, AG., Zurich. Do you know anything about this?

Sincerely,

To Tunny Gray

Atlantic Monthly Press

April 11, 1937

Dear Tunny Gray:

The Lincoln book came long ago, of course, and I found it most interesting despite the laboratory methods the author uses on the earlier sections.[1] Analysis isn't the best method in history. It's a little more convincing if you begin with the parts and reconstruct the whole,—something for the spectator or the reader to look at. In chemistry the process is, of course, the reverse.

Anyway, our author makes a very interesting story of the idea, despite his method, and if he had gone through some of the frontier manuscript material stuck away here and there, he would have found things, I'm convinced, that would have astonished even him. You see, we were often used as colonies, (*we* meaning the frontier regions). Anyone found embarrassing to the powers in high places could always be sent to the Indian country, where he might conveniently disappear. I run across odd bits here and there that might grow into something very tangible on the Lincoln murder if pursued. On the other hand it might vanish between the fingers, as such things sometimes do.

The author's characterization of Stanton may not suit Ida Tarbell but it fits perfectly into the picture a study of the Indian war of 1864 builds.[2] First, propaganda was spread through the papers that the Confederates were stirring up the Indians. Then here and there annuities, never too prompt anyway, didn't appear at all. A few Indians were accidently shot, despite their obvious "friendly" classification. Others were captured and locked up for this or that. Whole bands were not only starved but dogged by the military until the Minnesota massacre came off, 1863, completely forced upon the Indians. Many of the eastern Sioux fled Minnesota, with troops behind them parading with banners flying, through Dakota territory, which was all without permission of the Indians. Then the Cheyenne, gathered at Sand Creek for annuities that had long been overdue were massacred, men, women and children. That finished the business. Like a prairie fire the frontier blazed. The trails to the Colorado gold fields were closed; the Sioux and Cheyenne murdered and burned from Arkansas to Montana, including western Nebraska ranches long friendly and fearless in the Indian country.

And so, when the Civil war was pretty well shot there was a long, tedious Indian war on hand, never settled until the killing of Crazy Horse and my FLIGHT TO THE NORTH, with Fetterman's and Custer's commands wiped out.[3] All this was unnecessary. The Indian had to go before the white man but not one instance of Indian treaty breaking is on record. From the white man's appearance in this region until 1864 there had never been serious trouble with either the Cheyennes or the Sioux and it took Stanton a good long time to get them really stirred up. After that there was no peace until they were conquered, degraded to wards of the government.

But certain groups in the east, such as Belknap's[4] promoters, profited, and in the west too, fortunes were built up to take away to the Atlantic seaboard. So I suppose it was worth the scheming. . . .

Sincerely,

1. MS is probably referring to William E. Baringer's *Lincoln's Rise to Power* (Boston: Little, Brown, 1937).

2. Edwin Stanton (1814–69) was President Lincoln's and President Johnson's secretary of war. Ida Tarbell (1857–1944), a muckraking journalist, wrote the novel

In Lincoln's Chair (New York: Macmillan, 1920) and a history, *In the Footsteps of the Lincolns* (New York: Harper and Brothers, 1924).

3. Crazy Horse (c. 1842–77), the Oglala Sioux war leader, killed at Fort Robinson, Nebraska, September 5, 1877. Captain William J. Fetterman was killed with all his men in an Indian ambush at Fort Phil Kearny (Wyoming) on December 21, 1866. Lieutenant Colonel George Armstrong Custer (1839–76) was killed with all his men at the battle of the Little Big Horn (Montana) on June 25, 1876. "Flight to the North" was eventually published as *Cheyenne Autumn.*

4. William W. Belknap (1829–90), President Grant's secretary of war, was accused of corrupt handling of lucrative Indian Agency traderships.

To Alfred R. McIntyre

11th April, 1937

Dear Mr. McIntyre:

I'm sorry that I didn't know about the probable publication of OLD JULES in Switzerland in 1938 sooner.[1] I could have planned to go there this summer and avoided the unpleasantness that seems, at least in America, to go with the business of authoring. The Indians would have waited graciously.

Every letter from Boston reiterates your deliberate misconception of my concern over my work as a thing of money. This would be highly amusing if I didn't consider good understanding with my publishers so vital to my writing.

But evidently such an understanding is impossible. In the future I shall try to stick to the terms of our contract.

Respectfully,

1. *Old Jules* (Zurich: Atlantis Ferlag, 1937).

To Jacques Chambrun

May 20, 1937

Dear Mr. Chambrun:[1]

I'm sorry that the Atlantic mess got to you, as I've been sorry about the mess getting to me for the last two years. You see, it dates from the first letter from them. The telegram announcing the prize award to *Old Jules* set two conditions: that I let them change the name back to the original one (the one I always wanted) and that I cut out 15,000 words from the manuscript. I agreed. The prize was announced in all the papers. Then came the most appalling letter from Mr. Weeks, listing all the things I must do—in addition to the original agreement. Summed up they amounted to this: easternization of my entire writing vocabulary and the rotarianization of Old Jules. Leaving out all consideration of my integrity as a writer, the suggested prettification of Old Jules was an insult to the memory of the fine old Tartar that I couldn't stomach. Neither, however, could I face the unpleasant publicity the rejection of the prize would bring me. So I went to Boston, fought the issue out with them page by page, for ten miserable, sultry days. In the end, of course, I won, for as Louise Pound, sister of former Dean Roscoe [Pound], once said to me in a class of hers, "You are so sure of your ground, so persistent in your beliefs, that you can use any pronounciation you like and the rest of the world will come to it." Incidentally, she, a philologist, has always given me great encouragement in my use of the language of the people.

But to return to the squabble with the Atlantic: Hardly had I returned to Nebraska until portions of the battle won at Boston had to be refought, and were refought continuously until the book was finally out, and Mr. Weeks' pet bugaboos, the critics, praised the very honesty he bewailed. Was he convinced? He was not. Immediately he began the campaign to mould the next book to his measure.

Well, it's been a stupid business, particularly as they have no option at all on anything of mine. Knowing that I'm finally permanently disgruntled, they make a gesture of good will by buying RIVER POLAK.[2] And next week their abuse will begin again.

However, I tried to make the revisions they wanted, which were fortunately simple and while I don't think they improved the story, they were not unreasonable and served to preserve their right to object to my manuscripts as presented. What their further decision on this matter will be you will no doubt hear. Either way you will get your bit of commission.

About the man in Neuchatel who wanted to translate my stories: I had him looked up, an easy matter in well-regulated little Switzerland, bristling with relatives of mine, etc. The man seems to hang out much of the time at a place somewhat comparable to our local city mission. Evidently my suspicions of him were well-founded.

Forgive the verbosity, and the unpleasantness. It can always be dismissed as temperament on my part.

I'm glad to see Dorothy Thomas getting a foothold in the *Post*. Not that I admire it so much but she does so need a little financial security. The finest story of her whole repertoire is one she will never write: the story of the

Thomas family. It is a remarkable example of family solidarity, particularly amazing because every one of the lot is so highly talented.

Sincerely,

1. Jacques Chambrun was MS's literary agent for her short works and, for some time, film rights.

2. "River Polak" appeared in *AM* in September 1937.

To Laetitia Bolton

Atlantic Monthly Press

June 4, 1937

Dear Laetitia Bolton:

Your letter finds me going through SLOGUM HOUSE, reinserting the material cut out last summer on the strength of probable *Atlantic* disapproval. Now I don't give a good goddamn. Unfortunately the file of fragments went into a merry blaze in my cabin fireplace, a sort of burnt offering on the altar of New England conservatism. Now I have to rewrite it all.

I might have known that nose-thumbing is my forte rather than incense burning.

Anyway, I've put off delivery on my car and won't get to the Indians until later in the summer, and it won't be about Young Man Afraid. Two of my acquaintances here have been working on related biographies for years and while I know they will never finish them, my ethical compunctions compel me to put off my Sioux biography a while to give them more time. I anticipate difficulty in marketing their manuscripts if my book should appear first.

So I've been working on FLIGHT TO THE NORTH, a Cheyenne biography. It has one advantage for a first Indian book: the conflict is mostly external. In Young Man Afraid the great conflict is within the man himself and for that reason I believe the more familiarity I have with Indian psychology the better. . . .

About my itinerary: It was to be from Oklahoma to Montana, on to Saskatoon, Canada for my Indians, through Canada to upper Maine and down to Washington for a fall's look at the archives and then back to this region. Now there's no telling.

Besides, it seems that I (against my will and better judgment) have started an internecine war, as the enclosed clipping will show.[1] Just now I shouldn't run away. Incidentally, I wasn't talking about regional literature but the reporters are funny creatures here. (We have no Leo Rabbettes or Louis Hammonds here, nor any such newspaper men as your side-kick is sure to be). Anyway, the state lined up to my defense immediately, and the battle is going on, pro and con, with much of the sniping from beyond the borders. Last week, against my better judgment, I went down to an old settlers' homecoming and made the uncomfortable discovery that I've become the spokesman of all the underdogs—teachers and all types of dreamers and visionaries as well as the creatively inclined and the conscientious objectors to floodlighting our capitol building. Too bad Old Jules is dead. He did so love a good fight. In the meantime I'm trying to keep Mr. Wimberly's PRAIRIE SCHOONER from dying. . . .

I'm sorry that you won't get out into the hinterland this summer. However, we'll probably still be doing business here next year, and perhaps the next.

How is your nice mother—I often wonder whether she is in Panama. Somehow Panama always sounds romantic to me. Perhaps because of the yellow fever and Dr. Walter Reed, and Cuba and Fort Robinson. You see the ramifications.

Oh, I almost forgot—Mr. Ober writes me that OLD JULES has been chosen the Evening Standard Book for July, etc. My friends in London write me that a violent pro-American reaction has set in due to the persecution of [King] Edward by the Church of England. So evidently the book is to come out there at last. You probably know all this but if your employers keep information from you as they do their authors, there's no telling—

I'm still trying to talk myself out of a most uncomfortable hole my ignorance of the serialization of OLD JULES in *Atlantis* got me into in Switzerland.

And by this time you've another prize-winner to bother with. Lord, you must have a life.

Sincerely,

1. MS is probably referring to a debate carried on with Professor Lowry Wimberly about regional writing. She published an essay, "Stay Home, Young Writer," in *Quill*, June 1937. The debate, "Wimberly Thinks Regionalism Passe," "Mari Sandoz Defends Such a Theme," appeared in the *Lincoln Journal and Star*, May 23, 1937.

To Chancellor E. A. Burnett

University of Nebraska
Lincoln, Nebraska

June 11, 1937

Dear Sir:

The current issue of the PRAIRIE SCHOONER, with its tone of farewell, distresses me very much. Can it be that Nebraska's fine literary venture, her one encouragement to the creative writers of this region, and an outlet for the truly creative work of all the nation is to die so casually?

I realize that we of Nebraska have not always shown our full appreciation of the fine and faithful work of Mr. Wimberly, or of the cultural importance of the SCHOONER to us. Yet it was a matter of great pride to me that the magazine seemed of real moment in the eyes of the New Yorker or the Bostonian. Everywhere I went in the east I heard what a fine thing the state and the University were doing in maintaining a literary magazine of such high standards, particularly through the trying years of the drouth and the depression.

Are we to let the SCHOONER die now?

Sincerely,

To A. C. Booth

402 Shurtleff Arms[1]
September 10, 1937

Dear Mr. Booth:

Your letter came while I was hidden away, finishing my forthcoming book which may, incidentally, interest you, despite its being a novel. The theme is exploitation and lawlessness in the free land regions.

And in the meantime your most interesting and saddening letter went unopened. I wonder how shocking it must have been to run into your brother's tragic end in a book casually picked up.[2]

Unfortunately there is little evidence readily available on the case. What came out is suggested in the book. What was said by all the settlers, including those on the Spade payroll and on the coroners jury I tried to imply: that no man could hang himself with his throat cut enough to bleed through the blankets and into the dirt as George Booth did. Not one of the jury believed that, but he seemed to have died from hanging, or so the coroner seems to have said, although what he would know—. Strange verdicts have been reached in the sandhills, even recently. There was a case, some years ago in which, according to the newspaper accounts, the man tied a cement block around his neck with a wire and shot himself in the back with a shotgun and then jumped into an alkali lake, down near Ellsworth or Lakeside, I think. Unfortunately the lake wasn't so very deep and the man's foot stuck out. The verdict then was suicide too.

About your brother: Marquard Petersen, the foreman of the Spade at the time, lives at Alliance, and Wightman, bookkeeper for the ranch, is now postmaster at Ellsworth, Nebraska. Most of the others are gone. The ranch owners died; the ranch hands are scattered. Even those of us who listened to the story as children are in far places. Somewhere among my things out in the sandhills is a stamp picture of a young man in a fur coat with a big collar—a picture I kept because it was said to be of George Booth.

Have you the newspaper story of the time? It contains little of value but if you haven't got it, I can have it copied from the bound volumes of the Rushville *Standard* at the Nebraska State Historical Society. It's the typical controlled press story. You will understand that.

And thank you for writing, for sending me the copy of your verse. The world is a bad place for sensitive people.

Sincerely,

1. MS moved to Shurtleff Arms, a Lincoln apartment building at 17th and H streets, in August 1937.

2. A. C. Booth wrote MS for more details of the death of his brother George Booth, reported in *OJ*. Until he read the book he had not known of his brother's fate.

To Edward Weeks

September 26, 1937

Dear Mr. Weeks:

Yesterday the copy and proofs of SLOGUM HOUSE left for Boston by air express. I'm promised that the bundle will reach your office soon after nine Monday morning.

First of all I want to thank you for your fine tolerant and generous attitude toward the idiosyncrasies of my style and approach. I hope that it will prove justified. Because a sort of inner coherence that I strive for seems much more important to me than the surface unities, often even the alteration of a word at another's suggestion seems to tear and mutilate my work like a spade in a nasturtium bed. Yet I boldly walk in at my own impulse and throw dirt in all directions. I guess it's just a matter to test one's sense of humor.

About the book: Whole galleys make me sick to rewrite the book. I was appalled, too, when I saw the stupid things that got past me those hectic July days when we were making the final copy of the manuscript; me reading proof and three professional typists who admire Temple Bailey and Bob Taylor and can't read my revisions working day and night, on something that was just a foreign language to them. If I've missed anything this time don't hesitate to let me know. Some of those slips were awful.

Now about the queries on the proofs:

Galley 10: *Fetzelzüg* is a Swiss dialect word expressing impatience with inconsequentials, derived evidently from *Fetzen* rags or tatters, and *Zeug*, things or thing: a thing of tatters. I called the German department of the University and they confirmed my earlier findings that there was no authorized spelling for such words. To them *Fetzelzüg* seemed a good word and properly spelled to carry the meaning. None of them, however, is familiar with Swiss dialect.

Galley 10: distance from *Grossmutter* to River Haber: In my mind the place of the *G* is twenty miles NE of Columbus, [Ohio,] on Walnut river, where the timber, in early accounts, was thick and fine. The Habers were down the Scioto from town. Does my insertion on the proof seem sufficient, and in proper keeping with the times? All mail roads of the period seem to have been called Post Roads.

Galley 11: If the Atlantic policy is inflexible in the use of "had beens" instead of "was", make the change. However, I much prefer the modern trend to the "was" form in anything but formal writing. Further, "had been" suggests "had been there" to me, (gone now).

Galley 14: I never intended to imply that Ruedy neglected Fanny's letters. Is it clear now that Gulla never delivered the messages?

Galley 15: Leslie's *Weekly*. I made a special trip down into the magazine collections of the Historical Society to check up on my memory and notes. The files of the *Weekly*, scattered, a gift, cover the period 1893 to 1910, full name of the mag. is FRANK LESLIE'S ILLUSTRATED WEEKLY. My Encyclopedia was wrong too, as it is in most things that I can really check.

Galley 20: China silk, small c here, capital later. I think I cut them all down.

Galley 45: *To* and *at* mean different things to me. I wave *to* a man across the valley when I want help, *at* him in friendly greeting or joking derision, say, because he is working on a hot job while I'm going swimming. I wink *at* my sister if we're teasing Fritz, *to* her if I want her help against mother's wishes, etc. . . .

Bunchgrass. The only word, now that I'm reconciled to *plough* and *centre,* that really bothers me as you use it is *bunch grass.* That is no more my *bunchgrass* than *blue grass* is *bluegrass.* Even government bulletins on pasture use it as one word, making a distinction between the two usages. However, it's not a matter of life and death.

Well, that seems to cover everything I can think of. Thank you. You have been very grand.

Sincerely,

To Paul Hoffman

October 10, 1937

Dear Paul

You've had a month of Wyoming and have, I hope, got over into the Jackson Hole country, seen the Tetons, maybe crossed Ten-Sleep before the snow. That's always been one of my favorite names in American geography—Ten-sleep. Louise Austin, for years one of my nicest acquaintances, grew up at Shell, Wyoming and left there to become an artist. Her parents were in the cattleman-sheepman wars.

October 27

Somehow I didn't get my good intentions of the Tenth into any tangible form, what with a very bad jaw from the operation of the Saturday you came through Lincoln. Chips of jaw are still working out, with appropriate consternation on the part of the dental surgeon. Despite the constant pain I was tempted to try to get my car, (long ordered but not accepted for delivery because I had no use for it,) and take a jaunt through western Nebraska and up as far as Lame Deer, Montana, stopping at Bear Claw. However, my usual good judgment prevailed and here I still am, trotting down for treatments, x-rays, etc., every day or so.

Your account of the vacations and trips into the mountains sounds most exciting, particularly the elk hunt and the trip through Shell canyon. I'm glad that you saw the Custer battlefield. It was up that draw to your right, when you face the Little Big Horn, that Crazy Horse led his Sioux and cut off the retreat of Custer for all time. I pitched a tent just at the breaks of this draw at nine o'clock one night in July, 1930, and the next day, when the sun came up, there was my first view of the battlefield. I was once more overwhelmed by the astonishing helplessness of civilized man, (if not backed up completely by the mechanical juggernaut he has built) when brought face to face with the natural man in his own environment. Still it probably would have seemed worth the risk to Custer even if he had been able to appreciate the gravity of the situation. Had he succeeded that warm, dusty June day he would have been President.

I've been hoping that you wouldn't have to go into the publishing business again, even at Random House, where Harrison, my favorite Smith of all the Smiths, seems to work.[1] I wish he might have been my editor.

You can have no idea how glad I am to know that you've escaped the *Atlantic* and Boston, not the city but the people. As for taking a poke at E. A. and his like — it's not worth the bother for you and isn't for us. What we out here must do is free ourselves from the blight of economic colonialism thrust upon us by the Atlantic seaboard, and intellectual and cultural dictatorship they foisted upon us the day the first malcontent crossed the Alleghenies. We've let them build up a great edifice along the coast from our rich natural resources and let them tell us we must bow down before it, have no other gods —. And all this without as much protest from all of us in four generations as India can stir up in a month, Ireland in a day.

What started this outburst seems to be my anger at your possible return to a publishing office. To me they are like the desolate little prairie cemeteries scattered over knolls from the Missouri west.

Of course these months in Wyoming are not for writing, my dear Paul, but for the expansion of the soul. Wyoming seems to make one's little hopes and ambitions seem so very little. In the *Ecke* in Utica [NY][2] will probably be a better place for writing and if times get hard, as we say out here, while you're at it, there's always a little for spending stuck away in Postal savings that I can get at without fuss.

Tunny Grey stopped by and gave me a most pleasant lunch hour about a month ago. He's changed his whole point of view so much since going down to New Mexico that I feel like a crumb every time I recall how boisterously I laughed when he told me of his plans to shoot mountain lions with a bow and arrow. That was before he ever saw one, or New Mexico. He reported on your going-away visit at his house with obvious pleasure.

The *Atlantic* came today. Glancing through it I was glad that the *New Masses* arrived at the same mail. The violent smell of sweat on the latter kills some of the odor of a genteel corpse that clings to the former. I'm thankful to such gods as I can recognize that you've escaped and I'll always curse my damned western sense of obligation that held me to them when every legal bond was gone. I even hoped that they might try to sabotage *Slogum House* but I'm afraid they won't.

About who first recognized you at the Cornhusker—I don't think I ever knew.[3] By the next noon it was all over town. I'm sorry. You see, this is a village and everything just grows. I'm always eating with visiting firemen of one sort or another and everybody feels free to take a booth close and listen. One of us must have said something that gave them a clue. If you can stop off a while on the way home I'll see that you get a little blowout among your admirers. What I should like to have you do is stop off and go out to the folks. I'm planning to go home Thanksgiving but if you could stop by at Christmas time or New Years on your way back east, (Provided you go east then) I'd like to come out and go out there with you. Thanksgiving is nicer because there's no danger of getting snowed in, unless it be like the winter of '85–6, '96–7, '10–11 or '14–15. Last year we went out and had a great feast with all the outfit at the old place. Mother and the family would love it if you could come.

Sincerely,

1. Harrison Smith (1888–1971) was a reporter and author, later an editor and publisher. He was with Harcourt Brace, Cape and Smith, H. Smith and Robert Haas, Doubleday, and others.

2. *Ecke* is German for an alcove or study; Utica, New York, was Hoffman's family home. MS lent small sums of money to a number of friends over the years.

3. The Cornhusker was the leading hotel in Lincoln, its coffeeshop a popular meeting place. MS had a favorite booth there; after she moved from Lincoln she stayed regularly at the Cornhusker when in town. The owner-managers took a personal pride in her accomplishments.

To Alfred R. McIntyre

November 17, 1937

Dear Mr. McIntyre:

Thank you for the copies of the "trade" magazines containing discussion of *Slogum House*. Of course I am pleased and hoping that the book deserves the praise and your confidence.

As a novel [it] looks good—a nice solid-looking size. I've tried it out on two acquaintances who were a little appalled at *Old Jules*. They took *Slogum House* straight, without blinking and seemed astonished that a book with so much unpleasantness could leave one so "lifted." This reaction bodes good, I believe, for the book's reception among the more squeamish of our serious reading public.

Thank you again,

To Harold Ober

November 26, 1937

Dear Mr. Ober:

The arrival of the German translation of OLD JULES in two editions reminds me that I've never heard anything particular about the progress of the book in England. The fan mail from Australia is fine, the letters long and full of their own frontier accounts. Evidently their pioneer was similar to ours, as I, of course, suspected.

Beyond the fan mail and a few reviews I've heard nothing at all.

Sincerely,

To Chief Walter Anderson

POLICE DEPARTMENT
City of Lincoln, Nebr.

December 10, 1937

Dear Chief Anderson:

After the publication of *Old Jules* I had several threatening telephone calls, climaxed by the intrusion of a woman into my apartment threatening to circulate frankly concocted tales about me unless I bought her off. I called your office, an officer came at once, but of course the woman was gone, for she heard me call you. Anyway, after that the annoyance ceased.

Now, with another book and more public attention, the business begins all over again. Today a particularly annoying 'phone call, from an unctuous and elderly voiced man, warned me that concocted tales would be told about me, different tales, by the way. He also said he was "approachable" for a "settlement". When I laughed he added that I had better be serious about it, for I could be "picked off from an alley."

I'm certain that money is all such people want and yet there is always the possibility that they are cranks and really dangerous. For that reason I'm letting your office know of this annoyance.

Tomorrow, December 11, I'm to go to Omaha to autograph books, returning that evening, so there should be no trouble during that time. If, after that, there is anything more, I'll call your office immediately.

Thank you,

To Sophus Keith Winther

January 6, 1938

Dear Mr. Winther:[1]

The evening before your letter came I had Danish cookies and coffee at the Kristophersen's, assistant Librarian at the City Library here. Both of them were born in Denmark and their interest in what you are doing in your novels is very great. Although they have been in Nebraska only a few months they have already accumulated considerable local information about you. The books were read on appearance and both of them are waiting for more. To which I added the praise of my family to whom I sent the two books and repeated my complaint against the *Saturday Review of Literature* because they mutilated my review of *Take All to Nebraska*. Incidentally, they did as brutal a job on my review of the *Sod House Frontier*.[2]

Now I've learned my lesson well. Not that reviews seem important to me. I think books sell in spite of them, or don't sell in spite of them.

Your review of *Slogum House* is incredibly generous, and while praise of my books generally makes me uneasy because it may lead the reader to expect too much, I had a sneaking liking for yours because you obviously had fun doing it. There's entirely too little fun in the world anyway, and certainly too little for book reviewers. Miss Cather won't see what you said, and if she does she knows she's secure. There's only one *My Antonia*.

Don't be disturbed by my demand for nothing less than masterpieces from Nebraska. I'm more annoyed with my writing than with that of anyone else. My complaint with your books is not that they aren't good. They are, and the stories have stayed with me over dozens of novels read since. What I want is a Nebraska novel that will stand beside *Buddenbrooks*, beside *War and Peace* and I don't care who writes it. So lay to, Mr. Writing man, and I'll keep my eye out for your March publication date.

Thank you, and a good 1938 to both of you.

Sincerely,

1. Sophus Keith Winther (1893–1983) was a Danish-born immigrant. His best-known work was the Grimson Trilogy, which dealt with experiences of Danish

immigrants in Nebraska and which was generally based on his family's history. MS had reviewed the first book, *Take All to Nebraska* (New York: Macmillan, 1936): "Danes on the Prairie," *Saturday Review of Literature,* March 28, 1936.

2. MS reviewed Everett K. Dick, *The Sod House Frontier, 1854–1890* (New York: Appleton Century, 1937), in "Sodbusters," *Saturday Review of Literature,* December 18, 1937.

To Ann Gunnar

February 1, 1937 [1938]

My Dear Ann Gunnar:

You have a nice start in writing for a girl your age. At 11 I had had one children's story published in the *Omaha Daily News,* only one, I think, although it might have been two or three. The first one, when I was about 10, was under my name on the junior page.[1] That is the one that brought on the anger of my father against writing for me, and for which he locked me into the cellar. I think this is in the OLD JULES. After that I used a pen name, although I had never heard of pen names.

I used various ones, always with our mail box number on it, so if I ever won a book, the award for first prize, it would reach me. I never got beyond second prize, which was only the label, not until I was 16 and superannuated in the business of writing for junior pages. Sometimes I signed my stories Alice McCall, sometimes Ruth Norris, and a time or two I got fancy and used Anka Annis or something like that. There is no material published under my own name, not where father could have seen it, until he gave me permission to write his biography the day he died, in 1928. The three first serious stories I had published in the *Prairie Schooner* and the story that won honorable mention in Harpers Intercollegiate contest in about 1925 were all signed Marie Macumber.

None of these names or any other pen names appear on my work after the death of Old Jules in 1928.

You understand that I do not believe in trickery for personal gain. If it had been only trouble for me, I should have used my name at all times. Father, however, made things very difficult for all the family if he was displeased with one of us, particularly for our mother. So the use of a pen name saved the rest of the family from his explosive temper, although he did see the notice of the Harper Honorable Mention and was very angry over that, so angry that he wrote me the one sentence letter I quote in OLD JULES: "You know that I consider artists and writers the maggots of society." Or perhaps the letter read "writers and artists." You can check on this in your copy of my book. I copied the quotation there directly from the letter.

Some day, when you are in Lincoln, will you come in and bring me some of your writing?

Every success to you—

1. MS's first story, "The Broken Promise," appeared under her own name, Mary S. Sandoz, on the Junior Writers' Page of the *Omaha Daily News* on April 26, 1908. She was almost twelve.

To Jeannette N. Shefferd

February 25, 1938

Dear Dr. Shefferd:

Your letter followed me to Boston, New York, Washington and back home. This accounts for some of the delay in this reply. Still, writers don't like to write letters. Too much like work.

I'm sorry that *Slogum House* disappointed you. Did you by any chance read Celine's *Journey to the End of Night?* Most doctors here have. That is a Little, Brown book. Try it some time.

However, I'm still sorry that I disappointed anyone of your background and attainments. Not that anyone would want all tastes alike. But it should be possible, unless I've failed entirely, to dislike *Slogum House* and still see its serious purpose. For, of course, I wouldn't waste my time on anything without such a purpose. The novel grew out of my shock, as a child, that while the most despicable creature of my knowledge, the coyote, would steal from his kind upon occasion, only man, with all his pretence of superiority, produced individuals who lived entirely and deliberately off their own kind, stopping at nothing at all.

As I grew older and my interest spread into history, I learned of the terrific will-to-power that can grow up in an occasional individual who has been compelled to knuckle down. We see it in [John Jacob] Astor, for instance. The ambitious young German believed the accounts of freedom and equality in England, went there, then on to the land of opportunity, the new world, to old New York. But in this land of equality he found the most complete caste system of his entire experience. Here his ambition and his energy and skill were getting him nothing much beyond a clerkship and the right to get out of the way when the dwellers in the big houses came by. But there was anger in this young man, as well as ambition, and energy. The source material of the period shows this clearly. He wedged into trade, branched out towards China, then the American fur trade, and while he kept clear enough personally, nothing was beyond his henchmen, not thievery, degradation of the Indian with whiskey, bribery of senators, murder. Not even the prostitution of the talents of visiting artists and writers who were guests of his company. And so Astor built the finest house in New York and looked down upon those who had ignored his existence in a land of purported equality.

The story is old, old as man, but comes up very often in the modern world. The powerful dictators of today rose from nothing and take considerable pride in walking upon the faces of those who once despised them. It has happened many, many times in America, where land, timber, mineral, oil, etc., were handy for the ruthless.

Because I believe the writer can best vitalize a locale with which he is emotionally identified, and because I know that I must keep my canvas somewhere within the scope of my ability, I chose [a] composite of all the preyers upon the great trails west of the Mississippi, whether to Santa Fe, to Oregon, California or to the rangelands. I made up the Oxbow country and the people as I did because I wanted to keep the story within my own field, both professionally and as a human being. However, the story is still the story of the ruthless and their will-to-power, and the decay that is inevitable when the hand of the planner fails, for this is one thing that cannot be perpetuated. A good house, well-built, lasts many generations but an evil house, whether it be a government, a family or only a petty county political machine decays as the hand that guides it decays but that is not soon enough, for the time of man is short, and justice must come today, or it is too late.

If this shocks you I am sorry that you tried to read the book, not sorry that I wrote it.

Sincerely,

To Cassandra L. Bloom

February 28, 1938

Dear Cassandra Bloom:

I am answering this before the [Sandoz] coat of arms has arrived, mostly because if I don't reply immediately the letters just snow me under and I never get [to] them. I still have some of last spring to answer. . . .

I don't depend upon the Encyclopedia, anybody's, too much. There are so many errors in them all in the one field with which I am really familiar to place much importance upon their statements in other fields.

I'm amused at your comments on my writing. Has it ever occurred to you that you would not venture to suggest to even a failing bootblack how to run his business and yet you, every one of you, never hesitate to tell a writer, who may have spent his life studying his craft, developing and maturing his art,—may even have considerable natural talent for his work, what to do?

And for those of you who imagine that we go in for realism for the money—that is a most ignorant statement, if you really say it out where it can be heard. The money in writing is exactly in the same sort of thing that pays best in other fields, in the claptrappy, the sentimental and the mediocre, for that is understandable to the greatest number of people. It's the Amoses and the Andys who make the millions, year after year, and not the [Artur] Schnabels, the Temple Baileys and the Kathleen Norrises[1] in writing and not the [Theodore] Dreisers and the Katherine Anne Porters. I could write lying, romantic novels, one a year, and make a hundred times the money that the whole twenty years of thought and note-taking that went into *Slogum House* will bring me, just as Annette could and did make much more money than Libby.[2] But those who condemn the book without reading it won't understand that statement anyway.

However, while I'd be the last person on earth to deny anyone his preference and taste, I'm all for warning the complacent away from things that might disturb them, whether it is Powys THE MEANING OF CULTURE,[3] Celine's JOURNEY TO THE END OF NIGHT, or merely my *Slogum House.* And if, accidentally, one of these insulated souls should come across anything that threatens his self-erected isolation, I advise him strongly to run like everything in the other direction.

Sincerely,

1. Temple Bailey and Kathleen Norris were both prolific writers of light, popular fiction.

2. Annette Slogum was a prostitute in her mother's roadhouse. Libby, another Slogum daughter, preserved her moral character, although she was the housekeeper and cook for the family.

3. John C. Powys, *The Meaning of Culture* (New York: Norton, 1929).

To Louis Lightner

Judge, Sixth Judicial District
Columbus, Nebraska

March 3, 1938

Dear Judge Lightner:[1]

Your fine letter of so long ago seems determined to remain unanswered. Or perhaps it is really an old Teutonic kitchen devil at work around here. (Did the Romans have devils to offset the household gods? It seems reasonable.)

Anyway, your letter was acknowledged in that wild scramble before my forage into the east for material at Washington. But the pile of correspondence was so large and so messy that your card was lost and not mailed. Upon my return I found it and wrote you an answer to enclose with the card. My secretary addressed it to Columbus, Ohio, and today it came dragging back.

But if your patience hasn't been frayed as a gunny sack apron long before this I should still like to say how much I enjoyed getting your letter about *Slogum House*. I'm glad that you found it carried a convincing reality. A man from Kansas said he believed that the story was fiction right enough but he knew Gulla's twin sister down there. In the next county, of course.

I'm sorry I can't do anything just now about another novel. I'm deep in *Flight to the North*, the story of the Cheyennes' last revolt against starvation and malaria in Indian Territory and their desperate trek across Kansas and Nebraska with winter upon them, hoping at least to die in the land they loved. Why have so many people—kings, presidents, dictators, yes, even poets, failed to see this deeply ingrained identification of man with the land that bred him, or to appreciate its implications. Perhaps because modern man's hold upon a bit of soil of his own has been so precarious have the great migrations to new soil been possible.

So Dull Knife and his Cheyennes, (the old and the small were with the old chief) were shot to pieces by 12 pound guns in the gullies above Fort Robinson, Nebraska. But Little Wolf and his able-bodied men and women got away and finally obtained a home, an agency in the north, as they had been promised years before. But it cost them half their number, and the United States army a million dollars. The material is magnificent in both heroism and tragedy, and damning to the white man. Something of these things I hope to capture upon paper in a book length narrative.

In the meantime there are hundreds of letters from all the nation and from Canada demanding that I do another novel. Even my publishers think that my talent lies there. But I must do what I'm moved to—as I told the easterners when they tried to get me to take off time enough to make a play of *Slogum House*. . . .

There are a lot of wandering sons and daughters from Columbus, Nebraska, in the east. Joy Higgins called me up and told me some grand stories of early Columbus. It seems there was an informal baby derby of sorts there once, among the Higgins, the Turners, etc. Of course Columbus always has had a fascination for me—with its early position as an outfitting port for the soldiers, the Indians and the frontier in general. I've heard that the mud got hip deep in the early street. A little of that would go well now—.

Thank you for your patience. Now, with a look at this typing I'm convinced that I should go back to bed and put my cold through an old-fashioned treatment.

Sincerely,

1. Louis Lightner (1877–1963) was a district judge for twenty-five years. He was one of the many western history buffs with whom MS corresponded over a long period of years.

To Mr. Harold Becker

OMAHA PHILOSOPHICAL SOCIETY

March 18, 1938

Dear Mr. Becker:

Thank you for your invitation to speak to the Society. I've long heard of your organization, reports that make me anxious to take advantage of your invitation. Unfortunately, I speak very badly, know it, and don't seem to be interested in doing anything about it. That is a glaring deficiency in a writer—inability to go up and down the land speaking to any who will sit if not listen. My publishers keep reminding me how public appearances drive up sales. Not even that seems to stir me to action, or perhaps I might as well admit right at the start I'm not anxious to sell my books to people who are accustomed to Kathleen Norris and Temple Bailey. Yes, snobbery from the sandhills.

I'm interested in your Sioux county [Nebraska] origins. There's something exhilarating about the Panhandle country. Perhaps it's the altitude and the aridity.

Mabel Gillespie's remark that I consider myself an historian is true,—an historian of man's struggles in the Trans-Missouri country as a symbol of all the conflicts of man everywhere. *Slogum House,* which is really intended as the story of all ruthless will-to-power, is only placed in Nebraska by accident. I happened to be familiar with that locale. Its narrow scope was determined by my realization that a large canvas, say one large enough for a Rockefeller, an Astor or a Hitler, was beyond my talents. But the story, it seems to me, is the same. An ambitious underdog is given the insult that his pride cannot endure. . . . That [Astor] destroyed thousands of lives accomplishing his end, blighted many more and helped degrade a whole race meant nothing at all to him.

In *Slogum House* historical events permitted an optimistic note at the end: an actual, concerted move to curb such ruthless drive for power.

Oh — do forgive the flight on the tangent. And may I say that your 2500 poems appall me. You must really spout iambs.

Sorry about the talk.

Sincerely,

To Anne Ford

Publicity, Little, Brown and Co.

March 23, 1938

Dear Anne Ford:

Thanks for the good reports of my deportment in the east. . . . People were so nice to me in the east I almost forgot my Nebraska role of Big Sister.

But not for long. Hard upon my return to Lincoln our mortgage moratorium law was declared unconstitutional and my telephone began to ring, messengers to pound on the door. What was to be done? A thousand farmers would be dispossessed within a week or two. What *was* to be done?

Of course I had no solution to offer. Nothing short of another march upon the capital here could bring a special session and a new moratorium law. The papers are running pages of sheriff sale notices. Somehow the fight has gone out of us at last.

In the meantime I am writing, buried away in the archives, when I'm not nursing a migraine, or putting my material together in my booth at the Cornhusker Hotel here. It's the one booth that has no mirror opposite it, so those in adjoining booths can't watch me. Here I did one complete revision of *Old Jules,* mostly because the Cornhusker was one of the few air-conditioned spots here in those days, 1932. Much of the endless rewriting of *Slogum*

House was done in that same booth. But the spot has its drawbacks. Because of its easy accessibility it has become a sort of agony pocket.

Here men stop to tell me of the maneuvers to sabotage the T[ennessee] V[alley] A[uthority] or wonder who's going to run for state chief justice or for governor, or bewail the difficulties in getting a manuscript past the publishers' flunkies. Here women tell me of their fathers who have lost both jobs and investments, and now, after a life-time of protection and prevarication in the name of protection, their women folks, (usually the daughter, or daughters) are faced with foreclosure of the income property, often the very house roof itself, and left with a disgruntled parent in pauperism.

But spring must be here, for the old timers are crawling out of their hibernation. An 81 year old pioneer of South Dakota plodded up my stairs today and I found another just turned 75 from Kansas on the second landing, puffing, but determined. He had come to tell me about an old house he saw in Wyoming that was being advertised as the original of Slogum House. That makes five entries for the honor, with three of these from Nebraska and one from Kansas. Three seem to be capitalizing on their fancied resemblance and are taking in travelers who want to go away and say they slept at Slogum House.

Suggested originals for Gulla herself have reached fifteen entries, seven from Nebraska, the rest from Oklahoma, Kansas, Colorado, Wyoming and South Dakota.

Well, send along the Sarpy Creek book. It should be good. Montana has some grand locales.

Sincerely,

To Beatrice Blackmar Gould

THE LADIES HOME JOURNAL

March 23, 1938

Dear Mrs. Gould:

Now that I've come out of my archival investigations for a breath of air, I find a letter from you long, long unanswered.

You wished, apparently, for reactions to a series of articles on "What the Women of America Think". As I stem rather directly from the really not so remote frontier, where men and women fought for a living and a life from the wilderness side by side, I cannot think of people as divided into sexes so much as into types. To me there are only people, varying a great deal among themselves. Certainly there is less similarity between, say, John L. Lewis and

Robert Taylor than there was between Amelia Earheart [*sic*] and Lindbergh, or between Kathleen Norris and Mabel Luhan than there is between Amie [*sic*] Semple McPherson and Dale Carnegie.[1]

You gather that I wouldn't know any of the answers to your query.

Sorry,

1. John L. Lewis (1880–1969), president of the United Mine Workers' Union, also formed the Congress of Industrial Organizations. He was a militant unionist. Robert Taylor (1911–69) was a Hollywood film star; he was originally from Nebraska. Amelia Earhart (1897–1937) and Charles Lindbergh (1902–74) were both pioneer aviators. Lindbergh made the first solo nonstop transatlantic flight, from New York to Paris, on May 20–21, 1927. Earhart was the first woman to cross the Atlantic alone, on May 20–21, 1932. Kathleen Norris (1880–1966) wrote ninety books, as well as stories, a newspaper column, and a radio soap opera. Her books were light romances, often with contrived endings. Mabel Dodge Luhan (1879–1962) was a wealthy socialite and dilettante, who, together with her fourth husband, Tony Luhan, a Pueblo Indian, was instrumental in developing a colony of artists and writers in Taos, New Mexico. Her books include *Winter in Taos* (New York: Harcourt, 1935) and *Taos and Its Artists* (New York: Duell Sloan and Pearce, 1947). Aimee Semple McPherson (1890–1944) was a charismatic evangelist who traveled throughout the United States, Europe, and Australia to proselytize her religious beliefs. Dale Carnegie (1888–1955), a writer, lecturer, and entrepreneur, wrote *How to Win Friends and Influence People* (New York: Simon and Schuster, 1936) and conducted lecture series and study courses based on the precepts in his book.

To Edward Weeks

June 22, 1938

Dear Mr. Weeks:

I'm glad that the shingles have departed without leaving you with a jittery hangover, as they sometimes seem to. "Brother Charley" Bryan is still in no shape to run for office.

About Mr. Sedgwick's article in the *Atlantic:*[1] I think I understand something of the embarrassment of your position in the matter. However, Mr. Sedgwick should have accumulated sufficient editorial acumen by now to know that while the *Atlantic* can carry articles on almost any topic and any angle, even a pro-fascist one now and then, such an article over his name must label and damn the publication for a great many readers, for to them the magazine is Mr. Sedgwick and Mr. Sedgwick is the Atlantic.

Incidentally, I suppose you should be congratulated on your elevation to the editorship of the place but I suspect that it won't be the happiest position in the world.

About the Mummy Jones article: I enjoyed reading the clip sheets very much, although I did wonder how he happened to pick on *Slogum House* for his point of departure. Somehow it doesn't seem to ring quite the right note, perhaps because he seems to approve too much. However, that's his problem, I suppose, and not mine.[2]

About my writing a reply: I'm pleased to be asked, of course. However, a whole wall of circumstances stands in the way. First, I have to go home to sit with the family on the front row of the *Old Jules* production June 27th,[3] and I can't just tear back without going through the motion of a little visiting. I'm even making a talk or two to the local Rotarians, etc. Then Mother isn't well at all. (Her illness cut short my stay in Washington, somewhat.) I'm going to talk the matter over with her doctors and may take her to Rochester. But even beyond that, I'm far behind schedule in my Indian work. I wasted three months this spring on a novelette, written definitely for popular magazine publication.[4] Young Jules got himself into a land deal just before the late recession and this spring he needed more money than I could raise without touching my permanent investments. Now Chambrun tells me that the novelette is a classic of some sort and probably unsalable. I think he's wrong on both counts but it doesn't matter now. I've used pressure on the seller of the land and got Jules an extension of time without additional interest. The three months, however, are gone and I should really be in Montana this minute, interviewing.

Then, even if I had the time I wonder if answering Mr. Jones' gentle complaint wouldn't put me too far into the uncomfortable position of defending my work. I'll fight to the last ditch for the right to say a thing but once said, the statement must stand or fall on its own merits. If he had led off with, say, Hemingway, etc., I should have felt less embarrassment, perhaps, although I don't have any urge at all to take up the mud ball and the scatter gun against even the most articulate of the squeamish souls the times can produce. I suspect that the battle was an old one when the story of Cain and Abel got around. Surely someone pointed out that it was wicked to charge one half of the sons of man with murder and even if the charge should happen to be true, why write about it?

Mr. Jones' complaint seems to me a polite and gentlemanly version of that of all the tenderer souls who can accept violence well enough so long as it has become familiar by way of the acknowledged classic, — often even enjoy a little contemporary supply of blood and thunder in their reading, if the blood looks enough like red ink and the thunder sounds like the rumble of beer kegs bumping down the back cellar steps. Personally, I don't see why they shouldn't have their ink and their keg bumpings and their perennial fun denouncing those of us who try with perhaps indifferent success to capture, with the crude means at our command, something of the essence of this conflict called life. And perhaps a few writers will survive these onslaughts and go ahead, using such talent as they can muster to give significance and immediacy to their writing, even to the extreme of rendering personal and inescapable the realization of murder as a thing of horrible motivation and the consequences as a death and a dying.

Oh my! I guess it's just as well I didn't undertake to answer nice Mr. Jones. And do forgive my busi-ness and my haste in this letter.

Sincerely,

1. Ellery Sedgwick (1872–1960) was editor at *AM*. His article, "The Patron Saint of Andalusia," in the June 1938 issue was extremely laudatory of General Francisco Franco.

2. Howard Mumford Jones (1892–1980) was an English professor, a Pulitzer Prize winner, and a prolific writer on American literature, history, and criticism. His essay, "Relief from Murder," in the July 1938 *AM* used MS's *Slogum House* as a springboard for his complaint against too much violence in modern literature.

3. Alliance, Nebraska, for its fiftieth anniversary, presented a locally scripted and acted play based on *OJ*.

4. "Bone Joe and the Smokin' Woman," *Scribner's Magazine,* March 1939.

July 14, 1938

Dear Mr. Weeks:

Yes, I'm still here, at 105 above, and very cross about it too. But I keep running into the worst snags in my research. For example: I've accumulated three more "positive" eye-witnesses to the different killings of Dull Knife, two of these previous to the date of the Flight, and me with actual proof that the poor man lived to die on a white man's agency, half-starved, in 1884. Yet truly the man must have been feared in his day, to be reported dead so often by the military and the scouts. The difficulty is that I'm dependent upon some of these accounts for other material and how and when can they be trusted? But that's where the fun comes in, and while it takes time, it's all the better when it's done.

Incidentally, did I tell you that the young woman who has had the Crazy

Horse story preempted for years read *Slogum House* and decided to relinquish her claim to me. That is, of course, the most magnificent of all Indian material. I'd like to do a novel between the two Indian books. There's one seems to be simmering, back in my head somewhere. Maybe I'd like to try a play of S. House in between. Mr. Reid of Ober's office seems so generously convinced that I could do one. What do you think about trying it? Not this minute, of course; not until the Flight is done.

About the novelette—I'm rather ashamed to have you see it. It was so definitely an attempt at the slicks—a substantial theme treated superficially and obviously. You won't like it.

About the Old Jules Play, and that little town of Alliance did make a play of it, not a tableau or pageant,—a play that even pulled mother to the edge of her seat to say, "Yah, it is him; so he was!" Those amateur playwrights and actors really did a magnificent job. They had to, with old timers like Elmer Sturgeon down there in the audience. They even introduced me and gave me a mess of flowers a yard long, like those Galli Curci used to have handed to her in the old days. Mother, who seems much better, autographed programs by the hundred.

May the summer be nice to the Weekses.

Sincerely,

To Bernard DeVoto

July 27, 1938

Dear Bernard DeVoto:

Thumbing through all the Nebraska State Historical Society Library for my Cheyenne biography, I skimmed the bound volumes of *The Annals of Wyoming*. In Vol. 6, Nos. 1 and 2, combined, July–October 1929, I ran across a section called "Coutant's Notes in State Department of History". Among these, page 239, is a letter signed by O. P. Wiggins, giving a terse résumé of his life from the time he went to Fort Laramie, 1839, to his wounding in the Battle of Monterey, Sept. 23, 1847, also a list of the party of Mormons he says he and [Jim] Beckwourth guided to Salt Lake in 1846. He says Jack McGaa was first hired to go with Beckwourth but his wife was sick down in Taos, New Mexico, compelling McGaa's return there, and so Wiggins was hired to go instead.

If you haven't this and are interested, a photostat of the actual letter could be obtained, I'm sure, and Wiggins checked up on in the government list of troops and civilian employees in the battle's casualties. While I've never traced Wiggins, I'm very familiar with his name in the Fort Laramie region, also McGaa's. The first white child born in Denver was supposed to be Denver McGaa and in my childhood I knew a slew of the handsome Irish-Sioux breeds. The McGaas were the aristocracy of the Pine Ridge, South Dakota, reservation; wealthy cattlemen and the boys all grand dancers. Jack McGaa was a great uncle to some of the lot, I always understood.

But really I was moved to write this note because I had such fun reading your "On Moving from New York".

Sincerely,

August 28, 1938

Dear Mr. DeVoto:

Because I seem headed for the wilds of Montana in the near future, and may not be back here for months, I believe that it would be much better for you to send direct to the Wyoming State Historical Society for the photostat of the Wiggins' letter, or a photograph, if you intend to reproduce it. Besides, you'll probably manage to get more information from them on the problem. They may have much more material along the same line that hasn't reached print, since they are usually short of funds for publications. No one around in this part of the world has made any particular issue of the matter, so far as I know, and until someone does, the material may lay unpublished.

Have you ever run across Gleason's purported account and map of the trip? Just a suggestion, if you haven't. I've seen them listed in bibliographies but I can't make my mind disgorge the where and when nor have I seen either, so far as I can recall. This is a little out of my regular field of Plains Indians and Fur trade. However, I intend to spend some time in the Wyoming archives this winter and I'll keep my eyes open. I've begun to get quite an interest in the problem.

About Beckwourth's presence in the Mexican war: You know how ambiguous the frontiersman's position in the war was. Often he just "joined", quitting when it pleased him. Much of the personnel of that robber business seems to have been made up of romantic soldiers of fortune and scouts from up north who found life a little dullish, with the decay of the fur trade, etc. Have you tried a query to the War Department? I know what a mess the archives are but there's an old soldier over in a garage building who plods through bales of stuff to discover enlistments, etc. He uses the true researcher's nose and discovers some astonishing things by just "messing around," as he calls it. Garage is a Department of Interior building, about 21St & Virginia, if you've never been in that particular dumping ground, upstairs. And even if both of the chaps were in the war there may not be a scratch of evidence in Washington about it.

I wish you luck.

Sincerely,

To Carlton F. Wells

Department of English
University of Michigan

August 29, 1938

Dear Mr. Wells:

Thank you for confirming my verdict of *The Yearling*. I looked into the book when it first came out, decided it was another Penrod, over-sentimentalized, plus a lot of prettified nature-faking and I didn't bother to read it.[1] Wouldn't old wolf hunters hoot if they read the story, which they never will.

Incidentally, I suppose that you've read the various biographies, etc., of Audubon. My research in frontier accounts, letters and manuscripts, published and unpublished, convinces me that he was a much more convincing man than I can gather from the biographers. I can see why the prettifiers all soft-pedal the Missouri journey. There were some pretty lusty goings-on and mighty wild shows of temperament and what-not on that trip on the part of our Audubon.

I'm so pleased that you and Mrs. Wells liked my Polak story, particularly with your wife's ancestry and background. The story in the *Atlantic* fell pretty flat with their usual letter writers, I gather. Most of them live in New England and the natives there are on the defensive about Poles, probably as much about their imagination and vitality as about the economic competition. My river Poles were the finest playmates a child could ever have and out of those days have come four pretty good stories, with only "River Polak" published. I had plans for a novel on them too, once, but doubt whether I could get it past my publisher.

Most of my stories won't sell to magazines and while I still hope to get a volume of them together some day, there's a notion alive around publishing houses that volumes of short stories don't make money, which means they're *out*. Now I'm still on my Dull Knife and Little Wolf story, a composite biography of two Indian chiefs, Cheyennes. It's magnificent material and I hope I can master it. Neihardt's *Black Elk Speaks* and Linderman's *American* seem to me good books about Indians. I hope to make it three.

Thank you, and I hope that your own work is coming well.

1. Marjorie Kinnan Rawlings, *The Yearling* (New York: Scribners, 1938); Booth Tarkington, *Penrod* (Garden City, N.Y.: Doubleday, 1914).

To Jacques Chambrun

September 20, 1938

Dear Mr. Chambrun:

Because my mail contains many letters similar to the attached, I'm beginning to wonder about book publication for some of my short stories, particularly unpublished ones, that I like pretty well. I don't think I've heard any more about the possible acceptance of the one by the Yale *Review*. Then you have another one or two that is probably unsalable. In my files are about a dozen more, from which I might pick.

Not that I expect any publisher, least of all mine, to be enthusiastic about a volume of my short stories or that there would be any money in it. It would be purely a matter of pleasing me, and a few folks like the Wellses—and would get the stuff off your hands.

The first draft of THE GIRL IN THE HUMBERT is done—the most painful piece of writing I've ever compelled myself to do.[1] As a sort of bribe, I've promised myself that I'll take off time this winter to do a play that has haunted me for years, called, perhaps, STATE CAPITAL.[2] There is something dreadful about a midwest state capital, a completely parasitic growth, depending for its existence upon state taxes and bribes entirely. Perhaps not so much a parasitic growth as an actual parasite, like a flea or a tick on a dog, and very anxious that there be no changes, as a flea is probably not anxious that a dog shake himself. To be sure the topic deserves the genius of an Aristophanes. Yet, with all my conscious lack of ability at either satire or dialogue of any kind, I'm looking forward to the writing with zest. If you handle plays, might you be interested in looking at it, say along next spring some time?

Sincerely,

P. S. Indirectly I hear that my English publishers are not to take up their option on SLOGUM HOUSE. They consider the book anti-fascist and believe the British public would not be interested. From the results of the last month's activities in British government circles, I should say that they are right. But it's funny anyway.

1. "The Girl in the Humbert," *SEP,* March 4, 1939. MS felt the story was a potboiler, written for money.

2. "State Capital" evolved into the novel *Capital City* (Boston: Little, Brown, 1939).

To Helen McAfee

THE YALE REVIEW

October 17, 1938

Dear Miss McAfee:

I didn't realize that it was really "Bachelor Stork Party" that you were considering for publication. I sent the story to Mr. Chambrun several years ago, more to convince him that my work was not for periodical publication than for actual placing. In the meantime I've tightened up my prose considerably, depending more upon rhythm and less upon repetition.

Regarding the revisions you suggest: On the deletion of the repetitions I am with you. However, many of your changes carry us to the old battlefield fought over thoroughly at the Atlantic on the *Old Jules* manuscript: would the story be told in Boston English or in the language of the environment?

Most of that sort of thing in this short story could be adjusted. The thing that I must balk at is your suggested change in the ending. To me the end is inevitable. These people would not face a man acknowledged to be queer, armed with a gun and aroused to the point of shooting one of them before this. That, in the language of our country, would be "buying trouble" which is the sheriff's business and what he's hired for. Even in the old days there would have been the formality of rounding up a posse, and only then if the community had a definite grievance. Never for a grudge fight between two men. When the law came it was followed by a reluctance to be "horning in" on the sheriff's business, which never brought any good to anyone, as all remote communities believe very firmly.

I grant that the ending needs rewriting, and badly, but the outcome must remain what seems to me the inevitable one. If you wish me to see what I can do with the story under these circumstances, let me know. In any case, I'm sorry you've been put to so much trouble.

Sincerely,

To Alfred McIntyre

October 20, 1938

Dear Mr. McIntyre:

Every month or so since last January I recall that I promised Mrs. McIntyre a photograph of some sort for your collection. Somehow I never turn out anything but fantastic in my few encounters with the camera. I'm sorry.

But the picture is really incidental to my real purpose in this letter. Because Mother's uncertain health and my unfinished research prevented my departure for Montana until too late for camping out for my Cheyenne interviews, I'm left with the winter rather unoccupied. I might play, except that a growing uneasiness about some of the social trends in the middlewest, particularly in the capital towns, won't let me. So I decided upon a play, satire, if I could manage it, to be called STATE CAPITAL and started to go through my files of notes. Two weeks of this and the accumulation of material and the growing importance of the theme convinced me that I should put this into a novel—covering a short space of time, say two or three months, and immediately contemporary. The picture would not be of any special state capital and yet might be any one of all those that have little commerce, produce almost nothing—just live off the capitol and the adjacent university or agricultural college. In other words—a novel about a parasitic town, parasitic as Washington is, but small enough for me to handle, and without the international "glamour" to cloud the issue.

Barring actual serious illness for myself—I should be able to have this manuscript in good shape by the end of next July, if the Atlantic Press is interested. I've written about this to Mr. Weeks, and mentioned casually that I was writing you. I haven't forgotten that you were much more interested in my future as a novelist. Will you write me what you think of this?

Sincerely,

To Edward Weeks

December 3, 1938

Dear Mr. Weeks:

In my preoccupation with *State Capital* I forgot that your letter should have some sort of acknowledgement. Yes, I'm deep in the material. My dining table, a long one to accommodate maps, is spread across the living room and covered with little bunches of notes clipped to blue name tags—my characters, with name, description, background and their purpose in the book. In a file on a chair are the major incidents in folders, with dozens of notes for each one. And on the floor are stacks of the Topeka, Des Moines, Pierre, etc., daily papers with little bunches of clippings all around them, gleaned, ready for the files. On the radiator is a stack of chamber of commerce calendars from which I'm mapping a ten week progression of events: state fair time through election week.

On the wall is a map of the state of Kanewa, (accent hard on the first syllable, good midland American) which, if I don't undershoot my goose too far, shall seem, at least for the moment, more real to my readers than their own home state. Beside this is a map of Franklin, the capital city, complete from Grand Vista Country Club out on Boulder Heights, to Silver City, the Coney Island of the West, on old Mud lake, in the Polish bottoms, (both long ago glorified by new names by the chamber of commerce). Besides these is a sketch, much amended, of the state capitol building, a sort of hybrid North Dakota-Nebraska, Louisiana spire, a sugar stick for which, with the university, the State Hospital and the Penitentiary, the characters of my city have gradually given up all the initiative of their fathers and become parasites.

I hope this doesn't sound too dull. I'm having a most interesting time. See no reason why the book shouldn't be done in July.

Because I like Texas, at least the wilder portions that I've seen, I'm glad you took a jaunt down that way. Isn't it immense? Big enough for the tiny plots along the Rio Grande, and the private ranch of the Kings.

Vague rumors of an approaching holiday season drift into my hermitage. If these reports are not unfounded, may it be a happy one for all of you.

Sincerely,

To F. W. Hatterscheidt

February 12, 1939

Dear Mr. Hatterscheidt:

Thank you for the clipping about Estelle.[1] I wrote Ed Fry of Huron, South Dakota, and formerly of Knox County, Nebraska, when I was gathering material for the *Old Jules*. He knew of her, thought she had died. I'm glad Estelle found her acquaintances in South Dakota kinder to her than Old Jules was, or the people on the upper Niobrara evidently were. I asked about her among the old timers who were there when she came up. They evidently hadn't received her very kindly. Among Father's papers were several dozen letters from Estelle, and others from various people in Knox county about her. Old Jules was simply too much of a "natural" for her comprehension. Estelle wanted a weekly pay check, membership in a good church, some small security, as she saw it. To those things she had a right. But you don't get them by marrying an Old Jules. It was too bad, particularly for her. Set-backs and opposition are only further incentives to an Old Jules; they are heartbreaking experiences to an Estelle.

I'm glad you find my books interesting. I'd rather please one individual who is familiar with the situation as it was, and too frequently still is, in your region and in mine than all the critics in the world.

And may the grain grow tall around Aberdeen in 1939.

1. Estelle was Jules's first wife, whom he married in Knox County and then left when he went west to settle in Sheridan County, Nebraska.

To Jacques Chambrun

March 8, 1939

Dear Mr. Chambrun:

The check for Bone Joe received. I'll make you a carbon on *State Capital*, and decide then about trying the Serial market. My common sense is agin it.

There's a mess of fan mail coming in, particularly on the *Post* story, from people who obviously think that's tops in literature.[1] I liked the *Scribners* layout too. The magazine sold out here in a few days, I'm told, with reorders not yet filled. I'm convinced that Lincolnites don't like me, but they do read what I write.

There are still ten foot drifts of snow in the sandhill passes. Like old times.

Sincerely,

1. "The Girl in the Humbert."

To Robert Fox

March 21, 1939

Dear Mr. Fox:

Thank you for your grand letter. I'm glad Old Jules has given you something in time of need. I don't understand it, but I know that sometimes the simplest word is the right one. . . .

As a historian I am less pessimistic than you about the present obviously low state of the democratic forces. I deplore the present, I grow ill with impatience and anger at the stupidity that seems loose all over the world, and then I see that there have been such periods before, and that we have perhaps only plunged into an intensification of an old, old ailment of man. The intensification, I believe, is caused by the advance of science far beyond the dissemination of philosophy and sociology. The former has brought the world into a fence corner so far as space, communication and transportation are concerned; its advantages are enjoyed by every man. But we have been tardy in grasping the significance of these advantages, the changed relationship they necessitate, or the responsibilities they incur.

Perhaps I'm wrong. I don't feel too sure.

And why don't you want to publish your work? If you have something to say, and say it well and with force, why shouldn't the rest of us profit by it?

Sincerely,

To Mr. William T. Adams

March 21, 1939

Dear Mr. Adams:

Your projected book, HOW TO WORK YOUR WAY THROUGH COLLEGE, is interesting but may not be as commercially successful as you anticipate. The only article I ever wrote that did not sell was on working my way through college filling capsules. However, times have changed and even capsules are now filled by machine.

I doubt whether my experiences will be very useful to anyone, but if you will promise to use moderation and not quote me directly . . . I see no reason why you shouldn't use my experiences, limited as they unquestionably were.

Here, at the University of Nebraska, many women work their way, at least in part. Anyone in good health, with some initiative and adaptability could do it until along in 1923, when times got hard in most agricultural states. Many students, a good percentage of women among them, still manage it.

I started with just enough money for my fees, but I was better equipped than most. Even though I had no high school, I had some business college training, which I used very little, but had as a reserve.

The fall of my freshman year I got an afternoon job at a drug laboratory, filling capsules at 25 cents a thousand, about 25 cents an hour, if you drew the bigger jobs, aspirin, quinine, etc., usually five grain capsules and put out by the million. You took your turn on special formula jobs, which might be

100 capsules of one or two grain, with just enough of the formula to fill and no more. Then you didn't make over ten cents an hour.

With doctors among my ancestry back into the hazy days of the alchemist, and driven, for want of books, to reading father's *Materia Medica* in my childhood, I found the pharmaceutical field very interesting and was soon taken off capsule filling (later done by machine anyway) and put at straight laboratory work. Under the chemist's eye I mixed endless formulas that could not endanger health or life. I made fifty and hundred gallon crocks of salves, lotions, emulsions, elixers, syrups, etc., supervised their packing in jars, tubes or bottles, their labeling, wrapping, etc. I worked from noon to five-thirty, half day, Saturdays, for something like thirty-five dollars a month, with enough extra time during vacations to pay my fees. I sew rather well, and can, with a package of dye and scissors, make a fairly presentable new dress from an old one. Dental bills, however, set me back fifty dollars, that wasn't paid until I quit school. This could have been avoided if I hadn't spent so much time on my writing, which took stamps and brought in no return whatever in those days.

The next year the university added a short story writer to the staff and I enrolled for a night class. At the end of the semester he offered me a job reading freshman English papers and helping in the preparation of an extension course in short story writing. This brought in thirty or thirty-five dollars a month, with no vacation pay. Sometimes the checks were ten days late and those were pretty lean times. However, one always survives and the work with a man who kept the creating of literature always before me was invaluable.

The August before my senior year one of the editors of *The School Executive* magazine died very suddenly. I was hired to help with the editorial work, full time, at seventy-five dollars a month. Not much, but I was pretty ragged, and there was still no income from my writing. I took night courses, tried to keep up my writing but by September 1929 I saw I would have to give up the dreary field of editorial work in education if I was to get anywhere at all. So I quit, with enough saved to get on a few months. By 1929, I was doing a few feature articles for the local Sunday magazine sections, and working on the *Old Jules*. I decided that I needed more assurance in the field of frontier history, and returned to school for one semester. Afternoons I did research for the Nebraska State Historical Society and in addition I was sub proof reader at the two local papers, with Friday and Saturday night shifts. I won a state prize of fifty dollars on a short story, and a twenty-five dollar Chancellor's essay on "How to Choose a Profession" mainly on how to enjoy life outside of your work. The first prize, fifty dollars, went to, as I recall now, a young man who held a more orthodox view of professions. With three and one-half years college credit I quit.

By the time the *Old Jules* won the Atlantic prize, June, 1935, I had made $250 from published writings, $75 in prizes, and had a novel and 78 unpublished short stories on hand.

Whether this record is worth anything to you is doubtful, but there it is.

Sincerely,

To Edward Weeks

April 24, 1939

Dear Mr. Weeks:

Reporting on STATE CAPITAL:

Because I don't think I can have the manuscript in its best possible shape in your hands by July 1, I've taken to dreaming about the business and waking up with a hunted feeling. I'm as far as chapter seven the eighth time over, chapter ten the fourth time over, and chapter 14, (all the rest of the book) the second time over. The book promises to be pretty good, and certainly unlike anything that I've ever seen. It has grown so convincing to me I can hardly believe that it isn't the story of a real community, with items about its larger happenings in my evening paper. Not even the OLD JULES took on such actuality for me. Whether this is good or bad I don't know, nor does it matter at this stage.

There are two things that I can see to do: Send you a copy of it as it stands July 1, to give you an idea of what it might become, and work on the finish another month and thereby double your work, or I can work at it until the thing is done, and send it to you then, to be fitted into your publishing scheme as you can.

Have you anything better to suggest?

Sorry,

To Robert Gatewood

August 5, 1939

Dear Mr. Gatewood:[1]

At last my book is off to the publishers — with about two hours to spare on the deadline. Now I can take time for matters no less important but more deferrable.

Mrs. Leary stopped in to see me and we talked about her idea that I might do a book—a queer coincidence to rise out of my casual remark that there was a Cozad mystery in Nebraska's history, a vanished son, or so the story that floats about through early accounts puts it.

She told me of your difficulty in finding a writer and of those you mentioned to her, only Halburt would have had the historical perspective required. Of course, there's never any final telling. Sometimes talent lies completely latent in an individual and then suddenly flowers beautifully and vigorously.

I told Mrs. Leary that this story, as she tells it to me, is the best material lying idle in this region and it certainly should be done. Because its first impact upon the public will be the only one that will have a chance to do well, it should be done by the best writer you can get, one with the ability to ferret out significant detail, have sufficient historical background to make the times as well as the people live. In addition the writer should have a good understanding of both the creative temperament in general, the artist in particular, and know considerably of modern art.

Whether there is such a person living today I do not know. There are, however, several who could do the book much better than I, I'm sure.

But if you have no one else by the time my Indian book (already contracted for) is finished I should like to hunt you up and talk it over. Unfortunately this won't be until the fall of 1942.

Let me hear what you have to say.

Sincerely,

P. S. Nothing of this story will get out through me. I realize how important secrecy in this matter is—in addition to the ethical compunctions I would naturally feel.

1. Robert Gatewood was a nephew of John Cozad, the eponymous founder of the Nebraska town, and a cousin of Robert Henry Cozad, who later, under the name of Robert Henri, became the well-known artist who strongly influenced American art in the early twentieth century. Dr. Gatewood wanted Sandoz to write the Cozad story, which was finally published as *Son of the Gamblin' Man: The Youth of an Artist* (New York: Clarkson N. Potter, 1960).

To Edward Weeks

August 10, 1939

Dear Mr. Weeks:

. . . About my getting a Nebraska lawyer to look at the manuscript: First, there has never been, so far as my knowledge of state history goes, even one book libel suit in this state and no one knows anything about the precedent that might be followed in any decision. I found that out when I was writing the OLD JULES. Second, there's no way of my taking the matter up with anyone here in the state without precipitating a panic. I don't know just why but this book has everybody in a grand dither, particularly since the great Lincoln bank robbery has once more come to the foreground this summer. Of course I didn't bother with actual occurrences in anyway in the book. However things got so bad along in June that the *World-Herald* tried to calm the waters by giving me a good interview, in which I said that my state of Kanewa and its capital city with all its people were completely fictitious, as everyone will recognize when the book comes out, except that, as with SLOGUM HOUSE, everyone will think he knows who I had in mind, and end up with dozens of people for each character, as they did for the House. The interview settled the business a bit but I still got long distance calls from places as far away as Saint Louis from reporters gleefully hoping to get something spectacular to use in their papers. I've had threats of injunctions, etc, but nothing came of those either.

. . . [M]y business has been, of course, to give everyone for the time of the reading, an uneasy feeling of actuality. For that reason I decided against a too formal plot and too swift movement. You people in the East are probably not aware of the real danger of a growing fascist set-up in the middlewest, but let the book appear and see what a stir it will make.

I suspect that for my time this is the most important thing I have done or could do.

Sincerely,

To Jacques Chambrun

September 8, 1939

Dear Mr. Chambrun:

I'm sorry to take up so much of your time lately. No, I don't want CAPITAL CITY cut up, as you rightly surmised. That's what makes working with you such a joy,—you understand what I'd like to see done in American writing, by me or by others, just so it's done.

Anyway, unless there's been an unannounced change in publication plans the book is to come out November 21, although I've not seen anything of the galley proofs. However, Mr. Weeks seemed enthusiastic over the book, even called me long distance to say so, the first enthusiasm from Boston on anything I've ever written. I'll admit I was a little surprised, for there's no denying the leanings of Atlantic money. While there was no request for changes, they may still try to high-pressure me into some at this late time, and in spite of my mulish stubbornness about changing the economic and social implications in my work. There I've never given an inch with them, and never intend to. Other things, of course, I'm always willing to consider, and make the changes or not, as seems best to me.

If they fuss at me at all, I'll send back the royalty advance and send the book to Harpers, who have asked for it. Harcourt, Brace or Viking would please me even more, perhaps. However, there's not a chance in a million of getting the book back, no matter how stubborn I should happen to be about changes,—which, as I said, haven't been even suggested.

I'm making up the carbon of CAPITAL CITY, in case you want it for the moving picture people, which is probably unlikely, as I suspect they prefer proofs. However, RKO and MGM have both been friendly to me, and might like to get a look at something of mine they could use. With the war on, I suppose that the situation is unpredictable,—I still don't trust Chamberlain.

Notes for Polish stories are accumulating. We'll see what comes of them. There should be at least one that can be worked into a passable popular story and perhaps one or two better ones.

Gratefully,

To Edward Weeks, Editor

September 11, 1939

Dear Mr. Weeks:

I'm so relieved by your letter and the very pertinent queries of your attorney.[1] I'll admit I was steeling myself for the leading part in a nice bit of Eva-escaping-across-the-ice business, all the time knowing that it was my impulsive volubility that put me into my predicament, for while you could be excused for suspicion in 1935, you certainly should have no reason to doubt my dependability now. It was just another case of too much sharing of enthusiasm. . . .

But to the queries of your attorney: CAPITAL CITY is a thematic novel, as SLOGUM HOUSE was, with Gulla my personification of a will-to-power individual creating her environment. Hamm Rufe and his fellows are her opposite, parasites created by their environment, deprived of the power of positive action until it is too late. It would be nice if actual individuals could be found to illustrate such ideas. Unfortunately in life they are too complex, too confused with other urges. I have to make up all my characters, for thematic fiction. Therefore:

1. Kanewa and Franklin are wholly creatures of my mind. They are broadly general to the trans-Mississippi region—the land rises from the southeast west and north, the population and place names represent the world, the economy is predominantly agrarian, the political alignment is unpredictable, etc.; the capital cities rule but do not produce, they have some state institutions, none exactly those of Franklin, and all seem to have or had an old hotel where the actual governing of the state was carried on. Particularly, as in all art, I have had to simplify, to create means to my end. No capital city has the history of Franklin, none a Polish minority group of more than a handful; all have squatter regions, none a legalized one. All have state fairs, none a coronation, although Jefferson City and Lincoln would like to have those of St. Louis and Omaha. While all have some grandmother money control, as has even Boston, none has three distinct ones or three distinct families such as Franklin has been given.

2. Every character, except such names as Norris, etc., who wander through from the outside, is completely my own creation, made to fit a certain place in my theme and plot.

3. I know of no person living or ever having lived in Lincoln or any other place who could reasonably be taken for the original of Colmar Welles.

4. As above. Not existing, he could have no mistress, Polish or otherwise.

5. I know of no person who remotely resembles Mollie Tyndale any more than any pretty, serious, dark-haired girl might. The character, her family and all the incidents in which she figures are completely fictional.

6. A majority of any jury of Nebraskans would say CAPITAL CITY is Lincoln before they read the book, because I live here, and because few Nebraskans can conceive any other capital city as important as Lincoln. After reading the book they would be hurt that it isn't their city after all, for there are no recognizable incidents or individuals beyond the natural pattern into which man and his activities falls. There are leading families here, but

not three and not so distinct as I have made them, nor with the same back ground or the same personalities or appearances. There are influential grandmothers here, as in all the capitals, and other cities too, for women outlive men, but not three distinct dowagers, nor any with the appearance or origins I have given my characters. There are, I maintain, no recognizable characters in the book at all, among the Gold Shirts or otherwise.

I did not intend the clippings I sent you as evidence for the specific incidents of the book so much as evidence that these things are common to the region. I know as well as your attorney that repeating false tales is libelous; I know more, I know that repeating the truth with intention to harm anyone who has not placed himself deliberately into public life is just as libelous. . . .

Yes, I can make the unqualified statement that you are justified in printing in the book, CAPITAL CITY, the note:

> A few men and women who have played some part
> in the history of our times are mentioned by
> name in this novel. These apart, all characters
> are fictitious and all scenes imaginary.

If this reply is not satisfactory, let me know, and I'll try to clarify any vague points.

1. Atlantic Press feared that the publication of *Capital City* could make them subject to libel. Their attorney drew up a list of six specific questions for MS to answer.

[no date]

Dear Mr. Weeks:

. . . [A]nyway, today it occurs to me that I should know what changes you think advisable now that Mr. Chamberlain slipped a pamphlet war over on me when he was definitely slated to talk big and noble peace.

To include the September crisis in the book seems to promise nothing but confusion and serious clouding of the issue. However, if you think inclusion of the war advisable, it can be inserted as an established fact, perhaps already a year or two old, and failing to bring the expected prosperity to the agricultural regions any more than the 1914–16 years did. . . .

The actual situation here, and from the papers and the broadcasts in the other midwest capitals, is one of a weary sort of anger about the slaughter of the Poles and a bored, helpless annoyance with Chamberlain for waiting to declare war until there was no one much left to fight it and no place for the fighting, and then proceeding to do it like an elderly boy scout. That is, of course, not the attitude among the tories. I went to the horse show and a couple of the cocktail parties, etc., to find out, and I got the distinct impression of an almost hysterical admiration for Hitler. But along the street and in the eating places the denunciation of Senator Burke by the AFofL state convention was the big news here, and the AF rates somewhere below the Eagles in voting power, far below the Elks, in this non-industrial and un-unionized region.

Written originally as a sort of projection into the future, I should like to have CAPITAL CITY retain its pertinency for some time, and I think that is more likely if it is kept a peace-time picture, a conflict growing not out of an extra-ordinary situation but out of an ordinary one. However, I've not given this a great deal of thought. What do you think?

While I don't suppose there's much danger of any comparisons with *Grapes of Wrath* slipping into the publicity used for CAPITAL CITY, I feel that I'd better speak out. To me the Steinbeck book is a worthy and timely thing but sensationalized to the extent that the situation is pictured as a recent development of both the Okies and the vigilantes. It is having the expected effect: the growing notion that the problem can be met by locating the Okies in settlements, which isn't true at all, for the Okies have been settled a hundred times since the Northwest territory was opened. The problem is one of land ownership concentration and that must be the point of attack for any lasting solution. The *Grapes* is fine material for a novelette, it seems to me. I'd prefer it with the poetic, pseudo-social-historical portions deleted. Some are nice reading, like the one of the turtle, and that of the boys with the stick candy,—poignant. But the general effect is misleading.

Let me know what you think of the war in CAPITAL CITY.

Sincerely,

To Mr. F. E. Bredouw

December 16, 1939

Dear Mr. Bredouw:

Thanks for your nice note, and the clipping from the Kansas City *Star.*

Yes, I've read Benton's autobiography,[1] and also the stack of volumes by Mabel Dodge Luhan, a woman's version of the "telling all." Somehow I'm always reminded of George Jean Nathan's crack (it was his?) about adultery being the dreariest pastime known to man. Certainly reading an author's account of his love life, unless written by a genius, is one of the dreariest pastimes known to woman. So you will all be spared such an exhibition from my pen so long as I can stave off the brain softening of senility. After that, let the buyer beware.

In the meantime I wish you and us all a fine 1940 of peace with freedom and some dignity, even though it be presidential election year.

Sincerely,

1. Thomas Hart Benton, *An Artist in America* (New York: Robert M. McBride, 1937).

To Anne Ford

January 3, 1939, no, 1940

Dear Anne Ford:

Reports are coming in of a woman circulating down in Missouri among the women's clubs, etc., and claiming to be my sister, and, upon occasion, my sister-in-law. She gives a racy account of herself, and, I gather, of me, also. A man from the hills who knows all of us tells me he ran into her there last week and queried her rather closely. She didn't even seem to have read the *Old Jules*, worked entirely from a few publicity stories and her imagination. I don't know whether she's the same one who's been working Montana and North Dakota with the same game the last two years or not.

If you hear anything about her, let me know. In the meantime, have a good year all 1940.

Sincerely,

To Leonard Thiessen

The World-Herald
Omaha, Nebr.

February 26, 1940

Dear Leonard:[1]

Well, I got my migraine home Sunday, ran a doctor down, and am recovering today. Part of the recovery is due to two leisurely hours this afternoon down at the show, which is grand fun. I even had a fight with a woman over the Doris Lee mother and children group.

I'm enclosing the check for the "Oilcloth Bag" or whatever you call my picture.[2] When is your show? I'll be here another month and if you won't need the picture until after then, I'll take it home here and look at it for that length of time. Then you can have it back. However, if you are showing in March and want it for that purpose, that's ok too.

Let me know about this.

Sincerely,

1. Leonard Thiessen (1902–89), an artist friend from MS's university days of the 1920s in Lincoln, studied in Europe and had a distinguished career as an artist. Curator of a number of art museums, from 1938 to 1950 he was the art editor for the *Omaha World-Herald*.

2. MS never wanted to own things; Thiessen's oil painting was her only art purchase. (It is now in the Sandoz collection at the university.) Other artists lent or gave her paintings, however.

To Jacques Chambrun

February 26, 1940

Dear Mr. Chambrun:

By this time you will have "Peachstone Basket."[1] It's not much of a story, I suspect, for I worked at it until I went blind to the whole thing.

About the [*Saturday Evening*] *Post:* I've always been accused of having a very suspicious nature but perhaps in the future I had better be even more suspicious. Along in the fall Garet Garrett of the *Post* stopped by and took me to dinner and out for an evening of dancing at one of the suburban dance places. Old fashioned stuff, with nothing stronger than coffee and several square dances. He seemed to enjoy it very much and so did I. We visited freely, you know how easily one visits with me, and I talked of what I was working on, after some encouragement, the story of the Cheyennes. GG had been through the west Kansas region where these Indians raided and knew some of the stories told around about their doings. Among researchers it is unethical to touch a topic that another qualified worker has undertaken, at least until he has had six or seven years to do something with it, so I felt no necessity for secrecy. I didn't in New York two years ago. GG seemed to think the material fine, said it was a natural. Of course there was no talk of serialization, for ordinarily I'm against it with book material. I can always tell just what has been rewritten later and what not. . . . Now I am told that [Howard] Fast is something of a protégé of Garrett's.[2]

About the serialization that I suggested: I would have no difficulty in sustaining suspense. It is intrinsic in the material. However, I don't want to undertake the awful task of beating Fast to publication unless there is a good chance that the publication can be managed successfully.

Sincerely,

1. Published in *PrS* 17.3 (Fall 1943).

2. MS believed that Garrett, editor-in-chief of the *SEP*, suggested to Howard Fast that he write a novel about the Cheyennes, covering the incidents MS had been researching for her projected book. Fast contracted with Simon and Schuster to write it. *The Last Frontier*, however, was published by Duell Sloan and Pearce in 1941.

To Helen Blish

March 1, 1940

Dear Helen:

Yes, I know about Simon & Schuster putting a hack writer at my book, after I had a lot of publicity on it, and no ethical writer would have touched it. But I'm glad to have the clipping.[1]

It's bad, for I've put approximately three years of work and $2000 in cash into the book. In the future I'll do the unethical thing too, work in secret and let the other fellow worry. I dropped Young-Man-Afraid-of-His-Horse because the book was so closely related to Eleanor's Crazy Horse and Doctor Sheldon's Red Cloud. Because my book would make publication more difficult for both of them, I put it off until after the Cheyenne book.

Of course, with my publishers only advertising eastern writers, I can't compete with a Simon and Schuster book. Perhaps eight, ten years from now I can do it, when the taste of the bad job that Fast will do has died down a little.

But enough of this. I often wonder how your migraines are. Have you tried gynergen shots? They are wonderful if I get one in time. When are you coming by?

Sincerely,

1. Helen Blish had sent a *New York Times* article to MS about the Fast book. Blish (1898–1941) grew up on Indian reservations; her father was a teacher in Indian schools. She located a book of pictographs in 1926 at the home of Dolly Pretty Cloud, the sister of Amos Bad Heart Bull, a historian-artist, on the Pine Ridge Reservation. In 1927 Blish rented the book and received two grants from the Carnegie Foundation to

finance her fieldwork. She completed her thesis at the University of Nebraska in 1928 under the direction of Hartley Burr Alexander. The original book was returned to Dolly Pretty Cloud, the owner, in 1940, and later was buried with her. MS saw the book often while Blish was working with it. Blish was helpful to Hinman and MS when they first went to the Pine Ridge for interviews in 1930.

To Eleanor Hinman

March 1, 1940

Dear Eleanor:

After thinking over the Simon and Schuster deal on my Cheyennes, and verifying the rumor that they hired a hack writer and chartered a plane to beat me into print, I find I can't go on with the book, which would only be, at the very best, a more considered work on exactly the same events.

Are you still disinclined to go on with the Crazy Horse story? If you are certain that you don't want to do the book, and that you will not regret giving it up, do you mind my switching from Dull Knife to your old Sioux War Chief?

Sincerely

P.S. This time, no matter what I do, I'll not do the ethical thing of staking my claim publicly—not and have it jumped again.

To Dr. A. E. Sheldon

Nebraska State Historical Society
Lincoln, Nebr.

May 15, 1940
[Washington, D.C.]

Dear Doctor:

I put off answering your queries and those of Miss Poast until the end of my snoop through the archives, as the material from the Indian Bureau and the War department was moved in so recently that no one is very certain just what is there, and any day my nose might lead me to something important.

Now, in looking back upon the five very busy weeks there (I took no time to call anyone, not even Ruth [Sheldon]—I worked until ten every night) I have this incomplete report to make.

BUREAU OF INDIAN AFFAIRS

I took up the matter of a possible index (by which I suppose you mean a subject index) with the proper people and discovered that all they have is the common topical organization. The Indian material is in files like this:

Commissions	Com of Indian Affairs
Inspector	Superintendencies
	Agencies, etc.

with the various offices represented, if the records are complete, by Letter Books, sent and received, and the document files, including the telegrams, letters, vouchers, etc., sent to that particular office. The document files of the Commissioner are separated into agencies of origin, and are arranged alphabetically. From the files pertaining to Red Cloud [Agency], material on certain subjects has been collected into special files, such as the Marsh investigation, etc. I found, however, that this was not well and thoroughly done and the only way to be sure that everything on a given subject had been seen is to go through everything pertaining to the period. Another complicating factor is the apparent disappearance of so many documents. The official descriptive jacket is there, but the documents have been removed, very often without any memo of time, purpose or place.

All this makes for complicated research and no one understands this better than Mr. Holmes, in charge of the Dept. of Interior Archives. Some day he will have all this material perfectly organized, and in the meantime he and his staff are very helpful, and the work is going forward.

MILITARY RECORDS

These are collected by post, expedition, department, military division and War Department. The material of the '70's, from the Division of the Missouri, contains many special files, such as "Sioux War of 1876", "Little Wolf Papers", etc. Again, the collecting was sketchily done and I found some most important material loose among the mess of petty administrative detail papers. The researcher in the War Archives labors under another handicap: large files, like those of the Black Hills Expedition of 1876, for example, have not yet been located, and all that is available in these cases is the other end of the correspondence, etc. The Fort Robinson material is still at the post, but they write me from there that 1876–7 are missing. No one seems to know if these records were ordered to Washington or some where else for one of the endless investigations of the period, and lost or if they are still among the piles of material not yet unboxed at the archives. (The war records were moved very recently, some in 1940).

IDENTIFICATION OF PUBLISHED MATERIAL

Apparently the researcher is left to discover by actual comparison with the documents whether any given one has been published. A common practice seems to have been to publish a letter or report in the condensed form transmitted to higher offices rather than in the full version. About the Grattan Affair:[1] I suspect that all the material in the special file has been well pawed over if not published. Until the archives are really organized, the new material on such famous incidents will probably be that which the determined and lucky researcher turns up in unexpected places. The above seems to hold true for the Twiss material, and another. The breed descendants of Twiss, incidentally, seem to be called Twist, as you may have discovered.[2]

About the Richard tribe: I'm familiar with the outfit. Old Jules knew several of them and always compared them unfavorably to the Cuneys and the Ecoffeys.[3] Evidently the earlier Richards were mixed up in a lot of frontier activities besides running bridges and ferries, such as the liquor trade, hi-jacking freighting outfits, etc . . . I appreciate your offer to have my notes typed but it would be impossible for anyone to interpret my unique system of abbreviation and my handwriting in combination. I'll make notes for you this summer while I do my organizing. There is considerable Red Cloud material among them, much of it only more evidence for what you already have. However, there might be light or another light on this or that incident. We shall see.

I am enclosing some notes on the Sod Agency for you. The plat of the place is coming from Washington in a week or so. Of particular interest are [Colonel John Eugene] Smith's reports about the agency as he found it when he, as commanding officer of Ft. Laramie, took it over temporarily in 1871. Many of these citations, particularly the ones that seemed of special interest, I took with the actual document number so if you want to have the original photostated, done at cost by the archives, you can send in for the whole thing. I looked at every document in the Red Cloud files for 1871 to the removal of the Cheyennes, May 1877, and if you find any point upon which you think I might have discovered something special that I might overlook as being unimportant to you, tell me and I'll be glad to search my notes. I covered better than a ream of sheets with very condensed writing, both sides, so I must have stumbled upon something. The War Dept. Records were, in many cases, stuck tightly together with old rubber bands, said put on them over fifty years ago. Whole files had not been looked into since, chiefly, I suspect, because they were stored in garrets and basements and not available.

Sincerely,

PS I'll be in at the Society several days before I leave.

1. On August 19, 1854, at Fort Laramie, Wyoming, John L. Grattan, an inexperienced young West Point lieutenant, with twenty-nine volunteers, charged into a huge Indian camp. The soldiers were all killed. MS considered this episode the beginning of the Plains Indian wars.

2. Major Thomas Twiss was the Sioux Indian agent at Fort Laramie.

3. The Richards, Cuneys, and Ecoffeys were mixed-blood families.

To May V. Trovillo

June 11, 1940

Dear Miss Trovillo:

I don't see that I can give you any advice. You've discovered the essentials yourself—that writing is an art and demands a commensurate apprenticeship, that the agents who advertise are no better than advertising doctors, and that praise can mean absolutely nothing to the serious writer.

But I think your agent did you one unconscious service in telling you that *Colliers* was the only possible market for your story. To me that would mean that the story is built on the *Collier* formula, and of course a writer doesn't get into such magazines on formula alone. Anyone with normal intelligence and some ability in imitation can write such stories. What the slicks, with their huge advertising space, demand of a writer new to them is a substantial new reader following. It's much the same in the beauty operator business, I'm told.

There are, it seems to me, two ways of acquiring this reader following: by working up through the pulps, which carry almost no advertising and sell on story value to readers of a certain immaturity and unsophistication, or with a certain urge to escape reality, or, and the more difficult way,—through the little magazines, such as the *Prairie Schooner* and the quality magazines. Speaking as a serious writer the move up into the *Collier* type of magazine, or down to it, is a deplorable one, it seems to me. To attain the checks the writer has to give up the last bit of artistic freedom. If a bank account is all he wants there are easier ways of getting it, with shorter apprenticeship and with more security for an earning future. If you look through ten years or even five years of *Colliers* or such magazines you will find that few writers have survived that length of time, and if you put it up to fifteen years, they become scarce as presidents of General Motors.

On the other hand, substantial writers, such as Willa Cather, Dreiser, Anderson, etc., have a small but steady income from their reprints on books published twenty-thirty years ago.

There it is. All I can advise you to do is to write what seems most important to you, and revise, revise.

Good luck,

To Franklin Delano Roosevelt

July 7, 1940

Mr. President:

Presuming upon our correspondence of the past concerning irrigation, hydroelectric power, soil conservation and tree planting in our plains states, and later about the need for an archival building, I have another subject I should like to call to your attention.

Certainly you are cognizant of the work being done in so-called "atom splitting", in Germany by Hahn and Strassman as reported in *Naturewissenschaften,* January, I think, 1939, and a general report on various experiments in progress in a February 1939 issue of *Physical Review.*[1] Then there is Turner's article in Review of *Modern Physics* of sometime last winter,[2] and other discussions in many other magazines since.

Further, a relative of mine, a chemist in Berlin writes from a safe distance outside the *Reich* that two months ago there was considerable excitement, among the physicists he knew, over what he characterizes innocuously as "chain reaction".

I am certain that our great physicists have brought this all to your attention, and much more, but the possibilities of the latent power of the atom in the hands of Hitler is so overwhelming that I feel I must write you this.

Respectfully, and gratefully,

No acknowledgement, please

1. One of the articles MS probably referred to was J. R. Oppenheimer and G. M. Volkoff's "On Massive Neutron Cores," *Physical Review* 55.4 (February 15, 1939).

2. Louis A. Turner, "Nuclear Fission," *Reviews of Modern Physics* 12.1 (January 1940).

To Carl R. Raswan

Denver, Colorado
Robert Browning Apts.
July 8, 1940

Dear Carl Raswan:[1]

It was so nice to hear from you, and not nice at all of me not to answer sooner. However, I was in Washington, doing research in the archives when the letter reached Lincoln, and it followed me around some weeks before it caught up. Then I was packing books and storing filing cases for my move to this cooler, higher city.

Your invitation to New Mexico sounds very fine but I was down there in March. We put in several weeks, mostly around the Puye ruin country and Frijole Canyon, etc. Also took in the Pecos ruins. It was as well that I escaped then. I have seen the end of the world since the Spanish invasion when I was in the east, back in 1935. Unfortunately, a little training in history doesn't equip one to do anything about the world's mismanagement, just makes it clearer and more painful. I am wondering about your Arabian horse book. I don't suppose that it came out at all. Or did it?

I suppose that you are safe. Even if you can't get your Palestine book out, before the nazis take over America, (and they will, for there are the same people to sell us out as there were in Norway, Holland, Belgium, France, and England), you can still have it published. I have invested years and several thousand dollars in expense money on two Indian books, books about an inferior race! Perhaps I can save the manuscripts, somehow, and have them published in the future some time, say twenty, thirty years from now.

But enough of this. I wish you a fine summer, and phenomenal luck with your books. You deserve it.

Sincerely,

1. Carl Reinhard Raswan, an authority on Arabian horses, traveled extensively and wrote travelogues and reference books on Arabians, among them *Black Tents of the Bedouins* (Boston: Little, Brown, 1935); *Drinkers of the Wind* (London: Hutchinson, 1938); *Raswan Index and Handbook for Arabian Breeders* (Acapulco, Mexico: Equitacion, 1975). MS saw Raswan frequently at the Lazy VV Ranch near Boulder during her summers there.

To Alfred R. McIntyre, President

LITTLE, BROWN & COMPANY

August 21, 1940

Dear Mr. McIntyre:

I still think that my letter of July 23 was perfectly clear and adequate. However, I'll try once more to make myself intelligible.

About the man with the Connecticut accent and the so-called "list of contributors": I don't have the present name of the organization that he represents. I threw the man's literature out of the door with him, including the typewritten outlines of the articles and the interviews that I was to do. From his first words about his "organization" I thought I recognized it as the group that Senators Burke and Styles Bridges are supposed to be backing, one of the three approved by Westrich.[1] Later he verified my impression. Unfortunately I don't have the old name of the organization either, for I don't keep such information around since my apartment was entered several times last January and all my notes and my manuscripts pawed over. The man I threw out knew about those incidents, and of my being threatened with concentration camp, "when we take over," and suggested that "There might be leniency, considerable leniency" shown me if I did his work "in an acceptable manner."

About my reference to the possible sabotage of my books—that grew out of my talk with Mr. Weeks, only incidentally, and is a subject that I would never bring up otherwise. Because my files are in storage at Lincoln, I can't get at the Boston clippings on *Slogum House*. It doesn't matter anyway. As I see it you have the legal right to treat my books as you see fit.

But I'm the one to decide when my welcome is worn out.

1. Edward Burke was a Democrat senator from Nebraska, and Styles Bridges was a Republican senator from New Hampshire. Dr. Gerhardt A. Westrick, a German lawyer, was in America as commercial counselor to the German embassy. A mysterious figure, he was called "sinister" by *Life* (August 12, 1940), which reported some nefarious activities and called him a "salesman of appeasement."

To Edward Weeks, Editor-in-Chief

THE ATLANTIC MONTHLY PRESS

August 23, 1940

Dear Mr. Weeks:

Your letter of August 20 and that of Mr. McIntyre of the same date confirm my original impression that you are as disinterested in me as a writer as I am in you as a publisher.

So I once more assume that I am free to go on with my work.

Sincerely,

To Alfred R. McIntyre

August 30, 1940

Dear Mr. McIntyre:

Regarding your letter of August 28:

You can hold me to your option on my next book, but so long as you do, there will be no next one. . . .

To Chester B. Kerr

THE ATLANTIC MONTHLY PRESS

September 3, 1940

Dear Mr. Kerr:

I appreciate your kind letter and your very generous offer to make the long trip out here. But that sort of thing is never necessary with me, and, anyway, I have spared you the need to back up your suggestion. In my letter of August 30, to Mr. McIntyre, I agreed to save my publishers any further embarrassment from more Sandoz books, even under another imprint. I can and do fight to the last comma for a manuscript but I do not fight for myself.

It's too bad all this had to happen. With your experience we might have worked well together, if you can manage any freedom of action at all. You understand that I am not complaining of my publishers as individuals. They are, much more than any of their authors, the victims of their own organization.

I realize that it was my taking the initiative that annoyed them so, although I didn't act until I felt certain that it would meet only approval. If I could have waited a few more months I am sure they would have cast me off publicly, but I am a forthright person and I found I can only work in a forthright circumstance. The break is a great relief, even though it costs me my Indian books, on which I have worked so long. However, with my patience, I can certainly outwait a firm, already one hundred years old.

— — —

I do wish you luck in your new undertaking.

Sincerely,

Thank you for the Swiss *Slogum House.* It was a great surprise.

To Audrey Wood

Liebling-Wood Agency
Beverly Hills, Calif.

October 14, 1940

Dear Audrey Wood:

Of course I remember you. You are, or were, my favorite Manhattanite—an actual native of the island, and still living not only there but in the house in which you were born. I told the story only last week. Now I can tell it no more. Sad, isn't it.

. . . Irving Thalberg did have an option on OLD JULES when he had to give up production because of his health. Since then I've heard nothing more.

When SLOGUM HOUSE came out there were various good reports on it but no studio had anyone willing to undertake the part of Gulla. The Ma Joad would be excellent in the part, if she could be persuaded to do an unsympathetic role.[1] CAPITAL CITY also got good reports, but then the war picked up—

At the stressed advice of the Atlantic people I put the moving picture business into the hands of Harold Ober, who, I finally decided, is a gentleman and not a salesman. So I turned the books over to Chambrun, because he had been so energetic in his sales efforts with short stories from my region. His Hollywood representative is Abraham Lehr, Inc. They have had the books for over a year, without results. (*Capital City* since before publication last November)

If you think anything might be done I'll get a release from Chambrun. I don't think there will be any difficulty, there.

And I'm glad to hear from you, even at the cost of my good story.

Sincerely,

I'm mailing you a copy of the program of the play put on at Alliance, our trade town, of the OLD JULES. It was very well received, and good fun.

1. Jane Darwell played the role of Ma Joad in John Steinbeck's *Grapes of Wrath*, 20th Century Fox, 1940.

To *The Saturday Review of Literature*

October 14, 1940

Gentlemen:

May I ask a favor, please, of Bennett Cerf? I would like the name of the Mr. ..... who threw a cup of coffee in his publisher's face.

If such a man actually walks this earth, he deserves recognition, and I plan to see that he gets it.

Sincerely,

To Paul Hoffman

October 15, 1940

Dear Paul:

Your letter junketed around Nebraska and finally reached me here this morning. I've been away from Lincoln so long that even my forwarding address there seems to have been lost. But it's nice to hear from you.

Yes, I'm done with Boston—really have been done with them for five years. Only a warped sense of obligation held me so long. This summer I made the break final. Even if they could hold me to my option there would be no more books. So far I haven't done anything about another publisher. This time it must be someone who has, if not understanding, at least tolerance for my material.

All summer I plowed through the archives here, just so I could be certain that I wasn't overlooking anything. I have the Cheyenne and the Sioux biographies pretty well covered. These, with an eventual fur-trade novel and my published books will give me a High Plains Cycle from 1804 to the present. It's a nice set to think about, anyway, if I never get them all published. In September I went down through Nebraska to speak on irrigation and power and the implications of the coming Farm-Factory community unit. Just now I'm doing a couple of short stories for Chambrun. He's still nice about pushing my unknown friends. Then it's back to the Indians for me.

I found I absolutely could not write on them so long as I was tied to Boston. Perhaps it's the old Sioux chief who once told General Miles, "I can see that the Great Soldier Chief has a good heart, but behind him I smell the wagon guns that would shoot our women and children," that has kept me from getting on with my work.

But now I feel free, and there is no one standing behind me who would do damage to his women and children.

Don't you think that it's a nice coincidence that I ran across the cut of the Tetons in Sunday's Denver *Post?* It made me think of you and your Wyoming months.

I see nothing of your writing. Sorry.

Affectionately,

November 12, 1940

Dear Paul:

Your letter is very promising on all but one point—Suppose that you should sometime be gone from there, and I had to deal with an unknown, what guarantee have I that, after submission, I could ever get a manuscript back if I didn't want to make the changes insisted upon, or that I could even get a verdict on it at all? I know this sounds like unnecessary caution when dealing with people of integrity but that was the stick the Boston people always held over me. Once they had a manuscript I could either fight for it or let them butcher it; under no circumstances could I get it back. . . . So before entering into another contract I must have some sort of understanding about this. If, in a disagreement over a manuscript, no compromise can be managed, I get my manuscript back by asking for it.

Otherwise the offer you make is fine. I'm not interested in advances unless I happen to need the money, which may occur some time in the future, since I had to finance the home place at mother's death to keep it intact and in the family. However, I can probably always do a couple of short stories. I usually manage to get along.

About future books: I plan to have the Sioux biography ready in time for 1942 publication. The Cheyenne one would have been finished next spring but I foolishly talked freely about it to reporters in the east, considering my claim staked securely in the eyes of any researcher. Evidently it wasn't, for last winter Simon and Schuster hired Howard Fast to do the book, chartering a plane for him to go to Oklahoma and Wyoming. In two months he seems to have done the research (a problem that has taken me years, with all my background in Indians and Indian history) and the writing too. I understand it has been scheduled for publication in the Sat Eve *Post* all summer, but the war interfered. Anyway, I put the Cheyennes off until the Fast version is in the garbage dumps and moved the Sioux biography up.

Somehow I question the wisdom of two Indian biographies in succession. There seems some danger of becoming "typed". However, I'm willing to leave that to the publisher. I do have another story, my kind. One of America's foremost artists was born in Nebraska, son of a "colonel" who settled one of our midstate towns, named it for himself and made a fortune there in a few years in real estate, railroads, etc. He was an expansive, full-living man of the period, 1870–1900, and used to come to Denver for business and for fun. On one of these trips he shot a man in a place of gaudy aspect and reputation, was smuggled out, slipped back to Nebraska and in a few days had closed up his business and vanished, family and all, and was never heard from again.[1] The story of the killing never reached his town at all, and, so far as I know, never followed him into his new life.

Under a new name in the east the son grew up and became world-famous, rated many biographical sketches in art books and a book-length biography or two, all with a completely fictitious childhood and background. Now the family is almost gone and one of the few who remain wrote me last year (having discovered through something that I said to a mutual artist friend that I had inadvertently stumbled upon part of the story) and offered me the family's complete cooperation if I would write up the story with my characteristic frankness and feeling for lusty livers coupled with my strong interest in painting.

While I realize that this story may go to pieces completely upon a thorough investigation, I suspect, from my knowledge of the locales and the period, that it wouldn't. I could attempt this between the Indian books, or any one of half a dozen other books that have been simmering in my mind. That would make the Cheyenne book ready along about 1947–48.

There is one more thing, which the Knopfs probably have anticipated. The Atlantic and Little-Brown have an option on my next "work". After a lengthy fuss, this summer I finally wrote both Mr. Weeks and Mr. McIntyre that they would never get another book from me. Mr. Weeks admitted over the telephone that the option wasn't worth the paper it was written on. Mr. McIntyre never bothered to answer that letter at all.

I hope I haven't spoiled your plans.

Affectionately,

1. *Son of the Gamblin' Man.* MS's information on the killing is inaccurate here. Her later research placed the killing in Cozad; the man shot was a settler. MS's sources in UNA are extensive, consisting of interviews, correspondence, and original newspaper accounts. A small representative example includes interviews with "Hagadorn," January 1943, with Dr. Robert Gatewood, November 27, 1956, and with Charles E. Allen, c. 1955. Sample newspaper excerpts include *North Platte Enterprise,* June 20, 1874, July 18, 1874, August 8, 1874, September 5, 1874; *Dawson County Pioneer,* October 21, 1882; *Daily State Journal* (Plum Creek), October 21, 1882, December 30, 1882, April 24, 1883; *Cozad Local,* November 27, 1956, "Personal Diary of Robert Cozad" (between May and November 1880); and papers from Sidney and Kearney. She also had access to letters and journals of the period as well as court records, deeds, and land transactions.

To F. L. Williams

[*Lincoln Journal*]

December 10, 1940

Dear F. L.

It's nice of you to ask me for a "homecoming" letter, although I really don't feel that I rate one since I'm still in my Trans-Missouri country. Certainly I do not feel like a stranger in Denver, with the people so friendly. Then there's the goodly sprinkling of Nebraskans that keep bobbing up, many of them writing. For instance, there's the woman born at Grand Island who is working on a pioneer juvenile, and the daughter of Doctor Walker, formerly of Pine Ridge, (still in my country if across the Dakota line) who is arranging his Indian legends for publication. Last week I read Weldon Kees' novel manuscript, as finished and sensitive as his short stories and his poems always are.[1] At the Colorado Library Association I met Dr. Wyer of lean and distinguished profile. At Fort Collins I noticed two very familiar figures on the front row while I was giving one of my rambling talks. They turned out to be the Bruno Klingers, looking very hale. This fall the Neihardts were here and I got in my usual complaint that *Black Elk Speaks,* one of the finest Indian books, I think, ever written, is still out of print. We paid each other a few compliments and wished we could sit down with the Orin Stepaneks for one of their dinners, and the good talk afterward.

Earlier in the fall I stopped off in the sandhills to visit with my brothers and sisters. A driving hail had barked all Flora's young orchard, much of it experimental stock — following the lead of her father. We mourned the crippled young trees, but, true experimenter that Flora is, she was already planning replacements in the spring, her big brown husband grinning at the prospect.

With Jules, the scientific minded one of us, we went over the site of a prehistoric Indian village in one of the sandhill valleys. The wide site was covered with broken pottery and flint chippings, with some arrow heads and a few bone scrapers and decorated bone pieces among them. It lies on an elevation west of a broad sweetwater lake, with a marsh for muskrats, a stretch of meadow land for ponies and for game, second bottom for cornfields, and a chokecherry patch against the hill—altogether an ideal location.

The sandhills looked fine, grass-covered once more, cattle fat, and my brothers' hounds ready for the fall coyote hunts. There may be a better place to bring up a family than the sandhills of western Nebraska, but I've never seen it—particularly now that the highway is really coming through at last, bringing trading centers and good schools within reach.

I wish all the bedeviled of the world could have as good.

Merry Christmas.

1. Weldon Kees (1914–1955?) knew MS when a student at the university in the 1930s. He was employed at the city library in Denver during the years MS was there, and he went to New York at about the same time she did. A critic, essayist, poet, and artist, he disappeared (a presumed suicide) in San Francisco.

To Melvin Van den Bark

December 23, 1940

Dear Van:

This morning I awoke to your telegram. It was sweet of you—and I'm sorry you can't come, for it seems such a long time since we've had a good old talk-fest.

Neither can I come to look upon your Christmas tree. Somehow I've got myself hopelessly involved in a dozen situations. I don't seem to have the sense to keep clear of things any more. I suppose it's because of all those long unsettled months of fighting with the publishers, trying to clear up the difficulty so I can go on writing books with some chance of getting them published. To know that anything you write can be held up by a publisher until the copyright of your last book expires is maddening. There is no justice for the little fellow in this world and whoever claims there is is a damn liar, as you and I have always known.

Once, a couple of weeks ago, I had a Knopf contract on my desk—an impressive document reminiscent of the parchments that old Frank Watson showed us up in his office once, remember? And the K. contract had such convenient gadgets as a two month time limit on decisions on manuscripts submitted, etc. But I couldn't sign it with the old Boston option still hanging over me. So I had to return it.

In the meantime, and in desperation, I tried what I've often considered doing before, getting together a lease breaker—I hired in a crack typist and we worked a week, night and day and got together a volume of short stories. Unfortunately the hurry to get it out before the holidays didn't permit using our old "Fearbitten". It's still a good story but the sentence structure needs lengthening out into my present style. I'm sending you a copy of the title pagings and the contents of the manuscript, and while I hope the Atlantic Press turns it down, which will free me, I'm preparing myself for an acceptance. If they do the latter, may I write an inconspicuous dedication to you for it? If you object to my using your name, may I use Van or "MVdB"? Or something? There are several stories in it that won't shame you too much, I hope, and I do think the variety is good, both as to publication (on those that have been published) and the actual story content and treatment.

You won't say anything about the Knopf business to anyone, please, for I don't want to get them into difficulties. It is supposedly bad business practice to encourage an author to leave his publisher, and they didn't write me until a former member of the Atlantic staff told them I was breaking away, and his understanding that the Bostonians would be glad to be rid of me, because of my social and economic theories. However, they won't let me go, now that I can get a better publisher. What they really want, of course, is to suppress me, and they can only do that if I'm on their list.

In the meantime I've heard nothing at all of your book—and its scheduled sailing. When I was at Fort Collins, the Colo Ag school town, giving a talk, someone from the faculty asked about the slang book. I could give him much information on its contents and comprehensiveness and nothing on its probable appearance date.

Incidentally, have you read Hemingway—and Willa Cather? The latter seemed to me, despite all my loyalty, thin. Then there are the Farrell book, and the Wolfe. One book that surprised me was *World's End,* the new Upton Sinclair book.[1] Not a line that read like a tract, and an interesting, to me at least, portrayal of the pre-war, war and post-war European scene through the eyes of an adolescent son of an American munitions man and his giddy and yet generous and warm-hearted "wife" (she used his name, anyway). It has a lot of partying, intrigue and sudden seductions.

But for a little hilarity in this sad world, and baudy hilarity at that, I recommend the story of three tramps called *Walls Rise Up* by Geo. Sessions Perry. It's not as good in some ways as *Madame Toussaint's Wedding Day* but it's in some ways more hilarious and certainly more annihilating.[2]

Then Lady Hamilton is to be made into a movie. Won't that be a spectacle?

A merry Christmas to you, and a happy New Year—

Affectionately,

1. Ernest Hemingway, *For Whom the Bell Tolls* (New York: Scribner, 1940); Willa Cather, *Sapphira and the Slave Girl* (New York: Knopf, 1940); James T. Farrell, either *Counting the Waves and Other Stories* (n.p.: n.p., 1940) or *Father and Son* (New York: Vanguard, 1940); Thomas Wolfe, *The Web and the Rock* (New York: Harpers, 1939) or *You Can't Go Home Again* (New York: Harpers, 1940); Upton Sinclair, *World's End* (New York: Viking, 1940).

2. George Sessions Perry, *Walls Rise Up* (New York: McGraw-Hill, 1945); Thaddeus St. Martin, *Madame Toussaint's Wedding Day* (Boston: Little, Brown, 1936).

To F. B. Griffith

January 7, 1941

Dear Mr. Griffith:

Forgive the delay in this acknowledgement of your generous letter of last December about *Old Jules*. I'm always glad to hear from anyone who knows my region, and particularly pleased if anyone finds my portrayal passably good.

May the new year be a fine one for you, and for us all, and may it somehow bring peace with freedom to all the world.

Sincerely,

PS: I am enclosing a copy of a list of some of the things I have had published. I get word that my *Slogum House*, (my study of a Will-to-Power person which I wrote after being very disturbed by a chance reading of *Mein Kampf* along about 1930–31. Because I couldn't handle the large canvas of a world in flux, I placed my will-to-power individual in a western free-land region, where grabbing on a small scale was easy enough, and because I think men with dictator complexes are not sufficiently male, I made my will-to-power individual an ambitious woman) was the best selling American novel in Germany this Christmas season.[1] Ironic, it seems to me.

1. Beulah Rector, "Books in England, Italy, and Germany," *Watertown* (New York) *Times,* December 18, 1940.

To Vida Belk

January 20, 1941

Dear Vida:[1]

Don't you worry about *Capital City.* It may hold up better than you think. People, even many who know me, and some critics, said *Old Jules* was written by an embittered, vengeful daughter. Today I never hear that any more.

Some day *Capital City* may be recognized for what I meant it—a microcosmic study of the macrocosm that is our modern world. Every person in it, as in *Slogum House,* my study of a will-to-power individual, represents one particular aspect of the "system" under the lens. *Capital City* is my study of an organized society letting itself slip into fascism. Abigail and the artist are not 2 people but represent 2 aspects of the arts lost in a decaying society—one type makes the compromises necessary in order to get physical escape, the other withdrawing into her own little world of history and the business of mother confessor so she need not face the world going to pot around her.

When France fell I got many calls and letters saying, "Yes, we have Capital City all over the world." I still get an occasional such note.

Only the artist who is ahead of his time is worthy of the name, and because of that very fact, there is no telling, at any given moment, who are the artists among us active practitioners.

The above, all of it, serves to prove your point. This writer, at least, is an egoist, in the manner of George Meredith.

I'll call you when I get to Washington, which won't be now until the hubbub there quiets down some.

And thanks for the poem. As it implies, books are to "make us quite forget" but they are too, to make us "see". "Put all you value in a book * * * "

Sincerely,

1. Vida Belk, a South Dakota native, worked in the Government Printing Office in Washington, D.C. She and MS had a number of friends in common.

To S. Clarence Trued

March 3, 1941

Dear Clarence Trued:

I'm sorry about your flu, and pleased about the barbecue and the report on your general activities. You say nothing about the Nebraska novel. How is it coming?

About my Indian biography: I've settled my publishing difficulties. Now if America could be pulled out of the hands of our Quislings and Lavals[1] in time to stiffen some European backbones before England collapses, and we inevitably with her, I'll have my Indian book on the stands for fall 1942. If England falls there will be no book, for there will be no writing at all fair about an "inferior" race in my time of life.

Now that I have the material in chronological order, I am even more convinced that my material will make a fine modern opera. The story is tragic in the old Greek sense—a culmination of forces that will not be denied, with magnificent characters, dances and songs, from the naming song and ceremony in the first chapter to the death travois and the keening of the women to the end.

Are you interested in it?

Sincerely,

1. Vidkun Quisling (1887–1945), prime minister of Norway, and Pierre Laval (1883–1945), premier of the Vichy government of France, were considered to have betrayed their countries to Germany during World War II. Both were executed for treason.

To the Evan Stegers

March 3, 1941

Dear Children:[1]

There are four letters returned from various addresses that I was told would surely reach the Stegers in a bundle in my desk drawer. Then there are the notes for the Christmas letter that I never got to write you, what with the holidays in Denver being what they are. The town opens all its doors and I saw more people that I never saw before. In addition there was the stream of Rosebowlers, who looked me up, and if I wasn't home, just slipped a note under the door saying they'd be back at 2 or 3 am, and surely I would be home by then. I never in my whole life expectancy hope to drink with so many people that I never saw before. It was grand. Then Paul [Hoffman], from Knopfs, was here, and we did Central City and Berthoud Pass, and the Windsor hotel. There, in the old bar, with the water-stained old ceiling still untouched, under a bullet hole and a picture of Calamity Jane, we signed the [Knopf] contract. The Windsor hotel here, if you ever come, is the place where Tabor and his Baby Doe made their home for years. It's the home of old age pensioners and other loose-enders now, but the old bedstead, the diamond-dusted mirrors imported from France, eight and twelve feet high, some in birds eye maple, are still there. The gold knobs from the doors are gone but a reasonable facsimile has been kept on the ballroom. The Tabors were, as you will remember, the Silver Dollar Tabors.

By this time I suppose young Steger is well started towards teething and colic and Maggie should be accustomed to that, and able to do something on the side. There is a girl here who was chased out of her job as designer in Paris. She knows so many people in New York that Maggie used to mention. . . .

I wondered about Otho and Joyce [DeVilbiss].[2] I hope J is going on with her painting. She ought to be stimulated to it, with all the gallery opportunities. I feel perfectly jipped that I didn't get to come to New York this winter, and with the finest Indian show of all time at the Modern Arts too. Eric Douglas tells me it really was grand to have space, for once, for Indian things. Here he is very cramped. But he has some fine things in the city galleries here. . . .

Well, I must tie up the machine for the night and spread down a little hay for myself.

Love to all the menage. And do tell me that everybody's writing, etc.

1. MS first met Evan Steger in a Lincoln bookstore in 1938. She introduced him and his wife to many friends, and when they were transferred to the East she kept in touch for years.

2. Otho (1906–81) and Joyce DeVilbiss (d. 1985) were friends from Lincoln days. In the late 1920s and early 1930s, Otho was a reporter on the *Lincoln Star;* later he was secretary to Nebraska Governor Roy Cochran, then was in public relations in New York. Joyce studied sculpture with Angelica Archipenko. MS maintained her friendship with them until her death.

To Helen Blish

June 16, 1941

Dear Helen:[1]

By this time you are probably all set for a vacation. I hope it will be a nice one, and no migraines. And I hope, too, that your vacation will bring you in this direction. I have a fair-sized apartment, with a bedroom and an in-a-door bed (must have the floor space and the closets for my maps and files, etc) and no one sleeping in the beds but me. So if you're passing through there's place to throw your shoes.

I don't know whether Eleanor told you that she relinquished her priority right on Crazy Horse to me. She did it as a complete surprise to me, with her typical generosity and graciousness. I intend to dedicate the book to her, if she'll let me, after she's had some indication of what I am making of her beloved subject. I hope it won't disappoint her too much. The book has to be in Knopf's hands March 1, 1942, so I'm putting it together now. The story *is* tremendous, with all the cumulative inevitability of Greek tragedy, and I feel small and mean and incompetent, although I've done my best to get at the truth. If I can only pin it down on paper.

In the meantime there are still some points that I'd like to talk over with you and Eleanor. After over a year of intensive work on the material and a couple of months in Washington in the Archives, there are still gaps, discrepancies and contradictions, and what look like deliberate evasions and omissions, particularly in the family relationships. These are due, partly at least, I suspect, to the deep and permanent animosities of the old feud between the Smoke and Bear people [rival factions within the Oglala Sioux band], both in the early period and in the agency days, when most of the accounts got into print and into manuscript. To aggravate these animosities, there were all the later contributory splits, such as the killing of Grattan, the breed feuds, as that between the Janis and the Richard factions, up to the killing of Crazy Horse himself, and the aftermath. I'm going to Pine Ridge after I get done at the Writers Conference at Boulder, along in August, mostly for the Indian feel. Apparently the more reliable and the more communicative sources have died. Perhaps I can get at the family relationships that Nick Janis once worked out for the agency. Anyway, I suspect that by now you and Eleanor are better sources than any remaining on the agency, so I'd like to get at you with my relationship files—they're pretty fat and revealing and full of holes. If I don't manage to inveigle you into my web before, may I come through Detroit some time this fall with the file?

Incidentally, Eric Douglas says he's heard from you, which suggests to me that you may have some work you want to do here. I'll be up at Boulder for three weeks from July 21, and if you can use a hang-out here at that time, I'll let you have the key to my apartment while I'm gone. It's only 4 blocks from the capitol and the state museum, 8 from the city Library, with its good Western History department, etc.

Sincerely,

1. MS was not aware that Helen Blish had died earlier that year.

To Stuart Rose

THE SATURDAY EVENING POST

June 30, 1941

Dear Mr. Rose:

It was nice of you to remember "The Girl in the Humbert." I made some grand acquaintances through that story, actual acquaintances, I mean, folks who stop off to visit me whenever they come through the region.

About sending you another story: I'd like nothing better but just now I'm deep in a biography of the hostile Sioux of 1850–1880. I've been pointing for this book most of my life, and have been working on the interviewing and the research whenever possible since 1925. The last few years I began to worry about getting it out before a book favorable to another race might become taboo. Now at last I have all the tremendous material together and have let my publisher set a March 1, 1942 deadline for the book. In the meantime I've done little on anything else, nothing at all for a year except a short story, "Moochmouth and the New Schoolma'am" that crystalized out of my visit home to the sandhills of Western Nebraska last fall when the natives were sizing up their new crop of teachers.[1] Mr. Chambrun had this for a brief time and you may have seen it before I had to recall the story, temporarily, to help satisfy a book option. Since then I've done nothing about Moochmouth. He helped serve his purpose and now he is still in my lower desk drawer.

If you haven't seen the story, and think you might be interested, I'll send it on. Anyway, I have an idea or two I would like to take up with you when my Sioux are finished, if I may.

Thank you for writing,

1. In *"Victorie" and Other Stories,* ed. Caroline Sandoz Pifer (Crawford, Nebr.: Cottonwood Press, 1986).

To Louise Bechtel

August 7, 1941

Dear Louise:[1]

I'd love to see you Friday. Your letter sounds like you'll be a couple of folks stopping off in a hurry, so if you'll write me where and when to meet you, I'll be there. Anyway, from here on Capitol Hill, to the Depot, down along the crick, and at the other end of town will be all right. Unfortunately my kitchen is a big filing cabinet, with no space for cooking foolishnesses, so I can't have you up for food. And my telephone is disconnected, so you can't reach me direct. — More obstacles than the Stalin line.

But I do want to start you off on your northwestern junket with one last look at your smiling faces. If you can't let me know ahead of time where to meet you, and find yourselves with a few minutes to spare, call the Robert Browning manager, Keystone 0673, and say it's important and he'll hunt me up. I'll be ready for immediate starting. Or if no one answers that telephone, send a messenger, or come up. I'm only 4 blocks from the capitol, 1000 Sherman.

And do fend off the attackers in the corridors. There should be some holds barred.

Affectionately,

1. Louise Bechtel (1894–1985) was the head of the Juvenile Department at Macmillan from 1919 to 1934, the editor of children's book reviews for the *New York Herald Tribune Book Review* for several years, and a writer of children's books.

To Paul Hoffman

[Alfred A. Knopf Publisher]

May 14, 1942

Dear Paul:

I've had no postcard acknowledging the arrival of Crazy Horse at Knopfs but there was no plane wreck in that direction so I suppose you got the ms ok.

By this time I hoped to have the foreword, notes, etc., in your hands too, but when I got the ms off I went to bed and I've done little since but sleep. I did get together samples from my picture and map files and these you should have by now. They are, as I suggested on the page titled "Illustrations" more for you to glance at than for any other purpose. There is no picture of Crazy Horse. The one that appears in various pseudo-historical works like *Califor-*

nia Joe[1] is of a pathetic, black little Indian wearing a whiteman's shirt over his pants and a mangy old war bonnet—things Crazy Horse the First or Greatest never insulted his Indianness with wearing. On Pine Ridge I was told that the picture was of a Crazy Horse, Crazy horse Number 2, as he was called, an undistinguished little Indian who took the name after he married the Larrabee woman, sometime after Crazy Horse was killed. This practice—taking the name of your wife's dead husband—was considered a gesture of respect among the Lakotas. There are, however, good pictures available of the men listed with the manuscript. The cuts from the Neb. Hist. Magazine I sent you are only for your own visualization of the men, and for possible guidance for the book jacket, etc., if Knopfs take the book. I am trying hard to avoid the usual wild west show Indian on the jacket, with warbonnet and fringed buckskin. That alone would damn the book in the eyes of anyone who has a smattering of the truth.

I like the sort of thing that is used on the ceremonial lodges, crude but spirited. The lodge I borrowed would amuse you. The top is blue, for the sacred sky, the bottom green for the earth—both done in house paint with about an inch of oil-soaked rim beyond the color on both sides. The figures the art department people here told me were done by regular tube oil paint, which is unusual, for the Indians are so very poor. The land on Pine Ridge is very thin—the rainfall around six inches a year, and the space very limited. But don't the girlish features on the men amuse you? That is, of course, customary. The old Indians did look feminine. Notice Spotted Tail. He looked like my aunt Eugenie Pochon from Neuchatel. You will notice, too, that the face is unimportant in Sioux painting, less and less important as you go back. They all look alike in Bad Heart Bull's work and earlier than that they had almost no features at all.

When I get caught up on sleep I'll send the foreword, etc., if you still have the manuscript by then. I took yesterday evening off and went to an art talk with C. Bancroft.[2] She is just back from Central [City]. She takes her maps, etc., up there and hunts up the old timers. Seems to be going strong. I loaned her my *Deadwood Days*[3] and took a few notes on the art talk—on [John] Sloan, who was well acquainted with my main character [Robert Henri] for the Artist novel.

My, I'm still sleepy—

Affectionately,

1. Joe E. Milner, *California Joe* (Caldwell, Idaho: Caxton, 1935).

2. Caroline Bancroft (1900–1985) became a close friend of MS's during her Denver

years and remained so. A Colorado historian and newspaper columnist, she was an authority on many aspects of Colorado frontier life, her subjects including Baby Doe Tabor, Molly Brown, Cornish folklore, and mining. She was instrumental in the restoration of Central City. Bancroft often visited the Lazy VV Ranch near Nederland with MS.

3. Estelline Bennett, *Old Deadwood Days* (New York: J. H. Sears, 1928).

June 9, 1942

Dear Paul,

I am very disturbed by your silence on the threatening steal of my book.[1] I know there is something to the rumor because it included not only my title but the subtitle of the book, and I never let even my typist know what either of these were.

Is it going to be left to me to take action on this?

Sincerely,

1. MS had heard that Knopf had sent the book out to be evaluated and that it had been pirated. No other book on the life of Crazy Horse was published at that time.

June 12, 1942

Dear Paul:

I can see a little today, enough to type my own letter, and most of the pain is gone from the eyeball. In this clearer atmosphere, I have had to reconsider the whole matter of the book and its complications, and particularly the responsibilities I assumed when I took up the task of writing the Crazy Horse story. Now it is plain that the best thing for everyone is to call the whole Knopf deal off. I am, of course, ready to refund the advance.

My spiritual debt to my old Lakota friends, and to Crazy Horse himself, is much too great to compromise on this book for any reason, certainly never for a commercial one. Knopfs are in business for the money. There seems no possible meeting ground for us.

I'm sorry. I should have seen all this long ago.

Sincerely,

To Stuart Rose

THE SATURDAY EVENING POST

June 13, 1942

Dear Mr. Rose:

Thanks about the synopsis for a story. I hate to work that way too, would much rather submit the finished product. So I'll be working on something as time comes up.

It's nice of you to be interested in the Crazy Horse biography and I'm sending you a carbon. That's the best I can do. The original is at the publishers, accepted, apparently, but still under editorial consideration for notes, illustrations, etc., as well as publication date and other pertinent matters. In the meantime I've found some spots that I think should be revised, as I always do if I'm left alone with a manuscript.

If you run across anything in the book that interests you and for which you might like the source for your own historical work, let me know. I'll be glad to run it down in my file. The index to my notes runs to 15,000 cards—a big job to make but very useful for me and for others who want to know almost anything on the 1840–1880 trans-Missouri country.

Sincerely,

To Paul Hoffman

September 15, 1942

Dear Paul:

The proofs came and the book looked beautiful as a beaded robe in the sun, but one that proved, upon closer inspection, hacked and cut as with a sharp knife.

A great deal of damage can be done to a manuscript whose foreword plainly says that the idiom and the rhythm are of great importance. By changing all the *lays* to *lies*, the *ways* to *way*, etc., and inserting hundreds of *hads* I think the maximum possible has been done to mine, and all without a hint of a query to the author. Not even the very second rate textbook house where I worked a couple of years permitted such treatment of a manuscript.

Sincerely,

To Eleanor Hinman

September 15, 1942

Dear Eli:

Thanks for the nice letter, which I can't answer just now, but am writing this to explain my neglect of correspondence this summer.

After four months of battling, I seem to be winning my fight to keep Crazy Horse from being stolen from me, and put into print from my own manuscript. It seems that Knopfs have a lot of unworldly draft ineligibles who are new in their offices. At least somebody who knows nothing of the historical field had the bright idea to put my manuscript into the hands of an "authority" and so the manuscript was copied and a contract with another publisher signed to beat me into print with my own book, of course, under the thief's name. I would never have known about this if I didn't happen to have an admirer, (of my books,) in this second publisher's office, who saw the contract and was nice enough to risk his job by letting me know. I had, of course, no legal protection on an uncopyrighted book, and while Paul Hoffman, my editor, admitted that the manuscript got out of the office, etc., he was unwilling to do anything either, because he likes his job, etc. So all I could do was use what influence I could rake up with historians, etc.

Evidently the book is coming out under my name now and in time, November 9, to beat my "friend". It must look pretty safe or Knopfs wouldn't have invested the money to have it set up in type. I've read the proof on the book proper, finished yesterday. It's a nice job, seems to me, good type and attractive chapter headings. They did stick in about 200 "hads" but I couldn't have them taken out because of the delay it would cause and perhaps still be "beat" into print. So I let them go. Paper priorities seem to preclude extra galley proof copies.[1] At least I could only get one, which I must keep in case of last minute corrections by wire or telephone. I am sending you a carbon of the ms title page, dedication, and the table of contents. I'll try to get one of the sewed pre-publication page proof books for you. There's no time for me to be sent an actual page proof. But then I never had one before. . . .

Love,

1. Galleys are unpaged typeset copy. Page proofs are typeset copy organized into pages.

To J. R. dela Torre Bueno, Jr.

ALFRED A. KNOPF

September 16, 1942

Dear Bill Bueno:[1]

Sorry about the delay in this reply. I had the 134 galleys of proof to plow through, and the anger at having a couple hundred "hads" put in where I felt they were not needed and only broke up my sentence rhythm and gave a Barrett Wendell air to a book written deliberately in the idiom.

But finally I got at your things. Enclosed is an attempt, about the twentieth, at something for the War Bonds business.[2] I looked over a lot of samples of what other writers were doing and I knew I couldn't allow myself to do that sort of thing. I think it's time we quit talking idealistic drivel in magnificent generalities and talked tough and worked tough.

The photograph business has me going around in circles, as it always did Little-Brown. It seems impossible to get anything of me that isn't so simpering and prettified that it's disgusting or so realistic it scares people. I've a couple more poses coming up in gloss and will send them to you when they come in. Don't be too hopeful about them, either.

About names of people who might be interested in my book—I've never thought about my work in the light of people saying something for it. I've always been the one who said things about the work of others, particularly in the field of the frontier, fiction or fact. Often I've been one of the sources used. Anyway, I hate this getting books that I should approve in quotable words; too often they aren't worth reading. Good books, I'm convinced, are not handled that way. Stop me if I'm wrong.

About critics: After studying the Romance poets I've had little respect for the tribe. I seldom read reviews and not of my own books, although I recall that the Walton woman gave *Old Jules* and *Slogum House* an interesting dismissal in about six words. And Clifton Fadiman doesn't like my work—which I've always considered rank flattery. Oh, yes, there's Mummy [Howard Mumford] Jones—the *Atlantic* once gave him much space to denounce unpleasant books, conspicuously *Slogum House*.

Mostly the reviewers have been friendly, I gather, perhaps too much so, from Boston to San Francisco, notably Jackson in the latter town. Bernard DeVoto used to do very well by me. Clay, of a Winnipeg, Canada paper, said I had a sense of humor, which endeared him to me. [Lewis] Gannett, who was given the earlier ms by Knopfs, [Robert] Van Gelder, [Charles] Poore,

[Harry] Hansen, etc. have always been long on the space with reviews of my books. George Grimes of the *World Herald,* Omaha has, of course, been particularly friendly, even when he didn't know what I was driving at. Sterling North, too, etc.

A few people who might be interested in my book, and would have a special interest in the material are:

Prof. John Hicks, chairman, Dept. of History, University of Wisconsin, Madison. (He's the man who followed Paxson there, who had followed Turner, and is probably the top frontier history man in the country. Harvard has been after him for years, as they were, and got, Turner. I took my frontier history under Hicks at Nebraska.)

John G. Neihardt, *St. Louis Post Dispatch,* author of *Black Elk Speaks, Songs of the Indian Wars,* etc. His approach to the Sioux is mystical but I think he'd like my book anyway. He approved what I was trying to do. His Black Elk is the boy by that name who visits the Crazy Horse lodge.

[Oliver Wendell] Holmes, Department of Interior, National Archives, Washington, D.C. (who seemed very well posted on Indians)

Dr. Jesse Douglas, Records of the War Department, National Archives, Washington, D.C. (Whose field is Lewis and Clark and the upper Missouri-Yellowstone and Snake country, from what I gathered in months around him. He's intensely interested in Indian material of that region.)

About the Jacket: I'll leave that all to your judgment and I don't need to see it. Whatever you say about me or the book will be all right. Nobody ever bothered to read my manuscripts before the blurbs were written, so your method is a new high in my experience.

Is there anything else? (If you find the war bond material doesn't please everybody, write me and I'll try to redeem some of the other attempts.)

Sincerely,

1. J. R. dela Torre Bueno (1905–80), another editor who moved frequently, was the director of publicity for Knopf in 1942. He was also editor at Macmillan, Appleton-Century-Croft, and Wesleyan University Press during his career.

2. As was common during World War II, the *Crazy Horse* book jacket was to carry an appeal to buy war bonds.

To Emily Schossberger

[University of Nebraska Press]

[1943]

Dear Emily Schossberger:

Thanks for the nice letter. Yes, I received one of the notices of the Schooner Anthology but with a deadline on a novel, a short one, creeping up on me that was just one of the many things I was neglecting.[1] I have had, however, around a dozen calls and notes about it from people wanting to know about the possible contents, etc.

About The Vine—I've never liked the story as anything but satire and since I'm the only person who recognizes its satirical intention, I dislike having it published. However, since it was the first story in the first issue of the Schooner and so has some pertinency to an anthology, I don't object if you decide on that. Incidentally, it wasn't my first story published—that was in the junior page of the old Omaha Daily *News* when I was nine or ten. There were over a dozen stories in print before The Vine, two in the pulps. I just don't generally bring the subject up. But if this were put out in the anthology it would be a lie.

I'm sorry I haven't time to take up your offer to write you something new, as I should prefer. Instead, I am sending you a story I wrote back in the winters of 1939 and 1940 for inclusion in a volume of short stories of my own, some day. These are to be a series of quick looks at various Trans-Missouri communities at various times between 1900 and 1950. The one I am sending you is a picture of mid-America trying to evade the implications of the present (1940) through the glorification of the past.

If the story meets with the specifications the Press has laid down for the book, you are welcome to it, but I wish to reserve the right to reprint it in my own collection, with proper credit to the Anthology, of course. I'm sorry the ms is in such bad shape. It was never finished, of course, and here I have only my portable and no secretary and no time to type it over myself. I'm still trying to get my standard machine shipped east from Denver.

If the Peachstone won't do, I might send you a short section, 12–14 pages, of my autobiography. This section is a complete incident and very light and flippant.

I'm enclosing an order for four copies of the anthology.

Good luck

1. Lowry Wimberly, ed., *Prairie Schooner Caravan* (Lincoln: U of Nebraska P, 1943). MS's "Peachstone Basket" was the lead selection for the anthology.

To Korczak Ziolkowski

23 Barrow Street
New York City
March 25, 1943

Dear Korczak Ziolkowski (Have you taken on the American arrangement of your name?):[1]

After four months on trains and in hotels I've achieved a semblance of permanency here and am making an attack on my accumulated correspondence.

Today the joy of this method of procedure has been your letter about the Sioux and about Crazy Horse. I'm so glad that the old Sioux plans for a Crazy Horse memorial are to be realized and that you, with your vast talent and understanding for the task are to do it.

In the meantime, if you find a little time that has no definite label while you are in New York, come down. I'm just off Seventh avenue, below Sheridan Square, if you happen not to know the region—at the edge of the Italian push cart section, and my quarters are as unpretentious as they would be out on the ranch. There are easy chairs, ash trays and something to drink and while my Indian material is in storage in Denver, all except the two Sioux Painting folios containing works of Amos Bad Heart Bull and Kills Two, I have a good ear for stories about the Indians and the reservation, and about sculpture too. One of the things that brought me here is a book about an artist.

Sincerely,

1. Korczak Ziolkowski was a self-taught sculptor originally from New Jersey. Indians asked him to sculpt a monument to Crazy Horse in the Black Hills.

To Elaine Goodale Eastman

March 26, 1943

Dear Mrs. Eastman:[1]

. . . Today I struck your fine letter and review of *Crazy Horse* and the grey New York sky was gone and the blue of the Sioux country was once more over me.

Yes, I knew Dr. Eastman's books, knew them from my long interest in everything pertaining to Plains history and I always understood that you had part in the final flowering and no small part. I have a nephew who loves *Indian Boyhood.*[2]

I'm greatly pleased to hear about your play of Crazy Horse. I suppose that production must be put off until the war is done but after that it should go well.

Do you ever come to New York? If you do, look me up. I'm just off 7th avenue in the Village, if you happen not to be familiar with the immediate locale. My telephone is Chelsea 2-3043.

Thank you again for your generosity, and may good luck follow your tracks always.

Sincerely,

1. Elaine Goodale Eastman (1863–1953) taught in a number of government schools for Indians. She was at the school at Wounded Knee at the time of the massacre (1890). She married Charles A. Eastman, M.D., a famous Sioux doctor. See Kay Graber, ed., *Sister to the Sioux: The Memoirs of Elaine Goodale Eastman, 1885–1891* (Lincoln: U of Nebraska P, 1978).

2. Charles A. Eastman, *Indian Boyhood* (New York: McClure-Phillips, 1903; reprint, Lincoln: U of Nebraska P, 1991). Mrs. Eastman often assisted her husband in writing his books.

To Lynn and Rose Van Vleet

May 2, 1943

Dear Boss and our Rose:[1]

I'm sorry I'm such a dud about letters. I'll answer any crack brain from, say, California, who's sure he's a reincarnation of Chief Flying Bull but I never seem to get around to the people I like. Besides, it's devilish hard to get anything done around these slow-moving New Yorkers. I was almost two months getting settled, but then I always did find myself stepping on their heels. Unfortunately I'm stuck here for three, four years, and not a real day off between now and the first September.

But I often think about you all and the ranch and as the heat starts coming I'll think more frequently and more fervently. Last week I had dinner with the Ned Bechtels. He seems to be a lawyer and investment advisor and an expert on Doumier prints on the side; she's a former editor of children's books for Macmillans. He told me of a most beautiful sight he ran into in Arabia—one hundred white stallions in some sort of a parade. Carl [Raswan] may know what it was. Telling him about the Lazy VV [Ranch] and the horses helped get him over some very bad service and food at Charles and pleased Louise very much. She likes horses too, although some years ago she had a very bad fall, jumping in a flat saddle and receiving a broken hip and a limp for life. The horse was mistrained by a Russian nobleman, probably phony. The Bechtels go to Boulder now and then and after the war they intend to come up to the VV for a Sunday show. . . .

I'm working on two books here and been lunched the usual number of times by magazine and movie and radio people who think I might be induced to do this or that — all things that would scatter my activities and contribute nothing to my own goal. I'd like to be accommodating but my books call. I've done no short work, not even looked at "Death in the Ice Mine",[2] beyond an article for the *Writer* and a couple book reviews, one just now for the *Times*. The book was Charley Driscoll's story of his father in Kansas and I guess all the regular critics were afraid of it.[3] Driscoll with the old McIntyre column can just about destroy any of them if he wants to, they think. I consider myself immune from such easy destruction. Anyway, the joke's on everybody — the book is pretty good.

So far I've not looked up anybody much. I've gone to a few plays, seen the galleries, listened to a concert or two and seen Zorina for the first time. The most fun I had was meeting Agnes Smedley.[4] She's the woman who writes on China. She showed up at Blanche Knopf's ultra cocktail party, with such folks as the ex-president of Colombia, etc. present. Incidently his wife looks like a model for Vertes. Agnes came in one of those dollar chenile turban things wound around her head and plunked herself down. She's like a blowsy ranch woman from western Nebraska and as genuine and unpretentious. She told me she grew up in Oklahoma, is part Pawnee Indian and that her education was paid for by an aunt who had the looks and the gaiety for the customary business a woman with looks and gaiety could take up handily in those days in that country. While everybody else chattered in French and Spanish, Agnes and I talked our bald and bawdy frontier lingo. It was priceless and saved me from ever having to go to another one of those things so long as I live. New Yorkers aren't very subtle but when Agnes and I get together they seem to see that I'm not their kind.

Good night, folks.

Sincerely,

1. Lynn (Boss) and Rose Van Vleet, wealthy businesspeople from Trinidad, Colorado, owned the Lazy VV Ranch near Nederland and raised Arabian horses. Their ranch was a mecca for celebrities. MS spent several summers there. After they sold the ranch, MS often stayed with the family in Denver.

2. This was probably an early version of a novella MS wrote using the Lazy VV locale and including vignettes of a number of the guests. The focus of the story, however, was on the Arabian horses. Eventually titled "Foal of Heaven," it was not published during her lifetime.

3. Charles Benedict Driscoll, *Kansas Irish* (New York: Macmillan, 1943).

4. Agnes Smedley (1894–1950) was an ardent student of China. She published, among others, *Daughter of Earth* (New York: Coward McCann, 1929); *Battle Hymn of China* (New York: Knopf, 1943); *The Great Road: The Life and Times of Chu Teh* (New York: Monthly Review Press, 1956). Because of her views, she was accused of un-American activities.

To Louise Pound

June 2, 1943

Dear Doctor Pound:

Yes, the Robert Browning address still seems to find me, although I've been away from there for many months now.

I'm pleased that you're doing something more with the Nebraska Strong Men. I grew up on the Barada stories as told by the breeds from around Pine Ridge, brought up there, I suspect, by the Ruleaus, etc., who used to live on what's called the Breed Strip in S.E. Nebr. and still with relatives down there to visit in the early 1900's. Their story of the man's background was pretty much as told in the Nebraska folklore Pamphlet No. 8, as I recall. The University Library will have this, if not Mamie Meredith.

Antoine Barada seems to have been a breed, Spanish and Omaha, the son of Michael Barada after whom the town of that name in Richardson county was named. There was also a Michael Barada in the Custer county region for a while, I'm told, but this would need checking. Around 1934, while I was at the State Historical Society, a letter came in seeking information on the Barada family to settle, as I recall now, an estate. Whether this was another of the recurring Spanish inheritance hoaxes I don't know now. If anything about the correspondence got into the Nebraska History Magazine it would be easily traced through the "comprehensive" index in the Society offices at the Capitol.

About the stories: I've tried for two days to reconstruct some of them for you but I can recall only one in any semblance of entirety. (I wish I had something of the Pound memory!) The one I recall comes to me as a picture: a hook-nosed breed, French, but not further identifiable, sitting on our wood block over his pipe and telling the story something like this:

> Antoine Barada was a hurry-up man, always rushing, rushing, can't wait for anything. One time he got tired of watching a pile driver working along the Missouri, with the hammer making the up-down, up-down, the driver yelling, "Git up! Get up! Whoa! Back! Back! Whoa!" and then all of it over again and the piling going down maybe half inch. So Antoine he picked up the damned thing in his bare hand and swinging back, throws it high and far so it lights clear over in Missouri where it bounce and bounce leaving ground tore up bad for miles and making what the greenhorns call "Breaks of the Missouri". But at last it stop and if you dig down on them high ridges you find it is the damned pile driver with grass growing over him a little, poor soil, you understand but it seem to satisfy them that ain't never crossed the Miss [manuscript damaged] and don't know better.
>
> When Antoine have disposed of the Johnny Jumper hammer, he see that the piling that is left stands a mile higher than the rest, so he give it lick with his fist and it pop down into ground so deep it strike buried lake, the water flying out like from bung hole fifty feet high and like to drown out whole country if Antoine did not sit on hole fast.

A rather neglected group of strong man stories where mind rules over mere brawn and nature too, are the Moses Stocking stories. These were floating around western Nebraska in my childhood, always about a man in eastern Nebraska who ran sheep. Later I discovered there really was a Moses Stocking and, as I recall now, lived somewhere between Lincoln and Omaha. I don't remember many of these and know of no place where they reached print. All the great plant and animal stories were fastened to him, such as the squash vines that grew so fast they wore the squashes out dragging them over the ground, the corn that grew so tall a boy was sent up the stalk to measure it and was never heard from again except that they know he's still alive because they sell a train load of corn cobs every year from around the foot of the Stocking corn stalk, thrown down by the boy, who must be a grey haired man now, because the birds nests found in the corn leaves are made with grey hair, etc. There was also the story of how Stocking went into sheep. He had an acre of bottom land broke, (Stocking never did any of the work himself, you understand), and because it was late, he couldn't sow anything except turnips. The seed was bad and only five plants came up, one in each corner and one in the middle, but they grew pretty well, the corner ones squashed and flattened, of course, being so close together, and too puny for any real use, although they hauled one of them to the top of a hill somewhere along the Platte and when it was hollowed out and the wind dried it, it was used for a military academy and did very well for years to house the boys. Another one from the corners was used for the railroad depot at Omaha, since there would only be temporary use for a depot there. The other two corner turnips were wasted, as I recall, but the center one was worth saving and from it grew the Stocking fortune. After walking around it once and coming back footsore and with cockleburs in his beard, old Moses took the train for Chicago and bought up all the sheep at the stockmarket and for the next month there was a stream wide as the Missouri of sheep coming across Iowa to the Stocking place. They started eating at the turnip where Moses blasted a hole and lived there fat and snug all winter, not having to go into the blizzard cold at all, just eating the pulp out, the shell making a shelter for the sheep that were worth enough to keep Jay Cooke afloat for a whole year after he really was broke only the public didn't know it.

There's what I know about the subject at the moment, and I hope you will forgive the rough, unrevised versions. And if you come to New York in the near future, and think there might be anything around the Village you might enjoy, call me.

Sincerely,

Through his banking and railroad interests Jay Cooke came to represent all that was ruthless and rapacious to the western farmer and when the House of Cooke, after much propping up, finally crashed, September 1873, precipitating a great panic, his name became the symbol of the graft and skullduggery that had impoverished the country.

To Mamie Meredith

[before July 17, 1943]

Dear Mamie:

Hail to the new profession — which is what book selling is, if it's done right.

I'm so pleased that Fred Ballard liked *Crazy Horse*.[1] The book has brought me the most satisfactory response, not in numbers but in quality of letters, of any of my books and last month a mess of Indians, apparently northern Lakotas and Flatheads, mostly soldiers, came through and stopped off for a pow-wow. I'd never seen any of them, so far as I could find out, but one of them had a copy of the book in his sack and while they all sat around in my apartment he gave an old time harangue, in the sense of the word the French traders speaking of the Sioux orators used. It sounded like Lakota, although I couldn't be sure. Then there was probably the same thing in sign language, with bits of the book read here and there. All the while that circle of dark eyes never left my face, although here and there a glint of amusement came to the surface. And when it was done they solemnly gave me the double handshake, first the right hands on top, then the left and went formally away.

While it was funny at first, it got pretty awesome towards the last. Somehow those young men, none probably over 24, had all the dignity and high seriousness of the old buffalo hunters left in them. It was the finest thing that could ever happen in my house and I felt terribly small and insignificant for a week.

About Roberta Sandoz—I'm sure she's some sort of a relation; all of them are. There are, as I recall, Robertas in the Kansas branch that settled around Neuchatel, Kansas. Just where they came from to that place I've forgotten and my Sandoz files are in storage in Denver. She sounds OK, something like the legendary Sandoz woman who is said to have gone across northern Europe to Sweden after iron for watch springs during one of the usual upheavals, when any traveler was subject to robbery and death from wandering bands. She, legend says, picked the dullest looking youth from the village of Locle, our home village, and with him riding behind her, on a shabby horse, she started north across what is now Germany and got clear to Sweden and back. There's always been a saying among the Sandoz women that the Sandoz men can manage any woman but one of their own blood. I've not seen much of that spirit in the last generation, although one of our first cousins, the eye surgeon in Berlin, seems to have been put out of the way by the Germans. I suspect they have her in Russia doing eye operations, but not even her husband seems to know where she is, or if alive at all.

No, I've not seen the little U[niversity] of N[ebraska] press book of [Senator George] Norris' "Peace without Hate".[2] I know there is one, and I'm under the impression it's of his talk he gave at the university. When I got here people tried to commiserate with me about Norris' defeat, saying it was too bad to have such a blot against his career and they thought I was getting farfetched when I insisted that the blot was not against Norris. Humanity of his kind sheds all mud, no matter how accurately thrown.

Thanks, too, for the line about the Indian imagery. I looked it up when I was at the Library this morning, checking upon dates for songs that were popular in the post-civil war period for the first section of the short novel I'm doing for next spring publication. The article is good. Incidentally, the Library here has a complete set, or seems complete to my inexpert eye, of the Beadle Dime Union Song Books, published 1861, with some wonderful adaptations for the moment on old tunes, including several to the tune of Wait for the Wagon and a northern version of Camp Town races and one called "The Michigan Dixie," to the tune of Dixie, of course. There are, also, such songs as Annie Laurie, etc. No music, just the words. The books are board covered, vest-pocket size. Perhaps you ran into them in your study of Civil War slang. . . .

Leonard Thiessen was around here for about ten days. Now he's in England; the first V mail letter came yesterday. He's with a bomb group, looked fine and says he's sleeping, in the army, for the first time in years and years. I hadn't realized that he was cursed with insomnia. Sometimes I wish I were; sleep's such a waste of time. . . .

Thanks, Mamie, for all the thoughtful bits. And don't let the summer heat get you. Sterling North sends me a clip-sheet of his farewell to the Chicago Daily News. Coming to the Post here, permanently, three years anyway, he says. Wants me to agree to do an occasional review. I don't mind, if I'm not too busy and the books are something that interest me. etc.

Affectionately,

1. Fred Ballard (1885–1957), a playwright whose most successful work was *Ladies of the Jury,* had homesteaded in northwestern Nebraska. Successful in New York, he came back to Nebraska because of his ailing mother and never went back. A strong fan of MS's, he tried to get her works made into films.

2. MS admired Nebraska Senator George Norris (1861–1944) for his work on the Tennessee Valley Authority and for his liberal political views. He was a major promoter of the Nebraska unicameral legislature. When MS mentioned to him the lack of suitable archival storage for the national records, it was Norris who started the wheels moving for the National Archives Building.

To Florence B. Lennon

November 20, 1943

Dear F. B. L.:

Hurray! I'm very glad to hear that the biography has been accepted.[1] But, of course, the credit for all that is your own—the two years of work did the trick, not anybody's criticism.

The nice thing about writing is that the facility in revision learned on one book comes into fine service on the next, and so on. The difficult thing for the beginner is to be brutal enough about his manuscript. Somehow, changing it seems a good deal like chopping up his own baby. But, as you know, he has to get over that.

And now good luck with the book. May the sales still be going twenty years from now, as they will, and may the book have many brothers and sisters.

Sincerely,

1. Florence B. Lennon, *Victoria through the Looking Glass* (New York: Crowell, 1945). Later retitled *The Life of Lewis Carroll* in 1962. MS had first worked with Lennon at the Boulder Writer's Conference in 1941 and advised her until the book was accepted. This appears to be the first full-length book Sandoz helped to publication.

To Clifton Fadiman

FREEDOM HOUSE
WEVD, New York City

December 18, 1943

Dear Mr. Fadiman:

Accidentally I ran into WE SPEAK FOR OURSELVES Saturday and I was mighty pleased.

Frankly, I'd always considered your taste in books strictly for the salad dressing crowd until someone compelled me to read your review of *The Moon is Down*. Then I had to read the book again, to see if I could have been mistaken. But no, it was still hokum, and dangerous hokum.

Since then it seems to me that a native toughmindedness is coming out in you. I suppose that it is losing you a lot of old friends. Well, here's one that it's made, in her small way.

Sincerely,

To Joe De Yong

March 5, 1944

Dear Mr. De Yong:[1]

Almost a year ago you wrote me two fine letters, and although they brought me much joy, I was in the midst of a book and so couldn't answer. I know that sounds ungrateful and ungracious and temperamental but I either answer letters or I write books—never both.

But now I'm taking a breather and I want you to know how I treasure a reader like you for "Crazy Horse".

I know Frank Goings. He's a relative of the Mrs. Goings who was a sister of Frank Gruard. Goings married either one of Red Cloud's granddaughters (or nieces) or one of John Y. Nelson's daughters. He does a lot of "managing" of the full bloods. There is a Little Soldier family at Pine Ridge, a good family. One is a minister, preaches in Dakota.

Your knowledge of names of the Crazy Horse locale is certainly extensive. Cody, Nebraska is a little cowtown, with a lot of Indians trading from the old Brule agency (Spotted Tail's people) at Rosebud, South Dakota. Old Deurfeldt of Gordon, Nebr. is credited with killing the last deer (puns are out) in the Sandhills. His daughter married one of the Margraves, an old rancher in our country.

Now about your very fine Indian story. Why don't you write up the Mouse Lodge Story? And I am very pleased with your Indian name for me.

You have had a fine lot of experiences—growing up with Oklahoma Indians, working with [Charles] Russell and [Frank] Lindemann [*sic*]. I consider "The American" and Neihardt's "Black Elk Speaks" the best Indian books, best in Indian "feel".

No, my friend. I won't be tricked by Hollywood. I see that your advice about Crazy Horse is for the long trail, and good throughout the night. As you understand so well there are some things that are sacred and to be protected from the profane hand. I felt, years ago, when He Dog first called me his granddaughter, a sort of dedication to the man he looked upon as the greatest he would ever know. The things he gave me were put into my hands to make into the best I could, and always to protect. I couldn't fail He Dog, or Crazy Horse.

Sincerely,

1. Joe De Yong (1894–1975) was a traditional western painter and sculptor, writer of short stories, and later a consultant for Hollywood films. Brought up in Indian Territory, made deaf because of illness, he became an expert in Indian sign language. He worked in Charles Russell's studio for several years.

To Sgt. Martin F. Schmitt

War College Library
Army War College
Washington, D. C.

March 5, 1944

Dear Sergeant Schmitt:[1]

I'm pleased to know that some one is working on General Crook's Journal.[2] Unfortunately all my Indian notes and my bibliographies are in storage in Denver, but around the War Department I heard rumors of later memoirs than 1876, but evidently with some criticism of his superiors and the general war department policy from 1876 on, and I could never pin any one down as to the whereabouts of this material, or even get definitive word about its existence. Not that Crook's attitude was a secret from me. It was rather clear from the exchange of letters with both his superiors and his subordinates from 1876–1880. From time to time I've been shown letters from Crook to his friends, but I took no notes on these. Usually they had no direct bearing on my subject beyond establishing what I had come to suspect, the war department's annoyance with what they considered the general's tendency to procrastinate and what his defenders called his unwillingness to move half-equipped. The latter pointed out that Crook did understand the Sioux, and his detractors said, "yes, he was in fact over-friendly with them". Anyway, there was no denying that Crook's annoyance with bad ammunition, the grafting freighters and the ethically untenable positions he was sometimes forced into on some Indian problems was justified.

Some of the letter books covering the 1876 plus period are at Fort Crook, Nebraska, or were during the Historical Records survey (see mimeographed document list for Nebraska). More recently, I understand, a lot of Fort Robinson, Nebraska, material has been sent to the Nebraska State Historic Society. I saw this in 1930 at the post, in much the same shape as the war department material used to be over at Virginia Avenue before the National Archives was built. You may find something in this. The Society would be glad to tell you what they have.

Then there is the material in the Indian bureau, and perhaps in some of the various reports of investigations into the obtaining of signatures for dividing the agency lands at Pine Ridge, about 1883, the time Louis Bordeaux and Garnett, etc., got the information of the Crazy Horse betrayal to Crook's attention. The Ricker Collection, Nebraska State Historical Society, has material on this trip by Crook to Pine Ridge, told by men who were at the various conferences. It seems Crook was blamed for certain frauds and inequalities in obtaining names for the land division petition. I never investigated the matter. Material on this shows up in a lot of pamphlets, etc., and in, I think, a congressional investigation.

About Finerty and Bourke, you will have discovered that there are some variances between their books and their reports or private accounts—not so much as between Miles' *Recollections,* which he didn't write, and his reports, but some.[3] Bourke's official reports I have always found excellent.

I'm sure I know where there is more Crook material, but it doesn't come to mind just now.

For the present, I'm off the Indian material, but later I'll be back to Washington on another book, and then I'll be grateful to have you show me what you can.

And good luck,

1. Martin F. Schmitt, ed., *General George Crook, His Autobiography* (Norman: U of Oklahoma P, 1946). Schmitt (1917–78), a librarian, edited pioneer diaries and letters as well as western histories and library publications.

2. General George Crook (1829–90), a West Point graduate, was Commander, Department of the Platte, 1875–82, 1886–88, and Commander, Division of the Missouri, 1888–90.

3. John F. Finerty, *War-Path and Bivouac* (Chicago: M. A. Donahue, c. 1890); John G. Bourke, *On the Border with Crook* (New York: Scribner, 1891)—Bourke was Crook's aide-de-camp; and Nelson A. Miles, *Personal Recollections and Observations of General Nelson A. Miles* (Chicago: Werner, 1896).

To S/Sgt CHARLES THIESSEN

HQ Det 384 Bomb Gp (H)
APO 634, C/O Postmaster N.Y., N.Y.

March 6, 1944

Dear Leonard:

I've waited so long to get the information about the South Pass newspaper from Wyoming, etc., that I am ashamed to write at all. But I do wonder what you are doing, besides your army job—any painting or anything like that besides your Christmas card or any writing besides the paper? Have any of the war-slang dictionary people been after you? If you have half a dozen or so good new overseas army expressions, can you loan them to me for the last section of my book?[1] It's in semi-final draft at last. Was supposed to be finished last September, as you may recall.

The Armed Services Editions will include two of my books — *Old Jules* and *Slogum House*. If you see either one, let me know how they came out. I'll probably never see a copy, being only the author.

The Village is taking on a revival, it seems. Old artists that have been living out at Westport and such places moved in for the winter, due to the shortage of gas and heating oil. Volta Torrey's book is out and done pretty well by, so far.[2] I ordered a copy, which hasn't reached me yet, but it promises to be interesting. He left PM, is on *Popular Science*, or some magazine like that. He thinks he'll like it better.

Edith [Grobman] moved up to 10th street. She says it's so clean it makes her feel a little strange. Probably feels strange here in my apartment, which has reached its usual state of chaos that it always does when a book nears the end. Besides, I've decided to answer the last year of fan mail, and there are little piles of that all over the floor, sorted by those that a card will do, those that have to have information, and those that have to be encouraged. I see where one of my old friends of the Kills the Enemy family was inducted at Denver some time ago, and when he told his name, Charles Jonas Kills the Enemy, he was told to skip the fighting talk and give his name only. I bet his old grandfather is laughing in his braids, or he still wore braids the last time I was up on Pine Ridge Reservation. . . . Do you ever run into any of the newspaper correspondents? I hear Don Hollenbeck on the air now and then.[3]

Love —

1. *The Tom-Walker* (New York: Dial Press, 1947); at this time MS titled it "We'll Soon Have You Back Again."

2. MS may be referring to Volta Torrey's *This Island Earth* (Washington: NASA, 1944). Torrey was one of the students who launched *PrS* at the university in 1927. He was also editor of the *Daily Nebraskan* there. A reporter with Omaha, Chicago, and New York newspapers, he later became a publication specialist with the National Aeronautics and Space Administration.

3. A Nebraskan, Don Hollenbeck worked on the *Omaha Bee* and with Associated Press, then served as an announcer with NBC and CBS.

To Blanche Knopf

ALFRED A. KNOPF

March 15, 1944

Dear Mrs. Knopf:[1]

I am not surprised at your verdict on WE'LL SOON HAVE YOU BACK AGAIN. I predicted that to Bill Bueno over a year ago. To me it merely proves what I said then: that I am once more ahead of my readers, as a good novelist should be.

It was the same with *Slogum House,* a study of a will-to-power individual and all the techniques employed, as they have been since by Hitler, in reducing the opposition. If you were to read the book you would find them all there. Yet I made the first draft in 1933, and the Atlantic held the book up a year before they could bring themselves to take a chance on it. Now it has gone into another edition, summer 1943, and is going into the Armed Services Edition.

It was the same with *Capital City,* the microcosmic study of organized society selling itself out to fascism. That my publisher was afraid of it did not help make my grief any less when I was kept up all the night after France fell by people who called to tell me, tearfully, that I had predicted just how it would happen and that properly advertised the book might have saved, if not France, at least many thousands of lives in the struggle sure to come. Well, it came; unhappy people are still writing me about the book and its application to the times.

Properly finished and properly presented WE'LL SOON HAVE YOU BACK AGAIN might help save us from the chaos towards which we are certainly headed, unless all those of us who know the danger point it out, graphically and with passion. This speaking up in times of stress has always been the premise of the serious novelist; it shall always be mine.

As for your option on my work. I certainly consider this manuscript, now that it falls within the ninety thousand word or over class, as coming within its stipulations.[2]

Sincerely,

1. Blanche Knopf (1894–1966), the wife of Alfred Knopf, was vice-president and director of Knopf's from 1921 to 1957, president and director from 1957 to 1966, and director of Random House from 1960 to 1966.

2. Blanche Knopf wrote, March 28, 1944, "Our feeling . . . is that we should prefer, as was originally envisioned in our contract with you, to wait for your next non-

fiction book." MS believed that the contract referred to "work" and that *The Tom-Walker* would thus qualify.

To Richard G. Lillard

Indiana University
Department of English
Bloomington, Indiana

March 18, 1944

Dear Mr. Lillard:

... About my winning the Atlantic Monthly Non-fiction prize:

No, I did not write *Old Jules* for the prize contest, although I did begin reaching out towards literary prizes of a sort at the age of nine. I liked stories and I had none, so I began to write myself some. They were dull, uninteresting, and I wrote others, still bad. But by then I had discovered that not all published stories were good, and, too, that the Omaha Daily *News* offered a book as a prize each week for the best story in its junior page. I began writing for them and got several honorable mentions and second prizes (only honor) but never a book and when I was sixteen I was superannuated from that career and took up serious writing.

Before long I began to see that the best material of my experience would probably be my father and his community but he objected to my writing and wouldn't consent, not until just before he died. By then I had discovered something else—that for most beginning writers the material with which they have emotional identity is the best and easiest. So I began the book. By the time the five years of research and writing were done, I had added so many more rejection slips on other things to my collection that I had no illusion about getting a publisher easily. I made an alphabetical list of the dozen or so royalty publishers of good standing at the time and I started the manuscript out—A—Appleton, A—Atlantic. That happened to be 1933, an Atlantic non-fiction contest year, and so I entered the book. When it came back I went on through the list and by 1935 I was back at the A's, so I reentered the manuscript. I had, in the meantime, gathered a lovely set of rejection letters, every one with at least a hint of what the writer thought I might do to the book to make it more acceptable. By the time I had thirteen of these, all different, some five and six pages of single-spaced advice, I had one conviction fixed for life—publishers do not know what they want.

But evidently they knew one thing they did not want—*Old Jules,* and by then they had provided me with thirteen different reasons for their stand and about as many suggestions for making the book acceptable. Oh, yes, there was one more agreement. No one believed that the book was about an actual man. There were some, too, who indicated that I must be a morbid character to think up such a man and call him my father.

Well, I did none of the things any publisher suggested. I just kept on typing new pages for those who had cigarette burns on them or orange stains where the publishers' readers took time out for refreshments, revising these according to my own ideas. I even typed the whole manuscript over, changing all the names and calling it a novel. No results either. In the end I did cut out 15,000 words for the Atlantic, 1935, one of the prize conditions. It wasn't particularly difficult; easier than changing facts, as many suggested, or, as one publisher said, telling the story in the first person, with Old Jules the speaker, as in *The Journey of the Flame,* which was going well at the time.[1]

About prizes: I think they might encourage completion of some books that would otherwise just drag on forever. Perhaps some people even begin books with the hope of winning a prize. I never would. Winning a prize was good publicity for me, an unknown writer, but the prize seemed to cheapen my book in the very eyes I had hoped to please—the eyes of the historians, the sociologists, and students of man living in the mass. Now, with the prize forgotten, the book has appeared on the readings lists of many such courses. Students from as far away as Australia write me they have been assigned a look into it. Now and then the matter of the prize comes up inadvertently and brings on a frosty silence, indication to me that the little matter had been entirely overlooked or forgotten.

About the effect of the prize on my life: I doubt whether *Old Jules* would ever have been published without a prize award. After all, most of our publishers had put themselves on record in my files with the prediction that the book couldn't sell enough to pay for the publication. At the time I was nicely started as a historian of the frontier and I could have gone on in that way, and while *Slogum House* was already in rough draft and *Crazy Horse* might have been written too, I doubt whether either of these would have found a publisher with the situation in the publishing field what it was then, and is now. So far as being a happy person, I would have been that just as well as a historian, a happier one, perhaps. It was not until I began to deal with publishers that anyone ever showed any doubt of any statement of fact that I made. I had, in my small way, established myself as a person of dependability and judgment in my field, and I liked it and the people I dealt with. I don't have to have much money to live; in fact as a writer of serious books I don't make much.

This letter seems to suggest a dislike of prize awards. That is not true, except that I suspect prizes should be kept pretty well to the commercial field. I don't think literary prizes indicate literary merit to most people but popular appeal and a definite slanting towards good sales. I have always felt that *Old Jules* needed the defence of time to prove that it was not just a mill-run prize book. But perhaps I am just being proudful, as our old Kentucky neighbor used to put it.

1. Antonio de Fierro Blanco, *The Journey of the Flame* (New York: Houghton Mifflin, 1933).

To Blanche Knopf

March 28, 1944

Dear Mrs. Knopf:

This gets funnier and funnier. You say you are interested in my non-fiction and yet you were not interested enough in *Crazy Horse* so Brentanos, right here in New York, January 1943, knew there was such a book at all. Not until I pointed out that I was the author and in a position to know, would they bother to take an order for a couple of copies to be autographed and sent out.

The *Old Jules,* which I sent you at the special request of your Mr. McKie, was rejected over your own signature.

About the contract: My correspondence with Paul Hoffman is in Denver so I have no idea what there is in it that might be construed as your attorney says. Paul told me the word "work" was used to cover both fiction and non-fiction and a Denver attorney verified this, as did a New York one just recently.

However, that's a problem I'll solve when the need comes up, years from now.

Sincerely,

To Mr. C. Burr McCaughen

McCaughen and Burr
St. Louis, Mo.

March 31, 1944

Dear Mr. McCaughen:

Thank you for calling my attention to "The Attack on Crazy Horse", painted by Remington that you have for sale.

Unfortunately, my kind of writing does not permit the indulgence of a hobby that runs into much money. The best I can do is have all the unpublished maps, etc., that I need photostated, and pay my way from one archive to another. . . . I'm sorry that I can't think about such purchases, and I am very pleased that you liked *Crazy Horse.*

Sincerely,

To Thomas Hornsby Ferril

The Rocky Mountain Herald
Denver, Colorado

April 23, 1944

Dear Tom:[1]

So Chris Madsen is dead![2] I hadn't seen him since along about 1934, when he was up to Nebraska round about the time the marker commemorating the interception of the Cheyennes by [Wesley] Merritt and [Eugene] Carr, the day Yellow Hand was killed. I remember how hard the Bakers worked to have Buffalo Bill's name on the marker and how excited I got against the idea of the Historical Society sanctioning a lie like that, particularly with me as Director of Research. As I recall they put up their own little marker.

As a kid I knew half a dozen people who were either scouts or soldiers, or with the Indians in the contact that day of 1876. I heard the story many, many times with never any mention of Buffalo Bill; always it went something like this:

> The people, many old ones and women and children, were huddled together, afraid before the sudden appearance of the soldiers. A few of the young men went out towards the soldiers, singing, one, Yellow Hand, riding up and down before the soldier line. There was a roar of guns, about twenty little puffs of smoke, and the Cheyenne warrior fell and the people fled back towards Red Cloud agency.

Scouts with the soldiers said that no command to shoot had been given, that the excitement of the recent news of Custer's death and the fact that many of the soldiers were not only new to the frontier but new to the army caused the shooting. I went through all the Merritt and Carr reports of the campaign in the A[djutant] G[eneral's] O[ffice] records, Washington. These sustain the scouts' accounts to this point. The scouts had a further story for the campaign, that one of the soldiers scalped Yellow Hand and later got $5 from Buffalo Bill for the scalp.

I also went through the payroll of scouts, etc. Buffalo Bill was not listed, although everybody, including Chris, agrees he was along, pretty drunk much of the time, always lagging behind.

I think what makes this lie harder to nail than the others is [Charles] King's account of the Buffalo Bill version, quoted in story and book. To this I can only recommend that the skeptic look up the long denunciation of King as a liar in the *Army and Navy Journal*. I think that is the service publication; my biblio's not here. All this just to say why don't you finish the Buffalo Bill?

Sincerely,

1. Thomas Hornsby Ferril (1896–1988) was the author of several collections of poems and winner of a number of national poetry prizes, a columnist for *Rocky Mountain News* and *Rocky Mountain Herald*, and a drama critic for Denver newspapers. From a pioneer Colorado family (his grandfather rode with Jim Bridger), he had a great interest in western history.

2. Chris Madsen was a veteran of the Indian wars and later a U.S. marshal. He was a witness to the famous and disputed Buffalo Bill Cody–Yellow Hand battle near Fort Robinson in 1876. Homer Croy's *Trigger Marshall: The Story of Chris Madsen* (New York: Duell Sloan and Pearce, 1958) is an interesting, but not very accurate, biography.

To Alfred R. McIntyre, President

LITTLE, BROWN & COMPANY

June 15, 1944

Dear Mr. McIntyre:

Your letter saying the Army and Navy has discovered that the authorized plans for an Armed Services Edition of *Slogum House* fall under the political ban of the new Soldiers' Vote Act does not surprise me. Unfortunately this is only a very minor instance of the appalling ramifications of that repressive Act.[1]

Of course, most of us realized the implications of the Compromise Soldier Vote Bill during the weeks of debate but with no Norris or any other man conspicuous for goodwill toward his fellows in the Washington delegations from either Nebraska or Colorado there was nothing much I could do. Now, however, I cannot deny myself a bit of Aristophanic laughter when I recall that in 1940–41 anti-nazis in Germany were taking the risk of smuggling out letters to me praising the book as a study of a will-to-power individual and the development of the techniques of fascism.

Yes, the ban comes very pat just now, when I am finishing up a study of public intolerances and irresponsibilities as they manifest themselves in the war and post war periods of America's last three great conflicts: Civil war and the two World wars. There was plenty of proof even before the Soldiers' Vote Act that the picture I had been projecting for 1947–50 would work out entirely too true for comfort.

Incidentally, the day your letter reached me Cornelius Vanderbilt's column reported the rise of the Klan and of isolationism and racial and religious hatred and intolerance in Nebraska. He might just as well have included much of the region from the Alleghenies to the Rockies and said that it has been carefully nurtured for over twelve years. And probably still is. As late as November 1941 I ran into an organized covering of the state of Wyoming by agents peddling isolationist and hate literature, carrying it around in big sample trunks like book and stationery representatives. This on top of the isolationist and obstructionist tinge of most of the newspapers of the region, from the Chicago *Tribune* to the Denver *Post;* from the top to the least of the county papers, mostly boiler plate of the same color. The surprising thing is not that the people of the region have been contaminated but that with the billions of dollars spent in the work anyone has escaped the contamination at all.

I suppose that *Old Jules,* apparently safely published in the Army Services Edition before the Soldiers' Vote Act, stands a good chance of being held up.

Sincerely,

1. Title V of the Soldiers' Vote Act, passed by Congress in 1944, barred the publication of books for the armed services if they embodied political arguments. The four books banned were Catherine Drinker Bowen's *Yankee from Olympus* (Boston: Little, Brown, 1944); Charles Beard's *Republic* (New York: Viking, 1943); E. B. White's *One Man's Meat* (New York: Harper, 1942); MS's *Slogum House* (Boston: Little, Brown, 1937).

To Henry A. Wallace

Vice President of the United States

July 18, 1944

Dear Mr. Wallace:

Don't give up. You have the people on your side.

As for Senator Truman, has everybody forgotten how he was taken in by MR, Moral Rearmament?—a movement headed by Hess and Himmler, Hitler's notorious henchmen, as even the Saturday Evening *Post* finally had to admit in an article.

He is not the man we want in any high position during the next twenty years.

Hold fast, and good luck,

Author: *Old Jules, Slogum House, Capital City,* etc.

To Mr. E. A. Brininstool

May 21, 1945

Dear Mr. Brininstool:[1]

Thank you for the September 28 copy of WINNERS OF THE WEST with the Benteen story. I have it, along with the rest of your works in storage in Denver but it was nice to be remembered.

About a year ago a girl from NEWSWEEK talked to me about something you wrote them, something about old Bill Cody, I think. She didn't even know who Buffalo Bill was, let alone anything about the west. Here's where one finds the real provincials.

The old timers around here seem to be dropping off. I hear Mrs. Captain Deming is very ill, although getting a little better. A Sioux back from Germany stopped in the other day to talk about He Dog, from Pine Ridge. Crazy Horse's friend. I didn't know this boy but we were both adopted grandchildren of old He Dog, so it was fine. He said he didn't really appreciate the old buffalo hunters of his people until he was in a few months of war. Not so much because of their prowess but because of their philosophical outlook.

I suppose you knew Dr. Sheldon died. I worked under him so many years that it was like a member of the family going.

I don't suppose that you ever come east of the Rockies any more. I've been planning to go through the material at the Huntington library, about the only material in a public repository on my field that I haven't gone through, some time in the future. I'd like to look you up when I do. Seeing the Benteen story again reminds me of the two years I put in at the AGO records in Washington, going through the frontier records, many of them still bundled up with mule rope just as they came in from the posts. I ran into a lot of material that had no place in *Crazy Horse* but that had a place in another book I may do some day. *You* know how phony much of the frontier history written has been, with the republication of the old lies.

Good luck in whatever you're doing, and thank you again for the Benteen material, and for all the fine recording you have done for the west.

Sincerely,

1. Earl Alonzo Brininstool (1870–1957), western historian, reporter, and poet of cowboy and range life, was the author of many books and pamphlets on the history of the West during the Indian wars and frontier period.

To N. C. Abbott

Nebraska City, Nebraska

June 4, 1945

Dear Ned:[1]

It's so nice to hear from you, and to know you're still working for the collection, preservation and organization of the Morton material, and a lot of other material too.

About J. Sterling [Morton]—I know that my father carried on some correspondence with him while he was Secretary of Agriculture and later, but exactly what the times were and the topics I don't recall now. Old Jules' correspondence was so very voluminous and it's fifteen years since I went through it. How much survived to the time the book was published and I could convince my mother that such material was of value I don't know. Mother, with the good housekeeper's impatience with the accumulation of stuff that had been in her way for 30–35 years, threw most of it out into the meat house after my father died. The meat house was cooled by running water from the windmill, cooled and moistened. I found Old Jules' favorite heirloom, a hand written medical book of over three hundred years ago. It was the book of recipes the early medico-chemists in our family used. The paper was thick, hand-rolled stuff, the ink faded, the language old French and the recipes ribald and wonderful. When I got home and found it in the meathouse it was a block of grey mold. Not a page or even a fragment of a page could be saved. The letter files absorbed less moisture and I saved a large percentage of the correspondence that survived the two years from 1928 to 1930 and 1931, when I had the opportunity to go through it. I sorted out a couple thousand of the most important, so far as the book was concerned, and these I think are safe. The rest are in a dry place too, I think, but there are mice in the Hills. I tried to get them to a safer place but after all I'm only one of the children and have no right to thrust my ideas upon the rest.

However, when I get to Lincoln there may be notations of the letters, with dates and contents in my notebooks. If so, I'll see that you have at least that for the collection. I've been sitting here pounding at the typewriter hoping my mind would disgorge something more specific but it's no go.

The man you met at the Historical Society in 1900 sounds like Old Jules, although he was never considered small. True he was only a little taller than I, about 5 feet eight or nine inches, but he always gave the impression he was a large man until his sons shot up above six feet. But you are tall; perhaps it is to be expected that he would seem small. He always spoke with a distinct French-Swiss accent and with the speed of the FS. . . .

Well, perhaps something specific on the Morton letters will come to me when I get back on western material. If so, I'll make a notation for you. I suppose that you have noticed the similarity of the rhythm pattern of Morton's speeches and that of Churchill. I happen to be one of the scarce individuals who consider Churchill's type of oratory definitely nineteenth century and an offence to the modern ear. Morton spoke in his time, with the rhetoric of his time, and the generalizations and intolerances. I don't think the pattern fits our times. I've heard a student of Nineteenth Century American oratory say that Morton was a direct descendant of the Clay-Webster-Calhoun school.

Good luck, and do what you can for the Society, as I know you will.

Sincerely,

1. N. C. Abbott (1874–1960), a member of the Executive Board for NSHS, wrote extensively on the life of J. Sterling Morton. He was recognized as an authority on Morton and worked for many years to promote and popularize Arbor Day.

To Don Russell

THE CHICAGO DAILY NEWS

September 7, 1945

Dear Mr. Russell:

Returning from a summer in Colorado I find several notes about your letter to the Phoenix Nest, *Saturday Review of Literature,* regarding my interest in the killing of Yellow Hand.[1] Evidently the monument referred to in the articles you cite was the one dedicated September 9, 1934, at Montrose, Nebraska, to Col. Wesley Merritt and the Fifth Cavalry for the interception of the 800 Cheyenne and Sioux enroute to join the hostiles in the north, July 17, 1876. If you are interested in this dedication you will find a report of it in the *Nebraska History Magazine* Vol. XV, No. 2. I was director of research at the Nebraska State Historical Society at the time as well as associate editor of the magazine and it was my responsibility to correct and approve the wording on the plaque for the monument and to organize the day's formalities and speaking.

The Society spent considerable time the year preceding the dedication trying to verify the Captain King story of the killing of Yellow Hand. The findings gave Dr. Sheldon, superintendent of the Society (and a newspaperman at Chadron 1889–1899) no choice; he had to deny Mrs. Johnny Baker's suggestion that Buffalo Bill's name go on the plaque. Instead, she put up another monument a few rods away, without either Dr. Sheldon or Chris Madsen speaking there.

Prior to 1934 Dr. Sheldon and I had both carried on years of correspondence with Chris Madsen about the Sioux war of 1876. Never during all this correspondence, or during the talks before or during the dedication, or at any time since have I ever heard Mr. Madsen deviate from his story that Buffalo Bill had nothing to do with the killing of Yellow Hand. Certainly none of the 800 Indians on the Warbonnet that day thought so or Cody's life would have been mighty uneasy. As his partner, Captain Luther North told me, the Indians protected Bill's cattle from the northern raiders and made his beaded show costumes. I've heard Cody himself tell at our dinner table how the Cheyennes had carried him home when they found him drunk on the prairie. Never did I hear him say a word about killing an Indian.

But all this is foolishness. My purpose in running down such stories goes beyond my interest in the truth. What I am trying to do is to show that the technique for expropriating a minority is the same everywhere, in all times. Once the Sioux and the Cheyenne were a romantic, wondrous people, to be visited by foreign princes and lords and by sick and unhappy writers from Boston. Then came the time when the majority wanted their land. So we made them out as subhuman, as beasts, and men who killed them, or said they had killed them, became heroes.

Sincerely,

enc: Carbon of notes from Army and Navy Journal sent Tom Ferril Mar. 1944.

1. Buffalo Bill Cody claimed to have killed the Cheyenne warrior Yellow Hand at this skirmish in northwestern Nebraska. It was a claim contested by several eyewitnesses. MS never accepted it. See MS to Thomas Hornsby Ferril, April 23, 1944.

To Mrs. Richard E. Brenneman

September 17, 1945

Dear Mrs. Brenneman:

I'm sorry about your difficulties with "faunching". It's a very common word in various American vocabularies, in general use for at least fifty years in the High Plains region from Texas to Canada. It's even reached various dictionaries, although as a writer using a growing language I don't always restrict myself to words that have been used in print enough for that. I deal with life and with life situations, and so must use the vocabularies that my characters would use in life.

However, you will find "faunching" in *The American Thesaurus of Slang*, by Berrey and Van den Bark, meaning "angry" and in Wentworth's *American Dialect Dictionary*, meaning "to be angry, rage, storm, rant about."[1] In the sandhills of the story, where I grew up, it is used for man or beast and "faunching at the bit," "faunching of a cold morning," etc., are all good expressions. Incidentally, I've used the word before, often, in my writing, as recently as February 10, 1945 in the *Sat Eve Post.*

I'm sorry that profanity offends you. Many things in life offend me, man's inhumanity to man, for example, but as a writer dedicated to the portrayal of life as honestly and as wholly as I am able, I cannot cavil at profanity, or at anything else that I find intrinsic in human character. Nor is this a tendency developed in me or in other writers during the last six years. There is profanity in literature as far back as literature goes. In my case, the biography of my father, published in 1935, is full of profanity and rightly so, for he and his fellows lived through violent pioneering times and only strong men, men often of great faults as well as great virtues, could survive them and conquer our wilderness so we could, so far as they could provide, live our lives in softness and comfort.

But I am sorry that you were offended.

Sincerely,

1. Lester Berrey and Melvin Van den Bark, *The American Thesaurus of Slang* (New York: Crowell, 1942); Harold Wentworth, *American Dialect Dictionary* (New York: Crowell, 1944).

To William Rose Benét

[*Saturday Review*]

October 14, 1945

Dear Mr. Benét:[1]

Thank you for your nice note of long ago—.

About [George Bird] Grinnell on the Cheyennes: He's the best there is, and we could all be eternally grateful if someone had done as well for the Sioux, the Crows and the other Plains Indians. Now it is forever too late.

To be sure an occasional error creeps into Grinnell, as is inevitable with such voluminous detail, but mostly on matters that couldn't be checked, handily, until our western material in the National Archives is properly classified and organized. I ran into some such difficulties while plowing through the bales of AGO frontier records over on Virginia Avenue, Washington, above the old Department of Interior garage. Everything just as it came in from the dismantled frontier posts, some still tied with mule rope in 1936–40. Great fun, but very time-consuming.

Another difficulty in writing about the Cheyennes was the cleavage, even ritualistic, that was already developing by the 1850's between those who were adapting themselves to the Kansas, Oklahoma, Texas Panhandle country and then took up agency life early because the buffalo grew scarce, and those allied with the Sioux. I noticed this cleavage in 1930 on the Tongue River reservation, Montana, among the old buffalo hunters still alive. A couple of them came from the south to live with relatives. Their arguments over the old ways were something wonderful. Of course, with the coming of the horse so recent, and the resulting change from an agrarian to a hunting people, their ways had not become fixed in either case.

If you do not have WOODEN LEG, a Warrior Who Fought Custer, by Marquis, you might enjoy that personal account of a good man.[2] I think

WOODEN LEG, Linderman's AMERICAN and Neihardt's BLACK ELK SPEAKS are the three best books for the casual reader interested in the life and ways of the Plains Indians. Less battle business, more life ways, but that seems good to me.

Thank you again,

1. William Rose Benét (1886–1950) was a critic, editor, fiction writer, and poet. He helped found *Saturday Review of Literature* in 1924 and was associate editor and contributing editor there and elsewhere.

2. Thomas Marquis, *Wooden Leg: A Warrior Who Fought Custer* (Minneapolis: Midwest, 1931).

To Winston Bidwell

June 22, 1946

Dear Doc:[1]

No wonder I think you're one of the smartest, most discerning men alive—you see in my writing what I hope is there. And perhaps because you have that discernment you are doomed to dissatisfaction in your painting. It's an eternally damned state, but it's that quality that makes for real greatness in an art, so don't be discouraged by your gloom. Listen, now and then, to that objective little voice in the top of your head that says "you are more gifted with insight and therefore more difficult to please in your own work." Look at all the mediocre people who have a following among the mediocre. Would you be like they? Darling, you know you wouldn't. . . .

Here the weather has been with me, fine and cool; muggy, of course, to a highlander, but the best New York can do in June, and wonderful for the last pulls of the book. I'm off to Bloomington to the Writers conference in July. No Colorado for me this year. The Van Vleets generously asked me again this year, and I'd love it, but three months is a lot of time out of my life. . . .

The atomic control committee will work out just as far as the people want it to, and that means an informed public. I'm hoping—. If it works it won't be our figureheads who deserve the thanks. But that's usually the way with society—the ideas of some unknown save it. I'm not afraid of nations with the a-bomb as I am ambitious individuals. They can get power mighty fast now.

I like to think about Mary Chase having one of your paintings,[2] one of these days I'll get flush and buy one. Then I'll have two western painters to cart around.

You know, unintentional distortions in your work may be genius in you. Certainly many writers create better than they know—Wolfe, for one. His exaggerations were undiscernible to him, I'm sure, yet therein lies his art. Life raised to the nth degree—.

Affectionately,

1. Winston (Doc) Bidwell (1904–64) was the curator of oriental art at the Denver Art Museum and a reviewer for art journals. He struggled with his own painting for years; MS encouraged him consistently.

2. Mary Chase (1907–81), the author of the Pulitzer Prize–winning play *Harvey* and others, was a reporter and free-lance correspondent. Chase was a Denver resident, a friend of Caroline Bancroft's and MS's, and a frequent visitor to the Van Vleets' Lazy VV Ranch.

To Edward Weeks

August 15, 1946

Dear Ted:

Looking over the book since talking to you this afternoon I found some revisions I made on the train to Indiana. I've copied off a few pages and am enclosing them. I suspect that sharpening the last section will only make you more uneasy than you seem to be, now, about what you read since the other time you called.

As for libel: I suppose that's over such things as the possible parallel with the May business. The longer you delay the more of the book will come true, for what is created in art is verified in life. The whole business struck me with a bang in February 1943, on a wearisome train trip up to Schenectady. I had just seen Colonel Sandoz, directing Chemical warfare, and Cousin Young Paul, former reclamation engineer at Denver, helping build posts for the navy . . . and a mess of my old physics friends and former chemistry students under [Reuben G.] Gustavson (whom I helped talk into the chancellorship at Nebraska). It all crystalized on that trip—the whole story, in detail. . . .

Sincerely,

August 24, 1946

Dear Ted:

I've put in two nights and a day thinking about your verdict that the third section of THE TOM-WALKER is dull and predictable and that it be made into an epilogue or at least cut 30–40 percent—make an amputee of the story, and I've decided that it's just all too silly and reminiscent of the years I worked to market OLD JULES, when only my immoderate stubbornness saved the integrity of the book from just such suggestions. In fact, in all the publishers' divergent suggestions on OJ the one agreement was that it was dull and predictable, and only the Atlantic's printed rejection slip, I'm sure, saved you from being on the same record. Of course the book was, and is, dull and predictable, as are many books of greater importance, in fact all really important ones, because life is dull and predictable. I find it not unamusing that your verdict proves the point of the WALKER—that man never learns anything from experience, but always manages to avoid his learning in bigger and more spectacular ways—.

... The only Nebraskan, so far as I know, in the publishing field in the early Thirties, Frank Hannighen [*sic*], found OLD JULES too dull and predictable too, suggesting that I rewrite the whole thing, having OJ tell his story in one night around a dinner table, as in the then bestseller, THE JOURNEY OF THE FLAME. Drastic and appalling as that suggestion was, it was moderate compared to the one you make for the WALKER, that I not only destroy the structure and balance of the novel but that I completely destroy the whole theme and purpose of the book by eliminating its application and inevitibility in the contemporary scene.

My understanding is that you are not interested in the book without the amputation, so please have it returned. I'm writing Mr. Ober a note about this. He knows I wanted to come up for the manuscript after your second call.

Thank you,

To THE DIAL PRESS

New York City

Cornhusker Hotel
Lincoln, Nebraska
September 12, 1947

Dear Sirs:

I'm sorry I bothered you about the dearth in WALKERS, since obviously nothing can be done about that now.[1] The first crest of the demand has been wasted. But this is the fifth time I've had to see a book handled like that,—and after I suggested at our conference March 12 that the book would carry a 20,000 printing.

Here the shortage is not only at Miller and Paine (there's a new woman at Millers and she might expect to get through an autographing with 25 copies, when 230 would be the very least) but at Golds,[2] the Prairie Book store, the Lindell Book House and the American News, both here and in Omaha as well. All are out and have not received their reorders. Besides, I ran into the same complaint in Denver. Nor did I ever get my first order myself, which I mailed about Aug. 1. I assumed the books were sent to 23 Barrow instead of Wisconsin by mistake, and finally reordered. Those, second printing, reached me out in western Nebraska last week.

So far as I can see now the autographing is out. I have about a week's work in the archives here and with old timers and then I'll be heading back to New York. I'm sorry to miss the Emrichs' party.

Sincerely,

1. Dial Press published *The Tom-Walker* in 1947.

2. Miller and Paine was a leading department store in Lincoln, as was Gold's. Each had a strong book department. MS regularly held autographing sessions at both, as well as at the other major bookstores in Lincoln and Omaha.

[holograph letter (not sent)]
To Joseph Balmer

Freihofstrasse 33
Zurich 28, Switzerland

October 28, 1947

Dear Joseph Balmer:[1]

Now that my novel is off my hands I am digging into my back correspondence and I find your letter of March 1, 1947, with the criticism of my book by an easily identifiable writer. By this time you will have obtained my CRAZY HORSE and will have made your own decisions. The fact that there are no footnotes is not my fault, rather my sorrow. I have to make a living from my books and publishers, particularly under war-time paper restrictions, are not friendly to footnotes. I have them, thousands of them.

About the disorganization of the Indians when the buffalo was gone—was not the same disorganization evident in the Europe of 1939–1940? And with less desperation.

About the Indian societies, did I mention the ones put out by the American

Museum of Natural History? One on Oglala societies that should interest you very much. The museum is here in New York.

I understand there are several Swiss planning to come to America for the dedication of the Sioux Memorial in the Black Hills.

Sorry this answer has taken so long, and is so sketchy. I've never stooped to self-defence, and I'm not beginning now.

Sincerely,

1. Joseph Balmer, although Swiss, was a member of NSHS and an avid western history buff. He had a large western library and apparently carried on an extensive correspondence with many western writers. He sometimes questioned MS's methods, interpretations, and sources.

To Elmo Scott Watson

Medill School of Journalism
Northwestern University

February 23, 1948

Dear Mr. Watson:[1]

I am happy to receive your fine letter—which was, of course, not in any way expected from a busy man. I have a sort of casual exchange relationship about clippings and carbons of letters with a scattering of people across the country, by which we all receive an occasional bit that we might otherwise miss. No acknowledgement is expected, of course, again—

About the niece of Julius Meyer. Mrs. Levy (my notes on her material are in storage in Lincoln and I'm not even certain of the spelling of her name anymore) was living at the Lincoln Hotel, Lincoln, Nebraska, in the middle 1930's. She was a pleasant old woman then, but so crippled with arthritis that she could only write with great pain in tremendous scrawls. Nevertheless she was writing her notion of the life of Julius Meyer. She wanted me to collaborate on it, or at least help her get a publisher, but her version of the story was almost entirely from a lot of very romantic girlhood recollections, without any checkup, not even with the lot of material she had. There were boxes of this; sketchy memoirs of some sort, many letters, account books, too, I seem to recall, and many splendid photographs. When I pointed out some of the discrepancies between her story and the documentary material in her collection, the cited material vanished. I made suggestions for recasting and rewriting, just as a reader, not as a writer, but the poor soul was in such constant pain, and one does not become a biographer easily. Probably the woman is dead now. Her husband was a wine wholesaler. Perhaps that will help you locate the Julius Meyer material if Mrs. Levy *is* dead.

The Meyer brothers, in the period covered by *Crazy Horse,* seemed to be anxious to expand into the Sioux trade, since their old trade with the lower Missouri Indians, (Poncas and Omahas, as I recall now) had pretty well disappeared. This, with Julius' natural fondness for Indians (he seems to have had some sort of arrangement with both a Ponca and an Omaha girl), and his flair for display encouraged his spending money on the excellent photographs he had made of some of the Oglalas and Brules as they passed through. I went over all the material in the Indian Bureau on the traders with the Oglalas and Brules from 1851 to the fall of 1877 and I found only sketchy mention of the Meyers, as I recall. Perhaps they were aligned with some of the other Omaha trade outfits, or worked through agency traders. Mrs. Levy seemed to recall that Agent Saville of Red Cloud and Julius were friends. The firm petered out, losing a court suit about a wall falling on someone, etc., according to the material in Mrs. L's collection. I'm sorry I don't recall this more clearly, but perhaps you can [get something] from some of this. Realizing that I should put some of this material down as it occurs to me, I have a way of going on in letters, for the carbons for my own files. You will forgive it—

I'm happy to add your "Last Indian War" reprint to my files, which contain notes from the original appearance. I'll be very much interested in the whole study.

I was interested to find no mention of John Maher of Chadron among the correspondents who brought on the troubles of 1890–1 on Pine Ridge. I've never investigated this, but in my childhood all up and down the old Northwestern [Railroad], and among the Indians, his fantastic "space" pieces in the New York *Herald* were blamed for bringing the soldiers to Pine Ridge. About 1930 I interviewed him for the *Old Jules.* He was court reporter during the trials of my father and his vigilante gang, early 1890's, over the hanging of John Freese, and the only person still alive who knew about the troubles but was not involved on either side. I told him what I wanted, but at the mention of Old Jules, he went into an exaggerated tale of the snake bite incident. I interrupted, told him I was the daughter, and was with him when he was bitten. Old John stopped, focused his eyes on me. "The hell you are?" he exclaimed. "Well, it was a good story the way I was telling it—" Then he settled down and with the notes from the court records and the interviews with both sides, I got him to talking about the court scenes. Later I let him have his fun by listening to his story of how he started the "Ghost Dance War." He loaned me a sheaf of clippings from the N. Y. *Herald* he claimed he wrote. They sounded just like modern war scare reporting. He also told me about other deliberate hoaxes when news was short and he needed money: the petrified man, the soda springs and the "man who sank the *Maine*". You must have run into him personally, and probably found he was a total liar. I wouldn't be surprised, except that A. E. Sheldon and Charley Allen both told me that he did write for the *Herald* that fall. However, they may have depended upon his say-so.

Thank you for liking *The Tom-Walker* and for saying so in your generous way in the *Sun*. I'm happy that Mrs. Watson likes the book. And I'm more than happy that *Crazy Horse* bears rereading for you.

I'm sorry this got so long. We are both busy.

Sincerely, and in haste,

No reply—

1. Elmo Scott Watson (1892–1951) was a professor at the Medill School of Journalism, Northwestern University, an editor of *Publishers' Auxiliary,* a member of the Western Newspaper Association, and a member of the Chicago Corral of the Westerners.

To Russell Maloney

WCBS
New York City

June 10, 1948

Dear Mr. Maloney:

What do you mean, telling the public that authors write the blurbs of their books? I've had five books published—Atlantic-Little, Brown, Knopf and Dial, and never has anyone even suggested that I should have any interest in what goes into the blurb, much less write it.

In addition, not a one of my dozens of writing acquaintances ever acknowledged anything except appalled surprise at what appeared on the jackets of his books.

I enjoy your book talks, but please don't get those of us who have very personal contacts with the reading public into any more trouble than absolutely necessary. I've had dozens of complaints about my blurbs as misleading, coy and repelling. With one exception I've agreed with the complaints, and I try to make it plain to all my readers, and other people's readers as well, that some authors, myself for example, never see blurbs until the prepublication copies arrive.

Sincerely,

To Charles Heyl

Lincoln, Nebraska

May 15, 1949

Dear Charles:[1]

I'm deep in my Cheyenne book but there are still some things to clear up, some that my fall trip to the Cheyenne agencies will probably settle, and some that it may not. One of these is what happened to Yellow Swallow, claimed to be the son of General Custer, born to the Cheyenne girl he calls Monahseetah in his *Life on the Plains*,[2] and the Indians usually called Me-o-tizi or Me-otzi—one of the captives from the Washita fight, where her father, Little Rock, second to Black Kettle, was killed with the head chief.

The immediate reason I am writing you about this is a faded newspaper clipping that an old timer who used to work down in Indian Territory, was there as a boy in the 1870's, sent me to look at and return. The clipping was undated and unidentified but it told of a "Cap" Charley Heyl going through with a Cheyenne boy he called Yellow Locks. The clipping identified the boy as "the half breed son of Monaseetah" (sic) the Cheyenne maiden whose "charms are mentioned so warmy (sic) by General Custer" in his writing.[3]

This Charley Heyl may have been your father and the boy must have been Yellow Swallow, and so the one called Custer's son by Katie Big Head, the narrator of *She Watched Custer's Last Fight*,[4] by Marquis. Katie says she was a cousin of Me-o-tizi. Brill's *Conquest of the Southern Plains*[5] tells a similar story as related by two Cheyennes, Magpie and Little Beaver, with Kish Hawkins, grandson of White Antelope, killed at Sand Creek, as the interpreter. Brill says that Kish and John Otterby also knew Monahseetah well.

On the other hand there is some evidence that this boy may have been along with the Big Head lodge on the Cheyenne flight from Indian Territory 1878, and if so, apparently one of the boys killed in January 1879 in the outbreak from the barracks prison at Fort Robinson. He was born late summer 1869, so he would have been nine. By then his mother was married about three years and there are stories of his step-father's feeling against the boy, as well as some resentment from the Southern Cheyennes, since Custer killed Me-o-tizi's father, who was one of their famous men. There is still feeling against the woman, although she died along about 1921. There is, of course, also some pride in the fact that she was chosen by Custer from the entire captive camp for his tent.

Brill says the story was not told until Mrs. Custer died, and that is fairly accurate so far as books are concerned. I've seen the story in newspapers, however, and I can't remember when I hadn't heard the Sioux tell it. Probably the story was brought to them by the angry Cheyennes who fled north the summer and fall of 1869, and later. Big Head, a sub chief under Dull Knife, was an Oglala apparently married to the Cheyenne woman, Katie.

I wonder if you can throw any light on this matter?

Regards,

1. Charles Heyl was the son of an army man once stationed at Fort Hartsuff, Nebraska; he once had two books of Cheyenne pictographs.

2. George Armstrong Custer, *My Life on the Plains* (New York: Sheldon, 1874).

3. The boy was an Apache, not a Cheyenne.

4. Thomas Bailey Marquis, *She Watched Custer's Last Battle* (Hardin, Mont.: Custer Battle Museum, 1933).

5. Charles J. Brill, *Conquest of the Southern Plains* (Oklahoma City: Golden Saga Publishers, 1938).

To Mr. Rufus Wallowing, Chairman

Council of Northern Cheyennes
Tongue River Agency
Lame Deer, Montana

Address to September 1,
Lazy VV Ranch,
Nederland, Colorado
August 7, 1949

Dear Mr. Wallowing:

Superintendent John Hunter kindly sent me your name as Chairman of the Council and the man who can give me the names of some of the old Cheyenne who might be willing to assist me in getting as clear a picture as possible of the major events of the period from 1857 to 1880. I am enclosing a copy of my letter to Mr. Hunter.

You will see that I am particularly anxious to clear up some points on which the Cheyennes have been understandably reluctant to speak freely in the past. For example, there are such appalling attacks on them as the one on Sappa creek, April 1875, by Lieutenant [Austin] Henely and the buffalo hunters. Most of the accounts of this are from the white man's point of view. Grinnell makes only short mention of this fight, and Wooden Leg, in his story *The Man who Fought with Custer* [*sic*] gives only a side glimpse or two at this. Yet, according to my notes, these were the Cheyennes who fled from the attack in the sandhills in Oklahoma where the Indians retreated over the fighting when their men were being ironed for the trip to the prison at Ft. Marion, Florida, and that the survivors carried the Sacred Arrows to the north, and that some were in the Custer fight. If this is true, then the men in that Sappa camp in 1875 were important men, and important or not, such a brutal attack on the camp, with women and children there, should be told. According to my notes the Indians offered a flag of truce and were denied surrender but were shot down. Whatever the truth of this, I want it.

There are many other things I wish to know about, and many confusions in names and relationships to clear up. I hope that you and your people will find it in your hearts to help when I come up in early September. The Cheyenne story is the story of a noble people; I hope to measure up to its greatness as nearly as I can.

Sincerely,

To President Harry Truman

Washington, D.C.

October 18, 1949

Dear Mr. President:

Last night a long time friend, Otho DeVilbiss, Public Relations, BPOE, stopped in. He told me of his very pleasant visit at the White House last summer with the winner of the Elks' Americanism Essay Contest, and of your interest in the American Indian, and your extensive reading on the subject, including my book, *Crazy Horse.*

I am happy to hear all this, and regret that I did not know it earlier. I have just returned from an extensive cover of the old Plains Indian country, particularly the Tongue River Reservation of the Northern Cheyennes, where the calamities of the present compelled me to shift my interest from the old buffalo hunting days to the problems of the present.

After the appalling storms of last winter, the Reservation was struck by a devastating drouth this summer, followed by grasshoppers that destroyed even the small gardens. With no railroad and no good roads, hay costs around forty dollars a ton laid down on the reservation, so the Tribal Herds, in which the Cheyennes took so much pride, are having to be sold down far below even what survived last winter. This seems a final defeat to these people; one more defeat that the sons of the old fighting Cheyennes have to accept without a fight. During the last few years they had to see their agency discontinued, their reservation combined with that of their hereditary enemies, the Crows, and worse, see their new hospital stand closed, so the sick, the old of these 1800 people, many with tuberculosis, active or incipient, have to be hauled over the rough or snowbound roads to the already overcrowded hospital of the Crows. I went to see old Sand Crane, Keeper of the Medicine Hat, once as sacred an object to the Northern Cheyennes as the Cross of Christ would be to the Christian. He lay in a one room log hut, blind and bedfast. Could he be persuaded to go to die even in physical comfort among the Crows?

The situation, Mr. President, is very bad. The people are discouraged, resentful. It is true that they get small jobs, such as beet topping down in Wyoming, and so on, but seldom more than a few days. Their agency, too, has been reopened the last year, with a good, experienced man, Superintendent Hunter, in charge. But there is almost nothing from which the Indians can make a living. And always they reminded me of the hospital, closed, empty, a symbol of rejection by another economy-minded Congress that cut the appropriations of the small tribe of Cheyennes, as congresses have been doing since the 1850's. Back in the old days they could go out to hunt buffalo, join the hostile Sioux in their wars of protest, cost the government millions for the thousands congress saved. Now they must be grateful for every name that can get on the relief rolls. It is not good to see these people on relief, descendants of a tribe that produced some of the greatest warriors of the Plains, their women among the finest quill and bead workers, women considered by both whites and Indians as the most virtuous of any people on the continent.

I went to Billings to the Regional Offices of the Indian Service to protest the plight of the Cheyennes and was told there was no money to open the hospital, or apparently, for the means of a livelihood that, I am told by Superintendent Hunter and his staff, could be opened to the Cheyennes.

For, Mr. President, these Indians need not be in such straits even with all the forces of the elements against them. There is much work that needs to be done on the Reservation. First of all, everyone agrees, there should be a good highway. That would make work for many able-bodied men for a time. Then, in addition to the dream and hope of oil in the future, there is the immediate actuality of considerable timber, and a thirty foot surface vein of coal of good commercial quality. The Indians have a little saw mill going, and a small mine, enough to fill the local demand. With a good highway, some financing, and a training program in lumbering, mining and marketing, these Indians can once more become the independent, self-reliant people they were when they cost the United States government so much in money and lives to conquer.

I do not apologize for the length of this letter. I feel very strongly on what is happening to the Northern Cheyennes. I am certain you would feel as strongly if you had seen what I saw this summer.

****

Now to happier business. I am sending you an autographed copy of *Crazy Horse.* And if Margaret happens to be down in the Village and has a moment to spare, I'd like to have her drop in. I understand she had an uncle in Denver, my favorite town—

Faithfully yours,

To Charles J. Brill

Golden Saga Publishers
Oklahoma City, Okla.

December 28, 1949

Dear Mr. Brill:

In your most interesting book, CONQUEST OF THE SOUTHERN PLAINS, you speak of Yellow Swallow, the son of Custer and Monaseetah, daughter of Little Rock. You say nothing about the boy's later life. Do you know if he ever lived in the north?

In my childhood some Sioux friends of my father's used to bring along an old woman relative called Cheyenne Woman who was crippled from the outbreak of Dull Knife at Fort Robinson, 1879, the injury aggravated in her flight with the ghost dancers on Pine Ridge in 1890. Because she was so crippled and so old, she often remained as a visitor with us while her people went to pick potatoes or husk corn in the neighborhood. She spoke a rudimentary English and some French and told many fine stories of the hunting days and the battles. I recall her saying that the son of Custer was along with a relative of his mother's in the Dull Knife outbreak in Northwest Nebraska. "He lost; lotsa peoples lost—" she always ended the story.

Kate Big Head says the daughter of Little Rock married a white man named Isaac. Once I heard her say he was a man "mostly white, with one name Isaac." Now the Cheyennes tell me they know nothing of this boy being along with the outbreak, or living in the north or where he died.

I hoped to locate you the few days I was in Oklahoma City this fall, but failed. I anticipate that you are working on another book. There seems to be so much rich material down there.

I shall be grateful for whatever you have to say—

Sincerely,

January 4, 1950

Dear Mr. Brill:

I am most grateful for your prompt reply to my letter about Yellow Swallow.[1] I knew about the prevalence of syphilis in the Army of the Plains in the 1860's and 1870's. As you know, the Medical Records of posts like [Forts] Hays and Sill give a rather full picture of the situation, usually citing those treated by name and rank, Custer's among them. The venereal record is one of the items blocked out by the clerk who reads all notes taken from the AGO Records, National Archives, in all material pertaining, I think, to the period since 1860. I never ran into this censorship because I've never gone into the private lives of the whites involved, and I probably never will.

Now I am working on a book about the northern Cheyennes, the third volume of my six book study of the High Plains, from stone age man to the present. This is the second of the two book Indian section: the biography of Crazy Horse as a representative of the numerous Sioux and now this book on a small tribe—the northern Cheyenne.

Because I am so interested in what the past has to say to us, I am most anxious that every book possible be published on the region. Couldn't you manage to put a little time each week into your books? I realize that such books don't make money. My Cheyenne one won't pay for the years of work or even the cash outlay but one can always do other things to keep going. I wrote my *Old Jules* while I read proof on the night side of the Lincoln, Nebraska papers.

You certainly have material that must not be lost, and you make an interesting book. Not enough people know about your *Plains*. I found very few copies in the western Americana Libraries from Montana to Oklahoma and down when I made my last round this fall. Yet everyone was interested. . . . Incidentally, I am Miss Sandoz, but I seldom bother to indicate that. In the east a woman has to prove her ability to do work on outdoor subjects, and in the west I am either known or it doesn't matter.

Anyway, thank you again,

1. Brill confirmed Sandoz's contention that Yellow Swallow was General George Custer's son by a Cheyenne woman.

To Dudley B. Cloud, Director

The Atlantic Monthly Press

April 17, 1950

Dear Mr. Cloud:

I am indeed sorry to hear that there will be no more *Old Jules* with the Atlantic imprint.

It's sad there won't be any copies of the book around to sell, with the profile of me in the June *Flair,* using the paragraph from the front of the book as the point of departure for the article, quoted, and, by implication, for the whole American issue.

It's sad, too, that there won't be any copies around Lincoln when I'm out there to accept the honorary Doctor of Lit the University is giving me June 5. (announcement to come from the university publicity department)

I don't want the plates of the book destroyed. If nothing turns up by June 15, I'll have them sent to my storage. I'll let you know.

Sincerely,

To Mary Margaret McBride

May 31, 1950

Dear Mary Margaret:[1]

Thank you for your very gracious and neighborly card. I was fascinated to watch you work. I had never thought of you in relation to a microphone at all. You sound so direct; no one could be aware of a mechanical middleman. Of course I'll be happy to come again, any time you see something worth the time of your program.

By now I trust that you are completely recovered. The day after I was up there a very old Indian came slowly climbing up to my place. He was a Mohawk, he said, from the colony over in Brooklyn. His granddaughter had heard your program Friday and that you were ill and she was concerned. Jock is fond of his granddaughter and so he decided to make a little medicine for you, but he needed someone, preferably a woman, who had "The Powers." Perhaps I was such a person.

That kind of talk wasn't too new to me, since the old buffalo-hunting remnants among the Sioux always said I carried rain clouds in my tracks. (You know, go camping in a tent and it rains, and on reservations I usually live in a tent or shelter.) So old Jock went to work. I know nothing of Mohawk anthropology and so all I did was sit on the floor. I am a Left-Sitter, which apparently was also necessary. We smoked our cigarettes in silence, made the acknowledging gestures to the sky and the earth and all around and then the man went into his high, thin falsetto singing, with many gestures. He had an old medicine bundle about the size and shape of a young squirrel and with that he hopped around the room with great agility making monotonous chants. It was all very funny, and very impressive, too, and we both hope that you are well now.

Sincerely,

1. Mary Margaret McBride (1899–1976) was a writer, editor, radio broadcaster, syndicated columnist, and author of travel books. Beginning in 1934, she broadcast for Station WOR as Martha Deane; from 1937 to 1960 she was host on a national network as Mary Margaret McBride. MS was often a guest on her show.

[To Jacques Chambrun]

October 2, 1950

Dear Jacques:

Charlie Morton of the Atlantic writes me that the Cheyenne book is to be returned this week. Ted was to write me last Friday but I have no letter in today's mail, so he did not, and perhaps the return of the book will be delayed too.

I have some corrections in the wording of the material to go with the map, a foreword and revisions of the first four chapters to insert, with some checking through the rest. So I've written their manuscript clerk to send the book and the illustrative material direct to me, if the book has not already been returned. No use bothering your office further with this.

I have been feeling apologetic about the loss of time I have caused you, without return and I don't feel justified in taking any more. While Legerman's talk about the Duell, Sloan and Pearce deal was a good excuse to get action out of the Atlantic, I don't expect anything from that either. I'm sure a three book deal is possible somewhere but I suspect it will have to come through my own efforts, working personally, as my good book deals always have been managed.

There is only one year left ahead of me, financially, and I must do my best in this short time to get myself afloat again. I'm sure you will agree with the wisdom of this. If the FOAL is not out, I should like to pick it up too; at least for cleaning up the manuscript, when I get around to it.

You have been wonderfully patient, but I cannot expect you to go on, and I can't afford to let my career die unless it really must.

Thank you,

To Joseph Balmer

November 26, 1950

Dear Mr. Balmer:

There are great stores of letters, and so on of the stories and history of the Sioux up around Pine Ridge; the greatest accumulation was probably what was called the "Little Wound Paper", used a great deal by the Judge Ricker to whom I refer in my notes on Crazy Horse, but other Indians have trunks full. Since most of these are to or from the Indian Bureau or to government officials, army officers, or people around or connected with the region, there are usually copies or the wet book carbon copies that were made in those days. All the government end, and the private papers of Crook, etc., I have seen, and much of the Three Stars and the Little Wound, etc., material. The hostiles, of course, had much less, and theirs was mostly in picture accounts. He Dog's relatives are the best of these repositories, all things taken into account, and that means the fine picture history of Amos Bad Heart Bull that Helen Blish worked with. She had that down at Lincoln when we were undergraduates, (no, she was a graduate) where we worked on it a lot, and then, of course I had access to the whole voluminous manuscript of the interpretation the Indians gave her of the pictures.

The Eagle Hawks are or were relatives of He Dog's. The young one may be a descendant of the one who was a nephew of He Dog's, although Eagle Hawk was never an unusual name. I have five Oglala and Brule Eagle Hawks in my files, all alive around 1870, and not conspicuously related.

I saw a set of pictures, several, in fact, around the He Dog people at Oglala, of the Oglala history sort. Some were done by several people together, some individually, but that was in 1930–31 and now my notes are in Denver. However, the Indians have developed a habit the last forty, fifty years, of making copies of their history stories. There are various copies of the Sitting Bull autobiography and the owners all claim theirs is the original and the others all copies. And who's to tell now. I have a large, about 3½ by 4½ feet copy of Crazy Horse and He Dog guarding the Black Hills. It has a collection of peaks in the center, with He Dog on a horse with its head towards the hills on one side and Crazy Horse in similar position on the other. This was made from an Eagle Hawk painting, and enlarged, so perhaps you are speaking of the original. This painting was also used on a Crazy Horse tipi, etc., in 1934. This is in oil on canvas. How Doc Carver would get into this is beyond me. Carver as you will know, was a buffalo hunter and showman and had no contact with the hostiles while they were hostiles. He did know some of the agency Sioux, like Spotted Tail and some of the later wild west show Indians, and certainly Sitting Bull, I should judge, offhand.

There are various letters from Sioux and Breeds to Dr. McGillycuddy. Garnett, as you will know, was also called Billy Hunter, stepson of John Hunter. Garnett's father was the army officer at Ft. Laramie who went with the South in the Civil war and was killed. Offhand I seem to recall some of Garnett's letters being published various places.

I suppose you have the *McGillycuddy, Agent,* volume by Mrs. Mc. I saw this in manuscript and tried my best to check on her very old husband's memory to get the factual things straightened up, but she was certain he knew his dates and so the book is full of the most obvious errors. Every one's mind fictionizes and loses the relative position of what it does remember, and particularly a man as old and sick as McG. was when she got the material together. But historical writing is a technique that must be learned, and cannot be taught to everyone any more than anything else. She lost a very good opportunity to make a fine contribution. I regretted it very much; and I regretted the Nebraska History Magazine review of the book. It should have pointed out the errors that other reviewers did. Not all, of course, but it should, to be valuable historically, have suggested that while the experiences told therein are valid, there are evidences of faulty memory and of inadequate checking upon what the real situation was.

Yes, Roosevelt gave the northern Cheyennes a wonderful start. When I was there in 1941 the people were optimistic, so much happier than in 1930–31 and 1936. They had their tribal council functioning, the TB and other mortality rate was down, particularly among the young, partly through their good new hospital; their tribal herd was growing and they hoped to have the one million dollars borrowed from the government repaid by 1948. They did this before then, and had a good tribal herd of cattle left for a start out of debt, and soon they would be independent. Then came the economy congress of 1947 and like all such congresses since 1854, they drew a line through the Cheyenne appropriations and with that one stroke of the pen closed the agency, the hospital and the health and home economics and agricultural advisory services, with coming curtailments in education. Then came the winter of 1948 that cleaned out so many cattle herds of the west. (My brothers and sisters saved their herds but my niece teaching country school and her 13 pupils were lost for 23 days, until the 5th Army bulldozer broke through the snow and found them alive in a small one room ranch house.) This loss of their herd was no reflection on the Indians. Many old time cattlemen were cleaned out that winter. There is no railroad near the Northern Cheyenne reservation and no good road, so no feed could have been brought into the reservation for the cattle if any had been purchasable in the region. So they took the same appalling losses of other Montana ranchers. Then the summer after that winter there was no rain at all, and one of those terrible grasshopper scourges hit them. I was around the agency five weeks that late summer and fall and I never saw a region barer of grass, not even in the Red Desert of Wyoming. The grasshoppers even ate the onions out of the ground. Seventy percent of the families by then had some member with active TB and although an emergency agent had been brought in to handle the starvation region, the hospital was still closed, as it is today. All the Indians can actually count on for income is a couple of weeks a fall topping sugar beets down in Wyoming, and that means they must get there. Even their GI's, with many of superb war records, have no way of profiting from the GI education or training. I've tried to get a unit of forestry training set up there but congress still has appropriated no money, although, after five trips to Washington last winter, and several hundred letters, many telegrams, etc., on my part, and even more on the part of other people, we got the Cheyennes $100,000 relief last winter, in surplus commodities. Much of this came too late, and many people died and many are sick.

There is no need for the bad situation at all. There are 2000 people living in a lovely semi-bad-land region that would support perhaps 200 whites in ranching in a comfortable manner. To be sure there is a surface vein of coal varying up to 30 feet thick but there [is] no all weather road even to the agency, let alone to the mine sites, and no railroad, so they can't sell coal, particularly in a region where there are good railroad surface mines. However, with transportation facilities they could ship their coal to market as the white mine owners do. There are also good prospects of oil, but of course that only heightens the difficult situation for the Indians. It is the tools, the spokesmen of the coal and oil interests in our Congress that are against doing anything for these Indians. By the Northern Cheyenne charter, if enough of the Indians vote for it, the sale of all tribal lands can be managed, without government supervision, for whatever the whites will give the people, who would be starving. It's the old story of Indian expropriation. They have a few good friends in Congress, like Senator Murray of Montana, but very few.

Any coal or oil company can lease the land at the standard rate, such as is paid on other reservations, but the companies won't do this so long as there is a chance of getting the complete property for a song. The young GI's are very worried that starvation will lose the little property they have to pass on to their children.

School facilities were to be drastically cut this fall, but I marshalled a lot of pressure against that, with many people who are much more powerful, of course. There is not one college graduate on the reservation, breed or Indian, because, with Carlisle closed, there is no place an Indian can go to college without paying tuition unless he can win a scholarship and the one high school is so poor in equipment and general standards that only a genius could ever get through with a good enough preparation for a scholarship. There are only 45 high school graduates on the reservation, including breeds, many of whom go to Catholic schools. There is another strong missionary group on the reservation, Swiss Mennonites, but while their teaching is considered excellent by the Indians, making for moderation, something hopeless young people need to be taught, they are not strong in the teaching field. Evidently their teaching is limited to religious education.

One of the teachers up there is a Chippewa-Oneida woman who got her masters degree in Wisconsin this summer and lived at the same woman's hall as I did. I am trying to get a fellowship for advanced study in anthropology and sociology and education for her. She is the first graduate student who ever got a degree at the University of Wisconsin, one of our great schools.

Pardon me—I am sorry I got so long-winded, but you asked about the Cheyennes. And forgive the hasty letter. I am *very* busy.

Do you collect Indian phonograph records?

Sincerely,

[To Elizabeth Otis]

McIntosh and Otis

December 12, 1950

Dear Miss Otis:

Here is CHEYENNE AUTUMN, one of my six book study of the old trans-Missouri country, from stone age man to the present, as I keep telling everybody. OLD JULES and CRAZY HORSE are the two others done, with three left to write, one of the coming of modern man to the region with his iron and gunpowder, the other two reaching into the present. One is planned on a cattleman who grows into the packing business as it develops in Chicago and Omaha, the other of a man who develops the oil industry in the region, taking the story up to the present.

About the Cheyenne book: It was under option to Knopfs as a companion book to CRAZY HORSE. Before it was done I heard that Knopfs were withdrawing from many commitments and Ted Weeks wanted the Cheyenne book as the first of a three book series of mine they wished to take on, so I got a release from Knopfs. But I was two and a half months late with the book to the Atlantic, and Korea was upon us. After four months without a report I asked for a decision and when that didn't come either, I asked for the book back. By then Duell, Sloan and Pearce seemed to be toying with the idea of the whole series of six books, republishing OLD JULES and CRAZY HORSE as I was getting the plates for the former too. But that idea was done with last week.

So the manuscript is free, except that I promised Paul Hoffman (discoverer of OLD JULES, after everyone had rejected it, and whom I followed to Knopfs with CRAZY HORSE) that he could see the book for Westminister after it had been tried around a couple of places if he thinks they would be interested by then. This is also a three book deal and very tentative. I'll leave the selection of the couple of markets to your judgment and then we'll see, if you like, whether you want to send the ms to Paul [Hoffman].

I am still working on the Cheyenne manuscript and am willing to try any changes a publisher might like, provided the book is not cheapened below the standards set by my series.

About the OJ and CH: There are many requests for these from buyers and book dealers and I should like the books reissued. Preferably in regular editions by the publisher of the Cheyenne book, or, if not that, in pocket editions. OJ was in the Blue Ribbon once. The University of Nebraska Press would republish both these books, but I think I should have to give up all claim to reprints, etc., and I like to think of the books as property.

Now about shorter things: I have two short stories in casual progression. Stuart Rose asked for something again last August but I haven't done anything for him yet. Too involved in the dealings about the Cheyennes. If you are interested I'll send these in when I get them done. There are some articles too, that I've been to do so very long ago—

Let me know when you've made a decision about handling my work. Call Chel 2-3043.

Thank you,

List of items taken to Miss Otis:
Manuscript of CHEYENNE AUTUMN
roll of maps
envelope of other illustrative material
Copies of OLD JULES and CRAZY HORSE, with sample reviews
Folder with bibliography

***

January 12, 1951

Dear Elizabeth Otis,

Marguerite [Young][1] thinks I should have told you that Scribners are interested in my Cheyenne book, but it is so difficult for me to express a desire, even about my own work.

Scribners, or at least Wallace Meyer, seem to be interested in the theme of genocide in the Cheyenne book, and they seem favorable to a possible three book deal. Someone there liked OLD JULES well enough back before 1935 to hold it for many months. Besides, Scribners published the only good work by a regular publisher on the Cheyennes, Grinnell's FIGHTING CHEYENNES.[2] Fortunately this barely mentions the flight northward, because then the Indians would not speak of it, and Grinnell did not dig into the matter.

If you haven't sent the manuscript to Paul [Hoffman] perhaps you might think about Scribners. I don't know. There's another very serious aspect to the Westminister prospect: I have a novel, SON OF THE GAMBLIN' MAN, well started that the church tie-up of the press might well bar from the list because it has 1870–1880 river boat and gold camp gambling and drinking scenes. I should have to drop this book or have two publishers. It's a discouraging prospect. Perhaps I should withdraw my books from the market until times and markets change. Don't you think this might be better than get into the complications that I seem to be heading for the last mismanaged year or two?

I am sorry about Viking, more on your account than on mine. I have had a lot of preparation for such verdicts as theirs with OLD JULES. Most of the fourteen publishers' rejections on that book said it could only be published by a university press, and the rest implied this. Even Blanche Baumgarten echoed the "It won't sell a 1000 copies" plaint.

Besides I've been reading western manuscripts for university presses for twenty years and I know I wouldn't approve CHEYENNE AUTUMN as it stands for any of their lists. It would have to be completely rewritten, without any of the creative, imaginative work left in.

Perhaps everyone is afraid of the criticism of the army and Congress in the book, in these times. Then there's the problem with OLD JULES: So many publishers have an angry attitude about the book, since their rejection of it. That, I am told, was why Cap Pearce at Duell, Sloan and Pearce was against it now. He rejected it at Harcourt, Brace, and apparently Mr. Harcourt was not too pleased about it when the Book of the Month Club took it. Mr. Harcourt told me a lot about this once back in 1935, over a turkey carcass in the kitchen of Jimmie Reed, out at Darien.

Well, what do you think I should do? I am really not interested in any publisher who has no understanding or interest in what I am trying to do.

1. Marguerite Young, a poet and novelist, is the author of *Miss MacIntosh, My Darling* (New York: Scribners, 1965) and *Angel in the Forest* (New York: Scribners, 1966). MS encouraged her writing and found a number of grants and teaching positions for her.

2. George Bird Grinnell, *The Fighting Cheyennes* (New York: Scribners, 1915).

January 29, 1951

Dear Elizabeth Otis:

I have a letter from Greer Garson (I knew Buddy Fogelson[1] casually in Lincoln years ago and used to talk over frontier stories. She says):

> "I like your description of the Scotch-Irish pioneer woman doctor. With your permission I would like to show your letter to the head of the Story Department at Metro and see if I can develop some interest there but knowing how careful authors have to be of their original ideas I will not do this until I have a line from you saying that you have no objection."

I wrote Miss Garson today, giving her the permission she requests. In the meantime I have been toying with the idea of making a novelette of the story. What do you think? Here is what I wrote to Greer and Buddy:

"* * * there was a Scotch-Irish pioneer woman doctor along the old Oregon and Mormon trails in west Nebraska,[2] one who came out to the frontier in silks and brocades and was faced with the opposition of people everywhere to women doctors—people who would rather die than be treated by a female saw bones. Finally she became so beloved by her community that when she married and her husband wished her to give up practice, the community took it upon itself to divorce her from him, and did.

The doctor had worked herself through medical school and a year after graduation she was vice president of the county medical society of the college locale. Her stepfather, (Kentuckian, as I recall off hand) worked in frontier railroad building and so she went out to west Nebraska just opening to settlement. She was apparently a tall, handsome woman, with silken dark hair, a fine nose, mouth and chin, highish cheekbones, a free grace to her walk and a quick, humorous tongue. She drove dashing buggy teams or rode fine horses. She hung her silks and brocades in the one room sod house of her homestead, handy for her enthusiastic socializing: dances, literaries, and socials as more settlers came in. With her fine sense of humor she kept things endurable through prairie fires, blizzards, grasshoppers, drouth and epidemics of typhoid and diphtheria. Her practice, when it got started, consisted of Indians, cowboys and settlers and the victims of the cattle wars, and the gun fights of the old Sidney-Black Hills trail that went near her homestead. There was no railroad into the [Black] Hills then, where the Homesteak [*sic*] mine, the world's most productive gold mine, was giving up its great millions. She treated the miners, gamblers, prostitutes and the entire English cast of, I think, *The Mikado*. When caught in a blizzard she often unhitched her horses and got through in her buffalo coat, riding one of the horses, "in harness" as we used to call it. She is still remembered as the heroine of the epidemics.

Although the doctor could never kill a chicken for dinner, she was one of the first in the west to mend a skull, laid open by a well accident, with a hand-hammered silver plate from a silver dollar, the whole emergency operation carried out in a homestead shack without even a nurse to help. She even hammered the plate into the shape from the coin herself, on a piece of rail iron and a fencing hammer. The man lived to be eighty, the plate still well in place.

Gradually the doctor became so beloved, so much the refuge in joy as in woe and pain that when her new husband planned to take her away from the community, some of whom had denounced her so energetically, maneuvered the divorcing. It is an amusing story in itself, amusing on the surface, in a community and a time when divorce was no more popular that women doctors had been.

Do you think we could sell such a novelette to a popular market if I took the time to write it? I would frankly call it fiction, so I could fill in the holes, maneuver the plot, etc., to make the most of the material. I recall seeing the doctor in her old age; I know many people who recall her well and are full of stories about her.

Sincerely,

1. Greer Garson (b. 1908), a film star, won an Academy Award for her role in *Mrs. Miniver* in 1943. She also appeared in such well-known pictures as *Goodbye, Mr. Chips* (1939), *Madame Curie* (1943), *Random Harvest* (1942), and *Strange Lady in Town* (1955). Buddy Fogelson (1900–1987), her husband and manager, was a Lincoln, Nebraska, native. His own distinguished career included serving on General Dwight Eisenhower's staff during World War II. He also served on diplomatic assignments and was an oilman, rancher, and philanthropist.

2. Georgia Arbuckle Fix (1852–1918) was the first woman to graduate from the University of Nebraska Medical School, in 1883. She practiced in the North Platte River valley in western Nebraska for thirty years. MS's novel *Miss Morissa* (New York: McGraw-Hill, 1955) is based loosely on the life of Dr. Fix and two other western Nebraska women doctors.

To Jacques Chambrun

Febr. 8, 1951

Dear Mr. Chambrun:

I still do not have my FOAL OF HEAVEN. I want to pick this up as soon as possible. I have put my work, such as I wish to market, into the hands of McIntosh and Otis.

Sincerely,

To Mamie Meredith

May 21, 1951

Dear Mamie:

Ah, you are a sly one! Yes, everything I write always turns out to have larger implications, even a *Post* story, which, incidentally, was run a couple of months earlier than intended, to fill a hole that developed, and so got no publicity buildup, and had some material cut, to fit.[1] Not too much, but there is a little of the edge gone, and it didn't have too much at the start. I know my popular magazines by now, and don't try to get by with much substance.

Yes, I definitely planned the children to represent various kinds of upbringing, particularly the contrast of Maggie, who suffered in body from her poor childhood, and Olive, who suffered in spirit from her pampered one. Of the two I suspect the greater injustice is the soft upbringing. I know three young married women here in the village, the Walgreen drug heiress, and two from the Sears, Roebuck money. They did not finish school, that is college, they all dabble in the arts, and none have the real stuff to make what their abilities might permit. The Walgreen one had a very unhappy and shocking first marriage, and while that almost unseated her mentally, she seems now to be pulling out of her softness better than the other two. It reminds me of the rats Columbia university needed during the war for their psychological studies. Personnel and feed restrictions made them cut down on the extensive program of breeding their own test rats, and somebody had the idea to hire boys to trap them in the sewers. Great numbers were brought in, but they were useless. They didn't get neurotic or psychotic as the laboratory rats had. These sewer rats had had early frustrations and grew fat and sassy on what had driven laboratory rats crazy. Ha—

Anyway, the story was fun to do, and there have been several requests that I turn it into a short novel, with this the core. Showing the sweep of the storm, what happened in the various homes of the children, on the same pattern of study as in the shelter, and then the rescue. I won't do this until the story has been lost on most people's minds. I don't want them to start the book and then think: "I read this—" But some years later, perhaps. I have the great volume of blizzard material you all sent me, particularly your large amount and from Fred Ballard and Judge Paine.[2] If you ever run into the Judge, tell him this, will you?

I was up to the Botkins yesterday a week ago. They have two excellent young people, as you probably know. Never have I been exposed to such a questioning young woman as the daughter is, at least not in the east. The west still produces an occasional inquiring minded young person, but far too rarely two.

Ben is fine, your name came up, as did Miss Pound's, and almost everybody we knew in Lincoln.

My Indian school teacher candidate for a Whitney fellowship won it,[3] so that makes three since New Years, a Newberry, a Kaufman and a Whitney. A biography, a novel and a study of school and sociological problems in the Indian community. I feel happy about it.

What are you doing on your anecdotal history of MM?

1. "The Lost School Bus" (*SEP*, May 19, 1951) later was published as a book titled *Winter Thunder* (Philadelphia: Westminster Press, 1954). The idea for the story was generated by the experiences of MS's niece, Celia Sandoz, a country school teacher in the Nebraska Sandhills, and her pupils during a severe 1949 blizzard.

2. Judge Bayard Paine (1872–1955) was a justice on the Nebraska Supreme Court. Long active in Nebraska history, he was a member of Hall County (Nebraska) Historical Society and NSHS boards. He published *Pioneers, Indians, and Buffalo* (Lincoln: NSHS, 1935).

3. Gerry Harvey was a Menominee and Oneida Indian teaching at the Cheyenne reservation at Lame Deer, Montana. Her scholarship was the first ever given to an Indian for graduate work at the University of Wisconsin.

To Elizabeth Otis

Writers Institute,
Bascom Hall
University of Wisconsin
Madison, Wisconsin
July 16, 1951

Dear Elizabeth Otis:

Roberta Grahame of Wellesley is working in my advanced novel writing course, revising the novel you had for a while. I think it will work out well, if I can hold her to a complete rewrite, with much more characterization and sounder motivations. The class calls it the Agonizing Woman novel—

If anything materializes on the Cheyenne book by August 15, will you let me know immediately? I am having to decide on a permanent position that would prevent much writing in the future by then.

Sincerely,

To Alexander Lesser

Editor, THE AMERICAN INDIAN

February 18, 1952

Dear Doctor Lesser:

I feel very shabby that I have nothing at all for you. I did write an article on the Sioux and Cheyenne way of bringing up the eldest son, called "The Son." My agent sold it to *Readers Digest* for April, where it will be called What I learned from the Indians. The condensation loses much of the flavor and some of the material too, of course, but it does give the widest possible distribution. The article has been planted in the Rocky Mountain *News*, perhaps because of the short time left, or perhaps because I have friends there.[1] The Fosters are both old acquaintances of mine and Bob Chase is the husband of Mary Chase, of *Harvey*, and we are very old friends. The *News* is usually very friendly to Indian material.

Sincerely,

1. The article, retitled "What the Sioux Taught Me," was published in "Empire," the magazine section of the *Denver Post*, on February 24, 1952.

To Mr. D. H. Stroud, Jr.

June 11, 1952

Dear Mr. Stroud:

Old Black Elk I never knew, if by that you mean the famous old warrior against the Pawnees, the medicine man father of the Black Elk usually meant by the name. This latter one I can remember all my life but not when I first saw him.

Many of the Indians from around Manderson [South Dakota] used to come to the Niobrara and stop across the road from our house to visit with Old Jules long before I was born. I never was around Black Elk in the later days, after I went away to college. He wasn't old enough to know much of the pre-reservation life first hand and there were many still alive who went through the entire Sioux wars as adults. And these were the ones who knew the old life untouched by white man concepts. Besides, Black Elk was rather the find of [John] Neihardt, and so out of courtesy I was against cutting into his territory. Neihardt and Black Elk, both vague, visionary mystics, seemed so peculiarly compatible. You know Neihardt's *Black Elk Speaks,* of course, which I consider his most important book. This is the only creative first hand account of a Teton Lakota that we have, and with Wooden Leg's Cheyenne account, and Linderman's *The American,* old Plenty Coups, the Crow, make up the three good first hand accounts of Plains Indian life.

Your advice on the Cheyenne book is welcomed.[1] In fact a week ago my editor and I decided the same thing and when I return from Wisconsin, where I am in charge of the advanced fiction writing courses in their 8 week summer Writers Institute, I'll get at the pre-publication odds and ends, such as selecting illustrations, etc. Now I'm working against a desperate deadline on a novel which I must finish before I go to Wisconsin.

Sincerely,

1. Stroud had advised MS to publish *CA* immediately. She told him she hesitated because of similarities between situations in the book and events in the Korean War.

To Major Edward S. Luce

Custer Battlefield,
Crow Agency, Montana

September 15, 1952

Dear Major Luce:[1]

In filing away boxes of material accumulated the last three years I ran into your fine letter and lovely colored slides of my visit with you three years ago. I am sorry this has been neglected so long.

Someone sent me a copy of the run-over in the Billings *Gazette,* June 26, 1952, of your fine museum dedication. The first page wasn't included but the run-over shows that you had a fine blowout. I hear from Archie Teater, the artist with me in 1949 that he is about ready to start his large picture of the Custer battle. I sent him some material and a copy of Neihardt's BLACK ELK SPEAKS, and urged him to study the times, the various accounts of the battle, the life and war tactics of the Indians, and the history and personnel of the Seventh Cavalry. The ideal situation would be the coming together of a good historian and a good artist in one man, but there is no such individual so far as I know.

As you may know, the photographer, Harold Rodenbaugh, died. Unfortunately, in the final cutting of the *Flair* article the Custer battlefield photographs were discarded.[2] Not that your place, or you, need the advertising but I wanted as many people as possible kept aware of the place and time.

Thank you again, and greetings to your lovely wife and yourself.

Sincerely,

1. Major Edward S. Luce, U.S. Seventh Cavalry, Ret., Superintendent of the Custer Battlefield National Monument, wrote *Keogh, Comanche, and Custer* (St. Louis: John S. Swift, 1939).

2. "*Flair* Personified: Mari Sandoz," *Flair,* June 1950.

To Joseph Balmer

September 20, 1952

Dear Joseph Balmer:

You certainly are branching out into Indian collecting in a big way. And it has to be done soon, if at all. That is the old-time Indian things. I too, like the earlier Nebraska History *Magazine* better, chiefly because I prefer the primary source material, particularly first hand accounts, to the studies made by scholars and others interested in the field. But there is the constant trend in this country towards the prepared opinion, even in historical matters.

I'm happy that you and Mrs. Petter got together.[1] Her husband was certainly a serious worker in the Cheyenne field. I had read of her journey to Switzerland in the Miles City [Montana] papers.

About the Cheyenne book: It has been contracted for and the advance paid and spent long ago, but I held the book up because of the unpleasant reminder it might be of the Korean women and children caught between two fighting armies. For there is no denying that the Cheyenne women were shot down running over the hills and the shooting was done by the U.S. Army. I was afraid that the whole sympathy and impact of the book would be soured for the reader by the Korean fighting; in fact, the book might even tend to impede the Korean effort, as there is great division among us about the incident at all. Since the exposures of the last few days people are calling me up about my *Tom-Walker,* with its prophecy of a general who is taken in by a senator. First it was [Robert] Taft and now [Richard] Nixon. Although why anyone would expect our Republican vice presidential candidate to be honest now when he was not considered so before he was nominated is beyond me. Even his colleagues in the senate called him Tricky Dick. I was up in Maine last week, where the people are still angry because they found their

Senator [Ralph O.] Brewster in tricky dealings. But California is less stoney about ethics than the old hard-bitten, stubborn Mainer.

But back to the Cheyenne book: In June, before I went to Wisconsin, my editor pointed out that the Korean fight might go on twenty years, and so I agreed to a definite time limit for the publication, sometime before the fall of 1954, the exact time depending upon whether my light novel, MISS MORISSA, about a woman doctor on the Deadwood gold trail of 1876, is to come out first. These two books, with the complications of SLOGUM HOUSE going into pocket books, with an initial printing of 400,000, and my novelette in the Saturday Evening *Post* collection this year, etc., might saturate the market. A serious author's books must not crowd each other.

I'm sorry to hear about John Colhoff.[2] I'll write him a note through a mutual acquaintance in the Denver postoffice, who will see that it reaches John. Thank you for the information. With my years broken up with two months in Wisconsin, from one to three in the west and the rest in New York, I lose track of my acquaintances everywhere.

A good winter to you,

Thank you for the lovely block of stamps

1. Berthe Elise Schroeder Petter was the widow of a Mennonite missionary to the northern Cheyennes. The Petters were Swiss.

2. John Colhoff, Polish-Sioux, had been MS's interpreter during her trips to the Pine Ridge Reservation in the 1930s.

To Marguerite Young

Past midnight,
Nov. 10, 1952,
so must be typed on
allegedly noiseless
portable.

Dear Marguerite:

It's one of those nights that I would call you if you lived over on Gramercy, but since you're far away I'll drop you a note. Perhaps it was hearing Paul Engel's [*sic*] name[1] read out on the radio as being stopped from giving a talk somewhere by the American Legion because he's allegedly Red, along with Max Lerner, etc. I should be prepared for this, for I did forecast the unhep general, politically unhep, being elected by a wicked senator who takes over and his fascist rabble with him, but I still don't like what happens even though I knew it would. . . .

I think I wrote you that every time I see anyone over at McIntosh and O I am asked about you. Annie Laurie Williams was very eager for news from you.[2] She's such a darling. Gregory Ratoff has taken a six months option on *Crazy Horse* and I went out and bought a sealskin jacket with the money, and a little more, of course, for the option money wasn't much. The sealskin jacket was an old, old idea of mine but they were never available except at fabulous prices. Now they are fashionable and available in Union of South African seal. A nice, deep brown. I've let myself in for such a year of work on the Buffalo Hunters book for Hastings House that I can't be bothered looking around for a wardrobe, so I worked over my tweed greatcoat and with this I'm set. No suits, no dresses, no nothing—

Your barber turns his soft eyes my way every once in a while at the low counter drug and inquires about you. He surely has a case on you. Did you ever send him a postcard? He'd love it. A nice elaborate scene, please, to go with his personality. I discovered he's a little on the fey side, meaning used in the old sense. I think he believes in all kinds of special creatures floating and flying through solids, etc. I don't think the hairdressershop owner, Marie (same shop?) is back from Italy. She said one day last spring she was going and if she never got back, well, she never got back.

Wesley [Towner] wrote two nice children's books, but I don't know what he's doing with them. I had lunch with Arthur Wang last Friday, now at Wyn's new set-up.[3] They seem to be making a lot of changes over there, but I still recall what they did to Wesley's book.

The Custer Fighters have turned into something called the New York or eastern Posse of the Westerners. We meet such odd places as Wehawken or here in town at Rupperts Brewery. Want to come along?

Good night,
Mari

1. Paul Engle (b. 1908), a poet and editor, was a project director for the program in creative writing at the University of Iowa (Marguerite Young had a graduate assistantship there).

2. Annie Laurie Williams, the only motion picture agent of her time to operate from New York City, was associated with McIntosh and Otis. She sold a number of important books to film companies, including *Gone With the Wind, Magnificent Obsession,* and *Grapes of Wrath*. She was MS's film agent for years.

3. Arthur Wang (b. 1918), another editor who moved around, was with Doubleday, Knopf, Crowell, and A. A. Wyn. In 1956 he became president and editor-in-chief of Hill and Wang. Wesley Towner wrote *The Liberators* (New York: A. A. Wyn, 1946) and *The Elegant Auctioneers,* completed by Stephen Varble (New York: Hill and Wang, 1970), a book on the Parke Bernet galleries.

To John E. Parsons

Feb. 4, 1953

Dear Mr. Parsons:[1]

By this time you will have my notes mailed you yesterday. It's a joy to find someone who is really going into the history of any section or problem with such thoroughness as you. That's what we need, a real portrayal of our history, for a better understanding of it and of the future.

First about your John W. Smith. Somehow I got the impression you were looking for a John M. This is probably the Capt. John W. Smith who was post trader at Fort C. F. Smith in 1867, mentioned in a note, p 53, in Granville Stuart's *Forty Years on the Frontier,*[2] and probably the man who, the Indians told me, came back with Spotted Tail's Brule Sioux from their short sojourn up towards Whetstone, on the Missouri. I think one would be safe in saying that Smith was right in his opinion that Red Cloud and Old Spot had no influence over the hostiles. And safe, too, in going a step farther: that they had no desire to have any such influence. Both men were canny enough to know that the day the hostile power was broken the agency chiefs would lose their bargaining advantage. Red Cloud's son was in the Rosebud battle, as you will know, with the chief's inscribed gift rifle from [President] Grant in May 1875. You wouldn't assume that he was there without the father's approval.

About Durfee and Peck: I think the larger concerns were less likely to run into contraband trade, although their individual traders often took it on as a sort of sanctioned side-line. For instance, I've heard some old Sioux speak of Campbell's Houses on the Milk river as a place to obtain ammunition in the middle 1870's. Thos. Campbell was a Durfee and Peck man, but of course the trade may have been in the legal period. I understand he carried a large stock of discarded Civil War weapons at one time.

I think I am inclined to discount any substantial dealing in contraband arms by the larger outfits because small traders got such appalling prices for arms and even cartridges, as, say, a beaver hide, even a tanned robe for 1 rifle shell. Many of the better armed Indians went into the Custer battle with 3 to 7 cartridges for their guns, the latter the exception. So important was this figure that when I inquired about the ammunition of such and such a man of the Oglalas at Pine Ridge and then at the Northern Cheyenne, I was given exactly the same number of cartridges.

There are a couple of document files that might interest you if you haven't seen them. MIL DIV MO, Document Files, Box 169, Special, Sitting Bull Band covers the year 1876 and includes much hindsight reporting as well as such items as a report from Crook to the AAGenl, Department of Dakota, giving information from the interpreter that a party of breeds from Red River country in vicinity of Ft. Garry are and have been over a month encamped near the Black Hills, north of Bear Butte, carrying on an extensive trade with the Indians in ammunition. They had a council with the principal hostile chiefs etc. This is dated 4/19/76. Another file is the special one with a brief résumé of the papers relating to the Sioux war, giving date, subject, and number of each paper and very handy for the hurried researcher. This is MIL DIV MO, Special Document Files, Box 171, Sioux War, and certainly in the National Archives too now, although when I used it first it was in the stacks above a Department of Interior garage on Virginia Avenue.

I haven't been able to bring up the reference about the Custer pistols, but it may occur to me anytime. I've made a note of it.

Sincerely,

1. John E. Parsons and John S. Du Mont, both members of the New York Posse of the Westerners, were researching for their book on the weapons used in the battle of the Little Big Horn, *Firearms in the Custer Battle* (Harrisburg, Pa.: Stackpole, 1953).

2. Granville Stuart, *Forty Years on the Frontier* (Cleveland: Arthur H. Clark, 1925).

To Mr. W. S. Campbell

School of Journalism,
University of Oklahoma

March 9, 1953

Dear Mr. Campbell:

Thank you. I am happy to have your identification of the Roman Nose in the frontispiece of your WARPATH AND COUNCIL FIRE. Certainly George Bent was a thoroughly reliable informant.[1]

In my childhood the Indians around Pine Ridge and Rosebud, including the Cheyennes living among them, still had copies of many of the photographs of their tribes, copies that were correctly labeled. Somehow most of these have been lost by now, and as you realize, many of the younger Indians know very little of the past of their families. In going through the early inheritance files at Lame Deer, I found a lot of relationships and names of as recent as the 1880's that the old Indians seemed to have forgotten and the younger ones never knew. On the wall of the tribal council house at Lame Deer is an enlarged picture of the three Cheyennes Custer made captive in 1869, with his identification of one as Dull Knife. Even the remaining members of the Dull Knife family accept this as accurate now.

It's good that there are some people like you, who try to bring a little sense to the Plains Indian scene before it is too late. Archie Teater, the painter from Jackson, Wyoming, has been here all winter painting as authentic a picture of the Custer battle as he could manage from the accoutrements, etc. at the museums here. Of course there isn't enough smoke and dust in the picture. If he had been authentic in that there would have been little else to see.

Thank you again,

1. MS had questioned whether the Roman Nose in the frontispiece might not be a Sioux. Campbell responded that his picture had been identified by George Bent, a half-Cheyenne who had known Roman Nose.

To John S. Du Mont

April 16, 1953

Dear Mr. Du Mont:

It's generous of Mr. Parsons to mention my name. He gave the Westerners a good talk on the Custer battle guns. Your book should be a very interesting one.

About the legend among the Cheyennes of Custer's guns, the "white handled guns with writing on" as the Indians called them. I first heard of these, so far as I recall, from an old Cheyenne woman who, after the Cheyenne flight northward in 1878, remained with the Sioux at Red Cloud because, sent there with the wounded after the Dull Knife escape from Ft. Robinson, she couldn't bear to go on to the Yellowstone with the others now that there was not one relative left alive and barely a friend. Old Cheyenne Woman, as she was called, used to be around our place a lot, and in her pidgin English told me many stories, including this story of the man who brought back the "white-handled" guns from the Custer ridge. I heard this story again, in various versions, from some old Sioux who had been in the Custer fight, and then around the Tongue river reservation. None of these people are now alive, and if they were I could not give you their names because this would be considered a gross breach of trust by the Indians, and by me also.

However, there's nothing to keep you from working at this on your own. Contact Rufus Wallowing, head of the northern Cheyenne Tribal Council, Lame Deer, Montana, before you go out. He's one of the last of the Carlisle men and writes a good letter when so minded. He is anxious to get white understanding for the plight of his people and will put himself out considerably, particularly if he thinks you are honestly trying to get at the truth of anything concerning the Plains Indian wars. He is a relative of old Two Moons, a rising chief at the time of the Custer fight. He may very well know all the facts of this story, but he is a politician and understands his people. He will probably "know" nothing of this. But he will help you to see people over at Birney, the village of the less reconcilable old timers, and at Busby, etc. where others of the families from the Custer fight are living.

A good preliminary approach, both to Rufus and the others, would be to broach the larger subject: what were the arms that the Cheyennes in the fight carried, and be prepared for silence at first. There is still the old rumor that the government will deduct $1,000 from the heirs of each man who killed anyone in the fight on the Little Big Horn, that is, when they finally get paid for the illegal appropriation of their lands after their boundaries were established in the treaty of 1868. They may think you're a spy.

Rufus Wallowing won't think this, nor, probably, will the Birney people if they know I vouched for you. I send books and art materials to the Birney school and know the teachers there, the Wilbert Harveys. . . .

Well, these are my suggestions, and I wish you luck. I've always suspected that the white handled Custer guns, at least one of them, is in or around Birney village.

Good luck,

P. S. I am writing Rufus a note, introducing you.

To Rufus Wallowing

April 16, 1953

Dear Rufus Wallowing:

I am giving your name to John S. Du Mont of the Du Mont Corporation, Greenfield, Massachusets. He and John Parsons, a New York attorney, are writing a book on the weapons of the Custer battle. I heard Mr. Parsons give a talk on this almost entirely on the arms of the troops and so I suggested some sources for information on the weapons of the Indians. Now they wish to gather all the information that they can from the Indian side. Mr. Du Mont plans to come up to Lame Deer next summer. These two men are seriously interested in the Indians' side and perhaps some day, they can be useful to you. I think more men who have influence with the present Congress should be familiar with the situation of the Northern Cheyennes.

This week I have been going over the large map to go into my *Cheyenne Autumn* which will be published in the fall. As I promised, you will receive one of the first copies published.

Sincerely

To Mr. H. D. Wimer

Stratton, Nebraska

June 19, 1953

Dear Mr. Wimer:[1]

Thank you for all your trouble. I don't wish to go much deeper into the Hickok family matters. I don't want to cause any unhappiness or concern. All I was interested in knowing was if this Mrs. Barnes was really Lydia, a sister of Wild Bill's, or a sister-in-law, the wife of Lorenzo Hickok, who indisputably did call himself Bill Barnes upon occasion, as did Wild Bill, back in the Civil war, and a few times later, when an alias seemed useful. Wild Bill was known as Jim as late as his first Nebraska days, Dutch Jim and Dutch Bill, sometimes. It's true that almost nobody had fewer than half a dozen names in those days, but I think there is more to some of these things in the Hickok family than has ever been told. Wilstach, in his marginal notes on the copy of his book that he gave to the rare book section of the New York Public Library seems to hint that he had discovered some of them.[2] That's why I won't go into the matter; I won't need anything more of the family anyway.

I'm just interested in the buffalo hunting Wild Bill did in 1867 in the Republican [River] region. I found some nice items about his hide-hunting in the records of Sidney Barracks, 1867, much in the midst of hide-marketing as the Union Pacific moved westward. The U[nion] P[acific] never admitted to hauling many hides; didn't want legislation against the hide business, but there's plenty of evidence in the records, if one really gets to digging.

I am to have a conference with the art department about the illustrations for *Cheyenne Autumn* next Monday, May 25. There will, it seems, be a large general map of the whole flight region, one of the Lewis fight, a very good one, and one of the outbreak at Ft. Robinson. They plan some reproductions from Little Finger Nail's picture history that he made in the account book I told you about. In addition we have a good photograph of Little Wolf and Lieutenant W. P. Clark, to whom he surrendered. Schmitt, in his *Fighting Indians* etc. mislabels this as Little Hawk, not his fault, for there was an appalling tendency in the 1870–1892 period to mislabel Indian pictures in the various Washington bureaus and offices. Fortunately I have the whole story of the picture-taking at Ft. Keogh when Clark brought the Little Wolf Cheyennes in there. The photograph appeared in Frank Leslie's *Illustrated Newspaper* in June 1879, June, properly labeled.

In all the years I've been searching I've found no good picture that is indisputably Dull Knife, although I saw at least a dozen in my childhood. The one the Bureau of Ethnology used to put out as Little Wolf and Dull Knife is really Old Wolf and Lame White Man, two southern Cheyenne chiefs, as anyone who understands much of the accoutrements of the time would know. Unfortunately, although this was always identified as Old Wolf and Lame White Man by the Indians, somehow there was a mixup in the labeling and a few copies went out of the Bureau of Ethnology, after the final correction of 1938, with the *not* left out and now the misnaming once more goes on. Fortunately I have a copy of each labeling from the Bureau of Ethnology one saying it is *not* Dull Knife and Little Wolf, the other saying it is, and both saying the identification was made by the same Cheyennes.

We had a good series of photographs of the Oregon Trail taken by [Jack] Leermachers [*sic*] of the Eastman Kodak company with Paul Henderson and Pete Decker last summer—shown before the New York Posse of the Westerners. These will appear in a book soon, in full color.[3] Incidentally, if you ever come to New York let me know. You should speak to our group of the Westerners. And in the meantime, what have you done about getting your material into any publishable shape?

I often think of you and your fine, warm-hearted wife. I wish you both, and the young man of the family too, the best of everything.

Sincerely,

1. Henry D. (Doc) Wimer (1901–77), a longtime resident of the Trenton area in southwestern Nebraska and president of the Hitchcock County Historical Society, was an avid and knowledgeable collector of the historical material of his region. Contacting MS in 1949, he gave her valuable detailed information, including first-hand accounts, of incidents of the Cheyenne treks through northern Kansas and southern Nebraska, including both the 1875 massacre of Cheyennes at Sappa Creek and the 1878 retaliation by the Dull Knife–Little Wolf band. The Wimers, together with other history buffs from the region, guided MS to the locales of the killings and raids on more than one occasion.

2. Frank Jenners Wilstach, *Wild Bill Hickok: The Prince of Pistoleers* (Garden City: Doubleday, Page and Co., 1926).

3. Paul Henderson, *Landmarks on the Oregon Trail* (New York: Peter Decker for The Westerners, New York Posse, 1953). Photographs by Jack Leermakers.

To Jack Schaefer

July 7, 1954 [1953]

Dear Jack Schaefer:[1]

I'm very sorry I wasn't at The Westerners, after you made that awkward journey. It was the first meeting I missed but Sonia Levinthal of McGraw-Hill gave a party that night and you know about such things.

I have your CANYON. Anne Ford was going to send me a copy but it must have gone the way of many things in the mails now. Unfortunately I am in that stage of illiteracy that everyone seems to hit when deadlines push in on him. I've just turned in a manuscript to Hastings House and am deep in the business of the C. A. and still not reading. The book looks dramatic and I regret that [Stuart] Rose didn't take it for the *Post*.[2] I suspect that he is at least partly right about public taste. As you know part of the low level of public taste can be laid to the unwillingness of any popular medium to present anything that might elevate that taste. Oh, we get a bit of something now and then; not often.

No, you didn't talk too much. Of course there is good writing on western topics and material. You have a fine list. With the usual liberty one takes with anthologists, I wonder why Paul Horgan isn't on it, and Ambrose Bierce.[3] I wish you the best of luck.

About my stories: please don't use that "Sandhill Sundays" thing. I threw this together for Ben Botkin a long, long time ago, and largely to fit a special need at the moment, for his FOLKSAY. You're welcome to anything except those first stories in the *Prairie Schooner.* Those I prefer to bury. And no feelings hurt if you don't find anything. Oh, as an afterthought: I'm sure you wouldn't want the long school bus story. There's a deal on to make a novel of that.

I trust that you are deep in another creative job, in addition to the anthology.

Sincerely,

1. Jack Schaefer (1907–1991)—the author of *Shane* (Boston: Houghton Mifflin, 1948), "The Canyon" (1953), *Monte Walsh* (Boston: Houghton Mifflin, 1963), and other works—was assembling *Out West: An Anthology of Stories* (Boston: Houghton Mifflin, 1957). MS's "The Girl in the Humbert" was included.

2. Rose wrote that the public was not interested in Indian literature, although he himself thought *Crazy Horse* was one of the best biographies written by an American.

3. Paul Horgan (b. 1903) won the Pulitzer Prize for *Great River: The Rio Grande in North America History* (New York: Rinehart, 1954) and wrote other prize-winning histories and biographies. Ambrose Bierce (1842–1914?) was a writer of short stories, many set in the West.

[To F. H. Sinclair (Neckyoke Jones)]

[Sheridan, Wyoming]

November 11, 1953

Dear Neckyoke:

I owe you an apology. Back in June when your fine letter reached me I was deep in my advanced novel writing course at the University of Wisconsin, with 28 novels being worked on under my direction. Since I got back from there I had the last tag-ends of the page proofs, etc., of my *Cheyenne Autumn* to finish up. Now the book is coming out November 17, and I am finishing a manuscript on the buffalo hunters. I turned the next-to-the-last draft in to the publisher Monday and have been catching up on sleep since. I am very sorry about this delay in acknowledging your long letter.

I knew of Neckyoke Jones, of course, but I didn't connect your letter and the Indian Day notices with him, somehow. I had you over on the Missouri, somehow.

The work you and your wife are doing for the young Indians touches me very deeply. There's so little done for them in a constructive way — to help them develop into self-reliance, into self-confidence and responsibility. I trust your Indian Day went very well. Several of my acquaintances went out and sent back post cards but I've been too busy to visit with them and get the news.

Yes, I know of Julia Wild Hog. She *was* in the Outbreak. They wintered in Lost Chokecherry Valley, near the head of Snake river, a tributary to the Niobrara in northwestern Nebraska. The ranch of one of my sisters adjoins the Chokecherry. I put in a lot of time there reconstructing their camp of the winter of 1878–9 for *Cheyenne Autumn,* on the flight to the north. I ran into Julia in 1931, either at Katie BigHead's or some of the other Indians.[1] I recall that she was uncommunicative then. Fortunately I didn't wonder at their attitude; it was a very tragic time, that year and the things that led up to it. I wonder if my account might not help you get her story from her. I used to know one of her relatives, perhaps a great-aunt, very well, — the aunt of Little Finger Nail, one of the warriors killed in the last hole up in the Hat Creek bluffs above Robinson, with the Dull Knife people.

Yes, according to my files George Bent[2] belonged to the Chiefs Society of the Southern Cheyennes. You are really honored to be inducted by the Northerners. They shy from whites much more than the Southerners ever did, even from white blood, it seems to me. And it's not surprising.

I agree with you on the Crazy Horse statue being carved at the Black Hills. My European correspondents complain that Ziolkowski's conception is too Germanic, with the heavy-muscled, rounded chest figure, and the Germanic hair blowing back. But I'm still in favor of the statue, for we'll probably never get a good one if it is left too long, but if there is a commemorating figure, some one may come along later and get more of the Indian feeling into it. In the meantime we have something for Americans to remember. . . .

And do write some of your stories down. You owe posterity something for the privilege your eyes have had — seeing so many things that will never return.

And may the holiday season be a fine one for you and Mrs. Sinclair.

Sincerely, and in haste

1. Julia was a daughter of Little Wolf and daughter-in-law of Wild Hog, leaders in the Cheyenne trek from Indian Territory in 1878. She was with the group who attempted to escape from Fort Robinson in 1879 ("the Outbreak"). Katie Bighead, a northern Cheyenne, was a cousin of Monaseeta, the Cheyenne mother of Yellow Swallow, General George Custer's son, according to MS.

2. George Bent (1843–1917), a mixed-blood, was the son of the trader William Bent and a Cheyenne mother. See George Hyde, *The Life of George Bent Written from his Letters,* ed. Savoie Lottinville (Norman: U of Oklahoma P, 1968).

To Mary Abbot

McIntosh & Otis

December 20, 1953

Dear Mary Abbot:[1]

Thank you for the clipping from the Los Angeles *Daily News*. I'm happy to have Elliott Arnold's review of CHEYENNE AUTUMN, and to find that it praises my poetic presentation. Fortunately there is nothing in the book to indicate the heart-breaking two months I put in last spring defending my writing in this book, page by page, line by line, even word by word against editorial demands that I change the writing. Finally I was told that there were instructions I was to have the writing exactly the way I wanted it. Plainly this must have come down from Ed Aswell,[2] and I am very grateful. All over the west, where people know about Indians and the locale, the reviews have been the same, with conspicuous praise for the poetic quality of the writing and the successful conveyance of the sense and feel of the Indians. It would have been tragic had I given in to editorial pressure.

But it's always the same. Only Knopfs were content to assume that I was the one who knew how my book, in this case CRAZY HORSE, should be written. And always the critics and the fan mail praise exactly the thing I've had to fight for. So don't expect me to bow down before any editor. The fact that I've held two editorial positions doesn't increase my respect.

By this time you will have my note about the final draft of THE BUFFALO HUNTERS. Mr. Frese[3] did suggest another book, which I appreciate, but publishers have been suggesting that I do this or that book on everything from rivers, Powell's expedition down the Colorado, cattle, oil, and Galvanized Yankees, to a sort of series on the Grandma Moses of literature, the American primitives from manuscripts in the historical repositories. This started even before OLD JULES publication.

THE BUFFALO HUNTERS is going to turn out all right because nobody looked over my shoulders and I was allowed to do it my way. After all, I was able to write a pretty good book before I had an editor, although I later had to defend the writing almost as strenuously as I did in CHEYENNE AUTUMN.

Mr. Alsberg[4] made two major suggestions. First, the inclusion of an Indian buffalo hunt, which I once had in the manuscript but discarded as a break from the consistent white-man point of view. I'm putting this in. The other was that I write an introductory chapter on the pattern of the races-of-man one in Tolstoy's WAR AND PEACE. I refused this as entirely too pretentious, particularly for a book about buffalo hunters. Mr. Frese had already committed himself as against it before the matter was broached to me. I think every book should turn out to be more than is claimed for it at the beginning, not less. This is the usual conflict between the artist and the Broadway or Hollywood point of view. I was surprised to hear it from Mr. Alsberg, but editors are editors, I suppose. They all want to write the author's book. However, Mr. Alsberg was fine about this and didn't insist. I'm writing the foreword for him now, putting in the points he suggested. Also a couple of explanatory paragraphs he thinks the public should have somewhere in the first 60 pages of the book.

Thank you again,

1. Mary Abbot joined McIntosh and Otis in 1931; the agent for several noted writers, she worked closely with MS during the rest of MS's career. She initiated the meeting between the author and Hastings House that resulted in *The Buffalo Hunters* and subsequent books. In the various confrontations between MS and her publishers and editors, Abbot proved a valuable ally.

2. Edward Aswell (1900–1958), an editor MS first knew at Atlantic Monthly Press, was later at Harpers, at McGraw-Hill from 1947 to 1955, then at Doubleday.

3. Walter Frese (b. 1909), the founder and president of Hastings House, was later president of the American Institute of Graphic Arts. Hastings House specialized in Americana.

4. Henry Alsberg (1881–1970) was an editor at Hastings House. In the 1930s he had headed the Federal Writers' Project for the Works Progress Administration and was general editor of the state guidebooks. His work was greatly respected in the publishing world.

To J. Donald Adams

January 4, 1954

Dear Mr. Adams:[1]

I'm so sorry to hear of your illness. You seemed to be having such a stimulating, such a creative time, if one can still use the phrase to mean the sense of immediate life. I'll be happy to see the reviews, particularly the one of Dr. Alexander's *The World's Rim.*[2] I recall him so pleasantly from my days at the University of Nebraska. His office was down the corridor from my cubbyhole as English reader. He used to hunt me up when some particularly fine piece of Indian pottery or similar object came in. He couldn't bear to open such a package or barrel without a receptive eye to watch as the sweet grass was pulled away.

Surely you will be feeling well soon. You know what the westerners say: If you make it to grass you'll make it, meaning that it's not unusual to feel poorly on snowbanks. I shall be very happy to come up for a drink with you and your wife when it is convenient. I want to hear about your visits to the Indians and what you are doing.

Sincerely, and with best wishes for 1954.

1. James Donald Adams (1891–1968), an author, was the editor and contributing editor of *New York Times Book Review* from 1925 to 1964.

2. Hartley Burr Alexander, *The World's Rim* (Lincoln: U of Nebraska P, 1953). Alexander (1873–1939) was chairman of the Department of Philosophy at the University and an anthropologist. He was Helen Blish's advisor for her master's thesis, published in 1967 as *The Pictographic History of the Oglala Sioux*.

To Bess Streeter Aldrich

January 15, 1954

Dear Bess Streeter Aldrich:

Thank you for your fine letter. I'm happy you and Bob enjoyed it,[1] and I'm grateful to Mrs. Dobson for calling you.

Don't regret the fact that Abbie Deal was afraid of Indians.[2] The propaganda that made it possible to expropriate the Indian convinced people with much more time and sophistication—all, in fact, except those very closely connected with the Indians at the time. Besides, there were bad Indians just as there were bad whites, and it was important to be cautious, with the anger that all the Indians felt, and often heightened by the white man's firewater.

I don't see why the Arabs wouldn't like Abbie's story. There is a lot of remote living among them now, since the nomadic hunting patterns have broken up, and much that can pass as pioneering is taking place. I had a fine young Arab in my novel workshop at Wisconsin one summer. Although the son of a high official in the Egyptian government, he was engrossed in the material rising out of the fringe settlements of his country.

Bob's project for the WORLD-HERALD sounds fine. He'll make a real contribution. Mamie Meredith sends me clippings from their Sunday Magazine now and then but there are seldom bylines. Has the series started? Will you drop me a card telling me a word or two about this? The January 3, issue has an interesting unsigned article on paintings of Nebraska's past. Of course it's too bad that Bob's fiction career is arrested for the moment but that will be only temporary. These are not the best times for fiction anyway, with the shrinking markets and the deep concern with factual things of the present and the future.

I wonder how you are and what you have done on the autobiographical work you once spoke of doing. Unfortunately I've been deep in two books that required research, the Cheyenne and another to appear later this year. You will know what's happened to me — I'm illiterate. But I hope I didn't miss your autobiography.

Thank you again, and may you and Bob both have a splendid 1954.

Sincerely,

1. Bess Streeter Aldrich (1881–1954), author of short stories and best-selling historical novels set in Nebraska: *A Lantern in Her Hand* (New York: Appleton Century, 1928); *A White Bird Flying* (New York: Appleton, 1931); *Miss Bishop* (New York: Appleton, 1933); *Spring Came on Forever* (New York: Appleton, 1935); and others. She was a member of Quill in Lincoln. Bob was her son.

2. Abbie Deal was the major character in Aldrich's most popular novel about settling the Nebraska frontier, *A Lantern in Her Hand.*

To Oliver W. Holmes, Chief Archivist

Natural Resources Records Branch
National Archives and Records Service
Washington, D.C.

January 25, 1954

Dear Mr. Holmes:

Thank you for your nice letter. No, I didn't do my research for the Cheyenne book by mail. I worked on this the winter of 1937–8, much of it in the War Records over on Virginia Avenue, above the Department of the Interior garage. The Indian Bureau records were down in the basement of the Bureau offices, as I recall now, and a pleasant young Indian was among those who doled out the files to me there.

Later I worked in the Archives building, where a Mr. Holmes helped me with the Sioux records of the Red Cloud and upper Platte regions. Perhaps this was you, although somehow I seem to recall the first name as George. But anyway, this was a most earnest and helpful Mr. Holmes. At this time, 1940, up in the War Records Dr. Irvine was in charge and Dr. Douglas and Mr. Ballantine doled out files up there.

As a researcher who wants to see *everything* I prefer the old Virginia Avenue system, where I literally plowed through everything and uncovered many maps for the Cartographer in the great bales and boxes of material still just as it had come in from the dismantled frontier posts. Of course I knew that that system would not do for people of limited time, experience and ethics at all. I had been director of research for the Nebraska State Historical Society and was in charge of their Federal project that organized the material of sixty years accumulation, so Virginia Avenue was my dish. When I got to the Indian Records I had already seen much of the material in duplicate copy. However, every fire alarm in Washington used to bring me to the appalling realization that all those records over the garage might be gone in one fine smoking. I spoke of this once at dinner with the Senator George Norrises. The senator hadn't been aware that our records were so badly housed and soon we had an archival building.

Pardon the long letter—

Sincerely,

To John Parsons

February 2, 1954

Dear Mr. Parsons:

The M. I. McCreight book is CHIEF FLYING HAWK'S TALES. It has only one picture of a gun, I find, to my regret, but it is one of the several Crazy Horse carbines, and there is a good picture of one of the peace medals, this one of Washington, given out 1789, presented to an ancestor of Hollow Horn Bear, Sioux chief.

About pictures of Indians with guns (not scouts or peace Indians); these are rare because the pictures are usually of the chiefs and chiefs seldom carried guns, often owned none. The 2,3 warriors usually along were armed men, rather like our president and his secret service. . . . Your Ute Indians, Piah too, must have been friendlies. . . .

As for identifying Piah by his garments: whiteman made garments went to the frontier in big lots. Many alike. The only difference was in the eventual bead pattern some were given by the Indian women. Chiefs seldom bought their blankets; they got them as presents from the traders who found a welcome in their villages, and these presents had to be almost all alike. All to a certain social and political level had to be alike to avoid trouble. Since the Indians never recognized any one man as their sole chief, but always had several council or Old Man Chiefs, there were always several in every village with the same fine blankets, and anyone with the robes to trade could buy as fine.

Government representatives out to council carefully followed this custom, bringing ten or twenty fine blue blankets with white borders to be given out to the head men, the number depending upon the size of the conference, of course. Several times white blankets appeared, often from Canadian traders, visiting Britishers, or other foreigners, or the occasional government council, perhaps under the sway of some old Hudsons Bay employee, etc. But these always had to be in lots, enough for all the men of highest rank, and so on down.

Then there was the similar clothing worn by members of the soldier or chief societies to occasions when their membership was to be made conspicuous—much as white man occasions. Even warbonnets usually showed a man's rank and affiliations, although the bead designs (earlier the quill design, the paint) and sometimes the color of the base of the feathers, and so on, was different. Usually there were bits of the man's special medicine in the adornment.

When identifying Indian pictures I follow this rule: Look first for scars or special facial formations that do not change. Then remember that a man's face is slender in youth and in old age and broadens in from both ends of life towards middleage, if there is not conspicuous sickness or starvation. You can see this very clearly in the face of Red Cloud. Then look for special bead or paint designs, but these may be dropped entirely for special regalia, as the Shirtwearers' shirts, the Dog Soldier's crow feather (round) warbonnet, and the long striped "tail" or sort of flying panel reaching to his heels. This the warrior sometimes staked down and then he had to die there unless victorious. Or was rescued by a pal who dared rush into the fight and pull the stake.

But enough—According to the index to my notes, Crazy Horse carried a Winchester in the Custer battle. He Dog attested to this, I find, and [Stanley] Vestal's Sitting Bull, 173, agrees. He Dog said that the Winchesters were fine guns but it was hard to get ammunition, which was not yet anywhere, as older makes of ammunition were. Somewhere during the fight Crazy Horse evidently changed to a soldier gun, one with more plentiful ammunition. The

Department of the Platte Document File, April 27, 1877, reports that three lodges from Crazy Horse were disarmed at Spotted Tail agency, (Camp Sheridan). They had 1 muzzle-loader, 1 revolver and three bows. What they hid out or gave to those who stayed out a while longer no one can say.

Sincerely,

To Marguerite Young

March 5, 1954

Dear Marguerite:

Celebrations and Centennials! Marguerite has written!

I was at Wesley [Towner's] for a couple of hours Sunday evening and they hadn't heard, nor apparently had Jean, but Mary [Towner] said you had been on her mind for the last week.

I'm happy that you and Ray West[1] consider CHEY A fitting to be reviewed in *Western Review.* After all, there are so many volumes of poetry and novels on the new, the experimental side that might be given the space. No, don't send me a preview. That puts a taint of collusion upon it. . . .

Of course your book can't help but be a fabulous creation and I'm waiting with little patience for the volume in-the-hand. Mary Abbot asked about you and for once I was able to say I had heard. When will the books be done? I hoped soon, I said. And would I convey her best and Elizabeth [Otis's] also? I would, and do. Is there a tie-up between the ground floor of the little house within sight of the gold dome and the approaching finish of the book?

It's fine that you like the Wests, since you are stuck there for the rest of the year. I've never met Mrs. but Ray is a special kind of person, with serious and unexpected ramifications not too common on campuses, even among more creative people.

At lunch some weeks ago Arthur Wang was excited about the first section of Wesley's book. Even Wyn himself, I gather, has an enthusiastic reaction, and he's generally a chilly egg, I hear.

Jean Evans is excited about her new book, for which I gather you wrote an extraordinary appreciation.[2] I hope that the McCarthy business has died down a little before her publication date, so people can think about the problem of the delinquent and the mentally sick. However I suspect McCarthy is really the senator of my *Tom-Walker,* and that no one of the general's outfit will stop him.

Town's dull. Iowa City sounds better. Mary Pepper is still digging a little for Wesley. Benny at the drug store asks about you. I was over around Gramercy a week ago. Seems very dull over there.

Well, this is all—

1. Ray West (b. 1908) was a professor of English at the University of Iowa from 1949 to 1959; an author of essays, biographies, and critical evaluations; and the editor of *Western Review* from 1936 to 1959.

2. Jean Evans, *Three Men: An Experiment in the Biography of Emotion* (New York: Vintage, 1954).

To Dorothy McIlhatton

Secretary, Trade Book Dept.
THE WESTMINSTER PRESS

March 25, 1954

Dear Madam:

I am surprised that a birth date is required for a copyright. My six books were copyrighted by four publishers and if there is a birth date on these the publishers must have made it up. I couldn't swear to the year and there is no registration. It would be rather difficult to prove that I exist at all.

Even my annuities have no more than an approximate date, which we decided to put at 1898, marking it as uncertain. Can you do the same?

Sincerely,

To Mr. E. A. Brininstool

June 5, 1954

Dear Mr. Brininstool:

I am happy to hear from you.

Yes, indeed *Crazy Horse* is being filmed, and certainly without any permission from me, although I hear they are using much detail of the man's private life that is available only in my book. I hear from the Sioux on Pine Ridge that they really are to have some part in the filming. They assume that it is being done with my book, because they know about that and it would not occur to them that one steals such material.

I see reviews of your book with Stackpole all around, and find people of our New York Posse, the Westerners, talking about it. We have a lot of Custer fighters in our group. New York, particularly Wall Street, has a lot of Custer fight fans, men who spend their vacations plodding over the Little Big Horn battlefield.

Let me know if you hear anything more on Crazy Horse, although I suppose the picture will turn out to have no relation to actuality as to a person or event. Crazy Horse played by Victor Mature!

Sincerely,

To Irita Van Doren

Editor, BOOK REVIEW, New York Herald Tribune

October 3, 1954

Dear Irita Van Doren:

I'm sorry about the long delay in the reply to your note of September 15 and the letter from Oliver L. B. Rhodes criticising J. Frank Dobie's review of my *Buffalo Hunters*. I was out west.

Mr. Rhodes expressed a very common misconception basic in the "the only good Indian is a dead Indian" attitude. Of course Mr. Dobie is correct in saying that Big Foot's band of Sioux at Wounded Knee was even more scantily armed than clad.[1] In the War Records, now in the National Archives, I went through the itemized list of arms taken from these Indians at the surrender and picked up on the battleground afterward. It was a most miserable list, barely more than an armful of guns, mostly old muzzleloaders and singleshots. These Indians had been disarmed several times in their earlier surrenders to the reservation and what they had in 1890 were the few old guns they managed to get by the little trade they could work out, guns that were called "rabbit chasing" ones around the agencies of those days. My father, Jules Sandoz, went over the Wounded Knee battle ground the evening after the fight and left a long, angry account written that night to his sweetheart in Switzerland. He was a gunsmith, knew frontier arms and he said he didn't see a dozen really usable rifles in the whole lot that was gathered up from Big Foot's band.

The troops at Wounded Knee had four Hotchkiss guns and had set them up before the disarming, trained not on the surrendering men but on the tents where the women and children huddled. The whole story is available to anyone willing to look into the War Records in the National Archives, particularly the files gathered for the investigation by the Board of Officers after the fight. A readily available source is James Mooney's "The Ghost Dance Religion and the Sioux Outbreak of 1890," *Fourteenth Annual Report*, Bureau of Ethnology.

Contrary to Mr. Rhodes' complaint, Sitting Bull was really the first man to fall in the ghost dance troubles of 1890. He was shot by an Indian agency policeman, not Henry Bull, as Mr. Rhodes says, but Lieutenant Bullhead, after the arrest up on Standing Rock Reservation, December 15, 1890. It was the killing of Sitting Bull that alarmed Big Foot and his followers and caused their flight across South Dakota to Pine Ridge Reservation along the Nebraska border. Two weeks after Sitting Bull was killed Big Foot surrendered at Wounded Knee and was shot down with his people.

Sincerely,

1. Big Foot was the leader of the Miniconjou and Hunkpapa Sioux who were killed by Seventh Cavalry troops at Wounded Knee, South Dakota, on December 29, 1890.

To Henry Alsberg

[Hastings House]

December 20, 1954

Dear Henry:

It's generous of you to think of me for the book on the pioneer period of the Great Plains. Unfortunately I don't see how I could ever get around to it, with the cattle book only started, a novel on the modern art movement in America laid out for 12 years, the research mostly done and the plot and characters for the book all written out. Then there must be a book on the coming of iron and powder to stone age man in the Great Plains, the Number 1 in my own series, and then the one on oil to end up the series.

Do you think that I might live to be a hundred?

It's true that your book sounds like the game for my gun but if someone good shows up to do it, you better sign him up.

And in the meantime I wish you the best of years for this forthcoming 1955.

Sincerely,

I've just started the Zweig book.[1] I was startled by the first few letters. I didn't realize that women wrote the same kind of letters to authors that men do—. . . .

1. Stefan Zweig (1881–1942) was an extremely prolific Austrian novelist, playwright, essayist, and biographer. MS is referring to *Stefan and Frederike Zweig: Their Correspondence, 1912–1943*, trans. and ed. Henry G. Alsberg, with assistance of Emma MacArthur (New York: Hastings House, 1954).

To Annie Laurie Williams

February 12, 1955

Dear Annie Laurie:

For your temporary files:

Enclosed is a copy of the cast of characters, a synopsis and production notes of Universal-International's *Chief Crazy Horse*. The original has to be returned to a California friend.

As always, I am astonished at the pointless violences Hollywood commits on historical material. No factually true selection of events could have been less dramatic than what the boys made up for this picture, and along with the loss of drama they have made a lie of the whole.

They not only lost all the dramatic impact of the conflicts within the tribe; with the elements, the times and the white men; and within the man's own mind, but they have committed such shameless libels. By making Crazy Horse's wife the daughter of Spotted Tail, they are making his marriage incestuous in the Indian's meaning of the term. By making the killer of Crazy Horse a breed instead of a white soldier, they are libeling a whole class of people, by calling the breed Little Big Man, they are libeling a whole Indian family. Little Big Man was an Indian, not a breed. He did not kill Crazy Horse, and so on and on. No author would want to charge infringement of his copyright if this is an accurate portrayal of the moving picture. No one would admit putting such a story between book covers, let alone pretending that it was true.

The Westerners Brand Book of the Chicago Posse of The Westerners publishes the recent results of a survey made of experts in authentic literature of the west. Among the first ten, led by such books as Chittenden's *Fur Trade* and Parkman's *Oregon Trail,* etc., is my *Crazy Horse.* I hope to have the book back in print by 1956 or so. It has become one of the most-advertised-for books on the rare items list.

Well, stick this in your files for a while.

To the Reverend Peter J. Powell

Chicago, Illinois

February 20, 1955

Dear Father Powell:[1]

I am indeed happy to hear good news from you, and hasten to acknowledge your deeply evocative and most generous letter before it gets buried in the back mail that accumulates when I'm working against deadlines.

Surely no book could aspire to a finer use than that to which you, with your deep feeling for eternal meaning, put my Indian accounts. Certainly those brave ones, with their courageous selflessness, their passionate allegiance to a sense of the goodness, the wholeness of all things, touched a holy Something.

Yes, the little canvas lodge of the Sacred Medicine Hat of the Northern Cheyenne sits in the poor little village of log huts of Birney, Montana. The Sacred Arrows are in Oklahoma as the enclosed clipping for your files will tell you. I have a photograph of the Arrows, taken up at Bear Butte during this time of fasting. So far the Cheyennes have strenuously resisted all attempts to beg, borrow or steal these sacred objects of the tribe.

No, all the old time buffalo hunters of the Cheyennes and Tetons are all gone. Incidentally, Father Buechel (I'm not certain of the spelling any more) who spent most of his adulthood at the mission and school at Rosebud died in 1954. I hadn't seen him for over twenty years but the Indians often sent me word of him. . . .

Never apologize for your letters. There should be more communication between people of good will, particularly good will toward the Indian.

May the grass grow ever green where your moccasins pass.

1. Peter J. Powell, an Episcopalian priest, the founder and director of St. Augustine Indian Mission in Chicago, a Newberry Library Fellow, and a Smithsonian Fellow, is a recognized authority on Cheyenne religious life. He wrote *Sweet Medicine* (Norman: U of Oklahoma P, 1969). MS's Indian books were a strong encouragement to his own extensive research.

To J. W. Vaughn

Windsor, Colorado

February 26, 1955

Dear Mr. Vaughn:[1]

No, I don't say there is no picture of Crazy Horse, the Oglala war chief. I just say that the Indians who knew him well said he would never have one taken, and so far none that I've found or had called to my attention could possibly have been this Crazy Horse.

Crazy Horse, meaning Holy, Inspired or Mystical Horse, is a very common name among Indians. As I state in my short article on the burial places of Crazy Horse in *The Westerners Brand Book,* N. Y. Posse, vol. 1, no. 4, there were three of the name old enough and important enough to sign a Sioux treaty in 1889. In addition there was the one in the southwest, born sometime in the 1850's, who lived to be over 90 and whose photograph was often palmed off as *the* Crazy Horse. He usually wears the fur hat found among the southwest hunting Indians, and was sometimes called Crooked Nose by the Indians because there was a bend in the nose.

There was a Hunkpapa Crazy Horse contemporaneous to the Oglala war chief, see [Stanley] Vestal's *Sitting Bull.* This may be the subject of the Morrow photograph at South Dakota, the one in Brown and Schmitt.[2] This man is plainly part white and wears the slip knot hair tie of the northern Indians brought south by the returning Sioux from Canada in '81. The blanket coat is also northern. I am told that the Morrow picture is of Crazy in the Lodge.

Now to the most frequently encountered picture labeled Crazy Horse—the very dark little man in warbonnet, with his hands folded—The Indians told me this is of Greasy Head, known as Crazy Horse No. 2 after, by good Sioux custom, he took the name of his illustrious predecessor when he married Crazy Horse's widow, the Larrabee woman. The war chief was light coffee-colored, never wore a warbonnet, and died before this type of photography was discovered. And look at the clothing of the white men—long after 1877.

E. A. Brininstool has disowned this picture as not of *the* Crazy Horse long ago. You can reach him at 330 North Poinsettia Place, Los Angeles 36, California. Further, Lone Eagle wrote me this winter that he knew this was not the picture of the Oglala war chief.

I'm happy to know someone is working on the Rosebud battle. My bibliography on this is more than a thousand sources, big and little. Much comes from my own interviews, and much from the tremendous files in the

National Archives, both War Department and Indian Bureau Records, with much interview material there, as well as the official reports. There are many Indian accounts in various places. You could put a lifetime in on this one engagement, what led up to it, and the repercussions.

I'll look forward to your book.

Sincerely,

1. J. W. Vaughn (1903–68), a lawyer whose avocation was western military history, was the author of *With Crook at the Rosebud* (Harrisburg, Pa.: Stackpole, 1956), *The Reynolds Campaign on the Powder River* (Norman: U of Oklahoma P, 1961), and others.

2. Dee Brown and Martin Schmitt, *Fighting Indians of the West* (New York: Scribner, 1948).

To Edward Aswell

[McGraw-Hill Publishers]

March 8, 1955

Dear Ed:

Here's the first half of *Morissa,* with a map of the Trail for editorial edification.

I put in eleven hard days cleaning the manuscript up after all the editorial pencilings and my own revisions. I'll admit I paid scant attention to Mrs. Epstein's editing—not after her change in my subtitle: *The Doctor of the Gold Trail* to *The Doctor of the Dakotas,* which is not only a misstatement of fact, the North Platte Valley is not even near Dakota, but the alliteration is on a very low and tasteless level. Further, I certainly would not delete every bit of imaginative work, everything metaphorical and everything that makes the locale a worthy protagonist from the book. She wants this to be a love story on the thinnest, shallowest level, with both the characters and the setting two dimensional. That's fine for a certain type of book. What I have here is something vastly beyond that.

I read the manuscript through very carefully so far and did considerable revising, enough to require (with so many editorial markings that could not be erased cleanly) retyping 43 of the former 221 pages. Much of my revision is a return to my earlier, much terser version, which helped cut the 221 pages down to 209, with many of these short pages.

One result of this concentrated work is my firm conviction that for all the pressures brought upon us about this manuscript, I still have something here that will stand alone—the one worthy book in a field that has been almost completely neglected.

Sincerely,

To John R. Frame

April 16, 1955

Dear Mr. Frame:

Thank you for the nice letter about *The Buffalo Hunters.*

Your suggestion that I write a book on Custer is a genuinely flattering one, but I must beg off. The subject has been so mauled, pawed over and warmed over that I'm not interested in it. It is true that most of the books are merely rewrites of the sensational and sentimental newspaper accounts of the times, when the public had been led to believe that the Indians were blood-thirsty savages, without mentioning Custer was on land where, by treaty, no white man had the right to go, and that the charge of blood-thirstiness was certainly more applicable to Custer than to Crazy Horse, Sitting Bull, or the other leaders on the Little Big Horn.

Until 1940 it was difficult to get into the War Records because they were stored in old warehouses and so on in Washington, uncatalogued and without staffs or facilities to handle researchers. It is true I got in as early as 1937 for my *Crazy Horse* and *Cheyenne Autumn* but I had to wear down the War Department to do it. Now the Reno Inquiry has been published and the War Records are housed in the National Archives building and available to any serious researcher. Sooner or later some serious writer will undertake the real study of Custer possible now. Until then *The Glory Hunter*[1] and the various Custer sections of related books will have to do. Unfortunately the old Indians, the only survivors of the fight, are all dead now, so that source is gone forever, except the accounts some of us added to those the officers and others obtained for various archives.

But enough of this—I'm certain you have gone through the material in print. It is exciting.

Sincerely,

1. Frederick Van de Water, *Glory Hunter: A Life of General Custer* (Indianapolis: Bobbs Merrill, 1934).

To L. W. Van Vleet

May 14, 1955

Dear Boss:

. . . I didn't get any nearer to Denver than Scottsbluff, deep in a yellow dust storm. Now, instead of writing my article, I find the apartment house here has been sold to a big syndicate and they are already making trouble for me. I went to the Rent Commission today but as soon as they saw the name of the real estate outfit I was told, "They can make you take anything they want—" If I didn't have my time on an impossibly close assembly belt as it is I would fly to Denver or even Lincoln to find an apartment while packers threw my stuff into a truck. Never have I had one word with any landlord, but of course I never had gangsters for landlords before.

However, things will work out somehow—all I ask is that they don't destroy my lifetime accumulation of material while I'm gone to Wisconsin. I get more and more sympathetic to the vigilante leading Old Jules did.

But the wheat was green in Nebraska and even the dust was yellow and so plainly foreign—I trust the bean business will be the best ever.

Happy Days!

To Jack Leermakers

August 25, 1955

Dear Jack Leermakers:

Pete [Decker] and I were discussing future issues of *The Westerner* and the subject of old Fort Phil Kearny came up.[1] I wondered if you might not be interested in doing a sort of survey of the region and the action: the Fetterman fight, the Hayfield fight and the one called the Wagonbox. There's a lot of hokum in print about the Wagonbox affair, such as that it broke the back of Red Cloud's resistance (although he got the three Bozeman forts dismantled before he would sign the treaty of 1868, which suggests that it wasn't old Red's resistance that was broken). The usual story, as you know, is that the breechloaders (some accounts say the repeaters) of the troops were a surprise to the Indians. That's silly, as anyone can discover if he looks at the arms captured from the Fetterman fight the December before, which included two repeating rifles. The truth is that the Indians saw breechloaders before most of the troops did; visiting hunters brought them, and repeating arms were the fetish of the fur trader bigwigs. Some newspaper and magazine accounts put the Indian losses in the Wagonbox fight at 3000. There's nothing to back the killing of more than a handful in the reports in the War Records of the Archives, and even those couldn't be authenticated accurately, for the Indians dragged the wounded and the dead back alike, and the Indian was expert at lying motionless until rescued.

Another silly canard is the story of Portugee Phillips' lone ride through darkness and danger to burst in at the Christmas dance at Ft. Laramie with the chill of a blizzard wind. The fact is that Phillips rode out of Ft. Phil Kearny with two men along, had at least two along most of the way, and that the telegraph line was in service from up the trail and the news was sent ahead so when the men reached Laramie, it was well known among the head officers there that Fetterman had died. Further, the danger to the messengers is overrated. Both Phillips and one of the others, Dillon, as I recall now, (it's in my files) had Indian wives at the time and so were considered members of the tribe and were in no personal danger from Indians at all.

The curious thing about the Ft. Phil Kearny story is that no early writers bothered to take a good look at the terrain. Almost nowhere but at Lodge Trail ridge could Fetterman have been lured to his death so easily, and the death-trap would not have been so escape-proof, as you will know if you walked over the region. I went back up there December 1941, with the *Crazy Horse* manuscript, to take a look at the region with snow and ice on the Ridge as it must have been in 1866. It seems incredible that even a rash young Westpointer could have been tolled up to where he died. But it is true that each little gully looks so shallow, so harmless, and yet there was brush and rock enough to shelter the Cheyennes, the Minneconjous, the Brules and the Oglalas, as one discovers if he walks and slides down the icy slopes.

This is an important story, both as another annihilation of US troops, and because of the misconceptions that still linger in the minds of even some historians.

Sincerely,

1. Pete ("South Pass Pete") Decker was a member of the New York Posse of the Westerners and, for some time, the editor of their publication the *Brand Book*.

To Vardis Fisher

Hagerman, Idaho

September 24, 1955

Dear Vardis Fisher:[1]

I am grieved but not too surprised by the tribulations of the last five volumes in your Testament of Man series of historical novels. As you discovered long, long ago, any real departure from the ordinary can bring trouble for the author. Who would publish a modern Swift or Voltaire? I wish you and Alan Swallow every success with your books,[2] and wish I could subscribe to your special printing of the series, but such luxuries are not for the writers of serious books. You really are working on a monumental series. About your novel on Hudson's Bay: perhaps A. H. Greenly, 901 Hudson St., Hoboken, N.J., would be better than I. He is interested in the Hudson's Bay region, of which I know nothing. Your publisher can make suggestions to the *Herald-Tribune* as you know.

Of course, if the book is of the fur company, then it's more in my territory, and I'll be glad to undertake the review if the *Herald-Tribune* wishes me to do it. I never ask for a book; I leave the approach entirely to them.

May the sun shine warm upon
Hagerman [Idaho] this golden
time of autumn,

1. Vardis Fisher (1895–1968) was the author of the Testament of Man series and other books, often dealing with the Mormons. His *Children of God* (New York: Harpers, 1939) won the Harper Novel Prize for that year.

2. Alan Swallow (1915–66), professor, author, and publisher, established Swallow Press in Denver, specializing in serious western writing.

To Sonia [Levinthal]

[McGraw-Hill]

January 3, 1956

Dear Sonia,

Happy 1956:

Thanks for the clippings and the symposium of comments on MORISSA. You got delivery on the book everywhere, at least where I showed up. Even out at Scottsbluff. Mrs. Lyons there said the books came through in 7 days, a record for there.

I got back from the west in time for the event I fear most of all, a fire. At 1 am this morning a man burst from one of the little apartments upstairs 5th floor, with a great roaring blaze following him. I heard him, looked out into the horror, threw on a robe and began to pile the more irreplaceable files of my material on the window sills that open upon the fire escape. The firemen thundered up the stairs with a great pressure hose and water began to stream down the stair well and run along the ceiling. I rustled up all the tin waste-baskets and pans I could to catch most of the water but much ran on through the house so there were ponds all over, but I saved my material from damage.

Later I discovered that other people had sensibly dressed, pocketed their valuables and documents and retreated mostly to safe positions. If the firemen had been less swift I would have been left with nothing but a robe and slippers but, I trust, the most valuable of my files.

Happy 1956!

To Estelle Laughlin

Gering, Nebraska

January 8, 1956

Dear Estelle Laughlin:[1]

I'm so very sorry that you felt that your "song" had been taken from you. Of course it has not. Dr. Fix represents an entirely different period of time than my Morissa, and is a much saltier character than the composite that I made. Further, novels and biographies are seldom read by the same people, either the public or the publishers. Even a novel and a biography on the same individual, published in the same year, do not interfere with the sales of each other. The composite of frontier women doctors that Morissa is could never interfere with your biography, and only a very few people would ever see any connection. The whole environment of your Dr. Fix is so different, the community and even the medical practices.

The entire period of my book occurs before Dr. Fix came to the North Platte valley in 1886. The Northwestern railroad, the Fremont, reached Rapid City in 1886 and the Gold Trail was totally dead for over a year, along with the violence and the dire disease of it. Your doctor came into the country when all of Northwest Nebraska was organized into counties, with law and courts such as the period of Morissa's story never sees. Dr. Fix found settlers all through her region, with much less isolation, less stimulation to violence. The gold seekers were gone, the gold coaches and the big road agents too. Yet Dr. Fix managed to leave an imprint on the region such as no Morissa could ever have done.

In addition you have all the civic activities that took another kind of energy and courage—the work for temperance, for schools, a library and church facilities, as well as her own hospital. Nor was it always easy. I recall a great deal of malicious gossip that Uncle Paul said was probably started by those who were envious or fearful of damage to their nefarious businesses. Old Pat Dalton, living on the site of the old Pomroy ranch, where I boarded when I taught school up there north of Sidney, told endless stories about Dr. Fix and about coming across her on the range, perhaps on the way home from some night with a patient, the lines tied around the whipstock, the horses grazing, the doctor asleep in the old buggy. He told stories too, about some drunken driver who used to be considered "another of her husbands".

I have notes on a set of letters I saw years ago, written about Dr. Fix in California. There were comparisons in these to the New York woman, Doctor Blackwell, who pioneered in medicine and then turned to Christian Science, and to Clara Barton and her turn into Science and spiritualism. The letters spoke of a similar turn in the life of Dr. Fix. I never checked on these aspects for they had nothing to do with my composite of a woman doctor on the frontier. The dozen or so that I studied were all earlier than Dr. Fix, who was really very late for my frontier picture. Incidentally, I found some gruesome practices among these early accounts, as, for instance, the tanning of the skin of Big Nose George by a woman doctor up in Wyoming. These stories were at least in part canards but they indicate what the frontier thought of doctors, particularly women doctors.

You have so salty and energetic and engrossing a character that there will be no trouble finding a publisher for your biography if you write the story even passably well. My book will prove that the region exists and that there were women doctors out early. You, without experience with eastern publishers, have no idea how difficult these things are. No one would believe that there was still free land into the 1900 century when I was peddling my OLD JULES. That there is interest in the biographies of women doctors now is proved by the fact that since Morissa came out, I have been asked to do the biographies of all three of the women doctors I list in the front of the book. Of course I have no time or inclination for this. Just this last month I was asked to do a biography of Dr. Susan La Flesche Picotte, the breed Indian doctor of eastern Nebraska. I have no time for that either. But all this shows the interest that my book has aroused. You are in a position to capitalize on this.

I don't recall your letter about Dr. Fix. My correspondence (Oh, this typewriter! I've just had it repaired, too!) is between 1500 and 3000 letters a year, but I do recall one thing, that you are supposed to be a relative of the Chrisman here around New York who wrote TIN HORNS AND CALICO.[2]

I am happy that the Olive story is to be written. There is considerable material on these men in Texas. The late Mr. Vandale of Amarillo, Texas, a great collector of western Americana, told me about them once, and said they vanished up the cattle trail and were never heard of again. He was astonished when I sent him material on the Hastings, Nebr., trial. The Vandale collection, valued around $1,000,000, is now at the University of Texas and I'm going through it for my cattle book.

Oh, yes, about the illegitimacy of Dr. Fix: One of the Oberfelders told me about some legal tangles rising out of that a long time before the doctor died. I don't recall the ins and outs of it now. The personal blight aspects of the problem I got from the memoirs of a woman doctor in Kansas. She had her marriage to a prominent young Philadelphian broken up on her wedding day by the revelation of her birth out of wedlock. She fled west in the early 1870's but in her own mind never escaped the story, which really didn't matter to anyone except herself, out where most of the few women were prostitutes. I recall that the woman was accused of malpractice because an illegitimate child she delivered died, and so she had to move on, or thought she did, and started out in Nevada or Utah once more. I forget the exact state now. For my story it didn't matter.

I have heard that Dr. Fix was part Indian. Pat Dalton always called her "that hook-nose Indian medicine woman". I heard that one of her spirit controls in her psychic research was supposed to be the spirit of her Indian grandmother or great grandmother but I never tried to check on this. I recall an old faith healer and layer-on-of-hands at Sidney telling about this at the hotel once. I didn't listen too closely because I wasn't too interested. It was in that post-World War I period when everybody who had any emotional instability went in for spiritualism and so on.

About Calamity Jane—there were three of that nickname in the 1870's, but the one of the Deadwood time was apparently the one from Princeton, MO, the daughter of a son of well-to-do Iowa farm people who bought the son a place down in Missouri when he brought home a wife who shocked them with her promiscuity. This Mary Jane Canary is apparently the one who married a soldier at Sidney Barracks (I found the record of this in the material now in the National Archives, Washington, when I was working on Crazy Horse.) She bore the soldier a child but deserted it and followed the rest of her family to Alder Gulch. In the meantime there was another Calamity Jane operating in the south Wyoming and Denver region, etc. etc. This latter Jane died in the 1870's.

Incidentally Oberfelder once said he wondered if there really was much to the story that Georgia Arbuckle was a blood relative of the coffee Arbuckles, the people who bought ranch interests up toward Cheyenne and helped break a Cheyenne banker. He said one of the Arbuckle family stopped off at Sidney and seemed to be asking about Georgia. Seemed to know more about her than the Sidney people did, Old Oberfelder told me. I recall this curious conversation because Oberfelder once asked me if we saved the Arbuckle coffee coupons when I was small.

You see how much material there is on Dr. Fix just in my little cache. You must have a tremendous amount. Incidentally, there is a good half-tone portrait of Dr. Arbuckle in Tyler and Auerback's *History of Medicine in Nebraska* p 178, and a nice write-up, also a page picture of Dr. Fix in Watkins's *History of Nebraska* Vol III, 1st ed. bet. pages 710–711.[3]

I'm enclosing a copy of the outline of my course in advanced novel writing in the 8 weeks Writers Institute at the University of Wisconsin summers. The technique for a narrative biography is the same except that you must keep to the actual story, the actual people, incidents and background, and reproduce as faithful a picture of the actual people and the actual times as possible, no matter whether you like what was true or not.

If you do a passably good job we'll get your book published by a regular publisher but the book must be book length—75,000 to 95,000 words.

Every success to you—

1. Estelle Laughlin, a resident of the area in which Dr. Georgia Arbuckle Fix had practiced, had done considerable research and written articles about her but had never managed to publish the doctor's biography. Laughlin both congratulates MS and complains that her material has been taken from her in *Miss Morissa.*

2. Henry Christman, *Tin Horns and Calico: A Decisive Episode in the Emergence of Democracy* (New York: Holt, c. 1945).

3. Albert F. Tyler and Ella F. Auerback, *History of Medicine in Nebraska* (Omaha: Magic City, 1928); Albert Watkins, *History of Nebraska,* vol. 3 (Lincoln: Western Publishing and Engineering, 1913).

To Charles DeWitt O'Kieffe

Minneapolis, Minnesota

January 13, 1956

Dear Charles O'Kieffe:[1]

Your fine generous letter came in while I was away on a speaking trip from Chicago to Gordon and Scottsbluff Nebraska.

You *are* an authentic early Sheridan countyite. I recall the O'Kieffe name, particularly from the early files of the Rushville papers that I went through for *Old Jules*. I recall hearing about George O'Kieffe but I don't remember if I knew the Taylor family he married into. Was his wife a relative of Helen Taylor, who married Tommy Hare? Tommy came up in my visit with Pat Hooper when I was home two weeks ago. Tommy died early, but he was well-remembered by his fellow cowpunchers at the Spade [Ranch] when Pat rode for them.

I recall Clarence Mann and of course Johnny Jones. He went through a great deal of looking back for me in 1931 for the *Old Jules*. Afterward he laughed a little, admitting that he might not have spoken so frankly if he had realized that the girl who grew up barefoot on the Niobrara would really get the book published. Elmer Sturgeon, father's other fast friend is still alive; he was brought down to my brother Fritz's place December 28 to an open house given for me. He was in a wheel chair but still looked much the same as always. He was always a slight man, with pleasant manners, very mild. I see Judge Patterson's daughter now and then. She's married to a Greenslit in eastern Nebraska. Last year she sent me a painting Mrs. Asay made of some Sioux tipis. I was happy to have it. I recall Judge Westover and know some of the relatives in east Nebraska. I only saw Cody a few times although he was through our region very often in my childhood. The Gordon Community Chamber of Commerce gave a big dinner for me December 27, with people from all over the Panhandle there, and all my brothers and sisters. I saw people that I hadn't seen since I was five, six years old.

Yes, why don't you write the story of your life? Have you seen *Nothing But Prairie and Sky* by Bruce Siberts?[2] He didn't go west to the Dakotas until about 1890. You saw much more excitement, much more trying, and romantic, times.

To get your story started, why not try to put together a little of the Ghost Dance times and your herding cattle for Spring Lake [Ranch], or whatever else seems interesting to you? Just write it as it comes to you, plainly and as naturally as you would tell it. I'll be happy to look at it and perhaps make suggestions that are not to be taken too seriously, as you know. (I teach the advanced writing courses in the 8 weeks Writers Institute, University of Wisconsin, every summer.)

Perhaps you might like to join the New York Posse of *The Westerners*. I'm having the current issue of our quarterly sent to you and am enclosing a membership blank. No feelings hurt if you are not interested and in the meantime you will have a copy of the quarterly. There is a file of the publication at the Minneapolis Public Library, I suppose. Perhaps glancing over the articles, often first-hand accounts by nonwriters, will stimulate you to start on your memoirs or recollections.

I'm enclosing a preliminary map of the Old Jules country. You will have fun going over the region you once rode. If you are interested in the Sioux of Pine Ridge and the Cheyennes who broke out from Indian Territory in 1878, through west Nebraska, you might take a look at my *Crazy Horse* and *Cheyenne Autumn* at the library. I don't recommend them to you; they are hard reading, but they will carry you back to the old Indian region with just a glance into them, I think.

It was like hearing from a member of the family to receive your fine letter—

And may 1956 be a very fine one for you.

1. Charley O'Kieffe, *Western Story: The Recollections of Charley O'Kieffe, 1884–1898* (Lincoln: U of Nebraska P, 1960). O'Kieffe grew up near Rushville, Sheridan County, Nebraska, in the late 1800s. He consulted with Sandoz frequently during the writing.

2. Walker Wyman, from the notes of Bruce Siberts, *Nothing but Prairie and Sky* (Norman: U of Oklahoma P, 1954).

February 13, 1956

Dear Mr. O'Kieffe:

Your material is shaping up well. Go on as you have planned and begin to think of the material in scenes or incidents, each with a little beginning, middle and end. Or think of the book as a string of beads, each incident a bead, some smaller, some larger, some shining gold, or sky blue, some murky grey or dark as night. Or think of it as a row of marbles, well arranged, with agates and glassies, and between them, to set them off, those plain little glazed clay ones—what were they called?

But always remember to give the reader the story as it happened, by setting the scene, and characterizing the people. Let the reader see and hear, feel and smell it all. See notes on manuscript.

And best of luck,

To Ray Vickers

Wisconsin Rapids, Wisconsin

February 24, 1956

Dear Mr. Vickers:[1]

I am ashamed that your fine letter has been put aside so long. There was a speaking and autographing trip west as far as the edge of Wyoming, and since then the congestion of things that accumulated while I was away. There was also the back writing and the pressure to move my material to a less dangerous place. We not only lost our resident caretaker (the owner) but we have drunks around now who set the place afire. One was a big one, with water over everything, and I am afraid to be away at all, for fear I lose the accumulation of a lifetime of material, most of it irreplaceable.

I like your conviction that inspired writing has its drawbacks. It certainly does need whipping into shape later, for inspiration is usually a driving spurt of imagination, often without form or structure or any progression, perhaps.

The fact that you don't have the money to keep Miss Clyne at your work is not altogether a calamity. Services like hers are all right for mediocre writers but if she could operate on the imaginative level of your work she would be writing herself, not doing the rehash jobs that her work with writers demands, and for what is really pathetic sums, from the standpoint of a professional writer, or even a teacher of writing.

I suppose her sale of the $350 article to the AMERICAN JOURNAL WEEKLY is THE AMERICAN WEEKLY, the Sunday magazine section of the Hearst papers. They pay better than most such material commands but $350 sounds pretty high for the market. The articles must, of course, fit into the standards of Hearst readers, which is not your field, or mine.

Your novel of a blind young man sounds very promising because it comes out of material with which you have emotional identity. I look forward to seeing it this summer.

I've not done anything about getting any of my work into "Talking Books". *Miss Morissa* has gone into Braille. It's not a matter of money—I'm certain Talking Books go without royalties—but I don't feel that I want to push anything I write. I never do that!

The important thing for you, I think, is to get your feet set upon a path that makes the most of your rich imagination and your fine ear, with your sense of deep and subtle conflicts. Best of success to you.

1. Ray Vickers was a student in MS's summer fiction writing classes at the University of Wisconsin, Madison.

To Jesse Stuart

Riverton, Kentucky

March 31, 1956

Dear Jesse Stuart:[1]

By this time you will have heard from Ed Aswell and everything is truly fine. I know how Ed is. Although he is one of the few real gentlemen in the publishing business, one could wish he moved faster. Not that he can't, when necessary, but he can put off decisions for months and months. In the meantime you have at least one impatient reader. I gathered from Ed that this book was written during a slow recovery from an illness.[2] From his comments about it, I judge that your fine humor and humanity are all there, and a fine contemplative spirit.

No, I don't live in New York. I'm out all summer and most of the springs and falls too. I moved some of my files here during the war, when I put in time in home-front propaganda work, and somehow Denver never got uncrowded enough for me to return there. You are wise to stay right down in Kentucky, where you can feel that you are living as time passes, as well as writing. I count the time spent in New York as just so much lost from life.

I think we have convinced the University administration that the *Prairie Schooner* is worth the small investment from the appropriations. I don't need to tell you that it's always a struggle to talk down the pragmatic boys. Of course [Lowry] Wimberly's health is bad and may perhaps get no better, but certainly letting the *Schooner* die before his eyes would not have helped much.

I have always looked upon you as a friend, and I wish you complete restoration in body and spirit with the spring time. You know what the ranchers used to say, "If my cows make it to grass — "

Sincerely,

1. Jesse Stuart (1907–84), a novelist, teacher, farmer, and poet laureate of Kentucky, shared a concern for conservation with MS.

2. MS is probably referring to Stuart's *Plowshare in Heaven: Stories* (New York: McGraw Hill, 1958).

To the Reverend Father Peter J. Powell

August 25, 1956

Dear Father Powell:

It was fine to visit with you out at the lake front, and about Indians, at that. And thank you for the photographs. I'm glad to know that the Little Finger Nail picture book has been labeled Cheyenne.[1] The last time I looked it was still called Sioux.

About the Cheyenne delegation picture: I'll check on the list the next time I get to my Cheyenne material. All are conspicuous and familiar faces, and I shouldn't have much trouble when I dig into my files, and my mind. The one on the right with the leaf pattern at his waist is plainly not full blood Cheyenne, or else this is not his piece of adornment. Either he is part white, or of some tribe that took on what we call floral patterns. In fact, his regalia is such a conglomeration I wonder if he didn't do a lot of borrowing for this picture. The two men center and right in the back look like some of the Carlisle graduates. All are as familiar to me as old neighbors but I've been thinking in terms of novels and of cattle. (Incidentally, my *Horsecatcher* has been put off from Oct. 15 to March because the *Readers Digest* has taken an option on it.[2] If they buy it, Indians will get a lot of sympathetic publicity.)

I trust that your trip to Sheridan, etc., proved very interesting and profitable. I'm particularly anxious to have you make contact with the Keeper of the Sacred Hat, and others of the few mystics that remain.

Thank you again,

1. The Little Finger Nail book was a ledger book filled with drawings a Cheyenne Indian had made of events occurring during the Cheyennes' attempt to return from Oklahoma to their old home in Montana, 1878–79. Little Finger Nail was killed by soldiers near Fort Robinson in January 1879. The book later was given to the American Museum of Natural History but was mislabeled.

2. *The Horsecatcher* (Philadelphia: Westminster, 1957). *Reader's Digest Condensed Books* also published it in 1957.

To William E. Lemons

August 25, 1956

Dear Mr. Lemons:

Thank you for the very generous things you say of CHEYENNE AUTUMN and CRAZY HORSE. I put in as much explanatory note material as the publishers will permit. There's always the double complaint of high cost and possible antagonizing potential buyers. Books with notes or other explanatory material are said to seem too formidable to the average book buyer.

I suppose your friend Frederick Manfred (I am always stopped by that name. I much preferred his Dutch one [Feike Feikema]) has run into the same complaints from publishers. It's a difficult battle for the writer.[1]

Your enumeration of the cultural achievements of the American Indian in his native state seems a very fine one to me. It reminds me of my Harvard-bred editor at Knopfs. He remarked in astonishment: "But this Crazy Horse—I should say he was a man of superior culture!" A great deal for an easterner of this editor's back-ground to admit. You, much closer to the Indian in time and region, have a better opportunity for a discerning view. Still you are very exceptional in your appreciation of the meaning the Indian's way of life could have had, and still have, for us. I remember the first time I ran into the Greek idea of "the bit of mind stuff" that each human being was supposed to have and which, on death, returned to the great pool. It sounded so very much like the Plains Indian's idea of the spirit and of immortality before the white man pushed the phrase "Happy Hunting Ground" upon him.

I was out not too far from your region until last Saturday. I teach the advanced novel writing course in the 8 weeks Writers Institute, University of Wisconsin, every summer. Incidentally, are you of the same original stock as the Lemmon family of Nebraska and South Dakota?

Sincerely,

1. Frederick Manfred (b. 1912), a western writer, named his geographical focus—Iowa, Minnesota, and the Dakotas—Siouxland. His work includes farm novels with strong autobiographical overtones, such as *The Golden Bowl* (St. Paul: Webb, 1944), *This Is the Year* (Garden City: Doubleday, 1947), and *The Chokecherry Tree* (Garden City: Doubleday, 1948), as well as historical novels focusing on both Indians and whites, such as *Lord Grizzly* (New York: McGraw Hill, 1954) and *Riders of Judgment* (New York: Random House, 1957). His first seven books were published under his Frisian name, Feike Feikema, which he changed in 1954.

To Polly Richardson

September 15, 1956

Dear Polly Richardson:

I am happy to meet the sister of Tom Spence and the daughter of Karl Spence—the man whose independence, initiative and goodness of heart so many admired. . . .[1]

Of course you have to enumerate your qualifications, otherwise how could anyone know what you can do? There must be dozens of writers looking for just your admirable set of qualifications. Unfortunately I don't run a permanent establishment. I'm here one week, gone for three, four months, perhaps from Washington, D.C., to the Rio Grande and north to the Cache la Poudre and around by Topeka, of necessity having to change my plans as material or a possible source of material comes up. My research is, of course, *never* delegated. Only one with my lifetime in my work could analyze, understand and evaluate any bit of information for my work. I always work far beyond the fringes of the findings of others. I am just back from 2 days in the War Records of Old Fort Davis, Texas, double-checking some material for my cattle book.

I don't ever eat at home, and while all the world is looking for fine bakers of homemade bread, rolls and pastry, I value my waistline more than all the tasty food, and with it the alertness that, I hope, leanness of body brings. I do have a part time typist—the husband of a poet friend of mine originally from Omaha, and there are several others always available if needed. These all have other jobs and do not suffer if I am gone 4–5 months at a time.

But this should not discourage you. Your combination of talents is not common. If you want to get out of the Panhandle, you might try an ad in the *Saturday Review* (See the "Personals" on the enclosed page.) This is, as you know, read all over the country, particularly in the east here, the Chicago region and the southwest.

And may you have the very best of success.

1. Karl Spence, from Crawford, Nebraska, was a newspaperman, as was his son Tom. Polly Richardson later worked for MS as her secretary.

To Karl Shapiro

University of Nebraska Press

September 15, 1956

Dear Karl Shapiro:[1]

Of course I remember you and your charming wife from Wisconsin but I knew your poetry long before that. In fact we put your name on the list the fall before you came — as a promising man for the Writers Institute.

Yes, I knew you were at Nebraska. In addition, I saw Mrs. Shapiro a moment at the Cornhusker at breakfast time with Emily [Schossberger] when I was in Lincoln last May.[2]

I am very sorry that Dr. Wimberly couldn't bring out the 30th anniversary [*Prairie Schooner*] issue. It would have been such a nice rounding out of the years. But he has been ill a long time. I am happy to note that you will continue to stress fiction. The way most of the literary magazines have turned from creative work to almost complete concern with criticism, often with a strong coterie tinge, and too often what seems over-precious, disturbs me. In the meantime there is less and less space for writing on an artistic level.

Certainly I should not have bothered to take the time from my writing to help save the SCHOONER last year if I had expected it to become less a publishing ground for serious poetry and fiction. I hoped that the magazine could be made more receptive to the young writer with something special to say, or a special way of saying it. Of course, the writer from Nebraska or that part of the midwest and the High Plains, and work on the region, should be considered on a par with that of other writers and other regions. I have never, however, been much interested in regional literature *per se*. There must always, I think, be something universal in every piece of writing worth the time of a serious writer. Outside of a few short pieces for magazines, I've never bothered with regional material on that basis alone. (This, incidentally, is the reason that I'm not enthusiastic about Emily's selections from my work for the Nebraska volume. I don't think the selections could have been more diminuting.)[3]

About the piece for the winter issue of the SCHOONER: I'm four months behind on a book deadline, which is pushing the other three under contract back past their planned publication dates. All I could send you would be some section from the autobiographical accumulations I've been making for one of my editors, and I can't think of anything that seems suitable.

What do you think? It would have to be a sort of personal narrative, probably of some character who influenced me one way or another — at least enough to get into my files.[4]

I trust you are happy in Lincoln. The town used to be a trifle chilly to newcomers but it has changed considerably through the influx of new ideas the last fifteen years. Basically the people are good to know over the long stretch. Generally I prefer the Nebraskans from west of the 100th Meridian — there is less concern with the small out there where the horizons are far away, but Lincolnites can't be beat for loyalty and consistency — or so it seems to me.

October will be fine in Nebraska. Look at the blue sky of it once for me.

1. Karl Shapiro (b. 1913) a poet and professor, was editor of *Poetry* from 1950 to 1956, and editor of *PrS* from 1956 to 1966.

2. Emily Schossberger (b. 1908) was the editor of the University of Nebraska Press, 1941–58.

3. *Roundup: A Nebraska Reader,* comp. and ed. Virginia Faulkner (Lincoln: U of Nebraska P, 1957). Some of the selections were chosen by Emily Schossberger. MS was represented by "Wife of Old Jules" and "Sandhill Sundays."

4. "The Neighbor," *PrS* 30.4 (Winter 1956).

To Roger T. Grange, Jr.

Curator, Fort Robinson [Historical] Museum
Fort Robinson, Nebr.

November 3, 1956

Dear Mr. Grange:

Bertrand Schultz writes me they intend to use the Old Jules bear trap in a bear exhibit in their museum up at Robinson, so that's that.

I'm sorry to hear that Robinson material was destroyed in WWII. In 1930 Captain Ginsburg took Eleanor Hinman and me through the basement of the post HQ, stacked with the post records. Not organized, merely accumulated. By the time I got to the final work on the CRAZY HORSE this material, I was informed, had been "transferred." I found most of the letter books and a great accumulation of documents from the post in the AGO records over on Virginia Avenue, Washington (this was before the National Archives building). The Letterbooks of 1876, as I recall now, were at Fort Crook. You probably have these by now. An interesting item are the General Crook letters that were in the hands of an Omahan, whose name I never knew, that were loaned to me in confidence back about 1939. These included very frank expressions of Crook's disgust with the government's failure to keep so many of the promises he was ordered to make to the Indians, particularly the Sioux and Cheyennes.

My sister Flora wrote me a good account of what you are doing up at Robinson. I am very happy to hear of all this. I'll send the Little Finger Nail material when I get it together. You really should have a complete set of prints of the whole book. I suppose that you have a picture of the Red Bird shield, with its close tie to the Robinson locale.[1]

Best wishes,

1. MS writes of the Red Bird shield in *Cheyenne Autumn,* 196, 205, 244. When the Cheyenne Indians, incarcerated in the barracks at Fort Robinson, Nebraska, attempted to escape in January 1879, one of the warriors, Great Eyes, entrusted care of the shield, a family heirloom, to his nephew, Red Bird, aged thirteen. The boy survived the outbreak and saved the shield. It later became a museum exhibit in the East.

To Pat Hooper

January 19, 1957

Dear Pat:

I hope you are feeling your usual self again and that the new year is well started for both you and Julia and all the relatives.

Thank you very much for your recollections on points that will be useful to me in the cattle book, and the later one on Nebraska. I'm returning your copy of the 1884 Roundups. You may want it sometime and I have a copy in my Roundup collection, which covers many of the outstanding years from the Concho in Texas up into Canada. But there are still holes in it, and I'm happy for a look at any I can see.

I'll honor your request not to say much about the Hoopers. In fact there's not room for thousands of people who contributed to the growth of the cattle business.

I'm interested in your name for the brand Bartlett Richards brought down from the White river. The ranch, and often the brand, was called the Three Crow, because there was a third "crow" on lower hind quarter in addition to the two on the side.

According to the material in the museum at Canyon, Texas, the 101 out in the far western section of old No Man's Land had no connection with the

Miller 101 ranch at Ponca, Oklahoma. Rister in his NO MAN'S LAND[1] makes the same statement and there is no mention of any northern connection in the daughter's book of Zack Miller's old 101. The No Man's Land 101 ranch was running around 20,000 head of cattle there in 1883. I'm interested to know that their manager was Allen. Could this have been R. N. (Dick) Allen? In the Johnson County War time he was named as a short-time manager of the Western Union Beef Company, was in the attack on the KC and in the retreat to the TA ranch but left before they were surrounded to get word of their plight out to Cheyenne, etc. He seems to have been manager for a while of the Standard Cattle Company in the hills. I heard that he had bodyguards, but I didn't have their names. Most of those in the attack on the KC had bodyguards for years afterward. Billy Irvine, president of the 1884 Roundups, had one for years.

Yes, the Phil DuFran I'm trying to trace from 1873 to 1900 was the one in the 1884 roundups, and was stock detective in Wyoming for some years. He was arrested as an accomplice of the Olives down in Custer County, Nebraska, in 1878, went to Wyoming, apparently ran a saloon in the Big Horn Basin a while, and much later had one at LeBeau on the Missouri around 1904–5, etc. Curious character—always on fairly friendly terms with everybody, and in on about everything that happened from Kansas to the Yellowstone and the Missouri from around 1875 to 1905.

I'm certain you knew the two men I mean in Cherry County, or at least knew of them—Copsey or Popsey—down toward Brownlee. They were the talk of the region in my childhood because of their mysterious actions and their rumored connection with the Wyoming cattle war, 1889–92. One of them used to tell me bits about it. You probably knew them under other names. So far as I know they had no connection at all with the Jason Cole family. The Senator says he knows of none.

Yes, the Tate name is connected with what ranch bookkeepers called the "Protection Accounts," from Texas north. I have half a dozen of the name in my files, some probably duplicates of other first names.

I didn't know your father bought Texas cattle from Bratt. I have Bratt's book, a valuable cattleman account of the times.[2]

I suppose the Billy the Bear you mention as lost in the sandhills may be the same Billy, last name Iager or Yeager, who lived around Chadron for years after getting lost in a blizzard and having his feet and, I think, part of his fingers amputated.

About George West: Do you recall whether the one you knew about was an Englishman? I'm trying to decide whether the one in the sandhills was the same man as the West in Live Oak County, Texas who sold cattle to the XIT when they were stocking up the Capitol Lands in west Texas, and who tried to shoot his way through the Kansas State quarantine against Texas fever.

Incidently, in the records of the Sweetwater and Childress region down in the Texas History Center at Austin, I ran into some references to the Mericks. They were evidently pretty nice people down there too, which wasn't always true of some of the early Texans who moved north, as you know.

Well, I've taken enough of your time. I do thank you, and if something more occurs to you I should be happy to have it.

Sincerely,

1. Carl Coke Rister, *No Man's Land* (Norman: U of Oklahoma P, 1948).
2. John Bratt, *Trails of Yesterday* (Chicago: University Publishing Co., 1921).

To Eugene W. Horse

Pine Ridge, S. Dak.

February 9, 1957

Dear Mr. Horse:

So you are a grandson of Sitting Bull the Oglala, Sitting Bull the Good? I don't have to tell you that you come of a very fine family. The Little Wound family was famous for courage and honor, and your grandfather was the personification of both of these virtues.

As you may know, most white men, including western historians, made one man of your grandfather and the Hunkpapa Sitting Bull. In fact the gift rifle, which came to the Heye Foundation in the General Miles Collection, was labeled as the Hunkpapa's gun when I discovered it. I had been trying to trace the gun for some years, and while He Dog as well as other Oglalas told me the gun was lost to the Crows, and Miles' report to Washington indicated that he had the Crows disarmed, the gun disappeared, under the mislabeling. But I knew it the instant I saw it. The gun is on display now, properly credited, for the hundreds of thousands who come through the museum.[1]

For years I answered queries about the contradictions in the character of Sitting Bull made of the two men. Finally I put some of the evidence together and sold it to *Blue Book,* published in the November 1949 issue.[2] I don't know where you can obtain a copy. I have only the one in my files. Perhaps a letter to *Blue Book,* 230 Park Ave., New York, N.Y., might get you a copy if any remain, if you tell them who you are. Surely there is a copy at the South

Dakota Historical Society. I sent several copies to Pine Ridge in 1949, one, I think, to John Colhoff and one to the library of the Oglala boarding school there. But 1949 is long ago, and *Blue Book* is published on poor paper. . . .

I made a comparative map at the time, showing where the two men were at crucial dates from 1862 to the Good's death December 1876, but this *Blue Book* did not publish. Do you have a good photograph of your grandfather? I have a good one of him with Red Cloud and Spotted Tail etc., taken at Omaha on the way to Washington. The negative is in the Nebraska State Historical Society, Lincoln, Nebraska. There are several others in existence, when he was still called Drum Packer.

Sincerely,

1. The Museum of the American Indian, New York City.
2. "There Were Two Sitting Bulls," *Blue Book,* November 1949.

To Ronald Baxter

March 23, 1957

Dear Captain Baxter:

Your life sounds mighty interesting, and particularly when one considers that you are a grandson of old Henry Born, who was apparently a quiet, polite young German when he hit the west.

I'm happy that you liked THE BUFFALO HUNTERS. There is more about Custer in my Indian books, CRAZY HORSE and CHEYENNE AUTUMN, particularly the latter.

About one of your grandfather, Dutch Henry Born, see CHARLES GOODNIGHT by J. Evetts Haley, pp 287–88, 335–6. You will find a sort of synopsis of Henry Born's life on the Plains as one man estimated it. Also see W. E. Payne's "Dutch Henry's Raid near Ft. Elliott," *Frontier Times,* Jan 1924, pp 24–27, and skim through *Far West* etc.[1] Apparently he was a trooper with Custer in 1867. The War Records, National Archives, Washington, D.C., can check this for you if you haven't the information. This was during that bad march over north Kansas and to the Platte. The records should also show if he was merely a hired scout. My material on this is in storage and not available now.

See also QUEEN OF THE COW TOWNS, DODGE CITY by Stanley Vestal, pp 184, 206–8, and some of the [Charles] Siringo writings. There are, of course, hundreds of references to Dutch Henry, not all actually to Henry Born or Borne or Bohrn (for there was another man sometimes mixed up with Henry Born). I couldn't possibly have all my references copied out for you, even if there weren't the fact that material which is not available to other researchers, such as manuscripts, letters, etc., in private hands, and personal interview material is a matter of private property. Some of the Dutch Henry material was given me in strict confidence. Anyway you probably have most of it, and there is probably much more available to you. Have you looked through the index of the Kansas Historical Society Publications? Your public library can borrow many sources for you at the cost of transportation both ways from libraries that have it, etc.

Have you written to Sylvester Vigilante, now at the New York Historical Society, 77th Street & Central Park West, New York, N.Y.? He's the world's expert on western bad men, which include Dutch Henry because of his apparent Indian horse running activities. Apparently one of the Dutch Henrys was killed, and I don't think anyone knows for certain just how much of the outlaw activities belonged to each. That should be an interesting project for you. But remember that chattel rights were pretty loose and fluid in those days, even with the most honest of people.

Sincerely,

1. MS may be referring to Edmund Flagg, *Far West: A Tour beyond the Mountains* (Cleveland: A. H. Clark, 1906).

To Mary Abbot

April 5, 1957

Dear Mary:

Here's Walter Frese's copy of most of THE CATTLEMEN. The first seven chapters are next-to-last rewrite, the following chapters, on the yellow paper, will have to have much recasting and rewriting. The last chapter is in process of another revision and so marked up that only I can read it, so I'm not including that, only a very terse paragraph of what it will contain.

I think this whole idea of having me turn in an uncompleted manuscript is a fatal one. It's like pulling up a radish to see how it's growing. Under *no* circumstances will I ever do this again.

And do impress on Walter that I am coming up to get the yellow sections April 22.

Sincerely,

The carbon of the first chapters (the seven) is for your office, in case someone wants to glance into it before you get the carbon of the finished product.

To Donald Danker, Archivist

Nebraska State Historical Society

May 25, 1957

Dear Donald Danker:

About the Custer material Marguerite Merington has:

I've tried to run down some possible lead to a New York address for Mrs. Merington but everyone tells me that her home is apparently still Michigan and that if she's in New York it's only temporarily. In 1950, as you will know, Devin-Adair Co., New York, published her THE CUSTER STORY, the Life and Intimate Letters of General George A. Custer and his wife Elizabeth, edited by Marguerite Merington. Have you tried reaching her through the publisher? Devin is pretty unbusinesslike, as many semi-religious houses are, but they should be able to forward a letter. Mrs. Merington's book is interesting but flawed, I think, by her neglect to check dates and other factual statements. . . .

I should be happy to write some letters about this for you, but, of course, the hipped Custerites have little use for me. For them one must swallow the legend whole. You, uninvolved in the very tedious attempt by Mrs. Custer and Custer's idolators to keep anyone from going into the Custer material at all beyond what they want to dole out, should be able to get any material that has, for some perhaps deeply involved reason, escaped the avid Custer collectors.

I wish you luck,

To Virginia Faulkner

University of Nebraska Press

June 15, 1957

Dear Virginia:[1]

With the pressure of three books upon me, a dozen recommendations for candidates seeking various fellowships, and a talk on Indians to the Strawberry Festival for the New York Historical Society, my reply to your letter of June 3 has been sadly neglected.

You have done a lot of serious work on the project and for this I am grateful.[2] I might have spared you some of the searching. I have copies of all that you have not been able to locate.

Frankly, I still feel dubious about the project. First, if I wanted just my short stories published, this could have been done in paperback several years ago, and then the "Mist and the Tall White Tower," one of the few of my published stories that seems worth perpetuation, would have been included. I see the wisdom of your excluding this for the University of Nebraska Press, but so few of my more creative short stories were ever published that I dislike losing one of any merit. Most of my better stories were too *avant garde* for even the *Dial* in the middle Twenties. Now the only two that I didn't burn back in 1933 (when I tried to put all the writing business behind me, once and for all) sound like echoes of the experimental writing of the 1928–1935 period.

The only purpose I can see in an anthology of my writing would be to make the research articles available to the general public—pieces like "There Were Two Sitting Bulls." . . . Such articles, it seems to me, should be made available to the public, even if there is no creative historical vision in them, and some day these will be republished, preferably by some historical association or group. I do see the artistic unity in your plan for the short stories only, but I never thought they justified republishing—not even in paperback.

I regret all your effort. If I could have had a word with you in Lincoln you could have been spared a lot of work.

Sincerely,

1. Virginia Faulkner (1913–80), assistant editor at the University of Nebraska Press in 1957, was later editor-in-chief. Originally from Lincoln, she was a successful author, magazine editor, and screenwriter in New York and Hollywood before returning to Lincoln at a time when the future of the press was in doubt.

2. The project, Faulkner's suggestion to help the press's economic situation, was a collection of MS's short works. Faulkner edited the material that resulted in *Hostiles and Friendlies* (Lincoln: U of Nebraska P, 1959).

August 8, 1957

Dear Virginia:

The "Report" on my short writings came in this morning. I've just glanced over it with my coffee at the drug store. You have done an appalling amount of work and brought, so far as I can see now, some coherence and sense to the hodge-podge.

I am also struck again with the inadequacy of my short writings as any gauge to me as a writer, or at least I hope so. Certainly the writer of these pieces had no business giving up all the usual things in life for a career that produced only such results.

My immediate reaction was to drag down a box of old pieces, most of them discarded long before they got into any set form, for something that would give a little body to the volume you are planning so loyally. The only thing that could be called usable by any far jump would be the enclosed THE SMART MAN. This dates from the late 1920's and was out when I burned the rest. I don't think I would have burned it anyway, because it was not of the mood of the Twenties so far as my writing went; not entirely. It was a sort of transition stage into the OLD JULES. I once started to take a little of the Twenties out of it for some editor who had asked for something at a lit'ry tea. Yale Review, as I recall now. The softening of the bleak prose was not his idea so much as mine. Of course I never finished it. Nor did I ever do anything with FEARBITTEN, the story that was the honorable mention one in Harper's Intercollegiate Contest, 1925 or 1926. But that's not here. It's in storage. Further, it would require a lot of revision because in all the attempts to do what the Atlantic wanted done, all through the 1920's, I lost my original pretty good version entirely.

Anyway, look this over a bit.

Another thing: I have carbons of a lot of the stories you mention would have to be typed for real consideration and the printers. You can have these. But if we get together on this I want to do a little glancing over *everything*.

About the rights and copyrights; I have most of them in my safe deposit box here. I keep these things up as much as I can. Magazines die, and then there's trouble. I even have the rights to Sitting Bull; things as recent as that—

You've been noble—

To Jay Monaghan

December 16, 1957

Dear Jay Monaghan:[1]

Please forgive the delay in this reply to your letter. I was caught in a last minute rush to get my cattle book in, and I just had to leave my mail unopened. One writes books or answers correspondence—

Most of my Custer references are out west in storage but the enclosed may be of some help to you. Much of the personal material on Custer and other individuals that I ran into in the piles and bales of records from the dismantled frontier posts gathered over on Virginia Avenue, Washington, was classified when it was moved into the National Archives in 1940 or there abouts. I know that I've not been able to get another look at much of this, even though I had notes on the documents and the document numbers in many cases. I was told, as others were "No such material can be located." Time after time I've been left looking like a liar. Now the Moss Subcommittee is bringing out what happened to this material and much that I'm certain I never saw. Material that none of us know anything about. But I got what was important to me: Custer's relationship to the Cheyennes, etc. and the relationships of several other men to the western scene through their personal life.

I suppose you saw the report on the Moss investigations, but another reference won't harm you. I'm also enclosing a list (roughly done, in haste) of my sources on Custer and the mother of Yellow Swallow, so far as I could make it from the material available here.

Thanks for the kind words on my books. There are really so few of us who try to get at the truth of the West—

Happy holidays to all the Monaghans, and every power to your willing arm. There's a really fine study for you in Custer.

1. Jay Monaghan (1891–1981), historian, sheep rancher, and teacher, edited and wrote books on the American West, including *Custer: The Life of General George Armstrong Custer* (Boston: Little, Brown, 1959).

To Photographic Department,

SATURDAY EVENING POST

January 20, 1958

Gentlemen:

After the call from your department this afternoon I've decided to send you a short bibliography of material on "The Man Burner" I. P. Olive, called Print.[1]

1. DOCUMENTS IN APPEAL FOR CHANGE OF VENUE, Records, District Court, 5th Judicial Dist, State of Nebraska State Historical Society Archives. Most important single body of material, including depositions of all the important individuals involved, including Phil DuFran and Bion Brown, etc. giving story from beginning through the burning of men, and what followed, including the bribery attempts, the plans for killing officials, etc, with Texas background material.

2. OLIVE'S LAST ROUNDUP, by A. O. Jenkins, Loup City, Nebr., pamphlet, printed by Sherman Co, Nebr. *Times*. 1930
3. BOOK OF FACTS, concerning the Early Settlement of Sherman County Nebr., by Geo. E. Benschoter, Loup City, Northwestern Print, Loup City, Nebr. 76 pp, (apptly published 1897).
4. PIONEER HISTORY OF CUSTER COUNTY, S. D. Butcher, Broken Bow, Nebraska, 1901. From this come the pictures of Print Olive and Frederick Fisher in prison hair cuts, also picture of burnt bodies of Ketchum and Mitchell. (Note that bodies are misnamed. The one with leg cut off and arm burned is Mitchell, big, young body is Ketchum.) Posed pictures I sent in also come from this volume, as does the photo of first Custer County Courthouse.
5. Nebraska newspapers of 1878 through 1886 covering the killing of Print Olive, including Omaha Daily *Bee*, Grand Island *Independent*, six North Platte papers, of varying names during the period.
6. SNYDER PAPERS, J. W. and Dudley, Library, University of Texas, Texas History Center. HISTORY OF WILLIAMSON COUNTY, MA Thesis, Walton Hinds, Georgetown, Texas. Texas History Center WILLIAMSON COUNTY and related regions, Scrapbooks, Texas History center.
7. NO MAN'S LAND, Carl Coke Rister, Norman, Oklahoma, University of Oklahoma Press, 1948, for death of Bill Olive, son of I. P., Print, Olive.

Much of my material, and the checking on the holes in the above sources, and light on the contradictions comes from survivors of the man-burning period. Judge Goss[2] and Judge Bayard H. Paine, Supreme Court of Nebraska, both made considerable study of the Olive case, and gave me lengthy interviews on this. Judge Paine went to the Hastings trial as a small boy and saw the tents of the militia there to uphold the power of the court.

I am enclosing a photograph purporting to be of I. P. Olive in 1878, as you will note on the face of the print. This was given to the Nebraska State Historical Society by Robert Farriter of Broken Bow, Nebraska. I doubt the authenticity of this. First because Bob Farriter in his material has most of the dates wrong, even of the actual killing and the trial—the dates that are documented beyond a doubt. He also has the Olive family all mixed up. Further, I don't think either the accoutrements or the photography are of 1878 but much more recent. I asked Mr. Farriter for more information about the picture, pointing out that no ordinary trail outfit carried so much canvas, most of them nothing beyond bed rolls and perhaps a Sibley tent for the boss and his books. The man on the horse looks too young for I. P. Olive in 1878 and I wonder about the objects over toward the far river. They look like tile for culverts or irrigation and drainage to me. I suspect that the outfit is a road or drainage crew. The man does look like the Olive family, of whom I've seen several members, but I can't accept this as Print without more information. The hat, the chaps, etc., date it around 1886–1890 or later for me, depending upon when the items were purchased.

There is one more person who might be able to help you obtain photographs, Mrs. Grace Barmore, wife of the druggist at Lexington, Nebraska. She knows many of the old timers, is interested in the region. Lexington was Plum Creek in the Olive days, and changed its name later, partly to get away from the stigma of Olive Town.

Good Luck—

If Frank Johnson doesn't send you the Butcher [book] and you want to borrow my copy I'll lend it to you.[3]

1. *SEP* was preparing to publish "Tyrant of the Plains" (June 7, 1958), an adaptation of a section of *The Cattlemen* (New York: Hastings House, 1958). This list indicates the variety of sources MS would evaluate in addition to personal interviews and examinations of the actual sites.

2. Judge Charles Albert Goss (1863–1938) was chief justice of the Nebraska Supreme Court from 1926 until his death. He was noted for his research on judicial matters.

3. Frank Johnson (1897–1973), University of Nebraska regent and lawyer, was a Cozad native and practiced law in Lexington. He was particularly interested in the John J. Cozad story and gave MS considerable information about local history; he provided some of the photographs for the *SEP* article.

To Ralph Knight, Associate Editor

THE SATURDAY EVENING POST

February 4, 1958.

Dear Ralph Knight:

Please forgive the delay in my reply to your letter of January 27. I finally had to hide out to select the final minimal bibliography and body of notes for the CATTLEMEN.

About something to interest your readers: Even a bit is going to be difficult to scare up. Home life, as such, scarcely exists for me. Although I consider the sandhills of Nebraska my home and take great delight in my brothers and sisters and their homes and families, I usually have an apartment somewhere as a base of operations, at Lincoln, say, or Denver, or, the last years, in New York. Some place for the files of any particular work I'm doing. The rest of my files and notes are usually in storage out in Lincoln or Denver.

Often I'm in hotels four, five months at a time, Austin, Canyon, Texas, perhaps, or Dodge City, Topeka, Denver, Cheyenne, Laramie, or the old Crescent Hotel at Sheridan, Wyoming, or perhaps a tent on an Indian Reservation. I'm always at the Cornhusker at Lincoln for some time each year. Nine summers I spent at the University of Wisconsin. It's fun but it's not home life.

My hobbies are as unsatisfactory from your point of view. I have two compelling interests outside of my region — the Plains. One is avant garde writing, the experimental work of young writers or older ones who are somehow suddenly revitalized. Out of the experimental work of one generation often come the great writers the next generation adulates. The other interest is in art, avant garde too, from the wildest things one sees here, to the most slavishly representative or primitive tacked up in some cow country lunch room, the product of some old rancher or ranch hand. And after all [Jackson] Pollock was from the cow country once too —

As for my plans — I hope to fulfill my commitments to my four publishers, complete the rest of my Plains series and indulge my impractical dream — own a helicopter. I should like to go hovering over the Great Plains, spying out long lost historical sites. With a roll of maps, a camera, a pad of paper and a little shovel for a bit of digging I could have a wonderful time.

My, this all sounds so dull.

Sorry,

To Julia Luker

February 8, 1958

Dear Miss Luker:

I appreciate your kind letter about the *Horsecatcher*. I suppose that you read the story in the Readers Digest Condensed *Books*. In the full volume there is the following dedication:

Dedicated to the two great Cheyennes named Elk River, both council chiefs and peace men, one Keeper of the Sacred Arrows of the Cheyenne Indians, the other the greatest horsecatcher of all the High Plains.

Although Elk River (from the day when the Cheyennes first saw the Yellowstone, around 180–200 years ago, with so many Elk that they called the stream Elk River) has been a common name among them, there have been these two very prominent men, and since then their descendants or relatives that took their names. The horsecatcher of the dedication was a man of non-violence who became a chief, but for his wisdom and his honorable way, his great protectiveness toward the people, and his wonderful way with horses. Of course the one who became Arrow Keeper was also a man of non-violence by the time he became Keeper, and had to have the respect and admiration of the people. That Elk River was Keeper only one year and died, it seems, of some of the herbs the Arrow rituals demanded that he hold in his mouth. He swallowed the herb and died. He was remembered by many of his name. As keeper of the Arrows he followed Grey (White) Thunder, who was killed in the fight with the Kiowas much as the story is told in the *Horsecatcher*. The book is placed into the actual tribal history. You will find much of this in Grinnell's *Fighting Cheyennes,* reissued by the University of Oklahoma Press last year, but unfortunately with misnamed photographs. Grinnell knew that there were no photos that he could be certain were correctly identified.

Have you written up your Indian teaching days. Flora Gregg Iliff did in her *People of the Blue Water,* which I enjoyed.[1]

And thank you,

1. Flora Gregg Iliff, *People of the Blue Water: My Adventures among the Walapai and Havasupai Indians* (New York: Harper, 1954).

To Virginia Faulkner

February 16, 1958

Dear Virginia:

I'm sorry to hear that Emily [Schossberger] is leaving the Press, but certainly the Chicago job will be a much better one, particularly if my suspicions that things are getting worse at Nebraska are justified. I hope that you find you can make yourself stay, but I realize that you have your own writing to consider.

About the queries in your January 22 communication: (I let this get into the boxes of accumulated back correspondence. If you hadn't mentioned it, the matter might not have come to my eye for months, maybe years. I'm far behind in correspondence.)

Tentative title: seems fine to me.[1]

Contents: I see no place for suggestions. The groupings you work out seem fine to me.

The idea of a running commentary of "pertinent and enriching information" seems good to me.

The list of inclusions is all right. I guess I'll just not look into the *Bone Joe* piece and let you use it. I haven't the time to clear up the bad cutting in the Spike Eared Dog piece, and I don't want it used as it stands. Further, it hasn't much real substance at the best. So use the Bone Joe, if you want it.

Illustrations: Your suggestions seem good to me. If you want to use the funeral procession of Crazy Horse*, do credit it to *Frank Leslie's Illustrated Newspaper,* Oct. 13, 1877. I haven't much luck getting the *Westerners,* of the New York Posse, to abide by such rudimentary historical practices. (The funeral procession illustrates the complete ignorance of eastern artists about the accoutrements of the Sioux or their appearance. The horse wouldn't have a white-man's bridle, the mourners would be in tatters of mourning, the travoix is wrong, the saddle is wrong, etc. But that's not your problem.)

Have the photo pages grouped if you wish. That's become standard practice in these days of high production costs.

Author's revisions. Yes, I shall want to do this. Preferably here, with my index to my information, but I can do this out in Nebraska when I'm out there in May, if this is all right. . . .

Foreword: I'm against having one from the outside. I stood against this on the *Old Jules* and have never had any reason to regret my decision. Forewords from the outside are for newcomers to the field, for posthumous explanations and for people venturing into a field in which they are very definitely not expert. I maintain that so long as I am alive none of these hold. I do not consider [A. B.] Guthrie, [Walter Van Tilburg] Clark, or any one else you might name anything like the expert that I am in my field. [Wallace] Stegner is out too. He's a friend of mine and I wouldn't put him into such a difficult position, even if I approved of a contributed foreword. [Stanley] Vestal is dead, but nobody that I know would consider him an expert in my field. He never discovered that there were two Sitting Bulls until I pointed it out to him. He wrote the Hunkpapa's biography on a Guggenheim and never got much farther than to write me that there were certain discrepancies in the material, so far as I recall now. He was amazed when the story came out in

Blue Book; told me so. Etc. None of these people except Stegner works until he has everything he can possibly scare up, no matter what happens to his good story.

Publication date: At the present the schedule for my books goes like this: *The Cattlemen,* May 19, 1958; *Son of the Gamblin' Man,* not before fall 1959, if then; Harpers book on Nebraska, not before 1961. I got far behind, and am getting farther behind all the time.

Is that all you need to know now? I should like to work on the publishing of the work here, if it comes to that.

Sincerely,

*I have a glossy print of this if you wish to borrow it.

1. MS is discussing publication of *Hostiles and Friendlies.*

To Stuart Rose

February 20, 1958

Dear Stuart Rose:

Frederick Manfred (Feike Feikema) was in yesterday for a little visiting and to report how the winter is going in Minnesota. He spoke of the impending completion of three novelettes that everyone seems to like. I asked him about the subjects and treatment of these and it seemed to me that there is a chance you might like to see one of them, "Arrow of Love", around 30,000 words as it stands.

The agents are Curtis Brown.

Sincerely,

To Paul Hoffman

Editorial Offices
Hastings House

February 20, 1958

Dear Paul:

The Van Vleet material has come in.[1] Your letter suggests that you misunderstand the situation. I did not thrust this book upon Hastings House. Originally it evidently rose from a picture of Zarife that I sent young Diana Frese because she is such a horse lover and Zarife had one of the finest of the classical Arab heads. There was some talk about the ranch and the Boss' efforts to preserve the blood of the Arab at a time when it was vanishing from the regions that had built it up for 4000 years. Both Walter Frese and Henry Alsberg appreciated the Boss' story as the essence of the American Story, one of a time rapidly passing. I was urged to see if this couldn't be put into a book for Hastings House. Not by me but by someone. I never assumed that I was qualified to write this book.

I wasn't enthusiastic about asking the Boss for the personal material that would be necessary, or about the book itself without a fine creative mind to work on it. This book should be attempted by no one without an understanding of the deep philosophical and mystical implications of the material, the photographs selected with the same insight. After some urging I finally broached the matter to the Van Vleets.

Of course there was no predicting then that the decision would be yours to make, and that you would accept the character evaluation of the glossy mediocrity that a newspaper food columnist like Jan Owen must of necessity be.

It is, of course, preferable that this book need not go through your hands. To your advice that I avoid taking the time to write this book myself I can only say that I have no time to take if I had the qualifications to write it as it should be done. But you should understand that I consider no one equipped to advise me on what I should or should not write.

1. "Foal of Heaven."

To Mamie Meredith

2/21/58

Dear Mamie:

Just a note. . . .

About the *hostiles:* I've never heard it pronounced with anything but a long *I* as a noun meaning the hostile Indians, while they were effectively hostile. Curiously, old army men who fought them sometimes changed the *i* to a short one when they were captured. I recall old General Brown at Denver once speaking of "the captured hostiles" short *i* immediately after he had spoken of them with a long *i* under Crazy Horse at the Rosebud. I'm certain he wasn't conscious of this change in pronunciation. (Could this be unconscious agreement with *hostages?*)

I saw several people who asked to be remembered to you at the New York Alum dinner but because I am so *bad* at recalling faces, I never found out who they were, except that they are people I see every year at these dinners, and can't offend by asking who they are at this late date. It really is a serious handicap to be so bad about people. As is sometimes pointed out to me, I can recall thousands of Indians by name and pedigree—. . . .

I must run. I have to move as soon as the landlord gets a non-paying tenant out. I'll be at 422 Hudson (near here) with very good friends. I'll have the second floor of a house. The Wesley Towners'. Wesley is finishing up the exciting book on the Parke Bernet Galleries.[1] But I don't know when I can get in. There's no connection between their 3rd and 4th floor dwelling except that the hall of the stairs is the same one. I'll be completely independent, as their present tenants, a professor and then airplane hostesses, have been. . . .

Take care of those eyes. MS

1. Wesley Towner, *The Elegant Auctioneers,* completed by Stephen Varble (New York: Hill and Wang, 1970).

To Benn Hall and John Barkham

422 Hudson St.
New York 14,
April 5, 1958

Dear Benn Hall:[1]

It's very nice of John Barkham of the Saturday Review Syndicate to ask for some material on the influence of the west on my writing and the method that I use. Unfortunately the reply to such questions gets a little complicated, because both the west and the writing are really my life. You are both free to simplify, so long as the meaning is unchanged.

About the influence of the West: I suppose, with the exception of the Swiss discipline and folk-ways in our home, and the European culture in much of our immediate community, all the early influences in my life were western American. Much of our outlook on nature and man's relationship to his earth and sky, actual and mystical, came from the Indians, particularly the Sioux and the handful of Cheyennes who lived among them. Our place was never without some Indians around near in my childhood. In addition there were the old French and breed traders and their descendants. On the other hand were the cattle people, many of whom had come up on the cattle trails from Texas or sifted down from Wyoming after the Johnson County War of 1892 made that region less healthy for some of the more deeply involved, mostly men from the cattleman, the Invader, side.

Because our father, Old Jules, came rather directly from Switzerland to the unorganized regions of northwest Nebraska, what he knew of American ways were the ways left behind by the frontier—the techniques of hunting and trapping learned from the Indians and the old mountain men, and from the troops the winter of 1884–5 at Fort Robinson, where he lay with a broken ankle under the care of Dr. Walter Reed, post doctor, later famous for his work in yellow fever. Dr. Reed had been post surgeon in such places as Arizona before, and had the frontier physician's point of view.

I was born in the time when the region was changing rapidly from the law of the Winchester, in which my father led a vigilante gang and hanged a man and let him down to have them all arrested, to the final acceptance of the courts in most conflicts. I grew up on stories from the men who had roved the region when it was all Indian and buffalo country from the bend of the Missouri to the Rockies. In my early childhood much of our region was still public domain, and Old Jules a locater who found homes for thousands of landless homeseekers, homes too often deserted by those unable to stand the rigors of pioneering life. I saw the later phases of the cattleman-settler conflict and saw the last acre of public domain patented in our region, the last Texas steer disappear there, the Hereford and Angus take his place. I saw telephones come, and roads, radio, R[ural] E[lectrification] A[dministration] and television. I knew men like the Oglala Sioux brother chieftain of Crazy Horse—old He Dog—men whose lives spanned all the changes from the wild free buffalo hunting days up to the 1930's. I could not help but be aware of the swiftness of these great changes, the adjustments they demanded, the conflicts and tragedies, and the benefits too, that they brought. Long before the last of such men as He Dog died I was deeply involved emotionally in these changes, the people and region where the changes occurred. I wondered about them, and their implications. At the age of twenty I decided to write a six book study of the Great Plains region, from the coming of powder and iron to Stone Age man to the present. It looked much, much easier then than it does now, even after THE CATTLEMEN, the fourth of the series (or the fifth, counting THE BUFFALO HUNTERS.) After the cattle book one on the oil on the Great Plains remains to be written and the one that is perhaps the most difficult, the story of the coming of iron and powder to the region. But when I am done with the series I hope to know something of what modern man does to a region and what it does to him.

About my method of writing: the largeness of my undertaking, assumed back when I was too young to realize the vastness of the material and its implications, has thrust a slow and painstaking method upon me. My nonficion and much of my fiction crystalizes out of the research in the voluminous ecords in the various repositories on the Great Plains, in outside reposito-ies, and in the federal records, particularly the War Department, the Indian ureau and other divisions of the Department of the Interior, as well as the epartment of Agriculture. In addition I've plowed through vast accumula-ions of letters, manuscripts and documents in private hands, and dug into he memories of every participant left from the changing past of the plains hat I could find. I started keeping some sort of notes almost as soon as I earned to write words. The index to my material is a file of over 300,000 ards now, and growing.

When I decide upon a new book, as say, THE CATTLEMEN, I pull out all he index cards referring to the subject, dig out the filed material involved, go hrough all additional material and sources I can locate and then plan the ook. With a terse, synoptic rough draft I go back to the region, covering the important locales once more, to check on my memory of this site and that one in the light of my later, more intensive and clearer understanding of the events there. I make many, many changes and revisions until I hit upon a structure and an adaptation of my style that seems to tell the most, by implication, beyond the denotation and connotation of the bare words. This was particularly difficult in the Indian books, where so much of the story cannot be told in mere white man words, but must be suggested by other means: by the rhythm patterns, the unusual juxtaposition of words and ideas, etc.

None of my book[s] ever reach the heights envisioned in that first fine conception of it, but there comes a time when further polish seems to be at the expense of too much of the freshness and of that quality that I like to call *wonder*. When that time comes I try to stop, and then I find the proof reading a period of desperation, when I can no longer hope to rewrite the entire book or even any significant portion of it. So I let it go and never reread a word of the entire volume unless some one writes in to ask, perhaps, if on such and such a page the man might be a long lost uncle who went west and was never heard from again.

By proof-reading time I am always deeply involved in the next book, one which will surely come closer to my fine conception than others. I said this once in a talk to a Colorado audience and afterward a hearty, buxom farm woman came up to shake my hand. "I know just what you mean, always laying your hopes on the next book," she said. "We had eighteen children before we gave up getting a good one."

Mari Sandoz

1. Benn Hall (1911–62) formed Benn Hall Associates, an advertising firm, in 1946. This request may have been made by one of MS's publishers, possibly Hastings House.

To Melvin Van den Bark

April 13, 1958

Dear Van:

Thanks for the post cards. They are fine and colorful. Which reminds me: I wish you were here to take a glance at my new apartment before it becomes the typical dirty New York hole. It's fine and gleaming now. With wild slip covers on the only two pieces of actual furniture I own—the big couch and a big chair. I priced the stores for slip covers made to order, all taking four to five weeks, and most wanting to rebuild the pieces, coming to around $150.00 or $170.00. So I went to the basement at Gimbels, picked up 23 yards of seconds drapery material at $1 a yard, and did them myself. Everybody is kind enough to gasp a little, and then, when I admit they are homemade, add: "But we never realized you were *domestic*."

But I'm off for the west in a few days, as the enclosed route sheet will show you. Do you think you could slip up to Oklahoma City while I'm there? I'll soon know whether the Browns want me the 22nd or 23rd, and I'll let you know, in hopes— I enjoyed the Baltimore Book and Authors luncheon, sandwiched in between Bruce Catton and Cleveland Amory.[1] Catton was learned and a little dull. Amory was gossipy and funny. I played the part of the LITTLE GIRL FROM THE NIOBRARA. Both of the others were private school products. I played up the fact that I came from the rural schools, with the teacher usually teaching on a permit. People certainly woke up from the heavy lunch and Catton's solid talk. Amory brought them to a constant roaring with slightly off-the-record anecdotes of the Duchess of Windsor, etc.

1. Bruce Catton (1899–1978) was a professor of history and an authority on the Civil War. He received the 1954 Pulitzer Prize for history, as well as other accolades. Among his works are *Glory Road* (Garden City: Doubleday, 1952), *A Stillness at Appomattox* (Garden City: Doubleday, 1953), and *This Hallowed Ground* (Garden City: Doubleday, 1956). Cleveland Amory (b. 1917) was associate editor of *SEP*, 1939–41 and 1943, a free-lance writer and television commentator, and editor at large for *Saturday Review* and *World*. An animal-rights proponent, he wrote a syndicated column titled "Animal." His books include *The Proper Bostonians* (New York: Dutton, 1947), *Home Town* (New York: Harper, 1950), *The Last Resorts* (New York: Harper, 1952), and *The Cat and the Curmudgeon* (Boston: G. K. Hall, 1991).

To H. D. Wimer

April 19, 1958

Dear Doc:

Forgive this delay in my reply to your letter. I'm as busy as a farmer at planting time, getting all the tag-ends of THE CATTLEMEN off my hands, setting up my files and books in my new apartment so I can work, getting the material together for my research in the west, and lining up some logical route sheet for the talks and autographing the publisher scares up for me.

There is some material on Custer's son in the Wild Hog notes my father made to send to his sweetheart Rosalie in Switzerland, and the Indian's amazement that a man could make war on his woman's people, both down in the Texas Panhandle, when Custer made captives of the four emissaries, and up in the north, 1873, 1874, 1876, and Old Jules' cynical comment, "Modern war is for profit, and without profit there would be no modern wars."

Most of the notes are on what seemed very important to both of the men — the government's Indian policy, and the belief that Wild Hog finally could not escape the conviction that the Cheyennes were all to be killed, all wiped out. It was not surprising with all he had seen, with his own necessity to try suicide so his wife and children could go to Red Cloud's Sioux with the other widows and orphans. Wild Hog had a mystical turn too, and believed that somehow, somewhere, there would be just awards for good and for evil — but he thought it might be a long, long white-man time before that man would have to see his own women and children flee from an enemy as he had pursued the Cheyennes. Yet The Hog was certain it would come, and to the Cheyenne all things that happen in one place are of the same time. Some day I want to annotate these notes of my father's and publish them somewhere.[1]

I'll stop in at the Grove [bookstore] to autograph your book, and I wish I could come to Southwest Nebraska this Spring, but I am so desperately far behind in all my commitments. You are fine and generous to invite me and I appreciate it. The Wimers and the Suttons are on my list of favorite people and a junket to Bents Fort with you all would be a grand outing for me.

My regards to all the Wimers,

1. The Wild Hog notes were never annotated by MS and may no longer be extant.

To Mr. Frank A. Lundy, Chairman

Board of University Publications
The University of Nebraska

April 19, 1958

Dear Mr. Lundy:

Thank you. I am happy to know that the proposed HOSTILES AND FRIENDLIES has reached approval from the Board of University Publications.

At first I was doubtful of this venture, because I wondered whether the short pieces could ever be worked into a whole of any dignity and value. But Virginia Faulkner has done an unexpectedly fine editorial piece of work on the material and I should be pleased to have the book published.

I shall be in Nebraska a good portion of next May and available for any necessary editorial conferences.

Sincerely,

To W. D. Aeschbacher, Director

The Nebraska State Historical Society

June 16, 1958

Dear Doctor Aeschbacher:

Thanks for the attempt to apologize for me to Mrs. James J. Boblits. I prefer that you avoid this. First, you are not responsible for me in any way. Second, I'm a hard researcher and when I say a thing in my books of nonfiction it's, to the best of my knowledge, wholly true. . . .

I think I kept within the material and even followed Professor Fling's admonition "to hold a little back" when using historical material. I held back considerable in the Olive story, as some of the letters coming in point out to me.

Sincerely,

To Lewis Nordyke

Amarillo, Texas

June 22, 1958

Dear Mr. Nordyke:[1]

Your letter of June 9 was forwarded around to Oklahoma and Colorado and just came in. I regret the delay.

I don't know to what you refer when you say you "created many stories" in your CATTLE EMPIRE and ROUNDUP and "find much of this material" in my CATTLEMEN. I bought your books on publication and thinking they would interest the old Texas cowmen of our sandhills of Nebraska, I sent them right out to the libraries. I received many letters about your XIT [Ranch] story back around 1950 from old Panhandle Texans and their friends. Some were pretty mad but I assured them that the errors they seemed to detect were not, could not be intentional; that no reputable writer of nonfiction deliberately poisons the wells of history.

The only book on the XIT that I have is Haley's, which I kept to compare with the suppressed version.[2] I had run into some pretty strong meat in my XIT research, material that I did not use because I believe in a little understatement, and in a little handy reserve for emergencies.

As you of course know, my CATTLEMEN is the product of a life time of searching for all the information about everybody on the Great Plains. The ranches in our sandhills were almost completely manned by men from your Panhandle. There I began to accumulate the wonderful stories they told of the early XIT as soon as I could write, along with any other range material. However, my best body of material on your region, outside of the accumulations I found in Washington and in the repositories of Nebraska, Kansas, Colorado, Oklahoma, Illinois and Texas, was loaned me unofficially by Earl Vandale. Some years before his death he expressed a wish to know more about the Texas Olives who went north. In return for an extensive bibliography and copies of some manuscript material, he loaned me a box of manuscripts, letters and documents on the XIT and adjoining ranches. I also got a look at considerable material that was later put together for Mrs. Duke's collections.

Several biographies have been written from my CRAZY HORSE, with at least two-thirds of the entire book's material absolutely unavailable outside of my book—not just my conclusions or interpretations but the man's factual history. Of course I was happy that the books could be written. It is the duty and the privilege of the serious writer on historical subjects to collect and make available to the public as much new material as possible.

You state that you "looked at the facts and made" your "own interpretations" on the XIT and say you find the same conclusions in my book. If we looked at the same facts the conclusions should be similar but I am a little chagrined if my conclusions really are the same as those of a writer who admits he created stories in a book palmed off on the public as nonfiction. Still, you for your conscience, me for mine.

Sincerely,

I tried to find you May 1956 on my way north from Canyon, etc.

1. Lewis Nordyke (1905–60) wrote primarily about Texas and the Southwest: *Cattle Empire* (New York: William Morrow, 1949), and *The Great Roundup* (New York: William Morrow, 1955) are examples.

2. J[ames] Evetts Haley. *The XIT Ranch of Texas and the Early Days of the Llano Estacado* (Norman: U of Oklahoma P, 1953).

To Mary Abbot [not sent]

June 23, 1958

Dear Mary:

I've not heard any more about the book on the beavers for Hastings, and as things turned out, that's all to the good. I don't want to write any more books than the two already under contract. Two more will be enough to be killed by lack of stock at the publisher's just when the book is starting to sell well.

I made it clear to you and to Hastings House that I did not intend to go through this kind of thing with the cattle book. Yet here it is again, June 23 and no appreciable stock of books until Wolfs can run off another printing after they reopen in August from their month-of-July vacation closing.

I went to a great deal of effort and expense to get *The Cattlemen* well launched. Somehow we even overcame much of the muddle over the *Post's* delayed publication and the holding up of even publication day announcement advertising, which was most disconcerting out west. I'll even have to go to speak to the McClurg meeting at Chicago August 15 with no books on the market.[1]

I'm hard to discourage. If this were the first time this happened, or even the fifth or sixth, or seventh. But it always happens. I told Walter Frese this book would sell 50,000 copies with proper handling, and books in stock for prompt filling of orders.

Either my books are not worth keeping in good supply or all my publishers have been fools. It doesn't matter which now. I'm done. I'll write the two books under contract, knowing what to expect, and braced for it. But it will never happen more than twice more. Not to me.

Sorry,

1. McClurg, a Chicago book jobber, featured MS at its book and author fair in 1958.

To Morton D. Hull, Editorial Assistant

THE SATURDAY EVENING POST

June 24, 1958

Dear Mr. Hull:

I'm sorry that "Tyrant of the Plains" has stirred up such angry letters. I suppose they assume that nobody knows this story, or knew it before you published my article. Actually it's one of the most written-about topics, only nobody bothered to really run the story down from Mississippi around to Trail City and No Man's Land.

Of course I have good sources. . . . I work by understatement, no matter how lurid my accounts turn out. I always keep a little back in the name of art, and for special emergencies.

Mrs. Jenkins is wrong about my not having been in Custer County recently. I don't hunt publicity and never call the newspapers. I was in her region as recently as a month ago. I made a real junket through the county in 1955 while I was gathering a last look at the state for the NEBRASKA article for HOLIDAY and for a book I'm contracted to write for Harper Brothers eventually. But I got my Olive material back when people who lived through those days were still around.[1]

Sincerely,

1. Members of the Olive family were the "Tyrants" in the "Tyrant of the Plains."

To Olivia Pound

July 1, 1958

Dear Olivia,

You will know with what degree of sorrow all of us who were privileged to know you and your sister Louise heard of her death.

Those of us who were fortunate enough to have had Miss Pound as our teacher will never think of her as gone. The good teacher is immortal and if that is true, what can one say for the great teacher?

In sympathy,

To Walter Frese

July 9, 1958

Dear Walter:

Enclosed is a carbon of a letter I wrote to Mary Abbot March 11, 1957.

Before I let go of the manuscript of THE CATTLEMEN, I was careful to get a promise from Mary that she would do all she could to hold you to a large enough printing to assure a steady supply. I was under the impression that both you and Russell Neale promised me, right in your office, that you would keep a good stock of the book on hand all through the months of high demand.

As I reminded you in a recent letter, I told you then that THE CATTLEMEN was the final test. If you let it get short of stock while still selling well, as had happened to all ten of my earlier books, I was done with the whole business.

After 23 years my patience is gone. I don't want to hear another word about the whole matter.

Sorry,

To Mamie Meredith

July 21, 1958

Dear Mamie:

Thanks for the defense of THE CATTLEMEN against the Texans, but it's not necessary. Either the book stands like a rock in time with not even a memory of the dirty water that was spilled upon it, or it doesn't. Either way it's not my business to defend it. People all the way from Virginia Kirkus, in her preview out of New York, to Richard Dillon in the San Francisco *Chronicle,* and many Texans, have done the defending for me.

I think I know who the woman from Omaha is, the one who questioned one episode that I was supposed to have "misrepresented rather sadly." I'm sure the episode is the Olive story, which I really understated and everyone who really knows the story, the material, knows that I did. In fact I've had several complaints on that, as I have had on the Bartlett Richards story. But I believe in holding a little back, because in the condensation of a book the impact can be much greater on the casual bystander than it is by the slower impact of life. I gave Print Olive a little better deal than he had coming. I barely touched on the psychotic way that he treated any Texas youth who fell under his displeasure. They died, but very slowly. . . .

I'm enclosing verifax copies of two interesting letters that the Olive story brought in. Will you send them back soon? I don't want to lose these from my informational files.

Affectionately,

To Walter Frese

August seven, 1958

Dear Walter,

This business of THE CATTLEMEN would be very funny if it didn't come so close to the final destruction of a career to which I've dedicated my whole life. It all reminds me of an old mother saying piously over and over how well she had reared her son, and what a good boy he is, ignoring the niggling little fact that he's to dance on the gallows at dawn.

It was too bad to put your help to running down the information that there were no reorders from the probable jobber of the Hyannis [Nebraska] library. That's been my point all along: that nobody intended to reorder THE CATTLEMEN if there was any chance of this being another dreary repetition of the usual history of a Sandoz book—no copies available for weeks, perhaps months after publication date, not until all interest had pretty well died.

I don't know much about any particular jobber outside of an occasional one in the west, and they have been changed the last few years. I did get a lot of jobber reaction through small book stores and libraries. Some apparently told their customers that the book was out of stock and probably would remain so until fall. Some made no report at all, as you see from the Hyannis letter. One was quoted as saying that THE CATTLEMEN would be "out of stock for hell knows how long, and no profit handling a book that way."

This morning my typist cleaned up the last ten complaints from libraries and I am throwing away the twenty-year-old form letter for my apologetic reply to such complaints. I'm done explaining and apologizing.

And this *is* my last word on this whole matter.

Sincerely,

To Mrs. Elias Jacobsen

August 20, 1958

Dear Ethel Jacobsen:

It is fine to hear from one so long dedicated to the Indians of the Plains. Last week I met Susan Kelley at Chicago. She is secretary to Mr. Kendall, of McClurgs. She was born on Standing Rock, a descendant of the Hunkpapa chief, Two Bears, I gather—a fine, tall young woman, handsome, poised and intelligent.

I grew up among the Oglalas, so to speak, with many of the hostiles, the old Crazy Horse people, often camped across the road from our house on the river, the Niobrara. From these I heard the great stories told over and over—by men who had been in the fights. Then in 1930 and 1931 I went up to get the stories down clearly, and to check on many of the written reports. From such men as He Dog and Short Bull we got the details of the Crazy Horse dreaming, his medicine, the accoutrements these permitted him, and the rituals he followed and modified as he grew older, more mature. Under certain circumstances he wore the spotted calf skin shirt flying from his shoulders and his hair falling loose over it, as well as sometimes without the calf skin cape. I can lift my eyes from my typewriter here to a picture, a scene painted by Amos Bad Heart Bull, son of the historian of the Crazy Horse band of Oglalas, the Hunkpatilas, and historian in his own right. Later this was copied upon the sacred Crazy Horse lodge that is used now and then, or was, for ceremonials. In this painting Crazy Horse is riding his yellow and white spotted horse, carrying a shield and one of the sacred Oglala lances, in defense of the Black Hills. He is stripped to breechclout and moccasins, the spotted calfskin cape flying from his shoulders, and the usual one feather in his hair, which is flying loose. Several warriors wore it so into battle, old Two Strikes, for instance, particularly when he was the partisan. This is not chopped and ragged and full of ashes as for a Lakota mourning but blowing fine and free and long. Every old timer who had been in fights with Crazy Horse in the last ten years of his life agreed that he sometimes went in with loose hair, particularly if there was really dangerous leading to be done. But it did depend upon his meditations before the fight. If you want to see a lot of pictures of Lakotas with their hair loose, Lakotas obviously not in mourning, look into Neihardt's BLACK ELK SPEAKS.

About the spelling of Lakota or other Indian words: there has been so much discrepancy because our letters do no more than approximate the Indian pronunciation. Gradually writers have been accepting the spellings approved by the Bureau of Ethnology so far as their work covers the subject. I went over all the Lakota words very carefully with the old buffalo hunters, preferably with John Colhoff as interpreter. He was the only man left on Pine Ridge who had troubled to learn the old words and the old pronunciations of the pre-reservation days, which often varied from those of the younger Oglalas and even from those of the old Brules. There was such variety among the Tetons that one hardly dares say "This is the way they said it, not that." I recall a remark a Minneconjou made after he had lived with the Red Cloud Bad Faces for twenty years and then went back north to his relatives. "They look in my face and find it theirs, but my words they want put into sign talk."

In this chaos there had to be some attempt at uniformity, so we arbitrarily accept the Bureau of Ethnology whenever it seems logical. I listened very carefully to old He Dog and his brother speak of the Black Hills. There was no *ha* in the first word, just a stop after the *Pa. Hoppo* was pronounced as *Sappa* was, not on our system of vowel pronunciation, but *Hop po,* long *o; Sap pa* as two words, with broad a's. One finds each word spelled many ways but none give the exact sound that the old Oglalas produced. I recall an old Indian trying to teach me to speak a little Lakota, old Lakota. But I was a very slight little girl and he and his old cronies laughed heartily at my attempt. "Not enough belly!" they told me, in sign. . . .

But about you — have you ever written down anything of your experiences out among the Lakotas of Standing Rock? There must be many fine stories in your life out there. Those times will never return and it would enrich the future for our country a little if you would put down some of the things you saw and heard and endured and did. I think you might make a very readable account of it, if not for sale, then perhaps for one of the Historical Society magazines of say, the Dakotas, or Nebraska, or for one of the publications of the Westerners. Chicago has a fine group, the original one, as you will know.

It was fine to hear from you —

Sincerely,

To J. L. Norris

August 24, 1958

Dear Doctor Norris:

The Nebraska State Historical Society kindly forwarded your letter to me here, where I have a sort of outpost in the land of publication.

I am happy that a man from Lusk [Wyoming] enjoyed THE CATTLEMEN and that the doctor of 49 years of pill pushing thinks kindly of OLD JULES.

Your life should be a natural for a book. To write a volume of great artistic significance is not for everyone, not for the novice, but almost anyone with good material and the power of literacy can write an interesting book. Some doctors turn naturally to writing, and some even turn out to be really financial successes, such as Dr. Hertzler of the HORSE AND BUGGY DOCTOR[1] and in fields of the novel varying as much as those of S. S. Van Dine and Céline.

How will you write your book? Well, I've been working with new writers since my undergraduate days and I find the approach will vary as much as the individual and the material. In a case of reminiscences like yours I should suggest writing down any incident, any case, piece of dialogue, characterization or description that rises in your mind. Write it down on anything handy and pile these notes into a drawer, box or even a shopping bag hung in a closet by one of the loops to keep its mouth open and waiting.

One reason for preserving these items as they occur to you is that they won't come up when you start to write the book. Eventually you can sort them out and fit them into their proper places in the story.

Some day you will make up your mind to start the book in earnest. Dictate, write or type out the string of the story, the narrative, as fast as you can, to get movement into it. Then have it typed up on cheap paper, preferably triple-spaced, with room for insertions, interlineations, etc., Don't worry about a good beginning now. Most of us write the beginnings the very last thing; then we know what the beginning should do. How could I have known when I began OLD JULES that I should set the region before the reader and then show the man coming from the east in a wagon, driving hard?

Long before you get around to a good beginning you will have fitted those casual items into their places as seems advisable, pasting them in or on the back or stapling them to the page, with indications for proper insertions. With the manuscript retyped with these inclusions, you will begin to see what you have and your blood pressure will mount and your eyes perhaps blur a bit if you are doing a really good job. Later, after you've worked with the book, you will begin to get bored with it, but then you must remember that you are getting the objectivity needed. You are no longer reading into the book what you have not yet put down. Now add the necessary action, characterization, dialogue, description. Cut down the long-winded expository sections. Make something happen on every page. Don't make anything up, just cut down on the material between events.

Now is the time to revise, revise, until you can no longer improve the book. Go slow on showing the manuscript to friends. They aren't critics; they can't evaluate material in manuscript. They won't tell you the truth. Either they will feel they must say what you want to hear or perhaps even latent animosities will come out and they will make adverse criticism which may or may not be of any value.

Now, if you wish, send me a piece (first finding out where I am) and I'll be happy to look it over for the sake of the old days around Lusk.

Good traveling on all your back trails,

P. S. Your photograph suggests that you have a nice sense of humor. Use it on yourself as well as on the rest of the world. MS

1. Arthur Emanuel Hertzler, *Horse and Buggy Doctor* (New York: Harper, 1938).

To Ezra Warner

Aug. 26, 1958

Dear Ezra Warner:

At last a moment, but no more.

Mrs. Custer knew of the Yellow Swallow son of Custer. She came out to find him once, I heard, down in Oklahoma, but he was dead. He was always sickly. Lived only to about 17.

The conspiracy to keep the matter out of the press was nearly perfect in action. I'm working on a book now based on a world-renowned figure who lived under a fictitious biography, and not even at his death did the newspapers break the story, although everyone, including O. O. McIntyre, the columnist, (and a remote relative) ever broke the story. It has now come out so I feel free to do the book.

This has nothing to do with Custer, Indians or the military. I mention it only as another case of public silence to protect an innocent person.

Sincerely,

To Louis Lightner

September 26, 1958

Dear Judge:

I appreciate your very generous letter about THE CATTLEMEN. The material is certainly important and I hope that the book will stand up, in final evaluation, which won't be for forty, fifty years.

It is nice to know that Terence Duren is doing so well.[1] He's energetic and is taking on some fine side lines, like the Brownsville [Nebraska] project.

About my Bohemian life: It could only seem so through the romantic haze that Terence carries around with him. I avoid such Bohemianism as is left here, which isn't much. I live exactly as I would in Lincoln or Denver. Even an occasional old timer manages to find his way to my door. Last week George Werner, an old cowman from Spotted Horse, Wyoming, came drifting in to talk about the Johnson County War and the fight at old Suggs with the Negro troops. He went up there later, about 1902–3, I think, but got a bullet hole through one leg and into the other just the same — from a range "protector" who was to run him off his homestead or leave his carcass there. Fortunately the "protector" is long gone but George Werner is still right there.

I appreciate these old timers coming in or writing about their experiences in the cattle days. I got a fine letter from the daughter of Lawrence Ketchum down in the south. Her father died at her house as late as 1926, but she never knew anything much about the killing of Whit, as they called Ami Ketchum, her uncle. Lawrence was a one-time scout for the army, was up at Laramie at the time of the Olive troubles. After my book came out she went to the accumulation of material her father left in an old trunk and there was the whole story, even a letter from Conners, long before the trouble got so hot, warning Lawrence that the cattlemen were looking for an example to scare the other settlers out and he was afraid they had selected Ami Ketchum. Later Conners was among the defending attorneys. I wonder why the letter was never brought up. But of course it wouldn't have made any difference in the final result.

It was nice visiting you this evening, via letter. Give my regards to the lady of the house. Sincerely,

P. S. Nothing on movies of the CATTLEMEN.

1. Terence Duren (1906–68), an artist from Shelby, Nebraska, studied at the Chicago Art Institute, L'Ecole de Beaux Arts in Paris, and in Vienna. He exhibited in a number of major museums throughout the United States; he illustrated for the *Omaha World-Herald Midlands* magazine, *Fortune, Panoramic Review,* and others. He was also an accomplished muralist and set designer. His lifestyle and that of MS were considerably different.

To Mary Abbot

October 12, 1958

Dear Mary:

Within the next month or so I may have to make a drastic decision.

I've just agreed to make an eight week series of appearances, March 15 to May 15 under the auspices of University of Nebraska KUON-TV, talking about writing and my own materials, etc., the $2750 to be paid out of a Ford Foundation grant. I have to be in Nebraska for the Harper book around that time anyway and this will work out fine, I think.

But all summer there has been another matter brewing: a new panel show, on which I would be a regular, one of four members, over Mutual. Some time the next month I may have to say a definite "yes" or "No".

I am reluctant to leave my writing (after the present two books) so completely behind me as this new commitment and others that might follow (if the initial one was a success) would demand. Even at the substantial monetary sacrifice the writing would demand (and it has been so from the beginning. I refused a raise to $5000 a year on my editorial job back in the Twenties to write *Old Jules*) I should like to stay with it. But not unless you can think up some way to *insure* sufficient printings so I'll not have to face the humiliation and the loss of inadequate stock to fill the demands for a book right after publication day, as in the past.

The Atlantic sent Peter Davison, whom I knew as a most attractive boy, son of Ted Davison, the poet and director of the Colorado Writers Conference, long ago. They have a book or books they want me to do and while I was very pleased to see Peter again, and as a fine young man, I won't ever give them another chance at me. But as you know there are repeated offers of this kind and it's a shame that I can't get the assurance of a substantial first printing to take advantage of some of the ideas, let alone finish my own series.

Of course if I go on writing I have to do the beaver book for Hastings. Can you get something really binding from them about a substantial supply of books?

Or should I just take up the much more remunerative work on radio and TV as it comes along?

Sincerely,

To Fred Babcock

October 26, 1958

Dear Fred Babcock:[1]

Thanks for including THE CATTLEMEN in your list of books written by women.

It is true that I'm not much of a feminist. I'd rather be very far down in the whole human race than pretty high up in fractions of it. However, since people push you into making selections on the basis of sex, I'm happy to be included.

I trust that the fall is a fine one for the Babcock household.

Sincerely,

1. Fred Babcock (1896–1979) was a journalist, beginning at the *Nebraska State Journal* and eventually writing reviews for the *New York Times Book Review, Saturday Review, Nation,* and *Christian Century.*

To Mary Abbot

November 8, 1958

Dear Mary:

Thank you. I am sorry I have been such a troublesome client the last few months. I do seem to have lost much of my natural zest for writing, but perhaps it will come back if the matter can be settled. Anyway, I am willing to give it another run around the mulberry bush. Under your plan I'll sign up for the beaver book. I guess I still prefer to do what I've tried to train myself for—writing.

November 16 will see me back in town until the middle of March, I hope,—and I do appreciate all your effort.

Sincerely,

To Dr. Paul R. Stalnaker

November 8, 1958

Dear Dr. Stalnaker:

I appreciate your kind words about THE CATTLEMEN, and I am happy to have the brief biography of your uncle, Raymond Cloud. I have notes on him from the Texas History Center, from a dozen printed sources and from the files of early newspapers of Ellsworth and Wichita, etc., Kansas. Unfortunately I could only touch on a scattered few men in a book covering 400 years and thousands of individuals.

As I recall now, I have material on your uncle in my Buffalo Hunter files too, but this material is in storage out in Nebraska. That, too, was a way of making a little ready cash after the civil war, as you know.

I have no plans for further writing on the cattle trails. I am working on a seven-book nonfiction study of the Great Plains, from the coming of powder and iron to stone age man, to the present time. In this the cattle book was my attempt to treat the cow and her influence on the settlement and development of the region.

Chronologically this series is to contain:

1. The coming of powder and iron to the Plains. (To be written.)
2. CRAZY HORSE, the story of an Indian leader, from the buffalo days to the reservation period.
3. THE BUFFALO HUNTERS, the slaughter of the buffaloes.
4. CHEYENNE AUTUMN, a rebellion against the reservation system.
5. OLD JULES, a picture of a settlement period.
6. THE CATTLEMEN, the cow and her keepers, from Coronado to the present.
7. OIL COMES TO THE PLAINS. (To be written.)

Incidentally, has the story of your grandfather, the Reverend Cloud been recorded? That's important material.

Sincerely,

P.S. Your letter on a National Lottery and the reprint from the *Texas Journal of Medicine,* both of which I am returning, interested me. While none of us gamble with money, every one who went out upon the Plains in the old free land days was a gambler in a larger sense. As for medicine, there have always been Sandoz chemists and doctors, from back in the old alchemy days, as you well know.

To the Reverend Father Peter J. Powell

November 22, 1958

Dear Father Powell:

Your letters to Catton and Moe are excellent. I am certain you will have a fine response from both places.

Did you see Kaleidoscope on Channel 4 November 16, about the Indians, specifically the Blackfeet, but mentioning the destruction of the Menominee timber lands in Wisconsin, which disturbed me so two, three years ago, and the plight of the Northern Cheyennes? It was all right, but five, even eleven years too late. It was the economy Congress of 1947 that started the hatchet job on the Indians, followed by the steal of the Eisenhower administration. . . .

More power to you.

Sincerely,

To Walter Frese

Nov 24, 1958

Dear Walter:

It was fine to see you at the Westerners.

Since then I've given J. W. Vaughn of Windsor, Colorado, Hastings House's address. He's the attorney out there who wrote the book on the fight on the Rosebud (a week before the Custer battle), published by Stackpole. I wrote him that his new book, on the Dull Knife fight in the Big Horns, 1876, sounds a little too special perhaps for the regular publisher he is seeking, but if it isn't, you were a likely prospect. He does very careful research; in fact he keeps me busy checking Cheyennes through my files to be sure he doesn't mix them up.

Just now Charles Mills called up to remind me that his Crazy Horse Symphony is being premiered at Cincinnati Nov. 28 and 29, by the Cincinnati Symphony Orchestra under the direction of Max Rudolf. It is to be dedicated to me, he says. The next performance is by Szell, at Cleveland.[1]

I hope it will be performed here soon. It would be fun to go.

And I wish all the Frese household a fine Thanksgiving.

Sincerely,

1. Charles Mills (b. 1914) headed the Composition Department of the Manhattan School of Music, 1954–55, and was radio critic for *Modern Music.* Awarded a Guggenheim Fellowship in 1952, he concentrated on composition rather than performing. Max Rudolf (b. 1902) came to the United States from Germany in 1940. He conducted for many symphony orchestras, including the Metropolitan Opera, and was musical director of the Cincinnati symphony orchestra from 1948 to 1970. George Szell (1897–1970) studied in Vienna and conducted the Vienna symphony orchestra at sixteen. He came to the United States in 1939 and was musical director of the Cleveland symphony orchestra from 1946 to 1970.

To Mrs. M. F. Shickley

November 29, 1958

Dear Gail:[1]

It's fine to hear from you. I am reminded of a comment one of my New York friends who did a little typing for me between her own writing made: "Don't you ever let loose of your old friends?" It just occurred to me that you appeared in Van's class a very long time ago - - -.

About the *Dry Gulch* and *Saddle Wolf*, used in THE CATTLEMEN: As you know, I take special pains to use the vocabulary of the time in my writing, and I take notes on lingo as I gather the material. In addition, there is the wonderful 4 volume *Dictionary of American English*, which dates the Americanisms listed.

dry gulch

Gulching was long used as a term for catching or killing animals from a low place along their regular run, as deer, etc. See DAE. The term came into use politically too. In early Colorado, in the 1860's, gulching a politician meant rounding up opposition to him, more or less secretly, or among a special group or faction. The word was particularly pertinent if the gulching was done by a friend or supposed friend.

In the meantime *gulching* had come to mean ambushing a man too, and because this was usually from some waterless gulch, where there was less chance of leaving a track, the term *dry gulch* came into greatest use where there were many dry gulches, as in the higher Plains, and where *gulch* was more common than arroyo. I found the term used in a letter from a cowboy who went to the Colorado mines in the 1860's, and it appeared now and them among those in contact with Yankee cowmen in the Red River and upper Brazos country, etc., before the Civil War and after. Buffalo hunters were often said to have been *dry gulched* by hide thieves. In my childhood old trail drivers like Tom Milligan used the term right along, as did the hideouts from the Johnson County War among us. See Ramon F. Adams' WESTERN WORDS.[2]

saddle wolf

This term was well known to the old dragoons who rode up the Platte in the 1830's and appears in some of the more male accounts of the times. It was still used by old timers in Wyoming as recently as 1957, but because this is a sort of euphemism for the more vulgar terms meaning a saddle-galled bottom or, more precisely, chafed privates, it doesn't get into politer society or the dictionaries of our politer society. Often this was merely *wolf:* "I rode into

Miles, but I had such a hell of wolf from the trip that I stayed away from the girls", a cowboy wrote to a friend around 1883.

I wish you and Shick and all the Platte country a fine holiday season.

Sincerely,

P. S. Of course it's readers I'm after. I loan out my books to people myself.

1. Gail McCandless Shickley (1907–87) graduated from the University of Nebraska in 1929 and later lived in western Nebraska and in Colorado. She and MS kept in touch and occasionally met when MS was in Colorado.

2. Ramon F. Adams, *Western Words: A Dictionary of the Range, Cow Camp, and Trail* (Norman: U of Oklahoma P, 1944).

To Mamie Meredith

December 7, 1958

Dear Mamie:

I'm always amused at those recent people around the Historical Society. Of course I've seen [Erwin Hickly] Barbour's pamphlet on windmills. They don't seem to realize that I've seen *everything* except recent stuff. I'm a *researcher*. I wouldn't miss seeing anything like the Barbour pamphlet when I was working on the *Old Jules*. Fortunately we had that material at home, as we had most material applicable to the life of the region. Of course, mother in housecleaning after father died, burned up all such material, including the agricultural year books, the horticultural reports, etc. Very little escaped, but I was one member of the family who knew what was in those stacks of father's. I had read all of it that came while I was home.

Mother always reminds me of the Sydenhams, who, after the old father died, worked two weeks to burn all his accumulation of material around old Fort Kearny.[1]

I suppose it's the old animosity of the woman for the things that take her husband's attention from her—and clutter up her housekeeping.

I had Thanksgiving dinner with the De Vilbises. Joyce is one of the really rare cooks. Afterward we went over all the old days around Lincoln. We all worried a little about Helen Hayes. . . .

I'm enclosing excerpts from a review of the "Crazy Horse Symphony" by Charles Mills. He's a stranger to me, but he wrote me that the book was his inspiration. He has composed a lot, including some ballet material, but he considers this symphony his top work so far. I don't know when anything has pleased me more.

Well—it's time to push out to supper. So be nice to yourself and have a fine holiday season.

Sincerely,

1. Moses Sydenham (1835–1919) was postmaster at Fort Kearny, Nebraska, for fourteen years in the mid-1800s and was a noted local historian.

To Henry S. "Tom" Smith

Colton, California

January 12, 1959

Dear Mr. Smith:[1]

I am very grateful for your letter about the book banning and the witch hunt on authors in the Riverside [California] Library. So long as there are people who hope to benefit from a public kept in ignorance and benightedness there will be attempts to censor writers. I am not surprised that I am on that list. The mayor of Omaha banned *Slogum House* from the library there and Senator [Robert A.] Taft got *Slogum House* and *Yankee from Olympus,* the biography of Justice Holmes, banned from the Armed Services Editions until after the election of 1944. I have some of the mimeographed reports of the old Tenney Committee of California and their successors, and people send me literature on the general bannings all over the nation. I should be deeply ashamed if such people approved of my writing. As you know, we are liberals from way back, those of us who aren't just "aginners" in the rebellious years of youth. In our family my mother's people were liberals back in 1291, when the original Swiss confederation of three cantons was formed. On the Sandoz side liberalism goes back to pre-Reformation days, even before Peter Waldo. Some of the family were burned at the stake in northern Italy, some recanted, some fled to the woods, but our branch stepped across the line into France and when religious intolerance got going too strong there, they took another step, across the line into Switzerland, to Le Locle, back around 500 years ago.

Perhaps we wouldn't feel happy with much approval.

It is people like you, who not only see clearly but who are willing to act upon their insight that help keep some of the liberties for the people.

Happy 1959 to you and all your work—

1. Henry S. "Tom" Smith was an engineer with the Nebraska Department of Roads and Irrigation in the 1930s; he met MS when he worked in the state capitol building and she was there with the NSHS. When, in 1958, a member of the Riverside Library

Board proposed banning a number of works, including hers, he wrote her about it. (There were so many protests from library patrons that no banning occurred.)

To Virginia Faulkner

January 16, 1959

Dear Virginia:

Yes, the galleys A through 49 are nice and clean. I made few changes, only three of them of any importance and I hope these can be incorporated into the book. I added short footnotes, Galleys 2 and 3, to explain the discrepancy in the accounts of Uncle Emile's killing in the KINKAIDER piece and the NEIGHBOR. As I explain, when we went over this incident one evening in the family, my recollection was corrected. I don't see how I could have made the mistake in 1929. But with the deep research and interviewing for OLD JULES, a lot of incidents cleared up, became fresher in my mind. I am convinced that the mind forgets absolutely nothing, but our filing system, our association paths become dim. Given the right stimulation, the whole matter becomes sharp and clear as if it had just occurred. . . .

There's a lot of appallingly bad writing here, but I suppose it should serve as one of the Willa Cather stories from the *English Journal* long served me, as a writer and as a teacher of writing.[1] It is such an appallingly bad story, sentimental, old-fashioned, structurally incredibly amateurish, that it gives hope to almost anyone. Whenever my students thought I was over-optimistic about what they could learn to make of their material, I would read this story from a badly typewritten script and ask them to make little written criticisms on the spot. Then, straight-faced, I collected them and read them to the class. *Then* I showed them the story in print, with the author's name. It always made all my optimism very justified. Invariably the class fell on the early Cather story and buried it.

But enough. I'll be ready for the next batch. And if you can get the book out for Lincoln's Centennial week, I'll autograph at Millers as they have requested.

Happy days under the new regime.

1. No Cather story appears in *English Journal*. MS evidently has mistaken the publication source, but Cather herself was critical of some of her early stories.

To Robert Schlater, Program Manager

KUON-TV Channel 12
Lincoln, Nebraska

February 15, 1959

Dear Bob:

I am ashamed that your letter went unanswered so long. I had hoped to get through the bale of notes and the accumulation of articles, clippings, etc., that I've gathered the last ten months for your TV program.[1] Unfortunately there will be no time for me to give my entire mind to this before March 15, when I get out to Nebraska.

An hour ago I finished with the page proof of *Hostiles and Friendlies* which means that to this hour I've not been free to put all my mind on my novel that I had hoped to complete long ago, or to your material. The contract for the novel was signed five years ago; the book is 14 months late; I do all these other books for people by permission of my option publisher. I must get his book in. I have a single track mind. To have more than one task on it wastes my time and such ability as I may have. Of course I should not have consented to the H&F book at all, or to do your TV program, but unfortunately I am still so close to the pioneer period that any serious request for my time immediately takes on the aspects of a cow in the well and I have to go. (Incidentally, Virginia has done a fabulous job on that mess of stuff in the H&F.)

Of course I'll keep my appointment with you for the talks. I have never missed an appointment and never will so long as I am on my feet.

Now about the series of talks on "A People without history is like the wind on the buffalo grass." Whatever you decide should be done, I should like to entice my viewer-listener to look upon the story of people first and events second—to give him by illustration, etc., a new or renewed eye upon peoples of the past and the present and thereby upon events in which these individuals participated. The Plains are full of illustrations for this and most of them are not too generally known.

I should like to put in one session trying to restore a little of that native skepticism by which the illiterate hinterland American managed to protect himself against the political spieler and the lightning rod and medicine wagon man alike, whatever he was offering or is offering. I'd like by humorous and telling bits to bring to the viewer-listener's attention the validity of the old illiterate's question, "Whose mule's getting the corn if I believe what you tell me, yours, mine or everybody's?" A nice dose of the skepticism that saved the illiterate so often from the snake oil man could help save us from the demigogs, the Madison Avenue boys, the whole business of over-commercialization and of degraded values.

I should also like to insinuate the idea, without the flat statement, that it was not violence or taking the law into one's own hands that conquered any wilderness but the solid, determined people who respected the rights of others, could work with them in times of stress and prosperity. It was such people who stood off the outlaws and the Indians, the prairie fires and epidemics. It was the man with imagination who worked up the windmill and the irrigation ditch against the drouths. For instance, the Frenchmen and breeds at such places as the Cache la Poudre growing onions on their irrigated patches often did more to protect the troops and the travelers along the Overland Trails than guns and powder because more suffered and died of scurvy than from the Indians, and thousands more would have suffered and died if it hadn't been for the wagon loads of onions hauled up to the trails and sold.

Then there are the stories that men told each other to make calamities endurable. The story of the big turnip that fed and shielded all Moses Stocking's sheep one winter helped lighten many another hard winter. The one of the grasshoppers dropping enough pebbles into the Niobrara River to dam it and grow their own green stuff brought a little smile here and there to the grim faces during the grasshopper plagues.

Almost every community has or had some person or persons, known or unknown, who saved or helped save the early settlement, or is perhaps saving it now. Often too, it wasn't the community's finest citizen but that only improves the story.

I should like to stress the idea that if you know and understand the story of your community you will know and understand a great deal of the story of man, anywhere.

Sincerely,

PS: I've been listening to the David Susskind "Open End", Channel 13, while I wrote this. Faust of the Fund for the Advancement of Education, Ford Foundation; President McIntosh of Barnard; Professor Harris, Harvard Economist and President Taylor, Sarah Lawrence. Two hours of talk but nothing new, nothing we don't all know. Not even a nice little anecdote.

1. MS contracted to appear in two seven-segment KUON (Educational Television) series in Lincoln in April and May of 1959. One was titled "Mari Sandoz Discusses Creative Writing"; the other was "Mari Sandoz Looks at the Old West."

To Alice Marriott

February 17, 1959

Dear Alice:[1]

The chance air meeting with your delightful friend, Janet Rosenwald was a lucky bit for me. Your ears must have burned, the right one, of course.

I am happy that the Osages have some one so dedicated to do their research in support of their claims against the government through the treaties and land cessions 1808, 1813 and 1825. . . .

Unfortunately a great deal of my material on such subjects is in storage out in Nebraska and I didn't take Osage notes unless the Sioux or Cheyennes were involved. I do recall, without the source, unfortunately, that the Osages had several favorite spots for their early buffalo surrounds or traps, back in the stone implement days. One of these was on some rimrock country on the Neosho somewhere. The Osages, as you know, had the rather typical Siouan attitude towards women and had them prominent in their buffalo surrounds, both in the ceremonials and in the actual hunt, stationed along the big V that led to a natural cliff or rimrock, which, if not steep enough, was dug out.

When the Cheyennes pushed down into Kansas around 1800 they found Osages on the Arkansas just below the Big Bend, hunting.

Perhaps Nasatir has the material on the robe trade?[2]

I am happy that you found the map in THE BUFFALO HUNTERS good. It's, of course, not very detailed. You are certainly welcome to use it in your Osage Claims so far as I am concerned, and I'll send your letter over to Hastings [House] for their approval.

Sincerely,

1. Alice Marriott (b. 1910), a professor of anthropology at the University of Oklahoma, was a recognized authority on Southern Plains Indians. Her publications include *American Indian Mythology,* with Carol Rachlin (New York: Mentor, 1947), *Ten Grandmothers* (Norman: U of Oklahoma P, 1945), and *Saynday's People* (Lincoln: U of Nebraska P, 1963).

2. Abraham P. Nasatir, *Before Lewis and Clark* (St. Louis: St. Louis Historical Documents Foundation, 1952).

To Ed LaPlante

February 23, 1959

Dear Mr. LaPlante:

I am sorry you had trouble locating me. With so much research all over the country, I'm never anywhere for any length of time. Usually my publishers know or guess where I am.

Peters is a well-known name to me, and Anthony Peters might be the Tony Peters, son of Bill Peters, up on Mirage Flats, or a son of our rural mail carrier from Hay Springs, Nebraska, to Peters, and back.

I don't recall being in school with Tony. Our Peters neighbors ran to girls and the only Peters boy I recall in school was Steve. Could your friend be confusing me with the Emile Sandoz daughter, from South Dakota?

I had nothing at all to do with the appallingly bad movie, *Chief Crazy Horse*. Although the Sioux saw a copy of my *Crazy Horse* in the hands of the director, there was no sale of the book to them and apparently no real attempt to follow the book. A friend of mine in Hollywood sneaked a copy of the script to me. I was appalled not only at the lying picture they were making—having Crazy Horse not at Fort Robinson but at Fort Laramie, and killed through a personal feud of years' standing with a breed, instead of by a white soldier during a betrayal, first by the lies of the government officials who promised him an agency if he came in, and then through the lying misinterpretation of Frank Grouard, the Negro-French-Indian mixed blood who was wanted for murdering military mail carriers up in Montana and feared that Crazy Horse, who knew this, might expose him.

But worst of all, I think, were the liberties the movie makes with Indian relationships. Crazy Horse on his mother's side was a nephew of Spotted Tail, which, as you know, made Spotted Tail his "father". In the movie script Crazy Horse married a daughter of Spotted Tail—or, in other words, his own sister.

Jake Herman writes many good items about the Oglalas and about life up on Pine Ridge and for this we all are grateful. I don't know the younger Black Elk, but I used to see Old Black Elk, the fine old Dreamer, now and then around Gordon, and up around Manderson. I never knew him well. I recall a Gus Craven family up north-northwest of Rushville. There is a fine interview with Gus Craven about the early days up around Red Cloud Agency and Pine Ridge in the Nebraska State Historical Society at Lincoln. Is Doctor Craven a relative? I used Craven material in my *Cheyenne Autumn*, the Little Wolf and Dull Knife story.

It is good to have your new year's greeting, and by now I trust you have a fine running start on 1959.

Sincerely,

To Bruce Nicoll

[University of Nebraska Press]

To May 15:
Vance Apartment Hotel
[Lincoln, Nebraska]
March 27, 1959

Dear Bruce:[1]

I've been thinking about the possible surviving relatives of Amos Bad Heart Bull and realize that of course there would be no old timer, so there won't be any necessity for the old formal approach for your photographers in addition to the usual financial arrangement that would be made with any white owner of the picture history.

There were publishing arrangements, as I recall, signed with the Carnegie Foundation, but whether there was a time clause I do not recall.

The chief heir to Helen Blish's estate was, as I remember, an older sister, a Mrs. Doctor Joyner of Iowa. Eleanor Hinman may have the full name and address. In New York I have this for about 1937–8, which is pretty old. The Iowa Medical Association directory or better, the AMA directory may cut down the time consumed in tracing Dr. Joyner or his wife.

As I recall, the Carnegie people had the publication rights to both the pictures and the Blish narrative material but the time limit may have been reached.

Anyway, this is the most important single publishing venture, by volume, of the Great Plains. It is the fullest picture history in existence, so far as I know, with the greatest detail and artistry. Further, no other picture history has had anything like the intelligent and tireless interpretation by the old timers who took part in the events portrayed, events that include such fights as the Reno and Custer battles, etc., up to the battle of Wounded Knee, and inter-tribal fights. In addition there are many fine portrayals of ceremonials, with all the careful study and description by Helen Blish. All through this runs the philosophy and the religion of the Sioux, the Oglala Lakota, at his best.

I wish you every success—

in haste

1. Bruce Nicoll (1912–83) was the director of the University of Nebraska Press from 1959 to 1973. MS had known both Mr. and Mrs. Nicoll for some time; he had been assistant to the chancellor at the university, and Mrs. Nicoll was manager of the Miller and Paine bookstore. When Nicoll began the publication of Bison Books, MS recommended many titles the press accepted. One of the first was John G. Neihardt's *Black Elk Speaks,* published by the press in 1961.

To Mary Abbot

To May 18,
Vance Apartment Hotel
10th & L Sts.,
Lincoln, Nebr.
March 28, 1959

Dear Mary:

You are going to be cross with me but I can't help this now. I really am not very much interested in Ed Kuhn's opinion on *The Son of the Gamblin' Man.*[1] This book has very little to do with life as it was lived in the Platte Valley—only as it looked to the eyes of the youth who was, by the heat and pressure upon the matrix in which he found himself, being crystalized into the garnet that became Robert Henri.

About raising the dramatic presentation of the setbacks of John Cozad—I kept to the facts, which are psychologically true for the gambler. He really welcomes defeat and takes it quietly and with the sense of deserving it, as I tried to show before and finally in the ultimate defeat of his dream community when he has to flee into the brush. Everyone who knows gamblers of this type knows this. To others I recommend Dr. Bargler's study, published by, of all people, Hill and Wang, and the many earlier studies, some of which the Doctor mentions in his book.[2] I grew up around these old-time gamblers. I know how they respond.

This book of mine is a step by step development of the painter Henri in a family and a locale where such a talent had never shown itself. I was interested in his techniques and also in the great qualities of leadership that helped limit Henri as a painter but perhaps helped make a greater contribution to American art than if he had developed the painting potentialities of an angel.

You know that I've had to watch the strangulation of eleven books at birth by the publisher. For this I should go on mutilating my carefully worked-out manuscripts, my conception of what my books should be?

No — not any more. Minor matters I will consider, but I am done bothering with criticism from people who have no way of knowing either the potentialities of my material or my work.

Sorry, but you must admit that I've had an awful lot of foolish obstacles put into my path and I'm not the gambler to enjoy destruction,

I am enclosing a page that should clear up the family relationship.

1. Ed Kuhn (1924–79) was at that time an editor with McGraw-Hill; later he was with New American Library, with World Publishing, and then with Playboy Press.

2. Edmund Bergler, *The Psychology of Gambling* (New York: Hill and Wang, 1957).

From May 15 to June 13:
422 Hudson
New York 14, N. Y.
April 19, 1959

Dear Mary:

Oh, you are mistaken about my having any doubt over the form the *Son of the Gamblin' Man* was to take. You may recall the day you had lunch with Ed Aswell and me at the Harvard Club over the book, and that Ed tried to pressure me into making the book nonfiction and that I refused flatly. I said I could not fill in the necessary holes and that I wanted the form to be a written approximation of a Henri painting. Further, my nonfiction is really nonfiction. This side of the Hudson there is a difference.

My only structural problem in the book was the handling of the material of the 1883–1903 period. Fortunately the father's portrait was painted in a building that I know quite well, one I've visited many times, particularly the Allen Williams Studio, which had had no changes since the 1903 period.

I have no intention of making any material changes in the book and none in its classification. I consider the rewriting of books in publishing houses a major crime against the arts. It would be a crime even if the editor were a person of taste and information. A book worth the word, the term, is a product of the *writer*. I tolerated no such tactics from the Atlantic in 1935. My contempt for editors and publishers has not lessened, and McGraw, as I am in a position to know, are not even good business men, when it comes to trade books.

Even if I had written *Son of the Gamblin' Man* for money I would know that McGraw would not make it for me.

If you don't wish to handle the book, I should like to pick it up when I return to New York, May 15 or 16th.

Sincerely,

To Alfred Knopf

June 15, 1959

Dear Alfred Knopf:

You are very right to express dissatisfaction with writers on the west. There is so much to illuminate even the subtle depths of man's nature in western material, and to do that dramatically and with high adventure. But the artificial formula and the everlasting rewriting of the stock cliché has all but destroyed any chance for good writing with a western locale.

I suppose one reason for this was the early westerner's tendency toward action, leaving the writing to those who made a swift trip through the region if they got anywhere near it at all. Besides there was always the demand for the superficial and sensational—as if the truth of man in any locale weren't the most fabulously sensational of all.

There does seem to be another reason for the poor state of western writing—the curious notion rather common among younger editors that any author who works in such material must be a novice or a fool or both—one to be told just what the form and the detail is to be. So many do not understand that there is something more possible than the "western" of the pulps in the old days, the TV of the present. That western material can become literature would come as a great surprise to some editors in New York publishing houses [at] this moment. By now this is a joke to me but I realize that it is not a joke to a man with a family to support by his writing.

Incidentally, *Crazy Horse* has become a symphony, written by Charles Mills, from the book and premiered by Max Rudolf's Cincinnati symphonic orchestra last fall. I am told it will be presented here next fall. There is also a ballet and perhaps eventually an opera in progress. Charles Mills is from the Carolinas and stumbled upon the book by accident.

I trust that the summer will be a fine one for all the eastern regions. I'm heading west in a few days—

Sincerely,

To Mary Abbot

To July 25:
Cornhusker Hotel
Lincoln, Nebr.
June 29, 1959

Dear Mary:

While up at Fort Robinson, walking over the ground where Crazy Horse was killed and the Cheyennes made their desperate break over the snow, I suddenly struck upon an idea for a companion book for *The Horsecatcher.*

This would be the story of a young Sioux, son of the band historian, the man who keeps the tribal band history in pictures, back in the old buffalo hunting days. I plan to have the boy about six at the time of the Fetterman fight, 1866 and recall later, at the time of the book, that he had watched his father make the pictures of what happened there, saw the dead and the wounded at the time.[1] Then, around fifteen, when the last of the Sioux wars gets under way he has to make his final decision whether he will take up a full and heedless part in the fighting as a young warrior eager for coups and kills and other war honors, as all his fellows seem to be doing or will he hold himself aloof, keeping an eye out for as much of what happens as possible, even though in the attacks upon the village he must fight. As a band historian his personal exploits, outside of actually letting himself or his family and other helpless ones around him being killed, must always be subordinated to the observation of what is happening—to the stories of the people, and the practice to achieve as near perfection as possible in the pictorial portrayal of the events. The final decision comes in the Custer battle.

Of course before this there will be lesser fights with Indian foes and whites, and much village life, moving, sundances and other ceremonials to record and a great hunt on the Yellowstone and also the elevation of his father to the great Shirtwearers Society, men who vow to let no personal gain or feeling ever swerve them from unsullied allegiance to the public good.

This material is already in my notes and in my head. I'll make up a youth much like the famous storycatcher, Amos Bad Heart Bull, but he will have to be older, to see and take part in the fights of the 1870's, particularly 1875–6.

I should like to do this for Westminster; they did very well for us with the *Horsecatcher.* Perhaps they can do well with a story of storycatcher too. . . .

1. This is the first discussion of *The Story Catcher* (Philadelphia: Westminster Press, 1963). MS later changed the time of the story to the 1840s.

To Clarkson N. Potter

CLARKSON N. POTTER, inc., Publisher

422 Hudson St.,
New York 14, N.Y.
September 9, 1959

Dear Clarkson:

Here's THE SON OF THE GAMBLIN' MAN.

I've considered your very reasonable suggestions. There are short footnotes explaining the homestead law, etc., I've gone over the entire book, with enough changes, mostly my own that I had always planned to make, to necessitate recopying ⅔ of the manuscript. This time I typed it myself, avoiding the fantastic errors the typist had made and didn't correct. Unfortunately I was too pushed with my western deadlines to check on her. I am sorry.

About the scene with faro going: I included this in a short chapter, now VIII, that I omitted at the start because it is so perfectly action on the surface that I was afraid some editor, seeing this would want me to make a western of the book and wouldn't return the book on my demand. I went through all that at McGraw once and fortunately [Edward] Aswell was still there to save me. One of their editors volunteered to teach me how to write westerns. I gather he's in Wall Street now, and much happier.

I had had another motivation in VIII, but because you wanted faro, which had to be completely alien to the town of Cozad, to be consistent with the gambler's whole plan, I put it in this chapter, which is an alien intrusion from start to finish anyway.

In addition I cut one of the large chapters in the middle of the book into two parts, recast much of the center section and put the Cozad boys into the Platte river fire, as it turns out, only observers, primarily, but that's not known until the fire is over. They were in this fire, but I held this back too—I am so firmly convinced that I must find out whether an editor is sympathetic with what I am trying to write about that I am protecting myself, now that both Aswell and Paul Hoffman are out of editing. Fortunately Henry Alsberg at Hastings House is a priceless asset for my kind of writer there.

I've added various other dramatic bits that came up in my research for the Nebraska book last spring. Fortunately, all this, with the extra chapter, only made 11 additional pages in the book.

About pictures: Don't you think we should avoid them in this? For the jacket yes. For that there are the pictures of Cozad by Brady and Henri, as

well as a photograph of the 100th Meridian sign, etc. Some day, years from now, I should like this book brought out with Henri paintings, in color—
Sincerely,

To The Reverend Father Peter J. Powell

Sept 12, 1959

Dear Father Powell:

I'm happy that your summer was such a successful one. There will be a fellowship for you. Reapply for the Guggenheim. Very few people get it the first application.

About MEDICINE ARROW, ROCK FOREHEAD, STONE FOREHEAD, ETC:[1]

Most of my special notes are in fire proof storage and on those I can only give you my recollection, and what is in the book [*Cheyenne Autumn*].

I am convinced he was killed at the Sappa [River] but, as Grinnell agreed, there was no chance of getting any Plains Indians to talk directly of the death of such a personage by an enemy. He never was able to get a real account of the Sappa that he could use from them, as you will have discovered. Nor could anyone else. I took a lot of material to some of the old timers and only when I said I would have to use what I had, did any of them but Old Cheyenne Woman, in my childhood, open on that material, and none of the younger people seemed to have heard the story. Even then the material I got was under greatest secrecy, and never to be laid to the narrator's door. There is or was a set of pictures in an old account book made of the Sappa fight, much like the Little Finger Nail pictures. It was borrowed for me from the P[r]owers family (Mrs. John P[r]owers was a full blood Cheyenne, it is said, and niece of Medicine Arrow) by Rice, an old timer in north Kansas, whom I saw with the Wimers on my trip back to Cheyenne Hole, 1949. One of the pictures showed what the notes with the book identified as Medicine Arrow in front of the Arrow Lodge, going down before the bullets, a white rag still in his hand. The maker of the pictures was not identified.

I think the confusion is multiplied by Grinnell's "Great Mysteries" giving Black Hairy Dog's Arrow term as 1876–83 and saying Stone Forehead died in the north, 1876. R. I. Dodge says he became a drunkard and died on the Tongue River in 1874 OUR WILD INDIANS, p 120, etc.[2] And by the good old Cheyenne custom of giving a younger man, often a relative, the illustrious name of a man killed by enemies. There was a nephew of Stone Forehead, (blood nephew or adopted, and whether by white man term or Indian, I can't say,) on the Red Cloud rolls 1876–7. As I recall he went back south with Little Wolf, the Spring of 1877.

Mrs. John P[r]owers, Las Animas, Colo., the Cheyenne woman, called a niece of Rock Forehead, went into mourning for him when she saw some of his regalia in the hands of [Lieutenant] Henley's [*sic*] troops and buffalo hunters after the Sappa fight. There were a couple of lesser relatives of hers killed too, but she said that Henely would die before the year was out for killing Stone Forehead, and Henely was drowned. See Roenigk's PIONEER HISTORY OF KANSAS for some of this.[3] Ask the Indians who her arrow medicine man uncle was. You might also ask them where they think Stone Forehead died and what became of the body? Wild Hog told my father the Sappa story and I have much of it in rough draft, a rough draft of my father's letter to Rosalie, his Swiss sweetheart. According to Hog, they stopped at the place where Stone Forehead's body had been, in the bend of the Sappa, in a hole in the bluff, and taken away 1881–2, by Cheyennes coming through. Old Cheyenne woman verified this story when Old Jules asked about some of these things, one evening when a group of Cheyennes stopped, coming through on their way to Pine Ridge. We lived at the old Cheyenne crossing of the Niobrara, when they took the Spring creek valley up northwest, and crossed toward the creeks to the White river, making a short haul between water. I recalled very clearly the stern face on the old man along, stern that such things were talked about, I gathered.

You mention men who knew Medicine Arrow. They must be very old and were small children at his killing, even then. After all, the Sappa fight is long ago, 85 years next April, so even the 100 year olds would only have been fifteen at the time.

Now I must rush off—

Sincerely,

You've seen Street's acct. Kans. S[tate] H[istorical] S[ociety] collections reel X. p 368?. From Ben Clark.

I have half a dozen accounts from the buffalo hunters in the fight.

1. These were all names for the same man, the Keeper of the Sacred Arrows, who MS averred was killed in the attack by the army on a small band of Cheyennes on Sappa Creek in Kansas, in 1875. Her identification of Medicine Arrow is a major point in *Cheyenne Autumn* but is questioned by some historians.

2. Richard Irving Dodge, *Our Wild Indians: Thirty-Three Years' Personal Experiences among the Red Men of the Great West* (Chicago: A. G. Nettleton and Co., 1882).

3. Adolph Roenigk, ed., *Pioneer History of Kansas* (Lincoln, Kans.: A. Roenigk, 1933).

To Bruce Nicoll

October 25, 1959

Dear Bruce:

It was fine to see the Press going so well now, with a flood of manuscripts coming in. You certainly have put momentum into it, and direction.

In fact, you are far, far past needing me with the Wounded Knee book on your list. With this in mind I put in some time this week trying to come up with a good writer to take the book over, if you get the backing. If you haven't anyone in mind, I'll suggest a name or two. I am sure you can think of someone better. I've had Lott's novel on the Wounded Knee fight around here for many months.[1] The publishers apparently hoped I might say something about it for the promotion. I had no time the short periods I've been here since spring. Monday I did go through the book. The man writes pretty well but with an eye on Hollywood, where his first book landed. Whether he could do the sound research and the controlled writing for a good nonfiction account of the tragic events remains to be seen. His Indians are still really nothing more than the thinnest stock figures.

I suppose the best would be Alice Marriott or Jimmy Olson, when his RED CLOUD is done.[2] By then Jimmy will have completed much of the research.

Anyway, you don't need me now, and I can let my reluctance show. I just don't like to do books set up by anyone else and I have never accepted a grant of any kind, although the Museum of the American Indian (Heye Foundation) has always made it plain I could get grants for Indian books any time I wanted them. They always knew where such things could be managed, it seems. But I can't do books that way. Nobody gets to look over my shoulder.

I was ready to try to swallow my scruples if the Press needed the book. Now you don't, and so please, may I be excused? I'm certain nothing came of the attempts for a grant in this short time. All the writers I've named have had grants so I know there would be no trouble there.

Rain like a Wyoming gullywasher here yesterday. The day before I went to the Frank Lloyd Wright Guggenheim Museum. I think the critics who complained about it were startled by the amount of light that is concentrated on the pictures. This is the first eastern building that manages to get light and the sense of light into the picture and around it, where light should be. I wish the critics would go out to look into a Denver or a Santa Fe gallery.

Best wishes,

1. Milton James Lott, *Dance Back the Buffalo* (Boston: Houghton Mifflin, 1959).

2. James C. Olson was on the University of Nebraska faculty for twenty-five years, director of NSHS from 1946 to 1956, and later chancellor of the University of Missouri Four Campus System. He published over five hundred columns and six books, among them *Red Cloud and the Sioux Problem* (Lincoln: U of Nebraska P, 1965) and *History of Nebraska* (Lincoln: U of Nebraska P, 1955).

To Mrs. Ray C. Wiles

October 29, 1959

Dear Mrs. Wiles:

After eight months of research in the west and speaking from Colorado to Swampscott, Mass., I returned here to find boxes of mail that never caught up with me. Your postcard about the placement of the word *only* in a sentence in HOSTILES AND FRIENDLIES was among the accumulation.

All I can say is that I am sorry my writing reached your purist's eye. As a student of Dr. Louise Pound I consider English a living, growing language and like every creative writer, I try to use it as a live, dynamic instrument.

The formal essay can and should be written in formal English, in what we call Barrett Wendell English. Such essays are no more than an exercise in words as formal and limited as the formal ballet, *Swan Lake,* say. The language used in the personal account, the article, the narrative biography and particularly in the more creative forms — the drama and fiction, must rise out of the material and the life portrayed. Words are limited in meaning because they must carry approximately the same denotation to a great many people. The creative writer gives them special meanings by unusual usages and arrangements. This is particularly true of those of us who use rhythmic prose for special connotations and emotional impact. This means placement of words by ear as well as by eye.

Your card reminded me of the letter Dr. Weseen, head of Business English, University of Nebraska, once wrote to Willa Cather, one of the world's great stylists. He listed over 400 grammatical errors in one of her books. Her reply, paraphrased was, "Only that many?"

Why not reread Barrett Wendell on diction? You would like it.
Sincerely,

To Mildred Bennett

November 3, 1959

Dear Mildred Bennett:[1]

I want to thank you, not only for making my stay in Red Cloud [Nebraska] so pleasant but, much more important than anyone but you can see now, for the fine work you are doing with the Willa Cather Pioneer Memorial.

May the winter be a fine one.

1. Mildred Bennett (1909–89), a preeminent authority on Willa Cather, was instrumental in preserving Red Cloud buildings associated with the author's work, establishing archives, and organizing an annual Cather Conference in Red Cloud. Her publications include *The World of Willa Cather* (New York: Dodd, 1951), and she edited *Early Stories of Willa Cather* (New York: Dodd Mead, 1957) and *Collected Stories of Willa Cather* (Lincoln: U of Nebraska P, 1965).

To Ed Sutton

November 29, 1959

Dear ES:[1]

Just a hasty note about Billy Olive: You will find the most readily available sources in the CATTLEMEN, in the notes, pages 499–500. The most complete story on the killing of Billy, with considerable about his character is, as indicated in my notes, in Carl Coke Rister's NO MAN'S LAND, University of Oklahoma Press, Norman, 1948. This is a small book but should still be in print. See around page 112. . . .

Your Mr. Hurd must be pretty sentimental if he can doubt the Olive story. Print never denied doing any of the things he did, so far as I ever heard. There's no denial in the Texas trials nor in the Nebraska one. As for his inhumanities down in Texas, Dobie, in his LONGHORN. p 222, tells of Print Olive's use of the "Death of the Skins", the wrapping a man in the green hide of a critter and letting him die on the prairie. Sonnichsen, I'LL DIE BEFORE I'LL RUN, gives that and a lot more.[2] But I went to the trial records down there, and to the Texas papers, the Taylorville Times, for instance.

And as always, I held a little back. I always do, so nobody will drag me into court for fear I'll tell the rest.

Thanks for the photographs. They're mighty nice to have.

What are you going to do with your Kansas cattle story?

Greetings to Hazel and the rest—

In haste

1. Everette S. "Ed" Sutton (1893–1987), from Benkleman, Nebraska, was an amateur historian of southwestern Nebraska and northern Kansas. The Suttons, together with the Wimers and Mr. and Mrs. Arthur Carmody, escorted MS on several historical treks useful to her when she was writing *Cheyenne Autumn.*

2. J. Frank Dobie, *Longhorn* (Boston: Little, Brown, 1941). C. L. Sonnichsen, *I'll Die Before I'll Run: The Stories of the Great Feuds of Texas* (New York: Harper, 1951).

To Bruce Nicoll

December 6, 1959

Dear Bruce:

Going through my notes on manuscript material on Nebraska brought up the RECOLLECTIONS OF CAPT. L. H. NORTH,[1] by George Bird Grinnell, deposited in the Nebraska State Historical Society as well as in the Library of the Museum of the American Indian here.

I still wonder why this was never published. My notes reach to page 208 but the manuscript may be longer, and as I recall, the margins were rather small. At the end of my notes is the comment: With good editing and footnotes the manuscript would make a very good book with much material not in print elsewhere. It is true that the work with the Pawnee Scouts is pretty well covered in Grinnell's TWO GREAT SCOUTS AND THEIR PAWNEE BATTALION, Arthur H. Clark, 1928, but there's much, much, more of the life of the times, 1850's into the 20th century in this, including considerable about Buffalo Bill Cody, the Cody-North ranch, the Custer expedition into the Black Hills in 1874, with North and Grinnell both along, much about Major Frank North, who suffered from asthma, and a great deal about such characters as Buck and Baxter Taylor, brought up from Texas with a North trail herd, Bax who was the best broncho buster that L. H. North ever saw, Buck who went with Cody's show as "King of the Cowboys", etc., and about Billy Jaiger or Iager who got caught in a blizzard in the Wyoming region, lost both legs and most of his fingers and later was clerk of the district court at Chadron for years. (I remember Billy-the-Bear very well; he used to come down to our place and with a child's curiosity about deformities, I snooped around until I found out what had happened to Billy.)

There's much on the big ranchers of the Platte country too, considering the length of the book and considerable about nature at the time. I think this is a natural for Dr. Danker's editorial pen. I tried to get Dr. Sheldon interested in publishing this manuscript back in 1934, but the Society had no money and besides, the other North book was still in print.

There may, of course, be some restriction to publication but if so, I don't recall it. Mrs. Grinnell, the widow of the recorder was still alive a few years ago. She was a good friend of J. Donald Adams of the New York *Times* book section. I had her telephone number but not her address, as I recall. She wasn't a young woman, but not extremely old either the last time I visited with her.

About the Wounded Knee matter: I just can't see myself working under a grant. It's too foreign to my nature. Besides, I'm heading into the Canadian archives in the summer, with no telling how many months of work to get through there. If the situation is like the one I'm always running into in the USA, I'll have to do a great deal of organizing of material, let alone note-taking.

Well, the holidays are upon us. I'm farther behind than ever, but I wish all the Nicolls and the Press a happy and prosperous time.

Sincerely,

P.S. A friend sent me Perkin's write-up of *Molly* from R[ocky] M[ountain] *News*.[2] It's fine.

1. See Luther North, *Man of the Plains: Recollections of Luther North, 1856–1882*, edited by Donald E. Danker, foreword by George Bird Grinnell (Lincoln: U of Nebraska P, 1961).

2. Mollie Dorsey Sanford, *Mollie; The Journal of Mollie Dorsey Sanford in Nebraska and Colorado Territories, 1857–1866* (Lincoln: U of Nebraska P, 1959).

To Thomas W. Wright

Peabody College

December 11, 1959

Dear Mr. Wright:[1]

Thank you. I am happy to add another Oglala wintercount to my collection. They all vary a little, and agree in the larger tribal and natural events, such as the year of the smallpox, the year of the falling stars, etc.

I am amused to see the old Swan-feather stereoscopic view show up again. This photograph was never, so far as I know, identified as Crazy Horse before my book came out. In the old days, when this was a very common item in stereoscopic collections, it was usually labeled Red Shirt* or Short Bull or even Little Big Man, depending upon who was in the news or had been mentioned as being to Omaha or Chicago or, preferably, to Washington. Or having died. This was common practice. All the manufacturer had to do was run another name under the old view.

Are you certain that Mr. Hackett's copy of this is a tintype? It could, of course, be the original but tintypes were long out of style in 1877, when this would have to have been made. It is identified as a tintype in Vaughn's WITH CROOK ON THE ROSEBUD too, but it looks like a plate job to me, although I do not claim to be expert in photographic processes.

Further, the accoutrements of the picture would have been very unlikely for Crazy Horse. He could not, so far as He Dog, Red Feather, or the accounts of the summer of 1877, have worn the shell-core breast piece, and the feather piece is not the Sioux chief's one feather. That was always the black-tipped strong-quilled feather of an eagle, wing or tail, and usually worn erect at the back of the head. What your man is wearing is a swath of feathers from one of the white-feathered aquatic birds and usually termed Swan-breast among the Indians of the Plains and the traders. I can recall my father selling Indians such white feather pieces, not from swan but from white geese or brants. There were several other water birds with fine fall of white feathers. Often the side-back shield of feathers down toward the wing was used, skinned off, the skin tanned to hold the feathers in place. . . .

About the Joseph Eagle Hawk reminiscences of He Dog—Yours are probably the same as those with the Nebraska State Historical Society. I have around 200 pages of interview material with He Dog from the summer of 1930 and then a return in 1931, to check up on things that weren't clear in the first round, the weeks of 1930. I recall He Dog from my childhood, back when he used to come to the Niobrara to hunt and camped at our place. This was an honest man.

There are several fine untouched topics for anyone interested in old Fort Robinson. It was the most concentratedly dramatic post of our frontier. Just think of all that happened there from 1874 through to the spring of 1879!

* See Red Shirt, p 192, *Fighting Indians* Schmitt & Brown.[2]

Good luck,

1. Thomas Wright was writing a graduate paper on MS.
2. Schmitt and Brown, *Fighting Indians of the West.*

To Mary Abbot

January 17, 1960

Dear Mary:

Thanks for the carbon of the note to Wyeth about the Nebraska book.[1]

Friday I turned in all the galleys except the front matter for *Son of the Gamblin' Man.* I found Clark[2] and his office deep in stacks of jackets, etc., getting out the preliminary mailings. I had hoped they could change the jacket. It's pitiful, I think, like some poor vanity outfit's. I did get the front design changed from cards of six, seven hundred years ago to something that could be used in 1872–1882 but when Clark sent me a copy of the whole thing, I was really floored. It's not only that there's a blatant misstatement in the biographical matter of the back: I haven't taught school in Nebraska anywhere since the rural teaching I did back in the middle 1920's and a little English assistantship work the same time, but the photo was so appalling. I had never seen it, and I hope you haven't. It plays up my blind eye, which seems in very bad taste to me, and the mouth is shaped like a woman screaming in travail. In addition the thing seems to be printed by offset and very poorly.

Perhaps, if the book goes well, we can get Clark to change the back on some later edition, but the book will have to arrive at such a stage without any help from the jacket, in spite of the jacket. Fortunately I'm not committed to any public autographing. I couldn't face anyone over that book jacket.

But the type face is nice and if Clark will only print enough books and give it some announcement so people will know there *is* a book, perhaps all this misery over the jacket can be forgotten. He says there's wide interest in the story, even as far off as Japan. I think I told you Margit Varga at *Life,*[3] supervising all the art of an Americana nature, etc., was very interested in the story, amazed at it. Without reading it she thinks this must be the best thing done on an American artist. (It wouldn't have to be very good; there's fantastically little on our artists that's worth looking into.)

I suspect it will be up to you to get the book anywhere. Certainly its looks won't do anything for it.

Sorry, it's late and I'm cross—

1. M. S. "Buz" Wyeth, an editor at Harper and Row, worked with MS on *Love Song to the Plains* (1961).

2. Clarkson N. Potter (b. 1928) was an editor at Doubleday and Dial before founding his own company, 1959–76. Later he was with Brandywine Press; he was also a literary agent.

3. Margit Varga (b. 1908), an artist and author, was in charge of the art department of *Life* magazine in 1960.

To Jean Van Dorien

March 2, 1960

Dear Jean Van Dorien:

Thank you. I'm very apologetic about anything I do before the camera. It's the one thing in the world that I fear.

I wish there might be some way to determine genuine talent for writing. In my courses at the University of Wisconsin I often saw the writers of what seemed absolutely hopeless early manuscripts suddenly fired in the concentrated atmosphere of a creative group and become creative themselves. I've seen writers who did very well in commercial non-creative formula fiction suddenly, for no discernible reason, become creative, throw their remunerative careers away and start in on imaginative, significant writing. Barry Fleming is an outstanding example of this in his later CARNIVAL and in his forthcoming WINTER RIDE. True, there were signs of more serious intent in his FORTUNE TELLERS.[1] Besides he never wrote pure claptrap.

Anyone with the power of literacy and, as I suggested in my TV program, with the ability to see human conflict, can learn to write really artistic short stories. These may have to go to the quality magazines or the usually non-pay literary quarterlies. Greatness or even artistic excellence is not always easy for a writer's contemporaries. Often excellence in an art stands against popular acceptance in the artist's generation, as painters, musicians, poets as well as novelists sometimes find.

About your lack of a college education: Too much education can be a handicap to a writer if it happens to be in English literature. Unless the student has been writing as his taste develops, by the time he has obtained a doctorate his first writing will fall so far behind what he knows literature can be that he is discouraged. The ideal is of course, the combination of an excellent background in the literature of the world and a facility in good writing developed simultaneously. There is nothing in this to say that the familiarity with great literature must come from college courses. Few of our great novelists were ever in college.

Your statement: "I am realistic enough to know that if I do not have the talent or the ability to write my ambition could be the road to insanity." is pure nonsense. Writing, particularly attempts at serious fiction, is one of the most broadening, balancing of experiences. The consideration of human conflict it thrusts upon the writer tends to develop perspective, draw him out of the self-centeredness, the egocentricity and self-pity, with the resultant emotional immaturity, that lie at the core of so much mental illness.

You have my best wishes and my confidence—

1. Barry Fleming, *Carnival* (New York: Lippincott, 1953), *The Winter Rider* (New York: Lippincott, 1960), and *Fortune Tellers* (New York: Lippincott, 1951).

To Peggy H. Benjamin

April 13, 1960

Dear Madam:

Victor Hass of the *World-Herald* forwarded your letter about your father, James Daniel Haskell to me. . . . Obviously you have not read SON OF THE GAMBLIN' MAN or you would know that I portrayed him as a likable, intelligent and energetic young man of whom Robert Henry Cozad was very fond. . . . [W]hy don't *you* write your father's story?

As for Dr. Robert Gatewood asking me to write the Cozad-Henri story in the middle 1930's, I have his letters to prove it in my safe deposit box. The letters from John Cozad to my father in 1903 about starting a new town on the Short Line railroad planned to run up the Survey valley, through the sandhills, are also in existence. In these he refers to his son by name as the painter Henri. There are hundreds of letters with references to my queries about this story from 1936 on in my files. From the enclosed copy of a letter received just this week from Frank Johnson, former regent of the university and long-time attorney at Lexington, you will see that I have been working on this book since the 1930's, and spent a long period interviewing old timers around Cozad and Lexington in 1942, men and women who remembered not only the Cozads very well but your father, men like Stuckey, Hagadone, Koch (who knew your father very well), the Sheldons and dozens more.

You say you heard me assert at Red Cloud that I don't write for money. I also said that I never exaggerate, always hold back a little on everyone of whom I write.

To Walter Frese

May 1, 1960

Dear Walter:

Here's a copy of the little paper that Tom Ferril, the poet puts out. He used to be in charge of HARPER'S Easy Chair or whatever the department was called. See last page for DeVoto's estimation of him.

Of course, after [Elia] Kazin did a book of western literature, Tom could still do one, and the pieces wouldn't overlap much. Tom grew up in Denver, always in writing, knows the western writing, the good writing. True, he's a Harper author but they might not be interested in this and he might.

Another good man to do a western literary anthology would be Wallace Stegner, (Alberta, Canada; Utah, Iowa, Harvard, etc., excellent writer) now in charge of creative writing at Stanford University, California.

But Tom would be best, perhaps. Wallace wrote a fine book on Powell, the man who explored the Grand Canyon, BEYOND THE HUNDREDTH MERIDIAN,[1] and has worked with early writing a great deal. Either of these men know what the score is, and Kazin may by now, but remember the fantastic book that Van Wyck Brooks wrote on Mark Twain, before he knew anything about the west or western life? It developed into a grand feud with DeVoto, into which I was drawn, and was never forgiven by eastern critics for pointing out that Hannibal, Missouri, of Twain's boyhood was not *puritan,* as Brooks assumed and developed his thesis on Twain's hampering from that.

Later Brooks learned better, but the book is still in libraries and the real damage can never be calculated. Europeans always trot out that book to prove how dwarfed we are by puritanism, out west. Fortunately nobody uses *that* against me—not after OLD JULES.

1. Wallace Stegner, *Beyond the Hundredth Meridian: John Wesley Powell and the Second Opening of the West* (Boston: Houghton Mifflin, 1962).

To Caroline Sauer

[McIntosh & Otis]

Lincoln, Nebr
May 14, 1960

Dear Caroline:[1]

I was so disgusted with the whole publishing business when the Westminster contract came through that I couldn't get myself to look at it. Now, just back from an autographing in Omaha, after one here the 12th I wouldn't sign a contract with *anybody* for *anything*. Everywhere I'm reminded that I am offering a book that has had not *one* line of advertising, as one woman pointed out to me "Even Vantage Press does better than that." The general impression is that *Son of the Gamblin Man* must be a real stinker. I'd like to take a teaching job and never write another word.

Well, some day it will all be over.

1. Caroline Sauer was in charge of the Juvenile Department at McIntosh and Otis at this time. Later she became president.

To Bruce Nicoll

May 23, 1960

Dear Bruce:

Undoing the piles of mail that gathered while I was gone exposed the original of the enclosed "Wilderness Days on the Niobrara" by Elaine Goodale Eastman. That suggests another body of frontier material you might have someone look into for your paperbacks.

Elaine Goodale, as she says in the item, came as a schoolteacher from the east to Pine Ridge. She was there during the ghost dance troubles, and married Dr. Charles Eastman, Dakota (not Lakota but eastern Sioux) medical doctor who wrote books that are now out of print. He was always a little vague and cloudy about Lakota history, etc., but she was a better writer. She just died recently. There's quite a body of her writing around, mostly public domain, and from the journal section of this you can gather her style and comments. There's a good book in the lot of her writing, I suspect.

There's no date or source on the paper, but I suspect that it can be dated pretty well by an item that was on the back of the clipping: *Alice B. Toklas* was running in the Atlantic.[1]

And I am reminded of another book, not yet in the public domain, that will perhaps interest you: Elinore Pruitt Stewart's LETTERS OF A WOMAN HOMESTEADER, which ran in the *Atlantic* and then were published in book form 1914. She wrote from Burntfork, Wyoming, had a homestead there.

Must hurry on—

PS. Dr. Eastman was mostly Sioux, part white, brilliant man but ended up an alcoholic.

Greetings to the outfit. It was fine to see you all.

1. Gertrude Stein, "The Autobiography of Alice B. Toklas," *Atlantic*, May–August 1933.

To Mary Abbot

[before May 27, 1960]

Dear Mary:

I see that I'm to be blamed for the whole debacle over my book but since you will want to deal with Clark Potter in the future I think you should know some of the facts.

Far back in the winter he sat across my work table from me and urged me to go out west to autograph. I didn't want to, even before the picture deal because I had faced too many irate book people who didn't get their books in the past. Finally I did agree. "But I'll go only *after* the advertising and the reviews have had plenty of time to reach out there." With March publication, which I knew would be put off; my books always are, I wouldn't go before the two middle weeks of May and I said so right then. Clark promised the advertising would be made early, the review books go out early. I wanted it in writing but to me to ask this would be an insult and I let it pass.

I got the advertising *after* the autographing and not only the Lincoln *Journal* but even the Denver *Post* had to write in for a review copy, demanding it in a hurry because the autographing at May's was upon them. Perkin and Peckham both said they got the books barely in time to get the reviews in for May 15, the Sunday before I autographed, giving the country orders no time to get in, or the out of town people to make plans. This when review copies should go out a month before publication day, as everyone knows.

So far as I can discover there must not have been over a dozen review copies sent out all together. I'm tired of apologizing to newspapers about this. This scarcity of review books, coupled with an unknown and unadvertising publisher strengthened the growing rumor that the book was a piece of vanity publication, a book to let alone. The book sold well until after publication date, and then, with no reviews, no advertising the sales disappeared. The sales were 4500 six weeks before publication. Now you say they are 5000. The bookstores tell me that is the story with them. And it's not bad reviews, because there were none; nor bad word of mouth, because the reports are good, from those who read the book.

So now comes a full page in the New York *Times*. What a stupid waste of money, when half a page, even a quarter the Sunday before or right after publication would have served a thousand times better. Saved the entire situation. Everybody is mad at me. Even Lee Huff, of the Main Street Galleries, Chicago with the Henri show in the winter, ducked out when he discovered when I was coming, although in the winter he urged me to come in.

So Clark went in on the local autographing announcements? The business cost me practically two weeks of valuable time, $400 in money and thousands of dollars in goodwill and prestige. But Clark will pay too. He had a chance to show up as a real publisher with a book of mine; now he's just a bumbling vanity publisher in the eyes of the public. Of course I've lost the best paying prospect I've ever written, but that's apparently to be my lot.

To Bruce Nicoll

June 12, 1960

Dear Bruce:

Pretty gaudy stationery, what?

About the CRAZY HORSE: I don't suppose that there's any danger of you using a first edition for the off-set or whatever process you intend to use. There's an error on p 330—line dropped out. This is corrected in the later War Edition of Knopfs and, of course, in the Hastings [House] reissue.

I suppose you are using an off-set process for the paper backs, but if you want to use the original plates, they are in storage at Sullivans, in Lincoln, and I'd be happy to loan them to you, if you'll see that they get back.

I feel a little shame-faced about making any more suggestions to you, but recently when I suggested that a friend of mine use a copy of BLACK ELK SPEAKS, by Neihardt for some work she was doing on the Oglala Sioux, she had to pay $12 for a battered copy; a good copy would have cost $15. This was published 1932 by William Morrow & Co., New York, and remaindered very quickly. I paid 49 cents for my copy. Of course a reissue should include the colored drawings and black and white plates but the black and whites are printed on regular book stock and so could be included in a reissue. The book is 280 pages, not counting the plates. It is one of the three best and practically only first hand accounts of American Indians with any flavor of the old days left. The three are Marquis THE MAN WHO FOUGHT WITH CUSTER, the story of Wooden Leg, the Cheyenne; Linderman's THE AMERICAN, the story of Plenty Coup, the Crow chief, and Black Elk's story.[1]

The most poetic and in many ways the most valuable is this one that Neihardt took down with a poet's hand.

The people who wrote books and articles trying to "interpret" Black Elk's mysticism and medicine dreaming expose the shallowness of their preconceived Christian notions. Neihardt had sense enough to let Black Elk speak for himself.

Sincerely,

1. All three books were published as Bison Books by the University of Nebraska Press.

To Frank Johnson

June 12, 1960

Dear Frank Johnson:

Thanks for the letters and the evidence about the returned letter. Everybody knows everybody in Zone 14 — everybody who has had an address here as long as I, but the post office has become incredibly unaccommodating the last few years. Circulars addressed to 23 Barrow are sent here; first class mail not. . . .

At Denver three of Traber Gatewood's granddaughters came to the autographing and letters are pouring in from Gatewoods and Cozads all over the country.[1] The publisher mismanaged the book so badly (I had no books until long after the Omaha *World-Herald* review came out, which was dated for the earlier publication date, not for the final one) that we lost much of the natural sale but the book is getting around by word of mouth. I've had requests from five publishers to do books on the youth of other painters, which is significant, in itself.

I trust that you are feeling fine again. Last time I was through Lexington (Summer of 1958, with the rough-draft of my book, to check on the descriptions, etc.,) I was told that you had been ill and when I called your office I was told that you were out and not expected back for some days. On the way back from the west I got similar reports. I was sorry to miss you. I didn't want any publicity over my coming through but you are aware of the need for quiet procedure upon certain occasions. Mrs. —— is not the only person in the world who wants only her version of a story told, and I have to be free to make my own decisions. As a writer of integrity that is a necessity. . . .

Be nice to yourself,

1. Traber Gatewood was Robert Henry Cozad's uncle. He played a major role in MS's book. It was his son Robert who contacted MS in 1939 about writing the book.

To Hanson W. Baldwin

J. B. Lippincott Company

June 13, 1960

Dear Mr. Baldwin:[1]

Please forgive the delay in this reply to your letter of May 26, asking me to write the book on the Little Big Horn in your series of GREAT BATTLES (AND LEADERS).

I am immensely pleased to be asked to do this, particularly under your distinguished editorship, and I tried to work the book into my schedule. The problems proved too great. I have five publishers, with at least one book on each list for the future. True, most of these works have been on my own list for years, with much of the research and some of the rough draft work done, but even so the program is an appalling one, and would put your book entirely too far into the future.

As you know very well, the fight on the Little Big Horn is the most controversial battle of our history and much of the material that I discovered in the mass of stuff in the AGO Records over on Virginia Avenue back in 1937–38 had never been touched upon in any account that I've seen. As you say, the Indian victory was really an inexorable defeat from which he has not yet recovered. And behind this were the old feuds of the West Point days, which brought on such encounters as the fight on the Washita and the cumulative suspicions and angers of the Sioux as well as of the Cheyennes. Upon this came the greatest depression the nation had ever seen, with the need to get financing for the Northern Pacific railroad, which made Custer's 1874 junket into the Black Hills not only possible but apparently imperative, no matter who commanded the expedition or what ammunition this put into the hands of the angry young warriors against the peace plans of the chiefs. I am certain that if there had been no march into the Black Hills that both Sitting Bull and Crazy Horse would have surrendered that next winter, *come in,* as they put it. They both knew that the buffalo was about gone and that the roving end was near, but the 1874 expedition made life under the white man seem desperately hopeless.

On my wall here in New York is a canvas copy of one picture from the sacred Crazy Horse tipi. It is an allegorical painting of the fight to save the

Black Hills, which are a tree-sprigged mound in the center of the picture. On one side is He Dog on his black war horse, on the other Crazy Horse on his golden spotted horse, the calf-skin cape of the war floating from his shoulders. The two men bear the sacred lances of the Oglalas, and above, just over the Black Hills is the symbol of the buffalo, the buffalo skull, the symbol of the dead buffalo, the vanished buffalo. He Dog told me in 1930 that they were ready to come in to Red Cloud Agency when the snows of December 1874 came, but then the soldiers marched into their Black Hills and so their plans for the next winter were changed, had to be changed.

I wish I could suggest someone emotionally and artistically as well as factually equipped to do this book. Michael Straight has made an excellent approach to the situation on the Plains in his novel CARRINGTON, but he is very new to the field.[2] He hadn't discovered that Col. Chivington was involved in the failure of forage and ammunition to reach Fort Phil Kearny the fall of 1866, although the archives have a lot of material on this, as well as the Omaha, Nebraska, newspapers, from whence the grafting contracting company Chivington worked for hailed. (Oh my, I'm taking on the language of the time!) However, now that he has a better understanding of the necessity to see *everything* that might possibly apply to a problem, he could turn out to be the man to write the story of the Little Big Horn.

Anyway, I wish you great and good success.

Sincerely,

1. Hanson W. Baldwin (b. 1903) was a reporter, military and navel correspondent, and military editor for the *New York Times*. Winner of the Pulitzer Prize for journalism in 1942, he edited or coedited *Men and Ships of Steel* (New York: Morrow, 1935), *United We Stand! Defense of the Western Hemisphere* (New York: McGraw, 1941), and *Strategy for Victory* (New York: Norton, 1942). As editor for J. B. Lippincott's Great Battles Series, he was urging MS to write for that series.

2. Michael Straight, *Carrington* (New York: Knopf, 1960).

June 20, 1960

Dear Mr. Baldwin:

Your letter almost convinced me, particularly with the fight on the Little Big Horn a sort of garnet crystalizing naturally out of the matrix of my nonfiction series on the Great Plains.

It would be a treat to write for an editor who understands fluid frontier warfare on the enemy's own rugged terrain. . . .

Unfortunately you could not expect to get the Custer fight book for six, seven years unless some of my contracts were dropped, which never has happened. Practically all the research for the book you want is completed, and the interviewing too, fortunately, for much of this is with men, white and Indian, now long dead. All this material is cross-indexed by individual and activity, etc., and makes a solid section in the 350,000 card index to my notes. The work on the book would be largely a matter of the writing and 60,000 words is nice and short for me.

If this isn't an impossibly long editorial wait, I could start gathering the material as it comes up in my work already in progress—collecting it into one file. I always have several books underway at one time, contracted or not; a book seems to ripen in the back of my mind as the file grows.

Whatever your decision, I was pleased to be asked.

Sincerely,

To George Hart

July 13, 1960

Dear Mr. Hart:

I am sorry that you found my reply to your recent letter curt. It was the fifth Hickok letter that week, with three more to come, all eight at least two, three pages, and all eight from people who have written me about the very same points before, some repeatedly over the last twenty-seven years.

I have no desire to tell any of you what to think, but if you must ask me questions, why not get into areas of the Hickok character less well discussed in print, areas upon which I do have special material that is not closed, given me in confidence. Because all of you keep repeating practically the same questions I have had to adopt the practice of pulling a letter from the files that seems to answer most of the queries and having my typist copy it for you. Sometimes there are over 100 Hickok letters a month, particularly in summer and around New Year's—the silly seasons as historians call them, because that's the time when romantic figures stir the imaginations of their followers the most. I understand that German historians get floods of letters about Frederick the Great and now Hitler during those two seasons.

For the last 27 years, ever since I became director of research at the Nebraska State Historical Society, I have been swamped with Wild Bill correspondence. No one seems to remember that I have my own career to consider, my own living to make. . . .

I also found that I would have to deal with not only the mental difficulties one hears about Hickok's father, but the probably even more complex family situation, involving various perversions. I had had some hint of these from old timers in the west, men who tried to say that one could not put the Hickok family into a book. Two weeks [of research] in Illinois convinced me that I could not. I never write books that are without symbols of human normality, human idealism, no matter how depraved some of the characters may be. I could find nothing that was not pitiful in the Hickok story.

In haste —

To M. S. Wyeth, Jr., Editor

HARPER & BROTHERS

August 22, 1960

Dear Mr. Wyeth:

Thanks for the books. I'm enjoying the very occasional dip into the South Carolina.

I am sorry that you don't have NEBRASKA yet but the book is growing into something rather special and I want to work at it until this specialness is realized. It has taken on a subtitle that you may not like: LOVE SONG TO THE PLAINS. In the foreword I intend to refer to a scattering of tributes such as "Annie Laurie", "My Old Kentucky Home", "*Kennst du das Landt*", Hardy's Wessex books, and Conrad's of the open sea. Of course there will also be bits that remind one of "Jesse James", "Pistol Packin' Mama", and "Clementine".

Have you Thomas Hornsby Ferril for COLORADO?

Best wishes,

To Mary Abbot

August 23, 1960

Dear Mary:

Enclosed is a copy of my note to Wyeth at Harpers, and of a letter from [Stewart] Richardson of Lippincott and my reply.[1]

I've delayed replying to Lippincotts but I've had to reconsider the future rather carefully this summer, with the sad debacle of SON OF THE GAMBLIN' MAN and no chance of making enough to cover the actual outlay on the Nebraska book either. With the Beaver book a larger outlay too than I can expect Hastings to return to me, I have a rather slim prospect for any income the next few years.

In the twenty-nine months I've been here, at a much larger apartment outlay, I've realized only $600 from the writing I've done in that time, and that from the American Heritage article.[2] All the rest has been from past writing.

True there will be something from Clark Potter but probably not enough to cover the apartment rent here, let alone anything for my outlay gathering the material, or my living.

I tried writing the Indian article for READERS DIGEST to offset this situation but it's been more than two weeks since Elizabeth sent it over to them and I've heard nothing, so I suppose that's out. There are other offers to do articles but not enough to lay up anything for the lean years coming.

With the situation as it is, I've decided that I better commit myself to the book on the Little Big Horn for Lippincott. That will make a good seller for perhaps an article in the *Post,* and for paperback later, even if the publisher muffs it.

Sincerely,

1. Stewart Richardson, editor at Lippincott, was later editor in chief at Doubleday.

2. "Dakota Country" (discussion of the art of Harvey Dunn), *American Heritage,* June 1961.

To Bruce Nicoll

Sept 16, 1960

Dear Bruce:

So far as I know the map in *Crazy Horse* is factually o. k. I never liked all the shrubbery that the N. Y. *Times* man, who was hired by Knopfs to make an "artistic" job of my map put in, but that doesn't really matter. The material is mine. No one else could have got that together.

See you in early November—

To Mary Abbot

Sept 22, 1960

Dear Mary:

Thanks for the reviews of CHEYENNE AUTUMN. There are some that I didn't have. Usually I don't read reviews but if there's a bad one someone is sure to call me up and read it to me over the telephone. . . .

It's still strange to me that a book like Cheyenne Autumn should get such good reviews after nobody wanted it, as you and Elizabeth know. If it hadn't been for one of those everlasting luncheons I had with Ed Aswell when he wanted to talk over the tangle of his love-life, or I wanted to promote a student's manuscript, the book would probably never have been published, so thick is the provincialism of eastern publishers.

Enclosed is a copy of a bit from Hass of the Omaha paper.[1] Too bad he doesn't like novels. He is merciless to Wright Morris, who is a very talented man, but Victor can't see it.

Happy days—

1. Victor P. Hass (1910–88) was book editor for the *Omaha World-Herald* for over thirty-five years; his reviews also appeared in the *Chicago Tribune*, the *New York Herald Tribune*, the *New York Times*, and the *Saturday Review of Literature*.

October 16, 1960

Dear Mary:

I'm sorry about the delay in this reply to your letter. It has been a confusing time here, and difficult to make any estimate of time to complete anything. Last June when I returned from the west two months of concentrated work would have completed the Nebraska book. I got not one day of concentrated application on it. I should have hired a truck then and had my material hauled away somewhere far from the turmoil here but I kept hoping that four, five more days would clear up everything.

Unhappily I didn't really dare leave. The workmen left every door wide open day and night, and we little over a block from the center of the drug traffic, with the neighboring door here kicked in and the place cleaned out. In addition the workmen might break a water pipe any moment and flood the place, or even set it afire with their fantastic methods, and with Mary [Towner's] place piled high with all kinds of trash and junk from the tearing up—and unable to make decisions or to act, so even the workmen were confused and got little but tears.[1]

Now I have to work on the talks I'm to give. I planned these safely after the Nebraska book was done, or so I thought. Of course I'm being paid for this work, and I hope to get that two months of concentrated work in when I return, Nov 10. Certainly I should be able to get the book in by Jan 15 if the place stands up during the time that I'm gone. There is a new tenant where Miss Ward lived before her suicide so the house isn't entirely open to the wild winds. . . .

Sorry—

1. The matter of installing an air conditioner became complicated because of remodeling the building. A further disturbance came when a tenant committed suicide. MS remained in New York all summer. Mary Towner owned the building and lived in the apartment above MS's.

To S. Omar Barker

December 3, 1960

Dear Omar Barker:[1]

Enclosed are two copies each of a couple of tales out of the old west for the W[estern] W[riters of] A[merica] book Doubleday is to publish, also my release on the pieces.

You are free to use either or both of these pieces, but I must impose one condition. Kuebler says he wants these legends to "flow from one to another with some coherence." This suggests that the identity of the writer will be lost. I don't want to lose these pieces. Too much of my own material has already been lost to me.

Sincerely,

1. S. Omar Barker (b. 1894), a novelist, poet, teacher, and rancher in New Mexico, authored two novels, wrote or anthologized a number of books of poetry, and was editor and contributor to western anthologies. He edited anthologies for Western Writers of America: *Frontiers West* (Freeport, N.Y.: Books for Libraries, 1970) and *Spurs West: Legends and Tales of the Old West* (Garden City: Doubleday, 1962).

To John G. Neihardt

December 20, 1960

Dear John Neihardt:

You are, as always, most generous hearted. Thank you.

You must know that I wouldn't doubt your statement about anything including your sitting up alone with Tibbles and his dead wife, Bright Eyes.[1] I didn't mean only that the absence of her sisters and brother was unIndian but that it was unpioneer as well.

I know that the LaFlesches were aristocracy of east Nebraska, whatever the color. Those who were daughters of Mary LaFlesche, the daughter of Dr. John Gale, post surgeon at Fort Atkinson, were particularly cultured individuals, I suspect. These included both Dr. Susan and Bright Eyes, as you will remember.

Have you ever written this story up for publication? — not just included in Dr. Aly's biography, but as *you* tell it.[2] You should, you know.

We still hear fine words about your talk to the Westerners. It always startles the New Yorker to discover that there are still honest and sincere artists left in the world.

May 1961 be a magnificent year for you and in the good Sioux way, for everybody.

1. Thomas Henry Tibbles (1840–1929) wrote *Buckskin and Blanket Days* (Garden City: Doubleday, 1905) and *The Ponca Chiefs: An Account of the Trial of Standing Bear* (Boston: Lockwood Brooks, 1880). He was married to Susette "Bright Eyes" La-Flesche Tibbles, an Omaha Indian and a nationally known lecturer on American Indian problems.

2. Lucille Aly, *John G. Neihardt: A Critical Biography* (Amsterdam: Rodopi N.V., 1977).

To Boyd Carter

Department of Foreign Languages
Southern Illinois University
Carbondale, Ill.

February 11, 1961

Dear Boyd:

I am sorry that Peithmann's manuscript didn't fit into the requirements at the University of Nebraska Press. Books of protest do demand most complete documentation and great moderation of tone. . . .

Now about BROKEN PEACE PIPES: I'll gladly look at it sometime during the next few weeks, before my galley proofs, etc., come in but I will probably have to agree with McDowell on one thing: that the book probably won't sell enough copies for a royalty publisher to get his money back.[1] We *do not* want to face the fact of our inhuman treatment of the Indian. Even books like *Crazy Horse* and *Cheyenne Autumn* would never have reached publication if I had not had a name of sorts and a basic following. As it is, neither one has paid for the vast investment of travel and research expenses and my living costs during the long years involved in producing the books. That's all right; I'm happy to have done it, but I know the financial facts on such books. They are in print now (CA is being reissued this Spring) only for the prestige value to the publisher's list, not for the money they fetch him.

Beacon Press is excellent and well known for sound works of protest, but they seem to have curtailed their lists some the last few years. Paperback publication seems out for the PIPES unless the book is accepted for hard-cover. Paperbacks to pay without former publication usually must be particularly slanted to the popular reader, the escape reader. They must sell into the hundreds of thousands, unless on a University press list and if Dr. Olson questioned the book probably Oklahoma, Minnesota, Yale or even Indiana would. Indiana did bring out that fantastic hoax, CROW KILLER,[2] based, of all things, on the accounts of Doc Carver of Nebraska, than whom there was no greater and no less inspired liar. Anyone should have been able to tell what a lie this whole thing was from the internal evidence, without one speck of actual information.

If the book is really *very* good, and *very* soundly grounded, very moderate in tone, it should reach publication somewhere. So send it on and I'll see what can be done by me. But of course I'm not any last word either.

I trust that the Carters are flourishing—

1. Irvin M. Peithmann, *Broken Peace Pipes: A Four-hundred Year History of the American Indian* (Springfield, Ill.: C. C. Thomas, 1964).

2. Raymond W. Thorp and Robert Bunker, *Crow Killer: The Saga of Liver-Eating Johnson* (Bloomington: Indiana U P, 1958).

To Alvin Josephy Jr.

Feb 16, 1961

Dear Alvin:

I think your Indian book will be a fine one.

About the disposition of the body of Crazy Horse, see Neihardt's *Black Elk Speaks,* pp 148–9 and something of the flight of the Oglala hostiles to Sitting Bull on the march to the Yellow Medicine, fall 1877. The notion that the Crazy Horse body was cut in two came, He Dog and Short Bull (He Dog's brother, not the intellectual of the Ghost Dance) said rose out of the talk around the Oglalas that the two bayonet thrusts of William Gentles, the soldier who killed Crazy Horse "almost cut him in two", at least that was the only way they could account for the story, which they said rose the night the war chief died, flashed by fire signals all over the Indian west by morning.

There is a complete list of men who were with Sitting Bull in Canada and Crazy Horse's parents are not on it but they are on the annuity list every month while the Oglalas were near the Yellow Medicine the winter of 1877–8.* (These lists are invaluable; they even list the cast-off women of the army officers by the officer's name, as Mrs. Livingston, Mrs. Custer, etc. even a Mrs. Carr.)

About the photograph from which the line cut of the Clark and Little Wolf pic was made for Frank Leslie's, see p 200, Schmitt & Brown, FIGHTING INDIANS OF THE WEST, or my CHEYENNE AUTUMN. The photograph is credited to Barry, obtained from the Bureau of Ethnology, labeled W. P. Clark and Little Hawk, although why anybody should think that the knowing Clark would have his picture taken with anyone less than the Little Wolf whose surrender he obtained, I couldn't guess. Anyway, Little Hawk was what the Cheyennes called a "hill" man, that is, he squared himself off and held up nine men, two on each thigh, two on each shoulder and one on his head. He was a stocky, powerful man. The Indians still had prints of this photograph by Barry in my childhood and it was always shown as White Hat and Little Wolf.

Good luck—

* I had this from He Dog & Short Bull, also Red Feather brother of the Crazy Horse wife before this in 1930–31.

To Bruce Nicoll

February 18, 1961

Dear Bruce:

Of course . . . my New York editors have been [limited], all except Hoffman, from Utica, Aswell from Tennessee, Alsberg the Hebraic scholar and so from all the world. New York editors are always telling me that I don't know how to write westerns, as though I had any desire to do so. My contempt for the whole breed is icy. That's why I've had ten publishers, counting UNP.

About OLD JULES: I don't know what Hasting House would say to paperback publication. I suppose it will depend upon whether they think your CRAZY HORSE cut into their hard cover sales, etc.[1] Some sort of package deal on paperback for several of my books has been under consideration at Hastings all winter, but it never came to anything that I had to ok or refuse. Perhaps the doubt was on the quality of the paperback. I don't know. Perhaps it would include some of my novels which I control completely, and they want to get their hands on them before any deal, so they get half, etc. Business is business, and my agents are not business people, as I've discovered. Why not ask about OLD JULES? I'm willing if everybody else is.

The reports on NEBRASKA, *Love Song to the Plains* are enthusiastic from both Harpers and Carl Carmer, editor of the series but I'm reserving my enthusiasm until I know what the compliments are covering. At my fourteenth book, and being a westerner, I'm a little head shy about fine words. If they want any serious changes I'll be gone so fast they'll not even find any dust—

Maybe I'm heading for a fall. . . . I'm sure full of contempt. At the moment I am no longer helpless; several publishers have their hand out and open for the book if Harpers get domineering. But authoring is almost as uncertain as writing operas.

Best wishes,—hastily

1. *Crazy Horse* (Lincoln: U of Nebraska P, 1961); *Old Jules* (Lincoln: U of Nebraska P, 1962).

To Mary Squire Abbot

February 23, 1961

Dear Mary:

Today I had lunch and a short conference with Mr. Wyeth. My uneasiness about the whole matter is practically gone. There was none of the usual attack on what is special in my material or in my way of handling it. I am tired of fights.

There is a tinge of the Barrett Wendell school of writing about the copy editor who worked on a short section but I guess it won't be too bad. I was amused about the change of "Indian wife" to "Indian spouse". That's, of course, a completely uninformed substitution. On the Plains the word *spouse* is used only in ridicule of the east. Only the poorest, most pathetic, most frightened little missionary had a spouse. The legal husband of a high-toned madam — a man tolerated around the place to lend a little respectability, was also called a spouse. I'll never understand the arrogance of copy editors, actually trying to rewrite an author's work. I copy-edited the SCHOOL EXECUTIVE every month for two years, but I never assumed I knew the material better than the writer.

Fortunately Mr. Wyeth seems willing to let me use my own vocabulary.

There was a suggestion that the title be changed to LOVE SONG TO THE PLAINS, as less limiting. I think this is a good idea.

Apparently the book can be in the stores by mid-October, which would work out with my date in Lincoln for their first Book Week, November 5–10. I am to get the manuscript back to Harpers sometime between March 15 and 31. I plan on the 20th if I can get the original back in time. I'll revise on the master copy and retype what is necessary.

Sincerely,

My throat is still bad, but the doctor seems to think that warm dry weather will heal it.

To David Susskind

OPEN END
WNTA-TV
Newark, 1, N.J.

March 22, 1961

Dear Mr. Susskind:

During your Sunday Open End about that curious eastern and intellectual preoccupation, the battle of the sexes, will you please inquire of your guests why they concern themselves so much with this immature, this childish division of mankind down the middle?

Isn't the great modern problem the elimination of emotionalism over human differences, the development of a greater unity, greater solidarity in mankind? I recall an earlier program of this nature. It sounded like a lot of moderately polite bigots getting together to fight out their hatreds.

Sincerely,

To M. S. Wyeth

[Harper and Brothers]

April 14, 1961

Dear Buz:

Your kind words on *Love Song* are welcome but I have a feeling that I had better be protecting my jugular—

Of course the book has to be copy-edited. There are always slips, particularly when working under the tremendous pressure of that last working over. I did bring in much new material, openly and insinuated, in the latter part, as I felt I must, and could, under the enlarged title. The material was at my finger tips. The Plains are my home.

In addition to slips publishers all have special quirks, like the Atlantic's *plough,* even in *plough critter.* You seem to want *drought,* although this term means dry weather east of Illinois. West of the Missouri it is a plain affectation, See Craigie's *Dictionary of American English* for the difference in the word, regionally.[1] I'll receive a dozen letters on this change alone, with the charge that I am "selling out," Everybody realizes that I know better than to use *drought.*

I do want to say that I've made just about all the compromises on this book that I can honestly make. In fact, I made more in that first version you saw than I have any right to make, and I made more since, more than I can justify except that I suppose this crime follows naturally upon the primary artistic crime: writing a book that was not my own.

About awkward spots: Are you sure you understand what I am saying? My three distinguished books, *Old Jules, Crazy Horse* and *Cheyenne Autumn* are full of spots the editors considered unacceptably awkward but I persisted, though this scattered the books from the Atlantic to Knopf and McGraw. Fortunately, since publication the word *awkward* has not come up again, not on these books. If one has something special to say, ordinary words will have to have special arrangement.

About the Grattan repetition: This is only one of a dozen or so in the book, threads woven through to hold the divergent elements together. This one is the most important, the perfect symbol of the ignorant arrogance that causes generations of trouble in the colonies, whether in our west or south or in the Congo.

Sorry,

I know Barrett Wendell, got 92 and 96 in the two courses but this is dead language.

1. William A. Craigie, ed., *Dictionary of American English on Historical Principles* (Chicago: U of Chicago P, 1936–44).

To Robert S. Asplund

April 25, 1961

Dear Mr. Asplund:

Thank you for your kind words about OLD JULES.

I am always interested in reader reaction to this book, particularly those who consider him a bad father. This always brings up the question: what is a good father? How about a man who got all of his six children into adulthood whole in body and able to make good livings for themselves and their families, cooperative, law-abiding citizens of their communities.

Anthropologically, historically and sociologically speaking such a man is a good father. If in addition he gives them an independence of mind he is an excellent father.

It wasn't that Old Jules was against cattle. He was against cattlemen who hogged the public lands and kept out the homeseeker who had a legal right to the land.

As for farming, nobody in the sandhills runs cattle without some agriculture—alfalfa if nothing else. You may know that Fritz is a big grower of alfalfa, some kind of sorghum, corn, rye, vetch, etc. Some years he has a thousand or more acres under cultivation.

I don't think I ever met your wife but I knew Bill. Flora took me over to see his arrowhead collections, etc.

About our mother: you will find a piece about her in my collection HOSTILES AND FRIENDLIES, published by the University of Nebraska Press, reprinted from the old *Country Gentleman.* Your library may have a copy. There are some Indian pieces in this too, if Mrs. Asplund has her brother's interest.

Best wishes,

To Mary Abbot

May 20, 1961

Dear Mary:

Here are the corrections for the Lippincott Contract.

The copy editing of the manuscripts is done. At Harpers there is only the back and front material left. There was the usual set-to there over a rewriting copy editor, one who changed my dates and meaning right and left. She even gave the United States a boundary with Canada in the Montana region in the 18th century. I guess she had never heard of Spanish and French America, or the Louisiana Purchase. But to allow such a person the power to change a manuscript!

I rebelled and so they hired a Mr. McRee to do the copy-editing, a man who grew up in St. Louis, well posted and very good. I have a one-page foreword to do, from the galleys, as usual, and the index. This time I'm going to do it from the start, not spend days trying to work over a bad outside job and end up with a bad result and a bill to pay.

The Mary Bryan Forsyth chapter heading illustrations are coming along nicely, I think.[1] Buz Wyeth seems pleased. This leaves my magnificent sandhill pictures rather untouched for publication with a running description of the region, some day, as a special book.

Over at Hastings the copy editing is also done, nicely, and the manuscript may be at the printer by now.[2]

I am slated for Lincoln, Nebraska's first Children's Book Week, late October and early November, a sort of state-wide affair. Both of my books are supposed to be out by then.

Now you know all I know—

Sincerely,

1. Mary Bryan Forsyth, an artist and sculptor, was a granddaughter of William Jennings Bryan. MS first became acquainted when Forsyth gave her a picture of Crazy Horse, painted as she envisioned him after reading MS's book (the portrait is in UNA). MS recommended her to Harcourt to illustrate *Love Song*. When MS was inducted posthumously into the Nebraska Hall of Fame, Forsyth sculpted the bronze bust, now in the state capitol.

2. *These Were the Sioux* (New York: Hastings House, 1961).

To Stuart Harris

July 12, 1961

Dear Stuart Harris:[1]

Mr. Wyeth writes that you need my itinerary for the Lincoln-Omaha trip this fall. There are only two fixed elements so far:

BOOK FAIR, Lincoln, Oct. 30–Nov. 4, speaking dates not set.

First Autographing, MILLER & PAINE, date not yet set.

Perhaps the best time for this Miller autographing might be during book week, because there will be many out-of-towners in Lincoln, but I don't want to autograph until there are reviews out and some word-of-mouth publicity about the book. If you can make the October 11 publication date, the week of Oct. 30 will be fine, or even some date the week before, if Millers prefer. I plan to get the index into your offices Monday, if that will help.

Millers always want radio and TV appearances before the autographing but Norma Carpenter, Public Relations, usually manages these or at least helps the publisher. After Millers any others in Lincoln, Omaha or Denver can be considered if the requests materialize. Matthews, at Omaha, is a good place, and particularly for this book with all the material on [Fort] Atkinson and the Missouri River, etc., as well as Omaha.

I can, if necessary, go west the week of October 23, and stay through book week, or go sometime about October 26 and stay to November 12, whichever proves the best. That would give me time to run out to the sandhills for a visit of a couple of days with my brothers and sisters, even run up to Custer, S. Dak. perhaps, for a blowout that Ziolkowski, the man carving the Crazy Horse monument out of a mountain wants to give.

I'm pleased that we can use the Flair picture on the jacket—carries out the elegance of the meadowlark's breast on the front. . . .

Sincerely,

P.S. I'm sorry about the kind remarks from Mr. Wellman[2] about my book, sorry that I didn't make it clear enough in your questionnaire that such comments are not to be solicited for my books. They never have been. Such solicitation is a humiliation for the author of a first book, let alone a fourteenth. Besides, I consider myself the authority of the upper Plains; always have.

I suppose, with an out of town printer, there's no way of autographing books for stores that request this. Here in town I usually go and autograph a thousand or so, for those who want them for their stock.

1. Stuart Harris, publicity director for Harper and Row, was later director of advertising and publicity.

2. Paul Wellman (1898–1966), a western novelist and historian, wrote, among others, *Death on the Prairie* (New York: Macmillan, 1934), *Death in the Desert* (New York: Macmillan, 1935), and *Jubal Troop* (New York: Carrick and Evans, 1939).

To Margot Liberty

Custer Battlefield National Monument
Crow Agency, Montana

August 5, 1961

Dear Margot Liberty:

Indeed I recall your letter from the Birney school. I don't know where Eddie [White Horse] is. I am sorry about that. He had talent, but he would call long distance collect whenever he got very drunk and sad.

I'm happy to know about the research grant and the seasonal job as historian at the Custer battlefield. I'm happy that you found *Crazy Horse* interesting. I camped out on the point beyond the buildings there twice, once for almost two weeks, with a bundle of notes and maps from the War Records and the Indians who were in the fight. But what I got seemed outside and beyond the words — something that was in the June sun, the June moonlight.

I've heard of several carvings the Indians hinted were made by Crazy Horse, but as you know, such words are seldom actually said unless one comes with the information and demands their story of the occurrence, their view. Old Red Feather once said that "those places one does not go, with foot or tongue," meaning he, as an Indian, a respecter of Crazy Horse, could not, and I didn't push the matter. I saw some carving attributed to Crazy Horse from the summer of 1877, on the bluffs down from old Red Cloud agency.

These were in soft sandstone and well-weathered in my youth. All I recall was the curious movement in the drawings more even than in the Amos Bad Heart Bull work of the Reno fight.

The best source of the visions of Crazy Horse was old Chips, his mentor in such things. There's considerable on these things in the Ricker Interviews at the Nebraska State Historical Society. . . .

I have a great deal of scattered material on the Crazy Horse visions and dreamings in my interview notes, but this in storage out west.

Give John Stands in Timber my greetings, and take a look at the Montana sky for me.[1]

Sincerely,

1. John Stands-in-Timber (1884–1967) was a Cheyenne living on the Lame Deer Reservation near the Custer battlefield. With Margot Liberty he wrote *Cheyenne Memories,* based on tribal members' recollections of the era of the Battle of Little Big Horn. MS refereed one version for the University of Nebraska Press, submitting a six-page, single-spaced analysis. John Stands-in-Timber and Margot Liberty, with assistance of Robert M. Utley, *Cheyenne Memories* (New Haven: Yale P, 1967).

To M. S. Wyeth, Jr.

September 6, 1961

Dear Buz:

Love Song to the Plains has just arrived and I am doubly impressed. It's a nice looking book, but, more unusual in my experience, it's really on time.

The extra fold-in map comes as a nice surprise.

I hear eastern rumblings of disapproval of some of my versions of American history. I should hope so. There should be practically as much difference between the Atlantic seaboard version of the western expansion and ours, of the region overrun, as there is between the British and the Colonial version of early American history. I took my Frontier history under John Hicks who refused to follow the humbling path of [Frederick Jackson] Turner, from Wisconsin to Harvard, and went to California instead.

Anyway, thanks for a nice looking book on time.

To Mary Squire Abbot

October 4, 1961

Dear Mary:

Thanks for the copy of your letter to Walter Frese. *These Were the Sioux* is really a lovely piece of book making. I was down at the Hastings warehouse to autograph a batch for the stores that want them. The shipping head told me there was a fine start of orders. He seemed very pleased. . . .

I'm deep in *The Story Catcher* for Westminster—taking the manuscript with me up to Bear Butte, north of the Black Hills. The [Bear] Butte will have some significance in the story and I want to refresh my impressions.

Enclosed is my tentative route sheet Oct. 26–Nov 18.

Have a nice fall,

P.S. That Clarkson Potter business is really something. I don't think he can be planning to stay in publishing. Just hopes to get some authors to get in somewhere else, perhaps.

To Walter Frese

Oct 4, 1961

Dear Walter:

Mary Abbot sent me a carbon of her letter to you about the Sioux book. It *is* a fine job of book-making.

I mentioned the book to Harry Hansen yesterday. It was easy to do; there wasn't much else for me to say. Harpers hadn't sent him their book nor any material about it. I think Harry would really like a copy of the Sioux book. He said so and seemed to mean it. He thinks you are a very unusual man for the publishing field. We talked about you, but you could have overheard every word.

Enclosed is a sheet of my local commitments to the present, as you suggested, and the letter of May 24, 1960 from *Readers Digest* asking for a second article on the Sioux, second to the one they published May 1952. This second article, rejected about October 1, 1960, was the point of departure for THESE WERE THE SIOUX. As you will recall I sent a copy of the article to you about November 1, 1960, after some conversation about it at lunch. The contract was sent to me by Mary in December. Fast work.

The requirements for the *Digest's* condensed books are so much more flexible than those for the magazine that they might be interested in seeing the book. Besides, the attractiveness of the finished project may capture them.

Sincerely,

To Sam J. Ervin, jr., Chairman

Senate Judiciary Subcommittee on Constitutional Rights
United States Senate

October 15, 1961

Dear Senator Ervin:

Although I am not an Indian I appreciate the "Questionnaire to Individual Indians" that you sent to me. I grew up around the Sioux friends of my father, Jules Sandoz, and as an adult I made a close study of the Plains Indians from prehistoric times. I have spent considerable time on both the Pine Ridge and the Tongue River Reservations. I published various magazine articles on the Plains Indians and four books: CRAZY HORSE, the biography of the Sioux war chief, 1942; CHEYENNE AUTUMN, the story of the flight of Little Wolf and Dull Knife from Indian Territory in 1878–79, 1953; THE HORSE-CATCHER, a Cheyenne novel, 1957 and THESE WERE THE SIOUX, a short study of Sioux life and religion, 1961.

With this background I feel qualified to say that a serious study of the constitutional rights of the American Indian is well overdue. Unfortunately, in large areas it sounds a little like a search for the corn-ear worm in a field long choked with sunflowers, horseweeds and cockleburs. There are, it seems to me, some pertinent considerations beyond the strict legal interpretations of constitutional rights. For example, what is the proper constitutional protection for the Indian whose ancestors were:

1 Pursued by troops on the Indian's treaty-right territory until practically every man and boy of courage, intelligence and initiative died trying to protect the women and children from the soldier bullets.
2 Cheated out of their lands by treaties not kept or treaties thrust upon them by gun, stockade and cannon.
3 Herded to shrinking reservations so poor no white man of the moment wanted the land. Often unaccustomed to agriculture, they were to dig a living from the reluctant earth, the treaty-provided rations that were issued sustaining them barely above starvation levels, so the

Indian of today is the product of four, five generations of serious malnutrition. This is considered a sound reason for low energy and ambition in the East Indian, or in the southern share cropper but not in the American Indian.

4 Deprived of their religion, one which had fitted their environment and their temperament, and upon which their whole social, ethical and philosophical concept of the good life depended. Not only the ceremonials and the dances were forbidden but even the songs, despite the constitutional guarantees of religious freedom.

5 Deprived of the treaty-promised schooling, with the only real opportunity offered the penniless Indian youth for an education—Carlisle—closed in the face of the grandfathers. How many white children from illiterate, bookless homes, and from the poor reservation schools could hope to meet the requirements for college scholarships? How many young Indians are discouraged or actually shut out of the reservation high schools by the overcrowding? How many have no real opportunity for even a poor rural school education? Draft boards found and are finding men from reservations who never went to school long enough to speak passable English, let alone read and write it.

Decimated, starved, robbed of substance, of culture and religion, deprived of pride and dignity, both the ancestors and the Indian of today sought escape from the stark reality in any way open, whether in the Ghost Dancing of the 1889–90 period or the alcoholism of today. In many regions this situation was aggravated by the passage of H. R. 1063 in 1953. Often the Indian was victimized by practically any white man or group offering a whisky bottle, or, to the less compliant, something to tide the hungry family through the next winter in exchange for the earth, the coal, oil or other permanent wealth that had escaped the sharp eyes of the early reservation planners.

Unlanded and driven from the poor reservations by the ten thousands since 1953, too often without any training or preparation for existence in a modern town or city, the Indian today is frequently condemned to life in desperate privation in some squalid tenament or in a tar paper and tent colony at the fringes of an embarrassed town. With no employment open, and return to the reservation closed behind him, his land gone to a one-bid auction, often the only living that the Indian or his wife and daughter can eke out is by theft and prostitution, both offences that once brought ostracism—actual driving out—by many tribes.

What, I wonder, could one call the constitutional rights of such a man, a man of such condition in the United States of America today? It is true that the Indian needs to have his constitutional rights protected, but even more urgent is the rebuilding of his nutrition-starved body, his hope-starved mind. He needs training for a livelihood in white society, and the opportunity to use the intelligence, initiative, ingenuity and imagination that are his native heritage. Give him these weapons and the Indian will fight those who would deprive him of his constitutional rights as he fought Custer on the ridge of the Little Big Horn.

Sincerely,

To Harvey Little Thunder

Lincoln, Nebraska

November 20, 1961

Dear Mr. Little Thunder:

I've glanced through my index for material about your ancestor, Little Thunder, chief of the band struck at the Blue Water by General [William S.] Harney in 1855. The material is so voluminous that I'll mention only the more readily obtainable, with some of the military and Indian bureau records obtainable if you ever get to Washington, to the National Archives. It is true that these records can be copied for you by photostat or microfilm at no great cost, but even the obtaining is a task.

Much of this you will know, and some of this is contradictory, as you will expect. I leave the sifting to you:

1840–1, Little Thunder's brothers, 5, killed by Pawnees, in Battiste Good's Winter Count, *Bu. American Ethnology,* Vol 4, p 241 (Report)

1854 Little Thunder, Big Partisan and Man Afraid of His Horse among the soldiers when [John L.] Grattan ordered "Fire" at the Grattan fight. Nebraska State Historical Society *Publications,* Vol XX, 259

1855, "Reminiscences of the Indian Fight at Ash Hollow, 1855", by General Richard C. Drum. NSHS *Publications,* Vol XVI, pp 143–164 Calls Little Thunder the father of Spotted Tail, whether blood father or not does not say, p 147, etc.

1855, Little Thunder's niece, Wachema and 4 nephews captured at Ash Hollow (Blue Water). Wachema later married John Nelson. "Sketch of life of Dick Parr, by Louise Parr, his wife, *Annals of Wyoming,* Vols 8–9, (Watch this, Parr not very accurate in many spots. ms)

1855. Little Thunder deposed after Blue Water and Bear's Rib made chief in his place. *The City of the Saints, etc.,* Richard F. Burton, p 89, etc.

1855 Little Thunder's Brules captured and taken to Pierre, arrived Oct. 1855, made treaty March 1856, planned Indian police, etc., *A History of the Dakota or Sioux Indians,* by Doane Robinson, Vol II, 225. (Twelve had got away and beat Harney to Laramie after Blue Water fight.)

1855 Bat Good with Little Thunder among prisoners after Ash Hollow fight, 130 Indians killed. Bu Am Ethnology *Report,* 10, p 324

Little Thunder, Hoffman explains truce over Spotted Tail's imprisonment:

11-4-55, Laramie Letter Book 10A
12-13-55 " "
1-6-56 " " "
2-1-56 " " "
2-9-56 " " "
2-11-56 " " " Little Thunder agrees to go to Ft. Pierre but is very heavy to walk so far and the ponies are very thin

6-18-56 Laramie Letter Book 10A

2-19-56 Sioux Expedition Letter Book 9B, Little Thunder to come to Pierre

3-5-56 Sioux Expedition Letter Book 9B, turn over to Little Thunder all property captured on Blue Water

Is at Pierre.

Above Letter Book's in National Archives, Washington, as late as 1942

2-11-56 Little Thunder, Iron Shell and 400 lodges on Hat Creek, yesterday nephew of Red Leaf and Son of Black Hart, & another murderer of mail party brought in by large detachment of Brules, headed by Little Thunder and Iron Shell. Fort Laramie Letter Book 10A

4-14-65, Little Thunder and 60 lodges surrendered at Laramie, *War of the Rebellion,* 100[1]

2-10-67 Little Thunder succeeded man called Fighting Bear, later by disease, was no longer able to lead his braves in Battle. So asked Young Spotted Tail be put into his place. Rocky Mountain *News*

Little Thunder's Son:

6-15-65, 20 miles above Ft. Mitchell, mutineed, killed Fouts, also Standing Elk, Little Bear and Big Mouth (?) because wouldn't join in mutiny. Rocky Mountain *News*

6-15-65 Little Thunder's son led uprising against Fouts, etc. Rocky Mountain *News* (another item in same day)

End 2nd quarter, 1874, Red Cloud Agency, Little Thunder Jr., listed with Sioux on agency. Red Cloud Document Files (National Archives)

Uprising against Fouts: 6-15-65. Led by Little Thunder's son yesterday.

6-13-65, Dog Feast at Horse Creek, 382 warriors sat in secret council. Was taking Indians around Ft. Laramie to Ft. Kearny, with orders at the fort there to hang any Indians who tried to escape. Never got there, Indians killed Fouts and escaped across Platte on way (led by young Little Thunder) *War of Rebellion,* pp 101, 102, 971, etc.

Etc. etc. From the Indians I got much personal material on Little Thunder, much of it in confidence. I was told that some of Fout's officers kept throwing the small children into the Platte river to watch them swim out and that they took some of the young Sioux maidens to their tents at night. Out of this came the mutiny.

There's a good book in Little Thunder if you want to write it.

Sincerely, but in haste,

1. U.S. War Department, *The War of the Rebellion: A Compilation of the Official Records of the Union and Confederate Armies* (Washington, D.C.: Government Printing Office, 1880–1901).

To Kay Rogers

November 28, 1961

Dear Kay:[1]

It's fine to find your letter here on my return from the west. Thanks for the generous clip about the Harvey Dunn article, and I agree with Joe [Kay's husband] that the Frank Merriwell piece was more fun.

The doctoral robes I wore were rented, but the hood is mine, and that I'll gladly loan Joe for his graduation from Continental Classroom. I'll even throw in an admiralty in the Nebraska Navy. . . .

I haven't heard from Alida [Malkus] since before I left for the west.[2] I'll call her tomorrow. She'll be happy to hear from you, and I'll be happy to have breakfast with you and a walk when you're in town.

About the "Dispossessed". Allan Adler brought Saul Levitt, who wrote Andersonville, here to talk about a possible Indian trial for television.[3] I turned over such references as I had on Standing Bear when Saul decided on that trial. From that day CBS and Westinghouse were quivering bowls of jelly with fear over suits. They even changed Standing Bear's beautiful and dignified speech, although the actual one was published in all the papers in 1879. There was so much more sense to the actual speech, more poetry and significance. Standing Bear's speech is often considered next to the Gettysburg Address in beauty.

I was pleased with the serious attempt but I was sorry to discover how really cowardly and craven sponsors and TV companies can be. I'm happy I accepted no money for my ideas and bibliography and advice or I should feel besmirched.

The news of [James] Thurber's death reached me out in Colorado. It seemed like a personal bereavement. I felt that way over [Albert] Camus' death, and sorry about Hemingway, although I knew through the sister of my typist, who is married to a doctor at Rochester, that Hemingway would never recover.

The clip about Eudora Welty sounds like her old self. There's been very little writing from her for a long time. It's good to know she's on a novel (Damn this new typewriter; scallops the margins—)

See you around Christmas

1. Kay Rogers (d. 1990), a journalist and essayist, met MS shortly after the latter moved to New York. She often walked with MS when the medication taken for migraines required immediate exercise. The Rogers later moved to Washington, D.C.

2. Alida Malkus (b. 1899) published novels, biography, history, and geography books as well as wrote and illustrated children's books: *The Silver Llama* (New York: John C. Winston, 1939), *The Dark Star of Itza* (New York: Harcourt, 1930), *Meadows in the Sea* (Cleveland: World, 1960), and *Blue Water Boundary* (New York: Hastings House, 1960).

3. Saul Levitt (1911–77), a playwright and scriptwriter for Hollywood, wrote for "Westinghouse Theatre," "You Are There," and "Danger" for CBS and "Wide, Wide World" for NBC. He won an Emmy for "The Andersonville Trial," 1971. "The Dispossessed" apparently was to be based on the 1879 trial of the Ponca chief Standing Bear in Omaha. He and his followers had left their Oklahoma reservation without permission to bring his son's body back to their ancestral lands in Nebraska for burial. The trial was significant in that Indians were considered for the first time in law to have rights as human beings.

To M. S. Wyeth, Jr.

Dec. 31, 1961

Dear Buz:

The year is done, and LOVE SONG, for better or worse, labeled for all time. I want to thank you for backing me up against the initial and intolerable attempt at copy editing. I'm always grateful if I don't have to change publishers to save a book.

I don't know if I should be completely grateful to you for finding the book "lyrical", a quality practically every review now suddenly discovered in my work, although it's been there all the time if it's there now.

I trust some of the old "written with barbed wire on sand paper" quality isn't to be overlooked entirely in the future.

Anyway, thank you and I wish you and all your connections a fine 1962.

To John Grant Noll

February 1, 1962

Dear Mr. Noll:

Thank you. I appreciate your fine letter, and a look at the very interesting letter from Grant Reynard of the Montclair Art Museum.[1]

What a snug little world we live in! Mr. Reynard a student of [Harvey] Dunn's and president of an art museum that owns a fine portrait of a young Irish boy by Henri, you a fellow "land cruiser" over the west with Dunn, I with my interest in both Henri and Dunn and their backgrounds.

Of course I should like to have a good chin wagging dinner with you and Grant Reynard. I'm concentrating on the revisions of an Indian book so I can put a check mark on the margins of my manuscript practically any time that you men can get away from your less flexible duties. My telephone is CH2-3043 (in the phone book, as westerners usually are). I'll be in town most of the time the next two months except for a flying trip to Denver and Chicago February 7–9.

Sincerely,

P.S. Did you read that my Harvey Dunn article won the award of Western Heritage (and Cowboy Hall of Fame) as the best non-fiction piece on the west in 1961? I don't think they know anything about literature; probably were attracted by the pictures.

1. Grant Reynard (1887–1967) was a Nebraska-born artist and illustrator. With many shows and exhibitions to his credit, he also illustrated work for *SEP, McCall's, Ladies' Home Journal,* and *Redbook*. He was a friend of Willa Cather's.

To Henry Regnery

Henry Regnery Company, Publishers
Chicago 4, Illinois

February 4, 1962

Dear Mr. Regnery:

I've hoped for years that there might be good strong publishing houses scattered over the entire nation. The grip of the Atlantic seaboard on our writing has been a most unhealthy aspect of the cultural growth of our country. I'm less interested in regional publishers as such than I am in good strong publishers of significant creative writing, and that means, to me, a release from the kind of Atlantic seaboard regionalism that we have had to endure entirely too long.

This complaint is not a personal one. If any publisher demands changes of me that involve the integrity of my material or my writing, I just move to another one.

Unfortunately such high-headed freedom is often beyond the man with a family to support. This, in itself, is a commentary on the state of publishing, and of literature, in America today.

Do call me when you're in town—CH 2-3043 (in the telephone book). I am out west much of the time, but I plan to be in New York from the middle of February through April.

Sincerely,

To Hanson W. Baldwin

April 3, 1962

Dear Mr. Baldwin:

Thank you for the "Suggested Style Sheet" which I had not received previously, and the clipping about the cartridge cases in the Custer fight. I knew about these long before I ever walked over the ridge on the Little Big Horn. Some of the old Sioux had copper cases they had knocked out of guns obtained in the fight. Many warriors had carried willow ramrods for this purpose. The Indians all knew about the tendency of the cases to stick after a couple of fast shots.

Later I found a good handful of the swollen copper cases on the battlefield and was reminded of my father's refusal to reload copper shells because the metal was too soft. I reloaded thousands of brass cases in my childhood, and shot some of them. I still have one of Old Jules' reloading tools — one fitted to mould the bullet and to decap, recap, and reshape the case, and then set the bullet.

Incidentally, as you will know, General Crook fought for years against the worthless old ammunition issued to the troops on the Plains. He sent angry telegrams to Washington demanding the replacement "at once" — a replacement to be made in 1874, and delayed, in spite of all plans, so that both Crook and Custer went into their fights in 1876 with the same ancient powder, the faulty caps, and the swelling cases.

It's fine to hear that the series is well started. I still can't set an exact date for the delivery of my manuscript. I'm sorry.

Best wishes,

To Tom Fontaine

April 16, 1962

Dear Mr. Fontaine:

Your letter is one of hundreds I receive regretting the hiring of someone to revise their stories. Unfortunately, if you stopped to think you would realize that anyone able to write well enough to sell could make much more with his own stories than in rewriting the work of others. Really reputable periodicals, like *The Writer* for instance, do not carry advertisements from anyone offering revisions. Further, they do not carry advertisements from agents. A literary agent who advertises is in the same category as a doctor or lawyer who advertises — an admitted quack. I am enclosing an approved list of agents, investigated for reliability, solvency and experience. Approved revisors do not exist.

I have six books under contract, still to be written, and I never take on any revising, under any circumstances. Besides, you couldn't pay me what my writing time is worth.

The only thing for you or any writer to do is to *learn to write*. I'm enclosing a check sheet that will help you if you are willing to work.

Good luck,

To Mary Pfeiffer

Editor, Juvenile Books
WESTMINSTER PRESS

April 22, 1962

Dear Mary:[1]

I guess you're the boss about the publication date for *The Story Catcher* but that will mean the destruction of the book and with it endanger my following with the book stores of my region, where spring sales are travel, how-to's, and the lightest of romantic fiction for nice old ladies who can't go anywhere or do anything. There is no point considering eastern markets. Yesterday I had two requests for my new books and I couldn't give the name of even *one* bookstore in all of Manhattan that carries my most recent work. The enclosed copy of a review from the *National Guardian* reveals what fifteen books and ten publishers have done to get my work known here in the east. I spoke to the book and author gatherings at Westfield and Plainfield, N. J. recently. Apparently not one of the hundreds of women there had ever seen one of my books before. Why do you expect me to think you will do better on publicity or distribution on this book than you did on the earlier ones? Hadn't we better keep the markets that I built up for us through twenty-six years of hard work?

Your other authors may be able to live from library sales, which seem to mean a great deal to you. Library sales won't cover the actual money laid out in travel for research and locale searching and the typing of THE STORY CATCHER, let alone a cent for my office expenses and my time. As for prizes and awards, I hope my writing is above the mediocre level required of prize winners. I wouldn't think of reading an award book in any field and neither, I suspect, would anyone else with literary or even factual standards. It took twenty years and a new generation of historians—one too young to recall that OLD JULES was a prize winner—to get any historical recognition for that book. Only the last couple of years has there been any admission that I am a stylist, for naturally a prize winner could not write. Unfortunately the public had no way of knowing that the Atlantic didn't consider the book a prize winner in 1933 and wouldn't have in 1935 for all of Paul [Hoffman's] urgings, if there had been anything else possible among the entries.

As for THE STORY CATCHER at *Readers Digest:* I knew that was wasted effort. Why should they admit they take juveniles? Paul, as editor of adult trade books at Westminster and my editor, put THE HORSECATCHER into an entirely different category.

There's no reason why you shouldn't come here for any conferences, but I warn you I'll do no emasculating. In fact, I'm thinking about rewriting the book into the strong, bold thing it should be.

Sincerely,

1. Mary Pfeiffer (b. 1904), editor of the juvenile book section of Westminster, worked with MS after Paul Hoffman left the press. Pfeiffer felt a spring publication would give *The Story Catcher* a chance at the Newbery and other awards as well as more time for library and journal reviews. She argued that the biggest sales were to libraries.

To Bruce Nicoll

June 26, 1962

Dear Bruce:

While glancing through your fall 1962 catalog I noticed you're including *Home Below Hell's Canyon* which is good but a fairly recent book,[1] and it occurred to me that there are some others you might consider if they haven't been reprinted and haven't been considered by the Press:

First, there is *Checkered Years*, by Mary Boynton Cowdrey, excerpts from the Diary of Mary Dodge Woodward, written 1884–1889, while living on a bonanza wheat farm in Dakota Territory. This was published 1937 by Caxton Printers, Caldwell, Idaho. There was a connection with someone at Miller & Paine. Earl Campbell gave me the galley proofs to read. It is the best portrayal of the trials and triumphs of bonanza farming, with the dust, the drouths, hails, Dakota blizzard and wheat price gaugers. I think Virginia [Faulkner] or someone could think of a better title.

Then there's John Ise's *Sod and Stubble*, the story of his family homesteading in Kansas. You will recall John—an independent economist on the KU faculty until his retirement. I was told last week at Lincoln that he's still alive, a rare man—.

This book was published 1936 by Wilson-Erickson of New York.

Another book that I'm often recommending is Estelline Bennett's *Old Deadwood Days*, Scribners, 1928. She came to Deadwood as a child of five, the daughter of the first Federal Judge for the Black Hills, appointed as soon as the Sioux Treaty selling the Hills was ratified early in 1877. A few years later he brought his family out including Estelline, who, like most small children, found the prostitutes the most interesting people in town. But she treats them and all the rest circumspectly but with warmth and humor.

Sincerely,

1. Grace Jordan, *Home Below Hell's Canyon* (New York: Crowell, 1954; reprint, Lincoln: U of Nebraska P, 1962).

To Elizabeth Otis

June 28, 1962

Dear Elizabeth:

I'm back from Nebraska and the four day Homestead Centennial Symposium with speakers on all phases of land, from the Public Domain into the future, when there won't be foot room for anybody.[1] There was a delegation of over twenty land administrators, etc., from such places as Kenya, Madagascar, India, Paraguay, British and Dutch Guiana, Costa Rica, etc., with three interpreters — seeking ideas for the settlement of their remoter lands.

But what I'm really writing about is *Outpost in New York*.[2] I've had two anonymous calls threatening me, warning me not to have the article published. I suppose that's about the shooting that involved the man from the old Nut Club in the village. I made it clear at the time that I saw no faces, only legs and a man laying on the floor.

In view of these threats I think perhaps we should not try to sell the article. No magazine will have the courage to publish it, not that I'm afraid — I faced down violent men before I got into my teens, and the material will go into my book about New York. But magazine publishers aren't in a position for courage.

Have a good summer.

1. MS's presentation, "The Homestead in Perspective," was published in *Land Use Policy and Problems in the United States,* ed. Howard W. Ottoson (Lincoln: U of Nebraska P, 1963).

2. "Outpost in New York," *PrS* 37 (Summer 1963): 95–106.

To The Reverend Father Peter J. Powell

July 17, 1962

Dear Father Peter:

Yes, the Sandoz motel on Route 20 [Nebraska] is run by a relative, cousin Allie, who ran a ranch for years, was allergic to practically everything from hay to cow dandruff, so he went into the good old Swiss standby — innkeeping. (But it's never been in our family before).

I gathered from some remark at the annual meeting of the A[merican]

A[ssociation] of I[ndian] A[ffairs] this spring that the Cheyennes were to get a little financing. Why shouldn't you be a member of the Chief's Society? The Cheyennes have always been adaptable. That is why they managed so much poise and dignity in the face of such appalling massacres of their people.

Don't be too discouraged. You will find that there is much, much more coherence in your material than you suspect now. The subtle interrelationships don't reveal themselves until the creative process gets well under way. There will, of course, always be gaps, with the Cheyenne's swift transition to buffalo hunting from an agrarian life in Wisconsin, say. . . .

About my Cheyenne files in Nebraska: They're not in any form to be looked into. They are under lock and key, some under permanent seal. When I spoke of your looking into them I had hoped to have a large place somewhere, with enough room so all my files could be gathered and organized for researchers, all except the small section that can't be opened.

In my notes I found references to a band of Oglalas on the Yellowstone and the Tongue River around 1810, with some northern Cheyennes. An uncle of He Dog's was with the Cheyennes up there to around 1840 which was much of his life.

Give my greetings to all our friends in the Cheyenne country, and may you have the fine flashes of insight that I know will come to you as you write.

To Peter H. Davison

Executive Editor
The Atlantic Monthly Press

July 17, 1962

Dear Peter:

It's nice to find a letter from you in the mail that accumulated while I was out in Nebraska. It was my third junket west since early February. I started the trips with one to Denver. The mountains were glistening and beautiful in the February sun that warmed Denver to 65 degrees.

Yes, as you say, there is material for a good biography in Father De Smet, but it is not for me. There seem two possible approaches to the good little priest: the orthodox Catholic accepting all his writings and his accounts at face value; or the objective historical, frankly acknowledging the missionary's great fondness for the lurid and the horrible, and the ready tendency of frontiersmen, other missionaries, and the Indians, to feed this appetite. I suppose the very real hardships of missionary work seemed more justified if the Indians to be converted were sufficiently depraved. Yet not even this quite accounts for De Smet's practice of selecting the most lurid tales (many discounted by other travelers) to include in his writings, with all the horror elaborated and multiplied. Sometimes he told the same story several times, magnifying the gruesome detail with each retelling. A good example is the Pawnee human sacrifice story. It is known where he heard the story some years after its occurrence, and in what version. He piled melodrama and horror upon the account he was given, but even so it is mighty tame compared to his later rewrite of the story.

I have no desire to debunk the jolly little Belgian priest who was apparently a frustrated novelist of Gothic horror. He came west rather late, after Protestant missionaries had been established for some time, but he was much more colorful than any Baptist or Presbyterian forerunner. The Indians found him wonderful and delightful, and were still telling stories about him and laughing over them fifty years after his last visit. It is true that Father De Smet went to Sitting Bull's village in 1868 but then the Bull wasn't much of a hostile at the time — was, in fact, still going regularly to Fort Rice to trade while down south the Red Cloud war wasn't over. A few years later he would have found Sitting Bull's warriors less friendly although there seems no instance of the Indians of the Plains harming a priest or a minister — certainly not the Sioux.

But none of this need stop a De Smet biographer, although *American Heritage* has been looking for one. Personally I should find Father Pointe, the artist-priest, a little more interesting. He left an unpublished journal and a lot of pictures now in the archives at Loyola, but I have five books under contract in addition to the one on New York — one that is already bringing in anonymous telephone threats before one word of it is in print. Promises to be a good Sandoz fight.

Your father was a real genius with writer's conferences.[1] I've often thought of the time Eric Knight was there with the new royalty check, his first really big one, which he carried in his pocket constantly, even in his bath robe. And so soon afterward he was killed.

Thanks for thinking of me for De Smet, and take a look over the Public Gardens for me.

1. Edward Davison (1898–1970), a Scottish-born poet and educator, worked with English publications — *Cambridge Review, Guardian* — then came to the United States as a professor and was editor of "The Wits' Weekly" for *Saturday Review of Literature* (1928–30). The author of a number of books of poetry and a Guggenheim fellow, he directed the Writers Conference in the Rocky Mountains, 1935–42.

To Frank E. Sorenson, Director Summer Sessions

The University of Nebraska

July 27, 1962

Dear Dr. Sorenson:

You will recall that I brought up the subject of more stress on the Creative Arts in the University of Nebraska, particularly under the head of Continuing Education, or General Studies, or, as in the 1920's, Extension Courses offered on the campus at night.

I was a student in the Extension Course in Creative Writing originated in 1925 by Melvin Van den Bark, with meetings one night a week, by semesters. As a member of the class and then a reader for much of the time to 1935, I have retained some pleasant memories of the people touched directly, and indirectly, by the work, and something of the accomplishments that grew out of those years.

The enrollment which was generally large, included the following as I recall, with some of the consequent publications:

Marjorie Burcham Bayley	book by Coward-McCann, about 1937, also novelette and short stories.
LaSalle Gilman	*Shanghai Deadline*, 1936 (best seller, moving picture, etc.) *Dragon's Mouth*, 1954, etc.
Frank O'Connell (then state game warden)	*When Peace Comes*, 1930; *Farewell to the Farm*, 1962; articles and short stories.
Mari Sandoz	15 books; novelettes; stories and articles.
Marion Edward Stanley	(A.P., editor *Coronet* and *Esquire*, now with TV network) *Thomas Forty*, 1947; *The Rock Cried Out*, 1949, etc.
Pan Sterling	short stories, women's magazines and *Esquire* (her son, Tom Sterling is a successful novelist, living in Italy)
Dorothy Thomas	poetry, many short stories in *American Mercury, Harpers*, and popular magazines; novelettes; moving pictures; *Ma Jesters Girls*, 1933, Knopf, and *The Home Place*, 1936.
James Van Liew	short stories, one in *Story*.

Others in the class with, perhaps, less writing published: Lulu Mae Coe (*Star*): Marie Dugan (*Journal*); Edward Cole Fisher (later municipal judge); Helen Mary Hayes (*Journal*); Effie Hult (teacher); Anne Longman (*Journal*); E. Reye Merrill (secretary, state supreme court judge); Joseph Wishart (attorney) etc.

In the meantime there was a buzz of writing around the University outside of the class and around Lincoln. The writers included the following; with some of their publications:

Kwei Chen	(poet from China often into Van den Bark office) widely published; *Poetry*, etc.
E. P. Conkle	(playwright) *Creek Bottom Plays; Two Hundred Were Chosen; Prologue to Glory;* (young Lincoln); etc.
Loren C. Eiseley	(University of Pennsylvania) much poetry and poetic prose. *The Immense Journey*, 1957; *Darwin's Century*, 1953, etc., etc.
Virginia Faulkner	(now ed. University of Nebraska Press) *Friends and Romans*, 1934; *The Barbarians*, 1935; *My Hey-Day*, 1940, etc., etc.
Mildred Burcham Hart	poetry, one novel.
Weldon Kees	(painter-author) many quality short stories, 4 collections of poetry. *The Last Man*, 1943; *The Fall of the Magician*, 1947; *Poems, 1947–1954*, and a posthumous volume.
William McCleery	(now an editor of *Ladies Home Journal*) Plays: *Hope for the Best*, 1946; *Parlor Story*, 1947; *Good Housekeeping*, 1949; *Careful Harry*, 1951; *A Play for Mary* 1951; *The Lady Chooses*, 1952; *The Guest Cottage*, 1956; *The Family Man*, 1957, etc.
Weldon Melick (Don Weldon)	Jesse Lasky's *I Blow My Own Horn; Show Me a Miracle*, and many articles, etc.
Kenetha Thomas	(painter-writer) juvenile books and short stories.
Rudolph Umland	(came tired of shoveling corn to hogs) at least 25 satirical pieces in the *Prairie Schooner*, several reprinted practically world-wide.

And then there were the faculty members who wrote in the creative fields: Lowry C. Wimberly, founder and editor of the *Prairie Schooner,* published twenty short stories in such magazines as *American Mercury, Forum, Harpers,* and *Yale Review,* with many reprintings; Hartley Burr Alexander produced 2 volumes of poetry and several plays and pageants. Dean J. E. Le Rossignol wrote a novel and several stories of his Canadian-French background.

All these and many more were writing in creative fields in that teeming period of 1925–35 around the University. It was thirty years from the great creative period of the 1890's at the University to 1925. From 1935 –?

I think the time is ripe.

Sincerely,

To Mrs. Thomas M. Neal

July 30, 1962

Dear Ruth Neal:

Your interesting story of a relative of your husband's, a George Morehouse, middle initial C. falls into a rather general pattern of accounts of old timers. If you had had enough information to ask pertinent questions you could have, perhaps, obtained a more checkable story. As it stands, it could be any composite of Indian raid stories from the Atlantic seaboard to Oregon.

First, there were no Indian raids in Nebraska in 1876. There was an attack on freighters up near Red Cloud Reservation on the Sidney to Black Hills trail, up in the northwest corner of Nebraska, hundreds of miles from Red Cloud, the city. No violence against settlers. In fact there was very little attack on settlers in Nebraska except in the raiding of the summer of 1864, and I suspect George Morehouse was mixing these stories, as old timers do, into their own experience or their own families. Or, since the family came from Iowa, perhaps he retailed stories of the Spirit Lake Massacre of 1858, in which women and children were captured and killed. Red Cloud, the Oglala Sioux chief, had of course no knowledge of these things. And what a timber buyer would be [doing] passing through the regions that Red Cloud ever knew seems a puzzler. That's why people lived in sod houses; no timber. There was some timber in the Spirit Lake region, and even more in the region of the New Ulm, Minnesota, raids of 1863.

The only raiding in the Plains region in the 1870's of any consequence was in Kansas and the southwest. Perhaps George Morehouse got the stories of these raids confused. While 1876 was without Indian trouble in Kansas too, there was a Cheyenne flight through Kansas in 1878, with settler raidings in the Beaver region, but no women killed, only men. When the Cheyennes reached Nebraska they killed no more settlers, for Nebraska was notably free of "Indian hunters" and very few Indians were harmed by civilians in the state. Indians killed there were by soldiers. There was a Morehead killed up on the Morehead ranch on the Niobrara early 1879 by some of the Little Wolf warriors trying to get horses for the women and children. There were no women at those ranches in those days. See my CHEYENNE AUTUMN. . . .

I get requests to track down stories approximately like the one you present at least eight, ten times a year, and in every case so far they have always proved to be composites of several, often of stories that the old timer heard told, without any connection to his family at all. Memory fictionizes and must be checked upon, even with the young. If you could have had enough knowledge to say "But there were no raids in Nebraska in 1876," you might have made him check on his memory. Or if you had demanded the names of the people involved, the woman who came to help over the confinement, of their neighbors, where they went for their mail, where they voted, etc., you could have made him check on his story. I find it a complete waste of time to talk to an old timer about material completely new to me. If I know the general outlines, the geographic location, or something of the sort, I can jolt the narrator to search his memory. For instance, where did the family contact Red Cloud to get his account of what happened? Red Cloud was moved to the Missouri in South Dakota in 1877, and settled on Pine Ridge, South Dakota, in 1873, and was never down in the Red Cloud, Hastings, etc., region from 1875 on. He died blind in about 1909, on Pine Ridge.

The best newspaper files of Nebraska are at the State Historical Society, Lincoln, but there are no papers of the Hastings, Red Cloud, Juniata region in Indian raid days, 1864. The towns didn't exist. There are scattered copies of the early 1870's from North Platte, and there are always the Special Editions for anniversaries. The Juniata-Hastings fight for the county seat is in one of the Hastings special editions at the Historical Society.

Kansas seems a better bet to me for this Indian raid. There are good newspaper files at the Historical Society at Topeka. I've gone through much material there too, but do not recognize the raid your George C. Morehouse mentioned. There was serious Indian raiding in Kansas in 1864, 1867–9 and particularly in 1874. Most of this was along the trails, like the Smoky Hill, for instance. Then there were the people, men only, killed in the Cheyenne Raid of 1878 in the Beaver Valley, northern Kansas.

Sorry, but I am pressed with work—

To Museum

Earlham College,
Richmond, Indiana

August 15, 1962

Gentlemen:

In several sources on the American beaver, I find mention of the fossil skeleton of a giant seven foot two inch ancestor to our modern beaver in your museum.

I am working on the first, chronologically, (the final one in publication) volume of my six book series of the white man on the Great Plains. Because this earliest book of the series deals with the coming of powder and iron to the region I am deeply interested in the beaver, including the prehistory.

If it is possible to have a glossy photograph proper for good reproduction made of this giant beaver, please have this done and send the bill with the picture, including the proper credit line for use in the book.

Thank you,

To Caroline Sauer

August 19, 1962

Dear Caroline:

I think deletions of any reference to illegitimacy from books for high school students is very silly, and certainly without any regard for the facts of their lives. However, it's all right with me, and so far as I'm concerned, we may snag a permanent reader or two—

Hoping that you weren't dried out of house and home this drouthy year—

Sincerely,

Re: "The Neighbor" for Macmillan's Literary Heritage Series

To Editorial Office

WESTERNERS BRAND BOOK
New York Posse

August 22, 1962

Gentlemen:

Five years ago I asked to have my name removed from the Publication Committee of *The Westerners Brand Book* because I had no desire to thrust my historical training upon the other members and yet there were times when it was clearly my duty to point out where the historical evidence lay. Although I was given some assurance at the time that my name would be dropped "after a while" this has never been done.

Now I must demand that my name be taken from the list of the committee at once. There was an alarming amount of protest in my mail from historians when the [Don] Russell book on Cody was reviewed without any mention of the romantic fictions reiterated as fact.[1] The protests about the repetition of the fiction that Cody killed Yellow Hand have already begun to come in, although my copy of the quarterly just arrived.

I have no desire to censor anyone's writing but I have a duty as an historian and a writer of integrity to refuse the use of my name to give credence to this increasing tendency to infantile romanticism.

I expect immediate compliance with my request.

1. Don Russell, *The Lives and Legends of Buffalo Bill* (Norman: U of Oklahoma P, 1960).

To Daniel Willner

Follow-up Dept.
Memorial Hospital for Cancer and Allied Diseases
New York

September 28, 1962

Dear Mr. Willner:

Please forgive the long delay in this reply. Your letter followed me around my home region, the Great Plains, and got waylaid.

So far as anyone seems able to detect there seems to be no recurrence of malignancy. I had trouble healing the wound, and finally resorted to the method used by Colonel Dodge on the Kansas prairies in the 1870. Any soldier with a stubborn wound was put out into the air and wind with the wound bare. If he was able to ride, he was put into the saddle and got the full advantage of Kansas wind on the hoof.

I wasn't in Kansas but I discovered that sitting before a fan served the same purpose, a good tough scab and a fine healing underneath. In the meantime I've changed my diet radically and permitted no x-rays.

Thank you,

To Maynard Fox

Boulder, Colorado

October 14, 1962

Dear Mr. Fox:[1]

. . . About Willa Cather: She left the University of Nebraska before I was born and never made a public appearance in Lincoln there or elsewhere around town all the years I was in the vicinity. Apparently she carried a sort of grievance against certain people in Lincoln, and against the *State Journal.* So far as I know she always came through town secretly when she picked up Elsie, her sister, (teacher in Lincoln High) for the annual return to the old Red Cloud home. Willa was almost a recluse in my days both in Lincoln and during my years in New York. Elsie, a gay and stimulating acquaintance, is retired now, but still living in Lincoln.

You will have looked into the Mildred Bennett books, particularly the revised edition, and the half a dozen others about Miss Cather and her writing, as well as WILLA CATHER ON WRITING.[2] Don't miss Alvin Johnson's PIONEERS PROGRESS, Bison Book. He was around the University when Willa and Dorothy Canfield (Fisher) were writing stories together on the University campus, while [Dr. James Hulme] Canfield was Chancellor.[3] For some of my reaction to Miss Cather's work see my LOVE SONG TO THE PLAINS (indexed). . . .

Incidentally, are you the Mr. Fox who loaned me *The Hesperian* with the Red Cloud autobiography, through the Denver Library about 1941 for my CRAZY HORSE? I've always appreciated that.

Enclosed are copies of a few casual items from my Cather file, items you might miss. Don't return them.

Best wishes, but in haste,

1. Maynard Fox was a graduate student at the University of Colorado, writing a dissertation on Cather. He made a relatively common error in assuming that Cather and MS were contemporaries. Cather was a generation older (1873–1947).

2. Mildred Bennett, *The World of Willa Cather* (New York: Dodd Mead, 1951; rev. ed., Lincoln: U of Nebraska P, 1961); Willa Cather, *Early Stories*. Selected and with commentary by Mildred Bennett (New York: Dodd Mead, 1957).

3. James Hulme Canfield (1847–1909) was chancellor at the University of Nebraska, 1891–95. His daughter Dorothy and Willa were friends from the time of Cather's university years.

To Everette Sutton

October 15, 1962

Dear ES:

It's nice to hear from you and the Lady. I'm just back from a long junket through the Canadian archives and over the early route of powder and iron to the upper Missouri country. Turned out I had more on early Frenchmen to the region than the Dominion Archives, but in research much is a process of elimination. I got as far west as Winnipeg last week, and down, and then back here to get on with the final work on THE BEAVER MEN.

About the Custer material: I don't have the time to go into it now, and, even more important, after the beaver book I'm to do the LITTLE BIG HORN in Hanson Baldwin's series of decisive battles of the world. Then I'll go into the Custer material to the bitter end, and into all the lives of the men who were with him that June 25, 1876. I'm trying to get Antiquarian Press to reissue UPS AND DOWNS OF AN ARMY MAN by Armes, which covered the years 1866–69 in the Kansas region.[1] Armes was with another of the armies marching up and down across west Kansas those years of 1866–70. Wild Bill was their guide. Because Armes was always in trouble with his superiors, the book got very little distribution, as you will know, when it was published about 1890. . . .

Now back to the 17th Century and the Village of the Bearded Men, two Frenchmen whose names, white man names, I could not find, but men who lived out their lives among the Indians of the upper Missouri from 1640 on.

Greetings to the outfit,

1. George Augustus Armes, *Ups and Downs of an Army Officer* (Washington, D.C.: N.p., 1900).

To Mary Pfeiffer

October 25, 1962

Dear Mary:

Here is THE STORY CATCHER. As always I've done considerable last minute revision, largely without much consideration of the copy editing. It really had little pertinency to a book about Indians, told largely through the mind and eye of a young Indian. . . .

Now to some explanation of my objections to the copy editing:

I was taught copy editing through Rutterer of R. H. Donnelley of Crawfordsville. The first rule was: never change a factual point, whether statement or word. From the first page all through the book I found *Breaks,* a line of cliffs or associated spurs, *Webster* 3rd ed. changed to *brake,* which is a growth or vegetation. How anyone could read through the whole book without ever discovering that I was not writing about the bayou country, but about a broken region I'll never understand. The context made the meaning clear on the first page.

Another complaint is that this copy editor is what Dr. Louise Pound used to call, with much merriment, a *hadophile,* one who has a mania for the word *had* and sticks it into prose like telegraph poles along a railroad right-of-way. For the last hundred years, throwbacks in fiction have been established as such by an introduction of *had* or *had gone,* etc., to establish the time and then treated as plain past or present tense, as the writer finds most evocative. I was particularly annoyed by this hadophilia in a book told largely through the mind of an Indian youth, not a priggish old grad of Harvard in the Barrett Wendell days—when Barrett Wendell was already outmoded even for the formal essay.

There should be a course in the presentation of the elements of description for copy editors. Good description presents the elements of a scene as they appear to the eye, in the sequence of actuality. Close adherence to this principle gives my writing its high sense of actuality and immediacy, in spite of undiscerning copy editors. This principle holds true for the presentation of thought, and arbitrary rearrangement of the parts by copy editors is fatal to the studied effect the writer has produced. . . .

Sincerely,

To Walter Frese

Nov. 11, 1962

Dear Walter:

Thanks for *Gold Camp*.[1] It looks particularly interesting.

My Canadian trip proved one thing: that I had more information on the very early French penetration (17th century) of the upper Missouri region than there is in Canada, including the Dominion Archives or than they even suspected. I had material from the old Indian stories and from the Spanish records of New Mexico, where there was nervousness about these early Frenchmen. I was at Montreal, Ottawa, Toronto and Winnipeg and saw a great deal of the early fur routes, much of the region still pretty wild.

I trust everything is rolling along for you and that Diane loves Cornell.

Sincerely,

P.S. I was shocked to hear of Benn Hall's death. He was the only individual of his business I ever met who could work with reserve and taste and still get results.

1. Larry Barsness, *Gold Camp: Alder Gulch and Virginia City, Montana* (New York: Hastings House, 1962).

To Raymond DeMallie, Jr.

November 11, 1962

Dear Mr. DeMallie:[1]

I'm sorry the Indian Bureau people in the Archives didn't know what I meant by "Red Cloud Document Files. 1871–1875." They should have known. These were large file boxes over in the basement of the old Indian Bureau in 1937–1938, with no further identification, when I made my notes. If they have brought confusion to these records in the Archives building all I can say is that they must be following the example of the War Records Division, who seem to be making it practically impossible for anyone to trace references even when I give them the military department, the dates, names, and document numbers.

Spotted Elk is a very common name, particularly since the translation might mean White Elk, Pale Elk, Light Gray Elk, or Elk with Spots. There were two prominent Spotted Elks among the Sioux 1856–1877, one was apparently a Brule, brother of Conquering Bear. See Vestal's *New Sources,* etc. p213. This man is mentioned in the Susan Bordeaux Bettelyoun manuscript (I have a copy) as going to Leavenworth into prison with Spotted Tail, see my *Crazy Horse.*

Then there is the Spotted Elk also called Big Foot, who ran away from the agency about the same time that Bull Eagle left, but sent word he would come back if the horses and arms of his people were not taken away. 1-24-77, Col. Wood, 11th Infantry, Cheyenne (River) Agency, Dak. Ter., Document Files, Letters Received, 1877, Department of the Platte, War Records, National Archives, and the Spotted Elk, head of the Bull Dung Band, out in the hostile camp with Red Bear. 9-9-76, Lt. Col. Buell, 11th Inf., Special Document Files, Box 171, Sioux War, 1876. Military Division of the Missouri, War Records, National Archives.

I trust the above haven't been scattered since I saw them in 1938. These were also large file boxes.

About the children in Lone Horn's lodge: If you read *Crazy Horse* or *These Were the Sioux* you must know that these might or might not be blood relatives. The Horn might have been second father to any or all. They might have been children of a brother or sister of his or his wife's, and so also "sons" or "daughters," etc.

Crazy Horse had three women in his lodge when he came in. These might or might not have included the "old woman of the lodge" that was usually there. Agency personnel always called these women "wives" although making a wife of the "Old woman of the Lodge" would be as shocking as the same thing would be between your grandmother or grand aunt living in your home and your father. It was apparently this old woman that [General Jesse] Lee refers to as having died right after Crazy Horse was killed.

In the winter of 1876–77 the flight from the military reduced the number of men and of lodges so that there was a lot of doubling up. Some lodges had five, six middle-aged women who had lost their men in the fighting. All but the wives were guests. Don't fall into the glib pattern of agency clerks who called all these women (sometimes the man's mother or grandmother) wives.

On [George] Hyde you will have to draw your own conclusion. Compare the errors in the *Red Cloud's Folk* with the corrections he cites in Spotted Tail. You will find many of these corrected in my *Crazy Horse* (which he obviously consulted but omitted from the bibliography). Hyde was in a feud and wouldn't go to the Nebraska Historical Society, and lost prestige by the errors. But there is one thing to remember. For years he was practically blind, with only a small spot of sight in his eyes. Further, he really hates Indians.

Have you looked into *Sioux Chronicle*?[2] The Oklahoma Press sent me the manuscript which was appallingly incorrect. I pointed out all the glaring errors—misdating, etc. He made most of the changes but never forgave me.

The important thing is that corrections in historical writings are made, not who brings down ire for having pointed them out.

Sincerely, (and now to my own work for six months)

P.S. Iron Horse was some sort of a relative of Crazy Horse's wife, probably cousin or half brother, both of which would be called "brother."

1. Raymond DeMallie was fifteen when he first wrote Sandoz in 1961. Now a professor of anthropology at Indiana University, he has published many articles, coedited James R. Walker's *Lakota Belief and Ritual* (Lincoln: U of Nebraska P, 1980), and edited Walker's *Lakota Society* (Lincoln: U of Nebraska P, 1982) and *The Sixth Grandfather: Black Elk's Teachings Given to John G. Neihardt* (Lincoln: U of Nebraska P, 1984).

2. George Hyde, *Red Cloud's Folk* (Norman: U of Oklahoma P, 1935), *Spotted Tail's Folk: A History of the Brule Sioux* (Norman: U of Oklahoma P, 1961), and *Sioux Chronicle* (Norman: U of Oklahoma P, 1956).

To Walter Frese

November 16, 1962

Dear Walter:

It was fine to see you yesterday, looking so well and like yourself, and to catch a glimpse of the Eggenhofers.

I was, however, a little disturbed that I seem not to have made it clear to you what kind of a book I'm writing, particularly since you have paid out advance money on it. The following is a sort of description of it (and if you don't like the idea, no feelings hurt. You have an option on it, not I on you as publisher).

The tentative title is THE BEAVER MEN, *Builders of Empire*. That's exactly what they were, from prehistoric Indian times through the division of North America by the practical end of the beaver trade in 1833, and from the valley of the Micmacs in Nova Scotia to the very edge of the land at the Pacific. Whole sections of the Iroquois confederation and of their traditional enemy, the Algonquins, traced their origins to their paternal animal, the beaver. The Dutch, the English, the French and the Americans spread their territorial holdings for and with beaver, and if Spain had not been blinded by the glitter of hard gold she could have entrenched herself to the Great Lakes at the least, and westward to the Pacific with beaver gold.

The first chapter of the book shows the first actual coming of powder and iron to the beaver regions of the Plains, not merely carried through by Spaniards in search of gold, Coronado, Onate, etc., but actually brought to the life of the stone age Indians, and this by the French to the upper Missouri country. In chapter one there is also a description of the big drunken fur fair at Montreal, head of ocean navigation, where in the 1650–1660 period some of the Missouri furs are traded.

From that first fair to the one of 1833, with the beaver almost gone, the price broken by the fashion of the silk hat in Paris, the canny departure of Astor (a very late comer) from the trade and the influx of visiting outsiders to that rendezvous of 1833, men like William Drummond Steward, lies the shift of empire in North America, for and by the beaver. This is the book.

I think it can be very very significant. I shall try my best to make it so.

Sincerely,

To Harold Preece

Hastings House, Publishers, Inc.

December 18, 1962

Dear Harold Preece:[1]

It's nice to hear from you. Yes eventually I'm to write a book on Oil on the Plains, but this will go into the influence of oil on our foreign policy the last thirty years, particularly the last twenty. For this I shall have to get into the State Department archives, which are kept closed, or get Texas oil diaries available to me, much Tea Pot Dome material and much on Oklahoma, as well as what's in the Texas History Center at Austin. I've collected material on this since 1921. It's the latter part, the international end, that will be difficult.

As you will see, there's nothing in this to prevent you from doing a more personal Texas oil book. It's generous of you to offer your material but why don't you use it? . . .

The Harper editor of the Regions of America is M.S. Wyeth, Jr., a very pleasant young man. The last I knew they didn't have a writer for the Texas region. He'll be happy to see you.

Did you run across their NEW COUNTRY by Allan Bosworth, nonfiction account of one of those covered wagon families.[2]

May 1963 be a fine year for you,

1. Harold Preece (b. 1906), a member of the New York Westerners, specialized in literature and folklore of Texas. His books included *Lone Star Man* (New York: Hastings House, 1961) and *The Dalton Gang* (New York: Hastings House, 1963). In 1936–37 he was folklore editor of the Texas Writers Project; he also had charge of the Archives of American Folk Music for the Library of Congress in 1936–37.

2. Allan Bosworth, *New Country* (New York: Harpers, 1962).

To Walter Frese

January 28, 1963

Dear Walter:

Friday I signed a year's option on *Cheyenne Autumn* for a moving picture; $1,000 for the option. There's to be *no* publicity at all on this, but you will probably be approached for a quit claim on this if the matter goes any farther. I wasn't too anxious to let this fine piece of property go, but my name's to be included as the book author if the picture is made and that should stir up new sales.

Remember at our luncheon during the holidays, you said *The Readers Digest* people were at a table there? On my way home from the library after five that day I stopped in at Alida Malkus' cocktail party and ran into Grace Naismith of the *Digest* (she's married to one of the *N.Y. Times* nature editors). She asked for a piece. Recalling the *Digest*'s rejection of the article that I later made into *These Were the Sioux,* I mentioned something that would have sales possibilities at other magazines — "The Christmas of the Phonograph Records," when father spent $2000 of his $2100 inheritance for an Edison phonograph and thousands of the wax records when we needed overshoes and there was the inevitable mortgage due.[1]

I don't know whether the *Digest* will take it. If so, it will be good publicity for our books. If the editors decide against it, probably some other magazine will be interested, and pay me a good rate on it full length — more money than the *Digest.* Eventually the account would make a nice little Christmas book, for any Christmas. The article is about 5000 words now and could be lengthened to 6500 but not much beyond that without spoiling the terse, unsentimental, offhand tone that the amusing material demands. If you might be interested in this as a small book, perhaps with amusing line drawings, I'll send you a copy when I know what's to happen to the piece. In the meantime I'm enclosing a copy of the letter from Naismith at the *Digest.*

Alliance, Nebraska, which made a play of OLD JULES in 1938 for their

50th anniversary talks about putting the play on again for their 75th apparently coming up this summer. I'm inclined to give them permission as before. There would be fewer of the actual characters in the audience watching themselves played on stage this time. In 1938 mother was still alive and although very ill, she was completely enchanted, saying "Yah, that's right! That's how it was!" in her excitement.

I trust you have a fine running start on the new year—

1. *The Christmas of the Phonograph Records* (Lincoln: U of Nebraska P, 1966).

To F. H. Sinclair

February 18, 1963

Dear Neckyoke:

About Major Twiss:

Enclosed is a copy of my reply to Mrs. Twiss of Soda Springs, Idaho, who wrote me saying you suggested me as a source.

Most of the Twists of Pine Ridge went back to the correct spelling of their name after my *Crazy Horse* came out and they had verification of the Indian story of their name. . . .

For information have you looked in Trenholm? She mentions some possible sources for information, and Hunton's diary should contain material on the major.[1] A letter to some of the name descendants should scare up information of where the major died, if they are no longer too Indian to tell, or don't know. Too many of the present-day Indians remember only the stories told in the Wild West shows in which the present old timers took part and show publicity material.

There's a good story, even a book in Major Twiss.

Certainly Twiss never connived with [General] Harney to kill Indians. Too many Plains writers think Harney came down from Laramie to strike Little Thunder on the Blue Water. A look into the War Records would show that Harney's expedition left [Fort] Leavenworth Aug. 4, 1855, reached Ft. Kearny Aug. 20, left Kearny Aug. 24, reached Ash Hollow so. of Platte, Sept. 2, Sunday, camped on the North Platte that night, dragoons sent out to get behind Little Thunder's camp at 3 a.m. Sept. 3. The Indians wanted to parley but "as we had come for war and not for peace, we paid no attention to them." (correspondent with Harney for *Daily Missouri Republican*, Sept. 5, 1855)

That's all

encs: copies of letter to Mrs. Twiss and clips from Gordon and Rushville papers, mentioning current Twiss family [enclosures not identified].

1. Virginia Cole Trenholm, *Wyoming Pageant* (Casper, Wyo.: Bailey School Supply, 1958); Virginia Cole Trenholm and Maurine Carley, *Footprints on the Frontier* (Douglas, Wyo.: Douglas Enterprise, 1958); *John Hunton's Diary*, ed. L. G. Flannery, 6 vols. (Lingle, Wyo.: Guide-Review, 1956–63; Vol. 6, Glendale, Calif.: Arthur H. Clark, 1970).

To Walter Frese

March 4, 1963

Dear Walter:

Somehow I didn't finish what I started to say about the American novel Friday. Many of us were hopeful about Pelligrini and Cudahy out in Chicago. They seemed to have a good chance of escaping the eastern publishing clichés that even Alfred Knopf was having to accept in his difficulties in the inevitable post-war publishing slump.

I was uneasy when P & C moved into New York, with an apartment a couple of blocks from me in the Village. I didn't go to their sort of house warming that they gave, and the next thing I heard was that they had moved up town. I knew then that all hope of any individuality, any daring in publishing new and creative work was dead so far as P & C were concerned. Practically the only novels published in America worth reading are from foreign publishers.

This brings me to the novel you have under contract from me. May I suggest that I trade you a book of nonfiction for this? I should like to make my next novel the fourth in my allegorical novel series and that's obviously not for your list. It will probably have to start in Europe somewhere. I've had a couple of feelers from Great Britain. I'm unhappy about the poor sales on MISS MORISSA, certainly innocuous enough. My only reason for wanting this book reissued was in response to the requests from the librarians dealing with books for young adults. They wanted Morissa to fill the gap in their lists of book for young women. Unfortunately, MORISSA was not included in your catalog of books for young people, so the whole purpose was defeated.

There are a dozen topics on which I could write you a book of nonfiction instead of the contracted novel.

Sincerely,

To Bruce Nicoll

March 6, 1963

Dear Bruce:

Your paperbacks are a nice product, with excellent titles. They should reach distribution in England too, for prestige, at least. The titles are naturals for the British.

Oh, I'm always putting down autobiographical pieces — like the early two in *Hostiles and Friendlies*. Some day I'll shape them into a book but because I want to be free to be completely frank about publishers, etc., I've refused to give anyone a contract. I don't think it's for a university press — not that I'm out of sorts with the University — but I want to be free to say what I believe politically, too, and that would bring some of the anti-free speech boys up and yelling against you.

Anyway, we'll see — but thanks for asking.

To Walter Frese

March 11, 1963

Dear Walter:

I appreciate your saying that Hastings House would like to have all my books but I just can't afford that.

These research books invariably cost me in actual outlay of money, at least $10,000, including the research, the typing and postage, the books and maps, the apartment, telephone and telegraph for three years, the $500 to $700 that I always spend in the promotion — autographing trips, etc. The travel and hotel bills, etc., for the research on THE CATTLEMEN was over $2,200, not counting all the long years that I kept my eyes open, interviewed old timers, etc., for cattle when I was out on the Indian books, etc.

If it weren't for the selling genius of Paul Hoffman while he was at Westminster, I would have to give up writing the research books entirely. THE HORSECATCHER financed the work on both the CATTLEMEN and THE BEAVER MEN. I am not stupid enough to expect you to plan the selling of the beaver book well enough for me to get my money back from that either, no more than I did from the cattle book. So I have to try other publishers.

Take a look at my account on your books.

Sorry,

cc Mary Abbot

Dear Mary,
It seemed the time for a little plain talk to Walter.

To Mamie Meredith

March 13, 1963

Dear Mamie:

You're always so generous and reliable, and knowledgeable about how things should be done. Thank you.

No, I'm not surprised that Karl Shapiro is leaving the [*Prairie*] *Schooner.* My surprise was over his staying this long. He's always been migratory. He and Hayakawa used to be called the migratory birds of the English Departments, but Hayakawa's been at San Francisco State College since 1955. Anyway, his movings were less restlessness than conflicts over teaching methods and in one of his fights I was on his side. The others were always too far away for me to know the inside dope.

About Karl: I hear rumors about a return to Baltimore. This may be only a rumor so keep it in the bottom of the old tea pot.

I'm sorry you couldn't do the *Britannica* piece. They are so unreliable in so many fields. It's time they went to some who know what they are writing about. . . .

Thanks again.

Affectionately,

I'm so sorry about your eyes. My eye is all right. That Saskatchewan doctor said not to worry so long as there's no distortion, etc., that I would know of any serious change before any Xray could pick it up. Here the doctors are all for Xraying, which might just be the trigger to start trouble, but I have no intention of letting them at it. I have good vision in sunlight and bright electric light. It's just that the visual purple won't hold, never does in a snow-blinded eye.

To Caroline Sauer

March 19, 1963

Dear Caroline:

Indeed I won't have MUSKY cut, and cut like that! I should think *Scholastic* would be ashamed.

I don't believe in palming off a denatured world on children. No wonder they can't cope with the real thing when they have to face it!

And who would want such namby-pamby stuff connected with her name?

I'm sorry about your time wasted.

To Tyler Buchenau

Editorial Offices
W. B. Saunders Co.

March 27, 1963

Dear Tyler:

Several times the last six months I've thought about you and wondered how you are, and perhaps even where you are. Then today I opened *Harpers* for April and was faced by a seven page article "Harvard's Skinner, the Last of the Utopians" by Spencer Klaw. Much of this is based on the *Walden Two*.[1]

If you haven't seen this look into it. Do you remember the scramble over at Macmillans to make the manuscript even remotely publishable as a novel in order to get the book on psychology Skinner was working on and which he took elsewhere anyway. I hope Andy's still around somewhere, to get a laugh out of all the to-do. I still have a carbon of the long, page by page criticism and suggestions I made of *Walden Two* with the idea that the book could pass for a novel.

Have you been to Idaho lately? I plan to go to the Fort Hall region in September, just looking around to satisfy myself that I was accurate enough in *The Beaver Men* that I'm finishing this spring.

I was in Nebraska several times in 1962 but I didn't see anything of Olga Stepanek. The Raysors are still around, but scarcely anyone else of the old outfit.

Sincerely,

1. B. F. Skinner, *Walden Two* (1948; reprint, New York: Macmillan, 1962). This is the only reference in MS's letters concerning her work on Skinner's manuscript, a well-known incident to her friends.

To Kay Rogers

March 30, 1963

Dear Kay:

Your hope, like many others, was a little premature. The newspaper strike isn't over yet, and no telling how long it will drag along. I'm almost weaned off the local papers that are missing. With the *Post, The Wall Street Journal, The Christian Science Monitor* and magazines I'm learning to get along, particularly this busy time.

I'm sorry to hear about the Mrs. Fogle from Nebraska. I suppose I would recognize her maiden name. I knew Van's students from 1926 to 1938—was his English reader for three years. I suppose Lincolnites did call him my boy friend. Many thought we were married, but we weren't. We had a wonderful time, unmarred, so far as I know, by any regrets. We went everywhere together, even out home for Thanksgiving, etc. Mother took to Van immediately, partly because he had so much experience with mothers. He looked after his for at least twelve or fifteen bedfast years. My only qualms about those years of our friendship are that Van should have been finding a wife and raising his own children instead of putting his nieces and a nephew through school. I had a career to follow, and had to be free to go wherever the writing and the research demanded. He wrote beautifully, had a fine story in the O'Brien of 1924.

About the Oglala Sioux articles: I've been working quietly for better living conditions for them, and I stopped off the last time I was home to look over the progress in health and housing facilities. The progress is slow, but it took a lot of work to reverse the expropriation that had gathered such momentum under Eisenhower.

Spring will be really warming in Washington by now. Take a look at the lush greening for me, stuck here on dirty cement for a while longer.

My best to both of you,

To Gail Shickley

June 26, 1963

Dear Gail:

The book on the beaver detained this reply to you, and will keep on detaining things—

I feel with you on the ruining of the mountains. What an exchange—friendly, responsible beavers driven out for carousing summer campers.

I knew about the Lazy VV Ranch.[1] Rose told me it was better just not to think of it at all.

I don't think your target shooting victory is a minor one but it sounds more like me than like such a gracious lady-like person as you. I have an article on New York in the current *Prairie Schooner* that I withdrew from a market here because I was getting threatening telephone calls about it from the gangster element here. I feel safe with it in the *Schooner*. N.Y. gangsters will never see it, and couldn't care less. Here it is very easy to be picked off from an alley and I feel duty bound to do my best to finish the beavers—

Look to the mountains for me.

1. "Boss" Van Vleet had had to sell the Lazy VV Ranch because of ill health.

To Robert L. Sizer

Arthur, Nebraska

June 26, 1963

Dear Mr. Sizer:

Please forgive this long delay in this reply to your letter of June 2. I'm far behind on the deadline of my *Beaver Men*, my seventeenth book.

Your wish to preserve the stories of your region is a laudable one. The stories of the formative years of a region of a nation are very important to the understanding of what comes later.

You ask how I market my stories. It's a long trail. I wrote seventy-eight short stories before I sold a one. *Old Jules* was out to thirteen publishers before the Atlantic accepted it, the second time there. I started writing in my first year in country school. Had my first story published in the Omaha Daily *News* Junior page, so you see writing, like any other art requires a long apprenticeship. Now I have an agent, but I still make my own sales. Publishers come to me now, not I to them.

Your best chance with stories of old timers and early incidents is the local papers, then the magazine sections of such papers as the *World-Herald* and *Empire Magazine* of the Denver *Post*. I sold articles on prairie fires, well accidents and mad dog scares to the Lincoln and Omaha papers when I was in college. With fiction I had to start at the top—in what was then one of the most distinguished markets—the *North American Review*. That was, of course, because I had developed some artistry.

For your articles on old timers, remember that the material must have a beginning, a middle and an end, all pertaining to the same individual or incident. Start out at an interesting episode or characterization and never let down to the end. And *stop* when the story is told.

Good luck,

About *Slogum House:* It is still considered a very good novel. . . . There's such a thing as being a tenderfoot in reading as well as in ranching.

To Bruce Nicoll

July 7, 1963

Dear Bruce:

Thanks for the kind words.

About my I HATE NEW YORK book: Your kind offer is appreciated but I've been turning down offers for the work for years because I must keep myself absolutely free from all entanglements, free to say exactly what I believe about many things, including the destructive influence of publishers on the writing of 1940–1960's, and on the paucity of criticism in America except the monastic type from the colleges, written for other monastics and their employers.

(That's where the *Prairie Schooner* has been failing, I think. Wimberly was interested in the creative writer. As Van's reader I sat in on some of the pre-launching sessions in 1925–26 with Dr. Sherman, etc. The stress then was always on a quarterly for the creative. I tried to suggest this to Karl Shapiro in a letter Sept. 15, 1956. Of course he was under no obligation to pay any attention to my opinion but the letter does establish the consistency of my stand.)

About the Amos Bad Heart Bull book: I'm still shocked at the position the Carnegie Foundation took back in the early thirties etc. It seems to me that, since they will get the credit for financing Helen [Blish] in the interpretation, they would be happy to underwrite the expense of your publication. If you think it might not stir them up to claiming the right to the whole thing, I'll write them a note. I saw the correspondence; I as well as Helen and the Indians, thought they had committed themselves to publication. Of course no one needs to keep a promise to Indians, but I could surely rub that in if you feel your claim is ironclad.

See you in September—

To Gene Price

OUTDOORS POTPOURRI
Findlay, Ohio

August 25, 1963

Dear Gene:

Just a hasty note between bringing in THE BEAVER MEN (Book I in my Plains Series, the coming of powder and iron to the upper Plains) and a junket up through Wyoming etc., with a talk to the Historical Society fall meeting, Sheridan Sept 7.

According to Wm. D. Street, in Kansas State Historical Society *Collections*, Vol X, the Cheyenne massacre on the Middle Sappa, 1875, was on Sec 14, T5, R 33, Clinton Township, Rawlins Co., Kansas. There's a page map. It's almost straight south of Atwood and straight north of Colby. The world's expert on this is H. D. Wimer, Stratton, Nebraska. If you haven't been in correspondence with him you've missed several bets. He and Mrs. Wimer met me at Colby in 1949 and took me up for my first trip to the actual site.

The avenging of 1878 was on the Beaver and the Sappa. See pp 21–31, Kansas State Historical Society 18th Biennial *Report* and C. N. Constable's *History of Rawlins County*, etc., for the Kansas versions. The *Report* lists 20 killed in Decatur County and 12 in Rawlins. There is pretty good evidence that, as often happened, some white men took the occasion to kill off some enemies and blame it on the Indians. Certainly that was true in South Kansas and apparently for the one man killed in Nebraska.

The real source material on the 1878–79 flight is in the Ricker Collection at the Nebraska State Historical Society and the National Archives sources mentioned in my CHEYENNE AUTUMN. Old Jules got a great deal of the story, without much bias, from old Wild Hog before he died on Pine Ridge, (they were good friends,) in addition to the material I got from old Cheyenne Woman and in my interviewing and in the Darlington Agency records, etc.

The rarest is, of course, in the graves of the dead, and fortunately I have some of this in my files.

Why not bring your lady up to Sheridan for the Historical Society meeting the 7th and the historical junket through no. Wyo. and so. Montana the 8th?

Sincerely, and in haste,

To Caroline Sauer

August 25, 1963

Dear Caroline:

Well, the junket to the west for THE STORY CATCHER is lined up as the enclosed route sheet will show, but I face it without enthusiasm.

I finally had to look into the book. I was warned off by the jacket, pretty, but hybrid eastern Algonquin, not western Sioux. It can be discarded. The illustrations, unfortunately, cannot. Most of them are just babyish and mediocre, but the one of Chapter 2 is a serious triple anachronism. The youth shamelessly wears one erect feather at the back of the head—the mark of the highest Sioux council chiefs and *never* worn by anyone else. In addition the boy has a Cheyenne warrior's shell core choker of the 1870–1890 period, and the shell core breastplate worn by agency chiefs, not green youths, and not of the 1840's by anyone. All this after I went to the trouble of sending Westminster guide material—prints of Amos Bad Heart Bull's picture history, authentic work by the man to whom the book is dedicated. Who will believe that I, the Plains Sioux authority, was not consulted?

You will recall that I wanted you to try to buy the book back from Westminster when I brought the manuscript in—avoid throwing a good book down a rat hole. I knew at the time that I should have taken action myself.

To avoid a repetition of such embarrassment, and such misinformation being thrust upon the public, I shall sign no more book contracts without a firm clause forbidding the inclusion of any illustrative material without my approval, item by item.

Sincerely,

To Savoie Lottinville, Director

UNIVERSITY OF OKLAHOMA PRESS

August 31, 1963

Dear Savoie Lottinville:

Please forgive this long delay in my reply to your kind letter of July 30. I was hidden out to complete my BEAVER MEN.

My problem with the National Archives personnel is nothing personal, if I may put it so. I've had nothing but the most helpful cooperation from everyone there.

I completed much of my Plains research back in 1937–38 while the War Records were stored above the Department of the Interior garage over on Virginia Avenue. I made a complete survey of the material on the Plains and have been able, upon many occasions, to give file and document number to many seeking information on Plains topics. Sometimes, however, these inquirers are informed by Archives personnel that the material I suggested is "not available" and often this is construed to mean that I made it up.

A recurring example is the medical report on an examination of Wild Bill Hickok's eyes the spring of 1876 at Camp Carlin by the post surgeon. The full report appears in the Medical History of Camp Carlin, but inquirers are told that there is no such source available. I suppose that this means that the material has been classified since it reached the National Archives — suffered the treatment that roused Fred C. Othman to complain in his "Army Reveals Secret of Custer's Last Stand" in the N. Y. *World-Telegram,* Nov 19, 1957. This latter however, was an early case of classification but perhaps something similar has happened since the War Records were moved into the National Archives building. I know that there was a Military History of Camp Carlin in the post files over on Virginia Avenue the winter of 1937–38 and it should be in the War Records in the Archives now. There may have been what are considered reflections on the private lives of military men in the Military History — I don't take notes on such material unless it has special pertinency as the medical reports on Custer in 1868–9. If this is the reason for the classification of the Camp Carlin Medical History, those inquiring should be told this, and be given the opportunity to have the Hickok report photostated. He was no military man.

I suppose, making the complete search over at Virginia Avenue, that my notes contain much material that may be classified now. Surely the "not available" has reached several of my correspondents who obtained file descriptions from me.

I'm not objecting to the policy so much as the inadequate information offered the inquirer.

Sincerely,
copy to War Records

To Dr. Vernon C. Rockey, President

Crawford [Nebraska] Chamber of Commerce

September 25, 1963

Dear Doctor Rockey:

It's interesting that you should write me September 18. I came down through the Crawford region the tenth of September.

Yes, I understand how you feel about CHEYENNE AUTUMN, so intimately bound to Fort Robinson and the Crawford region, being made into a moving picture out in Utah, etc. Unfortunately, all my efforts toward having any of my books made into pictures set in their proper locales have failed—failed so that CHEYENNE AUTUMN is the first one to be made at all. The Crazy Horse picture of some years ago was, of course, not from my book.

For almost twenty-eight years, since Irving Thalberg took an option on OLD JULES for MGM, in case his health improved enough to make more pictures (which never happened) I've tried to keep some control over the background of any book that interested the moving picture people. Consequently none was ever sold. In the meantime the competition of television has cut the selling price of serious books to only a fifth, sometimes only a tenth of the pre-TV value. At my agent's urging that I sell the Cheyenne book before the value dropped even more, I signed the contract without any controls, which is customary. Picture companies don't want the author's finger in their pie. I had hoped for the impossible all those years.

The matter of locale is largely one of economy. A picture can be made in Africa, Spain, Italy, India or even Mexico, etc., for a fraction of the cost in the United States. Only the leading characters are taken over. Most of the rest of the cast are hired at a few cents value a day. Warner Brothers, to make the Cheyenne book, have sets in the western states named, with all the necessary accommodations, I am told, for any cast and extras, ready and paid for.

I am very sorry but there's nothing I can or could do.

Sometimes local people underwrite the production of a moving picture, hire a top Hollywood director, give him the free rein he must have on cast and production but keep control of the locale. Most pictures nowadays are made by one kind of independent or another and then handled under the aegis of some well-known moving picture company. I suppose that CHEYENNE AUTUMN should have been done this way but it was not my place to raise the backing and now it is too late.

About the trail book on the Crawford region that you suggest I write: The idea is a good one but too limited in sweep, scope—and significance—for me. I don't write river or trail books. That's more for people interested in the journalistic approach. I try to take an artistic view, with some significance far beyond the local, some significance for the understanding of man.

I recall that when I was on the Historical Society staff I suggested to Mr. Spence of the Northwest *News* that he write a book on the Crawford region in his spare time. As it turned out he had no spare time left.

Whoever does undertake the book you suggest, should not neglect the ancient Indian trails, those made before the horse—trails that had to follow the waterways rather closely, and the places of refuge.

The Crawford region looked fine two weeks ago—more fall green than I usually find there, the cattle fat and contented.

Sincerely,

To Tris Colket

T-T Ranch
Sheridan, Wyo.

October 22, 1963

Dear Tris Colket:[1]

Thanks for Erlanson's BATTLE OF THE BUTTE[2] with your note about the picture of Lieut. Clark and Little Wolf, and it is Little Wolf, not Little Hawk. Take a look at the enclosed photostat of a page of Frank Leslie's Illustrated *Newspaper* of June 28, 1879, with the story of Little Wolf's surrender and the cut made of this picture. It carries what I know is the proper caption, "Little Wolf, a chief of the Hostile Cheyennes, and his Captor, Lieutenant W. P. Clark. U.S.A." Anyone who thinks Clark would have had his picture published with anyone less than Little Wolf himself doesn't know the Plains Army or Clark. He was a good man but he knew how to get credit for his exploits.

I knew this picture from my childhood. Relatives of the Little Wolf of the Outbreak married into the Pine Ridge Oglalas had a print and treasured it.

As for the Indian in the picture being the uncle of Crazy Horse, Little Hawk, this isn't possible. First, there are several pictures around of him and he never looked like this. Further, he fled to Canada after Crazy Horse was killed in 1877 and came back with the Oglalas when Sitting Bull returned in 1881. See p 175, Fourth Annual *Report,* Bureau of Ethnology, and *McGillycuddy, Agent,* p 164. (The latter is very unreliable but the former isn't.) In 1930–31 He Dog, Short Bull, etc., verified the whereabouts of Little Hawk.

Often the Little Hawk supposedly in the picture is identified as the Cheyenne, which is not true either. That man was a stocky, blocky man, the anchor man of the "Cheyenne Hill" acrobatic stunt, with nine men on him.

In any case, Clark would not have settled for less than *the* Little Wolf.

This error is no reflection on Mr. Erlanson. Our Indian photographs are in an appalling state of mislabeling, and those of the Cheyennes the worst, as I knew before Grinnell wrote me about this in the 1920's. The picture on p 8 is also mislabeled. The man standing is Old Little Wolf, the Southern Cheyenne chief, as anyone who knows Southern Cheyenne accoutrements of the time would know. The fur hat was common among them and the Kiowas, etc. This Little Wolf was fighting the Kiowas back about 1828, died in 1886 at around ninety-two. See Grinnell's FIGHTING CHEYENNES p 39, Scribners edition, p 42 University of Oklahoma edition.[3] The Northern Cheyenne chief was called Few Tails until about 1856, as Grinnell indicated and as I found verified in the National Archives. The seated man in the picture p 8 was identified for me by the old Cheyennes and Sioux as Lame White Man, killed in the Custer fight.

There were dozens of men named Little Wolf on the Plains, many of them among the Cheyennes, north and south. I went through all the probate case records of the Tongue River Reservation before these were destroyed. In the two weeks, I got a comprehensive list of the Cheyenne relationships unequaled anywhere. Not even the Cheyennes know much about their involved personal histories. In the probate cases the real relationships, not the adoptive, were ferreted out.

More about Erlanson's booklet: The picture on p 24 is not Little Chief but a much younger man. See Brown and Felton's THE FRONTIER YEARS, p 21 for this picture of Huffman's, identified here as Young Spotted Eagle, who was at least the right age.[4]

On Page 26 is another picture identified as Little Wolf, and in this Mr. Erlanson can very well be correct. There were very many men of the name. It can't be of the Little Wolf in the outbreak, who never used the long pipe after he killed Lean Elk in about 1880, and never wore the upright one feather of the chieftainship any more. The jacket of the man is beaded in the Wild West Show style. Some time when you're up around Birney ask some of the old timers there, the old so-called heathens, why this picture should not be published.

Thanks for the booklet. I'm happy to have it and besides, this information about Cheyenne photographs should be put down, and only such an occasion would make me take the time to do it.

Greetings to Trudy and to you — The Byron and Newton pictures taken of me at the T-T Ranch are the best I've ever seen, meaning the most flattering, of course.

Sincerely,

1. Triss Colket, a rancher near Sheridan, Wyoming, was also a book collector.

2. Charles B. Erlanson, *Battle of the Butte: General Miles' Fight with the Indians on Tongue River, January 8, 1877* (N.p. 1963).

3. George Bird Grinnell, *The Fighting Cheyennes* (New York: Scribner, 1915; New Haven: Yale U P, 1923; Norman: U of Oklahoma P, 1956; New York: Cooper Square, 1962, introduction by MS).

4. Mark Herbert Brown and W. R. Felton, *The Frontier Years: L. A. Huffman, Photographer of the Plains* (New York: Holt, 1955).

To Walter Frese

Nov. 6, 1963

Dear Walter:

I'm off to Detroit today so I'm leaving the BEAVER MEN with Hastings. I've revised, recast and retyped about a third of the book, and expanded it a little here and there, with a few long pages and about three half-page insertions. The ending is developed more to the weight that I had in mind.

It's been difficult, with somebody in every day. When I get back from Detroit, sometime during the week-end, I'll start on the maps and finish up the notes, etc.

Marlon Brando called the other evening before he started around the world. Wants to do something about Indians. Says he'll stop off in about a month, when he's taken a fast trip around this far. I don't know what he has in mind. Talked about an hour but I couldn't decide just what he was driving at. We'll see. He's a little on the veering side, like a plains wind.

Sincerely,

To Don Beckman

Jan. 2, 1964

Dear Don Beckman:[1]

At last my maps for *The Beaver Men,* out next fall, are off my hands. . . .

Circle on the Square is a theatre here, and a good one. I wasn't aware there was a formal school connected with it. It's largely experimental, and gave Quintero his original reputation, or so it seems. I've been following its offerings from the time it was around the block from me when I lived at 24 Barrow.

Yes, I've read Genet, my only reservation is the rather formal religious message usually involved. Formal religion — church — was left behind us 700 years ago.[2] Our attitude has been that formal religion in the shape of creed and immortality is for arrested infantile minds. Not that we have any urge to interfere with anyone's beliefs — they just aren't necessary or tenable for us. Religion yes, but not anything of a set pattern.

Take notes, and do become aware of what luck you have to be present in a controlled environment where you could, in a novel, study your characters while free from outside infringement (as I was, for a small time, in *Winter Thunder.*)

A Happy and stimulating 1964 to you.

1. Don Beckman wrote MS first in 1954, while still a schoolboy, ambitious to be a writer. The correspondence continued until 1965. After her death he wrote two recollective articles: "Two Old Friends and a Shelf of Books" (*Gordon Journal,* January 24, 1968) and "The Pen Goes Dry" (*Gordon Journal,* February 7, 1968).

2. MS is referring to her Sandoz forebears.

To Ron Hull

Program Manager
University Television, KUON-TV
Lincoln, Nebraska

January 8, 1964

Dear Ron:[1]

Thank you for all the good wishes. May the Hull Productions thrive and prosper.

Yes, my *Cheyenne Autumn* is being made into a picture. It's a continuation of the sad run of circumstances in which the book was caught even before publication. When the news of my forthcoming book got out in 1939, a publisher (Simon & Schuster) hired Howard Fast to beat me into print. He wrote the book from the newspaper accounts, etc., without ever discovering that Indian Territory and Fort Robinson were in different military departments (like the present corps areas) and that a soldier who started after the

Cheyennes down at Fort Reno would not be with the troops at Robinson. The southern force was sent back at the Platte, because they were out of their department, with no replacements of stock or men available, or replenishment of the exhausted supplies. Department of the Platte (Gen. Crook's men) took over at the Platte.

The Atlantic people protested this technique to Simon & Schuster (it's customary to give an author seven, eight years on an announced research topic, as is done in physical research, etc.). They dropped the book. Duell, Sloan and Pearce took it up, made Literary Guild for it, sold it to the movies (never made in America but put together long ago in Russia). I put my book off to 1952. Fast's book is a lying libel, curiously on the theme that the Indians are a decadent and dying people but, with the Communist slant, that they, a minority, could do no wrong, shed no blood, although the Indians took pride in the fact that they fought back, no matter how hopelessly.

Lately Hecht-Lancaster hired a couple of writers to do a movie script on the Cheyenne outbreak from the newspaper accounts.[2] We got an offer, small, with no control or anything, from Smith for Warners, but with John Ford to direct. It was take that or lose the book entirely once more. Sadly I consented. At least there is to be a widely distributed paperback by Doubleday, of my version.

I'm sorry this got so long, but I did think this should be put down for my files, as a record of how things are done.

The Beaver Men is in, with good maps, etc., and considerable material on very early occupation of white men on the upper Plains, French, not Spanish. It's to come out in the fall and I'll be through Lincoln then. In the meantime I'll have to slip into town for some looking into the Ricker files again this spring probably.

Happy Days!

1. Ron Hull was KUON (public television) station manager in Lincoln, Nebraska, from 1955 to 1982; later he was program fund director for the Corporation for Public Broadcasting in Washington, D.C., before returning to KUON in 1988. He worked closely with MS when she made her two TV series in 1959 and remained a friend until her death.

2. The production company Hecht-Hill-Lancaster consisted of Harold Hecht, a producer, James Hill, a screenwriter and director, and Burt Lancaster, the actor. The company brought out such films as *The Young Savages*, 1961, *Taras Bulba* and *Birdman of Alcatraz*, 1962, *Cat Ballou*, 1965, and *The Way West*, 1967.

To Mary Abbot

January 20, 1964

Dear Mary:

Nothing I ever heard about the arrogant tastelessness and rank indecency of Hollywood exceeds the suggestion that I let that corrupt hack, Jack Webb, make a novel of *my* CHEYENNE AUTUMN.[1]

Only the knowledge that Hecht-Lancaster were doing the story from newspaper accounts and that lying book that Howard Fast was hired to write to beat my Cheyenne volume into print ever got me to agree to an uncontrolled sale of a book that contains so much that is sacred to a people.

I find myself in the position of a virtuous woman who foolishly conducted herself so the villain feels free to make his proposition, and in the most offhand manner, like volunteering to leave a dirty dollar bill on the washstand.

I suspect that there may very well be some Warner trickery, in spite of the prior sale of the book to paper back publication. I still have the correspondence about MISS MORISSA, which I wrote at the request of Clark at MGM for Greer Garson, who then went to Warners with the outline and made the lady doctor picture for them. While MORISSA isn't of the caliber of CHEYENNE AUTUMN the story is a masterpiece compared to Warner's STRANGE WOMAN IN TOWN. I saved all the Clark and Garson letters, and the notes on the arrogant letter Jack Warner wrote to Annie Laurie when she reminded him that the woman doctor story was my work, requested for, and by, Garson.

Still, it's all material for my autobiography, and I'm just that gal to tell the bald truth.

Sorry—

1. MS meant James Webb, a scriptwriter for Warner Brothers. His work includes *Charge at Feather River,* 1953, *Phantom of the Rue Morgue* (co-writer), 1954, *Trapeze,* 1956, *The Big Country* (co-writer), 1958, and *How the West Was Won,* 1963, for which he was awarded an Oscar. See MS to James Webb, July 25, 1964.

To Jim [James Carr]

Jan. 29, 1964

Dear Jim:[1]

I plan to be back from the hospital Thursday afternoon, 30, with the menace stood off once more, for a while.[2]

I wrote a substantial piece of rough draft that needed redoing for the Custer book and went all the way through *Crazy Horse* for your indexes. I think it might be nice to work on the index gradually as your help has time, and I happen to be in town.

Mari

1. James Carr, a rare-book dealer, became a friend of MS's after he read and praised *The Buffalo Hunters*. After her death he started a *Festschrift* for her, but he did not publish it.

2. The menace was a recurrence of cancer. MS had her second mastectomy the week of January 20, 1964.

To Allie Sandoz [not sent]

Merriman, Nebraska

February 13, 1964

Dear Allie:[1]

It's fine to hear from you and I appreciate your generous offer of a refuge for my manuscripts and data. I think Caroline plans to make a sort of small fireproof Old Jules museum of Flora's freezer house. This is fine and I plan to send some Old Jules material, etc., out there.

As for my total collection, except for university libraries, I could not consider any place except the Old Jules site, with a Sandoz Foundation to back it, to make the material permanently available for research and for the use of any creative writing. My collection is recognized as one of the great ones on western and American Indian materials, much of it from people now dead. In addition there is a large amount of material and advice for creative writers, particularly in the higher levels of artistic fiction, preferably of the newer, the more experimental, the avant-garde — with no connection at all to the western or Indian material.

Practically every great university library has approached me for my collection, including Yale, Virginia (started by Jefferson), Syracuse (which has been making a Sandozia collection for over ten years), Texas, Colorado, Wyoming, Nebraska, etc. All these offer fire proof space, with trained personnel to manage the collection, and air-conditioned office space for me the rest of my life.

I know that my material should go to what will some day be a monument to the Sandoz name on the Old Jules place, but probably this will be allowed to drag along as the site of Ft. Atkinson on the Missouri above Omaha was. The site was long government property and could have been made a national monument site at no realestate cost. Now it is in private hands and the last I heard, $75,000 must be raised for the approximately ten acres of worthless (except for historical purposes) land. As an historian I know the same will happen to a site on the Old Jules place some day, when we are all dead, and my material, at the best, will be permanently assigned to the care of some library, if it has not been dissipated to the wind by my heirs. Then the national monument or park can only be something to mark the spot—nothing more.

But that is probably inevitable. Nobody sees the value of his contemporaries, particularly not his contemporaneous relatives. Nobody listens to the historian.

Thanks anyway, and have a fine spring.

1. Allie Sandoz was a grandson of Jules's brother William and a close family friend.

To Walter Frese

March 12, 1964

Dear Walter:

About illustrations for THE BEAVER MEN, in addition to the 24 I brought to the office:

Your desire for a type of illustration that just does not exist for the 1609–1834 period alarms me. I'm afraid you will let someone insert shockingly anachronistic and false pictures that discredit my careful work permanently. A bad picture pops out at the potential reader as he thumbs through a book, so the truth of the text is never discovered. I'm still embarrassed by the sentimental and totally false picture in THE BUFFALO HUNTERS, opposite page 183. Even the cut line there is false and contrary to all my Indian writing.

My hesitation about the Catlin, Bodmer and Miller pictures is not only that even the first two are really picturing the post-1834 period, the day of the romantic travelers, instead of the period of the beaver, but that most of the items have appeared at least fifty times in books, pamphlets, magazines and newspapers, (articles and advertisements) the last few years. My readers know this as well as I, and using much from the three artists would not only verge on the false for this book but would label it as a rehash of the trite and hackneyed.

About a picture of Champlain in the attack on the Iroquois in 1609: there is one, a line drawing made by someone who had not even bothered to read the accounts. See page 46 of La Farge's AMERICAN INDIAN for a similar cut of the attack on the Onondaga village in 1615.[1]

I've marked some possible pictures in the enclosed La Farge book and in Morgan's INDIAN JOURNALS.[2] Go slow on the Catlin, Bodmer, etc., pictures. Bodmer's mouth of the Yellowstone is not so well known, nor are a couple of the others, the one of the toboggan, for instance. Rindispacher [*sic*] is early and not so hackneyed, but also far from the authentic.

Pick something from those I've marked but try to avoid the shop-worn, and do let me write the cut lines. I know what I'm doing in this matter.

Sincerely,

1. Oliver LaFarge, *American Indian* (New York: Crown, 1956).

2. Lewis Henry Morgan, *Indian Journals, 1859–62*, ed. Leslie A. White, illustrations selected by Clyde Walton (Ann Arbor: U of Michigan P, 1959).

To Lyle McCann

March 14, 1964

Dear Lyle McCann:

What a lovely letter! Thank you, and your kind-hearted lady.

Mother lived until 1938, long enough to see a local play made of *Old Jules*. She loved plays, and was really carried away by what was really an amateur production of Alliance. Yes, most of the bills were paid before she died. She was that kind of woman.

Old Jules is buried up near Alliance with Mary beside him. I would have preferred father's choice—a grave overlooking the orchard, but the rest thought it wouldn't look right.

Yes, I go home at least once a year. Often several times. Nebraska is my home, but I mean I go to the Old Jules place. . . .

I don't think we considered our childhood a time of hardship. It was our life and therefore normal until we discovered others were more pampered, but by then I think we understood that pampering was not preferable—.

Best wishes to both of you,

To Raymond DeMallie

March 14, 1964

Dear Raymond DeMallie:

Of course you can find *Annals of Wyoming,* the quarterly of the Wyoming Historical Society. The files are vast and important.

The Indians are difficult to contact effectively. They feel they have been cheated of everything else and are unwilling to put their history into the hands of the careless white man. Besides, you're not ready for any help from them if you've not looked through such obvious sources as the *Annals.*

You can't mix up Elk that Hollow Walking, and Lame Deer. Look up the sources. The latter was a hostile Elk with Spotted Tail 1867. See Vol X. Bu. of Ethno *Reports* in the winter counts. See also Vestal's books.

One does not ask to see a researcher's interviewed material or any other unique material.

Sincerely,

To Bruce Nicoll

May 11, 1964

Dear Bruce:

Since [Nebraska] Governor Morrison was in New York late last month I've thought about the state centennial coming up. It seems to me that those of us who are interested might work out something within our speciality or art—the composer, say, compose, the writer write.

While I have a genuine distaste for the chauvinistic, the overtly patriotic, I could be interested in writing something like the following:

> A TURN OF THE YEAR, the Beauty and the Terror (tentative title). This could be a special little book of about 40,000 words with four sections, one for each season, not strictly Nebraska but of the middle plains and not of any one year but of any season between prehistory and 1967, whatever works in. I think this might give a heightened sense of place, the earth and the sky, the flora and fauna and man as seen by a sort of disembodied spirit roaming.
>
> It might begin with the melting snows of spring, the pasques and the Easter daisies pushing up in the dead grass, the spring winds and prairie fires and pleasant rains and floods and tornado scares and reality, with all creatures and man moving out into enlarged life. There could be the

sun and the thunderheads and hail and chokecherries, the young antelope in the bull tongue cactus patches, the ripening harvest, with the scythe, the binder, horse-power thrashers and the staggering of combines down the golden fields, the canneries tamping lids on fancy green peas and on chicken stew, with man at work or hunting the buffalo and the deer or sailing on the lakes, old and new.

Then there would be fall, with its hurry for provisions and shelter from the coming snows, with the elk gathering in the sandhills to the change to snow tires, winter working hours and winter air schedules. Perhaps there might be an incident back at the lone pine tree in west Cherry county on a high cluster of blowouts where no prairie fire could destroy it. It had seemed destined to become the Christmas tree of some ax-toting settler, and threatened to bring violent turmoil in the new community, perhaps even murder, with one settler watching the tree, rifle ready. In the end it became the standing Christmas tree of all the half dozen families, still on its ancient roots.

For one Indian bit I might include the following:

EVENING SONG

(from several versions of the song of a chief, winter 1876–77, among the Cheyennes and Kiowas imprisoned at Fort Marion, Florida, for resisting the encroaching whites on their treaty lands of the Plains)

Sun-Going-Down!
Sun-Going-Down!
From our prison we call you, O Sun,
Look in pity upon our barred faces,
see our chained feet, our ironed hearts.

Sun-Going-Down,
Sun-Going-Down,
Soon you will shine
Into the winter faces of our deserted Ones.
Light them, comfort them, warm them
with the love you see in my face,
the water standing red upon my face.

Sun-Going-Down,
Tell them of this — but
not of the irons trapped on my hands,
the ball hard as the blacksmith's

iron rock upon which he hammers,
rooting my feet.

Sun-Going-Down,
Speak to them of the eternal earth,
Shine on them as they place my young son
upon his first pony, teaching him to ride,
selecting well the second father to guide
him.

The time is long and we must learn a new road.

Sun-Going-Down,
Sun-Going-Down,
Touch the cheeks in that far country,
Touch the cheek of my wife,
the brown cheek of my unknown son.

Then come the thaws, the blizzards, the pasques and Easter daisies, the buffalo and deer with their young, the irrigation water flowing, the stock growing new hair, the cities changing once more, for the year has turned.

If you have nothing better in mind and are interested, there's a germ of an idea that I might work on.

Sincerely,

June 4, 1964

Dear Bruce:

Now you've hit upon a real book for the Nebraska Centennial. Get Wright Morris to do it in picture and text.[1] This would be a fine contribution and I could go on with my own work. . . .

I don't know why I didn't think of Wright Morris for the Nebraska book in the first place. He will make a fine unified job of it. I like books where the writing and the illustration are by the same individual. . . .

Sincerely,

1. Wright Morris (b. 1909), a native Nebraskan, won the National Book Award in 1956 for *Field of Vision* (New York: Harcourt Brace, 1956). A prolific writer and excellent photographer, he used a Nebraska setting for many of his books. Wright Morris, *The Home Place* (New York: Scribner, 1948), was made up of short prose

paragraphs accompanied by his own photographs taken near Central City and Chapman, Nebraska.

June 14, 1964

Dear Bruce:

Just a hasty summing up before I take the plane this evening for Oregon: I still think the Wright Morris book is a good idea for the Nebraska centennial. It is true, however, that both his writing and his photography, being distinctly an art product of the 1960's, will date, as all self-conscious art, as well as all art innovations date. I see so many fine photographic shows here, evocative, artistic work, but fifteen, even ten years later they are dated, which doesn't matter in photography but as illustration for a book it can.

I've worked hard ever since my early undergraduate days to avoid the literary affectations of the moment, all the self-conscious artistic approaches so dear to English departments. I've tried to produce an experience for the reader, with, I hope, sometimes an evocation beyond the actual occurrence. Further, I should like, at rare moments, of course, to stir in the deep unchartered areas of racial memory that lie in all of us but are overlaid by hard, forbidding strata so early in life. There is art that does this, not always the greatest, but sometimes, as the Belvedere Apollo of which Benjamin West said, when he first saw the Apollo, "A Mohawk, by God!"

Among photographers W. H. Jackson is perhaps the nearest to a timeless worker, usually in scenery but not always. A Londoner, shown Jackson's photo of Washakie exclaimed "The Henry James of the American Indian!" It's the most acute remark ever recorded about the Shoshoni chief—hypersensitive and sophisticated, a little foppish, an expatriate in his own time. Or take one of the [Matthew] Brady photographs of Mary Todd Lincoln, exposing her egocentricity, her shallow vanity, her almost fatal extravagance in dress. It's all as clear in one glance as it was in 1861—when she was somehow suspicious of Brady. An occasional photograph of Halsman's will probably be timeless[1]—not the Einstein, which is too much the one man, in the one time and therefore dated. But there are some from the earlier period—the French years.

I realize that I am aiming at some sort of universality and that I probably won't achieve it in the writing any more than in a photographer or artist, but just in case that I might manage some lasting sense or quality—not lasting as fossils are the remains of a period but with timelessness, I shouldn't want it dated and fossilized by association.

It is much easier for a photographer to catch this timeless quality than for a writer, if the photographer is willing to shoot for the essence of the subject rather than for the fashionable showiness of the moment.

This book could be a fine little volume, fine for generations. Whether I could achieve this remains to be discovered, but I think there should be less doubt about the illustrator.

Sincerely,

1. Philippe Halsman (1906–79), named one of the ten best photographers in an international poll in 1958, was photographer for *Vogue, Vu, Voila, Life, Look,* and other publications. His portrait photographs of such figures as Winston Churchill, Dwight Eisenhower, and other notables are famous. MS was one of his subjects.

To [no addressee]

Re: Final script by James Webb for the moving picture made from my CHEYENNE AUTUMN, completed fall 1963, script sent to me June, 1964 for permission to make a novel, to be called *Cheyenne Autumn* from the Webb script.

June 28, 1964

It seems impossible that this greatest epic of American history could be reduced to a dull, static bore but here is the evidence. The greatest figures are drained of all character—of dignity, force and integrity. Then there is the incredible insertion of the white girl into the flight. She would have been driven out of camp and from among the fleeing Cheyennes, the Indians whipping her team at every jump. (The only way she could have gone along would have been on someone's race horse, carrying her food, to hurry out ahead each time she was driven back, to slip in among the Indians at night or while making their desperate stands, risk the bullet or the arrow of some angry young warrior.

As if destroying the main characters and inserting the girl and her wagon were not enough, dozens of stupid stock cardboard figures have been added: stock soldiers, gamblers, prostitutes and stock senators, all in dull, trite scenes that have no meaning or point and serve only to retard the action, kill the feeble interest aroused. Then there are the endless anachronisms. Plainly none except those completely ignorant of the region or the people would put sabers into the Army of the Plains in 1878 and ignore boundaries of military departments, taking troops from Fort Reno clear to Fort Robinson, when they were turned back at the Platte; put bib overalls on Indians and cries into the mouths of their babies (trained from birth not to cry) and have Cheyennes spy on bathers. Indians, men, women and children, bathed together and were free of the snickering white-man attitude toward the human body.

Pointless too, is the false combination of the Sacred Arrows of the Southern Cheyennes with the Sacred Bundle that Little Wolf bore from long before 1878 until it was passed on to another by week-long ceremonials years after the flight. Then there is the character assassination of Dull Knife and Little Wolf and their descendants through the fictitious wife-stealing and murder. Dull Knife's wife, Pawnee Woman, could have been dropped from the cast instead of giving her to Little Wolf, making him, by implication, a wife stealer. Encumbering Dull Knife with a fictitious son to steal the wife of his father's great co-leader, Little Wolf, seems overt libel to me, compounded by the spurious killing of this non-existent son by Little Wolf. This is like making a picture in which Madison is given a son to steal the wife of Jefferson, who kills him for it. Fortunately those great leaders were white and so protected from libel. It may be that the Cheyennes are tiring of character assassination too.

All this is Warner Brothers' concern, not mine. I can prove by my book that I carried out my responsibilities and obligations to the old Cheyennes who entrusted their stories, their secret rituals and religion, to me, and by my contract with Bernard Smith that I had no voice in the preparation of this script. I prefer to let the matter rest there.

Copy to Annie Laurie Williams

To Stewart Richardson

July 13, 1964

Dear Mr. Richardson:

I'm sorry that your letter was packed into the boxes of unanswered mail. It is completely impossible to care for my correspondence and write books too. The only remedy is to let my typist empty the mail box.

Unfortunately there are a hundred interruptions for my kind of writer. I wasn't discharged from my visits to the surgeon until mid-May. In the meantime the complications of dealing with copy editors, proof readers and cartographers have grown out of all reason. My forthcoming book, *The Beaver Men,* my 18th, involved me in more difficulties than all the earlier books together, from lost manuscript to three tries by the cartographer merely to follow the correct spelling of my place names.

Then there was the trip out to Portland for the Spur award for a Westminster book, added to radio tapings for a forthcoming paperback of *Cheyenne Autumn,* the reading of the script of the moving picture made from the book and my protest against a "novel" to be made from the libelous script. Now there are the plans for my usual western autographing junket for the beaver book, in October. In addition there are always the manuscripts of former students to consider, etc.

These are some of the factors that have delayed THE LITTLE BIG HORN, these and my desire to make the book an illusion of an actual human experience, poignant and immediate, and the most authentic study of the battle.

I must get the book in by the first of September if I can manage a few uninterrupted days—

I am sorry—

To Victor Gondos, Jr.

Chief, Army and Air Corps Branch
General Services Administration
National Archives and Records Service

July 25, 1964

Dear Sir:

Re: NMRA: 404 (copy enclosed)

My BATTLE OF THE LITTLE BIG HORN, in Hanson Baldwin's Great Battles series for Lippincott, is nearing completion. For the final draft I still need another look into the March-June 1876 records of Cheyenne Depot (Camp Carlin) Wyoming Territory. Perhaps the following will help your staff to locate this material:

> Cheyenne Depot (Camp Carlin) Wyo. Tet. March-June 1876; Capt. James Gilliss, QM officer in charge; Capt. Geo. K. Brady, with one company of 23rd Infantry.

This depot was a supply station from 1867 to around 1888 for all the military posts of the region, any armies in the field from there, and for the Indian Agencies of Red Cloud and Spotted Tail in northwestern Nebraska. These agencies alone included shipments as high as a million pounds at a time in the 1876 period. There were between 1000 and 1200 civilian employees at the depot the spring of 1876, usually with up to 25,000 animals.

I need information on the following points:

1. The amount of ammunition available for both infantry and cavalry arms for General Crook's expeditions of 1876 to shed light on the repeated orders that the general return his faulty ammunition from the field and his angry retorts that he could not comply until he received servicable ammunition in its place. He would not disarm his force in the midst of hostile country. This matter has direct bearing on Crook's delayed movements and on the results of the Rosebud battle, June 17, where a decisive defeat of the hostile Indians might have scattered the great Sioux camp and saved Custer and his men.

2. A possible bottleneck at Cheyenne Depot that delayed deliveries to the starving Sioux on the reservations and drove them out to the hostiles where there were still some buffaloes, and reinforcing Custer's adversaries.

3. Medical records of the depot, showing the diagnosis of glaucoma in the eyes of Wild Bill Hickok (civilian) possibly influencing his rejection as scout for Crook, and, it is said, his plans to apply to Custer's 7th Cavalry after Crook's rejection. (That Hickok was a civilian would not stop the post surgeon's examination. My father, a homesteader, spent eight months under the care of Dr. Walter Reed, post surgeon, Fort Robinson, Nebraska, 1884–5 with a crushed ankle.)

For many years the Archives staff has replied to queries from others, and from me, about material in the files of this Camp Carlin (Cheyenne Depot), with the remark that there was no such material available. This is, of course, rank nonsense. I have notes on the three headings above, all taken from the *Camp Carlin* files, some over in the old storage on Virginia Avenue in 1937–38 and some in the National Archives in 1940.

I plan to come to the Archives in about two weeks. By that time I expect word from you that the requested material is now available.[1]

Impatiently,

1. MS's penned note attached to this letter states: "Letter in reply to this says found them in Quarter Master files."

To Mr. James R. Webb

July 25, 1964

Dear Mr. Webb:

I appreciate the time involved in your long letter of July 20 explaining the script of CHEYENNE AUTUMN. Unfortunately it explains nothing.

About the sabers: I don't depend upon secondary material like Colonel

Todd's SOLDIERS OF THE AMERICAN ARMY when primary sources are available.[1] Back in the 1937–38 period, plowing through the U.S. War Records stored above the Department of the Interior Garage, Virginia Avenue, Washington, I ran across the telegram that went out to all the plains posts in 1873, banning sabers anywhere except for dress parade, sabers admittedly largely discarded as useless weight long before that.

Incidentally I am just completing the BATTLE OF THE LITTLE BIG HORN for Hanson Baldwin's Great Battles series, a subject that Mr. Baldwin knows I have been studying all my life, most of the research completed before the National Archives staff got their classifying hands on the material. *No sabers* on the Custer trek.

About bib overalls: I went through all the bids for goods issued to both Sioux and Cheyennes on reservations during the seventies. The trousers were all called worsted, but were really shoddy, recaptured wool from waste, old rags, etc. All this came out in the investigations into the graft in Indian contracts. Bib overalls were for artisans and later for hoe men. Not even the cowboys would wear them. When an Indian, during that hopeless period of 1890's to the first World War, got his hands on a bib overall to cover his nakedness, he cut the bib off and slit them up the front, with his breechcloth underneath.

About the crying Indian children—have you ever seen starving children? Then you know that their crying is silent, as Fitzpatrick knew very well. Army surgeons on the plains posts remarked in their reports about the silence of the children of the nomadic tribes, taught never to betray their camp to a skulking enemy. As late as Wounded Knee 1890, when practically every woman of child bearing age had reached maturity under the white man who forbade the old ways, the wounded children did not cry. The keening of the mothers of starving wounded children would have been much more effective in your picture than the fiction of a crying child.

Inserting spurious and momentary conflicts and drama in the picture proves to me that no one bothered to understand the real conflict of the book—the struggle to save some of the young people who might carry the nation on, and the brave hope of teaching them a little of the dignity of the Cheyenne way.

But all the foolish anachronisms could be overlooked with a contemptuous smile or perhaps the contempt tinged with ribald laughter as millions of us laughed at the remark in a teaser for HOW THE WEST WAS WON, about the calf that ought to be a big one because his father was the biggest *steer* on the Plains.

The unforgivable section of the picture is the libel on the two great men of the Northern Cheyennes—in the fiction of a Dull Knife son stealing a wife of Little Wolf's, and the leader killing the youth. True, Little Wolf later, much later, shot a man who had tried to seduce his wife years before and was then, when they were safely back on the Yellowstone, trying to seduce Little Wolf's young daughter. A Cheyenne wife is free to leave her husband, who must bear this with fortitude, but a young daughter must be protected from philanderers. Sober, Little Wolf could never have shot the man, even under this provocation. Sorrowing for all those killed at Fort Robinson, and full of the whiskey the soldiers at Keogh gave him to forget, Little Wolf pulled the trigger.

Your concoction is something entirely different. Has it ever occurred that you would never have dared take such liberties with the great men of any other minority—not Mexican, Jew or Negro, only with the American Indian? Perhaps this will prove the last time for such libel. I hope so.

In the meantime your face must burn with shame.

Sorry,

1. Frederick P. Todd, *Soldiers of the American Army, 1775–1954* (Chicago: Regnery, 1954).

To Don Ward

July 26, 1964

Dear Don:[1]

Re: a section of *Maheo's Children* by Henry W. Allen, (Will Henry, Clay Fisher, etc.)

The foreword or introductory bit tells one right off that the author knows nothing of Cheyenne religion. Let him read THE GREAT CHEYENNE MYSTERIES by Grinnell, or the two volume THE CHEYENNE INDIANS, by the same author.[2] All Allen offers here is the usual uninformed white man idea of sun, rain and earth gods. Living up on the Tongue [River] even a few days should have taught him better about the Cheyennes. If not, Allen can read, can't he?

Reading notes:

Page 1 Pawnees were never "rounded up" and put onto reservations. They were always white man allies from the start. They sold their lands gradually and as earth-house village Indians from prehistoric times lived on restricted ground. In the 1870's they were moved down into Indian Territory but they were still furnishing uniformed companies of scouts for the U.S. Army under the Norths as the Pawnee Battalion.

Dull Knife was always a peace Indian to the whites. He was enrolled on the agency of the Upper Platte from its creation, granted the treaty-guaranteed hunting privileges and was on the agency rolls from the creation of the first Red Cloud (Old Sod) agency, 1871, and moved with the Oglalas to Red Cloud Agency on White River, near the present Fort Robinson, 1873. He was there all the spring of 1876 except for a short hunt in the Platte country until long after the Custer battle. Starved out, he finally got away in late summer 1876 and was still out hunting buffalo when [Col. Ranald] Mackenzie struck him in November. Look in the key to the map in CHEYENNE AUTUMN and in CRAZY HORSE. These books of mine are true. There is no argument on any of the sites or dates. I am the authority in those fields, backed up by the records of the War department and the Indian Bureau.

The December 1875 government order to bring the hostiles running in to the agencies applied to the ones in Nebraska too, the Oglala agency at Red Cloud, the Brules at Spotted Tail. If the author wants to quote from this order, why not from the version sent to these agencies instead of Standing Rock, where no Cheyenne ever belonged, and no Oglala Sioux. Dull Knife and Two Moons were ordered to bring any of their bands still out to the Agency just like the others of Red Cloud, the Oglalas. Dull Knife was in; Two Moons wasn't coming, not to Standing Rock, but to what was supposed to be his agency, Red Cloud.

2 Crazy Horse was not a Bad Face but a Hunkpatila Oglala. He never sent scouts to spy on Standing Rock but to Red Cloud.

What has all this Sioux business to do with a book on the Cheyennes?

page 8. *Heyoka* does not mean fool in our sense of the word but a member of the Contrary Society, those who had thunder and lightning in their puberty dreams and must do everything backward to avoid being struck by lightning, and to make the people laugh when their hearts are on the ground.

9 Spotted Tail was *not* at Standing Rock but on his own agency. See enclosed map.

There was no Pine Ridge agency until late 1878, no school even started there until the fall of 1879 so Tonkalla, real or fictitious, could not have gone there before the spring of 1876.

That's enough of this hodgepodge. I don't see how Allen can permit himself to do such writing. If this is fiction then it should have a sustained conflict throughout with a central character or characters, or at the least a central idea that helps create the conflict. As for the falsification of Standing Rock, Crazy Horse, Dull Knife, etc., that's too much like applying real names of anti-godlin[?] characters, the Standing Rock too much like putting Washington, D.C. into Canada, or Mexico. A good novelist keeps his actual places in their real locales or makes up new ones, new names as well as new locales. One does not falsify widely known fact in fiction; one makes up a set to fit the story. Doling out such misinformation is never acceptable, and even bad fiction because it breaks the illusion.

If this book is to be considered nonfiction, then Allen better read *Red Cloud's Folk* by Hyde to find out where Red Cloud was, and Grinnell's *Fighting Cheyennes*. I'd just as soon he'd not read my books. I'm tired of misrepresentations of my stories, my carefully checked statements of fact.

I don't see how Hastings House or any other publisher except someone like Exposition Press could possibly put his imprint on such mishmash. What does Allen think Hastings House is?

Sorry,

1. Don Ward, an editor and writer, was another who moved from publisher to publisher. With the Western Publishing Company, Racine, Wisconsin, and New York, from 1945 to 1955, he was later with Hastings House and Dell; he also free-lanced. He edited *Bits of Silver* (New York: Hastings House, 1961), *Pioneers West* (New York: Dell, 1966), and the New York Posse's *Brand Book*.

2. George Bird Grinnell, *The Great Mysteries of the Cheyenne* (N.p., n.d.), includes reprints of articles from various sources.

To Stewart Richardson

August 16, 1964

Dear Mr. Richardson:

About THE BATTLE OF THE LITTLE BIG HORN:

At last, after many years of insistence, I managed to get the War Records Department, National Archives, to admit that the files from which I took notes in 1937–38 exist and that I can take another, more comprehensive look into the material on the Custer battle, now that I am writing a book on the subject. So tonight I am off to Washington, no telling for how long. Or what changes will be necessary in my manuscript.

About spring publication: Don't you think this will be a little close to my

BEAVER MEN, published October 5, 1964. This was the final volume that was contracted for completion before I signed to write the Little Big Horn for you. (see the enclosed bibliography).

One reason that spring publication seems too close to me is the rather intensive work that I do in the promotion of my books, see a copy of my route sheet for promotion of THE CATTLEMEN, the previous book of my Plains Series. . . .

For this fall, as I say, I am cutting down some on my itinerary: autographing here at Jim Carr's, interview at Chicago with Cromie for Krock & Brentano, Oct 14: Kupcinet, Oct. 17, two TV appearances out west, several radio interviews, autographings here and there, with a Mari Sandoz week in Nebraska, etc. Plainly the October junket is still in process of development.

My special customers expect this kind of thing, but spring 1965 is just too close to October 1964.

Sincerely,

To Walter Frese

August 23, 1964

Dear Walter:

About going to Cheyenne for the premiere of CHEYENNE AUTUMN: I wasn't asked but I couldn't go under any circumstances, unless the ending of the picture were changed. My presence there would give silent approval to the violence that the spurious, tacked-on ending does to the great men of the tribe.[1]

See the enclosed copy of my reaction to the script, far too late to do any good. Webb, the script writer, replied to this in a long, long letter, but he only proved how calloused those people are to human rights. As I told him, he would not have dared libel any other minority in this way, not Mexican, Jew or Negro, only the American Indian.

Sorry,

It is perfectly possible that some young Cheyenne carrying a little alcohol and a gun might take a pot-shot at me if he decided that I was guilty of the libel on his ancestors. I've had hair shot out of my head twice; the next time it might be closer. But the real barrier is the lie in the picture.

1. The *Cheyenne Autumn* film ends with a last-minute reconciliation of the U.S. Army and embattled Cheyennes. Historically no such scene took place. Some of the Cheyennes were slaughtered by army troops as they attempted to flee captivity at Fort

Robinson. The other group later surrendered to Lt. W. Philo Clark at Fort Keogh, Montana, without a battle.

To Ramon Powers

August 29, 1964

Dear Mr. Powers:[1]

Thank you. I am happy to know you found CHEYENNE AUTUMN worth reading.

You will have considered going through the records of the Cheyenne and Arapaho Agency in the Oklahoma Historical Society for your understanding of the situation there in the 1874–78 period. The staff is very cooperative.

Then there are the "Little Wolf Papers". Either K[ansas] U[niversity] Library or the Historical Society surely has had these microfilmed at the National Archives. This is done at cost. The same is true of the "Proceedings of the Board of Officers", which is a voluminous investigation into the outbreak from the beginning, with testimony from the Indian survivors at Ft. Robinson and the soldiers, scouts, etc. In addition there are all the Indian Bureau Records and War Records of the period in National Archives. You are not really conversant with the situation until you have seen them all, as I have.

The original of the "G. E. Lemmon" manuscript is either still in the family, (probably around Lemmon, S. Dak.) or in some historical repository. Mr. Lemmon gave me a carbon for my use but you can see that outside of my special use, the manuscript really remains the property of the family, as letters written to me do. The letters always belong to the *writer.*

H. D. Wimer's address is Stratton, Nebraska. Write him about the outbreak.

For the map of the Lewis Fight, write to the cartography Dept., National Archives, Washington, D.C., giving the complete description. A photostat will be run off for you at cost. There are many more maps of the outbreak and the military movements in the Archives, and in my files. The one of the five flights is, of course, mine. I put material together in the maps of my books. Each book has maps in my files. The publisher will not always go to the expense of using more than one or two, often not one.

You have a start, but only a start on the material of the flight. Just the cross index to my Cheyenne material runs to over 100,000 cards. I've been adding to this Cheyenne file all my life.

Sincerely,

1. Ramon Powers was a graduate student at the University of Kansas. He later published "The Kansas Indian Claims Commission of 1879," *Kansas History* 7.3 (Autumn 1984).

To F. H. Sinclair (Neckyoke Jones)

Continental Confederation of Adopted Indians
Sheridan, Wyoming

12 October 1964

Dear Neckyoke:

Thanks for the fine letter which I'll acknowledge hastily because I'm off to Nebraska this week.

Thanks too about the Continental Confederation of Adopted Indians. I've been a member for many years. My certificate of membership is in storage but as I recall, it was signed Blackhoop. The enclosed thermofax copy of your 1960 roster of members includes my name. Naturally you can't keep us all in memory. I don't recall which of my several Indian names that I gave. Perhaps Mouse Lodge, given to me after *Crazy Horse* was published.

I'm sorry about your surgery and trust that you are recovering very well. . . .

Yes, I know something of the sad story of Lydia Wild Hog.[1] Old Wild Hog was a good friend of Old Jules in the period between the Cheyennes' return to Pine Ridge about 1882 after the so-called trial down in Kansas. He died about 1889 of pneumonia. He never really recovered from the self-inflicted chest wound with the broken scissors in 1879. If he was dead his wife and the children could remain at Red Cloud, and, he hoped, be safe and fed. I have sheafs of notes Old Jules put down during his visits with Wild Hog. You will find these mentioned in the notes in *Cheyenne Autumn*. My understanding is that Lydia married one of the Wild Hog sons.

It's always difficult to get Indians to speak of any incident in which important tribal members died. They just don't know, or don't answer. Look at the years Grinnell worked with the Cheyennes yet he never got the story of the killing of women and children and Medicine Arrow under a white flag on the Sappa in Kansas, April 1875 by a few troops and a lot of buffalo hunters. Perhaps they swore him to secrecy as I was, on some subjects, but I had a lot of material from the white man's side and when the old Cheyennes refused to talk about "Cheyenne Hole" I frankly told them I would have to use the version I had unless they told me what happened.

That's how I got the story of the killing of Medicine Arrow, and the reason for the killing of the nineteen settlers in North Kansas in 1878, a settler for every Cheyenne man killed in 1875. I was told "There is no way to pay for women and children killed."

Greetings to the Lady of the House.

1. Lydia Wild Hog was impoverished and apparently received little help from any government agency. She was struck and killed by a car on a Sheridan street. Investigators found she lived in an abandoned truck body with two handicapped daughters and two younger relatives she was raising (see MS to Neckyoke Jones, November 11, 1953).

To Mary Abbot

November 8, 1964

Dear Mary:

I'm back, have been for a week but had to get over the appallingly hard trip. With politicians bumping me from the TV programs and even the recordings, the whole thing had to be rescheduled half a dozen times, making more night jumps, more hard day work with more interviews and speeches than I had planned on, more dinners, teas, etc.

My viral enteritis returned, so I was off my feed all the time, and finally I got what my doctor in Nebraska had predicted would happen sooner or later—I would have an attack of mother's lumbago.

Well, I'm eating again and the lumbago or whatever it was has yielded a little to hours of hot pads and sleeping sitting up.

This week I hope to have a thorough physical to see if this business can be kept from becoming chronic.[1] In the meantime the weather was beautiful, as I gather it was here, and most of the speaking and interviews and autographings went pretty well.

Happy autumn days—

1. The physical examination revealed recurrence of cancer.

To Richard B. Williams

Sturgis, South Dakota

December 1, 1964

Dear Richard Williams:[1]

It's nice to hear that there is to be some development of Bear Butte, but please try to keep it dignified. After all this is the single most sacred spot on the Plains to the American Indians, the Sioux and Cheyennes in later times but there are implications of its involvement in Comanche and Ree legends and even farther tribes. I'm certain that enough research would bring out allusions to the Butte in early accounts of far Indians.

About the article of your experiences at the ceremony with Baldwin Twins and the Arrows: outlets for such material have been diminished signally by the disappearance and curtailment of so many magazines. If you work up the material very thoroughly and well, hunt up additional pictures, Indian and white man, black and white and color, with a magnificant shot of Bear Butte, say with the morning sun coming over it, or from the air, perhaps you could interest *American Heritage*. I recall seeing a Sioux skin with a picture of the great camp circle of the annual summer conference of the Tetons on it, in color, with the bear brooding over it, in charcoal. Unfortunately I don't recall whether I ever knew who made it or where it is now. It was brought to the river place by some Indians long ago—perhaps the time Wounded Knee told us the story of his long-time hiding in the hole with the arrow in the back of his knee.[2] Perhaps the skin found its way to the Historical Society or to the Smithsonian.

About your article, when completed: just now I can't take the time to look at anything except the LITTLE BIG HORN, the book for Hanson Baldwin's series of great battles and this must be in by February. It is already a year late. Then I could glance over your article for suggestions for revision or extension, etc. Of course I never edit manuscripts for others. Editors are to creative writers as furniture handlers are to interior decorators—and most of them not that able. Anyway, serious writers don't edit for others.

No, I've spent no time at all on the picture CHEYENNE AUTUMN. The author is never welcome. . . . Unfortunately while there seems to be some awkward attempt at sympathy for the Indians, those who saw the picture at Cheyenne and in London say it was reduced to an awkward western. Too bad, but the sympathy is something.

Sincerely,

1. With Bob Lee, Richard Williams wrote *The Last Grass Frontier: The South Dakota Stock Grower Heritage* (Sturgis, S.D.: Black Hills Publishers, 1964).

2. This episode appears in *The Story Catcher.*

To Willis Blenkinsop

December 7, 1964

Dear Mr. Blenkinsop:[1]

You are a fine gallant man and I thank you for your spirited defense against [Dan Lincoln] Thrapp's attack on me in his review of the Adams book.[2] I haven't seen many reviews of the book and had missed this one entirely, but I did know about the abusive tone Adams used. He has had very little use for me since his WESTERN WORDS was published and I pointed out somewhere that he had fallen into the absurdities of a desk man writing about outdoor lingo, such as giving *coyote* the Spanish pronunciation when it isn't a Spanish word at all but Indian.[3] Without self-discernment he follows this with "coyotin' 'round", which could not possibly be pronounced *coyotay* as he gives it. Nor is a "dry-lander" a farmer of irrigated land, or a "Shorthorn" a breed of cattle with short horns "such as the Hereford". He says a sidewinder is a rattlesnake "which strikes by swinging its head and part of its body to the left and right." Evidently never saw a sidewinder's track in the sand. To him "split the blanket" means to share one's bed with another!—and a "Tom Horn" is a slang word for rope to him, while to everyone in Tom Horn country the expression means a dry gulching, a shooting from ambush, etc.

But the denunciations of Adams' kind really don't matter in the long run. A California paper published a most scathing review of my CHEYENNE AUTUMN, written by Burton Rascoe, who insisted that there was no such thing as a Cheyenne in the north at all. Now the book stands in its own right.

I'm happy that you like THE BEAVER MEN. My one regret about the book is the use of the small map instead of the large, comprehensive one I also made, with much fuller key—a key that is really a sort of historical outline of the fur and exploration frontier. But the map would have had to be a fold-in pocket job, with more expense loaded on the book and I bowed to the publisher's complaint on this, although I seldom listen to outside advice at all. Still, the map has gone into publication in four colors and is rather handsome and very enlightening or so it seems to me.

You are right. The decision of the Rees to drop all pretense of friendliness for the Americans was a final turning point in Upper Missouri trade and politics, and compelled the use of the Platte route, well known at the St. Louis waterfront from 1780 on, and before. . . .

Happy holidays, and grateful thanks!

1. Willis Blenkinsop first wrote MS in 1961, when he was a student, to verify an incident regarding General Custer and revenge claimed by the Cheyennes. Later he reviewed several of her books.

2. Ramon Frederick Adams, *Burs Under the Saddle: A Second Look at Books of the West* (Norman: U of Oklahoma P, 1964). Adams disputed Sandoz's accuracy in *The Buffalo Hunters,* challenging her source for Wild Bill Hickok's medical record at Fort Carlin, and criticized the authenticity of *The Cattlemen,* but he offered no evidence for his assertions.

3. Ramon Frederick Adams, *Western Words: A Dictionary of the Range, Cow Camp, and Trail* (Norman: U of Oklahoma P, 1944).

To Mr. Daniel Willner

Follow-up Dept.
[Memorial Hospital for Cancer and Allied Diseases]

[After December 10, 1964]

Dear Mr. Willner:

Thank you for this follow-up. December 1963 I noticed a retraction in the nipple of my remaining breast. I got in touch with Dr. Frank Adair again, but this time I was taken to Doctor's Hospital for the second mastectomy, week of January 20, 1964. The examination there and the preparation was not up to Memorial standards, but the wound is healed and Dr. Adair found nothing alarming at the last examination. This was, I am told, a number or scale 2 malignancy.

To Bente Hamann, Production

HASTINGS HOUSE

December 11, 1964

Dear Bente Hamann:

I've had several strong protests about the omission of the maps pages 2 and 24 from the list of illustrations. Please correct this in the next printing of BEAVER MEN.

One man returned his copy and demanded a "well-made" book in return, if there was one among my books. I sent him a copy of CHEYENNE AUTUMN.

There have been several comments on the break in the Missouri River on the endpaper map, see section between mouth of the Yellowstone and the Little Missouri.

This book, which caused me more trouble than all the rest together, should have been a more presentable product.

Sorry,

Bruce Nicoll

December 28, 1964

Dear Bruce:

Hurrah for the Amos Bad Heart Bull book!

I delayed replying to your letter until I had some of the results of tests I've been taking from the first of November. There will be more in January but the prognosis seems better than expected at first. Still, after two malignancies one learns to be prepared for anything, and promises very little for the future. If I'm alive I'll be happy to write the introduction for the book. Your suggestions are fine—very much what I felt should be done.

Unfortunately I still have all of January committed to THE BATTLE OF THE LITTLE BIG HORN. I really couldn't get free enough from pain and enteritis to do much on that book until the last two weeks, and there was almost two months of work left to do when I headed west in October. The academese "stipend" is fine. This is really a labor of love. I'm having the notes in storage in the west sent here, and about February 1 I'll go up to the Museum of Natural History to take another look into Helen's manuscript, that with my Sioux material, my letters and notes from Helen and my recollections should supply a good foundation for my introduction. I hope to get a visit with Mrs. Joyner when I'm down in Washington.[1]

Have you set a publication date?

—Wishing you and the rest of the Nicoll outfit and all the Press a magnificent 1965,

P.S. I didn't get to go home at all this year but Caroline sent me a big box of soapweed seed pod stalks, sprays of prairie rose hips and buckbrush berries, sulphur plant, wild flax pods, blue joint, trembling grass, etc. I made up a rather handsome Christmas spray for my door, but it only makes me homesick for the Hills.

1. Helen Blish had died in 1941. Mrs. Joyner was her sister and executor.

To Miss Blanche Yurka

Jan. 7, 1965

Dear Miss Yurka:[1]

At the suggestion of our mutual acquaintance, Melven Kritzler, I am sending you a copy of my SLOGUM HOUSE.

I apologize for this intrusion but Mr. Kritzler, as you may know, is an energetic promoter. He has a tremendous admiration for you and for your great talents and decided long ago that you should play Gulla Slogum of SLOGUM HOUSE, a fearless, avaricious, scheming mother ambitious for herself and her family. She uses the family to her ends—to gain the power and wealth to make the Ohio community of her youth accept her and her children. In the meantime she hates the cowardice of her gun-using sons, capitalizes on the promiscuity of her handsome twin daughters who corrupt the courts to save the brothers and Gulla. She despises her ineffectual husband and her eldest daughter who contemptuously refuses to take part in the lawless activities of the house but furnishes a good table and clean beds for the travelers patronizing the place.

Although the locale is the western cattle country of the early twentieth century to about 1930, the book is constructed on the general plan of the Thomas Hardy novels and received very serious consideration from the quality magazines as well as the usual review outlets, such as the New York *Times*, etc., and through its popular appeal, became a Dell paperback.

There have been several considerations of the book by moving-picture companies but there was never anyone to play the role of Gulla. Asked for some suggestions in the early 1950's, I mentioned your name but was informed that you had deserted the pictures.

Sincerely,

1. Blanche Yurka (1887–1974), a Shakespearean actress, had acted with John Barrymore, Katharine Cornell, and Alfred Lunt and Lynn Fontanne, among the finest actors of the time; she was also in such films as *Song of Bernadette* and *Woman from Hell.*

To Mary Abbot and Walter Frese

January 25, 1965

Dear Mary Abbot and Walter Frese:

About the possibility of putting together a sort of anthology from my work for the thirtieth anniversary of book publication: As you know I doubt the commercial prospects of volumes of short pieces, but there is the thirtieth anniversary, and my health, which may very well grow no better—

So, without committing myself, or either of you to the idea, I'm sending in some pieces that have had only very limited publication or none at all.

UNPUBLISHED:

"Snakes"

This was written while I worked on *Old Jules*. The ink sketches were made by an artist friend, Edo Anderson, who hoped to get publication with the article. I knew it wasn't done that way. The piece was never sent out.

"Coyotes and Eagles"

The history of this piece is similar to "Snakes" except that the guide for poisoning coyotes comes from Old Jules files, and the artist of the ink sketch is Burri.

PUBLISHED (Limited circulation)

"The Homestead in Perspective"

This was published in *Land Use Policy and Problems in the United States,* 1963, a compilation of the speeches and manuscripts offered at the Hundredth Anniversary of the Homestead Act. The experts were from all over the United States, and Canada, with observers from countries with new public domain problems to solve, men from Africa, South America, and island regions. I was the only program member who had ever lived on a homestead.

"Outpost in New York"

Experiences locating an apartment in New York, including a falling sliver of glass on my head from a ricocheting bullet, which reminded me of the old cattle-settler wars of my childhood. Published in the *Prairie Schooner* summer 1963.

Look the material over, Mary, and if you think the project might be worth considering, send the material and the ink sketches on to Walter.

Thank you,

Revised list of material sent for possible inclusion in 30th year anthology:

UNPUBLISHED:

EVENING SONG

SNAKES 4 ink sketches by Edo Anderson

COYOTES AND EAGLES 1 ink sketch by Burri

LIMITED PUBLICATION:

THE HOMESTEAD IN PERSPECTIVE

OUTPOST IN NEW YORK

THE DAUGHTER

INTRODUCTION TO GRINNELL'S THE CHEYENNE INDIANS

To Annie Laurie Williams

January 30, 1965

Dear Annie Laurie:

I trust that you have a fine running start on 1965, with your usual verve and charm.

Today I received another letter from Blanche Yurka, the third about *Slogum House.* She may be weakening on the part of Gulla Slogum. She asks "who has considered *Slogum House?* I am wondering if it would be anyone I know. I once had a most beautiful letter from John Ford, but he might not wish to repeat himself."

While I'm not certain what the last phrase means, I suspect she is interested. She says "as for my 'deserting the pictures' just let them test me out with a really good part and I can quickly disprove that rumor."

She ends up by asking me up for tea or a drink and I plan to go.

In the meantime I've scared up two copies of *Slogum House,* which I'm sending to you today.

The easter daisies will soon be coming out in Texas, and in Nebraska too, although a little later.

Affectionately,

To Walter Frese

February 11, 1965

Dear Walter:

Enclosed is a letter from Glen Dines about his biography of Crazy Horse, admittedly written from my book,[1] and a copy of my reply that this is the concern of Hastings House.

Will you have this answered please.
Sincerely,

1. Glen (Harry) Dines, a writer and illustrator, wished to write a juvenile based on MS's work. He published *Crazy Horse* (New York: Putnam, 1966).

To Harold Keith

February 20, 1965

Dear Mr. Keith:

Of course I remember you and the WATIE book very well.[1] I've even wondered a few times about your Comanche book.

What's the matter with your publishers, that they have to go to others for estimates about the probable sales of a book? I know what I would tell them, but then I have no one dependent on me and if I want to live small, no one else suffers for my independence. That's why I've had ten publishers, but I still have five of these, and even outsiders would like an Indian book for young people. I was under the impression that Indian books are high just now. Every publisher seems to have one on the spring list. Of course, most of them are bad and deserve to fail, although some of the worst won't fail at all.

THE HORSECATCHER has been paying for the travel and research for such nonfiction as THE CATTLEMEN, LOVE SONG TO THE PLAINS, and the BEAVER MEN. It's just as well, because these long research books never pay for themselves. I'm still in the hole on CRAZY HORSE, largely because Knopf had no paper in 1942, and by publication day the printing was sold out, not to be reissued for many years, etc. These long volumes of nonfiction have to be a labor of love.

THE HORSECATCHER is still selling some in the regular format. In 1963 Westminster followed it with THE STORY CATCHER, which was under contract to my good editor, but he was long gone by the time the book was done, and Westminster had withdrawn more and more into religion and uplift. Still, STORY CATCHER, a short novel of a Sioux youth in the 1840's, hasn't done too badly for the unhappy situation it was caught by. Grosset and Dunlap is bringing out a paperback edition and the book was half of a dual Spur award last spring, and the whole Levi Strauss Golden Saddle award. Not that awards make a book one word better but the awards pleased Westminster, and I'm sure there will be some STORY CATCHERS around for years, in one format or another. I've not found Indian books bad sellers, and even librarians have given them good reviews.

I don't understand your publisher's hesitation. It is true, as I said above, that most Indian juveniles are pretty bad, but yours can't be. There's such fine high adventure in the stories of the young Comanches, and you couldn't have mishandled it. I'll bet the librarians never read the book, know nothing at all about the Comanche material. Can you stick to your guns and surprise 'em?[2]

Good luck

1. Harold Keith, working with sports publicity for the University of Oklahoma, wrote prolifically in the fields of sports fiction and western juveniles. *Rifles for Watie* (New York: Crowell, 1957) won the 1957 Newbery award; *Susy's Scoundrel* (New York: New American Library, 1974) won the Spur and National Heritage Awards; *Obstinate Land* (New York: Crowell, 1977) won the Western Heritage Award.

2. Harold Keith, *Komantcia* (New York: Crowell, 1965).

To Donald F. Danker, Historian

Nebraska State Historical Society

April 6, 1965

Dear Donald:

Thank you for your comment from Dr. John D. Hicks' manuscript about me as an undergraduate, and that he liked OLD JULES.

I'm sorry that my predicament has become so severe, but there is not much I can do about writing for anyone. I still hope to do the introduction for the Amos Bad Heart Bull manuscript. It is the one thing I want to finish somehow for the University of Nebraska Press.

Sincerely,

To Volta Torrey

April 8, 1965

Dear Volta:

I was curiously excited to open your letter today. Almost thirty years ago your voice on the telephone from the *Omaha World-Herald* gave me the first outside notice that *Old Jules* had won the *Atlantic Monthly* Non-fiction Award. I had had a long, ambiguous telegram for several days, but because the news must not leak out at the telegraph or newspaper offices, it had been so vaguely stated that I didn't dare believe in it. Then, suddenly, at your voice, I found my heart pounding. I knew you had no way of knowing enough about the situation to compound such a hoax out of any impossible meanness of heart. At your words, "Didn't I have some news?" I realized the whole thing was true: that I had won the *Atlantic* Award. It is curious that nothing has ever had the same impact on me as your voice that day. I gave you the information you needed. I went to talk to my boss, Dr. Sheldon, telling him that I had won and that I would be resigning from my $15.00 a week job. At a glance at the telegram, Dr. Sheldon had turned pale. He said, "I congratulate you, but I hate to lose you." I sent notice to Mother and then I had to go to Van [den Bark's] place to tell him. He stood leaning on a shovel or a hoe in his back yard, and after a while he began to talk naturally again.

Now, a little less than thirty years later, your letter brought the same sense of reality to what is probably the end of the situation.

I'm glad Geneva liked *The Beaver Men* and I'm glad to know Tom is at Doane [College] in Crete, Nebraska.

You, Geneva and Tom have always seemed very close. I had hoped to write in my autobiography how close your voice was that day from the *World-Herald*.

Affectionately

To Liz Cashen

April 8, 1965

Dear Liz Cashen:

Thank you for the clipping about the *Cheyenne Autumn* movie and all the fine news about Mamie Meredith.

Your letter is the kind to start an answer of several pages, but unfortunately, I am down on my back in the hospital. I am told, as was my sister, Mrs. Pifer, when she was in the hospital here, that there can be no positive answer for some time. Either I come out feet foremost, or I come out for some interval, return for more treatment, etc.

There is no known cure, and no cause for grief—some people are struck by drunken drivers.

Sincerely,

To Elsa Spear Byron

Sheridan, Wyoming

April 14, 1965

Dear Elsa Spear Byron:[1]

It's fine to hear that both you and your sister are digging through your photographs and historical files. There's so much material in your possession tangibly and in your memories that must not be lost.

I can't look up the Thad Cole sources for my CATTLEMEN. Such material is in storage. Besides, I'm in the hospital with incurable bone cancer and while I may get some short intervals now and then, there is apparently more chance that I'll have no time for any real writing. In fact, a few weeks ago I was given about a 50-50 chance of getting out of the hospital alive for even a short interval.

So work hard with your material.

Sincerely,

1. Elsa Spear Byron (1896–1987) was a professional photographer who specialized in nature and landscape shots. A historian, she published numerous pamphlets and books about her region, particularly relating to the Fetterman Massacre at Fort Philip Kearny and events on the Bozeman Trail in Wyoming and Montana.

To Kay Rogers

April 20, 1965

Dear Kay:

You and Joe must stop sending me things—they cost money and energy and thought, and these are not necessary between us.

About the ailments—the violent internal bleeding has been stopped and most of the pain is gone for the time being, so the first and immediate necessity to get powers of attorney and make decisions on where my collections are to go are past, either done or not as urgent as a month ago.

The treatment—to hold the bone cancer in some abeyance and get time, seems to be having some success. My legs are still pretty worthless—due to anemia, I'm told. Otherwise I seem to be heading into a sort of cautious time, when I can operate like your friend.

Your flowers are the nicest I have, and the candy goes to others, Mary Ann if I can make her break her diet.[1]

Love,

1. Mary Ann Pifer, MS's niece, had come to New York from Nebraska to help with her aunt's manuscripts.

To Dr. Bernice Slote

April 22, 1965

Dear Bernice:[1]

Congratulations on the success of the *Schooner* as a trying ground for young writers. That's what old "Daddy" Sherman, etc., intended it to be when the idea arose. . . .

Names in fiction really have to be considered carefully. I worked for months for *Slogum*—pronounceable, with a suggestion of the characters involved, and certainly the name of no one. I went through stacks of telephone directories, including Omaha's.

Well, when [Mayor Dan] Butler banned the book in Omaha, wouldn't a family of the name crop up there? They took it as a joke, were certain I couldn't have known about them, and didn't like Butler anyway.

Best wishes,

1. Bernice Slote was the editor of *PrS,* replacing Karl Shapiro.

To Harry W. Brooks

April 26, 1965

Dear Mr. Brooks:

Please forgive the delay in my reply to your letter of February. I went through a hospitalization since then, with a long and not too promising convalescence ahead of me.

Do you really think there is a formula for success? First, I suppose, *success* should be defined and that would leave me out at the start. But if you did concoct a definition of success that could include my work, what formula could possibly include the prospects of a barefoot little girl on the Niobrara River with a language handicap, little country schooling and no opportunity to attend high school?

It isn't even brashness that carried me into the University. The fact is that I can out-wait practically anyone, including, it happened, the secretary of one of the deans at the University of Nebraska. Once in, I discovered that only the failures were scrutinized carefully. The same ability to wait got my OLD JULES published—the fourteenth time out to a publisher.

But this is not success, only a way of life for those of us who start very barefoot.

Sincerely,

To Governor Frank B. Morrison

State Capitol
Lincoln, Nebraska

May 14, 1965

Dear Governor Morrison:

Thank you for your energetic, and persuasive efforts in my behalf.[1] As you will know Commissioner of Housing Birns with his deputy and superintendent, marched right into the problem, came to see the layout and me. The Commissioner decided that my niece could move into the unzoned space in the house here to keep an eye on me while I attempt recuperation from illness, and help put my files into shape.

I think this is a nice, warm-hearted incident all around, and if not typical of New York, certainly typical of you.

Thank you again,

1. When Nebraska Governor Frank Morrison learned that New York's housing codes would prevent MS's niece from staying with her at her apartment building and acting as her secretary, he contacted authorities in New York, and the rules were waived.

To Bruce Nicoll

May 25, 1965

Dear Bruce:

So the White Bull pictographs are extensive enough for a book! About his killing Custer, that's a latter-day idea, fostered by Stanley Vestal and some newspaper men. I'm certain nobody, not Sitting Bull or anyone else at the Little Bighorn knew that Custer was there at all. A Cheyenne or two who had been at the Washita in 1868 recognized the insignia of the 7th cavalry on the clothing of Reno's men, but since the regiment was seldom together as a unit, that didn't mean Custer was there. The Hunkpapas saw the battalion under Reno when he went out to help guard the border survey; they saw some of it under Benteen at Fort Rice 1875–6. To the Indians Custer was Long Hair and with his hair cut off he wasn't Custer. Besides, he had had no contact for several years with the Hunkpapas. Even those few who went in to trade went to the small Fort Rice. Fort Abraham Lincoln seemed farther from their stomping grounds, more white-man territory.

Besides, if White Bull killed Custer why didn't he know it in 1933 and say so, permitting Vestal to say so in *Warpath?*

Sincerely,

To Mrs. Adah Landon

June 21, 1965

Dear Mrs. Landon:

Yes, Mrs. Custer was an interesting woman, but because she outlived practically everyone who knew her during her married life, and, as before Custer's death, she maintained a serious campaign to build up her husband's image, there was little written about her, really.

Of course I have seen all the Custer material available as well as all the related material and much not available to the general researcher. I knew many acquaintances of the Custers during their married life. There is no room for doubt that Custer usually had some young woman along on his campaigns, usually Indian or mixed blood. Look into the Fort Wallace [Kansas] records of 1867–68. The reason for Custer's deserting his command in 1867 was his wife's flight east when she heard about the girl Custer had along that summer. She later bore a girl baby considered to be Custer's. Then there was Yellow Swallow, born 1869 to the Cheyenne girl that Custer admits was married to him, Indian fashion, by Romero the fall of 1868. See *My Life on the Prairie.*[1]

The usual conclusion by experts on human relations is that Mrs. Custer was more an over fond mother or elder sister than a wife to her husband.

Sincerely,

1. George A. Custer, *My Life on the Plains,* ed. Milo Milton Quaife (Chicago: Donnelly, 1952).

To Mr. Hanson W. Baldwin

June 26, 1965

Dear Mr. Baldwin:

Thank you. I appreciate your kind words about chapters of THE LITTLE BIGHORN.

I've made some gain (temporary, of course, since there is no cure for bone cancer of this type) enough so I can work on the book. I've polished the first four chapters somewhere near my liking, and am working on the last three, which are in some shape but not yet finished.

My plans are to send in the manuscript as soon as it is finished and work on the maps afterward. There is to be a map of the Indian camp, with the location of the great council lodge with its eighteen foot poles — where most of the major chiefs were when Reno attacked. It was this conference lodge that both Gall and Crazy Horse were so anxious to protect with their movements along the river, that and of course the women and children. None of these conference lodges was ever captured by an enemy. Otherwise the mapping will be largely routine — there's really little that is new in the troop movements. I picked up a lot of cartridges, buttons, etc., when I camped on the ridge in 1930, and mapped out what seemed the movements then.

Unless there's a serious relapse, you should have the manuscript soon.

Sincerely,

To Mr. Douglas Fowley

August 4, 1965

Dear Mr. Fowley:

At your suggestion I watched *Bonanza* Sunday evening but the simple and obvious story didn't seem a fair test of either your acting ability or Frank Chase's talent as a story writer. I suspect that you may be a man of much greater sensitivity and power than the picture permitted you to employ.

As you will understand I am not interested in a picture of Old Jules as a character in a western. The pioneer setting in Western Nebraska is a sheer accident. He was a brother of all the young men of sufficiently undisciplined minds to dream great dreams in which they play the heroic part and are usually at least half defeated by their very lack of self-discipline. Old Jules, with the stubborn tenacity of the Swiss, was still full of the drive to build communities when he died in his seventies.

This conflict of the undisciplined dreamer is a rather universal one. Even when played against the rigors and predators of a new region it does not seem to me material for a western.

For a serious moving picture yes; not a western.

I appreciate your interest, and I am happy to have the pictures. The make-up as Old Jules would be no problem at all.

Sincerely,

To Bruce Riddie

August 6, 1965

Dear Bruce Riddie:

Now really, you didn't expect the War Record department to put out any information reflecting on the private life of an army officer, Custer or anyone else, did you? The way to get such material is to find it yourself, and *before* the archives get their hands on it, as I did, back in 1937–38. Read the notes in *Cheyenne Autumn* and look up the material still available, such as Brill, etc. Unfortunately the medical histories have vanished too.

Sorry,

I was in the National Archives last summer. Some of the documents on which I have notes for 1937–38, were no longer "available."

To Stewart Richardson

September 18, 1965

Dear Stewart Richardson:

Thank you, I'm happy that you found THE LITTLE BIGHORN good after your very recent visit to the region.

Of course I'll be happy to make a selected bibliography for the book, as Mr. Baldwin suggests, and I'm pleased that his wishes include a comprehensive all-over map for endpapers. I'm visual minded and love maps in my books. I'm putting the material for this together now and I'll make this as well as the other maps to scale for your cartographers. There's been entirely too little consideration of the larger motivations and implications of the whole May-June 1876 campaign against the Sioux.

Sincerely,

To Mary Abbot

September 30, 1965

Dear Mary:

Here's the Oil Book contract. I told Walter that I would try to do the Dog Soldier book, by blocking it out while I write the Sioux book for Harpers.[1] Unless my cancer moves into some soft tissue, usually lung, liver or brain, I'm told, I may very well have a couple of years—

Because the Dog Soldier (Cheyenne) book covers about the same period, and more, as the Harper book will, I'll be able to pile up a lot of book-notes as I go along.

The notes from Lippincott came just as I was leaving for the bank, so I've not looked at them yet. But we'll work it out, whatever they want. The bibliography is in their hands. So far there's still work to be done on the maps. My hands got painful.

Sincerely,

1. Neither book was completed. Probably MS did little beyond this preliminary planning.

To Mary Abbot

October 13, 1965

Dear Mary:

Enclosed is a copy of my letter to Stewart Richardson with the final map. I'm sorry this took so long but my hands have been pretty bad. I had to give up making tea because I dropped the teakettle with boiling water—

Sincerely,

To Francis W. Schruben, Assoc. Prof. of History

LOS ANGELES PIERCE COLLEGE
Woodland Hills, Calif.

October 24, 1965

Dear Professor Schruben:

It was kind of Mrs. Folsom to mention my oil book to you. Unfortunately this was to include a study of the part the Great Plains oil interests, through their eastern and near-eastern tie-ins, played, and play in U.S. foreign policy.

As the state department records are not open I knew the information must be obtained elsewhere and while I had set up some contacts, the development of incurable bone cancer precludes my further work on the book.

I regret this very much. The book would have shown the cycle of the Plains region, from empire barrier to the Western Sea and the China trade in the 17th and 18th centuries, to the root of power that conditions world politics.

Sincerely,

To Miss Elizabeth Otis

November 14, 1965

Dear Elizabeth:

The American Heritage offer to publish an excerpt from THE BATTLE OF THE LITTLE BIGHORN has its amusing side, particularly their comment "Although Miss Sandoz could not have access to tribal information about the suicide group revealed by John Stands in Timber***".

Of course I had access to half a dozen versions of the "suicide group", including Stands in Timber's own manuscript years ago. Margo[t] Liberty asked me to look it over and make suggestions that might make the material publishable. Because I am anxious to have the Indians write their stories, no matter how romanticized, I took a week off and worked up six pages, single spaced, criticism for Margo[t] Liberty. See the enclosed copy of the first page of the criticism, which I suggest you send to American Heritage.

I am willing to let them use the excerpt they want, but only if they delete the obviously false statement in their introduction. Of course I had access to John Stands in Timber's manuscript, as well as all the really valid material it contained but I got mine direct from the Northern Cheyennes, the old timers who took part in the fights of the 1870's, not at second-hand.

Thanks for all the bother—

Sincerely,

To Bruce Nicoll

November 19, 1965

Dear Bruce:

Now and then I recall the little book we once discussed for the Nebraska Centennial and although this never got to the contract stage, I do feel a little guilty about the matter. While I can't do the volume, if you are still interested in something from me for the Centennial list, you might be interested in a light, warmish and humorous section from my autobiography. The working title was "The Christmas of the Phonograph".[1] It happened the year after Old Jules' mother died in Switzerland and the $2,100 inheritance, which should have gone for the mortgage on the homestead and other debts, as well as for the first coats and overshoes we should have for the winter walk of almost three miles to school, father spent most of the money for the first Edison phonograph in the region and great boxes of six, seven hundred records apiece.

Not only was our family changed for all time by this phonograph but much of our community felt the impact, enough so one of the men Old Jules had promised a bullet through the head if he stepped foot on our land appeared at the fringe of the crowd the music drew night and day, that holiday season. (We even danced the kitchen floor so thin that chair legs went through it.)

The book would be a small one of the pre-1910 homestead period and fit into none of your categories but I think it captures much of another time and another mood in a region dominated by tall personalities. It could be an attractive, long time little seller.

If you are interested, write McIntosh and Otis, 18 East 41st Street, New York City, for the manuscript.

Greetings to everyone,

1. *The Christmas of the Phonograph Records* (Lincoln: U of Nebraska Press, 1966).

To Mr. E. T. Worley

December 24, 1965

Dear Mr. Worley:[1]

Thank you for a very fine letter, not so much because you found something with emotion in my books but for what the letter tells about you.

Surely you must know that you are by talent and desire a writer. All you need do is fill in the incidents included and implied in your letter from page 2½ on and you have a book.

Your kind of life can never happen again and you owe it to society and yourself, to put it down. Write it as frankly and openly as possible. Give the reader everything you can, so he *must* see and smell and hear and feel and sense as it all happened.

Make this a rounded account of all your family, and you, three dimensional, with the human flaws as well as the virtues included.

Keep largely to the chronological after you have established yourself as a boy with your grandmother.

Best wishes,

1. An Oglala Sioux, Worley had just read *Crazy Horse* and wrote a remarkable, detailed account of his growing-up under the influence of his grandmother, who had known Crazy Horse. He credited MS's book with helping him accept his Indian heritage with pride.

To Anais Nin

January 27, 1966

Dear Anais:[1]

We are all thinking of you, and wishing you the best and swiftest recovery.

In admiration and affection,

1. Anaïs Nin (1903–77), a feminist, author, and lecturer, wrote twenty-six books but is most famous for her seven-volume *Diary of Anais Nin,* ed. Gunther Stuhlmann, 7 vols (New York: Swallow, 1966–80).

* * *

Mari Sandoz died of cancer in New York on March 10, 1966.

Chronological Bibliography of Mari Sandoz's Works

The first date given is the date of composition, if known. Newspaper articles, book reviews, later editions, and excerpts are generally not included.

1908 "The Broken Promise" (short story, signed Mary S. Sandoz). *Omaha Daily News,* Junior Writers' Page, 26 April 1908.

1924 "The Prairie Fire" (essay, signed Marie Macumber). *Freshman Scrapbook,* University of Nebraska, 1 (1924): 19.

1925 "The Vine" (short story, signed Marie Macumber). *PrS* 1.1 (January 1927): 7–16.

1926 "Old Potato Face" (short story, signed Marie Macumber). *PrS* 2.1 (Winter 1928): 29–35.

"Dumb Cattle" (short story, signed Marie Macumber). *PrS* 3.1 (January 1929): 29–35.

1927–29 "Murky River" (novel). Unpublished.

1927–30 "The Kinkaider Comes and Goes" (article). *NAR,* April 1930: 422–31; May 1930: 576–83.

"Sandhill Sundays" (article). *Folk-say: A Regional Miscellany.* Ed. B. A. Botkin. Norman: U of Oklahoma P, 1931. 291–303.

1928 "The Smart Man" (short story). *PrS* 33.1 (Spring 1959): 32–43.

1928–35 *Old Jules* (biography). Boston: Little, Brown, 1935.

1930–32 "Musky, The True Story of a Foolish and Lovable Little Muskrat" (article). *Nature,* November 1933: 199–202.

1931 "Lives Risked for a Drink of Water." *Omaha World-Herald Sunday Magazine of the Midlands,* 10 May 1931.

1932 "Last of the Buffalo Bone Men." *Omaha World-Herald Sunday Magazine of the Midlands,* 14 February 1932.

"Pieces to a Quilt" (short story). *NAR,* May 1933: 435–42.

"What Should Be Considered When Choosing a Profession?" (essay, signed Marie Macumber). *Daily Nebraskan,* 3 April 1932.

1933 "The Daughter: A Recollection" (tale). *Midwest Review,* Spring 1961: 29–30.

"White Meteor" (short story). *Ladies' Home Journal,* January 1932: 12–13.

1933–37 *Slogum House* (novel). Boston: Little, Brown, 1937.

1933–38 "The Devil's Lane" (short story). *Ladies' Home Journal,* April 1938: 17.

1934–35 "The Birdman" (short story). *Omaha Sunday World-Herald Magazine of the Midlands,* 10 February 1935: 7–8.

1935 "I Wrote A Book" (article). *Nebraska Alumnus,* November 1935: 6–7.

"River Polak" (short story). *AM,* September 1937: 300–308.

1935–36 "The New Frontier Woman" (article). *Country Gentleman,* September 1936: 49.

1936 “Mist and the Tall White Tower” (short story). *Story,* September 1936: 41–50.

1936–39, 1949–53 *Cheyenne Autumn* (biography). New York: McGraw-Hill, 1953.

1937 “Old Jules Sandoz.” *Nebraska, Old and New: History, Stories, Folklore.* Ed. A. E. Sheldon. Lincoln: U of Nebraska P, 1937. 342–44.

“Stay Home, Young Writer” (article). *Quill,* June 1937: 8–9.

1938 “Foreword from a Friend.” *Tales of Pioneer Days in North Platte Valley.* Ed. A. B. Wood. Gering, Nebr.: Courier Press, 1938. 2–3.

1938–39 “Bone Joe and the Smokin’ Woman” (novella). *Scribner’s Magazine,* March 1939: 20–24.

Capital City (novel). Boston: Little, Brown, 1939.

“The Girl in the Humbert” (short story). *SEP,* 4 March 1939: 16–17.

1939 “The Far Looker” (Indian tale). *Sight-Giver,* February 1939.

“The Peachstone Basket” (short story). *PrS* 17.3 (Fall 1943): 125–36.

1940–42 *Crazy Horse: The Strange Man of the Oglalas* (biography). New York: Alfred A. Knopf, 1942.

1942 “To a Woman Who Made a Beautiful Garden” (paragraph in “The Editor’s Table”). *NH* 23 (April–June 1942).

1942–60 *Son of the Gamblin’ Man: The Youth of an Artist* (novel). New York: Clarkson N. Potter, 1960.

1943 “Anybody Can Write” (article). *Writer* 57.4 (April 1944): 99–101.

1943–47 *The Tom-Walker* (novel). New York: Dial Press, 1947.

1944 “Sit Your Saddle Solid” (short story). *SEP,* 10 February 1945: 26–27.

1945 “Martha of the Yellow Braids” (article). *PrS* 21.2 (Summer 1947): 139–44.

“The Neighbor” (article). *PrS* 30.4 (Winter 1956): 340–49.

“The Spike-Eared Dog” (short story). *SEP,* 11 August 1945: 24–25.

1947 “Yuletide Saga of a Lone Tree” (allegory). *Philadelphia Inquirer Book Review Supplement,* 7 December 1947.

1947–49 “Foal of Heaven” (short novel). Unpublished.

1948 “There Were Two Sitting Bulls” (article). *Blue Book,* November 1949: 56–64.

1950–51 “The Lost School Bus” (novella). *SEP,* 19 May 1951: 24–25.

Winter Thunder (unabridged version of “The Lost School Bus”). Philadelphia: Westminster Press, 1954.

1951 “What the Sioux Taught Me” (article). *Empire,* 24 February 1952; reprinted in *Reader’s Digest,* May 1952: 21–24.

1952 “To a Special Group of Blue Birds Who Are Soon to Become Camp Fire Girls” (letter). *Camp Fire Girl,* December 1952: 11.

1952–55 *Miss Morissa: Doctor of the Gold Trail* (novel). New York: McGraw-Hill, 1955.

1954 *The Buffalo Hunters: the Story of the Hide Men* (history). New York: Hastings House, 1954.

"The Indian Looks at His Future" (article). *Family Weekly,* 11 April 1954.

"The Look of the West—1854" (article). *NH* 35 (1954): 243–54.

"Search for the Bones of Crazy Horse" (article). *Westerners Brand Book* (New York Posse), Autumn 1954: 4–5.

"Some Notes on Wild Bill Hickok" (article). *Westerners Brand Book* (New York Posse), Winter 1954: 8.

"Some Oddities of the American Indian" (article). *Westerners Brand Book* (Denver Posse), 1955: 17–28.

1954–58 *The Cattlemen: From the Rio Grande across the Far Marias* (history). New York: Hastings House, 1958.

"Tyrant of the Plains" (article, adapted from *The Cattlemen*). *SEP,* 7 June 1958: 48–49.

1955 Acceptance Speech, Distinguished Achievement Award. *Westerners Brand Book* (Chicago Corral), January 1956: 81–83.

1956 *The Horsecatcher* (novel). Philadelphia: Westminster Press, 1957.

"December 2006 A.D." (article). Unpublished. Enclosed in cornerstone of KETV building, Omaha, Nebraska, to be opened in fifty years.

"Nebraska" (article). *Holiday,* May 1956: 103–14.

1957–59 *Hostiles and Friendlies: Selected Short Writings of Mari Sandoz* (recollections, short stories, articles, a novella). Ed. Virginia Faulkner. Lincoln: U of Nebraska P, 1959.

1958–61 *Love Song to the Plains* (nonfiction). New York: Harper and Row, 1961.

1959–62 *The Story Catcher* (novel). Philadelphia: Westminster Press, 1963.

1960–61 "Dakota Country" (article on the artist Harvey Dunn). *American Heritage,* June 1961: 42–53.

1961 "The Buffalo Spring Cave" (folktale). *Legends and Tales of the Old West.* Ed. S. Omar Barker. New York: Doubleday, 1962. 97–98.

"Climber of Long's Peak" (article). *Westerners Brand Book* (New York Posse), 1961: 70–71.

"Fly Speck Billie's Cave" (folktale). *Legends and Tales of the Old West.* Ed. S. Omar Barker. New York: Doubleday, 1962. 37–39.

These Were the Sioux (nonfiction). New York: Hastings House, 1961.

"Unavailable Documents" (article). *Westerners Brand Book* (New York Posse), 1962: 47.

1962 "The Homestead in Perspective" (article). *Land Use Policy and Problems in the United States.* Ed. Howard W. Ottoson. Lincoln: U of Nebraska P, 1963. 47–62.

"Love Song to Nebraska." *Omaha World-Herald Sunday Magazine of the Midlands,* 6 May 1962.

"Outpost in New York" (article). *PrS* 37 (Summer 1963): 95–106.

1962–64 *The Beaver Men: Spearheads of Empire* (history). New York: Hastings House, 1964.

1964 "Soft Gold." *Book News,* November–December 1964: 39.
Old Jules Country: A selection from "Old Jules" and Thirty Years of Writing since the Book Was Published (includes previously uncollected pieces: "Evening Song," "Coyotes and Eagles," and "Snakes"). New York: Hastings House, 1965.

WORKS PUBLISHED POSTHUMOUSLY

1963–66 *The Battle of the Little Bighorn* (history). Philadelphia: J. B. Lippincott, 1966.
1965 *The Christmas of the Phonograph Records* (recollection). Lincoln: U of Nebraska P, 1966.
1965–66 Introduction: *A Pictographic History of the Oglala Sioux.* By Amos Bad Heart Bull and Helen Blish. Lincoln: U of Nebraska P, 1966.
1966 "Letter for a Seventh Birthday." *PrS* 40 (Winter 1966): 285–88.

POSTHUMOUS PUBLICATIONS AND COLLECTIONS PREPARED BY EDITORS OTHER THAN SANDOZ

The Great Council. Comp. Caroline Sandoz Pifer. Rushville, Nebr.: News/Star Press, 1970.
Sandhill Sundays and Other Recollections (selected articles). Ed. Virginia Faulkner. Lincoln: U of Nebraska P, 1970.
The Making of an Author: From the Mementoes of Mari Sandoz. Ed. Caroline Sandoz Pifer. Gordon, Nebr.: Gordon Journal Press, 1972.
1925? "College in Capsules" (essay, signed Marie Macumber).
1925 "Fearbitten" (short story, signed Marie Macumber, Honorable Mention, Harper's Intercollegiate Short Story Contest, 1926).

"Ossie and the Sea Monster" and Other Stories (previously unpublished stories and articles, except for "The Daughter" [published 1961]). Comp. and ed. Caroline Sandoz Pifer. Rushville, Nebr.: News/Star Press, 1974.
1920s "Music" (poem).
1933 "Catching Eagles" (story).
"The Daughter" (story).
1941 "The Grubline Rider" (recollection).
"Junket through the Indian Country" (article).
1944 "Lineup at 39 Whitehall" (article).
1954 "Ossie and the Sea Monster" (story).
Untitled Poem.

"The Cottonwood Chest" and Other Stories (previously unpublished short stories and articles). Ed. Caroline Sandoz Pifer. Crawford, Nebr.: Cottonwood Press, 1980.
"Handy Andy" (recollection).

1920s "The Cottonwood Chest" (story).
"The Face of the Dying Monk" (story).
"The Woman in Grey" (story).
"Youth Rides into the Wind" (story).
1940–42 "The Road of the Strong Young Men" (story).
1958 "Boy Trail Drivers of Texas" (article).

"Victorie" and Other Stories (previously unpublished stories). Ed. Caroline Sandoz Pifer. Crawford, Nebr.: Cottonwood Press, 1986.
1929 "Victorie" (winner of the Omaha Women's Press Club Award, 1929).
1930s? "Second Honeymoon."
1934–35 "Coffee Shop."
1940s "Moochmouth and the Outside Woman."
1941 "Moochmouth and the New School Ma'am."

"Stranger at the Curb" (article). *Mid-American Review of Sociology* 13.2 (Winter 1988): 31–41. Editorial notes by Michael R. Hill.

Index of Addressees

Abbot, Mary Squire, 261–62, 296, 315–16, 324, 325, 337–39, 340, 350, 355–56, 361–62, 363–64, 369, 372, 376, 422, 441, 447–48, 458
Abbott, N. C., 216–17
Adams, James Donald, 262–63
Adams, O. W., 92–94
Adams, William T., 154–56
Aeschbacher, W. D., 313
Aldrich, Bess Streeter, 263–64
Alfred A. Knopf (publisher), 46–47, 187–88, 192–93, 208–9
Alsberg, Henry, 270
American Indian, The (journal), 247
American Indian Defense Association, 25–26
American Mercury (magazine), 24–25, 47–51
Anderson, Walter, 133–34
Army War College, 205–6
Asplund, Robert S., 371–72
Aswell, Edward, 274–75
Atlantic Monthly Press, 33–36, 80–83, 121–22, 125–26, 173–74, 234, 389–90

Babcock, Fred, 325
Baldwin, Hanson W., 358–60, 384–85, 456
Baldwin, Robert, 1
Balmer, Joseph, 224–25, 236–39, 249–50
Barker, S. Omar, 364
Barkham, John, 308–10
Barrett, Jay Amos, 97–98
Baxendale, Mrs. E. S., 94
Baxter, Ronald, 295–96
Bechtel, Louise, 187
Becker, Harold, 140–41
Beckman, Don, 419–20
Belk, Vida, 182
Benét, William Rose, 220–21
Benjamin, Peggy H., 352
Bennett, Mildred, 346
Bidwell, Winston "Doc," 221–22
Blenkinsop, Willis, 443–44
Blish, Helen, 165–66, 185–86
Bloom, Cassandra L., 137–38
Bolton, Laetitia, 125–26
Book Review (section of *New York Herald Tribune*), 269–70
Booth, A. C., 127–28
Botkin, Benjamin Albert, 26–27, 30, 37–38, 105–6
Bredouw, F. E., 162–63
Brenneman, Mrs. Richard E., 219–20
Brill, Charles J., 232–34
Brininstool, Earl Alonzo, 215–16, 268–69
Brooks, Harry W., 453–54
Buchenau, Tyler, 64–67, 74–79, 409
Burnett, E. A., 127
Byron, Elsa Spear, 452

Calhoun, C. C., 42–44
Campbell, W. S., 253–54
Carr, James, 422–23
Carter, Boyd, 365–66
Cashen, Liz, 451
Cather, Willa, 27–28
Century (magazine), 56–58
Chamber of Commerce (Crawford, Nebraska), 416–17
Chambrun, Jacques, xxix, 123–25, 149–50, 153, 158–59, 164–65, 235–36, 244
Chicago Daily News (newspaper), 218–19
Christie, Margaret, 3–11, 14–15, 16–18, 19–20

Clarkson N. Potter (publisher), 341–42
Clay County Sun (newspaper), 107–8
Cloud, Dudley B., 234
Colket, Tris, 417–19
Collier, John, 25–26
Council of Northern Cheyennes, 229–30
Custer Battlefield National Monument, 374–75

Daily News (newspaper). See *Chicago Daily News*
Danker, Donald F., 297, 450
Davison, Peter H., 389–90
De Voto, Bernard, 101–2, 110–13, 146–48
De Yong, Joe, 203–4
Dela Torre Bueno, J. R., Jr., 192–93
DeMallie, Raymond, Jr., 400–402, 426
Dial Press, 223–24
Dodd, Frank G., 29
Dodd, Mead and Company (publisher), 29
Du Mont, John S., 254–55

Earlham College Museum, 395
Eastman, Elaine Goodale, 195–96
Ervin, Sam J., 377–79

Fadiman, Clifton, 203
Faulkner, Virginia, xxx, 297–99, 304–6, 331
Fehr, Joseph Conrad, 18–19
Fehr, Mary. *See* Sandoz, Mary Fehr
Ferril, Thomas Hornsby, 212–13
Fisher, Vardis, 278
Fogelson, Buddy, 243–44
Fontaine, Tom, 385
Ford, Anne, 141–42, 163
Fort Robinson Historical Museum, 291–92
Forum (magazine), xxii, 2–3, 56–58
Fowley, Douglas, 456–57
Fox, Maynard, 397
Fox, Robert, 153–54
Frame, John R., 275
Frese, Walter, 317, 327, 353, 376–77, 400, 402–3, 404–5, 406, 407, 418, 424–25, 438–39, 447–49

Gannett, Lewis, 94–95, 103
Garson, Greer, 243–44
Gatewood, Robert, 156–57
Gold and Company, 23–24
Golden Saga Publishers, 232–34
Gondos, Victor, Jr., 432–33
Gould, Beatrice Blackmar, 142–43
Grange, Roger T., Jr., 291–92
Gray, Tunny, 121–22
Griffith, F. B., 181–82
Gunnar, Ann, 135–36

Hall, Benn, 308–10
Hamann, Bente, 444–45
Hanighen, Frank C., 51–52, 62–63
Harper and Brothers (publisher), 361, 370–71
Harpers Monthly Magazine, xxii, xxxii, 38–41, 101–2
Harris, Stuart, 373–74
Hart, George, 360–61
Hastings House (publisher), 270, 306–7, 403, 444–45
Hatterscheidt, F. W., 152–53
Hayes, Helen Mary, 71–73
Henry Regnery Company (publisher), 384
Herald-Tribune (newspaper). See *New York Herald-Tribune*
Heyl, Charles, 228–29
Hill, Edwin C., 45–46
Hinman, Eleanor, xx, xxiii, xxiv, 15–16, 58–60, 68–70, 166, 191
Historical Society. *See* Nebraska State Historical Society
Hoffman, Paul, xxviii, xxix, 130–32, 175–77, 187–89, 190, 306–7
Holmes, Oliver Wendell, 264–65
Hooker, William "Pizen Bill," 103–5, 115–18

Hooper, Pat, 292–94
Hornburg, L. A., 106–7
Horse, Eugene W., 294–95
Howard, Fred, 106–8
Hull, Morton D., 316
Hull, Ron, 420–21
"Human Side of the News, The" (radio program), 45–46

Indiana University, 209–11

Jacobsen, Ethel, 319–20
J.B. Lippincott Company (publisher), 358–60
Johnson, Frank, 357
Johnson, Will H., 92
Jones, Neckyoke. *See* Sinclair, F. H.
Josephy, Alvin, Jr., 367

Keith, Harold, 449–50
Kerr, Chester B., 173–74
Knight, Ralph, 302–3
Knopf, Alfred, 339
Knopf, Blanche, 208–9, 211
Knopf (publisher). *See* Alfred A. Knopf
KUON-TV (television station), 332–33, 420–21

Ladies' Home Journal (magazine), 142–43
Landon, Adah, 455
LaPlante, Ed, 335–36
Laughlin, Estelle, 279–82
Leermakers, Jack, 276–77
LeHand, M. A., 84–85
Lemons, William E., 288
Lenniger, August, 2
Lennon, Florence B., 202–3
Lesser, Alexander, 247
Levinthal, Sonia, 278–79
Liberty, Margot, 374–75
Liebling-Wood Agency, 174–75
Lightner, Louis, 139–40, 322–23
Lillard, Richard G., 209–11
Lincoln State Journal (newspaper), 60–61, 178–79
Lippincott Company (publisher). *See* J.B. Lippincott Company
Little, Brown and Company (publisher), 119–21, 141–42, 172, 213–14
Little Thunder, Harvey, 379–81
Longman, Anne, 70–71
Lorimer, George, 31–32
Los Angeles Pierce College, 458–59
Lottinville, Savoie, 414–15
Luce, Edward S., 248–49
Luker, Julia, 303–4
Lundy, Frank A., 313

McAfee, Helen, 150
McBride, Mary Margaret, 234–35
McCann, Lyle, 425
McCaughen, C. Burr, 212
McCaughen and Burr (art gallery), 212
McCreight, M. I., 114–15
McGillycuddy, Julia Blanchard, 101
McGraw-Hill (publisher), 274–75, 278–79
McIlhatton, Dorothy, 268
McIntosh and Otis (agency), 240–44, 246, 261–62
McIntyre, Alfred R., xxiii, 119–21, 123, 132–33, 151, 172, 173, 213–14
Maloney, Russell, 227–28
Marriott, Alice, 334
Memorial Hospital for Cancer and Allied Diseases, 396–97, 444
Mencken, H. L., xxii, 24–25, 47–51
Meredith, Mamie, 54–56, 200–202, 245–46, 307–8, 317–18, 329–30, 408
Merriam (editor), 28
Monaghan, Jay, 299–300
Morrison, Frank B., 454

National Archives and Records Service, 264–65, 432–33
Neal, Ruth, 393–95
Nebraska Credit Company, 53

Nebraska State Historical Society, 73–74, 166–69, 297, 313, 450
Neihardt, John G., 365
New York Herald-Tribune (newspaper), 94–95
New York Times (newspaper), 22–23
Nicoll, Bruce, 336–37, 344–45, 347–48, 354, 356–57, 362, 368, 387, 407, 412, 426–30, 445–46, 454–55, 459–60
Nin, Anaïs, 461
Noll, John Grant, 383
Nordyke, Lewis, 314–15
Norris, J. L., 320–22
North American Review (journal), 20–21
Northwestern University, 225–27

Ober, Harold, 114, 133
O'Kieffe, Charles DeWitt, 283–85
Omaha Philosophical Society, 140–41
Omaha World-Herald (newspaper), 163–64
"Open End" (television program), 370
Otis, Elizabeth, 240–44, 246, 388, 459
Outdoors Potpourri (magazine), 413

Parsley, C. P., 99–100
Parsons, John E., 252–53, 265–67
Payne, Kenneth Wilcox, 20–21
Peabody College, 348–49
Peterson, W. Keith, 96–97
Peterson and Barta (law firm), 96–97
Pfeiffer, Mary, xxvii, 386–87, 399
Police Department (City of Lincoln, Nebraska), 133–34
Potter, Clarkson N., 341–42
Pound, Louise, 198–200
Pound, Olivia, 316–17
Powell, Peter J., 272, 287, 326–27, 342–43, 388–89
Powers, Ramon, 439
Preece, Harold, 403
Price, Gene, 413

Raswan, Carl R., 171
Regnery, Henry, 384
Remarque, Erich Maria, 12
Richardson, Polly, 289
Richardson, Stewart, 431–32, 437–38, 457
Riddle, Bruce, 457
Rockey, Vernon C., 416–17
Rocky Mountain Herald (newspaper), 212–13
Rogers, Kay, 381–82, 410, 452
Roosevelt, Franklin D., 170
Rose, Stuart, 186, 306
Rosicky, Rose, 100
Russell, Don, 218–19

Sandoz, Allie (cousin), 423–24
Sandoz, Mary Fehr (mother), 84
Saturday Evening Post (magazine), 31–32, 79, 186, 190, 300–303, 316
Saturday Review of Literature (magazine), 175, 220–21
Sauer, Caroline, 353–54, 395, 408–9, 414
Schaefer, Jack, 258–59
Schlater, Robert, 332–33
Schmitt, Martin F., 205–6
Schossberger, Emily, 194
Schruben, Francis W., 458–59
Senate Judiciary Subcommittee on Constitutional Rights, 377–79
Shapiro, Karl, 290–91
Shefferd, Jeannette N., 136–37
Sheldon, Addison E., 73–74, 166–69
Shickley, Gail McCandless, 328–29, 410–11
Sinclair, F. H., 259–60, 405–6, 440–41
Sizer, Robert L., 411–12
Slote, Bernice, 453
Smith (credit manager), 23–24
Smith, Henry S. "Tom," 330
Sorenson, Frank E., 391–93
Southern Illinois University, 365–66
Stalnaker, Paul R., 325–26

State Historical Society. *See* Nebraska State Historical Society
Steger, Evan, 183–84
Stroud, D. H., Jr., 247–48
Stuart, Jesse, 286
Sun (newspaper). See *Clay County Sun*
Susskind, David, 370
Sutton, Everette "Ed," 346–47, 398

Tchanta Tanka. *See* McCreight, M. I.
Thiessen, Leonard, 163–64, 206–7
Torrey, Volta, 450–51
Trovillo, May V., 169–70
Trued, S. Clarence, 183
Truman, Harry, 230–32

University of Michigan, 87–88, 148–49
University of Nebraska, 127, 313, 391–93
University of Nebraska Press, 194, 290–91, 297–99, 336–37
University of Oklahoma, 26–27, 105–6, 253–54
University of Oklahoma Press, 414–15

Van den Bark, Melvin, 179–81, 311
Van Doren, Irita, 269–70
Van Dorien, Jean, 351–52
Van Vleet, Lynn, 196–97, 276
Van Vleet, Rose, 196–97
Vaughn, J. W., 273–74
Vickers, Ray, 285–86

Wallace, Henry A., 215
Wallowing, Rufus, 229–30, 256
Ward, Don, 435–37
Warner, Ezra, 322
Watson, Elmo Scott, 225–27
W. B. Saunders Company (publisher), 409
WCBS (radio station), 227–28
Webb, James R., 433–35
Weeks, Edward, xxviii, xxix, 83, 85–86, 88–90, 108–10, 118–19, 128–30, 143–46, 151–52, 156, 158, 159–62, 173, 222–23
Wells, Carlton F., 87–88, 148–49
Westerners Brand Book (journal), 396
Westminster Press, 268, 386–87
WEVD (radio station), 203
Wiles, Mrs. Ray C., 345–46
Williams, Annie Laurie, 271, 448
Williams, Frank L., 60–61, 178–79
Williams, Richard B., 442
Willner, Daniel, 396–97, 444
Wimer, Henry D., 256–58, 312
Winther, Sophus Keith, 134
Wood, Audrey, 174–75
World-Herald (newspaper). See *Omaha World-Herald*
Worley, E. T., 460–61
Wright, Thomas W., 348–49
Wyeth, M. S. "Buz," Jr., 361, 370–71, 375

Yale Review (journal), 150
Young, Marguerite, 250–51, 267–68
Yurka, Blanche, 446

Ziolkowski, Korczak, 195

Subject Index

AAA, 57, 58n. 1
Abbot, Mary Squire, xxvii, xxxi, 262n. 1, 338–39, 350
Adair, Frank, 444
Aeschylus, 102
Agricultural Adjustment Administration (AAA), 57, 58n. 1
Aldrich, Bob, 263–64
Alexander, Hartley Burr, 262–63
Alfred A. Knopf (publisher), xxvii, xxix, xxxii, 47n. 1
All Quiet on the Western Front (Remarque), 9, 12
Allen (editor at *Harpers*), 3
Allen, Charles, 227
Alsberg, Henry, 261–62, 307, 341
American, The (Linderman), 149, 204, 221, 248, 356
American Association of Indian Affairs, 388–89
American Educational Digest (magazine). *See School Executives Magazine*
American Indian (LaFarge), 425
American Indians. *See* Indians
American Speech (journal), 8, 9n. 2, 34
Amory, Cleveland, 311
Anderson, Edo, 447
Antony and Cleopatra (Shakespeare), 98
Argosy (magazine), 4
Aristophanes, 95, 102
"Army Reveals Secret of Custer's Last Stand" (Othman), 415
Arnold, Elliott, 261
"Arrow of Love" (Manfred), 306
Artist in America, An (Benton), 162–63
Ashbrooke, Harriet, 86
Astor, John Jacob, 136–37
Aswell, Edward, xxix, 261, 286, 338
Atlantic Monthly (magazine), 121n. 1
Atlantic Monthly Press, xxiii, xxvii, xxviii–xxix, 90n. 1, 91n. 7
Atlantic Nonfiction Prize, xiv
Attack on Crazy Horse, The (Remington), 212
Audubon, John James, 148
Austin, Louise, 29, 130
Austin, Mary, xxxiii

"Bachelor Stork Party" (M. Sandoz), 150
Bad Heart Bull, Amos, 188, 195, 319, 340, 375
Baker, Mrs. Johnny, 212, 218
Ballard, Fred, 200, 245
Balmer (Mademoiselle), 96, 97n. 1
Balmer, Joseph, 224, 249
Bancroft, Caroline, xxvi, 188–89
Banditti of the Plains (Mercer), 76
Barada, Antoine, 198–99
Barada, Michael, 198
Barbour, Ervin Hickly, 52, 53n. 3, 329
Barnes, Bill. *See* Hickok, James Butler "Wild Bill"; Hickok, Lorenzo
Barrymore, Ethel, 65
Battle of the Butte (Erlanson), 417–18
Battle of the Little Bighorn, The (M. Sandoz): bibliography for, 457; delays in writing of, 431–32, 442, 445, 456; form and style of, 432; maps in, 456, 457, 458; publication of, 437–38, 459; reactions to, 456, 457; research on, 358, 359–60, 432–33, 437; M. Sandoz on, 362
Baumgarten, Blanche, 242
Beacon Press, 366
Bear Butte, 442
Beaver Men, The (M. Sandoz): animals in, xvii, 395, 402–3; ecology in, xvii; illustrations in, 424–25; Indians in,

xvii, 402; maps in, 443, 444–45; plot of, 402–3; publication of, xxxi, 421, 437–38; reactions to, 402, 443, 444–45, 451; research on, 395, 398, 409; revisions of, 419; work done on, 398, 410, 411, 413, 414, 421
Bechtel, Ned, 196–97
Beckwourth, Jim, 146, 147, 148
Before Lewis and Clark (Nasatir), 334
Belk, Vida, 182
Bent, George, 253, 254n. 1, 260, 261n. 2
Bercovici, Konrad, 89, 91n. 4
Bessey, Charles Edwin, 52, 53n. 3
Beyond the Hundredth Meridian (Stegner), 353
Bierce, Ambrose, 258
Big Foot, 269, 270
Big Head, 229
Big Head, Katie, 228, 229, 233
Bison Books (publisher), xxx, 337n. 1
Black Buffalo Woman, 50n. 1
Black Elk, 247
Black Elk Speaks (Neihardt): as out-of-print book, 178, 356; publication of, xxx, 337n. 1; M. Sandoz on, xxx, 95, 149, 178, 204, 221, 247–48, 319, 356–57
"Black Hills Become a Stake in a $700,000,000 Lawsuit" (M. Sandoz), 25, 26n. 2
Black Hills treaties: and Calhoun, 42, 44n. 1; and M. Sandoz, 25, 26; signing of, 43; and Sioux, 25, 26, 42, 44n. 1; and Young Man Afraid of His Horse, 79
Black Kettle, 228
Black Shawl, 48, 49
Blish, Helen: death of, 186n. 1, 446n. 1; and E. Douglas, 186; and Hinman, 165n. 1; illnesses of, 185; research done by, 236, 336; and M. Sandoz, 165n. 1
Bolton, Laetitia, 88, 90n. 1
"Bonanza" (television program), 456
"Bone Joe and the Smokin' Woman" (M. Sandoz), 144, 146, 153
Booth, George, 127–28
Born, Dutch Henry, 295–96
Botkin, Benjamin Albert, 26–27, 34, 37
Boyd, Ernest, 38–41
Brady, Matthew, 429
Brando, Marlon, 419
Brewster, Ralph O., 249–50
Bridges, Styles, 172
Brininstool, Earl Alonzo, 268–69, 273
Bristow, Sarah Douglas, 29
Brod, Max, 78, 79n. 1
Broken Arrow (Gessner), 69–70
Broken Peace Pipes (Peithmann), 366
"Broken Promise, The" (M. Sandoz), 135, 136n. 1
Brooks, Van Wyck, 353
Brule Sioux, 226, 252. *See also* Indians; Sioux
Bruner, Lawrence, 52, 53n. 3
Bryan, Charles, 30n. 1
Buechel, Eugene, 20, 21n. 1, 272
Buffalo Bill. *See* Cody, William F. "Buffalo Bill"
Buffalo Hunters, The (M. Sandoz): animals in, xvii; ecology in, xvii; illustrations in, 424; Indians in, xvii; map in, xxx, 334; plot of, 326; publication of, xxxi; reactions to, 261–62, 269–70, 275, 295, 334, 423n. 1, 444n. 2; M. Sandoz on, 261; work done on, 251, 259
Bullhead (lieutenant), 270
Burk, Martha Jane Cannary. *See* Calamity Jane
Burke, Edward, 162, 172
Burnett, Whit, 89, 90n. 2
Burri (artist), 447
Burs Under the Saddle (Adams), 443
Butler, Samuel, 56

Calamity Jane, 281–82
Calhoun, C. C., 42, 44n. 1
California Joe (Milner), 187–88

Campbell, Thomas, 252
Campbell, Walter S. *See* Vestal, Stanley
Camus, Albert, 382
Canby, Courtland, 88, 90n. 2
Cannary, Martha Jane. *See* Calamity Jane
"Canyon, The" (Schaefer), 258
Capital City (M. Sandoz): Abigail in, 182; characteristics of, 151, 160; fear of libel regarding, 158, 159–61; as film script, 159; form and style of, 158; Lincoln, Nebraska described in, xvi, 149, 160–61; publication of, xxix, 159; reactions to, 158, 159, 161, 174, 182; research on, 151–52; revisions of, 156, 158–59; Rufe in, 160; M. Sandoz on, 156; satire in, 149, 151; theme of, 160, 182, 208; work done on, 151–52, 156; World War II in, xxiv, 161, 162
Carnival (Fleming), 351
Carr, Eugene, 212, 213
Carr, James, xxvi, 423n. 1
Carrington (Straight), 359
Carver, Doc, 237
Castle, The (Kafka), 78, 95
Cather, Willa: and East, move to, xxxiii; language usage of, 345; on pioneers, 87, 88; as recluse, 397; and M. Sandoz, 88, 134, 180, 331, 397
Cattle Empire (Nordyke), 314
Cattlemen, The (M. Sandoz): animals in, xvii, 326; ecology in, xvii; as film, 323; Indians in, xvii; lack of stock of, 315, 317, 318; language usage in, 328–29; B. Olive in, 346; I. P. Olive in, 317–18; plot of, 326; promotion of, 438; publication of, xvii, xxxi, 306, 315; purposes of, 326; reactions to, xvii, 314–15, 317–18, 321, 322, 325, 444n. 2; research on, 289, 292–94, 314, 328, 452; revisions of, 296, 312; M. Sandoz on, 322; work done on, 299, 302. *See also* "Tyrant of the Plains"
Catton, Bruce, 311
Caxton Press, xxii
Céline, Louis-Ferdinand, 120
Cerf, Bennett, 175
Chamberlain, Neville, 159, 161–62
Chambrun, Jacques: as agent, xviii, xxix, xxxi, 125n. 1, 158–59, 174, 175, 244; on "Bone Joe and the Smokin' Woman,", 144; on "Foal of Heaven," 244; and M. Sandoz, xviii, xxix, xxxi, 175
Chase, Frank, 456
Chase, Mary, xxvi, 221
Checkered Years (Cowdrey), 387
Cheyenne Autumn (film), xviii, 433–35, 438, 442
Cheyenne Autumn (M. Sandoz): Custer in, 295; film options on, xviii, 404, 416, 420, 421, 422, 430; illustrations and photographs in, 257; and Korean War, 249–50; maps in, 256, 257; Medicine Arrow in, 343n. 1; paperback edition of, 432; reactions to, xxiii, xxix, 241, 248, 261, 267, 288, 363, 439, 443; Red Bird shield in, 292n. 1; setting of, xxi; women in, 249
Cheyenne Autumn (Webb), 422, 430–31, 432
Cheyenne Tribal Council, 255
Cheyenne Woman. *See* Old Cheyenne Woman
Cheyennes: and Bear Butte, 442; and E. Carr, 212; characteristics of, 48; coal and oil on land of, 238–39; and Crazy Horse, 49, 51n. 3; and Crook, 292; and Crows, 231; and Custer, 300; divisions among, 220; education of, 238, 239; at Fort Marion prison, 230; at Fort Robinson, 292n. 1; Grinnell on, 220, 230; hospital of, 231, 238; illnesses of, 231, 238; massacre of, 122, 219, 230, 312, 413; and Merritt, 212; and pioneers, 87–88; poverty of, 231, 238, 239; and Powell, xxxii,

272, 287, 388–89; research on, 212–13, 389; and F. Roosevelt, 237–38; M. Sandoz on, 50, 230–32, 237–39, 388–89; and Stanton, 122; on Tongue River Reservation, 230–32; Wild Hog on, 312. *See also* Indians; Sacred Arrows
Chief Crazy Horse (film), xviii, 251, 268–69, 271, 335
Chief Flying Hawk's Tales (McCreight), 114, 265
Christie, Margaret: as agent, xxii, xxxi, 3, 4n. 1, 8, 14, 15, 16–17, 19–20; characteristics of, 3, 4; on "Fearbitten", 3; on "Kinkaider Comes and Goes," xxxi, 16–17; on "Last Ember," 14; on "Murky River," 11n. 2; and M. Sandoz, xxxi, 20; on "Victorie," xxii, 8
Christmas of the Phonograph Records, The (M. Sandoz), xxvii, 404, 459–60
Churchill, Winston, 217
Circle on the Square Theatre, 419–20
Civil Works Administration (CWA), 74n. 1, 77
Clark, W. P., 257, 417–18
Clark, Walter Van Tilburg, xxxiii
Cleveland, Grover, 104
Cloud, Raymond, 325–26
Cody, William F. "Buffalo Bill," 212, 213, 218, 219n. 1, 396
Cohn, David, 88, 90n. 2
Colhoff, John, 250, 320
Collier, John, 26n. 1
Colonel Pomroy (M. Sandoz), 68n. 4
Columbus, Nebraska, 140
Comanches, 442. *See also* Indians
Coming Struggle for Power, The (Strachey), 74
Compromise Soldier Vote Bill, 214
Comstock, William, 11n. 4
Condra, George Evert, 52, 53n. 3, 83
Conquering Bear, 118
Conquest of the Southern Plains (Brill), 228, 232, 233–34
Conrad, Joseph, 24
Conroy, Jack, 76
Continental Confederation of Adopted Indians, 440
Cooke, Jay, 200
Cornhusker Hotel, 132, 141–42, 290
Counting the Waves (Farrell), 180
"Cow Country Cure, A" (M. Sandoz), 8
"Coyotes and Eagles" (M. Sandoz), 447
Cozad, John J., 302n. 3, 352
Cozad, Robert Henry, 352
Crancer, Elinor Gustin, 72
Craven, Gus, 335
Crawford, Nelson Antrim, 71
Crazy Horse: ambush plans of, 49; background of, 48, 436; Brininstool on, 273; carvings by, 374–75; and Cheyennes, 49, 51n. 3; clothing of, 319; death of, xxii, 20, 22, 49–50, 51n. 2, 122, 123n. 3, 305, 335, 367; death of child of, 48; E. Eastman on, 196; fasting of, 48; and Gentles, 367; and Grouard, 49, 335; guns of, 266–67; and He Dog, 50, 115, 367; Hinman on, 20, 22, 26, 42, 69, 70n. 1, 166, 185; medicine of, 319; monument to, 195, 260, 373; name of, 273; and No Water, 48, 50n. 1, 51n. 2; and Old Red Feather, 374; opera about, 103; paintings and photographs of, 187–88, 237, 273, 305, 306, 319, 349, 359; rituals of, 319; M. Sandoz on, xxii, 20, 22–23, 48, 103, 204, 273, 319; and Short Bull, 367; visions of, 48, 49, 319, 375; wives of, 48, 49, 50; and Ziolkowski, 195, 260, 373
Crazy Horse (Dines), 448
Crazy Horse (M. Sandoz): background of, 185; and *Chief Crazy Horse,* xviii, 251, 268–69, 335; Custer in, 295; dedication of, 185; language usage in, 190, 191, 192; Little Big Man in, 32n. 2; map in, 362; pirating of, 189, 191; plot of, 326; proofreading of, 191; publication of, xxix, 190, 449; reac-

Crazy Horse (M. Sandoz) (*cont.*)
tions to, 190, 195, 200–201, 204, 211, 212, 224, 227, 230, 240, 251, 259n. 2, 261, 271, 288, 314, 374, 460, 461n. 1; reprinting of, 240, 271, 449; research on, 185, 190, 314; revisions of, 190; M. Sandoz on, 185; setting of, xxi; work done on, xxvi, 185, 187–88
Crazy Horse No. 2, 103, 187–88, 273
Crazy Horse Symphony (Mills), 327, 329, 339
Crazy in the Lodge, 273
Cronley, Marie, 71, 73n. 2
Crook, George, 204–5, 291–92, 385, 433
Crow Indians, 231. *See also* Indians
Crow Killer (Thorp and Bunker), 366
Cuney family, 168
Curly. *See* Crazy Horse
Custer, George Armstrong: characteristics of, 275; and Cheyennes, 300; death of, 45, 122, 123n. 3, 213; desertion of command by, 455; guns of, 253, 254–55; and Hunkpapas, 454–55; illnesses of, 233; and Little Rock, 229; and Monahseetah, 228–29, 232, 260n. 1, 300, 455; and Moss Subcommittee, 300; and Rain in the Face, 45, 46; research on, 299–300, 455, 457; M. Sandoz on, 275; and Standing Bear, 45; Vestal on, 454; and White Bull, 454–55; wife of, 455; and Yellow Swallow, 228–29, 232–33, 234n. 1, 260n. 1, 312, 322, 455
Custer Battlefield National Monument, 248–49
Custer Fighters. *See* New York Posse of the Westerners
Custer Story, The (Merington, ed.), 297
CWA, 74n. 1, 77

"Dakota Country" (M. Sandoz), 362
Dance Back the Buffalo (Lott), 344
"Danes on the Prairie" (M. Sandoz), 134–35
Darwell, Jane, 174
Davison, Edward, 390
De Smet, Pierre-Jean, 389–90
De Voto, Bernard, 102n. 1, 192
De Yong, Joe, 204
"Death in the Ice Mine" (M. Sandoz). *See* "Foal of Heaven"
Decker, Pete, 257, 276, 277n. 1
Deserts on the March (Sears), 105
Dessoulavy, Ida (grandmother), 96
Devil, The (Neumann), 56
DeVilbiss, Joyce and Otho, 184, 329
DeVilbiss, Otto, 230
"Devil's Lane, The" (M. Sandoz), 54–55
Dewey, John, 76
Dial Press, xxix
Dillon, Richard, 317
"Dime, The" (M. Sandoz), 3
Dimnit, Ernest, 12
Dinner at Eight (play), 65
"Dispossessed, The" (Levitt), 381–82
Doane, Gilbert, 65, 75
Dobie, J. Frank, 269
Dodd Mead (publisher), 53n. 1, 64
Dog Soldier book (M. Sandoz), 458
Douglas, Eric, 184, 186
Douglas, Jesse, 193
Drum Packer. *See* Sitting Bull
Du Mont, John S., 253n. 1, 255, 256
Dull Knife, 232–33, 254, 257, 436
Duren, Terence, 323
Durfee and Peck (store), 252
Dust (Haldeman-Julius), 12
Dutch Bill. *See* Hickok, James Butler "Wild Bill"
Dutch Jim. *See* Hickok, James Butler "Wild Bill"

Eastern Posse of the Westerners. *See* New York Posse of the Westerners
Eastman, Charles, 354
Eastman, Elaine Goodale, 196
Ecoffey family, 168

"Education on a Mountain" (Adamic), 102
Edward VIII (king of Great Britain and Ireland), 126
Eisenhower, Dwight D., 327, 410
Elegant Auctioneers, The (Towner), 308
Elk River, 304
Engle, Paul, 250–51
Erickson, Howard, 75
"Evening Song" (M. Sandoz), 427–28

Fadiman, Clifton, 192, 203
Far West (Flagg), 295
Farewell to Arms, A (Hemingway), 12
Farrar and Rinehart (publisher), 75
Farriter, Robert, 301–2
Fast, Howard, xxiii, 164–65, 176–77, 420–21, 422
Father and Son (Farrell), 180
Faulkner, Virginia: as editor, xxx, 297, 298, 305, 313, 332; on *Hostiles and Friendlies,* xxx, 298, 305, 313, 332; and M. Sandoz, xxx
Faulkner, William, 57, 58
"Fearbitten" (M. Sandoz), 3, 4n. 2, 5, 180, 299
Federal Emergency Relief Administration (FERA), 74n. 1
Fehr, Mary. *See* Sandoz, Mary Fehr
Feikema, Feike. *See* Manfred, Frederick
FERA, 74n. 1
Ferril, Hellie, xxvi
Ferril, Thomas Hornsby, xxv, xxvi, 353
Fetterman, William Judd, 122, 123n. 3, 276–77
Feuchtwanger, Lion, 64
Fighting Cheyennes, The (Grinnell), 241, 304, 418, 437
Fighting Indians of the West (Brown and Schmitt), 257, 273, 349
Filley, Horace Clyde, 59
Fisher, Vardis, xxxiii
Fitzell, Lenore, xxvi
Fix, Georgia Arbuckle, 243–44, 279–82
"*Flair* Personified: Mari Sandoz" (Young), 248–49
Flathead Indians, 200–201. *See also* Indians
Flight to the North (M. Sandoz). See *Cheyenne Autumn*
Fling, Fred, 102, 313
"Foal of Heaven" (M. Sandoz), 197, 198n. 2, 244, 306–7
Fogelson, Buddy, 242, 244n. 1
Foley, Martha, 89, 90n. 2
Folk-say (Botkin, ed.), 26, 34
Footprints on the Frontier (Trenholm and Carley), 405
For Whom the Bell Tolls (Hemingway), 180
Ford, John, 421, 448
Forsyth, Mary Bryan, 372, 373n. 1
Fort Marion, 230
Fort Phil Kearny, 123n. 3, 276–77
Fort Robinson, 232–33, 254, 291–92
Fortune Tellers (Fleming), 351
Forty Years on the Frontier (Stuart), 252
Freese, John, 226
Frese, Walter: and Abbot, xxxi; on *Beaver Men,* 402; on *Buffalo Hunters,* 262; on *Cattlemen,* 317, 318; as editor and publisher, xxxi, 317, 402, 406; on "Foal of Heaven," 307; on *Old Jules Country,* xxvii; and M. Sandoz, xxxi, 261
Freud, Sigmund, xix, 38, 40
"Frontier Days of an Immortal Man of Science" (M. Sandoz), 54
Frontier Years, The (Brown and Felton), 418
Fry, Ed, 152

Galleys, defined, 191n. 1
Gannett, Lewis, 88, 90n. 1, 192–93
Garnett, Billy, 31
Garnier, Little Bat, 31
Garrett, Garet, 164–65
Garson, Greer, xvii–xviii, 242, 244n. 1, 422

Gass, Sherlock Bronson, 10, 11n. 5, 98
Geddes, Alice, 64
General George Crook (Schmitt, ed.), 205
Genet, Jean, 420
Gentles, William, 367
"Ghost Dance Religion, The" (Mooney), 270
Ghost Dance War, 227, 232
Gillespie, Mabel, 140
"Girl in the Humbert, The" (M. Sandoz), 149, 150n. 1, 153, 186, 259n. 1
Glory Hunter (Van de Water), 275
Goings, Frank, 204
Gold Camp (Barsness), 400
Goss, Charles Albert, 301
Grahame, Roberta, 246
Grant, Ulysses S., 252
Grapes of Wrath, The (Steinbeck), 162
Grattan, John L., 168, 169n. 1
Greasy Head. *See* Crazy Horse No. 2
Great Council, The (M. Sandoz), 32n. 2, 37n. 5, 79. *See also* "Little Big Man's Heart is Bad"
Great Eyes, 292n. 1
Great Mysteries of the Cheyenne, The (Grinnell), 435
Great Plains series. See *Beaver Men, The; Buffalo Hunters, The; Cattlemen, The; Cheyenne Autumn; Crazy Horse; Old Jules*
Great Roundup, The (Nordyke), 314
Grey, Tunny, 131
Grey Thunder, 304
Grimes, George, 193
Grinnell, George Bird, 220, 230, 342
Grobman, Edith, 207
Grouard, Frank, 49, 335
Guggenheim Museum, 344–45
Gustavson, Reuben G., 222

Hall, Benn, 400
Halsman, Philippe, 429
Hanighen, Frank C.: as editor, 53n. 1, 64; on *Old Jules*, 62–63, 64–65, 223; and M. Sandoz, xvi, xxii, 64
Hansen, Harry, 88, 90n. 1, 193, 376
Harcourt (owner of publishing company), 242
Harney, William S., 379, 405
Harpers Monthly Magazine, xxx
"Harvard's Skinner" (Klaw), 409
Harvey, Gerry, 246
Hass, Victor P., 363
Hastings House (publisher), xxix–xxx, xxxi
Hayakawa, S. I., 408
Hayes, Helen Mary, 73n. 1
He Dog: background of, 48, 115; characteristics of, 349; and Crazy Horse, 50, 115, 367; death of, 115; on guns, 266; and Hinman, 22; painting of, 237, 359; and M. Sandoz, 20–21, 22, 115, 204, 349; and Sitting Bull, 115
Hecht, Harold, 421, 422
Hemingway, Ernest, 382
Henderson, Paul, 257
Henely, Austin, 230
Henri, Robert. *See* Cozad, Robert Henry
Herman, Jake, 335
Hertzler, Joyce, 25
Hess, Rudolf, 215
Heyl, Charley, 228
Hickok, James Butler "Wild Bill": aliases of, 256; as buffalo hunter, 257; and Crook, 433; illnesses of, 415, 433, 444n. 2; research on, 361, 444n. 2; M. Sandoz on, 360–61
Hickok, Lorenzo, 256
Hicks, John D., 35, 37n. 4, 193, 375, 450
Higgins, Joy, 140
Hill, A. T., 97, 98n. 2
Hill, James, 421, 422
Himmler, Heinrich, 215
Hindus, Maurice Gershon, 88, 90n. 2
Hinman, Eleanor: background of, 16n. 1; and Blish, 165n. 1; on Crazy Horse, 20, 22, 26, 42, 69, 70n. 1,

166, 185; and He Dog, 22; and Linderman, 42; and Neihardt, 42; research done by, 20, 42; and M. Sandoz, xx, xxiii, xxiv, 16n. 1, 20, 22, 26, 165, 166, 185; and Vestal, 42
Historical Society. *See* Nebraska State Historical Society
History of Medicine in Nebraska (Tyler and Auerback), 282
History of Nebraska (Watkins), 282
Hitler, Adolf, xxiv, 162, 170
Hoffman, Paul: on *Crazy Horse*, 240; as editor, xxvi–xxvii, xxviii, xxix, 91n. 7, 131, 176, 184, 240, 407; on "Foal of Heaven," 306–7; on *Old Jules*, 90, 91n. 7, 240; and M. Sandoz, xxvi–xxvii, xxviii, xxix, 91n. 7; in Wyoming, 130–31, 176
Hollenbeck, Don, 207
Holmes, Oliver Wendell, 167, 193
Home Below Hell's Canyon (Jordan), 387
Home on the Running Water (M. Sandoz). See *Old Jules*
"Homestead in Perspective, The" (M. Sandoz), 388, 447
Hooker, William "Pizen Bill," 117, 118
Horgan, Paul, 258
Horse and Buggy Doctor (Hertzler), 321
Horsecatcher, The (M. Sandoz), 287, 303–4, 449
Hostiles and Friendlies (M. Sandoz): proofreading of, 332; publication of, 304–6, 313; reactions to, xxx, 298, 305, 307, 313, 332, 345, 372; research on, 305, 307; M. Sandoz on, xxx, 407
"Hot Iron" (M. Sandoz), 15
"Hounds of Fear" (M. Sandoz). *See* "Fearbitten"
How the West Was Won (film), 434
"How to Choose a Profession" (M. Sandoz), 155
How to Work Your Way Through College (Adams), 154
"Hungry River" (Overbeck), 21
Hunkpapas, 454–55. *See also* Indians
Hyde, George, 401–2

"I Remember Lincoln" (M. Sandoz), xvi
I'll Die Before I'll Run (Sonnichsen), 346
Indian Boyhood (C. Eastman), 195
Indian Journals (Morgan), 425
Indians: and Bear Butte, 442; and Brando, 419; and buffalo, 224; clothing of, 265–66, 287; and Collier, 26n. 1; constitutional rights of, 377–79, 382n. 3; cultural achievements of, 288; decline of, 117–18, 327, 377–79; and Eisenhower, 327; and guns, 276; hearings regarding, xix; Hyde on, 401–2; on immortality and spirit, 288; Jacobsen on, 319; languages of, spelling of, 319–20; Lemons on, 288; and J. Meyer, 226; photographs of, 265; research on, 319; and Ricker, 31; M. Sandoz on, xvii, xix, xxxii, 47, 50, 79, 118, 319, 377; segregation of, 112; Truman on, 230; and women, attitude toward, 100; and Wounded Knee, 270n. 1. *See also specific groups of Indians and specific Indians*
Iron Horse, 402

Jacks, Leo, 4n. 1
Jackson, W. H., 429
Jacobsen, Ethel, 319
James, Henry, 65
Janis, Nick, 185
J.B. Lippincott Company (publisher), xxx
John Hunton's Diary (Flannery, ed.), 405
Johnson, Alvin, 89, 91n. 3
Johnson, Frank, 302, 357
Jones, Howard Mumford, 144–45, 192
Jones, Neckyoke. *See* Sinclair, F. H.
Josephus (Feuchtwanger), 64
Josephus, Flavius, 95

Journal of Fort Clark (Chardon), 111
Journey of the Flame, The (Fierro Blanco), 210
Journey to the End of Night (Céline), 136, 138
Jung, Carl, xix

Kafka, Franz, 78, 79n. 1
Kansas Irish (Driscoll), 197
Kazan, Elia, 353
"Keeping Posted" (M. Sandoz), xxvi
Kees, Weldon, 178
Kent, Rockwell, 12
Kills the Enemy, Charles Jonas, 207
Kills Two, 195
King, Charles, 213, 218
Kinkaid Act of 1904, 22n. 3
"Kinkaider Comes and Goes, The" (M. Sandoz), xxxi, 16–17, 21, 331
Kinkaiders, 22n. 3
Kirby, Rollin, 89, 91n. 3
Kirkus, Virginia, 317
Kirsh, Frederick Dwight, 86, 87n. 2, 90
Knopf (publisher). *See* Alfred A. Knopf
Knopf, Alfred, 47n. 1, 339
Knopf, Blanche, xxix, xxxii, 208–9, 211
Komantcia (Keith), 450
Korean War, 249–50
Kristin Lavransdatter (Undset), 9
Kritzler, Melven, 446
Ku Klux Klan, 214
Kuhn, Ed, 337
Kuse, Lorraine, 71, 73n. 3

La Gallienne, Eva, 65
LaFlesche family, 365
Lakotas, 200–201, 319–20. *See also* Indians; Sioux
Lame White Man, 257
Lancaster, Burt, 421, 422
Land Systems and Land Policies in Nebraska (Sheldon), 74n. 1, 83, 105
Landmarks on the Oregon Trail (Henderson), 257
Lantern in Her Hand, A (Bess Aldrich), 263
"Last Ember, The" (M. Sandoz), 14
Last Frontier, The (Fast), xxiii, 420–21, 422
Last Frontier, The (Sutley), 69
"Last Indian War" (Watson), 226
Laval, Pierre, 183
Lazy VV Ranch, 197n. 1, 411
Leermakers, Jack, 257
Lemons, William E., 288
Lerner, Max, 250
Letters of a Woman Homesteader (Stewart), 354
Levitt, Saul, 381–82
Liberty, Margot, 459
Life certificates, 39, 42n. 2
Life of Lewis Carroll, The (Lennon), 202–3
Lightner, Louis, 139, 322
Lincoln, Mary Todd, 429
Lincoln, Nebraska, xvi, xvii, 59–60, 291
Lincoln State Journal (newspaper), 73n. 1
Lincoln's Rise to Power (Baringer), 121–22
Linderman, Frank, 42, 44n. 2
Lippincott Company (publisher). *See* J.B. Lippincott Company
Little, Brown and Company (publisher), xxiii, xxviii–xxix, 121n. 1
Little Big Horn, 130–31, 358–59
Little Big Man, 32n. 2
"Little Big Man's Heart is Bad" (M. Sandoz), 31, 32n. 2. See also *Great Council, The*
Little Finger Nail, 260, 287, 292
Little Hawk, 367, 417–18
Little Rock, 228, 229
Little Thunder, 379–81, 405
Little Wolf, 257, 260n. 1, 417–18, 435
"Little Wound Paper" (collection of historical materials), 236

Lives and Legends of Buffalo Bill, The (Russell), 396
Longhorn (Dobie), 346
Lorimer, George, 32 n. 1
"Lost School Bus, The" (M. Sandoz). See *Winter Thunder*
"Lothario's Pajamas" (M. Sandoz), 15
Love Song to the Plains (M. Sandoz): Cather in, 397; dedication of, xxv; illustrations in, 372, 373; map in, 375; reactions to, 350, 351 n. 1, 361, 368, 370–71, 383; revisions of, 369, 370–71; M. Sandoz on, 361, 370, 375; setting of, xxi; title of, 369; work done on, 363–64
Lucian, 95
Luhan, Mabel Dodge, 162–63

McBride, Mary Margaret, 234–35
McCarthy, Joseph, 267
McCreight, M. I., 115 n. 1
McGaa, Denver, 147
McGaa, Jack, 146, 147
McGillycuddy, Valentine, 101
McGillycuddy Agent (McGillycuddy), 101 n. 2, 237
McGraw-Hill (publisher), xxix
McIntosh and Otis (agency), xxxi
McIntyre, Alfred R.: as editor and publisher, xxviii–xxix, 121 n. 1, 172, 173, 177; and M. Sandoz, xxiii, xxviii–xxix, 119, 172, 173, 177; on *Slogum House*, xxviii–xxix
Mackenzie, Ranald, 436
Macmillan (publisher), 13
Macumber, Marie. *See* Sandoz, Mari
Macumber, Wray (ex-husband), xv
Madame Toussaint's Wedding Day (St. Martin), 181
Madsen, Chris, 212, 218
Maheo's Children (Allen), 435–37
Maher, John, 226–27
Man, the Unknown (Carrel), 94
Man at the Mast (Kent), 12
Man of the Plains (L. North), 347–48
Man Who Fought Custer, The. See *Wooden Leg*
Manfred, Frederick, 288, 306
"Mari Sandoz Defends Such a Theme" (newspaper article), 125–26
"Mari Sandoz Discusses Creative Writing" (television program), 332–33
"Mari Sandoz Looks at the Old West" (television program), 332–33
Marriage and Morality (Russell), 12
Materia Medica (family heirloom), 155, 216–17
Mayor of Casterbridge, The (Hardy), 109
Meaning of Culture, The (Powys), 138
Medicine Arrow, 342, 343, 440
Mein Kampf (Hitler), xxiv, 181
Mellon, Andrew, 117
Mencken, H. L., xxii, 9 n. 2, 24, 25 n. 1
Me-o-tizi. *See* Monahseetah
Me-otzi. *See* Monahseetah
Meredith, Mamie, 55, 202, 307, 317, 408
Merritt, Wesley, 212, 213, 218
Meyer, Julius, 226
Meyer, Wallace, 241
Milligan, Tom, 69–70
Mills, Charles, 327, 329, 339
Mind and Society, The (Pareto), 95
Minnesota massacre (1863), 122
Mirror of Fools (Neumann), 56
Miss MacIntosh, My Darling (Young), xxvi, xxxii
Miss Morissa (M. Sandoz): background of, 244 n. 2; Braille edition of, 285; and Garson, xvii, 242, 422; Miss Morissa in, xxxii, 250; plot of, 250; reactions to, 279–82, 406; reprinting of, 406; research on, 280; revisions of, 274–75; M. Sandoz on, 243–44, 274–75, 279–82; and *Strange Lady in Town*, xvii–xviii
"Mist and the Tall White Tower" (M. Sandoz), 298
Modern Language Association, 9 n. 2

Mollie (Sanford), 348
Monahseetah, 228–29, 232, 260n. 1, 300, 455
"Moochmouth and the New Schoolma'am" (M. Sandoz), 186
Moon is Down, The (Steinbeck), 203
Moral Man and Immoral Society (Niebuhr), 75
Moral Rearmament (MR), 215
"More or Less Personal" (F. Williams), 61n. 1
Morehouse, George C., 393–95
Mormon Pioneer Cemetery, 110–13
Mormons, 110–13, 146, 147
Morris, Wright, 363, 428–30
Morton, J. Sterling, 216, 217
Moss Subcommittee, 300
MR, 215
Murky River (M. Sandoz), 2n. 1, 9, 11n. 2, 51, 53
Murray, William "Alfalfa Bill", 30–31
Museum of the American Indian, 294
"Musky" (M. Sandoz), 408–9
Mussolini, Benito, xxiv
My Antonia (Cather), 88, 134
My Life on the Plains (Custer), 228, 455

Naismith, Grace, 404
Nathan, George Jean, 162–63
National Recovery Administration (NRA), 57, 58n. 1
Native Americans. *See* Indians
Natoma (Herbert), 51, 103
Nazis, 171, 172, 214
Neale, Russell, 317
Nebraska History (journal), 74n. 1, 77n. 6, 79, 82, 218
Nebraska Sandhills. *See* Sandhills
Nebraska State Historical Society: background of, 97, 98, 99n. 3; editors of, 97; and M. Sandoz, 74n. 1, 86, 97, 99n. 3, 155, 212, 218, 265
Nebraska Strong Men, 198–200
"Neighbor, The" (M. Sandoz), 290–91, 331, 395
Neihardt, John G., 42, 44n. 2, 193, 247
New Country (Bosworth), 403
New York Posse of the Westerners: on Brininstool, 268–69; meetings of, 251; members of, 253n. 1, 277n. 1, 284; photographs viewed by, 257; purposes of, xix; and M. Sandoz, xix, 251
Nicoll, Bruce: on *Christmas of the Phonograph Records,* xxvii, 459–60; as editor, xxx, 337n. 1, 344, 407, 459–60; and M. Sandoz, xxvii
Nietzsche, Friedrich, xix
Nixon, Richard M., 249
No Man's Land (Rister), 293, 346
No Water, 48, 50n. 1, 51n. 2
Norris, George, 201, 202n. 2, 265
North, Luther, 218
North, Sterling, 193, 202
North American Review (journal), xxxi, 14n. 2, 21
Notes (Dawes), 89
Nothing But Prairie and Sky (Siberts), 283
NRA, 57, 58n. 1
"Nuclear Fission" (Turner), 170

O Pioneers (Cather), 88
Ober, Harold: as agent, xxv, xxxi, 90, 91n. 8, 114n. 1, 174; on *Old Jules,* 114; and M. Sandoz, xxv, xxxi, 90, 174; on *Tom-Walker,* xxv
Oglala Sioux, 226, 335, 410. *See also* Indians; Sioux
Oil Book (M. Sandoz), 458–59
Oilcloth Bag (Thiessen), 164
Old Cheyenne Woman, 232–33, 254, 343, 413
Old Deadwood Days (Bennett), 188, 387
Old He Dog. *See* He Dog
Old Jules (M. Sandoz): armed services edition of, 207, 214; background of, 19, 34–36, 80, 209; G. Booth in, 127–28; characters in, names of, 35,

80; film options on, 174, 416, 456–57; form and style of, xxii, 36, 62, 120, 321; Krauses in, 104; language usage in, 219–20; Old Jules in, xvii, 52, 63, 93, 104, 209–10; paperback edition of, 368; photographs in, 86, 87n. 2; pioneers in, xvii; as play, 144, 145n. 3, 146, 175, 404–5, 425; plot of, 326; populism in, 63; publication of, xvi, xvii, 51, 114, 123, 126; purposes of, 81, 92–93, 135, 209; reactions to, ix, 30, 33–34, 35, 37, 52, 62–63, 64–65, 85–86, 88, 89–90, 91n. 7, 92–93, 94, 97, 101–2, 106–7, 108, 114, 120, 124, 126, 132, 133, 146, 153, 181, 182, 192, 211, 223, 226, 240, 242, 321, 371, 405, 450; rejection of, 211, 242; reprinting of, 234, 240; research on, 13, 14n. 6, 29, 33, 35, 52, 81, 82, 93, 96, 98, 108, 152, 209, 216–17, 226, 283, 331; revisions of, 51, 63n. 1, 80, 82n. 2, 85–86, 108, 124, 141, 210; Richards in, 103–5; M. Sandoz on, xxii, 51, 86, 107, 156; serialization of, 126; setting of, xxi, 51–52, 120; Spade ranch in, 104; title of, 29, 63n. 1, 82n. 2; translations of, 121, 123, 126, 133; work done on, 155
Old Jules Country (M. Sandoz), xxvii, xxxi
"Old Potato Face" (M. Sandoz), 1n. 2
Old Red Feather, 374
Old Spot. *See* Spotted Tail
Old Wolf, 257
Olive, Billy, 346
Olive, I. P. "Print", 300–302, 313, 314, 318, 346
"On Massive Neutron Cores" (Oppenheimer and Volkoff), 170
"On Moving from New York" (De Voto), 147
On the Border with Crook (Bourke), 206
"Open End" (television program), 333
Osages, 334. *See also* Indians
Otis, Elizabeth, xxxi
Our Wild Indians (Dodge), 342
"Outpost in New York" (M. Sandoz), 388, 390, 411, 447
Owen, Jan, 307

Page proofs, defined, 191n. 1
Paine, Bayard H., 245, 301
Paine, Clara, 97
Parsons, John E., 256
"Patron Saint of Andalusia, The" (Sedgwick), 143
Pawnees, 435–36. *See also* Indians
Payne, Kenneth Wilcox, 14, 16, 20–21
"Peace without Hate" (Norris), 201
"Peachstone Basket" (M. Sandoz), 164, 165n. 1, 194
Pearce, Cap, 242
Penrod (Tarkington), 148
People of the Blue Water (Iliff), 304
Pepper, Mary, 267–68
Personal Recollections (Miles), 206
Petter, Berthe Elise Schroeder, 249
Pfeiffer, Mary, 386
Phillips, Portugee, 277
Picotte, Susan La Flesche, 280
Pictographic History of the Oglala Sioux, A (Bad Heart Bull and Blish), 21, 236, 263n. 2, 412, 450
"Pieces to a Quilt" (M. Sandoz), 1n. 2
Pifer, Caroline Sandoz (sister), xv, 14, 72
Pifer, Mary Ann (niece), 452–53, 454
Pioneers Progress (A. Johnson), 397
Plains Indian wars, 169n. 1
Plowshare in Heaven (Stuart), 286
Pointe (artist-priest), 390
Pollock, Jackson, 303
Poore, Charles, 192–93
Potato Eaters, The (van Gogh), 89
Potter, Clarkson N., xxix, 341–42, 350, 355–56
Pound, Louise: and Botkin, 27n. 1, 34; death of, 316–17; as editor, 8, 9n. 2, 34; on language, 8, 9n. 2, 345; and

Pound, Louise (*cont.*)
Mencken, 9n. 2, 25n. 1; on Nebraska Strong Men, 198–200; and M. Sandoz, 8, 34, 98, 124; as teacher, 98, 124, 317, 345, 399
Powell, Peter J., xxxii, 272, 287, 388–89
Prairie Schooner (journal): characteristics of, 290, 412; decline of, 126, 127, 286, 290; editors at, 34, 36n. 2, 408, 412, 453; purposes of, 453; M. Sandoz on, 126, 127, 286, 290–91, 412
Prairie Women (Beede), 37
Preston, John Hyde, 89, 91n. 4
"Protection Accounts", 293
Psychology of Gambling, The (Bergler), 337
Pursuit of Happiness (play), 65

Quill (writers' group): and Christie, 4n. 1, 15; members of, 70, 71n. 1, 73nn. 2, 3, 77n. 7, 264n. 1; purposes of, 4n. 1, 15n. 1
Quintero, Serafín and Joaquín, 420
Quisling, Vidkun, 183

Rain in the Face, 45, 46
Rascoe, Burton, 443
Ratoff, Gregory, xviii, 251
Raysor, Thomas, 64, 68n. 3
Rebel, The (Neumann), 56
Recovery through Revolution (Schmalhausen, ed.), 75
Red Bird, 292n. 1
Red Bird shield, 292
Red Cloud: as agency Indian, 48; capture of, 43; and Grant, 252; as Oglala Sioux chief, 44n. 3, 46; photographs of, 32, 79; resistance led by, 276; J. W. Smith on, 252
Red Cloud and the Sioux Problem (Olson), 344
Red Cloud's Folk (Hyde), 401, 437
Red Leaf, 43
Ree Indians, 442, 443–44. *See also* Indians
Reed, Carroll, 8
Reed, Walter, 86, 87n. 1, 90, 309, 433
Reid, James, 89, 91n. 4
"Relief from Murder" (H. Jones), 144, 145n. 2, 192
Remarque, Erich Maria, 12
Reynard, Grant, 383
Rhodes, Oliver L. B., 269–70
Rice, John, 102
Richard family, 168
Richards, Bartlett, 10, 11n. 4
Richardson, Polly, 289
Ricker, Eli, 31, 33n. 4, 35, 43, 236
Ricker Collection: contents of, 31, 33n. 4, 35, 42–44, 205, 375, 413; and M. Sandoz, 31, 33n. 4, 34, 35, 42, 44
Rifles for Watie (Keith), 449
"River Polak" (M. Sandoz), 87n. 3, 124, 125n. 2, 148
Rock Forehead. *See* Medicine Arrow
Rodenbaugh, Harold, 248–49
Rogers, Kay and Joe, xxvi
Roman Nose, 253, 254n. 1
Roosevelt, Franklin D., 82, 84, 85, 237–38
Roosevelt, Theodore, 104
Rosalie (Jules Ami's Swiss sweetheart), 312, 343
Rosat, Jeanne, 82, 84, 85n. 1
Rose, Stuart, 186, 190
"Rose for Emily, A" (W. Faulkner), xxii, 56–57
Roundup (V. Faulkner, comp. and ed.), 290
Rudolf, Max, 327, 339

Sacred Arrows, 272, 304, 342, 343n. 1. *See also* Cheyennes
Sacred Medicine Hat, 231, 272. *See also* Cheyennes
Sand Crane, 231
"Sandhill Sundays" (M. Sandoz), 10, 26–27, 259

Sandhills: characteristics of, 28, 61, 179; drought in, xvi; eastern ignorance about, xvi, xxii–xxiii, 2–3, 16–17; M. Sandoz on, xvi, 3, 28, 63, 179; F. Williams on, 61 n. 1; winds in, 105–6
Sandoz, Allie (cousin), 15, 16 n. 2, 388
Sandoz, Caroline "Peggy" (sister). *See* Pifer, Caroline Sandoz
Sandoz, Celia (niece), 238, 246 n. 1
Sandoz, Emile (uncle), 4–5, 10, 52, 82, 331
Sandoz, Estelle Thompson (Jules Ami's first wife), 97 n. 1, 152–53
Sandoz, Flora (sister), xix–xx, 14, 69, 72, 178–79
Sandoz, Fritz (brother), 72, 371–72
Sandoz, James (brother), 72
Sandoz, Jules Alexander "Jule" (brother), 72, 144, 179
Sandoz, Jules Ami (father): background of, 52, 81; and Barbour, 52; and Bessey, 52; and Bruner, 52; characteristics of, xix, 52, 309, 456–57; and Condra, 52, 83; correspondence of, 216–17; and J. Cozad, 352; on Cuney family, 168; death of, 135; on Ecoffey family, 168; emigration of, 24, 309; and Garnett, 31; and Garnier, 31; humor of, 52; and Maher, 226; marriages of, 80, 96, 97 n. 1, 152–53; and Morton, 216; and Old Cheyenne Woman, 343; and Reed, 309, 433; research done by, 312; on Richard family, 168; on Richards, 10, 11 n. 4; and Rosalie, 312, 343; and Emile Sandoz, 10; and Estelle Sandoz, 152–53; and M. Sandoz, xix, 17–18, 34–35, 54, 80–81, 92–93, 107, 135, 209, 371; and M. F. Sandoz, 81; and Sheldon, xiv, 34; and Sioux, 31, 247; as storyteller, 80; temper of, 135; as vigilante, 309; on war, 312; and Weeks, xiv; and Wild Hog, 343, 413, 440; and F. Williams, 33, 82; on women, 82; on Wounded Knee, 269; on writers, 81, 135–36
Sandoz, Mari: on agents, xxx–xxxi, 2, 169, 385; anthology of works by, 447–48; on art and artists, 73 n. 1, 81, 89, 182, 303; on atomic bomb, 170, 221; awards won by and honors given to, xiv, xxviii, 4 n. 2, 9 n. 1, 19, 31–32, 47 n. 1, 53 n. 2, 77 n. 6, 81, 83, 119, 123–24, 126, 135, 155–56, 209–11, 234, 283, 299, 373 n. 1, 383, 386, 432, 449, 450–51; banning of books by, 330–31, 453; birth of, xiv–xv, 268; on blurbs to books, 227–28; "bohemian" life of, 323; as book reviewer, 197, 278; bronze bust of, 373 n. 1; burning of manuscripts by, xxii–xxiii, 298, 299; on censorship, 330; characteristics of, xiv, xix, xx–xxii, xxiv–xxv, 18, 92; childhood of, xv–xvi, xxi, xxiii, xxxii–xxxiii, 2, 10, 17, 31, 38, 39, 54, 57, 80–81, 101–2, 155, 308–9, 319, 425; on Columbus, Nebraska, 140; on communism, 74–75, 76–77; on conversation, 66–67; cultural and social life of, xviii–xix, xxi–xxii, xxv, xxvi, 88–89, 188, 197, 311, 344; death of, xxi, xxv, xxvii, 461; on democracy, 153–54; depression, frustration, and stress of, xvi, xx, xxii–xxiii, xxiv, xxv, 59, 78–79, 107, 315–16, 317, 318; detachment of, xix, xxiii, xxv, xxxii, 15–16; on dust clouds, 105; on easterners and the East, 115, 116, 120, 131, 140, 141, 148, 159, 176, 245–46, 280, 288, 305, 344–45, 353, 363, 375, 384, 386, 406; as editor, 1, 2, 3–4, 12, 14 n. 3, 52, 62, 74 n. 1, 77 n. 6, 79, 82, 155, 242, 261, 369, 399; on editors and publishers, xxvii–xxx, xxxiii, 4, 13, 46–47, 54, 70, 77, 78, 109, 115, 119–21, 131–32, 166, 169, 173–74, 175–76, 179–80, 189, 209–10, 242, 245, 261–62, 274, 280, 288, 299,

Sandoz, Mari (*cont.*)
315–16, 324, 337–38, 353–54, 355–56, 357, 362, 363, 366, 368, 369, 372, 383, 384, 385, 399, 406, 407–9, 412, 442; on education, 6–8; education of, 1, 154–56; at family reunion, 65–66, 68, 69, 72, 132; on farmers, 57–58, 85; on fatherhood, 371; as feminist, 325; on films, 416; fire in New York apartment of, xiii, 279, 285; form and style of works of, xxv–xxvi, 128–29, 150, 310, 383, 399; friendships of, xxv, xxvi–xxvii, xxix, xxx, xxxii; on fur trade, 112; on grants, 344, 348; harassment of, 133–34, 158, 172, 388, 390, 411; on helicopters, 303; as housekeeper, 29; humor of, xxi–xxii, xxiii, 93, 94; as hunter, 67, 70–71, 92, 110; illnesses of, xvi, xviii, xx, xxvi, xxvii, xxviii, 84, 130, 140, 141, 163, 189, 369, 382n. 1, 396–97, 408, 422, 431, 441, 444, 445, 447, 450–54, 456, 458, 459; independence of, xvi–xvii, 20, 54, 58, 115, 119, 159, 169, 172–73, 176, 180, 337–38, 344, 357, 364, 370–71, 373–74, 384, 387; Indian names of, 440; language usage of, ix, 26–27, 150, 190, 191, 192, 219, 328–29, 345–46, 370; as lecturer, xiv, xxvii, 140, 175, 180, 283, 285, 297, 310, 312, 315, 345, 364, 372, 373, 388, 413, 441; as liberal, 330; on literary critics, 108–9, 192, 412; on literature, 9–10, 13, 29, 40, 55–56, 303, 406; on marriage, 18; marriage and divorce of, xv, xvi, xxi; marriage proposals received by, 18; as mentor, xviii, xxiii, xxxii, 13, 47, 75–76, 99–100, 101, 131, 132n. 2, 134, 135, 142, 154, 169–70, 178, 204, 205, 221–22, 233, 242n. 1, 246, 252–54, 257, 260, 267, 272n. 1, 276–77, 278, 280–81, 283–86, 289, 295–96, 300, 304, 306, 320, 321–22, 327, 342, 351–52, 365–67, 381, 389, 403, 411–12, 439, 442, 452, 460–61; on Mormons, 110–13, 146, 147; on music, 67, 68, 73n. 1, 74, 81; name change of, 11n. 1, 19, 52, 81, 135; on names of characters, 453; on Nazis, 171, 172; on New York and New Yorkers, 196, 197, 286, 365, 368, 454; on oil, 403; organizational skills of, xxv–xxvi, xxvii, 102n. 2, 348; on photographers and photography, 429–30; photographs of, 151, 192, 350; on pioneers, 87–88, 332–33; poverty of, xvi, xx, xxiv, xxv, 14–15, 23–24, 53, 54, 77, 155, 212, 233, 236, 246, 324, 361–62; on promotion of works, 411–12, 438; as proofreader, 19–20, 27, 30, 129, 155, 233, 310; pseudonyms of, 135; on psychology, 55, 245; as radio and television personality, xiv, xxxii, 234, 235n. 1, 324, 332–33, 351; on regional writing, 125–26, 290; on religion, 16, 420; research collection of, 423; on sex and gender, xxxi–xxxii, 38–41, 142–43, 325, 370, 395; "shack" built by, 64, 67, 68–69, 71; on short stories, 13; as speechwriter, 68; on success, 453–54; on Talking Books, 285; as teacher, 29, 30, 58, 62, 98, 155, 246, 248, 259, 263, 282, 284, 288, 331, 350, 351; and television, opinions on, 416; temper, opinionatedness, and reactions of, xxiii–xxv, 59, 60, 110, 123–24, 138, 172–73, 175, 190, 211, 307, 315–16, 317, 318, 338–39, 350, 355–56, 360, 370–71, 373–74, 385, 393–95, 414, 425, 426, 433–35, 436, 445; on Texas, 152; on war bonds, 192, 193; on Western literature, 339, 353; on westerners and the West, 308–10, 365; on World War II, 183; as writer, xv–xvi, xx–xxi, xxv, xxx, 5, 11n. 2, 12, 31–32, 56, 62, 82, 109, 126, 153,

185, 202, 208, 284–85, 298, 309–10, 313, 315, 316–17, 321–22, 337–38, 347, 351–52, 386, 399, 411–12, 416–17, 429, 460–61. *See also specific works and specific headings*
Sandoz, Marie (sister-in-law), 72
Sandoz, Mary Fehr (mother): death of, 176, 425; illnesses of, 144, 146, 151; on *Old Jules,* 146, 405; and Jules Ami Sandoz, 81; and M. Sandoz, 6, 12, 14n. 6, 67, 72
Sandoz, Roberta (relative), 201
Sappa River battle, 230, 342–43, 413
Sapphira and the Slave Girl (Cather), 180
Saturday Review of Literature (magazine), 102n. 1
Scaife, Roger L., 84
Schoen, Marie von, 121
School Executives Magazine, M. Sandoz at, 1, 2, 3–4, 12, 14n. 3, 52, 62, 155, 190, 369
Schossberger, Emily, 304
"Sex in Biographies" (Boyd), 38–41
Seymour, Edmund, 104–5
Shadows on the Rock (Cather), 28
Shapiro, Karl, 408
She Watched Custer's Last Battle (Marquis), 228
Sheldon, Addison E.: background of, 33n. 3; death of, 215; as editor, 31, 33n. 3, 34, 97; and Madsen, 218; on Maher, 227; and Merritt memorial, 218; as politician, 33n. 3, 34; and Jules Ami Sandoz, xiv, 34; and M. Sandoz, xiv, 31, 34, 42, 74, 82, 83, 97, 165; and Weeks, xiv
Sherman, Harry, 88–89, 90n. 2
Sherman, Lucius Adelno, 98, 99n. 4
Short Bull, 367
Sinclair, F. H., 440
Sioux: and Bear Butte, 442; and Black Hills treaties, 25, 26, 42, 44n. 1; and Calhoun, 42, 44n. 1; characteristics of, 117; clothing of, 305; and Crook, 204, 292; decline of, 47–48; and McCreight, 115n. 1; massacre of, 122, 219; Neihardt on, 193; opera about, 47–51; paintings by, 188; and pioneers, 87–88; and Jules Ami Sandoz, 31, 247; M. Sandoz on, 25, 47, 50, 117; and Stanton, 122; weapons of, 384–85; and women, attitude toward, 103, 117. *See also* Brule Sioux; Indians; Lakotas; Oglala Sioux
Sioux Chronicle (Hyde), 402
Sioux War (1876), 218
Sitting Bull: in Canada, 50; and Carver, 237; characteristics of, 294; death of, 270; and He Dog, 115; name of, 294–95, 305; photographs of, 295; Vestal on, 305–6; visions of, 45
Sloan, John, 188
Slogum House (M. Sandoz): Annette in, 138; armed services edition of, 207, 208, 213; background of, 136, 137; banning of, 330, 453; Dodie in, 109; Fannie in, 109; as film, xviii, 174, 446; flashbacks in, 109; form and style of, 63, 64, 69, 120, 446; Gulla in, 160, 174, 446, 448; Libby in, 109, 138; paperback edition of, 250, 446; as play, 140, 446; plot of, 63, 64, 137, 141, 181–82, 208, 214, 446; proofreading of, 129–30; reactions to, xxiii, xxvii–xxix, 90, 108, 109, 120, 132–33, 134, 136, 137, 138, 139, 144–46, 149–50, 174, 182, 192, 213, 214, 330, 446, 448; research on, 129, 138; revisions of, 109, 110, 119, 125, 129, 141–42; Ruedy in, 109; M. Sandoz on, xxiii, 86, 119; serialization of, 90; setting of, 120, 137, 181, 446; and Soldiers' Vote Act, 213, 214; translations of, 174; Ward in, 109; work done on, 67, 69, 73, 138
"Smart Man, The" (M. Sandoz): Pahl in, 54; publication of, 5n. 1, 9n. 4; rejection of, 4; revisions of, 8, 299; M. Sandoz on, 299

Smedley, Agnes, 197
Smith, Harrison, 131, 132n. 1
Smith, John Eugene, 168
Smith, John W., 252
"Snags in the Missouri" (Bodmer), 111
"Snakes" (M. Sandoz), 447
Sod and Stubble (Ise), 387
Sod House Frontier, The (Dick), 134, 135n. 2
"Sodbusters" (M. Sandoz), 134, 135n. 2
Soldiers of the American Army (Todd), 433–34
Soldiers' Vote Act, 213–14
"Son, The" (M. Sandoz). *See* "What the Sioux Taught Me"
Son of Earth (Erickson), 75
Son of the Gamblin' Man (M. Sandoz): advertising of, 355–56, 357, 361; background of, 157, 177; characteristics of, 241; Cozads in, 337, 341, 352, 358n. 1; form and style of, 338; Haskell in, 352; illustrations in, 341–42, 350; plot of, 177, 337; publication of, xxix, 157n. 1, 306; reactions to, xxv, xxix, 337, 338–39, 341–42, 350, 354, 355, 357; research on, 178n. 1; revisions of, 341; work done on, 241, 350
Soskin, William, 88, 90n. 1
Spade Ranch, 11n. 4
Spengler, Oswald, 76
Spotted Elk, 400–401
Spotted Tail, 32, 49, 79, 188, 237, 252
Spotted Tail's Folk (Hyde), 401
Stalin, Joseph, xxiv
"Stalking the Ghost of Crazy Horse in a Whoopie" (M. Sandoz), 20–21, 22–23
Standing Bear, 45–46, 381–82
Stands in Timber, John, 459
Stanton, Edwin, 122
State Capital (M. Sandoz). See *Capital City*
State Historical Society. *See* Nebraska State Historical Society
"Stay Home, Young Writer" (M. Sandoz), 125–26
Stefan and Frederike Zweig (Alsberg, trans. and ed.), 270
Stegner, Wallace, 353
Stepanek, Orin, 51, 53nn. 1, 2, 64
Stocking, Moses, 199–200, 333
Stolberg, Ben, 88, 90n. 2
Stone Forehead. *See* Medicine Arrow
Story Catcher, The (M. Sandoz): background of, 340; illustrations in, 414; paperback edition of, 449; plot of, 340; publication of, 386; reactions to, 386–87, 449; revisions of, 387, 399; work done on, 376
Strange Lady in Town (film), xvii–xviii, 422
"Stranger at the Curb, The" (M. Sandoz), 25
"Striped Pajamas" (M. Sandoz), 15
Stuff, Frederick Ames, 98, 99n. 5
"Sunbeams" (Howard), 107n. 1, 108
Susskind, David, xxxii
Sutley, Zachary Taylor, 69
Swallow, Alan, xxvi, xxxiii, 278
"Swan Song, The" (M. Sandoz), 4, 28
Sweet Land (Gannett), 103
Sydenham, Moses, 329
Szell, George, 327

Taft, Robert A., 249, 330
Take All to Nebraska (Winther), 134–35
Talking Books, 285
Tarbell, Ida, 122
Tchanta Tanka. *See* McCreight, M. I.
Teater, Archie, 248, 254
Tenney Committee, 330
Testament of Man series (Fisher), 278
Thalberg, Irving, 174, 416
"There Were Two Sitting Bulls" (M. Sandoz), 294, 298

These Were the Sioux (M. Sandoz), xxxi, 372, 376–77, 404
Thiessen, Leonard, 202
This Island Earth (Torrey), 207
Thomas, Dorothy, 77, 124–25
Thompson, Estelle. *See* Sandoz, Estelle Thompson
Three Men (Evans), 267
Thunder in the Morning (M. Sandoz). See *Old Jules*
Thunderer, The (M. Sandoz). See *Old Jules*
Thurber, James, 382
Tin Horns and Calico (Christman), 281
Tobacco Road (Caldwell), 89
Tobacco Road (Kirkland), 89
Tom-Walker, The (M. Sandoz): fear of libel regarding, 222; language usage in, 206–7; publication of, xxix, 224 n. 1; purposes of, 208, 222, 223; reactions to, xxv, 208–9, 222–23, 227, 249, 267; revisions of, 222; M. Sandoz on, 208; World War II in, xxiv
Tongue River Reservation, 230–32
Towner, Wesley, 251, 267
Trails of Yesterday (Bratt), 293
Truman, Harry, 215, 230
Turn of the Year, A (M. Sandoz), 426–27
Turner, Frederick Jackson, 37 n. 4
Turner, Martha, 97–98
Twiss, Thomas, 168, 169 n. 2, 405
Two Great Scouts (Grinnell), 347
Two Moons, 255
"Tyrant of the Plains" (M. Sandoz), 300–302, 313, 316. See also *Cattlemen, The*

"Under the Lion's Paw" (Garland), 24
Ungirt Runner (M. Sandoz). See *Murky River, The*
University of Nebraska Press, xxx. *See also* Bison Books
Ups and Downs of an Army Officer (Armes), 398

Van den Bark, Melvin: and M. Sandoz, xxv, 64, 68 n. 6, 98, 410; as teacher, 68 n. 6, 98, 391–93
Van Gelder, Robert, 192–93
Van Gogh, Vincent, 89
Van Vleet, Lynn, xxvi, 197 n. 1, 306–7, 411
Van Vleet, Rose, 197 n. 1, 411
Vandale, Earl, 314
Vanderbilt, Cornelius, 214
Varga, Margit, 350
Vaughn, J. W., 327
Vestal, Stanley, 42, 44 n. 2, 305–6, 454
Victoria through the Looking Glass (Lennon), 202–3
"Victorie" (M. Sandoz), xxii, 8, 9 n. 1, 24
Vigilante, Sylvester, 296
Viking Press, 75
"Vine, The" (M. Sandoz), 1 n. 2, 2, 194

Wagonbox fight, 276–77
Walden Two (Skinner), 409
Wallowing, Rufus, 255, 256
Walls Rise Up (Perry), 181
Wang, Arthur, 251, 267
Warner, Jack, 422
Warner Brothers (film producers), xviii
Warpath (Vestal), 455
War-Path and Bivouac (Finerty), 206
Warpath and Council Fire (W. Campbell), 253
Washakie, 429
"We Speak for Ourselves" (radio program), 203
We'll Soon Have You Back Again (M. Sandoz). *See Tom-Walker, The*
Web and the Rock, The (Wolfe), 180
Webb, James R., xviii, 422, 430–31, 433–35, 438
Weeks, Edward: on *Capital City*, 158, 159, 161; as editor, xxix, 83, 85, 144, 173, 177; illnesses of, 143; on *Old Jules*, 85–86, 108, 124; and Jules Ami

Weeks, Edward (*cont.*)
Sandoz, xiv; and M. Sandoz, xxviii–xxix, xxxii, 98, 173, 177; and Sheldon, xiv; on *Slogum House,* xxviii–xxix, 108, 109; telegram from, 83n. 1; in Texas, 152; on *Tom-Walker,* 222–23
Wellman, Paul, 373–74
Welty, Eudora, 382
West, Ray, 267
Western Words (Adams), 443
Westerners Brand Book (journal), 271
Westminster Press, xxvii, xxix
Westrick, Gerhardt A., 172
Wharton, Edith, 65
"What I Learned from the Indians" (M. Sandoz). *See* "What the Sioux Taught Me"
"What Makes Teachers Cranky" (Judd), 6, 7, 9
"What the Sioux Taught Me" (M. Sandoz), 247
White Bull, 454–55
White Horse, Eddie, 374
White Thunder. *See* Grey Thunder
Whiting (editor), 90
Wiggins, O. P., 146–47
Wilcox (editor), 13
Wild Bill Hickok (Wilstach), 256
Wild Hog, 260n. 1, 312, 343, 413, 440
Wild Hog, Julia, 260
Wild Hog, Lydia, 440, 441n. 1
"Wilderness Days on the Niobrara" (E. Eastman), 354
Willa Cather Pioneer Memorial, 346
Williams, Annie Laurie, 251, 422
Williams, Frank L.: as editor, 33; on *Old Jules,* 33–34, 35, 52; on Sandhills, 61n. 1; and Jules Ami Sandoz, 33, 82; and M. Sandoz, 29, 60, 61n. 1, 82
Wimberly, Lowry: as editor, 34, 36n. 2, 412; illnesses of, 286, 290; and Mencken, 25n. 1; and M. Sandoz, 34, 36n. 2, 125–26
"Wimberly Thinks Regionalism Passe" (newspaper article), 125–26
Wimer, Henry D., 258n. 1, 413
Winners of the West (Brininstool), 215, 216
Winter Quarters, 110–13
Winter Rider, The (Fleming), 351
Winter Thunder (M. Sandoz), xxxii, 245, 246n. 1, 420
Winther, Sophus Keith, 134–35
With Crook on the Rosebud (Vaughn), 349
Wolf Solent (Powys), 11–12
Wolfe, Thomas, 222
Wooden Leg (Marquis), 220–21, 230, 248, 356
Woollcott, Alexander, 117
World of Willa Cather, The (Bennett), 397
World War II, 183
World's End (U. Sinclair), 180–81
World's Rim, The (Alexander), 262
Wounded Knee, South Dakota, 269, 270n. 1
Writers Conference at Boulder, 185
Wyeth, M. S. "Buz", Jr.: on *Love Song to the Plains,* 350, 351n. 1, 361, 370–71, 383; M. Sandoz on, 369
Wyoming Pageant (Trenholm), 405

XIT Ranch, 314–15
XIT Ranch of Texas, The (Haley), 314

Yankee from Olympus (Bowen), 330
Yearling, The (Rawlings), 148
Yellow Hand, 212, 213, 218, 219n. 1, 396
Yellow Swallow: and Custer, 228–29, 232–33, 234n. 1, 260n. 1, 312, 322, 455; death of, 322; illnesses of, 322; and Monahseetah, 260n. 1; Old Cheyenne Woman on, 232–33; research on, 312
You Can't Go Home Again (Wolfe), 180
Young, Marguerite: on *Cheyenne Au-*

tumn, 267; and M. Sandoz, xxvi, xxxii, 241, 242n. 1; and A. Williams, 251
Young Man Afraid of His Horse: as agency Indian, 48; and Black Hills treaties, 79; characteristics of, 36, 106, 125; and Conquering Bear, 118; death of, 36, 106; Hooker on, 118; name of, 118; photographs of, 32, 79; M. Sandoz on, 36, 37n. 5, 44, 82, 106, 115–16
Yurka, Blanche, xviii, 446, 448

Ziolkowski, Korczak, 195, 260, 373

www.ingramcontent.com/pod-product-compliance
Lightning Source LLC
Chambersburg PA
CBHW020931310726
48980CB00007B/722/J